Security and Strategy Models for Key-Solving Institutional Frameworks

Marios Panagiotis Efthymiopoulos
Neapolis University, Pafos, Cyprus

Andreas Masouras
Neapolis University, Pafos, Cyprus

IGI Global
Scientific Publishing
Publishing Tomorrow's Research Today

Vice President of Editorial Melissa Wagner
Director of Acquisitions Mikaela Felty
Director of Book Development Jocelynn Hessler
Production Manager Mike Brehm
Cover Design Jose Rosado

Published in the United States of America by
IGI Global Scientific Publishing
701 East Chocolate Avenue
Hershey, PA, 17033, USA
Tel: 717-533-8845
Fax: 717-533-7115
Website: https://www.igi-global.com E-mail: cust@igi-global.com

Library of Congress Cataloging-in-Publication Data

Names: Euthymiopoulos, Marios-Panagiōtēs, editor. | Masouras, Andreas, 1980- editor.
Title: Security and strategy models for key-solving institutional frameworks / edited by Marios Efthymiopoulos, Andreas Masouras.
Description: Hershey, PA : IGI Global Scientific Publishing, [2025] | Includes bibliographical references and index. | Summary: "Entrepreneurship is intricately connected to social and cultural changes. Successful entrepreneurs are those who can identify and respond to shifts in societal values, preferences, and expectations, aligning their ventures with the evolving needs of their target audiences"-- Provided by publisher.
Identifiers: LCCN 2024053535 (print) | LCCN 2024053536 (ebook) | ISBN 9798369355831 (hardcover) | ISBN 9798369355848 (paperback) | ISBN 9798369355855 (ebook)
Subjects: LCSH: Organizational change. | Entrepreneurship.
Classification: LCC HD58.8 .S439 2025 (print) | LCC HD58.8 (ebook) | DDC 658.4/062--dc23/eng/20250201
LC record available at https://lccn.loc.gov/2024053535
LC ebook record available at https://lccn.loc.gov/2024053536

British Cataloguing in Publication Data
A Cataloguing in Publication record for this book is available from the British Library.

Table of Contents

Detailed Table of Contents

The global strategic, security, and political landscape is transforming significantly. A new security architecture is on the way to be established. The current chapter examines complex shifts in our attempt to exploit the current environment that is genuinely volatile and unclear. This chapter assumes that we all seem out of any global ideological purpose, considering the evolution of international affairs, including operational choices and a balance of power. This chapter explores how emerging forces use geopolitical realignments to technological innovations, politics, and demographic changes to redefine global power structures and possible solutions or challenges for the near or future positions. Are we in the West in decline, or is Western-centric dominance? Are we seeing the rise of new power centers? The chapter assesses current governance methods and the availability or absence of current organizations or institutions (based on our case studies). The role of energy resources, the impact of trade disputes and power balance, and technological advancements are reshaping international relations. New dynamics and new political realities are on the rise.

This chapter explores the profound disruptions to globalization and trade liberalization caused by the resurgence of trade wars in the 21st century. Driven by geopolitical rivalries and shifting economic power dynamics, these conflicts have led to a restructuring of global supply chains through reshoring and friendshoring strategies. The chapter also examines the dual role of technological advancement as both a driver and a casualty of trade wars, with export controls and decoupling efforts reshaping global innovation. Additionally, it highlights the growing significance of energy security, focusing on resource access disputes, rare earth elements, and the geopolitical implications of fossil fuel dependency. Offering critical insights for policymakers, businesses, and scholars, this chapter provides a comprehensive analysis of the evolving landscape of international trade, economic competition, and global stability in an era of intensifying geopolitical tensions.

This chapter examines the connection between human rights and foreign direct investments, focusing on the potential impact of foreign investments on human rights. It explores the relationship between human rights and international investment law, highlighting that these legal fields are not isolated but interconnected. Through the analysis of investment treaties and case law, the chapter demonstrates how human rights issues increasingly arise in investment arbitration. Ultimately, the chapter argues that embedding human rights considerations into investment frameworks and dispute resolution mechanisms is essential for addressing societal challenges and achieving sustainable development.

This chapter addresses the comprehensive set of United Arab Emirates' policies focused on deterring military aggression, combatting extremism both domestically and regionally, and on fostering stability as a crucial condition to achieve its vision for the future based on security and economic growth. It discusses key aspects of the foundation of the country in 1971, its vision for the future towards the Centennial of its independence and explains the security challenges posed by state and non-state actors. Finally, it focuses on the analysis of both domestic and foreign policies to promote stability, and it argues that the success of these policies will depend not only on sustained and conscious efforts, but also on a complex set of variables beyond the control of the UAE.

The electoral choices of a nation, combined with the practices of its political establishment and institutions, are a significant factor in the functioning of democracy, prosperity and the overall prospects of the state. Moreover, both political institutions and the surrounding political environment, on the one hand, and the communication

Diversity and Inclusion: Harnessing the Power of Inclusivity for Business Success" examines how integrating diversity and inclusion (D&I) into business practices can drive competitive advantage and align with societal expectations. The chapter explores the strategic benefits of D&I, such as improved customer loyalty, enhanced innovation, and broader market reach. It provides practical strategies for embedding D&I into organizational culture, marketing, and product development, supported by real-world case studies. Challenges like resistance to change and policy gaps are discussed, along with strategies to address them. The role of leadership and institutional policies in promoting inclusivity is emphasized. The chapter also looks at emerging trends and offers guidance on how businesses can adapt to stay competitive in a diverse market. Overall, it provides actionable insights for business leaders and policymakers to leverage D&I for greater organizational success.

Consecutive economic and health crises have reshaped the global markets with their impact to be clearly visible on small and medium enterprises (SMEs) which are facing serious obstacles in the attempt to ensure sustainable development. These problems are clearly identified at a larger scale in SMEs than large companies as the latter have the appropriate knowhow as well as the relevant productive resources to overcome these challenges and increase their market resilience. Further, several geopolitical developments such as the war in Ukraine have put more pressure on SMEs on both microeconomic and macroeconomic levels requiring from national authorities to provide the appropriate support in order to ensure uninterrupted supply chain management which leads to a major impact on food security.

This chapter examines how digital technologies transform social entrepreneurship, creating opportunities and challenges. Social entrepreneurship addresses societal issues by merging social and economic goals but often faces regulatory and resource limitations. Digital tools such as AI, big data, and blockchain enhance efficiency, transparency, and value co-creation, helping social enterprises expand their reach and financial sustainability. Case studies from Greece and beyond highlight how digitalization fosters resilience and collaboration, particularly during crises like COVID-19. While digital transformation offers new growth pathways, it also raises ethical concerns about access, privacy, and disparities. This study proposes a framework linking digitalization, value co-creation, and social entrepreneurship, offering insights for policymakers, researchers, and practitioners seeking innovative and sustainable business models.

This chapter explores the linkage between the Total Quality Management (TQM) and customer satisfaction, in the context of academic service quality. Using Deming's theory as a theoretical background, this study examines how TQM principles can improve academic quality services, with the goal of increased customer satisfaction. It is sought to reveal the possible impact of TQM in upgrading academic services through the empowerment of academic community members, students, faculty and staff. From the literature review path, it seems that there is strong evidence of the positive impact of TQM on academic services, with an emphasis on long-term benefits for all members involved. TQM offers a powerful framework for the improvement of academic quality services, while, concurrently, achieving high levels of customer satisfaction. The successful implementation of TQM seems to have a beneficial effect on all members, contributing to the overall effectiveness of the academic organization. The study concludes with recommendations on the dynamics of TQM in enhancing academic services.

Sreelal Bhagyabhavanam, Indian Institute of Management, Ranchi, India
Shilpee A. Dasgupta, Indian Institute of Management, Ranchi, India
Prashant Maurya, Indian Institute of Management, Ranchi, India
Shubh Majumdarr, Indian Institute of Management, Ranchi, India

In this chapter, the authors examine Corporate Social Responsibility initiatives to empower Indian women, emphasizing that sustainable development is unattainable without their active participation. The study employs a non-probability purposive sampling technique to analyze secondary data from CSR reports of Indian companies from 2014 to 2018, including sources such as the High-Level Committee-2015 (HLC-2015), the CSR Reporting Survey 2019, the National Health Survey of Families Health, and the top 10 women empowerment projects through CSR initiatives in 2018-19. Utilizing percentage analysis, the chi-square test, and ANOVA, the study assesses the impact of CSR initiatives on women's personal and professional growth in both social and economic spheres. Furthermore, the chapter proposes a conceptual framework to enhance women's development through CSR. This chapter contributes valuable insights into the role of CSR in fostering women's empowerment in a developing economy like India.

Stalo Georgiou, Neapolis University, Paphos, Cyprus

In the rapidly evolving landscape of education, distance learning has emerged as a pivotal modality, necessitating the strategic application of educational frameworks to ensure effectiveness, engagement, and communication. This article explores the integration of strategic models within distance education and educational communication to optimize learning outcomes. Among these models, the Community of Inquiry (CoI) framework emphasizes the importance of cognitive presence, social presence, and teaching presence in creating an interactive and meaningful learning experience. Additionally, the ADDIE instructional design model provides a systematic approach to course development, ensuring that learning objectives, content delivery, and assessment are aligned with student needs. The blended learning model offers a flexible solution, combining online and face-to-face instruction, while Competency-

Preface

In a world increasingly defined by complexity and rapid change, institutions are under constant pressure to adapt. Security concerns, strategic interests, and evolving governance frameworks intersect in ways that demand innovative responses. As global systems shift, the need to design models that offer practical and sustainable solutions to institutional challenges has never been more urgent.

This book, *Security and Strategy Models for Key-Solving Institutional Frameworks*, brings together scholars and practitioners from diverse fields to explore how institutions can confront uncertainty with resilience and foresight. The chapters investigate a range of pressing issues, from geopolitical strategy and digital transformation to human rights, economic sustainability, and educational reform. By addressing these topics through a strategic lens, the volume seeks to offer tools that are not only theoretical but also applicable in real-world contexts.

Our motivation as editors was to foster interdisciplinary dialogue around the question of how institutions can remain effective, secure, and ethically grounded amid turbulent times. Whether considering the redesign of governance models, the role of entrepreneurship in resilient economies, or the ethics of emerging technologies, our contributors aim to inform decision-making processes that prioritize long-term stability and social good.

Chapter 1: Geopolitical Security, Technology and Business Strategy: How Should Business Approach Geopolitics

This chapter underscores the growing importance of geopolitics for global businesses navigating complex and volatile environments. It explores how geopolitical events, shifting alliances, and technological developments can directly impact supply chains, production, and demand across continents.

By examining the dynamics of a multipolar world, the author emphasizes the need for strategic foresight in business decision-making, especially in anticipating geopolitical shifts. Technological integration and resource management emerge as critical tools for resilience.

The chapter ultimately argues that businesses must adopt agile, globally informed strategies that account for emerging geopolitical risks and opportunities to remain competitive in today's interconnected economy.

Chapter 2: Continuous Monitoring and Updating of Security Strategies Based on the Evolution of Threats in Contemporary Geopolitical Relations

This chapter investigates whether continuously updated security strategies can effectively respond to evolving geopolitical threats. It critiques static security models that fail to adapt quickly, leaving institutions vulnerable.

Through case studies and expert insights, the authors illustrate how real-time threat data and adaptive policies enhance organizational resilience. Their analysis points to the benefits of agile frameworks not only in defense but also in sectors like healthcare.

Ultimately, the chapter calls for integrated, continuously evolving safeguards across institutions to meet the challenges of an unpredictable global environment.

Chapter 3: Geopolitical Challenges: The Global Influence or Decline of Western Society: A New World Order or Rising Volatility?

This chapter explores the fluid and complex shifts in the global security and political landscape, with a particular focus on the role and future of Western dominance. It considers whether we are witnessing a decline of the West or a transformation into a new power balance.

The author evaluates how emerging political, technological, and demographic forces are reshaping global power structures. Special attention is given to institutional effectiveness, energy politics, and trade dynamics.

The analysis concludes that the world is entering a phase of increasing volatility and fragmentation, calling for reimagined governance structures and renewed strategic thinking.

Chapter 4: Trade Wars and International Relations: Implications for Global Supply Chains, Technological Advancement, and Energy Security

This chapter analyzes the resurgence of trade wars and their disruptive effects on globalization, supply chains, and technological collaboration. It discusses reshoring and friendshoring as strategic responses to geopolitical friction.

Technological innovation is shown to be both a driver of conflict and a victim of decoupling policies, while energy security emerges as a parallel battlefield marked by rare earth competition and fossil fuel dependency.

The chapter provides a timely assessment of how global economic and political instability is reshaping trade and innovation ecosystems, offering insight for business and policy stakeholders.

Chapter 5: Human Rights and Foreign Direct Investments: Addressing Societal Challenges

This chapter explores the intersection of human rights and foreign direct investment (FDI), advocating for integrated legal and policy frameworks. It reveals how investment arbitration increasingly involves human rights concerns.

The author uses treaties and case law to show how the legal spheres of human rights and international investment are interconnected, not siloed.

The chapter concludes that embedding human rights in FDI mechanisms is essential for addressing societal challenges and ensuring equitable, sustainable development.

Chapter 6: Integrating Economic Inclusion and Empowerment into Investment Strategies: Promoting Equitable Growth

This chapter emphasizes the growing importance of aligning investment strategies with social equity goals. It explores how economic inclusion and empowerment can be embedded in decision-making processes to foster equitable growth.

Through case studies and practical frameworks, the authors demonstrate how inclusive investment strategies enhance long-term returns, community resilience, and stakeholder trust.

The chapter concludes that promoting equity is not only a moral imperative but a strategic advantage in navigating the evolving global investment landscape.

Chapter 7: Measuring Social Return on Investment in Inclusive Investment Strategies

This chapter presents a comprehensive methodology for assessing the social return on investment (SROI) in inclusive finance initiatives. It defines SROI as a multidimensional approach that quantifies social, environmental, and economic value creation.

The authors provide a framework for applying SROI across sectors, highlighting its usefulness in guiding strategic choices and enhancing transparency.

By linking investments to measurable societal outcomes, the chapter positions SROI as a powerful tool for promoting accountability and sustainable impact in institutional frameworks.

Chapter 8: Inclusive Business and Social Entrepreneurship in Institutional Contexts

This chapter examines the role of inclusive business models and social entrepreneurship in addressing institutional and societal gaps. It defines inclusive businesses as those that integrate marginalized populations into their value chains as producers, employees, and consumers.

The author explores how social entrepreneurship can complement state and market mechanisms, especially in delivering essential services and creating jobs.

Through institutional analysis, the chapter shows how enabling environments—such as policy support and access to capital—are key to scaling inclusive initiatives and fostering systemic change.

Chapter 9: Public–Private Partnerships for Inclusive Growth and Economic Development

This chapter investigates how public–private partnerships (PPPs) can drive inclusive economic development. It argues that well-designed PPPs can leverage private sector efficiency alongside public sector oversight to achieve social goals.

Case studies illustrate successful models in infrastructure, healthcare, and education, with a focus on equity, transparency, and accountability.

The authors propose governance principles and performance metrics to ensure that PPPs contribute meaningfully to inclusive and sustainable growth.

Chapter 10: Integrating Quality Management Systems into Business and Institutional Strategies for Sustainability and Resilience

This chapter explores how quality management systems (QMS) can be embedded into institutional frameworks to support sustainability and resilience. It discusses standards such as ISO 9001 in the context of strategic planning, risk management, and continuous improvement.

The author argues that QMS tools not only enhance operational efficiency but also build trust, adaptability, and stakeholder alignment.

By linking quality to resilience and long-term viability, the chapter makes a strong case for systematic integration of QMS into organizational strategies.

Chapter 11: Empowering Social Entrepreneurship and Social Enterprises Through Digital Technologies: Opportunities and Challenges

This chapter explores how digital technologies reshape the landscape of social entrepreneurship by enhancing efficiency, transparency, and scalability. It analyzes tools such as AI, big data, and blockchain, showing how they enable social enterprises to overcome regulatory and resource barriers while expanding impact.

Case studies from Greece and beyond highlight how digital transformation fosters resilience, particularly during crises like the COVID-19 pandemic. The authors also address ethical concerns, including digital inequality and data privacy.

A proposed framework links digitalization with value co-creation in social enterprises, offering guidance for policymakers and practitioners aiming to build sustainable, tech-enabled models for social impact.

Chapter 12: Total Quality Management (TQM): A Linkage to Customer Satisfaction Through Academic Quality Services

This chapter examines the role of Total Quality Management (TQM) in enhancing customer satisfaction within academic institutions. Using Deming's theory as a foundation, the authors explore how TQM principles empower academic stakeholders—students, faculty, and staff—to drive continuous improvement in service delivery.

The study draws from literature to show a strong correlation between TQM practices and long-term service quality in education.

By positioning TQM as a strategic tool for academic excellence and stakeholder satisfaction, the chapter offers actionable insights for institutional leaders seeking to elevate educational outcomes and operational performance.

Chapter 13: Women Empowerment Through CSR in India: A Review of Indian CSR Initiatives and Framework Development

This chapter investigates how Corporate Social Responsibility (CSR) initiatives in India contribute to the empowerment of women, a critical component of sustainable development. Using secondary data from CSR reports and national surveys, the authors evaluate programs implemented between 2014 and 2018.

Statistical tools such as ANOVA and chi-square tests assess the social and economic impact of leading CSR initiatives, especially in health, education, and employment.

The chapter culminates in the development of a conceptual framework aimed at strengthening CSR's role in women's empowerment. It provides evidence-based recommendations for companies and policymakers focused on inclusive development in emerging economies.

Chapter 14: Applying Strategic Models in Distance Education and Educational Communication

This chapter analyzes the strategic use of educational models to enhance the effectiveness of distance learning and communication. It highlights frameworks such as the Community of Inquiry (CoI), ADDIE, blended learning, and Competency-Based Education (CBE).

Each model addresses key aspects of instructional design—ranging from fostering presence and engagement to aligning content with student competencies.

By integrating these models, educators can deliver flexible, interactive, and outcome-oriented learning experiences. The chapter underscores the importance of strategic planning and model selection in the evolving digital education environment.

We believe the perspectives in this volume contribute meaningfully to ongoing debates about institutional security and strategy. Each chapter highlights a different facet of this conversation, revealing the layered interdependencies between policy, technology, ethics, and leadership. Collectively, they offer a roadmap for navigating future crises while strengthening institutional integrity.

While the contexts and challenges may differ, a common thread runs through all contributions: the recognition that security is not merely a defensive posture but a proactive and strategic enterprise. Resilient institutions are those that anticipate change, embrace innovation, and maintain clarity of purpose in the face of adversity. This volume reflects that ethos and invites readers to think critically and constructively about institutional transformation.

We hope that this book will serve as a valuable resource for academics, policymakers, and professionals who are shaping the next generation of institutional frameworks. It is our belief that by bridging theory and practice, we can better equip institutions to act with agility, accountability, and vision.

Marios Panagiotis Efthymiopoulos
Neapolis University, Pafos, Cyprus

Andreas Masouras
Neapolis University, Pafos, Cyprus

Chapter 1
Geopolitical Security, Technology, and Business Strategy: How Should Business Approach Geopolitics?

Josef Demergis
https://orcid.org/0000-0001-6906-7308
Neapolis University, Pafos, Cyprus

ABSTRACT

Geopolitics deeply matter for modern businesses since events around the globe may have serious and long-lasting effects to production, supply-chains and general demand for products and services. The existence of an interconnected world has supply chains stretching into many continents while actions of local actors may pose geopolitical risks far beyond their immediate physical reach. A world where the geopolitics and geoeconomics seem to be shifting towards a multipolar world, albeit in nuanced and complex ways makes for new ways and best practices for how should business approach geopolitics. Strategic foresight of geopolitical events, technology and resources are all key when formulating a sound business strategy.

DOI: 10.4018/979-8-3693-5583-1.ch001

INTRODUCTION

Geopolitics and security are two concepts that come hand in hand when dealing with the intricacies of explaining the behaviour of international actors while trying to navigate around such common themes as resources, technological applications, and supply chains.

A highly inter-connected world where supply chains may stretch into many continents and countries and where commercial clients may be from next door to afar, means that business needs to have a sound understanding of prevalent geopolitics.

It also means that business must be able to take such decisions that will allow it to cater for both mediums of stability and instability in global affairs that may have an effect on its operations.

The diffusion of technology along with the recognition of what constitutes geopolitical risks and geopolitical transformation should be within the risk-assessment employed by business when approaching geopolitics and be part of their strategic foresight process.

The Importance of Geopolitics

Geopolitics do matter. Such events as the invasion of Ukraine by Russia, the Hamas attack on Israel and the resultant Israeli response in Gaza, Iran's drone and missile attack on Israel, the interdiction of shipping by the Iranian-backed Houthis in the Red Sea, are all part of an intricate geopolitical chain.

The importance of such a chain spans through geographical and political divides and has an effect on economic affluence, shifting of power and business endeavours.

A practical example of the importance of geopolitics in business are the international events of March 2025. US President Donald Trump imposed measures that raised a flat duty on "steel and aluminium entering the US to 25% and ends all country exemptions to the levies" (Silva, 2025).

With the US being one of the world's major importers of aluminium and steel, such a move was bound to have major repercussions to exporters of these materials that are crucial to manufacturing and to business at large. This "flat duty" being a tax charged on good imported by other countries and in our case from the European Union, it was inescapable that geopolitical tensions would rise and that countermeasures would be taken from the international actors affected.

The European Union an intergovernmental organisation that amongst other activities facilitates free trade and is involved in various transnational initiatives (Piroska & Epstein, 2023) had to take action in order to protect its financial interests and duly answered the US tariffs with imposing tariffs of its own on €26bn worth of US goods (BBC, 12/03/25).

Other exporting countries of aluminium and steel to the United States, like Canada (Guardian, 12/03/25) were similarly affected.

In a usual geopolitical twist that ties geopolitical events, business, imports, exports and consumer behaviour, the European Union, the United States and the West in general are not averse to employing countermeasures when public perception demands it.

The Chinese steel industry has been targeted concerning its working conditions, environmental practices that tend to be questionable along with inferior steel quality (Patrice & Mamadou, 2024) leading to pressure from the public and indigenous competitors to take appropriate measures. Such instruments of policy as the European Commission are forced to take action while simultaneously being influenced by other political actors that thus manage to have geopolitical, global reach.

NGOs for example may have an effect on consumer behaviour and may influence corporate behaviour (Fioretti et al., 2024) and thus directly or indirectly exert political pressure that will have a geopolitical effect.

The process of defining geopolitics and thus defining their relationship with security, technology and business strategy is still fluid since "geopolitics as a subject of scholarly inquiry has passed through various phases and stages" (Sarpong, 2021).

Mackinder's Heartland Theory (Mackinder, 1904), Spykman's Rimland Theory (Spykman, 2007), Critical Geopolitics (Tuathail, 1996), are attempts to understand how the different forms of power are projected globally while influencing and being influenced by geography and the nature of prevalent politics.

In our case geopolitics and geopolitical security are defined by the most precious commodity to humanity since the beginning of history, resources. Resources, however they are defined, are the reason for local and global competition in human history (Bretschger & Pittel, 2020) and this competition produces geopolitical risks and security issues that are interconnected with economies, technology and business. Trade protectionism has both been sustained and sometimes expanded as a global trade policy adjustment tool as the competition for resources globally creates geopolitical risks (Shen & Yang, 2024).

Some scholars have expressed the view that economic power and influence is slowly transitioning towards the East (Landesz, 2023), without this being a given.

The complexities of geopolitics make the rise of new regional powers a start for new global alliances and a potential source for conflict and geopolitical risks.

Geopolitical security thus encompasses not only the interplay between politics, international political actors and geography but also of the assets each international actor brings to bear that has an effect on geopolitical security.

The economic repercussions of global security have been studied for well over a century now with geopolitical tensions influencing business and economic growth, with "economic uncertainties and tensions disrupt(ing) the supply chain, production and other economic activities, resulting in fluctuations across business cycles" (Jha et al., 2024).

Disruptions in manufacturing, in shipping, in a part of a long supply chain that extends around the world, may have a deleterious effect on business and it unavoidably has an impact on both investment intentions and the customer's willingness to pay for goods and services.

Business may even be impacted on them using or being used, unawares in illegal supply chain methods.

Illegal supply chain methods are regularly used in global geopolitics from such diverse actors as crime syndicates, rogue states, states that are sanctioned heavily because of their recent actions, as is the case with Russia after its invasion of Ukraine.

Technology plays a huge role in such situations since it is both an enabling factor for a transaction to be made, enabling and bringing together commercial partnerships and exchanges around the globe, but also being the highly - sought commodity one seeks to sell or purchase.

It is also a stabilising factor in business, allowing for innovation to combat disruptions within the supply chains (Stern, 2024). This worldwide competition, in the various strands that will be presented, shapes in its way the suitable business approach to geopolitics and how to examine and interpret geopolitical security.

The search for geopolitical security in a business strategy should consider that security in international relations refers to the protection of states, individuals as well as many other political actors, economic entities and global systems from threats that could undermine their stability and existence.

It encompasses business strategy as relating to geopolitics, economic security, internal security, personal security, etc. and is called upon to address traditional and non-traditional threats, such as those that may arise from the introduction of emerging technologies.

Geoeconomics and Business

A mention should be made about geoeconomics where the the main area for rivalry between international actors is envisaged to be economic rather than military.

It also encompasses the mutual interplay of economics and geopolitics. Global economies and financial markets have a strengthening dependence due to the expanding international trade, access to markets and the infrastructures needed to conduct financial and other types of exchange. Geoeconomics is also about the natural resources contained in a region and the politics on how to control and exploit those resources.

Geopolitical security comprises of a lot of facets of risks to business, like war, cyber-attacks, clandestine, asymmetrical warfare and others that threaten economic activity. Such security risks nevertheless lead “to a rise in demand for security-related goods and services and the involvement of the government and business sector” (Bardalai, 2024).

Economic developments have geopolitical impacts i.e. the declining power of a specific state.

Geopolitical change, for example territorial conquest, influences economics while peripheral conflicts may either hinder or on the contrary promote economic goals.

A good example of this is the establishment of the Nord Stream II pipeline between Russia and EU with Russian geoeconomics being successful over the years in fracturing its dealings with the European Union by dividing its member states(Vihma & Wigell, 2016).

The Nord Stream II pipeline was built in order not only to further the capacity of the exported Russian gas to Germany but also, in the geopolitical context, to avoid using other transit avenues passing through countries that Russia, as the guardian of the Soviet Union’s legacy has considerable bad history with, years before its invasion of Ukraine.

Covid 19 is another example where business was affected due to the disruption of the global supply chains and manufacturing with “serious supply chain shortages in critical commodities such as microchips” (Rosenberg, 2024).

Shortages in medicine, medical-related supplies and various foodstuffs was also prevalent with business severely curtailed in many sectors.

Tied into the theme of global power and thus economic and business influence migrating from the West, there is research that suggests that the G7 countries, in comparison to the states comprising the BRICS alliance, “have demonstrated lower resistance to geopolitical uncertainty” (Nazir et al., 2025), while ASEAN bloc countries exhibit caution in geopolitical events that may cost them in the long run.

The Houthi, Global Business and Geopolitical Security: A Small Case Study

The Houthi attacks on global shipping have disrupted the global trade in a significant manner, posing both a threat to maritime security, stability of the supply chains and irregularities with broader economic repercussions. The Houthi attacks are part of a much bigger geopolitical nexus that involves, Russia, Iran, Israel, Saudi

Arabia, many other Arab and Sunni states and the MENA region at large as well as such western global actors as the European Union and the world's only superpower.

Through their war against the Saudi Arabian led coalition intervention of 2015 and through Iran's policy of enabling armed groups and non-state actors through the Middle East in order to achieve strategic depth, the Houthi emerged not only as a local actor within Yemen but as a non-state actor with regional and global importance (Juneau, 2024).

Yemen's geography makes it a chokepoint for international trade due to the presence of the Bab el-Mandeb Strait (Comments,2018), located between Yemen, on its eastern edge, and bordering with Eritrea and Djibouti.

The strait is 20 mile wide and 70 mile long and is one of the most vital passageways along the world's main shipping route between Europe and Asia.

By connecting the Red Sea to the Gulf of Aden and to the Arabian Sea, a huge transit of oil carrying ships takes place every day making it one of the more significant global energy routes.

Beyond the direct impact on shipping, the Houthi attacks have wider economic consequences. Supply chain disruptions, particularly in industries reliant on timely deliveries of raw materials and finished goods, could result in production delays and rising costs.

Sectors such as automotive and electronics, which depend on just-in-time inventory systems, can also be affected.

The global trade has been under great pressure since Hamas' attack on Israel and the resultant war, with the actions of the Houthi making shipowners face "higher insurance premiums as the risk of losing a vessel has dramatically increased, above all, in the Red Sea" (Kaufmann, 2024). With much of the Red Sea trade being rerouted around Africa, adding to the shipping cost and time (Kaufmann, 2024) with geopolitical security and instability being the main driver of change behind relevant business strategies. The World Bank in its October 2024 MENA report mentions that due to the conflict in the Middle East centred in Gaza "supply chain disruptions and economic disorganisation, higher costs of finance, and a decline in investment" (World Bank, 2024) were contributors to the general cost of conflict in the MENA region.

Complicating the geopolitical security picture was a reported deal that both Russia and China entered agreements with the Houthi (Bloomberg), to ensure the safety of their merchant ships in contrast to Western-owned ships. According to a September 2024 analysis by Lloyd's List no Russian-owned ships were targeted by the Houthi in their area of operations for the past nine months, with only a single Chinese ship coming under attack (Bockmann, 2024). Hellenic owned ships, on the other hand accounted for more than 30% of the vessels attacked by the Houthi with various weaponry.

The European Union is currently engaged in a military operation for the protection of freedom and navigation and maritime security of merchant vessels in the Red Sea, the Indian Ocean and the Guld under the auspices of the EU Common Security and Defence Policy in another example of how business, in this case maritime commerce, engages with geopolitical security concerns. The EUNAVFOR ASPIDES (EU, 2025b) as this military operation is called could not have found the necessary political backing if there were not significant geoeconomic and geostrategic interests at play.

One of the more fascinating facets of this mini case study is the employment of technology by the Houthi in order to further their agenda and curtail economic activity. The Houthi, through Iranian state support use "missiles and armed drones with ranges up to 1500 Km" (Mutschler et al., 2024) with such weaponry targeted at ships and being intercepted and destroyed in a twist of fate by the Hellenic Navy warships of the ASPIDES operation (Reuters, 2024).

The Russia-Ukraine war, the BRICS, China and a new World Order

An enduring and well-established idea in Russian strategic culture and operations mindset is its "perceived vulnerability to external attack" (Götz & Staun, 2022) and its vulnerability against the West. The way the Russian political and military elite understand geopolitics are both deeply rooted in both geography and history. Russia is a large territory with long borders, that are also shared with China, another major geopolitical actor.

It has experienced many invasions over the centuries such as the invasion from Napoleonic France that resulted in its joining the Quadruple Alliance (Dwyer, 2008), two World Wars (Levy & Mulligan, 2017; Wegner, 1990) and various other incursions.

Many international actors and in our case, business understand geopolitics and international affairs as contained within a regulated system of order.

The war in Ukraine and the resultant Western support has broadly been depicted in the West as "a stand for rules-based international order" although the West has not been averse to violating international law if it serves its purposes (Narine, 2023).

Russia's invasion is undoubtedly a completely illegal and violent act that is not unprecedented in international historical events, and which has so far isolated Russia from the Western world and has promoted multiple changes within Russia.

What matters to the question on how should business approach geopolitics, comprehend geopolitical security risks and formulate a suitable business strategy in the case of the Russia-Ukraine war is another function of geoeconomics.

The war itself has managed to exhibit profound effects on the global economic and financial landscape, as well as on the geopolitical balance of power. Major western economies, such as that of the United States and the European Union, have exhibited evident signs of strain.

Russia's invasion of Ukraine, the conflicts in the Middle East and the economic crisis that now seems to be affecting Europe are preludes to geostrategic upheavals worldwide, where the management of discourse and the washing out of aggression are neither sufficient nor appropriate.

China and Russia seek another role within international affairs, the first perhaps with more impetus behind it although Russia is not to be excluded. The world order and its geopolitical nature seems to be changing from a system of one superpower to a multipolar system with the resultant power shifts. The alliances of nations into partnerships of an economic nature are "commonly utilised mechanisms to promote collaboration and trade, often within a common geographic area" (Cochrane & Zaidan, 2024).

Such alliances produce business dynamics, opportunities and geopolitical risks based on their rise or decline or at least the global perception of it that indirectly influences business and consumer behaviour. For example, macro-economic data shows the relation of two such alliances or political and economic blocks that are major drivers of business globally.

The Group of Seven (G7:United States, United Kingdom, Japan, Germany, Italy, France, Canada), broadly representing Western geopolitical influence and the BRICS+ (Brazil, Russia, India, China, South Africa, Iran, Egypt, Ethiopia, the UAE and on January 2025 added Nigeria and Indonesia to its members) that seek to take the geopolitical lead from the Western countries with Saudi Arabia still hedging its commitment to this group (Stuenkel & Treadwell, 2024).

Saudi Arabia has been engaged by the second Trump administration to play a role in the negotiations regarding the Russia-Ukraine war in a geopolitical bid, amongst others, to keep the huge Saudi influence on energy production away from the BRICS+.

The sixteenth annual BRICS+ conference held in Kazan, Russia on October 2024, is ostensibly a challenge to the dominance of the West as manifested by organisations such as the IMF and the World Bank.

A domination both financial and political, spread across the globe, having a heavy footprint in geopolitics and dominating infrastructures critical and necessary to a country's and international actor's presence on the international stage.

The use of specific currencies, systems of inter-banking, bring political and economic pressures that are no longer accepted by the emerging regional powers, both by rivals of the West as well as by smaller countries, that want to keep their options open in terms of affiliation to larger organisations of political and economic influence. Business strategies must be aware of such differentiating factors and trends in world politics and plan accordingly.

The BRICS+ countries represent about 54% of the world's population and 42.2 of global GDP (Norton, 2025) at a time when the West, influenced by unproductive ideas, is literally committing suicide by not promoting the growth of its population, a population that is ageing and will have major problems in the future in terms of the global geopolitical game and in being competitive in business.

A smaller population means less production where it is needed, and less investment in critical infrastructure in the transport part of the supply chain (ports, railways, airports, road networks).

This results in less competitive sufficiency and reduced geopolitical influence if the existence of indigenous human resources, with common education, shared ideals and continuity, is not made a priority.

In any case, the BRICS+ and the many other countries that participated in the 16th conference of this group, such as Turkey, the only NATO member state to participate, do not necessarily share common goals and common geopolitical interests on many issues but are a manifestation of global fluidity.

Available macro-economic data shows “the relative rise of the BRICS+ and the relative decline of the G7” (Cochrane & Zaidan, 2024).

If one is to offer a single comment about China’s role within the geopolitical infrastructure is that the US failed to integrate it into its notion of a “rules-based order” while it is most clear that the liberal dictum that economic interdependence limits the possibility of open confrontation with the West does not hold true any longer, if it was ever the case.

The strategic realignment the second Trump administration wishes to make in the position of the US versus its potential major competitors has China clearly marked as the main competitor. Such a clear strategic shift, while being lost within a media frenzy of what the US administration will do about Russian aggressiveness and its prospects against Europe, should and cannot be lost by business leaders when planning ahead.

China may be a major geopolitical player and manufacturer of goods but has also heavily engaged in “debt-trap diplomacy as part of its Belt and Road Initiative (BRI) (Bardalai, 2024). It has gained direct or indirect control on many resource-heavy locations around the world and has emerged as geopolitical competitor to the West while being heavily invested in doing business with it.

NATO has addressed the Chinese conundrum since the 2019 London Declaration that recognised Chinese growing influence in world affairs.

The NATO Secretary General was very clear when stating that "it was not NATO that had moved closer to China, but rather China to NATO through activities in the Arctic and in Africa, through investments in critical infrastructure in Europe, as well as activities in the cyber and information space" (Kaim & Stanzel, 2022).

Such acknowledgements of the geopolitical status of China have direct correlations to business and many times may have deleterious effects on business practices.

Chinese Telecom giant Huawei was blacklisted by the US with several EU countries following suit to "impose restrictions on telecom suppliers that are considered high-risk, such as Huawei and ZTE, for 5G network infrastructure" (Kroet, 2024). Constructing a business strategy in a western company at that time, that would involve the use of Huawei or ZTE telecommunication products would have been deleterious if the considerations at board level did not take into account the evolving geopolitics and the risks associated with buying Chinese telecommunication equipment.

Similar considerations are evident in the technology cybersphere where social app Tiktok, a favourite amongst users of the internet and a prime target for indirect marketing from businesses making viral videos, was met with US governmental disapproval. The Biden administration in 2024 enacted a law that required its Chinese parent company, Bytedance, to sell "its Tiktok app to an American buyer or be banned" (Chukwuma et al., 2024).

US national security, accounts of misinformation and disinformation, mental health, data privacy were cited, with the final decision getting a reprieve until April 2025 by the new US administration.

Such concerns of course are cited for other internet social platforms such as Facebook, Youtube, Instagram etc that are nevertheless controlled by the US and which have a huge financial turnover as well as great influence on their users while collecting statistics about their usage.

The intersection of geopolitical security and business strategy is again laid bare.

Geopolitical Business, Energy and Raw Materials

Natural resources play a central role in geopolitics and the resulting actions to attain them are of critical importance when dealing with global events and practices and how should business approach them. The modern global economy could absolutely not work without resources while a special category of materials, called Critical Raw Materials are of great importance to digital transformation, energy transition and technological development.

Critical raw materials (CRM) are raw materials of high economic importance to the EU, with a high risk of supply disruption due to the high degree of supply concentration and the lack of adequate and affordable substitutes.

The European economy is very vulnerable because of its extreme dependence on China to procure them and according to the European Commision CRM's are "of high importance to the European Union (EU) economy and of high risk associated with their supply" (Gómez et al., 2024).

Such Critical raw materials are lithium, vanadium, phosphorus, nickel, helium, strontium, graphite, cobalt and many others, with thirty-four of those identified by the EU (EU, 2025a). Certain CRM's have complex production requirements with evolving need of use, making their supply chain much higher in risk.

As far as business strategy is concerned CRM's are used in many products ranging from everyday appliances to major hardware that all play a role in everyday life and are commodities of great interest to the business commodity, whether in the manufacturing or commercial or other sectors.

Electric vehicles for example use lithium, cobalt, nickel amongst others, semiconductors use silicon metal, while aeronautics manufacturing uses magnesium, scandium amongst others. Such hardware necessary to energy transition as wind turbines use boron and strong magnets for generating power and "require significant quantities of CRMs such as neodymium and praseodymium, dysprosium, niobium, borates, and cobalt" (David et al., 2021).

Indicatively and in order to show the geopolitical considerations at play, China provides 100% of the EU's supply of heavy rare earth elements, Turkey meets 98% of the EU's boron needs while South Africa meets 71% of the EU's platinum needs(EU, 2025a).

Those international actors that supply such difficult to find commodities will have a disproportionate geopolitical leverage to other international actors and their behaviour will have to be catered for.

China for example can leverage the supply of these critical raw materials in order to influence global trade, favourable trade practices and foster diplomatic relations while making inroads to markets that may have been far less generous in allowing Chinese influence if their needs in CRM's did not dictate such a cooperation.

The global market for critical raw materials (CRMs) is heavily reliant on China, which holds a dominant position in their production and supply. China accounts for 100% of the world's heavy rare earth elements (HREEs), 91% of magnesium, 94% of gallium, 86% of tungsten, 85% of light rare earth elements (LREEs), 83% of germanium, 79% of phosphorus, and 76% of silicon metal (European Commission: Directorate-General for Internal Market, Entrepreneurship and SMEs et al., 2023).

As the primary supplier of more than twenty different CRMs, China maintains a major strategic position in the global market and global affairs while leveraging its dominance to strengthen its diplomatic influence on the international stage.

A similar situation also applies to clean energy technologies with components of solar and wind energy that are in need of CRM's that can be supplied by China.

A characteristic example of the geopolitical volatility and associated business risks involved in such a market is that export quotas set by China on neodymium and dysprosium, both key materials for offshore wind installations "in 2011 led to an increase in their prices by more than 1500% and 3500% respectively" (Gomez & Basterra, 2024).

Such arrangements leave China with disproportionate negotiating business power and leverage while allowing it to even hinder technological development in other countries that may require these CRM's in ample quantities in order to further their technological knowledge in a specialised field, let alone manufacturing on a large scale of suitable products for the market.

Technological innovation is thus also controlled by CRM availability.

The growing global focus on critical raw materials (CRMs) is closely tied to the increasing interest in the role green hydrogen may play in the energy transition. Produced via electrolysis with the aid of CRM-based technologies, green hydrogen can be entirely sustainable. According to the International Energy Agency (IEA), low-emissions hydrogen "can help to decarbonise a range of sectors, including heavy industry and long-distance transport, where it has proven difficult to reduce emissions" (International Energy Agency, 2025).

Geopolitical Risks and the Business Approach

Trade wars and tariffs have an immediate impact on supply chains, as countries may impose tariffs, create barriers or being generally recalcitrant to external trade. These restrictions force businesses to adapt their sourcing and shipping strategies, often resulting in higher costs and delays.

They also force businesses to reorient themselves as to their prospective markets leading to possible loss of short-term income and the need for new investment to execute the re-orientation. Businesses find it harder to plan and manage their supply chains.

Similarly, political instability and sanctions can significantly disrupt supply chains. The US-China trade war is a prime example of this (Chukwuma et al., 2024). Government changes and political unrest create uncertainty, while sanctions imposed on certain countries compel companies to seek alternative partners, routes, and markets.

Pandemics, as exemplified by COVID-19, demonstrate how health crises can severely disrupt global supply chains. Covid 19 "impacted supply chains, organisations and industries as a whole creating severe risks" (Younis et al., 2023).

Production slowdowns, transportation challenges, and shortages of essential goods highlight the vulnerability of interconnected markets during such crises.

Natural disasters also play a crucial role in supply chain disruptions. Extreme weather events—such as hurricanes, floods, and wildfires—can halt production and disrupt transportation networks. As climate change intensifies, these weather-related disruptions are expected to become more frequent and severe.

Energy shortages present another critical challenge for the global supply chain, affecting the production, transport, supply, and consumption of both goods and services. In addition to these factors, illicit financial flows and broader geopolitical tensions further complicate supply chain stability, influencing trade policies and market access on a global scale.

A Geopolitical Approach to Business

It is now evident that geopolitics does matter to business and their long-term prospects. Nevertheless, business owners, board members, CEO's are not in place because they are political scientists, deeply versed to the minutiae of geopolitics.

They are professionals invested in their profession without necessarily any knowledge of the greater things that influence their business on a global scale.

Certain best practices can be implemented in how should business approach geopolitics.

Geopolitical analysis should be incorporated into major business decisions to mitigate risks associated with such issues as political instability, trade regulations and tariffs, problems to the supply chain.

Leadership should be educated accordingly and kept current of vital current events that may shape the future and affect the way their business interacts with the rest of the world.

Directors, board members, experts within the company, owners, should be prepared and schooled over geopolitical risks.

While it is improbable that they will become masters of it, since this is not their primary function, such education will enhance organisational resilience and allow them to better evaluate the markets they are competing in.

The evaluation of the markets a business is engaged in according to their geopolitical significance and emerging risks is another facet of a best practice for business to promote its operations and prioritize investment of resources.

Strategic foresight is another best practice that should be employed by business that understands the nature of geopolitics. Modelling various scenarios according to geopolitical tensions, either presently evolving or probable, addressing supply chain disruptions, consumer demand are all part of a sound business approach in protecting its market position and its prospects.

The integration of technology as an agent of change, with digital emerging technologies set to revolutionise many aspects of human activities, with Artificial Intelligence for example set to bridge the gap in incomplete information among actors in the international system(Sticher, 2024) is another best practice for businesses influenced by geopolitics.

Future proofing and managing the geopolitical security shifts, potential trends and changes is the name of the game for a resilient business circumnavigating the modern global business environment.

REFERENCES

Bardalai, A. K. (2024). On the Geoeconomics Drivers of International Conflicts Global Political Economy, Geopolitics and International Security: The World in Permacrisis. In Mishra, O., & Sen, S. (Eds.), (pp. 93–112). Springer Nature Singapore., DOI: 10.1007/978-981-97-2231-0_6

Bockmann, M. W. (2024). *China, Russia ships get free pass from Houthis to transit Red Sea.* https://www.lloydslist.com/LL1150561/China-Russia-ships-get-free-pass-from-Houthis-to-transit-Red-Sea

Bretschger, L., & Pittel, K. (2020). Twenty Key Challenges in Environmental and Resource Economics. *Environmental and Resource Economics*, *77*(4), 725–750. DOI: 10.1007/s10640-020-00516-y PMID: 33082623

Chukwuma, N. A., Ngoc, L. M., & Mativenga, P. (2024). The US-China trade war: Interrogating globalisation of technology. *Cogent Social Sciences*, *10*(1), 2365509. DOI: 10.1080/23311886.2024.2365509

Cochrane, L., & Zaidan, E. (2024). Shifting global dynamics: An empirical analysis of BRICS + expansion and its economic, trade, and military implications in the context of the G7. *Cogent Social Sciences*, *10*(1), 2333422. DOI: 10.1080/23311886.2024.2333422

Comments, S. (2018). Strategic rivalries around the Bab el-Mandeb Strait. *Strategic Comments*, *24*(4), viii–x. DOI: 10.1080/13567888.2018.1485341

David, M., Lyth, S. M., Lindner, R., & Harrington, G. F. (2021). Critical Raw Materials Future-Proofing Fuel Cells: Critical Raw Material Governance in Sustainable Energy. In David, M., Lyth, S. M., Lindner, R., & Harrington, G. F. (Eds.), (pp. 15–33). Springer International Publishing., DOI: 10.1007/978-3-030-76806-5_2

Dwyer, P. G. (2008). Self-Interest versus the Common Cause: Austria, Prussia and Russia against Napoleon. *The Journal of Strategic Studies*, *31*(4), 605–632. DOI: 10.1080/01402390802088440

EU. (2025a). *An EU critical raw materials act for the future of EU supply chains.* https://www.consilium.europa.eu/en/infographics/critical-raw-materials/

EU. (2025b). *EUNAVFOR ASPIDES.* https://www.eeas.europa.eu/eunavfor-aspides_en?s=410381

Fioretti, M., Saint-Jean, V., & Smith, S. C. (2024). *NGO Activism: Exposure vs. Influence.* In. https://arxiv.org/abs/2411.06875

Gomez, J. F., & Basterra, M. L. (2024). Critical Raw Materials and Strategic Relations between the EU and China: The Role of the EU Critical Raw Materials Act. In Li, Y., & Leandro, S. (Eds.), *The Palgrave Handbook on China-Europe-Africa Relations*. Palgrave. DOI: 10.1007/978-981-97-5640-7_13

Gómez, J. F., Basterra, M. L., Sánchez, J. M., & Mosquera-López, S. (2024). Critical Raw Materials and Strategic Relations between the EU and China: The Role of the EU Critical Raw Materials Act The Palgrave Handbook on China-Europe-Africa Relations. In Li, Y., Leandro, F. J. B. S., Tavares da Silva, J., & Rodrigues, C. (Eds.), (pp. 271–300). Springer Nature Singapore., DOI: 10.1007/978-981-97-5640-7_13

Götz, E., & Staun, J. (2022). Why Russia attacked Ukraine: Strategic culture and radicalized narratives. *Contemporary Security Policy*, *43*(3), 482–497. DOI: 10.1080/13523260.2022.2082633

International Energy Agency. (2025). *Hydrogen*. https://www.iea.org/energy-system/low-emissions-fuels/hydrogen

Jha, S., Bhushan, S., & Nirola, N. (2024). Is geopolitical risk always detrimental to economic growth? *Economic Change and Restructuring*, *57*(2), 25. DOI: 10.1007/s10644-024-09585-1

Juneau, T. (2024). How War in Yemen Transformed the Iran-Houthi Partnership. *Studies in Conflict and Terrorism*, *47*(3), 278–300. DOI: 10.1080/1057610X.2021.1954353

Kaim, M., & Stanzel, A. (2022). The rise of China and NATO's Strategic Concept. *04*.

Kaufmann, D. (2024). *Rising shipping costs hit global trade hard*. https://www.dw.com/en/rising-shipping-costs-hit-global-trade-hard/a-69586965

Kroet, C. (2024). *Eleven EU countries took 5G security measures to ban Huawei, ZTE*. https://www.euronews.com/next/2024/08/12/eleven-eu-countries-took-5g-security-measures-to-ban-huawei-zte

Landesz, T. (2023). Future of Geopolitics. In *Future Intelligence*. https://library.oapen.org/bitstream/handle/20.500.12657/76732/1/978-3-031-36382-5.pdf#page=50

Levy, J. S., & Mulligan, W. (2017). Shifting power, preventive logic, and the response of the target: Germany, Russia, and the First World War. *The Journal of Strategic Studies*, *40*(5), 731–769. DOI: 10.1080/01402390.2016.1242421

Mackinder, H. J. (1904). The Geographical Pivot of History. *The Geographical Journal*, *23*(4), 421–437. DOI: 10.2307/1775498

Mutschler, M., Bales, M., & Meininghaus, E. (2024). The impact of precision strike technology on the warfare of non-state armed groups: Case studies on Daesh and the Houthis. *Small Wars & Insurgencies*, *35*(7), 1123–1150. DOI: 10.1080/09592318.2024.2319216

Narine, S. (2023). The problem of a "rules-based international order": The significance of the non-Western world's restrained response to the Russia-Ukraine war. *Canadian Foreign Policy*, *29*(3), 301–316. DOI: 10.1080/11926422.2023.2193420

Nazir, S., Sohag, K., & Mariev, O. (2025). Geopolitical Risk and Trade Reorientation Dynamics: A Comparative Study. *Emerging Markets Finance & Trade*, •••, 1–22. DOI: 10.1080/1540496X.2025.2451188

Norton, B. (2025). *BRICS expands to 54.6% of world population by adding Nigeria, Africa's most populous country*. https://geopoliticaleconomy.com/2025/01/19/brics-expands-population-nigeria-africa/

Patrice, C., & Mamadou, T. (2024). How does consumer quality misperception change European Union antidumping actions? *Review of World Economics*, *160*(4), 1247–1275. DOI: 10.1007/s10290-024-00553-5

Piroska, D., & Epstein, R. A. (2023). Stalled by design: New paradoxes in the European Union's single financial market. *Journal of European Integration*, *45*(1), 181–201. DOI: 10.1080/07036337.2022.2154344

Reuters. (2024). *Greek military ship intercepts two Houthi drones in the Red Sea*. https://www.reuters.com/world/greek-military-ship-intercepts-two-houthi-drones-red-sea-2024-04-25/

Rosenberg, M. (2024). Geopolitics and Business Strategy The Palgrave Handbook of Contemporary Geopolitics. In Cope, Z. (Ed.), (pp. 1037–1054). Springer Nature Switzerland., DOI: 10.1007/978-3-031-47227-5_52

Sarpong, S. (2021). Geopolitics of Natural Resources The Palgrave Handbook of Corporate Social Responsibility. In Crowther, D., & Seifi, S. (Eds.), (pp. 1131–1151). Springer International Publishing., DOI: 10.1007/978-3-030-42465-7_15

Shen, M., & Yang, M. (2024). Are Geopolitical Risks Fuelling Trade Protectionism? *Defence and Peace Economics*, *35*(8), 1120–1140. DOI: 10.1080/10242694.2024.2364320

Silva, J. D. (2025). *Trade war escalates as Trump metal tariffs take effect*. https://www.bbc.com/news/articles/cx2r3md0j84o

Spykman, N. J. (2007). *America's Strategy in World Politics: The United States and the Balance of Power* (1st ed.). Routledge., https://doi.org/https://doi.org/10.4324/9781315082431

Stern, R. (2024). Technology Combats Supply Chain Disruptions. *Research Technology Management*, *67*(5), 2–4. DOI: 10.1080/08956308.2024.2370224

Sticher, V. (2024). War and peace in the age of AI. *British Journal of Politics and International Relations*, •••, 1–9. DOI: 10.1177/13691481241293066

Stuenkel, O., & Treadwell, M. (2024). *Why Is Saudi Arabia Hedging Its BRICS Invite?*https://carnegieendowment.org/emissary/2024/11/brics-saudi-arabia-hedging-why?lang=en

Tuathail, G. Ó. (1996). *Critical Geopolitics The Politics of Writing Global Space*. Routledge.

Vihma, A., & Wigell, M. (2016). Unclear and present danger: Russia's geoeconomics and the Nord Stream II pipeline. *Global Affairs*, *2*(4), 377–388. DOI: 10.1080/23340460.2016.1251073

Wegner, B. (1990). The road to defeat: The German campaigns in Russia 1941–43. *The Journal of Strategic Studies*, *13*(1), 105–127. DOI: 10.1080/01402399008437403

World Bank. (2024). *Growth in the Middle East and North Africa: MENA upadate*. https://www.worldbank.org/en/region/mena/publication/middle-east-and-north-africa-economic-update

Younis, H., Alsharairi, M., Younes, H., & Sundarakani, B. (2023). The impact of COVID-19 on supply chains: Systematic review and future research directions. *Operations Research*, *23*(3), 48. DOI: 10.1007/s12351-023-00790-w

KEY TERMS AND DEFINITIONS

Geopolitics: The study of how geography, politics, and power interact on a global scale, influencing international relations and strategic decision-making. It examines territorial disputes, resource control, and global influence.

Geoeconomics: The use of economic tools, policies, and strategies to achieve geopolitical objectives, such as sanctions, trade agreements, and infrastructure investments.

Geopolitical Risks: Potential threats to stability and security on the global level that impact economies, markets and global relations.

Critical Raw Material (CRM): A raw material essential for economic and technological development, with high supply risks due to scarcity, geopolitical factors, or limited production sources.

BRICS: An economic and loose political alliance between Brasil, Russia, India, China, South Africa initially that had more members added.

Tariffs: Taxes or duties imposed on imported or exported goods by governments to regulate trade and protect domestic industries. Tariffs are also employed as tools in trade wars and thus have a geopolitical impact.

Multipolar: A view of the world where global order is distributed between multiple global actors with global influence, rather than having a superpower dominating the world system.

Chapter 2
Continuous Monitoring and Updating of Security Strategies Based on the Evolution of Threats in Contemporary Geopolitical Relations

Eldar Šaljić
https://orcid.org/0000-0002-5751-3419
American University in the Emirates, UAE

Dusko Tomic
https://orcid.org/0000-0001-8551-098X
American University in the Emirates, UAE

ABSTRACT

This dissertation investigates a pressing challenge: whether keeping security measures under constant review helps counter the ever-evolving threats from today's geopolitical shifts. Many current security setups fall behind, often too slow in catching new threats, putting both national and international safety at risk. Instead of sticking with rigid models, the study blends case studies with expert insights from international relations and security studies. It shows that gathering timely threat data and making on-the-fly policy tweaks strengthens our response. The findings suggest that organizations relying on flexible, continuously updated security frameworks build better resilience and respond more nimbly to sudden geopolitical twists. The impact of these strategies stretches beyond defense, hinting that similar approaches could

DOI: 10.4018/979-8-3693-5583-1.ch002

benefit fields like healthcare, where rapid reactions to emerging crises are crucial. This research argues for continuous monitoring not only for defense but also in public health, advocating for an integrated safeguard in today's unpredictable world.

INTRODUCTION

Global security isn't what it once was. Nations now interact in ways that blur old boundaries, and this fresh reality mixes cutting-edge tech with challenges like cyber attacks, terrorism, and power struggles in ways that upend the traditional playbook (Perera C et al., 2013). Over the past few decades, this blend of modern technology and shifting threats has exposed flaws in outdated security setups, leaving both national and international defenses vulnerably exposed (King G et al., 2013). In many cases, the existing systems simply don't catch up fast enough when new dangers show up, which is a serious worry (Emerson K et al., 2011). This research takes a closer look at whether keeping an eye on these changes and tweaking our strategies on the fly might be the answer; essentially, it explores a new plan that uses real-time data collection paired with flexible policy adjustments—an approach that aims to tackle the surprise factors of today's risks (Kraay A et al., 2010).The study also tests out this idea by diving into real-world examples, blending case studies and chats with experts in international relations and security studies (Weeks J, 2008). Its significance comes twofold: it lays down a theoretical base to argue that security can't be rigid while also offering down-to-earth tips for decision makers trying to preserve national safety amid modern challenges (N/A, 2022). With threats growing ever more tangled and connected, rethinking how we plan and apply security measures is clearly needed. By nurturing a mindset that's open to constant change, the findings might even cut risks down more effectively and contribute to a safer global scene. Ultimately, this dissertation isn't just about pushing academic debates on security strategy—it's also about providing real, usable insights for those on the frontlines tasked with protecting national interests in these uncertain, rapidly shifting times (Yogesh K Dwivedi et al., 2022).

LITERATURE REVIEW

National security these days is in a real state of flux. Threats seem to come from all sides—cyber attacks, terrorism, even health crises like COVID-19—and that means our old, rigid defense plans just don't cut it anymore. Instead of relying solely on military might, today's challenges call for blending in public health measures and smart technology solutions (Monitoring C and Updating of Based SS on the Evolution of Threats in Relations CG, 2025). Many researchers now stress that keeping our security plans under constant review is vital if we're to protect our national interests.Studies keep hammering home the need for proactive measures. They show that state-backed cyber intrusions and fake news campaigns are undermining both stability and public trust (Thomas P Boeckel V et al., 2015). When you look at institutions like the UK's National Cyber Security Centre or the impressive digital identity innovations out of Estonia, it becomes clear that integrated, flexible security models offer a way forward Christopher M Weible et al., 2020). Plus, emerging tools such as artificial intelligence are proving to be game changers in spotting risks early. All this evidence suggests that a multidisciplinary, tech-savvy approach—one that mixes defense with health expertise—is increasingly essential (Weeks J, 2008).Of course, even with these advances, there are some obvious blind spots. Researchers seem to focus a lot on technological fixes and top-down government strategies, while international cooperation often doesn't get nearly as much attention. In our tightly connected world, a piecemeal response won't suffice; what's really needed is a collaborative framework that pools expertise and resources across borders (Yogesh K Dwivedi et al., 2022).

And as threats keep evolving, there's a noticeable lack of long-term studies to show whether these adaptive strategies work well across different geopolitical settings (Fawzy S et al., 2020).In the sections that follow, I'll explore several big ideas from the literature. For instance, security setups must now be agile and ready for change—they're not just about stacking up military defenses but also about embracing frameworks like the NIST Cybersecurity Framework to boost threat detection (Christopher M Weible et al., 2020). Pulling together widespread research paints a picture of current practices while underscoring why a continual process of evaluation and revision is absolutely key.

As countries work to remain resilient in a global village, addressing these research gaps could offer priceless guidance for policy makers and security experts (Margaret E Kruk et al., 2018)(Sangam L Dwivedi et al., 2017). Ultimately, this discussion aims to deepen our understanding of how evolving international ties impact national security and why constant vigilance is non-negotiable (Nazarenko S et al., 2024). If you look back at earlier work, it's interesting to see how notions of security have morphed over time. Not long ago, the focus was squarely on traditional military threats and fixed defense postures (Emerson K et al., 2011).

But starting in the late twentieth century and moving into the new millennium, scholars began to recognize that non-traditional hazards—like cyber warfare and terrorism—demand fresh strategies (Emerson K et al., 2011). By weaving in insights from fields as varied as technology and public health, researchers have gradually shifted toward advocating for more nimble security frameworks (King G et al., 2013). Recent work demonstrates that cutting-edge tech, including artificial intelligence, plays a pivotal role in enhancing our ability to detect and respond to threats (Weeks J, 2008), Estonia's digital identity system is a prime example of modern cybersecurity in action (Yogesh K Dwivedi et al., 2022), and the UK's approach via the National Cyber Security Centre shows a real commitment to keeping security agile and responsive (Christopher M Weible et al., 2020).The COVID-19 pandemic only made it clearer that the way we think about security needs to break free from traditional boundaries. When crises cross borders, strategies must also—mixing health insights with security planning becomes essential (Margaret E Kruk et al., 2018). A number of studies now insist that solid international cooperation is the only effective way to meet these transnational challenges, advocating for a proactive stance that builds societal resilience amid rapidly shifting threats (Stevan E Hobfoll et al., 2017).

The research timeline unmistakably shows an increasing call for constant adaptation in our security approaches, especially in an ever more interconnected world. There's no shortage of themes running through this body of work. Researchers keep returning to the idea that modern security is an intricate blend of different elements—public health concerns intermixed with the threats from cyber warfare and terrorism (King G et al., 2013).

Numerous case studies underline that staying on one's toes through regular updating and using advanced tech like artificial intelligence is critical for spotting threats and mounting effective defenses (Emerson K et al., 2011). In one study, for example, a proactive, flexible posture is described as vital for protecting national interests and strengthening community resilience (Perera C et al., 2013).Cybersecurity urgency is a constant refrain, particularly when you consider the rising tide of state-sponsored attacks and disinformation campaigns. Estonia's secure digital systems frequently serve as a model for what modern cybersecurity should look like (Weeks J, 2008). Equally, frameworks like the NIST Cybersecurity Framework offer a structured way to build robust defenses against shifting threats (Yogesh K Dwivedi et al., 2022). International collaboration, too, gets a nod—many scholars argue for a united approach to transnational challenges as the only way to secure a stable future in a closely linked world (Christopher M Weible et al., 2020). These varied insights come together to stress that adapting our security strategies is not optional but essential in today's volatile geopolitical arena.Researchers have tapped both quantitative and qualitative methods to shed light on these issues. Data-driven analyses make a strong case for agility—statistical monitoring proves crucial when anticipating risks like cyber warfare or pandemics such as COVID-19 (King G et al., 2013). Meanwhile, qualitative case studies—like the deep dive into Estonia's digital identity system—offer rich insights into how modern technologies can strengthen security frameworks (Kraay A et al., 2010). Combining these approaches gives us a fuller, more nuanced picture of the challenges and potential responses in the security domain.Studies that blend numerical data with narrative detail show just how critical a multilayered view of security is.

Adding technological assessments to in-depth case studies creates a richer understanding of what's needed on the ground (Perera C et al., 2013). Frameworks like NIST not only provide theory but also offer practical guidelines for ongoing threat monitoring and response building (Weeks J, 2008). Ultimately, these mixed methodologies underline the growing need for collaborative, smart, and proactive security strategies.A final, recurring point in the literature is that no nation can face modern threats alone. There's a clear insistence on sharing data and working together, which is seen as vital for mounting any effective defense (Yogesh K Dwivedi et al., 2022).

This mix of methods and ideas neatly encapsulates how our security challenges are evolving—and why only an adaptive, cooperative approach can hope to keep pace.Reflecting on the broader theories behind these trends, it's evident that flexibility is more than a buzzword. Scholars widely discuss the need to continuously update security measures, a call echoed by ideas that weave in public health as part of the national security fabric (Perera C et al., 2013). In the classic debate between realism and constructivism, realists argue that nations are forced to refine their strategies nonstop in a fiercely competitive world (Perera C et al., 2013), while constructivists remind us that social and political contexts deeply shape the nature of security threats (King G et al., 2013).

Estonia's success story in proactive cybersecurity, for instance, clearly shows that understanding local context can make a significant difference (Emerson K et al., 2011).Theoretical frameworks like the NIST Cybersecurity Framework lend weight to the argument for using predictive analytics and artificial intelligence as key tools in our security arsenal (Kraay A et al., 2010). What emerges from combining these perspectives is a strong case for a multidimensional security strategy—one that goes well beyond traditional military concerns to address new, global challenges. Many researchers argue that relying on just one approach is simply inadequate in our interconnected world (Weeks J, 2008).To bring it all together, the bulk of the literature makes a compelling argument: we need to overhaul our security strategies by embracing flexibility and advanced technology. With threats ranging from state-sponsored cyberattacks to global health emergencies like COVID-19, there's a pressing need for security frameworks that adapt quickly and efficiently (Monitoring C and Updating of Based SS on the Evolution of Threats in Relations CG, 2025). The integration of new technology—notably artificial intelligence—with tried-and-true military tactics is seen as a key step in building more resilient defenses (Perera C et al., 2013) Real-world examples, like Estonia's digital identity systems and the UK's NCSC, highlight how an integrated, adaptive approach can meet the challenges of today's dynamic threat landscape (Kraay A et al., 2010).

The overarching takeaway is that national security isn't just about military strength anymore. It's a complex mix that involves public health, technology, and even economic factors—all interacting in unpredictable ways (Yogesh K Dwivedi et al., 2022). Research strongly advocates for global cooperation, arguing that sharing expertise and resources is essential for tackling cross-border threats (Christopher M Weible et al., 2020).

Yet, despite all the progress in research, some significant gaps remain. Much of the current work zeroes in on technological and governmental solutions, with community engagement and public trust getting far less attention. Besides, there just aren't enough long-term studies to prove how well these adaptive measures work in various geopolitical settings (Margaret E Kruk et al., 2018). Looking ahead, future research should put more focus on building collaborative frameworks—ones that bring different stakeholders, including civil society, into the conversation about security policy.

It would also be smart to examine how social and economic conditions affect community resilience in the face of emerging threats (Sangam L Dwivedi et al., 2017). Plus, more empirical studies are needed to see how well public health measures mesh with national security plans when preparing for crises like pandemics (Brian C O'Neill et al., 2016). Researchers suggest that combining both quantitative data and qualitative insights will be the best way to capture the messy, interconnected picture of modern security (Chan A-W et al., 2013). In short, the research not only informs us about today's security challenges but also lays the groundwork for future strategies. Embracing an adaptive, technology-driven approach—and acknowledging that our world is more interconnected than ever—is key to navigating modern threats. As our geopolitical environment continues to shift, there is a persistent call for constant improvement, urging policy makers and practitioners to stay vigilant and proactive even when times get a bit messy (Nazarenko S et al., 2024). All these findings serve as a kind of roadmap for developing security frameworks that meet the intricate demands of the 21st century.

METHODOLOGY

Global security is changing fast these days, and keeping up with it isn't a simple task. With unexpected challenges like cyber attacks or even major health crises—think COVID-19 (Monitoring C and Updating of Based SS on the Evolution of Threats in Relations CG, 2025)—our current systems sometimes lag behind. This study digs into the core issue that many security setups just aren't quick enough when new, shifting threats hit (Perera C et al., 2013). The main aim is to build a plan that keeps a constant eye on security efforts, making national policies more agile and effective, in most cases (King G et al., 2013). It reflects today's idea of security that goes beyond one-dimensional fixes by mixing tech leaps, public health insights, and global teamwork (Emerson K et al., 2011).This approach stands out by blending hard numbers with real-life examples, using a mixed-methods formula that genuinely adds to security studies (Kraay A et al., 2010). We pulled together previous research, digging into extensive literature reviews and real-world data to spot what really works (Weeks J, 2008). For instance, looking at examples like Estonia's digital ID system and the UK's National Cyber Security Centre strategy offers a glimpse into how diverse security measures can be integrated successfully.

The analysis also crunches statistical data—sometimes a bit messily—to track threat trends with guides like the NIST Cybersecurity Framework (Yogesh K Dwivedi et al., 2022). Moreover, this method dives deep into entrenched vulnerabilities that have long hampered effective responses (Fawzy S et al., 2020), and it emphasizes, in most cases, how vital international collaboration is when handling threats that cross borders (Christopher M Weible et al., 2020. By involving various stakeholders, the study moves theoretical debates forward while giving policymakers practical insights to tweak security adaptations (Margaret E Kruk et al., 2018). Ultimately, mixing qualitative impressions with solid quantitative analysis paints a comprehensive picture of today's evolving threat landscape and offers well-rounded recommendations for future policies (Stevan E Hobfoll et al., 2017)(Sangam L Dwivedi et al., 2017). This methodology section lays out a roadmap that not only fills current gaps but also breaks new ground with flexible, integrative checks for ongoing security assessments(Nazarenko S et al., 2024).

RESULTS

Today's world pushes nations to keep a constant eye on their defense plans because threats seem to shift from one moment to the next, coming from both state groups and rogue players. You can see this in how issues range wildly—from cyberattacks to health crises like the COVID-19 outbreak—which have pretty much turned old security ideas on their head (Monitoring C and Updating of Based SS on the Evolution of Threats in Relations CG, 2025). Research tends to show that security systems able to adapt quickly are key; data even suggests that countries using flexible threat models end up less exposed to attacks, which is pretty compelling (Perera C et al., 2013). Adding new tech, especially artificial intelligence, into the mix also seems to boost the system's knack for spotting risks early so that responses are more about prevention than scrambling after the fact (King G et al., 2013).

It's interesting, for instance, that when you compare different approaches, Estonia's focus on digital defenses appears to help it dodge major risks far better than those clinging to outdated, static policies (Emerson K et al., 2011).Many reports point out that while governments are aware of these shifting dangers, they often fall behind when it comes to updating their defenses, leaving noticeable gaps in protection (Kraay A et al., 2010).

Some analyses even show that when agencies join forces and work with private partners, the overall resilience grows considerably, even if the collaboration isn't always seamless (Weeks J, 2008). There's also a strong argument for more investment in cybersecurity infrastructure and public education about threats—steps seen as crucial in building a real culture of security within communities (Yogesh K Dwivedi et al., 2022). In fact, earlier studies have even estimated that failing to update cybersecurity measures can cost regions tens of billions annually, a figure that really stresses the need to act fast (Fawzy S et al., 2020).All these insights aren't just theoretical musings; they offer a practical roadmap for decision-makers.

Generally speaking, using detailed data to craft adaptable security strategies might be the ticket for nations to shore up their defenses better (Christopher M Weible et al., 2020). Overall, pulling these threads together paints a picture of modern states emerging from political pressures with security setups that are both tough and flexible, ready to face changing challenges (Sandra Díaz et al., 2019). And as things keep evolving, the conversation about security, tech integration, and forward-thinking policy is likely to keep adding new, valuable perspectives to the ongoing global debate (Margaret E Kruk et al., 2018).

DISCUSSION

Security issues in today's global scene simply don't stand still. Nations, it turns out, must keep changing gears constantly because threats are just as quick to evolve—especially as tech keeps shifting and shaking things up. One study shows that security strategies tend to work a lot better when their setups are looked over and tweaked on a regular basis. In many cases, countries that lean into flexible threat assessments and mix in modern tech like artificial intelligence not only seem less open to attacks but also get better at spotting risks before they fully unfold, pushing them to act early rather than scrambling later (Perera C et al., 2013). This kind of idea kind of echoes earlier work that points out how important it is to use tech for managing and diffusing dangers (King G et al., 2013).

A good example is Estonia's digital setup; its proactive, sometimes gritty, measures show, in no uncertain terms, that being ready in advance can really guard national interests (Emerson K et al., 2011). Then again, lots of studies have noted that many nations tend to drag their feet when it comes to adapting, which generally leaves them unprepared for a mix of challenges—be it cyberwarfare or even health crises like the COVID-19 situation (Kraay A et al., 2010). In fact, the research even highlights a kind of gap in current practices, suggesting that places with robust cooperation among agencies and a genuine handshake between the public and private sectors tend to manage risks better and come out more resilient Yogesh K Dwivedi et al., 2022).On a broader note, these findings speak to both the theory and the on-the-ground application of security measures.

They hint that better teamwork in government and beyond is key when handling issues that cross borders (Fawzy S et al., 2020). Also, it seems reasonable to say that rethinking security to include not only military readiness but also health and cyber aspects opens up fresh avenues for improvement (Christopher M Weible et al., 2020). When you consider the staggering economic consequences of being unprepared—billions lost due to underinvesting in resilience, really—it underscores why moving towards flexible security is so urgent (Sandra Díaz et al., 2019). Plus, the research suggests that, without real commitment to beefing up cybersecurity infrastructure and spreading threat awareness through education, nations might just be leaving their doors wide open for attackers (Margaret E Kruk et al., 2018).All in all, this study lays out a kind of blueprint for why constant updates in security policies are non-negotiable, nudging policymakers to put resilience and cooperation at the top of their agendas in today's rather unpredictable geopolitical world (Sangam L Dwivedi et al., 2017). When you put these insights together, they offer a useful guide for future research and strategic planning—basically, showing that with combined efforts and steady watchfulness against emerging threats, nations might manage to carve out lasting stability amid all the unpredictability (Thomas P Boeckel V et al., 2015). In the end, tackling these issues will demand a real commitment to innovative practices and a dash of international cooperation to navigate the messy complexities of modern threats (Brian C O'Neill et al., 2016).

CONCLUSION

Continuous monitoring and updating of security plans is something our research keeps hammering home. Today's world—swirling with cyber warfare, terrorism and even health crises—demands that countries stay nimble rather than stick to old routines (Monitoring C and Updating of Based SS on the Evolution of Threats in Relations CG, 2025). The study dug into these emerging dangers in a way that wasn't just textbook; it mixed case studies with hands-on tech assessments to show, quite clearly, that blending in new tech like artificial intelligence is key to keeping our defenses sharp (Perera C et al., 2013). It turns out that nations wedded to flexible threat models tend to work through complex dangers more predictably—just take Estonia's digital security setup as a real-world example (King G et al., 2013). The findings really shake up our traditional view of security, nudging both scholars and policymakers to see public health and cybersecurity as part of the same family, not separate issues (Emerson K et al., 2011). In most cases, this means rethinking how we mix proactive planning with everyday societal needs, which might lead to a more rounded and practical response to looming threats (Weeks J, 2008).Looking ahead, researchers are generally encouraged to expand on this work by exploring real-time data monitoring systems and boosting collaboration between government bodies and private partners—if not, our national resilience might just lag behind emerging challenges. There's also a nudge towards forming new frameworks that make international cooperation a reality, paving the way for resource-sharing and knowledge exchanges across borders (Yogesh K Dwivedi et al., 2022). These next steps are as much about enriching our collective understanding as they are about arming policymakers with practical strategies. The idea is clear: craft security frameworks that can shift quickly as new threats pop up, making them both effective and responsive (Christopher M Weible et al., 2020). Fine-tuning adaptive strategies is crucial, especially now that threats in our globalized era evolve so rapidly—research in this area could really fill the existing gaps (Sandra Díaz et al., 2019). Ultimately, the goal remains to build lasting stability with a proactive security posture that isn't just stiff or outdated; it's a living, breathing approach to handling the messy, complex challenges of modern threats (Stevan E Hobfoll et al., 2017).

REFERENCES

Chan, A.-W., Tetzlaff, J. M., Gotzsche, P. C., Altman, D. G., Mann, H., Berlin, J. A., Dickersin, K., Hrobjartsson, A., Schulz, K. F., Parulekar, W. R., Krleza-Jeric, K., Laupacis, A., & Moher, D. (2013). SPIRIT 2013 explanation and elaboration: Guidance for protocols of clinical trials. Volume(346), e7586-e7586. *BMJ (Clinical Research Ed.), 346*(jan08 15), e7586. Advance online publication. DOI: 10.1136/bmj.e7586 PMID: 23303884

Core Writing Team, P. (2014). Climate change 2014: synthesis report. Contribution of working groups I, II and III to the fifth assessment report of the intergovernmental panel on climate change, 151.

Díaz, S., Settele, J., Brondízio, E. S., Ngo, H. T., Agard, J., Arneth, A., Balvanera, P., Brauman, K. A., Butchart, S. H. M., Chan, K. M. A., Garibaldi, L. A., Ichii, K., Liu, J., Subramanian, S. M., Midgley, G. F., Miloslavich, P., Molnár, Z., Obura, D., Pfaff, A., & Zayas, C. N. (2019). Pervasive human-driven decline of life on Earth points to the need for transformative change. Volume(366). *Science, 366*(6471), eaax3100. Advance online publication. DOI: 10.1126/science.aax3100 PMID: 31831642

Dwivedi, S. L., Van Bueren, E. L., Ceccarelli, S., Grando, S., Upadhyaya, H. D., & Ortíz, R. (2017). Diversifying Food Systems in the Pursuit of Sustainable Food Production and Healthy Diets. Volume(22), 842-856. *Trends in Plant Science*. Advance online publication. DOI: 10.1016/j.tplants.2017.06.011 PMID: 28716581

Dwivedi, Y. K., Hughes, L., Baabdullah, A. M., Ribeiro-Navarrete, S., Giannakis, M., Al-Debei, M. M., & Dennehy, D.. (2022). Metaverse beyond the hype: Multidisciplinary perspectives on emerging challenges, opportunities, and agenda for research, practice and policy. Volume(66), 102542-102542. *International Journal of Information Management*. Advance online publication. DOI: 10.1016/j.ijinfomgt.2022.102542

Emerson, K., Nabatchi, T., & Balogh, S. (2011). An Integrative Framework for Collaborative Governance. Volume(22), 1-29. *Journal of Public Administration: Research and Theory*. Advance online publication. DOI: 10.1093/jopart/mur011

Fawzy, S., Osman, A. I., Doran, J., & Rooney, D. W. (2020). Strategies for mitigation of climate change: A review. Volume(18), 2069-2094. *Environmental Chemistry Letters*. Advance online publication. DOI: 10.1007/s10311-020-01059-w

Ferreira, F. H., Messina, J., Rigolini, J., López-Calva, L. F., Lugo, M. A., Vakis, R., & Ló, L. F. (2012). *Economic mobility and the rise of the Latin American middle class*. World Bank Publications.

Hobfoll, S. E., Halbesleben, J. R. B., Neveu, J.-P., & Westman, M. (2017). Conservation of Resources in the Organizational Context: The Reality of Resources and Their Consequences. Volume(5), 103-128. *Annual Review of Organizational Psychology and Organizational Behavior*. Advance online publication. DOI: 10.1146/annurev-orgpsych-032117-104640

King, G., Pan, J., & Roberts, M. E. (2013). How Censorship in China Allows Government Criticism but Silences Collective Expression. Volume(107), 326-343. *The American Political Science Review*. Advance online publication. DOI: 10.1017/S0003055413000014

Kraay, A., Kaufmann, D., & Mastruzzi, M. (2010). The worldwide governance indicators: Methodology and analytical issues. *World Bank Policy Research Working Paper*. Advance online publication. DOI: 10.1596/1813-9450-5430

Kruk, M. E., Gage, A., Arsenault, C., Jordan, K., Leslie, H. H., Roder-DeWan, S., Adeyi, O., Barker, P., Daelmans, B., Doubova, S. V., English, M., García-Elorrio, E., Guanais, F., Gureje, O., Hirschhorn, L. R., Jiang, L., Kelley, E., Lemango, E. T., Liljestrand, J., & Pate, M. (2018). High-quality health systems in the Sustainable Development Goals era: Time for a revolution. Volume(6), e1196-e1252. *The Lancet. Global Health*, *6*(11), e1196–e1252. Advance online publication. DOI: 10.1016/S2214-109X(18)30386-3 PMID: 30196093

Nazarenko, S., Sharyi, V., & Kifin, O. (2024) Prospects for the Integration of Ukraine's National Security Mechanisms with the Collective Security Systems of the EU and NATO. Economic scope. doi: https://www.semanticscholar.org/paper/7185f2e034463f4b11b8caa56f232a0f0091014b

O'Neill, B. C., Kriegler, E., Riahi, K., Ebi, K. L., Hallegatte, S., Carter, T. R., & Mathur, R.. (2013). A new scenario framework for climate change research: The concept of shared socioeconomic pathways. Volume(122), 387-400. *Climatic Change*. Advance online publication. DOI: 10.1007/s10584-013-0905-2

O'Neill, B. C., Tebaldi, C., Van Vuuren, D. P., Eyring, V., Friedlingstein, P., Hurtt, G., & Sanderson, B. M. (2016). The scenario model intercomparison project (ScenarioMIP) for CMIP6. *Geoscientific Model Development*, *9*(9), 3461–3482.

Perera, C., Zaslavsky, A., Christen, P., & Georgakopoulos, D. (2013). Context Aware Computing for The Internet of Things: A Survey. Volume(16), 414-454. *IEEE Communications Surveys and Tutorials*. Advance online publication. DOI: 10.1109/SURV.2013.042313.00197

Van Boeckel, T. P., Brower, C., Gilbert, M., Grenfell, B. T., Levin, S. A., Robinson, T. P., Teillant, A., ... (2015) Global trends in antimicrobial use in food animals. Volume(112), 5649-5654. Proceedings of the National Academy of Sciences. DOI: 10.1073/pnas.1503141112

Weeks, J. (2008). Autocratic Audience Costs: Regime Type and Signaling Resolve. Volume(62). *International Organization*, *62*(1). Advance online publication. DOI: 10.1017/S0020818308080028

Weible, C. M., Nohrstedt, D., Cairney, P., Carter, D., Crow, D. A., Durnová, A., & Heikkila, T.. (2020). COVID-19 and the policy sciences: Initial reactions and perspectives. Volume(53), 225-241. *Policy Sciences*. Advance online publication. DOI: 10.1007/s11077-020-09381-4 PMID: 32313308

Chapter 3
Geopolitical Challenges: The Global Influence or Decline of Western Society: A New World Order or Rising Volatility?

Marios Panagiotis Efthymiopoulos
https://orcid.org/0000-0002-2277-0941
Neapolis University, Pafos, Cyprus

ABSTRACT

The global strategic, security, and political landscape is transforming significantly. A new security architecture is on the way to be established. The current chapter examines complex shifts in our attempt to exploit the current environment that is genuinely volatile and unclear. This chapter assumes that we all seem out of any global ideological purpose, considering the evolution of international affairs, including operational choices and a balance of power. This chapter explores how emerging forces use geopolitical realignments to technological innovations, politics, and demographic changes to redefine global power structures and possible solutions or challenges for the near or future positions. Are we in the West in decline, or is Western-centric dominance? Are we seeing the rise of new power centers? The chapter assesses current governance methods and the availability or absence of current organizations or institutions (based on our case studies). The role of energy resources, the impact of trade disputes and power balance, and technological advancements are reshaping international relations. New dynamics and new political realities are on the rise.

DOI: 10.4018/979-8-3693-5583-1.ch003

INTRODUCTION

The global strategic, security, and political landscape is transforming significantly. One that already impacts former balances, ideologies, and ways we comprehend security. We will eventually adapt to new realities. These realities will season for the years to come. The complex environment has given way to new security and strategic opportunities or further challenges and eventual change. Some may say a new security architecture is forthcoming. We have yet to define the exact outcome of this new security architecture. What will it comprise, who will the actors be, and who will benefit? Will this new security architecture result in an unbitter ceasefire at various levels and possibly peace? Or whether it will be one that will result in further instability and resentfulness? Will we witness pivoting in global politics with new actors and new landscapes?

The chapter examines some of these complex shifts. Global Affairs paradigm shifts that are taking place even while this chapter is being written. Volatility and constant change overrule current balances and current political situations. Time feeds volatility. Imbalances feed time.

By completing the current chapter (April 2025), I was concerned that any work written below may become obsolete. I consider that 'time has folded.' The scientific capability to analyze has been shortened. Considering the statements, this current chapter analysis is based on the shortest information gathered at a time scientific knowledge challenge competed by limited time to test things as they progress or develop. Any analysis or information as such may be disturbed the following day or become obsolete by unforeseen or unexpected variables and new paradigms from the global arena that may disrupt the strategic thinking of what is analyzed below.

In our attempt to understand the current environment, which we consider volatile and thus unstable, I believe that ideologies we all grew up with and many believed in have become ever more complex and possibly obsolete. Global political developments have led us to conclude that current political ideologies may no longer be relevant. Our world has become so complex (dependency and non-dependency simultaneously) that the world may not care about ideologies. Marking it as a world without ideology, political affiliation, or attached strings. Private interest is the leading actor—a world of individualism and, indeed, a world without social or global balance, respect, and possibly justice.

Per our topic of concern, I seek to examine, in effect, ways of governance, leadership, and decision-making to achieve a political understanding of what is happening around us. We are in dire need of an actual global balance of power. We may not know whether we need a bipolar or multipolar world whole of actors as things progress from the second trump presidency onwards (Donald Trump being the 47th Elected US President). But we need to comprehend the current environment in front of us concretely and ahead of us, which tends to become more complex than ever before. We must seek solutions in a specific timeframe as complexities and challenges multiply and become multidimensional (Lindberg, 1970).

In this chapter, I attempt to explore, at a strategic-holistic level, how current or emerging forces use geopolitical realignments to their national or alliance-based activities and interests. While individualism may take place. Interests change, or interests are short of the needs of an alliance or a collective of powers with a common objective or threat.

Technology's extensive use and innovation have given ample space and ways to further or deepen the above-mentioned political change and constant challenge—an actual challenge to the current state of societal structures, laws, and beliefs.

We should be cognizant that demographic changes (negative or positive) also influence us. It does influence global power shifts in the long term. Hence, many powers consider that demographics may eventually change the balance of power. Look at the IMEC agreement and India's relations with the EU (Banerjee, Singh, 2024), the Gulf Middle East (Das, 2024), and Israel and the US (Levitan, Reich, and Rynhold, 2025).

Demographic increase or decrease may define or redefine power politics, now and in the near future. Power structures seem to change positively, like India (Underwood & Paul, 2025), and others to be in question, such as the European Union (Leruth, 2024). Hence, what are the possible near or future positions or solutions for establishing a concrete world order? One that will be based on a collective approach rather than individualism? Will we, in turn, look at multipolar or bipolar collaborations and options, considering ongoing national and international security, safety, opportunities, challenges, known or not known variables, and paradigm shifts?

The chapter delves into current and new contexts and real-world examples in time. The chapter asks for a detailed overview of possible mechanisms of new drives of change to serve international affairs in practice in the near or long-term future.

This chapter could be a reasonable basis for further vital research. It seeks to expand further in various levels and chapters at the first opportunity. These are the new pillars of approach to international political affairs as fragility and volatility surround the chance for a secure and safe world, but that is undoubtedly not the case.

VOLATILITY VS. OPPORTUNITY

Strategic volatility, having made its appearance, threatens the balance and, more so, peace. The Western world is affected by it. Where-ever it may come from. Volatility creates constant instability. At the EU level, it also created reluctance to face challenges in its near abroad practically. To act. The EU has yet to ensure, both at home and overseas, lasting safety and stability, and hence, stable progress, regional or territorial, or near its proximity. As things in international affairs have progressed, we wanted to allow instability to flourish. And although an actual opportunity to establish a new security architecture is there, one that would possibly or at least regionally bring a balance, we are still reluctant to act.

Europe sees that any action for security may include foreseeing a 'supposed opportunity' (Jopp, Pollak, 2024), but there is an immediate need to secure non-traditional challenges. But again, our actions and moves are slow. Decisions are visionary and optimistic but do not reflect immediate security and strategic needs.

It can be said that Europe 27 is merely reacting to challenges in a very short-sighted way. Europe does not have foresight challenges and does not design the future well. Although visionary, it is not realistic in terms of needs. We wish to engage non-traditional allies but without specifications or requests. On the other hand, the opposite sides do come with requests and exchanges Oğurlu, 2024).

Europe is neither preventive nor pre-emptive in its approach to practice and actions. It considers strategic volatilities around the Western world that borders the European Union (which we are concerned with). However, the aim is not to solve the issue in the long term. These challenges have negatively affected the European Union overall, with continued financial inflation among other and popular negative opinions on the rise on and about moderate actors and political parties. Hence, we may see extreme political electoral parties coming into the forefront of their national politics sooner rather than later, as well as in EU-level designated politics.

Foreign challenges have become perpetually internalized. Europe has 'digested' outside issues and has become a European issue. And we wonder if this is a "trojan horse" to the EU. The EU needs a "political push" for a more globalized and more involved Europe. While challenges eventually brought to the surface the ill-readiness of Europe to act as an actual global actor and not solely as an international financial power, it is not too late to act and take firm national decisions for more Europe, with a more active approach and less of a bureaucratic approach. We have yet to see the European Union deciphering its capability from a financial power to a political and military power on a global scale.

The problem is that Europe seems to be re-active. Not pro-active. It lacks swift decision-making. We lack the actual leadership and vision of the future of what possibly could challenge stability and development. At this point, the security matrix's Strategic design and architecture do not stem from the European Continent and, therefore, the EU 27 member states. At the same time, dissatisfaction and disorientation between Western countries progress due to political emerged competition. We 'battle' between Western countries for financial, trade, and military power and might.

While the US has a new Presidency, the first moves by the 47th President of the USA, Donald Trump, such as proposing the annexation of Canada and Greenland, were not well received. It should also be considered no surprise with projected Trump policies ahead of things in case he is elected. Hence, a new order of things (at least as an attempt from the US side) was coming. The outputs of the USA's latest financial and political status versus the world do not leave room for thinking otherwise (Lammert, 2025). President Trump's actions are clearly 'unorthodox,' business-based, and lack the diplomatic 'language skill sets.' More so, he seems to enjoy the ways and levels of decision-making (Bell, 2025).

During his first cabinet assembly, President Trump stated that the EU was created to defeat the US presence (Fayet, Futter, Kühn, Kulesa, van Hooft & Bruusgaard, 2025). And as a European, I say we should be concerned. He sees Europe as a competitor, not an ally. He wants to reshape the trade balance and assumes that trade partition is no longer the game without the US controlling the overarching trade. Hence, renaming the Gulf of Mexico to the Gulf of Americas and taking control of sea trade straights such as the Panama Canal is only the start. There is yet more to come.

Trump attempts daily to "shock the markets." The world balances (if any), and at the same time, disturbs the collectivity of any alliance, the ethics, and morals in this case of the Euro-Atlantic and transatlantic relationships. However, the latter may not yet be the case. He assumes that US power is declining and, consequently, Western dominance, which entails a "Pax Americana," is no longer there. His actions testify to how one reshapes bilateral relations and trade collaborations by utilizing in its full capacity the mediation capabilities of power. It seems that regionally, President Trump wants to re-negotiate and re-ignite all US trade and presence in the European Continent, extend with non-EU regions, extending to the European Continent, the Euro-Atlantic area, and slowly make way to other regional ways and affairs in the Southeast Mediterranean, the Middle East, and beyond. With a later view of the fast East, looking at China.

It can be safely assumed that the European Union did not do its 'due diligence' on current and future challenges, coming right at the EU average citizen and governments. The European Union, being the area for the "Game of Thrones" for significant powers (China, Russia, and the USA), must be able to rely on its powers (Groitl, 2025). To self-be protected at all levels, both political and operational. Europe must realize its power and envision its future capabilities.

A possible Trump escalation of political, economic, and trade affairs, along with ongoing volatility around us and wars holding and spreading in our near abroad, may further jeopardize what the EU is meant to do in its region. We may not have faced the current situation and what may become a reality. The European Union lacks an immediate decision-making process and immediate practicality put into action. And any possible opponent knows about it. This chapter estimates that considering the lack of actual involvement as a powerhouse stemming from Europe will ultimately be seen as a point of extreme political parties on the rise that may require more sovereignty, more protective approaches, national safety, and exclusion from the 'current state of affairs'.

President Trump probably knew about the ill-competence of solid decisions by the Europeans at the time of his second election as the 47th US President. And he is making great use of it, reminding us who is "in control." However, we can never be sure of his actual intentions. However, as earlier said, he and his government are unorthodox. Nonetheless, His actions testify towards an "aggressive policy in the world affairs and more so versus powerhouses like the European Union of the 27 and more.

One may say that he "orchestrated change." It is a clear signal of change. But not entirely in the best way and in the best interests of his country. Leading states and leaders to assume that the time has come safely, more than ever, to overrule current balances and build on new solid strategic security grounds. But how can this be achieved in a specific timeframe? That is the question.

Trump should have been aware of the lack of bureaucratic competence and capability in governance from Europe and beyond. This would, in turn, mean opportunity. To attempt to control Europe regionally or bilaterally.

The US probably knew the lack of competence in detecting failing states or areas and failing to commit to safety, stability, and social development near the European continent and, at times, within the European states to practically commit to national safety and fighting out illegal migration, among others. The new US administration also knew that this would ultimately give rise to other or new political powers that would project their capability to reinstate 'own sovereignty.' A probability is that we may also see countries denounce at times diverse alliances where needed (Brexit) or through example cases like Hungary, Melony's Italy (Italy), and more recently, Greenland[1]. The story may develop more in the near future, assuming that the US will now pivot to establish a 'solid political rhythm,' in essence, claiming US power over Europe as it once did post-World War II Marshall Plan.

Not far away from Europe, in its near abroad, in the Middle East, Sharaa, known as the interim leader of Syria, is considered a transitional leader -one claim that the author of this chapter disagrees with seems to be favored by Europe. In essence, the reason for acceptance is to relieve Syria and Syrians of further degradation and deprivation and provide them the choice of returning to their homeland with safety. War, instability, and volatility have raged in Syria since 2012 (Neep, 2025) Following atrocities that took place in neighboring Iraq.

Nonetheless, Sharaa's actual life background stipulates the opposite: He is a known terrorist. And it is safe to say he does not believe in the actual rule of law and democracy. He claims he does, and people claim he meets "a possible list" as ironically "the best leader choice." Is he a leader's choice? Or his followers? Is he a terrorist, or is he not? Why did he 'level into becoming the leader of Syria'? The answer is simple, as referred to above: to end possibly massive migration flows from Syria and surrounding states. Granting him, if promised to do so, the opportunity to 'redeem himself from the error acts he committed. This is a great opportunity for him and his followers to be seen as peace-makers in a new security environment (Hall, 2025). Establishing "a national security and governance framework from the beginning" only meets the "checklist of standards" that neighboring foreign powers seek. Surely, with the help of neighboring Türkiye and a similar plan that took place recently in Afghanistan in 2020, with the withdrawal of the US and the introduction of Turkey and Qatar as "guarantors" of stability (Parker, 2025). Hence, the same will be done in Syria.

Based on the above, sound moral and ethical questions are suddenly emerging: are we seeing the decline of Western-centric dominance? Are we now actually splitting again between the Western powers? Did the War between Ukraine and Russia in 2022 affect us all in a very structural way? Was the terror atrocities in Israel in October 2023 the turning point? Does this coincide maybe with the societal and trade requirements and outcomes of what COVID-19 caused? Or is it pure -to blame the new US leadership- for its 'unorthodox ways'?

The ill-equipped readiness and practicality of solving key issues for the Euro-Atlantic leadership (Reference), the ill-capability and capacity to terminate and not sustain a war that should have been avoided first, have now adapted to new European realities and challenges. European leadership allowed it to become a problem of "its own." A problem that, while Europe needed to react or even prevent it, European leaders were never ready to do so or never anticipated such action.

Politically, this resulted, and still moves forward into a faster rise of new power centers and speeded up the rise of extremes. An eventuality or characteristic that is seemingly not over yet. Europe lacks today's effective decision-making process. Neither does a timeframe of action and a chronology of events that can provide tangible results for safety in Europe. Europe may see another lost opportunity to play a pivotal yet global role. While things have become more convoluted, there is still an opportunity to render Europe more powerful, but now only in the long term and not the actual short term (Parscariu, 2025).

Western powers, overall, never saw a proximity war coming into the European continent by 2022: That the Ukrainian War would be making an impact on the security and stability of Europe. And rightfully so. Russia ultimately exploited the opportunity laid ahead of it. Time worked well for Russia. We should have known:

2006 Estonia, 2007 Georgia, 2014 Crimea (Schulze, & Pupcenoks, 2025). And the list goes on. Illegally controlling areas in the Caucasus, influencing the Black Sea, and continuing to attempt to control Balkan areas while increasing or re-shuffling its presence in the Middle East and Central Asia, Africa, and South America. Competition has increased, and a new approach to security and volatility continues to grow.

On the other hand, Ukraine pivots precisely and clearly to become a member of the EU while aspiring to become a full member of NATO. Membership would provide safety and, in essence, mean actual security and, more so, re-construction. Without sovereignty, security, and safety, there cannot be stability, progress, development innovation, and, more so, international positioning. That was also made clear.

It is true that Ukraine meets moral and ethical standards and is the newest member of the EU. And yet, realities and questions persist: Where do the borders of the EU stop? The actual realities ahead of the westernization of Ukraine to join the Euro-Atlantic family may not be meeting the financial, political, or even sociological standards to join the EU just yet. It may, however, meet the military standards. What about the overall Acquis Communautaire? On the other hand, it is the right of the Ukrainian people and its leadership to aspire and seek membership to the EU if it wants to, like a proportion of the Georgian population and more so for security reasons, which has also been the case for other states in the past and will potentially be for the future.

THE DAWN OF A NEW GOVERNANCE FORMAT THROUGH PERMANENT CAPACITY BUILDING

Governance availability, capability, and capacity building are in question. Primarily due to the constant regional or international instabilities and volatilities and the lack of strong, steadfast decision-making with a proven track record in application. So what are to expect? How do we manage change? The direct answer to global instabilities may be permanent methods of security resilience and business continuity capacity building. Institutionally, this allows us to adapt to a constantly changing environment, where while we are required to be vigilant of the challenges arising, we also need to foresee joint capacity building between allies that face similar or the same challenges in international affairs. Maybe there is no actual applicable and effective decision-making. Currently, representative institutions are at odds with their members. Face significant challenges regarding their contemporary objectives and lack of fiscal or ideological support.

Considering the stakes and the necessity for a firm European or Euro-Atlantic safety and security institutionalization that is modern and contemporary to the needs and future objectives, a strategic necessity to re-draw and build on a new security architectural design is required. If Europe wants to pivot outside the European "near abroad" and " go global, " European interests are now settled. While Europe goes global, Europe deepens its integration processes and methods.

The technological and digital ecosystems and the combined advancements between the two 'ecosystems' have facilitated communication and capacity building in methods of security, safety, and combined applied strategies. It has more so facilitated direct international relations formats. New dynamics and new political realities are on the rise. We are looking at applied methods of approach to subjects. This is the dawn of an ecosystem that we need to invest in. AI and Generative AI are only the beginning. Cloud computing is only the beginning. The bigger picture includes Robotics, genetics, outer-space colonization, outer-space exploration, health, and their respective combined industries. The new digital ecosystem meets market requirements and needs. It may be suitable for businesses to include digital currency and fintech, as well as defense, security, and safety. For all the above to develop, we require safety, security, and resilience to all dimensional methods nationally and abroad, wherever possible. Trade affects us all; therefore, with instability and without actual framed orientation, we may be unable to make it.

This is the dawn of a new era, defined by intense competition, complete with conflicts in the short run and more with solutions in the possible longer run. These are the new dynamics ahead of us. To be fair, the new dynamics need to be processed more scientifically. This chapter requires more than several thousand words to define or decipher the vast examples and realities ahead of us in defense, security, and their volatilities or insecurities. We need to do more to offer possible readers a comprehensive understanding of the current and future dynamics that are still on the rise, to foresight, and eventually, future affairs. A new balancing order is on the rise. As said in the beginning, we are unsure how it will end. We are unaware of prevailing forces but instead emerging forces that threaten the existing order and opportunity forces (Vicuña, 2025).

To remind us that this chapter is only a first attempt to raise scientific awareness of the importance of the subject at hand. To actually "make room" for new research. New research is needed for the dawn of an era where strategic orientation is not yet defined, but we still need to assess risk. Through actual analyses of the events, as they proceed, we must elevate ourselves to a policy outcome that will make people concretely aware of what is happening. What are the actors, who, and what is the good and bad side, if any, and for which purpose?

We envision the Middle East differently: Africa South, North and Central, and Western Africa. Differently, we lay our foundational comprehension in foreign affairs based on geographic needs or proximity. New alliances are to be forged while some common denominators are still pending or are influenced by short-term interests (Efthymiopoulos, 2019).

So, for the chapter to enlarge and enhance its strategic posture, one needs to complete further primary research, which requires practical and applied participation, collaboration in writing, and much more. It involves coordinating regional and topical issues that explain well to all professionals, scholars, decision-makers, and policy crafters what is now and what is expected soon.

According to what was analyzed above, if we briefly explain what is taking place today, one could say that the changing strategic landscape is now based on a constantly changing environment that is completely volatile. This is the actual modus vivendi. We are seeing a great deal of regional new approaches. A new security architecture attempt is on the rise. But we are not there yet to define new possible alliances. Alliances tend to be short-lived. We do not know the destination of the latest architectural design. We do not see what changes may take place. We estimate. Unfortunately, we do not have an ideological or strategic orientation. We do not expect to have a new balance or framework of security. We only have levels of business security and continuity in the making. We have expectations and consider our environment volatile; indeed, alliances are fragile.

The main questions remain: Are we looking at Western fragmentation? We are misapplying or mis-concepting on various levels. Things change daily: Ideologies and practices, alliances and allies, and interests, among others. We are unsure how to examine things from a scientific, ethical, or philosophical point of view. How to demonstrate economic shifts, trade disputes, and demographic trends. Based on which current data can we foresight strategic assumptions on risk? Can we even make long-term assessments? What are, if any, illustrations that result in opportunities for a possible new order in the making rather than considering that all volatile actions are actual challenges of the current world order?

This chapter provides a multidisciplinary approach that draws on political science, international economics, international law, security affairs, and strategic moves. It is a real-politic-based chapter, and based on pragmatism, we need to structure a safe, sound, and secure environment.

We don't know any new alliances in the making, the actors, or the presumed great powers. We struggle to adapt to fragility and volatility. Current and/or new circumstances may produce even more volatility and possibly instability. We struggle to see if any current emerging powers are filling a possible vacuum left or created if current powers find the current global phenomenon to reshape the world order or if they wish to any longer and others to commit to fulfilling this power vacuum.

SHIFTING THE GLOBAL PARADIGM: EMERGING FORCES AND GLOBAL REALIGNMENTS

The strategic paradigm may also change depending on the political choices governments and leaders may make. It should be to our leaders' "best of their knowledge," as one may say, that leaders take, or have taken, the appropriate decisions or steps to protect and serve our nations and protect our interests.

So far, it has come to the point where the COVID-19 virus first made its "official appearance" in 2020. I consider it to be a turning point. The concern is not physiological. It is psychological. It soared toward financial, political, and ideological change. It caused, among others, a global moral, ethical, social, and economic crisis, a constant recession that we still struggle to battle against (Reference). It was a pivotal moment that left governments worldwide with a strategic paradigm of specific choices. Safety and security will be improved; in the long term, a new possible framework of choices (challenges and/or opportunities) will be created. For others, it led to a chance for emerging power and global realignment (Brands & Gavin, 2020).

Goodman stated in 2020 that "the world is almost certainly ensnared in a devastating recession delivered by the coronavirus pandemic" (Goodman, 2020). A crisis that is now sociological and political but also trade-fiscal and is still ongoing. Policy alignments are different. Causes differ. Objectives are rules-based and differ.

A global shift of balance of power is ongoing. Power vacuums are seen, and the emergence of new powers is also acknowledged. New realignments have been achieved or are yet to be completed. Current and emerging forces are entangled by elements that provide volatility. Economic data, productive methods, technological agility, dependency or independence to others, regional and global approaches to security, international trade affairs or wars, and the quest for opportunity to enlarge, grasp land, or exploit natural habitat and natural resources.

Covid-19 provoked an "end to an era." It also projected a 'new era'. Global architecture shift. It projected opportunity and, as we mentioned multiple times, volatility. None of us was ready to face potential socio-economic and security consequences. We swiftly drifted away from the possible threat and the immediate ban we all held in the living conditions in our natural habitat, at least for a short period. The result brought many questions to the surface. Opened an "appetite" for a "new dawn of world political affairs." Geostrategic challenges never ceased to exist. None of the current difficulties phased out. Covid-19 did have strategic challenges and opportunities that were somehow reshaped. Ongoing wars resumed (Koyama, 2024).

Fragmentation of ideology and strategic value added to the fact that they could not protect themselves from safety and security issues became a prominent characteristic in Africa and Central Asia. At the same time, new wars emerged between

Russia and Ukraine in 2022. Multiplied in Africa, Sudan in 2021, Gongo-Rwanda in 2022, and the list continues. Not withholding the Middle East, which was always in turmoil, one way or another, as previously described and analyzed. In contrast, the terror attacks on October 7, 2023, in Israel subverted the Abrahamic accord that was ongoing for further expansion/recognition and practical effect through business and trade achievements. (Codish, Frenkel, Klein, Geftler, Dreiher & Schwarzfuchs, 2024).

Wars have been marking new realities since 2023. This is a new 'milestone'. A new paradigm shift. Offering short results like in Syria, with the fall of the Assad regime, whose new regime provides a solution to, among others, the illegal flow of migration and a normalization and rebuilding phase. Such effects "canonicalized a new security paradigm: where war methods, actions, and possible unconventional attacks became the new normality: from Ukraine in 2022, to Azerbaijan-Armenia in 2023, to terror and Iran attacks to Israel and vice-versa to the attacks on Gaza on Hamas and Hezbollah in Lebanon (Agubamah & Theresa 2025). Attacks from Houthi Rebels to Israel and vice-versa, to Somalia, to terror groups leading the way (ironically so) to: 'extremist redemption and capacity to lead to power,' like in Afghanistan, now into Syria and beyond. A Türkiye, amazingly, utilizes the opportunity to take steps for political expansion while demonizing the West and keeping the West somewhat alive, stating that it can do it on its behalf and saying that Europe or the West cannot do without.

At the same time, the Gulf States emerged as the 'land of opportunity through safety.' While becoming a beacon of hope, it also became a place for business and mediation, with an abundant methodology of security and safety through a new method of ruling and participation in the dialogue with the world community (Abdulla 2013).

CONCLUSION: METHODS AND RULES FOR A NEW WORLD ORDER

A shift in global politics is, therefore, a reality. Realignments are here. Now. New expectations emerge. New alliances are to emerge. Others call it a new security architecture. Others a new strategic reality. There are too many issues to be examined, analyzed, and discussed. There are significant issues to be negotiated and mediated. There are just too many balances to be kept. Short, based interests are the new canonical framework. Leaderships are now learning how to survive over small or few exchanges, giving validity and causality to the long-term cause: to figure out whether the end of those political ideologies will give way to a new framework set of new ideologies. What we have yet to see, we need to figure out. Our methods of approach in security and strategic affairs have yet to change. Based on security and safety, we can design financial stability volatility to turn into opportunity and discuss designated development. Time is against us. All things change. And at this pace, we move; balances are just not there. There is no practicality, not visible outcome that can testify about stability and prosperity, global or regional, ahead of us.

Eventually, a new world order will emerge. We are yet to find out whether this will be a bipolar or multipolar world. Who will be the leading actors? We have yet to see whether strong values, ethics, morals, checks, and balances will characterize this world. Without them, we cannot ensure safety and security—reconciliation and peace.

We are to see many political/ideological changes as challenges grow. New alliances will be shaped and will be delivered on short-term visions. There is a military armament process that testifies to the need for internal and regional security and safety to start with. There are and will be many fiscal changes to take place, as well as energy loops, always keeping technological agility and research and development of technology at the forefront, overlooking the race and rise to power.

As we stated at the beginning, a new security architecture is on the way. To a certain extent, the current chapter examined many complex shifts, seeking ideological understanding and philosophical yet pragmatic/realistic understanding of what is going on. This chapter was created in our attempt to comprehend the current environment, which is genuinely volatile and unclear. With a specialized ideological and geopolitical risk analysis, we seek to understand the evolution of global affairs, including operational choices and a new balance of power that may be on the rise. This chapter explored how emerging forces used to date geopolitical realignments to technological innovations and politics. While we know that, among others, demographic changes are also redefining global power structures and, hence, possible near or future political interests or conflicts.

To the greatest extent possible, each statement and case analysis can be examined separately and further considered, considering the ongoing changes ahead. We are not sure how each day will turn out to be. However, we require authentic, agile, resilient leadership that balances our global society.

REFERENCES

Abdulla, A. (2013). The Arab Gulf moment. In *The Transformation of the Gulf* (pp. 106–124). Routledge.

Agubamah, E., & Theresa, O. S. (2025). Hezbollah Involvement in Israel-Hamas War: Causes and Implications 2023-2024. *Kashere Journal of Politics and International Relations*, *3*(1), 15–21.

Banerjee, S., & Singh, S. (2024). Examining the India-Middle East-Europe Economic Corridor (IMEC) as a collaborative infrastructure for transcontinental policymaking: An ICIO-LP analysis. *Asia Europe Journal*, *22*(4), 481–506. DOI: 10.1007/s10308-024-00712-1

Bell, D. A. (2025). The Age of Trump and Musk: Reflections on the Election of 2024. *Society*, *62*(1), 109–111. DOI: 10.1007/s12115-024-01045-w

Brands, H., & Gavin, F. J. (2020). *COVID-19 and world order*. Johns Hopkins University Press. DOI: 10.1353/book.77593

Codish, S., Frenkel, A., Klein, M., Geftler, A., Dreiher, J., & Schwarzfuchs, D. (2024). October 7th 2023 attacks in Israel: Frontline experience of a single tertiary center. *Intensive Care Medicine*, *50*(2), 308–310. DOI: 10.1007/s00134-023-07293-4 PMID: 38172298

Das, D. (2024). Revisiting the contours of the evolving Middle Eastern order through the India-Middle East-EU Corridor: Mapping India's scopes and limitations. *Asian Journal of Political Science*, *32*(1), 35–56. DOI: 10.1080/02185377.2024.2322498

Efthymiopoulos, M. P. (2019). Hybrid Alliances: Efficiency, Business Continuity and Future Foresight in a World of Challenges. In Smart Technologies and Innovation for a Sustainable Future: Proceedings of the 1st American University in the Emirates International Research Conference—Dubai, UAE 2017 (pp. 187-193). Springer International Publishing.

Fayet, H., Futter, A., Kühn, U., Kulesa, Ł., van Hooft, P., & Bruusgaard, K. V. (2025). Forum: European Nuclear Deterrence and Donald Trump. *Survival*, *67*(1), 123–142. DOI: 10.1080/00396338.2025.2459011

Goodman, P. (2020, April 1). New York Times. Retrieved April 1, 2020, from https://www.nytimes.com/2020/04/01/business/economy/coronavirus-recession.html

Groitl, G. (2025). *The good, the bad, and the ugly: What Donald Trump's return to the White House means for US strategic competition with Russia and China*. Z Politikwiss., DOI: 10.1007/s41358-025-00403-2

Hall, N. (2025). With the Fall of Assad, Can Syria Rise? *Survival*, *67*(1), 45–54. DOI: 10.1080/00396338.2025.2459015

Jopp, M., & Pollak, J. (2024). Introduction: The EU's Geopolitics—Where Ambition Exceeds Ability. In Jopp, M., & Pollak, J. (Eds.), *The European Union's Geopolitics. The Future of Europe*. Springer., DOI: 10.1007/978-3-031-74587-4_1

Koyama, T. (2024). Who Restarts Violent Conflict? Post-Conflict Government Policy and Two Types of Conflict Recurrence. *Defence and Peace Economics*, *36*(2), 200–226. DOI: 10.1080/10242694.2024.2308473

Lammert, C. (2025). *The USA after the election: economic and social policy implications*. Z Politikwiss., DOI: 10.1007/s41358-025-00400-5

Leruth, B. (2024). Political long-termism and the European Union: Five research questions for the future. *Contemporary European Politics*, *2*(2), e70000. DOI: 10.1002/cep4.70000

Levitan, N., Reich, A., & Rynhold, J. From Conflict to Connectivity: The India-Middle East-Europe Corridor Amidst Geopolitical Turbulence (January 30, 2025). Bar Ilan University Faculty of Law Research Paper No. 5117805, Available at SSRN: https://ssrn.com/abstract=5117805 or DOI: 10.2139/ssrn.5117805

Lindberg, L. N. (1970). Political Integration as a Multidimensional Phenomenon Requiring Multivariate Measurement. *International Organization*, *24*(4), 648–731. DOI: 10.1017/S0020818300017501

Neep, D. (2025). Rebuilding the State in Post-Assad Syria. *Journal of Democracy*, *36*(2), 68–77. DOI: 10.1353/jod.2025.a954564

Oğurlu, E. (2024). Changing Nature of the European Union - Turkey Relations: From Civilizational Project to Transactional Cooperation. *Ankara Hacı Bayram Veli Üniversitesi İktisadi Ve İdari Bilimler Fakültesi Dergisi*, *26*(1), 33–54. DOI: 10.26745/ahbvuibfd.1363956

Pascariu, G. C. (2025). Resilience: From Theoretical Thinking to a New Paradigm and Normative Approaches in EU' Foreign and Security Policy. In Rouet, G., & Pascariu, G. C. (Eds.), *Resilience and the EU's Eastern Neighbourhood Countries*. Palgrave Macmillan., DOI: 10.1007/978-3-031-73379-6_2

Schulze, J. L., & Pupcenoks, J. (2025). Securitizing Russian-speakers in Estonia and Latvia: The Frame-Policy Nexus before and after Russia's Invasion of Ukraine. *Nationalities Papers*, •••, 1–25. DOI: 10.1017/nps.2024.97

Tyler, B. (2025, June). Parker, Accepting Appreciation: Partner Perceptions and Major Non-NATO Ally Designations. *Journal of Global Security Studies*, *10*(2), ogae047. Advance online publication. DOI: 10.1093/jogss/ogae047

Underwood, E., & Paul, T. (2025, January 22). Rising India. *Oxford Research Encyclopedia of Politics.* Retrieved 6 Apr. 2025, from https://oxfordre.com/politics/view/10.1093/acrefore/9780190228637.001.0001/acrefore-9780190228637-e-2163

Vicuña, F. O. (2025). "Chapter 15 International Law and World Order: In Search of Rebalance". In International Law in Search of Rebalance. Leiden, The Netherlands: Brill | Nijhoff. DOI: 10.1163/9789004721388_016

ENDNOTE

1 Referral to Greenland is due to the interest of the 47th US President Donald John Trump, to buy from Denmark the autonomous region. In recent elections, Greenland elected party seems to be a right wing party for the independence of the territory.

Chapter 4
Trade Wars and International Relations:
Implications for Global Supply Chains, Technological Advancement, and Energy Security

Georgios A. Deirmentzoglou
https://orcid.org/0000-0003-1687-0708
Neapolis University, Pafos, Cyprus

ABSTRACT

This chapter explores the profound disruptions to globalization and trade liberalization caused by the resurgence of trade wars in the 21st century. Driven by geopolitical rivalries and shifting economic power dynamics, these conflicts have led to a restructuring of global supply chains through reshoring and friendshoring strategies. The chapter also examines the dual role of technological advancement as both a driver and a casualty of trade wars, with export controls and decoupling efforts reshaping global innovation. Additionally, it highlights the growing significance of energy security, focusing on resource access disputes, rare earth elements, and the geopolitical implications of fossil fuel dependency. Offering critical insights for policymakers, businesses, and scholars, this chapter provides a comprehensive analysis of the evolving landscape of international trade, economic competition, and global stability in an era of intensifying geopolitical tensions.

DOI: 10.4018/979-8-3693-5583-1.ch004

1. INTRODUCTION

1.1 Background and Context

The prevailing global economic order, once characterized by the progressive advancement of globalization and trade liberalization, has undergone a period of significant disruption, marked by the resurgence of trade wars in the 21st century. While often framed as disputes over economic fairness, these conflicts are deeply rooted in geopolitical rivalries and shifting power dynamics (Bown, 2021). A prime example is the ongoing U.S.-China trade war, which commenced in 2018 when the United States imposed tariffs on billions of dollars worth of Chinese goods, citing concerns over intellectual property theft, forced technology transfers, and trade imbalances (Mavroidis & Sapir, 2021). However, this conflict is not an isolated event; it is part of a broader trend of strategic economic competition, where countries such as India, the United Kingdom (post-Brexit), and the European Union have engaged in their own trade disputes, often in response to national security concerns or supply chain vulnerabilities.

Trade wars are not merely economic disruptions; they reflect deeper geopolitical tensions. As Allison (2017) argues in *Destined for War*, the rise of China as a global power has created a "Thucydides Trap," increasing the likelihood of conflict with the established hegemon, the United States. The U.S.-China trade war is as much about technological dominance and strategic influence as it is about trade imbalances. The U.S. government's restrictions on Chinese technology firms such as Huawei and ZTE, as well as efforts to limit China's access to advanced semiconductor technology, underscore how technology has become central to modern trade conflicts (Bown, 2020). The U.S. CHIPS and Science Act (NSF, n.a.) and the European Union's push for technological sovereignty through the European Chips Act (European Commission, n.a.) illustrate how governments are actively reshaping global technological supply chains rather than passively accepting fragmentation.

The implications of these trade wars extend beyond immediate economic costs, fundamentally reshaping global supply chains. Companies are increasingly adopting strategies such as "reshoring" (bringing production back to domestic markets) and "friendshoring" (relocating supply chains to politically aligned countries) to mitigate risks and reduce dependency on adversarial partners (Charpin & Cousineau, 2024; Gur & Dilek, 2023). This shift is evident in industries such as semiconductors, pharmaceuticals, and critical minerals, where reliance on single-country suppliers has been identified as a strategic vulnerability. While these adjustments increase resilience, they also introduce inefficiencies, higher costs, and potential bottlenecks in global trade.

Concurrently, technological advancement has emerged as both a catalyst and a casualty of trade wars. In this context, nations are engaged in a fierce competition to dominate pivotal sectors such as artificial intelligence, 5G, and quantum computing. This pursuit is driven by the recognition that technological leadership is indispensable for enhancing economic and military prowess (Mori, 2019). However, the emergence of "technological decoupling," marked by the imposition of export controls and the curtailing of collaborative efforts among nations (Zhang, 2023), portends a deceleration in global innovation and scientific progress. In response to these challenges, novel technological alliances are emerging. A notable example is the U.S.-led CHIPS 4 Alliance, which includes Japan, South Korea, and Taiwan, with the aim of increasing semiconductor production domestically. Moreover, the European Union (EU) is implementing measures to mitigate its reliance on external semiconductor production, underscoring a transition towards self-sufficiency and regional collaboration in technological governance.

Energy security has also emerged as a pivotal theater in the ongoing trade wars. Access to critical resources, such as rare earth minerals, which are essential for high-tech manufacturing and renewable energy, has become a major geopolitical concern (Overland, 2019). China's preeminence in the production of rare earth minerals has endowed it with considerable leverage in trade negotiations, compelling countries such as the United States, the European Union, and Japan to explore alternative supply chains and domestic production (Barteková & Kemp, 2016). The transition to renewable energy has introduced new geopolitical complexities, as nations compete to secure access to materials and technologies essential for the green transition (Meckling et al., 2015).

The geopolitical dimensions of trade wars are exemplified by the evolving tensions between Russia and the European Union over energy security. The 2022 Russian invasion of Ukraine fundamentally reshaped Europe's energy strategy, forcing the EU to rapidly diversify its energy sources away from Russian natural gas and accelerate investments in renewables (Deirmentzoglou et al., 2024). The Nord Stream 2 pipeline, once a symbol of European-Russian energy interdependence, has been effectively abandoned, and sanctions have targeted Russian energy exports (CRS, 2022). The United States has also played a role by imposing sanctions on Russian energy projects and increasing liquefied natural gas (LNG) exports to Europe as an alternative (Hosoe, 2023; Lambert et al., 2022).

Beyond these significant conflicts, trade restrictions have emerged as a strategic instrument of foreign policy. The United States has utilized economic sanctions not only against China and Russia but also against nations such as Iran and North Korea, thereby shaping international alliances and economic flows (Chivvis and Keating, 2024; Walterskirchen et al., 2022). A notable illustration of this phenomenon is the case of U.S. sanctions imposed on Iran, which have given rise to considerable tensions with European allies. This has led to a predicament where businesses must decide between accessing the U.S. financial system and maintaining operations in Iran. Disagreements between the U.S. and the EU concerning tariffs on steel, aluminum, and digital taxation further underscore the intricacies of trade relations among allies (Walterskirchen et al., 2022).

In this context, trade wars must be regarded not merely as economic conflicts but rather as instruments of geopolitical strategy, reflecting the complex interplay between economic interests, national security, and global power dynamics. As nations confront these challenges, the future of global trade will hinge on their capacity to balance competition with cooperation while sustaining the advantages of globalization. The reinforcement of multilateral institutions, such as the World Trade Organization (WTO), and the development of novel mechanisms for economic coordination may prove pivotal in the effective management of future trade conflicts.

1.2 Objectives of the Chapter

This chapter explores the multifaceted implications of trade wars for global supply chains, technological advancement, and energy security. It situates these issues within the broader context of international relations. The objective of this chapter is to provide an in-depth analysis of the manner in which trade wars disrupt global supply chains, thereby precipitating shifts in production and sourcing strategies. To this end, the chapter will focus on case studies from industries such as semiconductors, automotive, and pharmaceuticals. It also examines the role of technological competition in fueling trade wars, exploring the consequences for innovation, global collaboration, and the future of technological leadership. Furthermore, the chapter explores the nexus of trade wars and energy security, with a particular emphasis on the geopolitical dynamics surrounding the competition for critical resources and the transition to renewable energy. Finally, it provides a comprehensive understanding of how trade wars are reshaping international relations, including the role of alliances, institutions, and diplomatic strategies in mitigating or exacerbating trade conflicts. By addressing these objectives, the chapter contributes to the growing body of literature on trade wars and their implications for the global economy and international relations. It also offers valuable insights for policymakers, academics, and industry leaders navigating the challenges and opportunities presented by this new era of economic and geopolitical competition.

1.3 Structure of the Chapter

The chapter is organized as follows. Section 2 establishes the theoretical framework, drawing on international relations and economic theories to contextualize trade wars. The subsequent section, Section 3, undertakes a detailed analysis of the interplay between trade wars and international relations. This analysis considers the role of alliances, institutions, and diplomatic strategies. The subsequent section, Section 4, examines the repercussions of trade wars on global supply chains. This examination involves the use of case studies, which highlight instances of disruption and adaptation. The subsequent section, Section 5, explores the role of technological advancement in trade wars, focusing on issues such as export controls, technological decoupling, and the race for innovation. The final section, Section 6, delves into the ramifications of trade wars for energy security, with a particular emphasis on geopolitical tensions over critical resources and the renewable energy transition. Finally, Section 7 discusses policy implications and offers a forward-looking perspective on the future of global trade and international relations.

2. THEORETICAL FRAMEWORK

2.1 International Relations Theories and Trade Wars

Trade wars are not merely economic conflicts; they are deeply embedded in the broader context of international relations. To comprehend their dynamics, it is imperative to draw upon seminal theories of international relations, including realism, liberalism, and constructivism. Each of these theoretical frameworks offers unique insights into the origins, consequences, and implications of trade wars.

2.1.1. Realism

Realist theories, as articulated by scholars such as Hans Morgenthau and Kenneth Waltz, underscore the anarchic character of the international system. In this framework, states are primarily concerned with survival and power (Waltz, 1979). In this context, trade wars are regarded as a logical progression of geopolitical competition, wherein states employ economic instruments to augment their relative power and diminish the standing of adversaries. A notable illustration of this dynamic is the ongoing U.S.-China trade war, which can be interpreted as a component of a larger struggle for global hegemony, with the United States endeavoring to impede China's ascent as a dominant global power (Allison, 2017). In addition, realists emphasize the concept of "relative gains," which posits that states prioritize gaining an advantage over rivals over achieving mutual benefits (Grieco, 1988). This perspective lends credence to the notion that trade wars frequently escalate despite their economic costs, as states prioritize strategic interests over economic efficiency.

2.1.2. Liberalism

In contrast to realist theories, which emphasize the importance of power and politics in international relations, liberal theories prioritize the potential for cooperation and mutual benefit in international trade. Scholars such as Robert Keohane and Joseph Nye contend that institutions, norms, and economic interdependence can serve as mitigating factors in the occurrence of conflicts, thereby fostering peaceful relations (Keohane & Nye, 1997). For instance, the World Trade Organization (WTO) was established to provide a rules-based framework for resolving trade disputes and reducing tariffs. Nevertheless, the recent rise of protectionism and the undermining of multilateral institutions like the WTO underscore the limitations of liberal approaches in an era of great power competition. Liberals also emphasize the role of domestic politics in shaping trade policies, as interest groups, corporations, and voters influence government decisions (Milner, 1999). This dynamic helps to elucidate why trade wars often emanate from domestic pressures, such as the demand to protect jobs or industries.

2.1.3. Constructivism

Constructivist theories, advanced by scholars such as Alexander Wendt, emphasize the role of ideas, identities, and norms in shaping international relations. According to this perspective, trade wars are not merely about material interests but also about competing visions of global order and national identity (Wendt, 1999). To illustrate this point, one need look no further than the ongoing U.S.-China trade war. This conflict is, at least in part, driven by differing ideologies and narratives about economic governance. On one side is the United States, which advocates for free markets, and on the other is China, which promotes state-led development models. Constructivists further emphasize the role of historical grievances and perceptions in exacerbating trade conflicts. For instance, China's perspective of the trade war as an attempt by the United States to contain its rise reflects a broader narrative of Western dominance and resistance (Callahan, 2016).

2.2 Economic Theories of Trade Wars

Economic theories offer further insights into the etiology and implications of trade wars, emphasizing subjects such as comparative advantage, protectionism, and the economic costs of trade barriers. These theories facilitate a more nuanced understanding of the factors that precipitate trade wars and the reasons why they frequently result in unintended consequences.

2.2.1. Comparative Advantage

The principle of comparative advantage, first articulated by David Ricardo in 1817, posits that countries derive benefit from specializing in the production of goods in which they possess a relative efficiency advantage and trading for other goods. However, the principle is subject to challenges, as evidenced by the repercussions of trade wars. These wars have been shown to distort market signals and curtail the benefits derived from trade (Krugman, 1987). A notable illustration of this phenomenon is the imposition of tariffs on Chinese goods by the United States, which has resulted in increased costs for American consumers and disruptions in global supply chains (Amiti et al., 2019). Economists contend that trade wars diminish global welfare by impeding countries from capitalizing on their comparative advantages.

2.2.2. Protectionism

Protectionist policies, including tariffs, quotas, and subsidies, are frequently justified on the grounds of safeguarding domestic industries, preserving employment opportunities, or addressing trade imbalances. However, economists contend that protectionism is often counterproductive, resulting in inefficiencies, retaliation, and diminished economic welfare (Cho, 2004; McGee, 1992). A notable historical example of the potentially deleterious consequences of protectionism is the Smoot-Hawley Tariff Act of 1930, which exacerbated the economic downturn known as the Great Depression (Eichengreen, 2002; Nivola, 1986). Contemporary trade conflicts, such as the U.S.-China dispute, have also resulted in elevated prices, diminished market access, and augmented uncertainty for businesses (Fajgelbaum et al., 2020).

2.2.3. Trade Barriers and Economic Costs

The imposition of trade wars has been demonstrated to exact a substantial economic toll, encompassing elevated consumer prices, constrained market access for exporters, and augmented business uncertainty. This, in turn, can occasion a diminution in investment and economic growth (Bown & Crowley, 2013). The adverse effects of trade wars are not evenly distributed, as some industries and regions suffer disproportionately, particularly those reliant on global supply chains or heavily dependent on exports (Autor et al., 2016). For instance, U.S. farmers have experienced considerable financial distress due to China's retaliatory tariffs on agricultural products, resulting in declining exports, surplus production, and increased reliance on government subsidies (Morgan, 2022). Furthermore, retaliatory measures have the potential to disrupt long-standing trade relationships, compelling businesses to seek alternative markets, often at a higher cost and with reduced efficiency.

2.3 Interdisciplinary Approach

In order to comprehend the multifaceted nature of trade wars, it is imperative to adopt an interdisciplinary approach that integrates insights from political science, economics, and technology studies. This methodological framework enables a more comprehensive examination of the intricate dynamics among economic interests, geopolitical rivalries, and technological competition.

2.3.1. Political Economy

The field of political economy is the study of how political forces shape economic outcomes, and vice versa. A prime example of this dynamic is trade wars, which are driven by both economic interests (e.g., protecting domestic industries) and political considerations (e.g., maintaining national security) (Gilpin, 2001). For instance, the United States government's restrictions on Chinese technology companies are driven by concerns regarding both economic issues, such as intellectual property theft, and security concerns, including espionage risks. The political economy paradigm underscores the pivotal role of domestic politics in the formulation of trade policies, as governments endeavor to harmonize the divergent demands of diverse interest groups.

2.3.2. Technology and Innovation

The contemporary era is characterized by technological advancement (see Deirmentzoglou et al., 2024; Kourkoumelis et al., 2024; Deirmentzoglou and Deirmentzoglou, 2022) and the growth of innovation (Agoraki et al., 2024a; Agoraki et al., 2024b). Technological advancement has been identified as a primary catalyst for trade wars, as nations engage in a competitive pursuit of dominance in critical sectors such as artificial intelligence, 5G, and semiconductors. Concurrently, trade wars have the potential to disrupt global innovation ecosystems by impeding collaboration and knowledge sharing. A notable illustration of this phenomenon is the ongoing technological rivalry between the United States and China, which has resulted in the fragmentation of global supply chains and the emergence of parallel technological standards. This phenomenon, termed "technological decoupling," has the potential to impede the rate of innovation and erode the collective advantages derived from global scientific collaboration.

2.3.3. Energy and Resource Politics

Energy security constitutes an additional critical dimension of trade wars, as access to critical resources, including rare earth minerals and renewable energy technologies, becomes a source of geopolitical tension (Overland, 2019). The transition to renewable energy introduces new complexities, as countries compete to secure access to the materials and technologies needed for the green energy transition (Meckling et al., 2021). For instance, China's preeminence in the production of rare earth minerals has endowed it with considerable leverage in trade negotiations, compelling other nations to explore alternative sources and cultivate their own competencies.

3. THE INTERPLAY BETWEEN TRADE WARS AND INTERNATIONAL RELATIONS

3.1 Geopolitical Alliances and Rivalries

Trade wars are not merely economic conflicts; they are deeply intertwined with the broader dynamics of international relations. A notable consequence of trade wars is their effect on geopolitical alliances and rivalries. In the context of trade conflicts, nations often seek to fortify alliances with like-minded states while concurrently isolating their adversaries.

The dynamic shifts in global alliances have profound ramifications for the global balance of power. On the one hand, these shifts create opportunities for countries to form new partnerships and strengthen existing ones. Conversely, these shifts can also lead to an escalation of geopolitical tensions and an increased likelihood of conflict. A notable illustration of this dynamic can be observed in the escalation of tensions in the South China Sea, where the United States and China, both of whom have competing claims over territory in the region, have engaged in a trade war (see Gomez, 2025). This underscores the close connection between trade wars and broader geopolitical rivalries.

The Russia-EU relationship offers a compelling illustration of how trade wars and energy dependencies can lead to the restructuring of alliances and rivalries. The European Union's (EU) reliance on Russian natural gas has been a point of geopolitical contention, particularly during periods of conflict, such as the Russia-Ukraine war. In response, the EU has intensified its efforts to reduce its reliance on Russian energy by diversifying its energy sources and investing in renewable energy (Deirmentzoglou et al., 2024).

This shift has not only altered the dynamics of the Russia-EU relationship but also created new opportunities for the EU to strengthen its energy partnerships with other regions, such as the United States and the Middle East. Nevertheless, these endeavors have concomitantly resulted in elevated energy expenditures and economic challenges for European nations, underscoring the intricate trade-offs inherent in the management of energy security and geopolitical alliances.

3.2 The Role of International Institutions

International institutions play a crucial role in mediating trade conflicts and promoting cooperation among nations. Nevertheless, trade wars frequently impede the efficacy of these institutions by eroding trust and weakening the rules-based international order. The World Trade Organization (WTO), for instance, has encountered challenges in addressing the ramifications of the U.S.-China trade war. On occasion, both nations have circumvented the WTO's dispute resolution mechanisms and imposed tariffs unilaterally (e.g., BBC, 2020). This phenomenon has given rise to concerns regarding the future of multilateralism and the capacity of international institutions to effectively manage trade conflicts in a global context characterized by increasing polarizations.

At the same time, trade wars have spurred efforts to reform and strengthen international institutions. For instance, the European Union has advocated for reforms to the World Trade Organization (WTO) to address issues such as state subsidies, intellectual property theft, and forced technology transfer (Directorate-General for Trade and Economic Security, 2020; Blenkinsop, 2018). These endeavors underscore a discernible acknowledgement of the pivotal role that international institutions play in ensuring global economic stability and averting the escalation of trade conflicts into more profound geopolitical confrontations.

The Russia-EU energy dispute further illustrates the challenges faced by international institutions in managing trade conflicts. The EU's attempts to reduce its reliance on Russian gas have been hindered by the absence of a cohesive energy policy among member states and the geopolitical intricacies of energy trade. For instance, in October 2024, EU energy ministers met to address the escalating imports of Russian liquefied natural gas (LNG), the energy shortages in Ukraine, and strategies to balance energy prices among member states. This meeting highlighted the persistent challenges in harmonizing EU energy policies and ensuring energy security in the face of geopolitical tensions (Payne, 2024). Notably, despite the imposition of sanctions intended to curtail Russia's energy revenues, investigative findings have exposed substantial loopholes in these measures. These investigations have exposed ongoing trade in Russian oil through complex schemes involving offshore companies and illegal cargo transshipments. This highlights the need for enhanced enforcement mechanisms to ensure the effectiveness of international institutions (Le Monde, 2024).In summary, while the EU has made progress in reducing its reliance on Russian energy, the intricate interplay between trade conflicts, energy security, and geopolitical rivalries remains a complex challenge. This underscores the necessity for the development of more robust and effective international institutions capable of effectively navigating these challenges.

3.3 Soft Power and Diplomatic Strategies

Trade wars have been shown to have significant implications for soft power and diplomatic strategies. Soft power, defined as the ability of a nation to exert influence over others through attraction and persuasion rather than coercion, is frequently undermined by trade wars. For instance, the ongoing U.S.-China trade war has adversely impacted the soft power of both nations, as their assertive trade policies have led to the alienation of allies and the erosion of their reputations as proponents of free trade and globalization (Nye, 2023). Consequently, the European Union and Japan have emerged as potential beneficiaries, able to position themselves as defenders of the rules-based international order, thereby attracting support from other nations.

The geopolitical landscape is intricately interwoven with economic dynamics, with trade wars serving as a pivotal element in the strategic calculus of nations. In this context, states endeavor to harness their economic might to achieve political objectives. For instance, the United States has utilized trade sanctions as a form of coercive diplomacy, targeting countries such as Iran, Russia, and North Korea to exert pressure on them to modify their conduct (Walterskirchen et al., 2022). A similar dynamic can be observed in China's use of economic leverage to shape the policies of other countries, particularly in developing regions where it has substantial investments (Bräutigam, 2020). These strategies underscore the intricate interconnection between trade conflicts and broader diplomatic aspirations.

The Russia-EU relationship offers an additional illustration of how trade wars impact diplomatic strategies. Russia's strategic employment of energy exports as a geopolitical tool has compelled the EU to adopt a more assertive diplomatic posture, encompassing the imposition of sanctions and the cultivation of alternative energy partnerships (Deirmentzoglou et al., 2024; Goldthau and Sitter, 2021). These actions are indicative of a broader trend in which countries employ economic instruments to attain political and security objectives in an era of escalating geopolitical competition (Deirmentzoglou et al., 2024; Goldthau & Sitter, 2021).

4. TRADE WARS AND GLOBAL SUPPLY CHAINS

4.1 Disruptions to Global Supply Chains

The global supply chain, a critical component of globalization, is particularly vulnerable to the disruptions engendered by trade wars. These disruptions, which have been documented by numerous scholars, are often attributed to the implementation of tariffs, export controls, and geopolitical tensions. These factors, when considered collectively, have the potential to engender uncertainty and increase costs for businesses. A notable illustration of this phenomenon is the profound impact of the U.S.-China trade war on global supply chains, as evidenced by numerous studies (see Mao & Görg, 2020). A similar dynamic can be observed in the case of the geopolitical tensions between Russia, the European Union (EU), and the United States, which have further complicated global supply chains, particularly in the domains of energy and critical materials.

Tariffs imposed during trade wars directly increase the cost of imported goods, compelling companies to either absorb the higher costs or pass them on to consumers. For instance, the tariffs imposed by the United States on Chinese goods resulted in substantial price increases for electronics and machinery, sectors that depend significantly on Chinese components (Amiti et al., 2019). These cost increases have the effect of disrupting supply chains by increasing the cost of sourcing inputs, which in turn reduces profitability and delays investments. Beyond tariffs, trade wars engender a climate of uncertainty regarding future trade policies, impeding businesses' ability to plan and invest. This uncertainty often results in delays in capital expenditures, reduced hiring, and slower growth (Handley & Limão, 2017). During the period of the U.S.-China trade war, many multinational corporations postponed investments in new factories and supply chain infrastructure due to fears of further escalation. U.S. firms with direct supply partnerships in China encountered heightened challenges, marked by declines in performance, inventory management issues, and diminished profitability (Fan et al., 2022; Liu et al., 2022).

A salient example of these disruptions can be seen in the semiconductor industry, which is highly globalized and dependent on complex supply chains. The restrictions imposed by the United States on the exportation of semiconductor technology to China have had a significant impact on global supply chains, compelling companies to seek alternative suppliers (Khan, 2020). This has resulted in increased costs and delays in production, thereby underscoring the fragility of global supply chains in the face of geopolitical tensions.

The Russia-EU energy dispute offers an illuminating case study of how trade wars can disrupt global supply chains. Russia, a significant supplier of natural gas to Europe, has strategically employed its energy exports as a means of exerting geopolitical influence, particularly during periods of heightened tension, such as the conflict in Ukraine. In response, the EU has endeavored to mitigate its reliance on Russian gas, pursuing strategies such as diversifying its energy sources and investing in renewable energy infrastructure (Deirmentzoglou et al., 2024). However, this transition has been accompanied by substantial challenges, including the need for substantial investments in novel infrastructure and technologies, which has resulted in increased energy expenditures for European consumers.

4.2 Reshoring and Diversification Strategies

In response to the disruptions caused by trade wars, many companies and countries are adopting strategies such as reshoring and diversification. Reshoring, a term used to describe the return of production activities to the home country or nearby regions, is a strategy employed to mitigate risks associated with geopolitical tensions and tariffs. For instance, to evade tariffs and mitigate exposure to trade uncertainty, certain US and Chinese companies have relocated their production to Mexico (Grant, 2024; Towfighi, 2024). However, reshoring is not without significant challenges, including higher labor costs, infrastructure limitations, and workforce training requirements, making the transition both costly and time-consuming.

Instead of relocating production, some companies have opted to diversify by sourcing inputs from multiple countries to avoid overdependence on a single supplier. The electronics industry exemplifies this trend, with companies diversifying their supply chains by sourcing components from Vietnam, India, and Malaysia to reduce reliance on China. While diversification enhances supply chain resilience, it concomitantly introduces operational complexities, requiring firms to manage multiple regulatory environments, logistics networks, and quality control challenges.

The automotive industry exemplifies the manner in which reshoring and diversification strategies are reconfiguring global supply chains. Given its substantial reliance on a highly integrated global supplier network, the automotive sector has been particularly affected by trade disruptions. In response to these developments, prominent automotive companies such as General Motors and Ford have been compelled to realign their production operations in accordance with the provisions of the United States–Mexico–Canada Agreement (USMCA) to mitigate the risks posed by tariffs. In light of these developments, the Trump administration recently declared a one-month reprieve from the recently implemented 25% tariffs on automobiles and automotive components imported from Canada and Mexico. This decision, influenced by appeals from major U.S. automakers—Ford, General Motors, and Stellantis—provides short-term relief to an industry deeply integrated across North America. (Buchwald, 2025).

In Europe, the Russia-Ukraine conflict has led to an acceleration in efforts to diversify energy supply chains and reduce dependence on Russian gas. The European Union (EU) has augmented its imports of liquefied natural gas (LNG) from the United States and other suppliers, while concurrently allocating resources to the development of renewable energy and energy storage technologies (Deirmentzoglou et al., 2024). This broader trend of regionalization reflects a strategic effort to build resilient and self-sufficient supply chains in response to geopolitical risks.

4.3 Long-Term Implications for Globalization

The disruptions caused by trade wars are reshaping the structure of global supply chains and challenging the traditional model of globalization. A salient trend is the transition from globalized to regionalized supply chains. In response to the heightened risks associated with global trade tensions, companies are progressively relocating their production and sourcing activities within regional blocs. For instance, the European Union's substantial internal trade network, accounting for approximately 70% of its exports and imports, functions as a buffer against external disruptions, reducing exposure to hostile trading partners and increasing supply chain resilience (Economic Impact, 2025).

However, this fragmentation of global supply chains is associated with significant costs. This phenomenon invariably leads to a decline in efficiency and an escalation in costs, as companies forfeit the advantages afforded by economies of scale and specialization. This phenomenon has the potential to impede economic growth and result in increased consumer costs (Rodrik, 2018). For instance, the reshoring of production to high-cost countries like the United States could result in higher prices for goods and reduced competitiveness in global markets. Furthermore, geopolitical uncertainties have prompted firms to reevaluate their supply chain strategies, with many opting to relocate production operations into the EU to enhance resilience. A survey conducted by the European Central Bank revealed that nearly half of the surveyed firms identified geopolitical risks as a significant factor influencing their decision to relocate production into the EU (Attinasi et al., 2023).

The pharmaceutical industry offers a powerful example of these long-term effects. The ongoing global pandemic has brought to the forefront the vulnerabilities inherent in the pharmaceutical industry's supply chain, which is heavily reliant on China and India for critical inputs. The ongoing U.S.-China trade war has further exacerbated these vulnerabilities by disrupting the supply of active pharmaceutical ingredients (APIs) and other critical inputs (Global Data, 2018).

A similar dynamic can be observed in the Russia-EU energy dispute, which has brought to the forefront the risks of over-reliance on a single supplier for critical resources. The EU's endeavors to diversify its energy supply chains and invest in renewable energy represent a broader trend toward regionalization and self-sufficiency. However, it must be noted that these endeavors necessitate substantial investments and coordination. The success of these initiatives hinges on the capacity of nations to harmonize economic efficiency with geopolitical resilience.

5. TRADE WARS AND TECHNOLOGICAL ADVANCEMENT

5.1 The Role of Technology in Trade Wars

Technological advancement has become a central battleground in modern trade wars, with nations vying for dominance in critical sectors such as artificial intelligence (AI), 5G, and semiconductors. This heightened competition can be attributed to the acknowledgement that maintaining technological leadership is imperative for achieving economic growth, enhancing military capabilities, and expanding global influence.

The ongoing trade tensions between the United States and China exemplify this intense rivalry over emerging technologies, characterized by export controls, investment restrictions, and other strategic measures. The United States has implemented comprehensive export controls to restrict China's access to advanced computing and semiconductor technologies (BIS, 2024). These measures are designed to impede China's capacity to develop and manufacture state-of-the-art semiconductor technology, with the objective of safeguarding U.S. national security and foreign policy interests.

The strategic importance of technology in trade wars is evident in the U.S. government's restrictions on Chinese tech companies such as Huawei and ZTE. These restrictions, which include bans on the sale of U.S. technology to these firms, are motivated by concerns over national security and the misappropriation of intellectual property (Bown, 2020).

This technological rivalry has significant implications for global innovation ecosystems. On the one hand, it has led to increased investment in research and development (R&D) as countries seek to achieve self-sufficiency in critical technologies. Conversely, it has also resulted in the fragmentation of global innovation networks, as countries implement export controls and restrict collaborative efforts. This phenomenon, termed “technological decoupling,” has the potential to impede the rate of innovation and erode the collective advantages derived from global scientific collaboration.

5.2 Technological decoupling

Export controls represent a pivotal instrument within the technological dimension of trade wars, as they empower nations to impede the dissemination of critical technologies to their competitors. The term "technological decoupling" is defined as "the undoing of cross-border trade in high-tech goods and services" (2021). Throughout history, national security has been a driving force behind competition and conflict among global powers. The cycles of globalization and decoupling frequently coincide with the emergence and ascendancy of superpowers. The initial phase of globalization, spearheaded by the United Kingdom in the 19th century, was marred by the disruptions wrought by World War I, which saw Germany emerge as a major competitor. A subsequent period of decoupling ensued during World War II, coinciding with Germany's recovery and the ascent of the United States. The Cold War era witnessed a divided world, with globalization unfolding within separate blocs led by the United States and the USSR. The second wave of globalization commenced in 1991, following the dissolution of the USSR, enabling the United States to propel unparalleled global economic integration (Zhang, 2023).

In the contemporary global economic landscape, the United States is confronted with a substantial challenge from China. In response, the U.S. is reverting to a strategy of decoupling. Restrictions on technology transfer and export controls have been observed to disproportionately affect China's welfare, with the primary negative effect stemming from limitations on technology access rather than trade barriers. It is anticipated that both the U.S. and China, in conjunction with other nations, will encounter economic setbacks as a consequence of this decoupling. However, the magnitude of these losses is expected to remain relatively moderate provided that containment remains bilateral (Jinji and Ozawa, 2024).

5.3 Innovation and Self-Sufficiency

While trade wars and technological decoupling pose significant challenges, they have also spurred efforts to achieve self-sufficiency in key technologies. In this context, countries are allocating substantial resources to domestic R&D initiatives and fostering innovation with the objective of enhancing autonomy in technology. Beyond the U.S.-China rivalry, the broader geopolitical landscape is increasingly shaped by technological competition. In light of these developments, nations are undertaking a re-evaluation of their reliance on foreign technology and directing increased investments in domestic innovation with the aim of enhancing resilience and reducing vulnerabilities.

China's "Made in China 2025" initiative aims to transform the country into a global leader in advanced manufacturing and technology by investing in sectors such as robotics, artificial intelligence, and renewable energy (Conroy, 2022). The nation has been making rapid progress in the field of AI research, as evidenced by the development of its AI model, DeepSeek, which has garnered the attention of the U.S. government since 2023 (Tan, 2025).

The United States has initiated several programs, including the CHIPS for America Act. This initiative allocates a sum of $52.7 billion to the goal of increasing U.S. semiconductor manufacturing, with the aim of reducing the nation's reliance on foreign supply chains. The funding is earmarked for the construction and expansion of chip production facilities, research initiatives, and workforce development programs. The initial phase of funding was initiated in 2023 with the objective of enhancing domestic semiconductor capabilities (U.S. Department of Commerce, 2023).

Concurrently, the European Union is undertaking measures to augment its semiconductor capabilities, with the objective of reducing its reliance on Asian suppliers. This initiative is part of a broader shift toward achieving technological self-sufficiency. The European Chips Act, a legislative initiative, aims to mobilize €43 billion in public and private investments to support research, innovation, and manufacturing activities. The act emphasizes the development of advanced chip technologies, the attraction of skilled labor, and the enhancement of Europe's global competitiveness in the semiconductor sector (European Commission, n.a.).

These endeavors to attain self-sufficiency have the potential to stimulate innovation and generate novel opportunities for economic growth. Nevertheless, these endeavors give rise to concerns regarding the duplication of efforts and the inefficient allocation of resources. For instance, the parallel development of technological standards in the U.S. and China has the potential to result in redundant investments and hinder the pace of innovation. Furthermore, an overemphasis on self-sufficiency has the potential to hinder the collaborative nature of scientific research, which has historically been a significant catalyst for technological advancement.

6. TRADE WARS AND ENERGY SECURITY

6.1 Energy as a Geopolitical Tool

In the contemporary geopolitical landscape, energy security has emerged as a pivotal dimension of trade wars, as the access to energy resources and technologies has become a source of geopolitical tension. Energy is not merely a vital input for economic growth; it is also a strategic tool that countries employ to exert influence and achieve political objectives (Overland, 2019). A notable illustration of this phenomenon is the ongoing U.S.-China trade war, where both countries have strategically employed their energy resources and technologies to gain a competitive edge in their broader geopolitical rivalry. A similar dynamic is evident in the Russia-EU energy relationship, where Russia strategically utilizes its dominance in natural gas supplies to exert political pressure on European nations (Deirmentzoglou et al., 2024; Goldthau, 2016). The European experience during energy crises highlights how economic policies, including fiscal adjustments and regulatory frameworks, are crucial for maintaining stability amid resource access disputes (Patsoulis et al., 2022).

The strategic importance of energy in trade wars is evident in the competition over critical resources, such as rare earth minerals. These minerals are essential for the production of high-tech goods and renewable energy technologies. China, a major player in the global rare earth market, strategically utilizes its dominant position to exert leverage in trade negotiations. For instance, during the U.S.-China trade war, there were concerns that China might restrict rare earth exports to the United States, which would have disrupted supply chains for industries such as electronics, defense, and renewable energy (Overland, 2019). A similar dynamic can be observed in Russia's strategic use of its natural gas supply to Europe, which has afforded it considerable leverage in its geopolitical interactions with the EU, particularly during periods of heightened tension, such as the conflict in Ukraine (Deirmentzoglou et al., 2024; Goldthau, 2016).

Energy security is also closely linked to the renewable energy transition, as countries compete to secure access to the materials and technologies needed for the green energy transition. The notion of energy security has only recently garnered significant attention in academic discourse, despite its initial conceptualization in 1975 (see Augutis et al. 2011). The ongoing U.S.-China trade war has led to heightened tensions in this domain, as both nations strive to dominate the global market for renewable energy technologies, including solar panels, wind turbines, and batteries. This heightened competition has far-reaching consequences for global energy markets and the rate of the energy transition.

6.2 Case Studies of Energy-Related Trade Conflicts

The nexus between trade wars and energy security is exemplified by numerous prominent case studies. A noteworthy example is the U.S.-China trade war, in which both countries have imposed tariffs and restrictions on energy-related goods and technologies. For instance, the United States has imposed tariffs on Chinese solar energy resources, including solar polysilicon, wafers, and cells (Kennedy, 2025), while China has retaliated with tariffs on liquefied natural gas (LNG) from the

United States, coal, and crude oil (Race and Espiner, 2025). These measures have precipitated a disruption in global supply chains and engendered a state of uncertainty for businesses in the energy sector.

A notable example is the energy dispute between Russia and the EU, which has been characterized by tensions over natural gas supplies and pipeline projects. Historically, Russia has strategically leveraged its dominant position as a natural gas supplier to Europe to exert significant geopolitical influence, a factor that was particularly evident during the Ukraine conflict. In response, the European Union (EU) has actively sought to reduce its dependency on Russian gas by diversifying energy sources and investing in renewable infrastructure (Deirmentzoglou et al., 2024). The situation escalated following Russia's invasion of Ukraine in 2022, leading to significant shifts in energy dynamics. The European Union imposed sanctions on Russian energy exports, leading to a precipitous decline in Russian gas supplies. Consequently, the share of Russian pipeline gas in EU imports has experienced a substantial decline, from over 40% in 2021 to approximately 8% in 2023. When pipeline gas and LNG are considered collectively, Russia's contribution to EU gas imports remains below 15% (Council of the European Union, 2025).

6.3 The Transition to Renewable Energy

The transition to renewable energy has emerged as a pivotal factor in the nexus between trade wars and energy security. As nations endeavor to reduce their reliance on fossil fuels and address the challenges posed by climate change, they are increasingly engaging in competition to secure access to the materials and technologies necessary for the transition to green energy. This heightened competition has far-reaching consequences for global energy markets and the overall pace of the energy transition.

The competition over rare earth minerals constitutes a pivotal element in the transition to renewable energy. Rare earths are vital components in the production of advanced technologies and renewable energy sources. China exerts significant influence over the global supply, maintaining a substantial share of the market. During the period of the U.S.-China trade war, there were concerns that China might restrict rare earth exports to the United States, which would have resulted in a disruption of supply chains for industries such as electronics, defense, and renewable energy (Crownhart, 2024). This case study underscores the strategic importance of critical resources in trade wars and the challenges of achieving energy security in a globalized economy.

A recent study by Deirmentzoglou et al. (2024) provides a comprehensive analysis of the interplay between international economic relations and energy security, particularly within the European Union (EU). The study's findings indicate a growing emphasis on renewable energy sources, particularly hydrogen, as evidenced by recent research. The EU's objective to achieve climate neutrality by 2050, with clean hydrogen playing a pivotal role in this transition, is further supported by the European Commission (2022). While the EU's Hydrogen Strategy is dependent on imports, the hydrogen market is expected to exhibit greater diversification compared to other energy sectors, thereby reducing the risk of supply disruptions. In light of the energy crisis triggered by the Russian invasion of Ukraine, the REPowerEU plan underscores hydrogen's potential to enhance energy security and decrease reliance on Russian energy (Dejonghe et al., 2023). Nevertheless, achieving domestic renewable hydrogen targets remains challenging, necessitating the establishment of international partnerships to facilitate progress.

7. POLICY IMPLICATIONS AND FUTURE OUTLOOK

7.1 Policy Responses to Trade Wars

Trade wars have far-reaching implications for policymakers, who must navigate the complex interplay between economic, geopolitical, and technological factors. A salient challenge confronting policymakers is the economic cost of trade wars, which encompasses higher consumer prices, diminished market access for exporters, and heightened uncertainty for businesses. To address these challenges, policymakers can implement measures such as targeted subsidies, tax incentives, and support for affected industries. For instance, the U.S. government has allocated financial assistance to farmers experiencing the repercussions of the U.S.-China trade war, aiding them in coping with lost export markets and declining commodity prices (The Guardian, 2019).

Another salient policy response is the diversification of trade relationships, which is intended to reduce the country's dependence on any single nation. This objective can be accomplished by means of regional trade agreements, such as the Comprehensive and Progressive Agreement for Trans-Pacific Partnership (CPTPP) (DFAT, 2025) and the Regional Comprehensive Economic Partnership (RCEP) (ASEAN, n.a.), which promote economic integration and mitigate the risks of trade wars (Baldwin & Evenett, 2020). Furthermore, the diversification of trade relationships entails the reinforcement of domestic industries and supply chains, thereby enhancing resilience in the face of global disruptions.

The Russia-EU energy relationship offers a compelling illustration of how diversification can bolster energy security. In response to Russia's strategic use of energy exports as a geopolitical tool, the EU has accelerated its efforts to diversify its energy sources. This includes increasing imports of liquefied natural gas (LNG) from the

United States and investing in renewable energy infrastructure (Deirmentzoglou et al., 2024). These endeavors are indicative of a broader trend of regionalization, as nations seek to establish more resilient and self-sufficient supply chains in response to geopolitical risks.

7.2 Strengthening International Institutions

The emergence of trade wars has underscored the necessity to reform and fortify international institutions, such as the World Trade Organization (WTO). The WTO's dispute resolution mechanisms have been inundated with the magnitude and intricacy of contemporary trade conflicts, giving rise to calls for reforms that address issues such as state subsidies, intellectual property theft, and forced technology transfer. The reinforcement of the WTO and analogous multilateral institutions is imperative for sustaining a rules-based international order and forestalling the escalation of trade conflicts into more expansive confrontations.

In addition to the reform of existing institutions, policymakers should explore new forms of international cooperation that address emerging challenges such as technological competition and climate change. For instance, the Paris Agreement on climate change establishes a framework for global collaboration to reduce greenhouse gas emissions (UN, n.a.). Initiatives such as the Global Partnership on Artificial Intelligence (GPAI) promote collaboration on ethical AI development (GPAI, n.a.). These initiatives exemplify the capacity of international institutions to tackle intricate global challenges and mitigate the risks associated with trade wars.

The Russia-EU energy dispute further illustrates the challenges faced by international institutions in managing trade conflicts. The EU's attempts to reduce its reliance on Russian gas have been hindered by the absence of a cohesive energy policy among member states and the geopolitical intricacies of energy trade. The EU has endeavored to utilize international institutions, such as the Energy Charter Treaty, to enhance energy security. However, these endeavors have yielded only limited success, largely due to Russia's reluctance to adhere to international norms. This underscores the necessity for the development of more robust and effective international institutions that can effectively navigate the intricate dynamics among trade disputes, energy security, and geopolitical rivalries.

7.3 Recommendations for Sustainable Global Cooperation

In order to promote sustainable global cooperation in an era of trade wars, policymakers must adopt a multifaceted approach that addresses the root causes of trade conflicts while fostering resilience and collaboration. A critical initial step is the promotion of economic resilience through the diversification of trade relationships, the strengthening of domestic industries, and the investment in critical infrastructure, thereby reducing a nation's dependence on any single country or region. This strategy not only mitigates the risks of supply chain disruptions but also enhances a nation's ability to withstand external shocks. In addition, the reform and strengthening of international institutions, particularly the World Trade Organization (WTO), is imperative to address contemporary trade challenges, including state subsidies, intellectual property theft, and forced technology transfer. The revitalization of multilateral frameworks is instrumental in upholding a rules-based international order, thereby averting the escalation of trade conflicts into more widespread conflicts.

At the same time, fostering technological cooperation is essential to address growing competition in emerging technologies such as artificial intelligence, 5G, and semiconductors. It is incumbent upon policymakers to promote international cooperation in research and development while addressing the risks of technological decoupling. The latter is a phenomenon that threatens to fragment global innovation networks and decelerate the pace of progress. Integrating climate objectives into trade policies is another imperative, as the transition to renewable energy and the fight against climate change require coordinated global action. Initiatives such as the Paris Agreement provide a foundational framework for these efforts; however, further efforts are necessary to align trade policies with sustainability objectives.

Furthermore, cultural differences play a pivotal role in the shaping of business relations (Deirmentzoglou et al., 2024), economic policies, and diplomatic negotiations. The acknowledgement and respect for disparate cultural viewpoints have the potential to enhance communication efficacy, avert misunderstandings, and cultivate trust among nations. In the context of trade diplomacy, cultural awareness is particularly important because different attitudes toward business ethics, negotiation styles, and regulatory frameworks can affect the outcomes of economic agreements.

Finally, enhancing diplomatic engagement is vital to de-escalate trade conflicts and build trust among nations. By prioritizing dialogue and cooperation, particularly in regions such as the Indo-Pacific and Europe where geopolitical tensions are high, countries can mitigate the risks of conflict and foster a more stable and prosperous global order. The implementation of these strategies offers a multifaceted approach to navigating the intricacies of trade conflicts and fostering sustainable global cooperation in an era of increasing interconnectedness.

8. CONCLUSION

8.1 Summary of Key Findings

This chapter has examined the multifaceted ramifications of trade wars for global supply chains, technological advancement, energy security, and international relations. Trade wars, such as the one between the United States and China, are not merely economic phenomena; they are deeply intertwined with geopolitical rivalries, technological competition, and the global energy transition. The ramifications of these trade conflicts have reconfigured global supply networks, compelling corporations and nations to adopt strategies such as reshoring and diversification to mitigate risks. Concurrently, the competition over emerging technologies has intensified, resulting in increased investment in innovation but also the fragmentation of global innovation networks. Energy security has emerged as a critical dimension of trade wars, with countries competing to secure access to critical resources and technologies needed for the green energy transition. These dynamics have profound implications for international relations, as trade wars reshape alliances, undermine international institutions, and challenge the rules-based global order.

The Russia-EU relationship offers a compelling case study in how trade conflicts intersect with energy security and geopolitical strategy. In the context of the Russia-Ukraine conflict, Russia's strategic exploitation of energy exports as a geopolitical tool has compelled the EU to expedite its efforts to diversify energy sources and invest in renewable energy infrastructure. These developments are indicative of a broader trend of regionalization, as countries seek to establish more resilient and self-sufficient supply chains in response to geopolitical risks. A similar dynamic is observable in the U.S.-EU trade relationship, which has been strained by disputes over tariffs, subsidies, and digital taxation, highlighting the challenges of managing economic competition among allies.

8.2 Broader Implications for International Relations

The escalation of trade conflicts carries profound ramifications for the future of international relations. As nations increasingly employ trade as a geopolitical instrument, the probability of confrontation and instability is anticipated to escalate. This phenomenon is particularly evident in regions such as the Indo-Pacific, where the U.S.-China rivalry is reshaping the geopolitical landscape. Concurrently, trade wars have catalyzed endeavors to reform and fortify international institutions, such as the World Trade Organization (WTO), and to cultivate novel forms of cooperation that address emergent challenges, including technological competition and climate change. These developments underscore a discernible acknowledgement of the pivotal role that multilateralism plays in ensuring the stability of the global economy and averting the escalation of trade conflicts into more profound geopolitical confrontations.

The dynamic interplay between trade wars and international relations underscores the necessity for a more nuanced and strategic approach to global economic governance. It is incumbent upon policymakers to achieve a balance between the promotion of economic resilience and the preservation of the benefits of globalization. Achieving this balance necessitates addressing the underlying causes of trade conflicts, including economic inequality and technological competition. This can be achieved by fortifying international institutions and cultivating collaborative efforts on matters such as climate change and cybersecurity. Adopting a multifaceted approach that integrates economic, geopolitical, and technological considerations is a prerequisite for reducing the risks of trade wars and promoting a more stable and prosperous global order.

The Russia-EU energy dispute further illustrates the challenges faced by international institutions in managing trade conflicts. The EU's attempts to reduce its reliance on Russian gas have been hindered by the absence of a cohesive energy policy among member states and the geopolitical intricacies of energy trade. The EU has endeavored to utilize international institutions, such as the Energy Charter Treaty, to enhance energy security. However, these endeavors have yielded only limited success, largely due to Russia's reluctance to adhere to international norms. This underscores the necessity for the development of more robust and effective international institutions that can effectively navigate the intricate dynamics among trade disputes, energy security, and geopolitical rivalries.

8.3 Final Thoughts

The future of global trade and international relations will be shaped by the ongoing tensions between globalization and nationalism, cooperation and competition, and innovation and fragmentation. While trade wars present considerable challenges, they also create opportunities for countries to rethink their strategies and build new partnerships that promote economic resilience and geopolitical stability. The transition to renewable energy sources, the emergence of novel technologies, and the imperative for global collaboration in addressing climate change present opportunities for cooperative endeavors that can ameliorate the deleterious effects of trade wars and promote sustainable development.

In Europe, the Russia-Ukraine conflict has led to a acceleration in the efforts to diversify energy supply chains and reduce dependence on Russian gas. The European Union (EU) has augmented its imports of liquefied natural gas (LNG) from the United States and other suppliers, while concurrently allocating resources to the development of renewable energy and energy storage technologies. These measures are indicative of a broader trend of regionalization, as countries seek to establish more resilient and self-sufficient supply chains in response to geopolitical risks.

The capacity of nations to successfully navigate the intricacies of trade wars is contingent upon their readiness to embrace multilateralism, allocate resources to innovation, and prioritize diplomatic engagement over confrontation. Addressing the underlying causes of trade conflicts and fortifying international institutions is a strategic approach that policymakers can adopt to mitigate the risks of trade wars and foster a more stable and prosperous global order. The insights garnered from contemporary trade conflicts, such as the U.S.-China dynamic and the Russia-EU energy dispute, offer invaluable guidance for shaping the future of global trade and international relations in a progressively interconnected and competitive global landscape.

REFERENCES

Agoraki, K. K., Deirmentzoglou, G. A., Psychalis, M., & Apostolopoulos, S. (2024). Types of innovation and sustainable development: Evidence from medium-and large-sized firms. *International Journal on Management of Innovation & Technology*, *21*(02), 2450013. DOI: 10.1142/S0219877024500135

Agoraki, K. K., Deirmentzoglou, G. A., & Triantopoulos, C. (2024). Cultural Values as Catalysts of Technological Innovation for a Sustainable Future. *Sustainability (Basel)*, *16*(5), 2064. DOI: 10.3390/su16052064

Allison, G. (2017). *Destined for War: Can America and China Escape Thucydides's Trap?* Houghton Mifflin Harcourt.

Amiti, M., Redding, S. J., & Weinstein, D. E. (2019). The impact of the 2018 tariffs on prices and welfare. *The Journal of Economic Perspectives*, *33*(4), 187–210. DOI: 10.1257/jep.33.4.187

Attinasi, M. G., Ioannou, D., Lebastard, L., & Morris, R. 2023. Global production and supply chain risks: insights from a survey of leading companies. https://www.ecb.europa.eu/press/economic-bulletin/focus/2023/html/ecb.ebbox202307_01~2a0bcf0b48.en.html?utm_

Augutis, J., Krikštolaitis, R., Pečiulytė, S., & Konstantinavičiūtė, I. (2011). Sustainable development and energy security level after Ignalina NPP shutdown. *Technological and Economic Development of Economy*, *17*(1), 5–21. DOI: 10.3846/13928619.2011.553930

Autor, D. H., Dorn, D., & Hanson, G. H. (2016). The China shock: Learning from labor-market adjustment to large changes in trade. *Annual Review of Economics*, *8*(1), 205–240. DOI: 10.1146/annurev-economics-080315-015041

Barteková, E., & Kemp, R. (2016). National strategies for securing a stable supply of rare earths in different world regions. *Resources Policy*, *49*, 153–164. DOI: 10.1016/j.resourpol.2016.05.003

BBC. (2020). US China tariffs "incosistent" with trade rules says TWO. https://www.bbc.com/news/business-54168419

Blenkinsop, Ph. (2018). EU expands WTO case against Chinese technology transfers. https://www.reuters.com/article/us-eu-china-wto/eu-expands-wto-case-against-chinese-technology-transfers-idUSKCN1OJ1AP/

Bown, C. P. (2020). How the United States marched the semiconductor industry into its trade war with China. *East Asian Economic Review*, *24*(4), 349–388. DOI: 10.11644/KIEP.EAER.2020.24.4.384

Bown, C. P. (2021). The US–China trade war and Phase One agreement. *Journal of Policy Modeling*, *43*(4), 805–843. DOI: 10.1016/j.jpolmod.2021.02.009

Bown, C. P., & Crowley, M. A. (2013). Import protection, business cycles, and exchange rates: Evidence from the Great Recession. *Journal of International Economics*, *90*(1), 50–64. DOI: 10.1016/j.jinteco.2012.12.001

Brautigam, D. (2020). A critical look at Chinese 'debt-trap diplomacy': The rise of a meme. *Area Development and Policy*, *5*(1), 1–14. DOI: 10.1080/23792949.2019.1689828

Buchwald, E. 2025. Tariffs on cars from Mexico and Canada delayed by one month. https://edition.cnn.com/2025/03/05/business/tariffs-autos-mexico-canada-paused/index.html

Callahan, W. A. (2016). China's "Asia Dream": The Belt Road Initiative and the new regional order. *Asian Journal of Comparative Politics*, *1*(3), 226–243. DOI: 10.1177/2057891116647806

Cerdeiro, D. A., Mano, R., Eugster, J., & Peiris, M. S. J. (2021). *Sizing up the effects of technological decoupling*. International Monetary Fund.

Charpin, R., & Cousineau, M. (2024). Friendshoring: How geopolitical tensions affect foreign sourcing, supply base complexity, and sub-tier supplier sharing. *International Journal of Operations & Production Management*. Advance online publication. DOI: 10.1108/IJOPM-01-2024-0067

Chivvis, C. S., & Keating, J. (2024). How Evil? Deconstructing the New Russia–China–Iran–North Korea Axis. In *Survival: December 2024–January 2025* (pp. 51-66). Routledge. DOI: 10.1080/00396338.2024.2432198

Cho, S. (2004). A dual catastrophe of protectionism. *Nw. J. Int'l L. & Bus.*, *25*, 315.

Conroy, G. (2024). How 'Made in China 2025' helped supercharge scientific development in China's cities. https://www.nature.com/articles/d41586-024-03522-y#:~:text=The%20overarching%20goal%20of%20MIC2025,ocean%20engineering%20and%20aerospace%20equipment

Council of the European Union. (2025). *Where does the EU's gas come from?* Retrieved [date], from https://www.consilium.europa.eu/en/infographics/where-does-the-eu-s-gas-come-from/

Crownhart, C. (2024). China banned exports of a few rare minerals to the US. Things could get messier. https://www.technologyreview.com/2024/12/12/1108568/china-export-bans/

CRS – Congressional Research Service. (2022). Russia's Nord Stream 2 Natural Gas Pipeline to Germany Halted. https://crsreports.congress.gov/product/pdf/IF/IF11138#:~:text=On%20January%2019%2C%202021%2C%20the,in%202020%20(PEESA%3B%2022%20U.S.C.

Deirmentzoglou, G. A., Agoraki, K. K., & Patsoulis, P. (2024). The nexus between cultural values and perceptions of corporate sustainable development. *Social Responsibility Journal*, *20*(2), 224–242. DOI: 10.1108/SRJ-09-2022-0373

Deirmentzoglou, G. A., Anastasopoulou, E. E., & Sklias, P. (2024). International economic relations and energy security in the European Union: A systematic literature review. *International Journal of Sustainable Energy*, *43*(1), 2385682.

Deirmentzoglou, G. A., & Deirmentzoglou, E. A. (2022) September. Pest analysis of the e-commerce industry: The case of Greece. In *Business Development and Economic Governance in Southeastern Europe:13th International Conference on the Economies of the Balkan and Eastern European Countries (EBEEC),Pafos, Cyprus,2021* (pp. 315-323). Cham: Springer International Publishing.

Deirmentzoglou, G. A., Vlassi, E., & Anastasopoulou, E. E. (2024). DDMMO Website Quality, Destination Image and Intention to Use Metaverse Platforms. *Platforms*, *2*(4), 180–192. DOI: 10.3390/platforms2040012

Dejonghe, M., Van de Graaf, T., & Belmans, R. (2023). From natural gas to hydrogen: Navigating import risks and dependencies in Northwest Europe. *Energy Research & Social Science*, *106*, 103301. DOI: 10.1016/j.erss.2023.103301

DFAT – Australian Government – Department of Foreign Affairs and Trade. (2025). *Comprehensive and Progressive Agreement for Trans-Pacific Partnership*. CPTPP.

Directorate-General for Trade and Economic Security. (2020). EU, US and Japan agree on new ways to strengthen global rules on industrial subsidies. https://policy.trade.ec.europa.eu/news/eu-us-and-japan-agree-new-ways-strengthen-global-rules-industrial-subsidies-2020-01-14_en

Economic Impact. (2025). Europe's path to resilience and responsibility in a fragmented world. https://impact.economist.com/projects/trade-in-transition/regional-analysis-europe/

Eichengreen, B. (2002). The political economy of the Smoot-Hawley tariff. In *International Political Economy* (pp. 37–46). Routledge.

European Commission. (2022). A Hydrogen Strategy for a Climate-Neutral Europe. https://energy.ec.europa.eu/ system/files/2020-07/hydrogen_strategy_0.pdf

Fajgelbaum, P. D., Goldberg, P. K., Kennedy, P. J., & Khandelwal, A. K. (2020). The return to protectionism. *The Quarterly Journal of Economics*, *135*(1), 1–55. DOI: 10.1093/qje/qjz036

Fan, D., Zhou, Y., Yeung, A. C., Lo, C. K., & Tang, C. (2022). Impact of the US–China trade war on the operating performance of US firms: The role of outsourcing and supply base complexity. *Journal of Operations Management*, *68*(8), 928–962. DOI: 10.1002/joom.1225

Gilpin, R. (2001). *Global political economy: Understanding the international economic order*. Princeton university press. DOI: 10.1515/9781400831272

Global Data. (2018). Is the biopharma industry safe from the US-China trade war? https://www.pharmaceutical-technology.com/comment/biopharma-industry-safe-us-china-trade-war/?utm_source=chatgpt.com&cf-view

Goldthau, A., & Sitter, N. (2021). Power, authority and security: the EU's Russian gas dilemma. In *Renegotiating Authority in EU Energy and Climate Policy* (pp. 107–123). Routledge. DOI: 10.4324/9781003173106-7

Gomez, T. (2025). Philipine defense chief warns allies will fight if China restricts flights over South China Sea. https://apnews.com/article/philippines-south-china-sea-defense-secretary-gilberto-teodoro-air-defense-zone-4c63b28b674c63b1730a22d-c9faa5f22

Grant, W. (2024). How Chinese firms are using Mexico as a backdoor to the US. https://www.bbc.com/news/business-68825118

Grieco, J. M. (1988). Anarchy and the limits of cooperation: A realist critique of the newest liberal institutionalism. *International Organization*, *42*(3), 485–507. DOI: 10.1017/S0020818300027715

Gur, N., & Dilek, S. (2023). US–China economic rivalry and the reshoring of global supply chains. *The Chinese Journal of International Politics*, *16*(1), 61–83. DOI: 10.1093/cjip/poac022

Handley, K., & Limão, N. (2017). Policy uncertainty, trade, and welfare: Theory and evidence for China and the United States. *The American Economic Review*, *107*(9), 2731–2783. DOI: 10.1257/aer.20141419

Hosoe, N. (2023). The cost of war: Impact of sanctions on Russia following the invasion of Ukraine. *Journal of Policy Modeling*, *45*(2), 305–319. DOI: 10.1016/j.jpolmod.2023.04.001

Jinji, N., & Ozawa, S. (2024). Economic consequences of US-China technological decoupling: An illustrative quantitative analysis. https://cepr.org/voxeu/columns/economic-consequences-us-china-technological-decoupling-illustrative-quantitative

Kennedy, R. (2025). US government raises tariffs on Chinese solar polysilicon, wafers, cells to 60%. https://www.pv-magazine.com/2025/02/05/us-government-raises-solar-polysilicon-wafer-and-cell-tariffs-from-china-to-60/#:~:text=Imported%20solar%20energy%20resources%2C%20including,from%2025%25%20to%2050%25

Keohane, R. O., & Nye, J. S. (1997). *Power and Interdependence: World Politics in Transition*. Longman.

Khan, S. M. (2020). *US Semiconductor Exports to China: Current Policies and Trends*. Center for Security and Emerging Technology, October. DOI: 10.51593/20200039

Kourkoumelis, A., Anastasopoulou, E., Deirmentzoglou, G., Masouras, A., & Anastasiadou, S. 2024, September. Artificial Intelligence and Managerial Decision-Making in International Business. In *European Conference on Innovation and Entrepreneurship* (pp. 363-369). Academic Conferences International Limited. DOI: 10.34190/ecie.19.1.2573

Krugman, P. R. (1987). Is free trade passé? *The Journal of Economic Perspectives*, *1*(2), 131–144. DOI: 10.1257/jep.1.2.131

Lambert, L. A., Tayah, J., Lee-Schmid, C., Abdalla, M., Abdallah, I., Ali, A. H., Esmail, S., & Ahmed, W. (2022). The EU's natural gas Cold War and diversification challenges. *Energy Strategy Reviews*, *43*, 100934. DOI: 10.1016/j.esr.2022.100934

Le Monde. (2024). Western sanctions on Russian oil have too many loopholes. https://www.lemonde.fr/en/opinion/article/2024/10/31/western-sanctions-on-russian-oil-have-too-many-loopholes_6731133_23.html

Liu, R., Zhang, J. J., & Vortherms, S. A. (2022). In the middle: American multinationals in China and trade war politics. *Business and Politics*, *24*(4), 348–376. DOI: 10.1017/bap.2022.14

Mao, H., & Görg, H. (2020). Friends like this: The impact of the US–China trade war on global value chains. *World Economy*, *43*(7), 1776–1791. DOI: 10.1111/twec.12967

Mavroidis, P.C. and Sapir, A. (2021). China and the WTO: why multilateralism still matters.

McGee, R. W. (1992). An economic analysis of protectionism in the United states with implications for international trade in Europe. *Geo. Wash. J. Int'l L. & Econ.*, *26*, 539.

Meckling, J., Kelsey, N., Biber, E., & Zysman, J. (2015). Winning coalitions for climate policy. *Science*, *349*(6253), 1170–1171. DOI: 10.1126/science.aab1336 PMID: 26359392

Milner, H. V. (1999). The political economy of international trade. *Annual Review of Political Science*, *2*(1), 91–114. DOI: 10.1146/annurev.polisci.2.1.91

Morgan, S., Arita, S., Beckman, J., Ahsan, S., Russell, D., Jarrell, P. and Kenner, B. (2022). The Economic Impacts of Retaliatory Tariffs on US Agriculture.

Mori, S. (2019). US technological competition with China: The military, industrial and digital network dimensions. *Asia-Pacific Review*, *26*(1), 77–120. DOI: 10.1080/13439006.2019.1622871

Nivola, P. S. (1986). The new protectionism: US trade policy in historical perspective. *Political Science Quarterly*, *101*(4), 577–600. DOI: 10.2307/2150795

Nye, J. S. (2023). *Soft power and great-power competition: Shifting sands in the balance of power between the United States and China*. Springer Nature. DOI: 10.1007/978-981-99-0714-4

Overland, I. (2019). The geopolitics of renewable energy: Debunking four emerging myths. *Energy Research & Social Science*, *49*, 36–40. DOI: 10.1016/j.erss.2018.10.018

Patsoulis, P., Psychalis, M., & Deirmentzoglou, G. A. (2022). Stability and Growth Pact: Too Young to Die, Too Old to Rock 'n'Roll. *Journal of Risk and Financial Management*, *15*(12), 608. DOI: 10.3390/jrfm15120608

Payne, J. (2024). EU energy ministers discuss Ukraine energy crisis, Russian LNG. https://www.reuters.com/business/energy/eu-energy-ministers-discuss-ukraine-energy-crisis-russian-lng-2024-10-15/

Race, M., & Espiner, T. (2025). How is China hitting back against US tariffs? https://www.bbc.com/news/articles/czj31l4p7vzo

Ricardo, D. (1817). *On the Principles of Political Economy and Taxation*. John Murray.

Tan, K. W. K. (2025). The US has been watching DeepSeek since late 2023 and still has a way to beat it, Biden's former AI advisory says. https://www.businessinsider.com/biden-ai-advisor-us-watching-deepseek-since-late-2023-2025-3?utm_

The Gurdian. (2019). US government to pay farmers hurt by China trade war $16bn. https://www.theguardian.com/business/2019/jul/26/us-government-to-pay-farmers-hurt-by-china-trade-war-16bn

Towfighi, J. (2024). Manufacturing in Mexico is having its moment. The US is buying in—and so is China. https://edition.cnn.com/2024/04/28/business/us-china-mexico-manufacturing-nearshoring-hnk-intl/index.html

U.S. Department of Commerce. (2023). Biden-Harris Administration Launches First CHIPS for America Funding Opportunity. https://www.commerce.gov/news/press-releases/2023/02/biden-harris-administration-launches-first-chips-america-funding

Walterskirchen, J., Mangott, G., & Wend, C. (2022). Sanction dynamics in the cases of North Korea, Iran, and Russia. *Objectives, Measures and Effect*. Springer.

Waltz, K. N. (1979). *Theory of International Politics*. Addison-Wesley.

Wendt, A. (1999). *Social Theory of International Politics*. Cambridge University Press. DOI: 10.1017/CBO9780511612183

Zhang, K. H. (2023). US-China economic links and technological decoupling. *Chinese Economy*, *56*(5), 353–365. DOI: 10.1080/10971475.2023.2173399

Chapter 5 Human Rights and Foreign Direct Investments: Addressing Societal Challenges

Eleni Gavriil
https://orcid.org/0000-0003-4112-8329
Neapolis University, Pafos, Cyprus

ABSTRACT

This chapter examines the connection between human rights and foreign direct investments, focusing on the potential impact of foreign investments on human rights. It explores the relationship between human rights and international investment law, highlighting that these legal fields are not isolated but interconnected. Through the analysis of investment treaties and case law, the chapter demonstrates how human rights issues increasingly arise in investment arbitration. Ultimately, the chapter argues that embedding human rights considerations into investment frameworks and dispute resolution mechanisms is essential for addressing societal challenges and achieving sustainable development.

I. INTRODUCTION

This chapter examines the relationship between human rights (HR) and foreign direct investments (FDIs). Traditionally, human rights and international investment law (IIL) are regarded as two separate regimes. However, the two legal branches are not isolated; they interact harmoniously and in conflict. This chapter addresses social entrepreneurship by examining the trend of incorporating human rights in

DOI: 10.4018/979-8-3693-5583-1.ch005

foreign direct investments. The specific objective of this chapter is to examine how international investment law addresses emerging societal challenges. By doing so, the chapter will indicate how much human rights are incorporated in FDIs. It aims to analyse whether human rights have a place in foreign direct investments. It will interpret specific investment treaties and investment arbitration cases to reach general conclusions about how IIL deals with human rights issues.

International investment law has been criticised for protecting foreign investments while excluding other interests such as the environment, health, access to essentials and human rights (Sornarajah, 2015). According to Gao (2021), this potential conflict stems from the lack of coordination between HR and IIL. States are obliged to protect foreign investments and, at the same time, safeguard human rights (p. 15). Consequently, it is imperative to address the conflict between these two legal fields and explore the tools to mitigate these tensions (Schill & Djanic, 2018). The minimisation of conflict and the achievement of equilibrium can allow foreign direct investments to foster economic growth while simultaneously advancing sustainable development. Sornarajah (2015) highlights that "the old view regarding the inflexibility of investment protection as the basis of law had to undergo a change" (p. 61). These efforts aim to reform IIL by incorporating rules from various legal fields (Sornarajah, 2015).

This chapter consists of five sections and proceeds as follows. Part II overviews the relationship between human rights and international investment law. It will discuss the interconnection between the two fields to provide a general understanding of their fundamental elements.

Part III will explore existing international investment agreements (IIAs) referring to human rights. The nature of treaties began to change, and the new trend of bilateral investment agreements (BITs) paved the way for investments that will address societal challenges. These BITs respond to the public criticism of existing investment agreements and implement new sustainable policies (Sornarajah, 2015). The latest models recognise the broader impact of foreign investments on society and the environment (Arcuri & Montanaro, 2018). By giving attention to human rights and environmental issues, IIAs look beyond the mere protection of investments and support multinational corporations in developing business models that prioritise social impact alongside financial success. Schill and Djanic (2018) highlight that states can establish new BITs to make them more "sensitive to issues of public interest", such as human rights (p. 43).

Part IV will examine the role of the Non-Governmental Organisations (NGOs) as emerging actors in IIL, concerned with the impact of FDIs on human rights. Prior to proceeding, an analysis of the role of non-governmental organisations in human rights law will be conducted. Investor-state arbitration is not limited to corporations and states; notably, NGOs are increasingly involved in these proceedings, primarily as *amici curiae*. *Amicus* submissions by NGOs are of significant importance as they facilitate the introduction of human rights concerns into investment arbitration (Wiik, 2018).

II. HUMAN RIGHTS AND INTERNATIONAL INVESTMENT LAW

While human rights and international investment law appear to have developed apart and are often treated as distinct areas of law, there is evidence of their convergence. Notably, IIL has expanded significantly during the era of globalisation. During globalisation, human rights started to operate beyond national borders and gained increased importance (Radi, 2018).

The idea that the individual is something more than a mere subject of the ruling prince emerges from the idea that the act of governing is not an entirely arbitrary occupation but is, itself, subject to and limited by law. After the end of the Second World War, a more coherent concept of the rights of citizens against the state emerged, as reflected in the establishment of the United Nations Declaration of Human Rights (UDHR) in 1948 (Nordenfelt, 1987). Human rights law, as understood today, was born in the 1940s. Before the Second World War, human rights were systemically violated and rarely discussed internationally. In contrast, the treatment of nationals was regarded as an internal issue. Over time, human rights have become a recognised code of conduct, making their way into a majority of contemporary constitutions and providing a standard for relations between the state and the citizens (Osiatynski, 2014).

The role of human rights is to ensure that every human being has the freedom needed as a moral agent to pursue goals and objectives of his or her own choosing (Cragg, 2012). The key values of human rights are human dignity and equality. Human rights can be understood as defining those basic standards that are necessary for a life of dignity, and their universality is derived from the fact that all humans are equal. According to the Council of Europe (2021) their main three characteristics are:

- Human Rights are inalienable and thus inherent to all human beings. It is accepted that, in some cases, they may be suspended or restricted.
- Human Rights are indivisible, interdependent and interrelated.
- Human Rights are universal. In particular, every individual is entitled to enjoy his or her human rights without distinction of "race" or ethnic background, colour, sex, sexual orientation, disability, language, religion, political or other opinion, national or social origin, birth or other status.

International investment law is considered a new legal field since it has expanded in the last decades (Miles, 2013). Nevertheless, foreign investment protection is an old concept which originated from the principle of protection of aliens (Radi, 2012). The development of IIL can be divided into three periods: the colonial, postcolonial and global eras.

During the colonial era, only a few agreements were investment-related, and the primary means of protecting foreign investment was customary law. Thus, most economic agreements are concerned with trade relations rather than foreign investments (Valdevelde, 2009).

The next era in the history of international investment law began with the end of the Second World War and continued until the collapse of the Soviet Union. During that era, states that liberalised barriers and promoted foreign trade entered into multilateral agreements such as the General Agreement on Tariffs and Trade (GATT). Notably, multilateral agreements did not include investment protection issues at that point (Trakman & Ranieri, 2013).

During the global era, there was an exponential growth in the conclusion of BITs. This was mainly due to economic liberalism prevailing in developing and developed states. Over time, some provisions of investment agreements have remained unchanged, but their content hasn't stayed entirely still. Indeed, today, the purpose of investment agreements is not only investment protection but also the liberalisation of investment flows (Valdevelde, 2009). Currently, there is a trend to reform IIAs to ensure coherence with societal concerns such as environmental issues and human rights issues by incorporating investor responsibility (Gao, 2021).

From a historical origin and content aspect, IIL and HR have significant differentiations. In fact, the two regimes are not simply considered different but antagonistic. Foreign investment protection preceded the recognition of fundamental human rights with the adoption of the United Nations (UN) Charter and the UDHR. Some authors argue that while International Human Rights Law (IHRL) has evolved within the public law sphere, investment protection focuses on private law (Hirsch, 2010, p. 107).

The most fundamental difference between the protection of aliens and the protection of individuals is that the legal status of aliens is directly linked to the state of their nationality (Dupuy, 2009). *A contrario*, in IHRL, individuals are protected regardless of their nationality. Human rights are linked to human existence without conditions, while foreign investors are protected under specific conditions. While the protection of foreign investments depends on the reciprocity of inter-state relations, this is not the case in human rights law (Dupuy, 2009). Moreover, individuals whose rights have been violated by states usually need to exhaust all local remedies as a condition to resort to the relevant international human rights *fora*. In contrast, in IIL, investors have direct access to international arbitration (Tomuschat, 2009).

Despite their different development era, international legal rules protecting individuals and foreign investors both grew from the law of state responsibility for injuries to aliens. General principles originally pertaining to the protection of foreigners have later been transferred into human rights frameworks. The most fundamental feature between the two regimes is the asymmetrical legal relationship between the sovereign state and individuals/investors, where the state is in a superior position (Hirsch, 2010, p. 98). Investment tribunals and human rights mechanisms serve the analogous function of providing judicial review of government conduct. Thus, both legal regimes protect individuals from the arbitrary actions of states (Ehsassi, 2010).

In recent years, investment agreements and investor-state arbitration claims have exploded. This increase has resulted in more complex legal questions. International investment agreements hold that tribunals should consider international law as applicable. Investment tribunals, thus, often have to examine non-investment issues such as human rights and environmental issues. These interconnections between IIL and other areas of international law can cause conflicts and raise complex issues.

This view is supported by investment arbitration awards such as *Urbaser v Argentina*. In this case, arbitrators noted that that account is to be taken of "any relevant rules of international law applicable in the relations between the parties". The BIT cannot be interpreted and applied in a vacuum" (*Urbaser SA v Argentina*, 2016, para. 1200). The Argentinian crisis and the large number of arbitration cases against Argentina demonstrate that societal challenges are raised in investor-state arbitration (Burke-White & Staden, 2010). In recent times, arbitration tribunals must deal not only with pure investment issues but also with issues of human rights and environmental issues. The increasing prevalence of these societal challenges in foreign direct investments further complicates the field.

The case law shows that human rights claims are increasingly emerging in investment arbitration. Arbitral tribunals provide a neutral forum for the settlement of investment disputes. Human rights considerations are essential guidelines for states, investors, and arbitral tribunals (Scheu, 2017). Even though arbitral tribunals are reluctant to assess human rights considerations, they have referred to the jurisprudence of human rights courts (Butler, 2017).

Human rights are often invoked by host states against foreign investors. This happens when foreign investments interfere with the economic and social rights of the population, as well as indigenous people's collective rights or environmental rights. The criticism against FDIs revolves around the fact that investment instruments rarely impose substantive binding obligations on foreign investors. In contrast, "they focus exclusively upon the obligations of host states vis-à-vis foreign investors" (Amado et al., 2018, p. 108).

Host states may be required to prioritise human rights obligations over investment treaty commitments when the latter negatively impacts the rights of local populations. Human rights treaties can provide oversight and remedy when investment treaties conflict with or violate human rights standards (Ghouri, 2019). Importantly, states not only have to respect foreign investments but also protect human rights from threats. These threats can arise from actions associated with foreign investments. In that sense, in *Suez v Argentina,* the latter argued that the measures that injured the investor were adopted to safeguard the human right to water. The tribunal, in its decision, noted that the "host state's human rights obligations and its investment treaty obligations are not inconsistent, contradictory, or mutually exclusive" and "it must respect both of them" (*Suez and Vivendi v Argentina*, 2010). *Suez* is an illustration of cases where host states used human rights as a defence against investors for violating BITs' provisions.

In cases where host states do not make use of human rights arguments, *amicus* briefs are the only way by which human rights arguments enter investor-state arbitration (Gavriil, 2024). Their purpose is to represent the affected nationals of the host state. It is noted that tribunals in the last decade have been faced with *amicus curiae* submissions from various actors of civil society (Schadendorf, 2015). Civil society, while addressing human rights concerns, has resorted to the institution *amicus curiae,* which enables non-parties to raise human rights and environmental and social concerns during the arbitration proceedings. It is noted that even though *amicus curiae* can influence the reasoning of awards, they have not been given adequate consideration by arbitrators (CCSI et al., 2019). Nevertheless, they can serve as a valuable resource for arbitrators in balancing investment protection with human rights and addressing matters outside their expertise. This mechanism also enhances transparency by allowing NGOs to participate in the proceedings (Gavriil, 2024).

Kriebaum (2014) believes that the integration of human rights offers the potential to solve many of the problems in the context of an interaction between non-investment obligations and international investment law (p. 1030). Ortino (2009) mentions that human rights considerations are essential in strengthening the legitimacy of international law on foreign investments (p. 366).

III. HUMAN RIGHTS IN INTERNATIONAL INVESTMENT AGREEMENTS

International investment agreements are usually silent on human rights. As a result, investment tribunals do not have consistent approaches when human rights are raised in the proceedings. However, in recent years, several countries have signed BITs that refer to human rights and corporate responsibility. In response to the imbalance of IIL, states are revising their BITs to promote socially responsible foreign investments as part of sustainable development (Baltag & Dautaj, 2021). The UN Guiding Principles on Business and Human Rights holds in Article 9 that IIAs may constrain states from fully implementing new human rights legislation. Therefore, states should ensure that they retain adequate policy and regulatory ability to protect human rights while providing the necessary investor protection (*United Nations*, 2011). BITs are often criticised for safeguarding the interests of foreign investors without establishing any obligations. This asymmetry has resulted in the conflict between HR and IIL. This research suggests that the inclusion of human rights provisions in IIAs can address the legitimacy issues of foreign direct investments.

The BIT signed between Morocco and Nigeria is considered an innovative agreement that is aligned with the need to reform FDIs. The BIT, in its preamble, recognises the contribution of investments to sustainable development and the furtherance of human rights and highlights the needed balance among the state parties and investors. Article 15 further states that parties shall provide for a high level of human rights protections that are consistent with the international human rights agreements. Under the BIT, foreign investors have specific obligations to comply with environmental, labour and human rights standards. Article 18 requires foreign investors to uphold human rights and not operate in a manner that circumvents environmental and human rights obligations (*Morocco-Nigeria BIT*, 2016). The Morocco-Nigeria BIT is an excellent example of an investment agreement that can rebalance investment protection and human rights.

Another IIA that refers to human rights is the Common Market East Southern Africa Investment Agreements. Article 2 states that COMESA provides an overall balance of rights and obligations between investors and member states (*COMESA Investment Agreement*, 2007, pt. two). In addition, according to Article 7, the CCIA Committee of the Agreement is responsible for making recommendations to the Council on any policy issues, such as human rights. Further, COMESA refers to existing international law. Article 22 particularly mentions that the agreement does not preclude member states from applying measures that are necessary under the United Nations Charter (*COMESA Investment Agreement*, 2007). Within the African region, the Southern African Development Community Model BIT also follows a similar language. Article 13 holds that investors shall comply with environmental and social criteria. Also, it provides for impact assessment that includes the impact on the human rights of the persons in the areas potentially impacted by the foreign investment. According to Article 15, investors have a duty to respect human rights and shall not commit acts that breach human rights (*SADC Model BIT*, 2012).

The Canada-Côte d'Ivoire BIT in Article 15 encourages foreign investors to recognise standards of corporate social responsibility in their practices, such as human rights. It also holds that it is inappropriate to encourage investments by lowering health, safety and environmental measures (*Canada-Côte d'Ivoire BIT*, 2014).

Similar provisions are found in Brazil's investment agreements. For instance, the Brazil-Chile Agreement holds that investors should develop their best efforts to comply with the OECD Guidelines for Multinational Enterprises of the Organisation for Economic Cooperation and Development. Foreign investors should respect internationally recognised human rights and refrain from seeking or accepting exemption other than those established in the law of the host state with respect to human rights and other matters (*Brazil-Chile CFIA*, 2015, art. 15). The Brazil-Malawi BIT mentions in Article 9 that investors should respect the human rights of those involved in the company's activities, consistent with the international obligations and commitments of the host state (*Brazil-Malawi BIT*, 2015, art. 9). A number of IIA also refer to human rights in their preamble. The preamble is not binding, but it can guide tribunals when interpreting the relevant agreement (Goldstein, 2017).

Model BITs provide the framework for future investments, and thus, the inclusion of human rights provisions is vital. For instance, India's model BIT states that investors should endeavour to incorporate internationally recognised standards of corporate social responsibility in their practices that address, amongst others, human rights (*India Model BIT*, 2016, art. 12). Another example of a Model BIT that mentions human rights is the Italian. The agreement states in Article 5 that parties reaffirm the right to regulate within territories such as human rights. In addition, according to the BIT, investors are subjected to and must comply with the legislation of the host state relating to human rights as set forth in the UDHR (*Italy Model BIT*, 2020, art. x).

The 2019 Netherland Model BIT is an innovative agreement that aims to achieve sustainable investments. The model BIT opens the way for investments that focus on sustainable development, incorporation of human rights and gender equality. It holds that parties have a duty to protect against business-related human rights abuses and reaffirms the obligation of the parties to protect and respect human rights. The BIT states that the members of the tribunals shall have expertise in public international law, including HR and IIL. In article 5, the Dutch model BIT obligates contracting parties to "take appropriate steps to ensure, through judicial, administrative, legislative or other appropriate means, that when such abuses occur within their territory and/or jurisdiction those affected have access to effective remedy." In connection, it makes specific reference to instruments on business and human rights. The BIT further addresses gender equality by referring to the "important contribution by women to economic growth through their participation in economic activity, including in international investment" (*Netherlands Model BIT*,

2019, arts. 5–7, 20). Significantly, the treaty endorses the view that human rights have a place in international investment law, and tribunals must be ready to address the relevant issues that arise.

In the modern era, FDIs do not have mere economic aims, but they address sustainable development. The chapter suggests that the new model for IIAs is moving in the right direction to strike a balance between investors and states. Such developments are very positive for the relationship between HR and IIL, contributing to their rebalancing. The restructuring of IIAs can help bridge the asymmetries in the field of investment law.

IV. NGOS AND INTERNATIONAL INVESTMENT LAW

In *Methanex v United States* in 2001, the tribunal accepted three civil society organisations to submit briefs as *amici curiae* (*Methanex Corporation v United States of America*, 2005). By accepting *amicus* submissions, the tribunal opened the way for non-governmental organisations to intervene in investment arbitration due to the public interest issues as stated. In general, non-governmental organisations have sought to take part in investment arbitration cases that concern human rights issues (El-Hosseny, 2018, p. 27). This section will examine the involvement of NGOs in international investment law by referring to the submission of *amicus curiae* in investment arbitration aiming at promoting human rights norms in IIL. This section aims to determine how *amicus curiae* submissions by NGOs can influence IIL by incorporating human rights considerations. It addresses the social responsibility concerns in foreign direct investments and examines the goal of aligning FDIs with societal objectives.

Foreign direct investments focus on economic liberalisation and, for that reason, have been strongly criticised. Sornarajah (2010) notes that IIL often clashes with groups that have non-economic concerns, such as NGOs. IIL's critics support reforming the field to focus on sustainable development and consider social issues, including human rights (p. 67). Accordingly, NGOs may contribute to a more balanced international investment law (Mann, 2011). That said, this part of the chapter will explore the role of NGOs in international investment law, especially in investment arbitration. The focus will be on human rights NGOs due to their prominent activity in this field and their connection with IIL. Notably, an increasing number of investment disputes raise public concerns about human rights, environmental issues, the right to water, etc.

A. NGOs in Human Rights Law

Firstly, it is essential to explore and provide an understanding of the "non-governmental organisations" concept. It is important to note that there is not a single definition of an NGO. The World Association of Non-Governmental Organizations (2021) defines NGOs as "non-state, non-profit orientated groups who pursue purposes of public interests". The World Bank (1995) defines NGOs as "private organisations that pursue activities to relieve suffering, promote the interests of the poor, protect the environment, provide basic social services, or undertake community development".

International NGOs act as social, cultural, legal and environmental advocacy groups (Koster et al., 2019). They have an important role in the human rights context and have been described as "the conscience of the world" (Cassese, 1990, p. 115). The UN, along with NGOs, has contributed to the development of human rights and has influenced the field dynamically (Stephan, 2019). NGOs are a relatively recent phenomenon and have been a part of international law since the nineteenth century. During the start of globalisation after the end of the Cold War, their activities and roles have been strengthened dramatically. Over time, NGOs have transformed into essential actors in international law, and their role has been critical in several institutions.

NGOs are not only concentrating on governmental actions but also on corporate practices. For that reason, they have been described as "watchdogs of large multinational corporations" (Koster et al., 2019, p. 484). When corporations engage in human rights violations, NGOs seek to address these violations and constrain the conduct of the corporation. According to Hasan (2013), NGOs' activity in exposing abusive practices has forced multinational enterprises to become more socially responsible and comply with ethical standards (p. 42).

Amnesty International and other NGOs (2018) have suggested elements for a European Union (EU) action plan on business and human rights. NGOs are urging the EU to take concrete steps to make the UN Guiding Principles on Business and Human Rights a reality. They highlight that the EU must ensure that its investment policies are not harmful to human rights and that investment agreements adequately safeguard human rights that are at risk because of FDIs. The report also notes that affected people and communities must have access to remedies (Amnesty International et al., 2018).

The UN gave voice to NGOs under the establishment of the United Nations Charter. According to Article 71 of the Charter, "the Economic and Social Council may make suitable arrangements for consultation with non-governmental organisations which are concerned with matters within its competence" (*UN Charter*, 1945). Based on Article 71, the Economic and Social Council (ECOSOC) adopted the 1996/31 resolution, which concerns the consultive relationship between the UN and non-governmental organisations. Under the ECOSOC, different NGOs have different rights. NGOs may sit as observers and potentially speak at public ECOSOC meetings, propose to place items of special interest in the provisional agenda or submit written statements (*Economic and Social Council,* 1968).

In general, the role of human rights NGOs is to promote and protect recognised human rights. Their goal is to monitor governmental and corporate behaviour and create mechanisms to end human rights violations. In some cases, they cooperate and consult with governments. Nevertheless, they often clash with the latter when they violate human rights, especially in non-democratic states (Stephan, 2019).

The role of the NGOs can be traced to three categories: legislative, administrative or adjudicatory (Woodward, 2011). Their ability to initiate or to intervene before international courts or tribunals is limited. However, they can participate by submitting *amicus curiae.* In the early 1990s, courts changed their hostile position and started to accept *amicus* submissions, mainly by NGOs. In the European Court on Human Rights (ECtHR), the participation of NGOs as *amici* has significantly increased (Farber, 2019).

Direct NGO participation in international *fora* is relatively limited, and its standing is mainly in domestic litigation. However, NGOs have, in certain cases, direct access to international proceedings as parties (De Brabandere, 2011). For instance, the European Convention on Human Rights (ECHR) allows for the submission of non-governmental organisations if they allege that they are victims of a violation of rights included in the Convention. NGO's can also represent the victims of human rights violations (Smyth, 2012).

NGOs have influenced international law by contributing to the drafting of international treaties and declarations. Indeed, NGOs have influenced drafting the Universal Declaration of Human Rights and the International Covenant on Civil and Political Rights (ICCPR) (Spiro, 2008).

B. NGOs in International Investment Law

NGOs' concerns in regard to IIL are that the field emphasises investment protection without considering human rights and environmental concerns. According to them, the field of investment protection must be more balanced and must hold investors accountable when they violate environmental and human rights standards (Sornarajah, 2010, p. 145). Therefore, NGOs' role is crucial to ensure the transformation of FDIs. NGOs participate in investment treaty arbitration for the following reasons:

firstly, to interpret an investment treaty according to human rights and secondly, to analyse subject matters of their expertise (Saravanan & Subramanian, 2016).

The relevant case law shows that NGOs have participated in investment arbitration to introduce human rights arguments that otherwise would not be addressed. NGOs, by submitting *amicus*, have sought to strike a balance between investors' rights and host states' population rights. The involvement of the civil society is justified by the fact that often states, to protect foreign investments, take measures that affect the society (Wiik, 2018).

In light of this, *amicus curiae* submissions are the only way to represent the interests of the affected population. The representatives of the affected society are usually NGOs. NGOs have contributed to the emergence of global public policy, and their pressure can be significant in the context of corporate social responsibility (Puvimanasinghe, 2007). One of the main arguments in support of NGOs' participation is that they can bring into investment arbitration their research capabilities, technical information and specialist knowledge in fields like human rights (Knahr, 2011, p. 335). Human civil society actors are crucial to exposing human rights abuses, providing support to victims of abuse and identifying business-related human rights impacts (Amnesty International et al., 2018). Thus, the involvement of NGOs in foreign direct investments can align FDIs with broader societal and environmental objectives.

Amicus curiae have the ability to harmonise HR and IIL. They can bring human rights issues that might otherwise go unvoiced to the attention of arbitrators. *Amicus* briefs are accepted in many international judicial bodies, such as the ECtHR, the Inter-American Court of Human Rights (IACtHR) and the World Trade Organization (WTO). Even though they appear to be different in various courts, they are used to address additional legal claims, provide certain types of information, and present arguments made by the parties in an alternative way (Farber, 2019). Their participation includes written submissions, presentation of evidentiary material or participation in oral hearings (Born & Forrest, 2019).

In the context of investment arbitration, the only mechanism that allows for the participation of third parties is *amicus curiae*. NGOs have used this mechanism to participate in arbitral proceedings as *amici*. According to the relevant case law, foreign investments have affected indigenous people and local communities, as well as users of public utilities such as water. Wiik (2018) refers to NGOs that submit *amicus* as a link between the court and the public (p. 50). This tool is essential for cases that involve matters of public interest; otherwise, the tribunals could risk their legitimacy. Nevertheless, the case law suggests that tribunals do not have a uniform approach towards *amicus* submissions. Some tribunals have been more accepting of human rights claims than others.

The involvement of NGOs in investment arbitration through *amicus* briefs can address the social challenges of the field and help the latter deal with human rights issues that are outside the arbitrators' expertise. Investment arbitrators are reluctant when considering human rights norms due to their commercial orientation (Mikadze, 2016). Although arbitrators primarily focus on commercial issues, they often handle cases that extend beyond commercial concerns and involve matters of public interest. This aspect of public concern in IIL has highlighted the need to pay attention to human rights issues in investment arbitration proceedings. By adequately considering public law aspects, arbitrators can contribute to the reform of the field by applying human rights norms where appropriate and promoting the social responsibility of investors (Schill, 2010).

In order to participate in investment arbitration, the relevant NGO has to prove that the FDI negatively affects the purpose for which it was created (Gomez, 2012, p. 558). By submitting *amicus*, NGOs mainly provide relevant information on points of fact or law. The system has not been designed to grant a compelling voice or protection to those whose rights are being affected by foreign investment. Third parties do not have the right to intervene in a significant way in the proceedings, and they can only assist the arbitrators in their decision-making (Columbia Center on Sustainable Development, 2019).

Some IIAs explicitly allow for the acceptance and consideration of *amicus curiae* briefs. However, historically, *amicus* was not expressly addressed either by investment agreements or by the ICSID Arbitration Rules and the UNCITRAL Rules. More recently, these instruments have been amended to allow *amici* to participate in investment treaty arbitration. Following their amendments, these instruments now give arbitrators the discretion to permit *amicus* under specific requirements (Born & Forrest, 2019). When the relevant applicable treaty is silent, some tribunals have required the consent of the parties to permit *amicus* participation. Accordingly, in *Aguas del Tunari v Bolivia*, the tribunal provided that "it does not, absent the agreement of the Parties, have the power to join a non-party to the proceedings, to provide access to hearings to non-parties" (*Aguas Del Tunari SA v Bolivia*, 2003).

The question of admitting *amicus* was first asked in the North American Free Trade Agreement (NAFTA) under Chapter 11. The tribunal in *Methanex* noted that "no provision of NAFTA limits a tribunal's discretion to accept written submissions from a person or entity that is not a disputing party. This participation of non-disputing parties is based on NAFTA Chapter 11". Arbitrators in *Methanex* highlighted the need for a more transparent field (*Methanex Corporation v United States of America*, 2005, para. 27).

Transparency is a critical component in the evolving trend towards social entrepreneurship and foreign direct investment models that aim to address societal challenges. This emphasis on transparency is a key factor considered in the examination of *amicus* submissions. For example, in *Biwater v Tanzania,* the tribunal noted that its willingness to receive *amicus* submissions might support the process of the field to be perceived as more open or transparent (*Biwater Gauff Ltd v Tanzania*, 2008, para. 358). The lack of transparency in IIL is one of the primary reasons for allowing third-party involvement, particularly when disputes have the potential to impact public and societal interests (Butler, 2017).

Amicus curiae were not regulated by ICSID Arbitration Rules until the 2006 revision. Rule 37(2) provides that "a non-disputing party can file a written submission regarding a matter within the scope of the dispute". The provision allows non-disputing parties to attend or observe the hearings (*ICSID Convention*, 1966). Nevertheless, NGOs attempted to participate as *amici* before the 2006. The tribunal in *Suez/ Vivendi v Argentina* was the first ICSID tribunal that accepted *amicus curiae* by NGOs' expertise in human rights and the environment. The tribunal based its acceptance on Article 44 of the ICSID Convention (*Agues Argentinas SA Suez Sodedad General de Aguas de Barcelona SA and Vivendi Universal SA v Algerine Republic*, 2005, para. 10). The tribunal noted that an *amicus* is not a party, but its role is to "help the decision maker to arrive at its decision by providing expertise that the parties may not provide". The tribunal accepted that the case potentially involves matters of public interest, including human rights considerations and thus, the NGOs' perspective will help arbitrators to arrive at a correct decision (*Agues Argentinas SA Suez Sodedad General de Aguas de Barcelona SA and Vivendi Universal SA v Algerine Republic*, 2005). In *Biwater v Tanzania*, the "public interest" criterion is also taken into account (*Biwater Gauff Ltd v Tanzania*, 2008, para. 358). Public interests include human rights issues, environmental concerns, and more specific interests such as the right to water.

Obadia (2007) notes that ICSID amended its rules, and NAFTA issued an integrative statement of rules as a response to NGOs (p. 354). This development is characterised as remarkable because it gives NGOs access to investor-state arbitration to represent non-state interests (De Brabandere, 2014).

Other tribunals that accepted *Amicus* based their decision on the potential assistance they could provide by offering expertise, knowledge or insight. In that sense, NGOs must present arguments that are limited to the subject matter of the dispute and be beneficial to the court by providing information (De Brabandere, 2011). As an illustration, in *Apotex v US*, the tribunal noted that "this Panel has considered *inter alia*, whether the Applicant's submission could provide a different perspective and particular insight on the issues in dispute, based on either substantive knowledge or relevant expertise or experience that go beyond or differ in some respect from, that of the Disputing Parties themselves" (*Apotex Inv v The United States of America*, 2011, para. 22).

In sum, tribunals take into account three basic criteria for the acceptance of *amicus curiae*: (i) the public interest issues of the case, (ii) the expertise and perspective of the *amici* and (iii) the expectation for increased transparency and legitimacy (Harrison, 2009, p. 416). The purpose of these conditions is to prevent NGOs from submitting *amicus* automatically (Obadia, 2007).

V. CONCLUSION

The divergence between human rights and foreign direct investments has led to a cautious approach by investment tribunals in addressing human rights issues. However, the study indicates that the distance between the two branches is progressively narrowing. The proliferation of IIL has given rise to increasingly complex issues, including those related to human rights. As these challenges continue to evolve, the appropriate way to face them involves a focused assessment of the social impact of FDIs.

The societal issues arising in some instances indicate that foreign direct investments should not be regarded merely as private agreements. In *Urbaser v Argentina,* the tribunal affirmed this perspective and highlighted that the BIT cannot be interpreted in isolation. It was underlined that human rights considerations are relevant and applicable to the parties involved in the dispute.

As illustrated, the majority of international investment agreements lack specific provisions addressing human rights. However, contemporary IIAs incorporating human rights are a significant achievement towards sustainable development. Amending investment treaties to include such provisions is crucial for fostering a more balanced field with reduced tensions. Investment agreements serve as a great means by which states can agree to establish specific standards that respect both investment and human rights. The inclusion of human rights provisions in IIAs provisions can have multiple benefits. It can enhance the confidence of foreign investors because the inclusion of such provisions will help mitigate possible disputes. It can also help entrepreneurs develop business models that will address societal challenges.

Critics of IIL have consistently argued that the field must account for the human rights of local populations. In this context, it has been shown that *amicus* briefs can represent public interests. The participation of NGOs as *amici curiae* in investment arbitration is regarded as a significant development. NGOs, in their role as *amici*, possess the potential to open the field to human rights considerations and to bridge the gap between the two regimes. The role of NGOs is pivotal for the future development of international investment law. NGOs have exerted considerable influence in the field of human rights. Therefore, their participation as *amici* also has the potential to impact foreign direct investments. The case-law analysis demonstrated that *amicus curiae* submissions serve as a mechanism for including human rights claims in investment arbitration, potentially enhancing the transparency and legitimacy of FDIs. The tribunal in *Biwater v Tanzania* specifically noted that *amicus* can support the field and be perceived as more open or transparent.

Current trends suggest that foreign direct investments have the potential to be socially responsible in maintaining an equilibrium between the rights of foreign investors and the rights of the host state's population. Overall, human rights considerations are becoming increasingly prominent, arising in discussions about the future of foreign direct investments.

REFERENCES

Aguas del Tunari SA v Bolivia ICSID Case No ARB/02/3 Letter by NGO to Petition to Participate as Amici Curiae. (2003).

Agues Argentinas SA Suez Sodedad General de Aguas de Barcelona SA and Vivendi Universal SA v Algerine Republic ICSID Case No ARB/03/19 Order in Response to a Petition for Participation as Amicus Curiae. (2005).

Amado, J. D., Kern, J. S., & Doe Rodriguez, M. (2018). *Arbitrating the Conduct of International Investors*. Cambridge University Press., DOI: 10.1017/9781108235051

Amnesty International. Actionaid, ECCJ, Campaign, C. C., Anti-Slavery, & FIDH. (2018). *Suggested Elements for an EU Action Plan on Business and Human Rights*. https://www.amnesty.eu/wp-content/uploads/2018/11/suggested-elements-for-an-eu-action-plan-on-business-and-human-rights_8-june.pdf

Apotex Inc v The United States of America ICSID Case No UNCT/10/2 Procedural Order No 2. (2011).

Arcuri, A., & Montanaro, F. (2018). Justice for All? Protecting the Public Interest in Investment Treaties. *Boston College Law Review. Boston College. Law School*, *59*(8), 2791–2824.

Baltag, C., & Dautaj, Y. (2021). Promoting, Regulating, and Enforcing Human Rights Through International Investment Law and ISDS. *Fordham International Law Journal*, *45*(1). https://www.fordhamilj.org/volume-45-issue-1/2021/10/19/promoting-regulating-and-enforcing-human-rights-through-international-investment-law-and-isds

Biwater Gauff Ltd v Tanzania ICSID Case No ARB/05/22 Award. (2008).

Born, G., & Forrest, S. (2019). Amicus Curiae Participation in Investment Arbitration. *ICSID Review*, *34*(3), 626–665. DOI: 10.1093/icsidreview/siz020

Burke-White, W., & Staden, A. V. (2010). The Need for Public Law Standards of Review in Investor-State Arbitrations. In Schill, S. W. (Ed.), *International Investment Law and Comparative Public Law*. Oxford University Press. DOI: 10.1093/acprof:oso/9780199589104.003.0022

Butler, P. (2017). Red Riding Hood: Is Investor State Arbitration the Big Bad Wolf? *Penn State Journal of Law & International Affairs*, *5*(2), 328–373. https://elibrary.law.psu.edu/jlia/vol5/iss2/5

Cassese, A. (1990). *Human Rights in a Changing World*. Cambridge University Press.

Columbia Center on Sustainable Development. (2019). *Third Party Rights in Investor-State Dispute Settlement: Options for Reform*. UNCITRAL. https://uncitral.un.org/sites/uncitral.un.org/files/media-documents/uncitral/en/wgiii_reformoptions_0.pdf

Council of Europe. (2021). *What are Human Rights*. https://www.coe.int/en/web/compass/what-are-human-rights-

Cragg, W. (2012). Business and human rights: A principle and value-based analysis. In Cragg, W. (Ed.), *Business and Human Rights*. Edward Elgar Publishing Limited. DOI: 10.4337/9781781005774.00007

De Brabandere, E. (2011). NGOs and the Public Interest: The Legality and Rationale of Amicus Curiae Interventions in International Economic and Investment Disputes. *Chicago Journal of International Law*, *12*(1), 85–114. https://ssrn.com/abstract=1992939

De Brabandere, E. (2014). *Investment Treaty Arbitration as Public International Law: Procedural Aspects and Implications*. Cambridge University Press., DOI: 10.1017/CBO9781107589216

Dupuy, P.-M. (2009). Unification Rather than Fragmentation in International Law? The Case of International Investment Law and Human Rights. In Dupuy, P.-M., Petersmann, E.-U., & Francioni, F. (Eds.), *Human Rights in International Investment Law and Arbitration* (pp. 45–62). Oxford University Press. DOI: 10.1093/acprof:oso/9780199578184.003.0002

Ehsassi, A. (2010). Cain and Abel: Congruence and Conflict in the Application of the Denial of Justice Principle. In Schill, S. W. (Ed.), *International Investment Law and Comparative Public Law* (pp. 213–242). Oxford University Press., DOI: 10.1093/acprof:oso/9780199589104.003.0007

El-Hosseny, F. (2018). *Civil Society in Investment Treaty Arbitration*. Brill Nijhoff., DOI: 10.1163/9789004349131

Farber, S. (2019). The Amicus Curiae Phenomenon—Theory, Causes and Meanings. *Transnational Law and Contemporary Problems, 29*(1). https://ssrn.com/abstract=3341963

Gao, R. (2021). Bridging Separate Worlds—Application of Human Rights Law in Investment Treaty Arbitration. *SSRN*, *42*(1), 1. DOI: 10.2139/ssrn.4075407

Gavriil, E. (2024). Protection of Property under Human Rights and International Investment Law: A Case-Law Analysis. *Laws*, *13*(1), 1. Advance online publication. DOI: 10.3390/laws13010006

Goldstein, J. (2017). Bringing BITs Back from the Brink. *Denver Journal of International Law and Policy*, *45*(3). https://digitalcommons.du.edu/djilp/vol45/iss3/5

Gomez, K. F. (2012). Rethinking the Role of Amicus Curiae in International Investment Arbitration: How to Draw the Line Favorably for the Public Interest. *Fordham International Law Journal*, *35*(2), 510–564. https://ir.lawnet.fordham.edu/ilj/vol35/iss2/3

Harrison, J. (2009). Human Rights Arguments in Amicus Curiae Submissions: Promoting Social Justice? In Dupuy, P.-M., Francioni, F., & Petersmann, E.-U. (Eds.), *Human Rights in International Investment Law and Arbitration* (pp. 396–421). Oxford University Press. DOI: 10.1093/acprof:oso/9780199578184.003.0017

Hasan, R. (2013). Reflections on Foreign Direct Investment and Development with Reference to Non-Governmental Organizations and Corporate Social Responsibility. *Critical Sociology*, *39*(1), 37–43. DOI: 10.1177/0896920511414067

Hirsch, M. (2010). Investment Tribunals and Human Rights Treaties: A Sociological Perspective. In Baetens, F. (Ed.), *Investment Law Within International Law: Integrationist Perspectives* (pp. 85–105). Cambridge University Press., DOI: 10.1017/CBO9781139855921.008

Knahr, C. (2011). The New Rules on Participation of Non-Disputing Parties in ICSID Arbitration: Blessing or Curse? In Brown, C., & Miles, K. (Eds.), *Evolution in Investment Treaty Law and Arbitration* (pp. 319–338). Oxford University Press. DOI: 10.1017/CBO9781139043809.022

Koster, M., Simaens, A., & Vos, B. (2019). The Advocate's Own Challenges to Behave in a Sustainable Way: An Institutional Analysis of Advocacy NGOs. *Journal of Business Ethics*, *157*(2), 483–501. DOI: 10.1007/s10551-017-3674-4

Kriebaum, U. (2014). The Rompetrol Group N.V. v. Romania. *The Journal of World Investment & Trade*, *15*(5-6), 1022–1031. DOI: 10.1163/22119000-01506011

Mann, H. (2011). Civil Society Perspectives: What Do Key Stakeholders Expect from the International Investment Regime? In Alvarez, J. E., & Sauvant, K. P. (Eds.), *The Evolving International Investment Regime: Expectations, Realities, Options* (pp. 22–29). Oxford University Press., DOI: 10.1093/acprof:oso/9780199793624.003.0004

Methanex Corporation v United States of America UNCITRAL Final Award. (2005).

Mikadze, K. (2016). Uninvited Guests: NGOs, Amicus Curiae Briefs, and the Environment in Investor-State Dispute Settlement. *Journal of International Law and International Relations*, *12*(1), 35.

Miles, K. (2013). *The Origins of International Investment Law*. Cambridge University Press., DOI: 10.1017/CBO9781139600279

Nordenfelt, J. (1987). Human Rights—What They Are and What They Are Not. *Nordic Journal of International Law*, *56*(3), 3–8. DOI: 10.1163/157181087X00093

Obadia, E. (2007). Extension of Proceedings Beyond the Original Parties: Non-Disputing Party Participation in Investment Arbitration. *ICSID Review*, *22*(2), 349–379. DOI: 10.1093/icsidreview/22.2.349

Ortino, F. (2009). Non-Discriminatory Treatment in Investment Disputes. In Dupuy, P.-M., Francioni, F., & Petersmann, E.-U. (Eds.), *Human Rights in International Investment Law and Arbitration* (pp. 344–366). Oxford University Press. DOI: 10.1093/acprof:oso/9780199578184.003.0015

Osiatynski, W. (2014). The Historical Development of Human Rights. In Sheeran, S., & Rodlev, N. (Eds.), *Routledge Handbook of International Human Rights Law* (pp. 9–24). Taylor and Francis., DOI: 10.4324/9780203481417-4

Puvimanasinghe, S. F. (2007). *Foreign Investment, Human Rights and the Environment*. Brill | Nijhoff.

Radi, Y. (2012). Realising Human Rights in Investment Treaty Arbitration: A Perspective from within the International Investment Law Toolbox. *North Carolina Journal of International Law and Commercial Regulation*, *37*(4), 1108–1185. DOI: 10.1525/sp.2007.54.1.23

Radi, Y. (2018). Introduction: Taking Stock of the Societal and Legal Interplay between Human Rights and Investment. In Radi, Y. (Ed.), *Research Handbook on Human Rights and Investment* (pp. 1–11). Edward Elgar Publishing., DOI: 10.4337/9781782549123.00007

Saravanan, A., & Subramanian, S. R. (2016). The Participation of Amicus Curiae in Investment Treaty Arbitration. *Journal of Civil & Legal Sciences*, *5*(4). https://ssrn.com/abstract=2840614

Schadendorf, S. (2015). Investor-State Arbitrations and the Human Rights of the Host State's Population: An Empirical Approach to the Impact of Amicus Curiae Submissions. In Weiss, N., & Thouvenin, J.-M. (Eds.), *The Influence of Human Rights on International Law* (pp. 167–181). Springer. DOI: 10.1007/978-3-319-12021-8_12

Scheu, J. (2017). Trust Building, Balancing, and Sanctioning: Three Pillars of A Systematic Approach to Human Rights in International Investment Law and Arbitration. *Georgetown Journal of International Law*, *48*, 449–504.

Schill, S. W. (2010). Crafting the International Economic Order: The Public Function of Investment Treaty Arbitration and Its Significance for the Role of the Arbitrator. *Leiden Journal of International Law*, *23*(2), 401–430. DOI: 10.1017/S0922156510000117

Schill, S. W., & Djanic, V. (2018). Wherefore Art Thou? Towards a Public Interest-Based Justification of International Investment Law. *ICSID Review - Foreign Investment Law Journal, 33*(1), 29–55. https://doi.org/DOI: 10.1093/icsidreview/six025

Smyth, S. (2012). NGOs and Legitimacy in International Development. *Kansas Law Review, 61*(2), 377–440. https://ssrn.com/abstract=2129399

Sornarajah, M. (2010). *The International Law on Foreign Investment*. Cambridge University Press., DOI: 10.1017/CBO9780511841439

Sornarajah, M. (2015). *Resistance and Change in the International Law on Foreign Investment*. Cambridge University Press., DOI: 10.1017/CBO9781316156339

Spiro, P. J. (2008). NGOs and Civil Society. In Hey, E., Bodansky, D., & Brunnée, J. (Eds.), *The Oxford Handbook of International Environmental Law*. Oxford University Press., DOI: 10.1093/law/9780199552153.001.0001

Stephan, H. (2019). Human Rights, Role of Non-Governmental Organizations. In *Max Planck Encyclopedia of Public International Law*. Oxford University Press., DOI: 10.1093/law:epil/9780199231690/e816

Suez and Vivendi v Argentina ICSID Case No ARB/03/19 Decision on Liability. (2010).

Tomuschat, C. (2009). The European Court of Human Rights and Investment Protection. In Binder, C., Kriebaum, U., Reinisch, A., & Wittich, S. (Eds.), *International Investment Law for the 21st Century: Essays in Honour of Christoph Schreuer* (pp. 636–656). Oxford University Press. DOI: 10.1093/acprof:oso/9780199571345.003.0034

Trakman, L. E., & Ranieri, N. W. (2013). Foreign Direct Investment: A Historical Perspective. In Trakman, L. E., & Ranieri, N. W. (Eds.), *Regionalism in International Investment Law* (pp. 14–26). Oxford University Press., DOI: 10.1093/acprof:oso/9780195389005.003.0002

United Nations. (2011). Guiding Principles on Business and Human Rights: Implementing the United Nations "Protect, Respect and Remedy" Framework A/HRC/8/5.

Urbaser SA and Consorcio de Aguas Bilbao Bizkaia, Bilbao Biskaia Ur Partzuergoa v Argentina ICSID Case No ARB/07/26 Award. (2016). **Secondary Sources**

Vadi, V. (2018). *Proportionality, Reasonableness and Standards of Review in International Investment Law and Arbitration*. Edward Elgar Publishing. DOI: 10.4337/9781785368585

Valdevelde, K. (2009). A Brief History of International Investment Agreements. In Sauvant, K. P., & Sachs, L. E. (Eds.), *The Effect of Treaties on Foreign Direct Investment: Bilateral Investment Treaties, Double Taxation Treaties and Investment Flows* (pp. 3–36). Oxford University Press. DOI: 10.1093/acprof:oso/9780195388534.003.0001

Wiik, A. (2018). *Amicus Curiae Before International Courts and Tribunals*. Nomos., DOI: 10.5771/9783845275925

Woodward, B. K. (2011). The Role of International NGOs: An Introduction. *Willamette Journal of International Law and Dispute Resolution*, 19(2), 203–231. https://www.jstor.org/stable/26211687

World Association of Non-Governmental Organizations. (2021). *Overview of NGOs—NGO Handbook*. https://www.wangohandbook.org//index.php?title=NGO_Overview

World Bank. (1995). *Working with NGOs A Practical Guide to Operational Collaboration between the World Bank and Non-Governmental Organizations*. Operational Policy Department.

Chapter 6
Chasing the Future:
The UAE's Quest for Stability and Resilience in a Turbulent Region

Agustin Maciel-Padilla
Independent Researcher, Mexico

Saul Sandoval Perea
CETYS Universidad, Mexico

ABSTRACT

This chapter addresses the comprehensive set of United Arab Emirates' policies focused on deterring military aggression, combatting extremism both domestically and regionally, and on fostering stability as a crucial condition to achieve its vision for the future based on security and economic growth. It discusses key aspects of the foundation of the country in 1971, its vision for the future towards the Centennial of its independence and explains the security challenges posed by state and non-state actors. Finally, it focuses on the analysis of both domestic and foreign policies to promote stability, and it argues that the success of these policies will depend not only on sustained and conscious efforts, but also on a complex set of variables beyond the control of the UAE.

DOI: 10.4018/979-8-3693-5583-1.ch006

INTRODUCTION

Figure 1. Map<Fig_Large></Fig_Large>

Source: Maceda, C., "How Google is showing Arabian Gulf on Maps", Gulf News, August 2, 2015, available [online]: https://gulfnews.com/going-out/society/how-google-is-showing-arabian-gulf-on-maps-1.1560237

The United Arab Emirates (UAE) is a young nation that in a short period of time has achieved remarkable social and economic progress. It has reached a 0.937 level on the United Nations Human Development Index, close to that of advanced countries such as Canada, the United Kingdom and Belgium (UNDP, 2024). From an external perspective, the UAE is considered a model of rapid development, economic and political stability, world-class infrastructure, and as a trade, transport and logistics center, which together makes it an attractive investment center (Export Council Australia, 2021). The driving force behind its accomplishments is partly its leadership's strong sense of direction and vision for the future. As a relatively newcomer to the international system, the country focuses on its future goals and ambitions.

For a nation with vast oil resources but a small population, from the outset of its independence it became evident to the UAE's leadership that opening its society to immigration was key to having access to labor, as local workforce was scarce. For instance, in 2020, immigrants represented 88.1% of the UAE's total population of

10,032,213 (CIA, 2024). A restrictive immigration policy, in comparison, would have been an obstacle to taking advantage of economic opportunities provided by significant energy resources. The UAE holds the world's fifth-largest oil reserves (113 billion barrels) (World Population Review, 2024), the seventh-largest proven natural gas reserves (Slav, 2023) and earned US$94.6 billion from oil exports in 2022 (OPEC, 2022).

The opening of society was complemented with a strategic shift away from oil and towards the diversification of its economy. The country's leadership recognized that mono-dependence on oil was not convenient in the long run as this resource is not infinite. Therefore, the purpose of economic diversification was to foster "post-oil" stability, to remain competitive, and to absorb external shocks (Talwar, 2022; Patel, 2019). This strategy generated growth based on finance, tourism, and real estate services, as well as logistics and light industries. For instance, *Emirates Global Aluminum* is the world's largest "premium aluminum" producer and one of the main Emirati industries (Mubadala, 2024). As a result of economic diversification, 53% of the gross domestic product (GDP) is generated by non-oil activities (ADMO, 2024), and the UAE has become the third-largest economy and one of the wealthiest countries in the region (per capita), with a 2022 GDP estimated at US$507 billion (World Bank, 2022). Moreover, the UAE's leadership aligns its "over-the-horizon" perspective that emphasizes innovation, technology, and knowledge-based sectors, with diversification as part of its vision for the future (Antwi-Boateng and Al Jaberi, 2022).

Nevertheless, to maintain momentum and sustain progress, the UAE requires stability at home and abroad, which is threatened not only by a variety of state as well as non-state actors, but also by the fragility of the international order in terms of trade disputes and everything that is related to the functioning of the political economy that is also vital to the geopolitics of the region. For instance, conflict in the Pacific or Indian Ocean, or in the Mediterranean, would be negative news for the UAE, let alone the Gaza and Israel-Iran tensions. In this context, volatility and turmoil are the main obstacles to realizing its vision for the future. The analysis of these issues calls for the inclusion of domestic and international considerations to better understand a country's foreign policy preferences (Alons, 2007; Rickly and Almezaini, 2016). Indeed, some scholars argue that a country's likely success in advancing foreign policy goals heavily hinges on "getting its domestic affairs in order" (Antwi-Boateng and Alhashmi, 2022, p. 208). As such, the UAE is an example of a federation in the Middle East (Almezaini, 2011, p. 21) that has been successful in getting its house in order. The delivery of effective governance, a solid economic foundation, significant investments in education, and a culture of tolerance, are factors that give the country domestic and international legitimacy (Antwi-Boateng and Alhashmi, 2022). These developments, in turn, have allowed the UAE to explore and use different soft and hard power tools, that is, "smart power", to advance its stability-based national interests in the region. The UAE's successful efforts to promote domestic and international stability are challenged by state and non-state actors, and therefore the country has become more active in international affairs and a more influential actor, in fact becoming a small state with a considerable power, something akin to the city-state phenomenon of Singapore.

Within the broad international relations context, it is important to consider this a time of flux. The international "disorder" reaches far into the domestic affairs of states, perhaps as much or more than the Cold War. This is not always evident in terms of a direct transgression of traditional elements of sovereignty but the clash of cultures (not civilizations), based on consumption and the all-encompassing nature of social media which have indeed made the world (at least the urbanized part of it) into Herbert Marshall McLuhan's "Global Village. In this context, culture is the foundation of civilization, which is the external manifestation of human progress. Cultures can exist within civilizations, and civilizations can encompass multiple cultures (Hofstede, Hofstede and Minkov, 2010). National States impose law and order within a territory, while the internet-driven world does not respect the traditions of international law. This caveat may be obvious, but it is not like the Realist and other paradigms that tend not to consider factors such as these, even when smart power is invoked. That is, Nye addresses the virtues of influence but is unable to see "inside" each actor's particular "organic evolution" in response to its own realist and smart power forces it is subject to (consider influence operations, or cyber) (Nye, 2008).

The purpose of this chapter is to analyze the comprehensive set of UAE policies focused on deterring military aggression, combatting extremism both domestically and regionally, and fostering stability as a crucial national interest to achieve its vision for the future based on security and economic growth. The first section of this chapter addresses the theoretical framework for this study based on perspectives provided by the foreign and security policies of small states. It also addresses key aspects of the foundation of the country and its vision for the future. The second section explains the security challenges posed by state and non-state actors. Next, the focus is on the analysis of both domestic and foreign policies to promote stability. The last section presents the conclusions.

1. BACKGROUND

1.1. *Analytical Framework*

Defining a "small state" is not a straightforward issue, as there is no consensus on the parameters to consider in the definition. Moreover, the analysis of small states' foreign and security policy has not been central to International Relations theory, which is paradoxical, given the fact that most states in the international system can be classified as "small" in comparison to "great powers", which are only a handful. In general, it can be argued that this category of peripheral states has been "deemed irrelevant" in terms of foreign and security analysis (Rickli and Almezaini, p.8).

The reason for this neglect lies in International Relations theory, specifically in political realism's focus on "great power" politics. For instance, the core of the realist perspective is based in Hans Morgenthau's second principle that conceptualizes and defines national interest in terms of power (Morgenthau, 2005). These ideas are also present in Henry Kissinger *A World Restored* (Kissinger, 2017). This contrasts with one of the main characteristics of a small state: its insufficient capabilities, particularly military power, which is a relevant differentiation aspect according to Kenneth Waltz's structural realism (Waltz, 1979, p.82). Although other theoretical perspectives provide additional elements for analysis, the study and understanding of small states have remained limited. For neo-liberals, the key to understanding small states lies in the influence they exert within international institutions, even though it is recognized that their impact is not significant when acting alone or in small groups (Keohane, 1969, p.296). For constructivists, smallness is a matter of "self-perception" (Hey, 2003). From their perspective, interests result from social practice, and the definition of small state is a matter of perception. Therefore, the definition can be based on size - which is relative-, role and influence, or perception.

An alternative way to look at small states is to focus on power, not the power they possess, but the power they exercise in two dimensions: influence and autonomy. Influence refers to the capacity to affect the behavior of other states, while autonomy refers to the capacity to prevent their behavior from being defined by others (Goetschel, 1998). This approach is relevant for small states that are unable to shape the international agenda due to their limited power. On the one hand, influence can be augmented through alignment, either by "band wagoning" or balancing, to create alliances or less formal structures such as coalitions to confront threats (Walt, 1987). While band wagoning offers an opportunity for gain, balancing offers an opportunity to prevent losses. On the other hand, instead of focusing on alignment, small states can choose to protect their autonomy. However, the risk involved in being left alone is also being isolated by great powers during times of need, as evident in a policy of neutrality. Another option is to adopt a hedging strategy, characterized by ambiguity regarding alignment with great powers. This is a convenient alternative for small states in contexts of uncertainty (Lim and Cooper, 2015). Non-alignment with great powers can be a disadvantage for small states if those same great powers gain preeminence in the future, given the fact that small states may be perceived as lacking commitment. However, the advantage of a hedging strategy is to allow the state to remain relatively well-positioned regardless of future developments. Additionally, small states have the advantage of engaging in niche diplomacy (Rickli 2008; Taulbee, 2014), which involves using their resources rationally based on a clear set of priorities to maximize their impact and achieve the best results. This could include exploiting their soft power in areas such as "peacekeeping, institution building, conflict prevention, mediation, human rights promotion or sustainable development" (Rickli and Almezaini, p.16). Soft power involves the ability to get others to do what they otherwise would not do through means that do not involve the threat or use of force. For instance, it can be argued that the European Union (EU) has significant influence or weight, which the North Atlantic Treaty Organization (NATO), despite its military might, does not have. In this context, the micro-members play very different roles though they are members of both.

The analysis of small states' foreign and security policies also benefits from the perspectives provided by neoclassical realism, which is useful to see "what happens within the black box"; that is, the possibility of understanding both external and internal factors (Rickli and Almezaini, p.19). This approach can be relevant to the analysis of Gulf states as they represent an "anomaly" in the international system. This peculiarity arises from their origin as states (they were created by the British), their "rentier" economies (oil-rich countries), their active regional foreign policies (facilitated by financial resources), their distinct political systems (relevance of domestic politics) and being based on tribal politics (which is central to national leadership) (Rickli and Almezaini, pp.21-22).

As will be discussed below, several elements of analysis for small states' foreign and security policy apply to the UAE. These include the importance of internal cohesion for maintaining domestic stability in the face of a significant expatriate population, the opening of society based on tolerance and gender equality as key aspects of its soft power, its international activism both in supporting military operations and providing foreign aid, and its adoption of a hedging strategy in response to uncertainty regarding the extent of the US commitment to the region. This strategy reflects the sophistication and diversification of UAE's foreign policy, by recently strengthening and deepening ties with countries such as Russia and China. The UAE also has financial clout beyond foreign aid (investment) and it uses that efficiently.

1.2. *An Independent Nation*

After centuries of Ottoman Empire (1299-1922) rule over the Middle East ("Near East"/*Le Proche-Orient*), regional politics were transformed when France and Britain divided the area into spheres of influence after World War I (WWI) through the Sykes-Picot Agreement. This agreement "arbitrarily created 'nation-states' out of people unused to live together" (Marshall, 2015, p.150). Since these artificial demarcations did not acknowledge tribal divisions, this generated disputes that have lasted until today. This colonial legacy is of course shared by other regions and contributes to the friction that drives the principal force that realism identifies as inherent to state survival, and that is the need for survival by any means. It is however, complicated by an overlay of a patchwork of the attributes of the "people unused to live together" that are all a part of cultures that can, but may not easily coexist. In addition, the role of historical "branching" as each political unit evolved differently makes friction with neighbors within this paradigm more rather than less likely.

The area became of relevance to Britain in the 19th Century as a connecting point between the British Isles and India. British presence in the Middle East was motivated by the need to secure and protect the route to India, which is evident in the secret purchase by Benjamin Disraeli's government, in 1875, of 44% of the shares in the *Suez Canal Company* (Gordon, 2018, p.473). Protecting this route was fundamental for the *East India Company* (EIC) for trade as well as for geopolitical reasons. The EIC was a British trading enterprise established in the early 17th Century to trade in the Indian Ocean region, including the Middle East. In this area, the EIC traded in textiles and spices, and established posts along the Arabian Peninsula and the Arabian Gulf. These locations served as crucial intersections for EIC's trade with the Middle East, facilitating the exchange of products between the region and British colonies in India and the Far East.

The activities of a politico-religious alliance, the Wahhabis-Saudis, present in the central and eastern Arabian Peninsula in the second half of the 18th Century, pushed several tribes towards the western shores of the Arabian Gulf. There, with British support, they established several principalities ruled by Bedouin sheikhs. These sheikhdoms, which spread along the southern coast, made a living out of fishing, except for Bahrain that excelled at pearling (Belcher, 2024). It was in this context that around 1820, the British signed treaties with the sheikhdoms attaining peace through truces among them (Rafeq, 2005, p.236). These local tribes became the Trucial States, and they were part of a British protectorate.

With the gradual decline of the British Empire after WWII in the Gulf, the Cold War invited in the United States and the Soviet Union, and especially Iran. That external dynamic shaped the world and brought about several events such as the

Suez Crisis in 1956, the Iraq Revolution in 1962, rebellion in Oman in 1963, accession to power of a socialist government in Yemen in 1967 and led Prime Minister Harold Wilson to withdraw from the area in December 1971. This decision created the opportunity for the UAE to become an independent nation. Between the end of 1967 and the beginning of 1968, Britain was experiencing an economic crisis. Several Arab leaders suspected that Britain had secretly supported Israel in the June 1967 Six-Day War and, as retaliation, the Gulf states sold off their reserves of British sterling, producing a devaluation of the currency. Under pressing economic circumstances, Wilson ended British obligations in the Middle East, where Britain had been a prominent actor since the 18th Century (Ghafoor and Mitchell, 2022).

In December 1971, the UAE was established as a small state with significant energy resources. After becoming independent, the country took advantage of oil to invest in public works and services across its territory, which also facilitated the consolidation of the federal pact among its seven Emirates: Abu Dhabi, Dubai, Sharjah, Ajman, Umm Al Quwain, Ras Al Khaimah, and Fujairah. Oil exploitation allowed the country to increase its economic and defense capabilities, thus embarking on nation-building, led by the best endowed of the Emirates, Abu Dhabi. Today, the UAE is a successful country in the Middle East in terms of political stability and development. This is evident in Dubai's economic performance, which is based on its thriving service sectors. This success is further explained by its capacity to attract foreign investment in different sectors (Ahmed, 2023), notwithstanding the external shocks produced first by the global economic crisis of 2008 and, to a lesser extent, by the 2019 COVID-19 pandemic, whose impact was minimized due to previous investments in health and education (Mirzaei, 2019; Rizvi, 2020). Oil exploitation allowed the UAE to accumulate massive capital, which in turn is the basis of sovereign funds that are invested abroad and in domestic projects, such as in the case of Mubadala and Abu Dhabi Investment Authority (ADIA), to further foster economic growth and development (Nyarko, 2010).

Currently, the UAE is an active state in the region, and this international engagement is supported by soft power, hard military power, a solid economy, religious tolerance, and an open - liberal and secular - society that guarantees gender equality, which together represent the foundation of the so-called "UAE Model" (Salisbury, 2020, p.2). As such it has a reach and influence that far extends beyond its immediate borders and even region. This has given the UAE the ability to play a role on the international stage that it has carefully developed and cultivated in what, during the Cold War, may have been called a "non-aligned" manner. As diplomacy plays a large role in what the UAE does, it can leverage its internal stability far beyond its borders as indicated. That is a major accomplishment in and of itself. It is also a magnet for so-called "spoilers" seeking to destabilize the international and regional order.

1.3. *Vision for the Future*

The UAE Model provides the country with a source of soft power, generated to promote economic, diplomatic and cultural objectives (Antwi-Boateng and Alhasmi, 2022), and one of the main characteristics of the Emirati leadership is its forward-looking mindset with a constant focus on the future. This is reflected in the fact that the country has developed a series of strategic plans such as the 2021 plan, the 2030 plan, the 2050 plan, and the 2071 plan, the latter to commemorate 100 years of its foundation. The UAE 2071 Centennial plan, for instance, is based on four main pillars: a) a government with a long-term vision emphasizing prosperity and optimism about the future; b) an education system based on science, technology, and innovation; c) a diversified and competitive knowledge-based economy fostering productivity and innovation; and d) a "happy society" based on tolerance, cohesion, humility, respect, and loyalty to the UAE (UAE, 2024).

The UAE's National Agenda translates these plans into specific targets, focusing on the development of smart services and learning, enhancing safety, increasing per capita gross income, and achieving global leadership in logistics and infrastructure, among others. For instance, Dubai World Central (DWC), *Al Maktoum International Airport*, started cargo operations in June 2010, followed by passenger flights three years later in October 2013, with an initial capacity for 5-7 million passengers. Once completed, DWC is projected to be a sprawling complex, potentially accommodating over 160 million passengers annually and serving as a multi-modal logistics hub handling up to 12 million tons of freight (Dubai Airports, 2024), linking the UAE to its wider neighborhood in East Asia and East Africa, on top of its existing connections to Europe. Making the UAE a logistics hub also represents a significant effort to move away from the carbon economy (even if COP 2024 in Brazil was not conclusive and the big oil producers were not onboard with the move away from carbon) and shows the UAE willingness to contribute to address global issues such as climate change.

To promote prosperity, security, and to build infrastructure for world-class business and logistics status, stability is crucial for the country. Achieving these objectives requires a strategy that considers goals, means, and potential obstacles to attaining these goals. Stability, both domestic and regional, is the foremost requisite to meet these targets (UAE, 2024). However, stability is challenged by a diverse source of threats from state and non-state actors, or a complex combination thereof, and therefore the UAE has been willing to offer its good offices abroad to foster stability.

2. CHALLENGES

2.1. *Context*

The UAE is in a highly complex and volatile region characterized by political and social dislocations, which were further exacerbated in 2011 by social movements. In December 2010, Mohamed Bouazizi, a Tunisian national, set himself on fire in protest to his government (Khalil, 2020). This tragic event produced widespread social mobilization across the Middle East and North Africa, resulting in the downfall of some established regimes. Ironically, while the uprisings brought about limited political, social, and economic change to the region, they also contributed to violence and repression, and to displace populations (Robinson and Merrow, 2020).

One of the most significant consequences of these movements, however, was the opportunity for social divisions to be exploited by anti-government Islamist groups. The grievances of those rebelling against the authorities were based on a strong record of a lack of respect for human rights, difficult economic conditions due to the fall in oil prices, corruption, poverty and high unemployment, especially among the young population. Despite social mobilization, the situation did not improve, as the official response was further suppression of freedom (e.g. social media facilitated social activism and exposing government abuse), displaced population due to civil war, and foreign military intervention that intensified violence and disorder (Robinson and Merrow, 2020).

Another significant consequence of social activism was the alteration of the internal and external balance of power in an already divided region (Al Shaikh, p.28). This division manifested itself in two discernible camps: one comprising quasi-alignments among Israel, the UAE, Saudi Arabia, and the United States; and another involving Iran and its loyal groups. These dynamics occurred in the wider context of differences between Sunni-majority Saudi Arabia and Shia-majority Iran, which have been present elsewhere in the region in countries suffering domestic disruptions such as Libya, Syria and Yemen (Al Shaikh, p.13). These are examples of structural conditions that escape the diplomatic abilities of the UAE, even though it has attempted to maintain neutrality and to foster stability.

Despite being a small state, yet one determined to become an influential player in regional power politics, the UAE responded to regional change and the gradual US withdrawal from the area by strengthening regional security through foreign policy, soft power and, only, when necessary, military power. This represented a complement to, and a higher level of sophistication in the country's foreign policy which has traditionally been grounded --and continues to be founded—on the principles of sovereignty, given that the whole weight of the UAE's efforts is firmly settled in this foundational concept of the international regime that establishes statehood and the need to assure the survival of the state. The emphasis is placed on sovereignty given the fact that most of the other, if not all institutions and principles of international law rely, directly or indirectly, on State sovereignty; it suffices to mention, for instance, the relationship between the conditions and attributes of statehood or the principles of territorial or personal jurisdiction, immunity, and non-intervention, on the one hand, and considerations of sovereignty, on the other (Besson, 2011).

However, according to an insightful perspective, while social change altered the regional balance of power by creating power vacuums that led to civil wars, and by enabling extremist groups to spread disruptive ideologies that eroded stability, two earlier events were critical in shaping regional security. Firstly, the 2003 US invasion of Iraq and, secondly, the ascent of Bashar Al Assad in Syria (Al Shaikh, pp.30-31).

On the one hand, the US invasion of Iraq further intensified social differences, leading to the emergence of the Islamic State of Iraq and Syria (ISIS) and facilitating the growth of Iranian presence in the country. On the other hand, the death of Hafez Al Assad in Syria on June 10, 2000, and his succession by his son, Bashar Al Assad, apparently represented a smooth transition within the Syrian regime. Bashar came to power promising political and economic reforms, which soon contrasted with his autocratic style (Rais, 2004, p.144). By 2004, the US government labeled Syria "an unusual and extraordinary threat" and, under the *Syria Accountability and Lebanese Sovereignty Restoration Act*, prohibited the export of US products other than food and medicine to the country. Financial transactions were suspended, and assets of Syrians suspected of involvement in terrorism or weapons of mass destruction (WMD) development were frozen, which increased conflict in the country (Labott, 2004). This underscores why the characterization of social activism in 2011 as the turning point for instability in the region does not tell the whole story (Al Shaikh, 2022, pp.30-31). Security challenges stem not merely from domestic social discord but from "external actors seeking to engineer change through local proxies" (Al Shaikh, 2022, p.32). These are "structural" issues that escape the efforts to establish stability in the region that the UAE undertakes. Nevertheless, it does offer "good offices" and neutral spaces for dialogue and the peaceful resolution of conflicts. It is a leader in the promotion of confidence-building measures. For instance, the UAE actively participates in, and is a member of, the Conference on Interaction and Confidence Building Measures in Asia (CICA) since 2008, where it has contributed to various initiatives aimed at enhancing regional security and cooperation (CICA, 2024). This is an example of how the UAE is proactively seeking to reduce regional friction and tension.

In this context, the UAE supported the governments in Bahrain and Yemen as part of the Gulf Cooperation Council (GCC), collaborated with Egypt against Islamist militias in Libya, and participated in US-led coalitions against ISIS in Syria to fight extremism. The UAE had diplomatic differences with Qatar over its support revisionist groups in the context of regional social change, and because *Al Jazeera*'s Arabic and English-language broadcasts were perceived as spreading division (Salisbury, p.16). This situation lasted until 2021 when the GCC solved its differences with Qatar. Also, Iranian activity in the Strait of Hormuz, facilitated by like-minded groups such as the Houthis in Yemen, has further affected freedom of navigation in the area (Scarr et.*al*, 2024). This situation has been further complicated by drone attacks against Saudi Arabia and missile attacks on Abu Dhabi (Yadlin, 2022), the latter aimed at persuading the UAE not to support the government in Yemen, and more recently by the conflict between Hamas and Israel. This has been further exacerbated by the intervention of Israel in Lebanon, which under a two-month truce still represents an expansion of frictions.

Even though the UAE and the United States remain close allies, the latter's gradual disengagement from the region has been concerning to the former, as reflected in President Donald Trump's decision in 2019 to withdraw US forces fighting ISIS in Syria. This withdrawal not only weakened anti-terrorist efforts but also increased competition among regional actors vying for influence on that country. For instance, at the same time Arab governments tried to foster stability in Syria, Russia also emerged as a mediator in the conflict (IISS, 2019). This situation was compounded by the US retreat from Iraq under the Obama Administration in 2011, and from Afghanistan under the Biden Administration in 2021, which in part explains why the UAE became more concerned about regional security. The full extent of the security implications for the Middle East from the developments described above is reflected in weak governance, humanitarian crises, economic hardship, but especially in the spread of extremism. Within this context, the UAE has become an increasingly active regional actor fostering stability as one of its national interests, including shielding its society from extreme ideologies and safeguarding the integrity of its oil industry, whose main facilities are located close to its borders (Al Shaikh, p.33). Of paramount importance has been to keep open the Strait of Hormuz, the 21-mile-wide channel through which 21% of global petroleum consumption travels (USEIA, 2023).

2.2. *State-centered*

The UAE is in a unique geographic position, located amidst regional flashpoints that pose internal and external challenges. Since its creation, the UAE has faced a challenging international environment, first from Saudi Arabia, and stemming from longstanding territorial negotiations. Early issues included efforts by Sheikh Zayed bin Sultan al-Nahyan to secure recognition for the UAE post-independence from Britain. A significant event regarding these boundary concerns was the 1974 Treaty of Jeddah (UN Treaty Collection, 1993), where Saudi Arabia relinquished claims to the oil-rich Al-Rimi area between Oman and the UAE in exchange for territories like the Shaybah oil field. However, negotiations over Shaybah and Al-Yasat, a marine reserve near Abu Dhabi's southernmost point, were not conclusive. The UAE's approach shifted in 2004 under Sheikh Zayed's successor, his son Sheikh Khalifa bin Zayed al-Nahyan's, who prioritized renegotiation regarding the Jeddah settlement, though these issues remain unresolved. Discussions resumed in 2019 when the UAE expanded the Al-Yasat Marine Protected Area, prompting Saudi Arabia to include in the dialogue the UN and the GCC in 2024.

In historical and structural terms, the main state-centered, strategic, issue is Iran, which on November 30th, 1971, one day before UAE's independence, occupied three Emirati islands in the Arabian Gulf—Abu Musa, and the Greater and Lesser Tunbs.

Figure 2. Map<Fig_Large></Fig_Large>

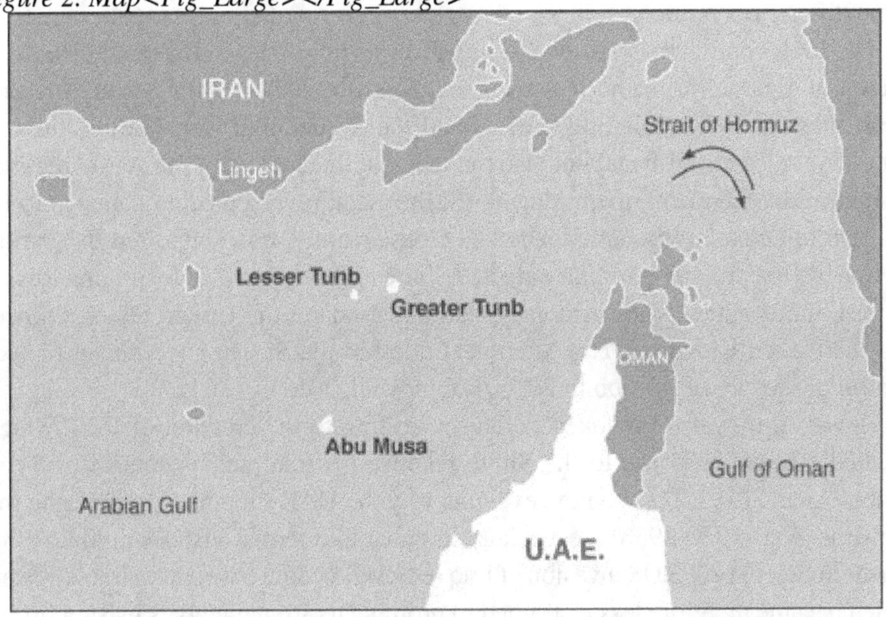

Source: Embassy of the United Arab Emirates in Washington, DC, Occupied UAE Islands, Unofficial Map. For Illustrative Purposes Only, available [online]: https://www.uae-embassy.org/discover-uae/foreign-policy/occupied-uae-islands

Pressure had been building up since the 1930s when Iran attempted to influence Bahrain. The situation continued to be complicated in the 1970s when Iran did not agree with the formation of the Emirati federation, as it was considered as an attempt to annex Bahrain. Following Britain's 1968 announcement of withdrawal from the Gulf, differences between Arab leaders and Iran over Bahrain and the three islands in the Strait of Hormuz persisted. At that time, the Shah of Iran accepted to recognize the independence of all the Arab-ruled territories in the Gulf except "that island" (Bahrain) (Ghafoor and Mitchell, 2022). Iran historically claimed Bahrain and the three islands, asserting they were "stolen" by the British. Through secret diplomacy, Arab rulers, Britain, and the Shah, agreed to transfer the three disputed islands to Iran. According to a confidential note from the Iranian foreign ministry dated June 1970, the Shah informed Britain's Foreign Secretary, Sir Alec Douglas-Home, that "these islands belong to Iran and must be returned to Iran... No matter what, we will take these islands" (Ghafoor and Mitchell, 2022). Despite British officials publicly stating that the islands belonged to the Trucial States, declassified cables revealed that Sir William Luce, a British colonial administrator and diplomat, privately accepted the Shah's claim to the islands. Iran took control of the three islands, and the Sheikh of Sharjah later reached a last-minute agreement with Iran to share administration of Abu Musa. This agreement lasted until 1992 when Iran took full control over the island (Ghafoor and Mitchell, 2022), in a context in which some differences remain.

The UAE continuously assess the impact of its proximity to Iran and the latter's pursuit of regional primacy (Robinson and Merrow, 2024). Iran's posture became clear after the 2011 social movements and the Syrian civil war. The reason was not only a rejection of Israel but also the fact that the decline of the Assad regime, dominated by members of an Alawite (Shiite) sect, represented a challenge to its position in Lebanon through Hezbollah. Consequently, Iran supported the Syrian regime by first providing military aid and Shiite militias, and then by joining Russia against Sunni states (Saudi Arabia, Qatar, and Jordan), the United States, France, and the United Kingdom. This alignment allowed the Syrian government to take control of the city of Aleppo in 2016 (Rabinovich, 2019).

However, this also provoked defiance, leading to the creation of ISIS, which became a Sunni response to the Shiite takeover in Iraq and its control of Syria (Rabinovich, 2019). This context explains why the UAE supported Iraq during the Iran-Iraq War (1980-1988), "especially in economic terms" (Bonesh, 2022, p.3). Furthermore, the 2003 US invasion of Iraq removed a counterweight to Iran's power, which became therefore less restrained to promote its strategic goals by supporting like-minded groups such as the Houthis in Yemen.

Iran has also remained in the UAE's foreign policy radar due to the Emirates' close ties to the United States, Iran's security concern, even though the US presence in the region has been recently declining. Iran's nuclear program is an outstanding issue because Iran's potential acquisition of nuclear weapons is a concern for the GCC states. This stems from the idea that the region cannot take for granted the US security umbrella, which could lead both the UAE and Saudi Arabia to increase self-reliance. In fact, Saudi Arabia has not ruled out the possibility of obtaining nuclear capabilities (Borger, 2023). This situation would be troubling for the UAE, given the fact that a nuclear stand-off could go beyond Iran-Israel to include Saudi Arabia and Pakistan.

The UAE has been attentive to Iran's nuclear program (Iran International, 2023), promoting improved bilateral relations. In fact, the UAE and Iran have been fostering confidence building measures to improve their bilateral relations (Kamrava, 2024). While the UAE has resorted to military power to promote its interests only when it has been necessary, it in general opposes conflicts that could increase regional instability and in particular in the Strait of Hormuz (Al Shaikh, p.127).

2.3. *Non-State-centered*

Non-state threats attract the attention of the UAE at both the domestic and international levels, especially after the 2011 movements. As in different parts of the world, radical ideologies threaten the domestic legitimacy of the government and the successful UAE Model. Internationally, they contribute to regional instability. The movements, initially fueled by public discontent, were later exploited by extremist groups to gain power. In the UAE, *Al-Islah*, the local branch of an Egyptian-based group, was categorized as a threat as early as the 1990s when it began to emulate its Egyptian sponsors and attempted to strengthen ties between "Islamist and liberal currents in the UAE" (Al Shaikh, p.131). In 2014, the UAE classified this group as terrorists, interrupting diplomatic ties with Qatar over alleged support for this organization (Salisbury, p.16).

The UAE is concerned about the spread of radicalized Islam in the region, due to the potential impact of its ideology in a country that upholds tolerance in a modern society. In this context, the Emirati government's objective is to prevent extremist views to take hold in the country (Jacopo et al., 2023). As mentioned above, the whole culture of development is premised on modernization as an effort to promote a non-sectarian and open society with tolerance for Islam as a peaceful and accepting faith. Radicalization is precisely the threat that is the strategic objective to avoid through education, tolerance, gender equality and an open society.

In addition to being considered an important issue at the level of state actors, Iran supports groups that potentially affect both regional and UAE's stability. For both the UAE and its allies, such as the United States and the GCC, Iran not only represents an issue because of its nuclear program but also an asymmetric matter due to the activities of its proxies in the region, the so-called "Axis of Resistance" (Akbarzadeh and Azizi, 2024). Instability allows state actors and their loyal groups to gain influence, and Iran is known for supporting organizations such as Hamas and Hezbollah. Through these groups, Iran promotes its interests by being present in countries such as Iraq, Syria, and Yemen, and it has also been assisting Shiia groups in Bahrain.

This explains UAE's support to the Saudi-led actions in Bahrain in 2011, responding to a call for help from the government, "where the Shi'ite Muslim majority complains of discrimination by the Sunni Muslim royal family" (*News Wires*, 2011). Saudi Arabia's military deployment was driven by Bahrain's strategic importance, being just twenty miles off Saudi Arabia's eastern coast. Bahrain's proximity has an economic, tribal, and geopolitical impact. It is near Saudi Arabia's Eastern Province, a major oil-producing region (holding one-quarter of the world's proven oil resources) and center of most of Saudi Arabia's Shiite population, where radicalization could potentially spread to the rest of the country with geopolitical consequences, given Iran's long-standing territorial claim over Bahrain (Bronson, 2011).

Iran's support for non-state actors to advance its regional objectives has had an impact on stability. For instance, in the context of the Yemen War, the Houthis have been able to disrupt shipping lines by targeting oil tankers in UAE's territorial waters in the Strait of Hormuz. Some of these incidents occurred in May 2019 when four ships were hit (Almezaini, 2020, p.206). This group has also targeted Saudi Arabia. Additionally, there is evidence of Iranian support to militias in drone operations, including the 2018 incident in Abu Dhabi International Airport and then again on the same target in 2022 (Batrawi, 2022), as mentioned above.

The relationship with Iran is paradoxical in a broader context where the UAE and this country maintain stable economic exchanges, and where there is a sizeable Iranian business community in Dubai. For instance, in May 2024, there was a meeting of the UAE-Iran joint economic commission in Abu Dhabi, the first in 10 years. Even though the UAE limited its diplomatic ties with Iran after Riyadh suspended relations with Tehran in 2016 - following the attack on the Saudi embassy in Iran by protesters over the Saudi government's decision to execute a Shiite cleric-, the UAE resumed dialogue with Iran in 2019. Dubai has long been one of Iran's main windows to the outside world. Iran imported $20.8 billion of goods from the UAE in its past fiscal year ending in March 2024, making the UAE its top source of imports. In the same period, the UAE was Iran's third top export destination, with $6.6 billion worth of goods exported (Reuters, 2024).

The UAE is also vigilant, as other countries in the context of globalization, regarding other non-state actors such as criminal organizations, which could take advantage of Dubai's openness and favorable investment conditions, as well as of its financial and communications infrastructure (Page, 2020, p. ix). According to a report, preventing organized crime operations in Dubai is crucial because of its international ramifications, given the close relationship of the UAE with the United States, the United Kingdom, and other prominent countries in the international financial network. This is not only because the UAE is a key security and trading partner in the region but also because of Dubai's close ties to Iran. It is important to prevent illicit activities from deepening conflict, transnational organized crime, terrorism, and poor governance in the region and the world (Page, 2020, p. x). In the past decades, even before becoming an economic powerhouse, the UAE was already the target of several terrorist incidents on its own soil, such as the 1973 hijacking of a *Japan Airlines* flight diverted by the Palestinian Liberation Organization (PLO) and the Japanese Red Army to Dubai; the 1974 PLO hijacking of a *British Airways* flight forced to land in Dubai; explosives discovered in a Jordanian aircraft in Dubai airport in 1985; bombs going off at the *Syrian Airlines* office in Abu Dhabi in 1986; and explosives discovered in 1999 at one of the major shopping malls in Dubai, Deira City Centre (Davidson, 2009, p.26). The intensity of events such as these has been reduced due to intelligence efforts by the UAE and its allies, and also because the geopolitical realities have changed as well.

The UAE has achieved significant economic progress in just a matter of five decades, as previously mentioned, and one of its key national interests is to continue as a stable, secular, country with a clear path to the future. The UAE is required to confront multiple sources of instability due to its openness, rapid economic development and, consequently, its greater exposure to the international economy. In this context, stability is paramount because the country needs to present itself as a safe destination to continue attracting foreign investment. However, the financial, real estate, and tourism markets can be easily disturbed by conflict, and this makes stability a primary political and strategic objective.

3. STABILITY-PROMOTION STRATEGY

One of the UAE's key advantages in addressing potential security issues is its internal cohesion and domestic support for the government (BTI, 2024, p.6). In recent years, the country has built up significant soft power, enabling it to become an attractive investment center. A primary focus has been to create strong partnerships in the region and beyond promoting openness and collaboration. The UAE played a leading role in the Abraham Accords, the groundbreaking agreement that normalized relations between the UAE and Israel. According to H.H. Sheikh Abdullah bin Zayed Al Nahyan, Minister of Foreign Affairs and International Cooperation, in a speech at an official reception in Tel Aviv on September 16, 2022:

The Abraham Accords were based on a simple premise: that diplomacy and communication would promote greater stability, prosperity, and hope. Today, we can say with great confidence that the premise was correct… we are building a brighter future together by expanding opportunities for our peoples, and people across the region. The UAE's founding principles of coexistence, tolerance and inclusiveness form the basis of our vision for a more peaceful and prosperous region (Embassy of the United Arab Emirates, 2022).

Even though the Abraham Accords have not been universally accepted in the region (El Kurd, 2023), and perceived as producing for the UAE and Saudi Arabia an unwelcoming reaction from groups not supportive of dialogue and peace (Rahman, 2023), this initiative has made a significant contribution by setting the stage for other Arab countries to promote moderation, such as Bahrein, and therefore to contribute to regional stability.

In terms of the UAE's interest in maintaining domestic stability, the country has achieved this objective through its cohesive federal structure under the leadership of Abu Dhabi, and the autonomy of each of the Emirates to decide on local economic and social matters, except on foreign policy issues (BTI, 2024, p.4). This stability has facilitated economic prosperity, as is evident in the country's high GDP-per capita income. The UAE has also diversified its economy through its sovereign wealth funds, as mentioned above, which guarantee reinvestment to ensure greater economic sustainability. However, regional instability threatens these interests and, therefore, the UAE has become increasingly active in stability-promotion strategies abroad.

3.1. External

Since its independence, the UAE has pursued a steady foreign policy based on the defense of sovereignty, which has helped build its reputation as a predictable and reliable partner. Defense of sovereignty has meant for the UAE to resort to diplomacy and uphold the principle of non-interference in the internal affairs of other states. Within this perspective, UAE's actions are legitimate in the context of the international regime. The UAE has increased its role as a security guarantor, primary in diplomatic terms, but in some cases also militarily in the region in response to radical Islam, which gained momentum after the 2011 movements. These kinds of movements pose a challenge to the UAE, potentially harming its status as a safe tourism destination and investment center, as it aims to further diversify its economy. This underscores its interest in addressing religious extremism.

Furthermore, in response to increasing US disengagement and the resulting political vacuums in Iraq and Afghanistan, the UAE has complemented its existing soft power capabilities with hard power to achieve "smart power" (Janardhan, 2019). Over the last decade, the UAE has invested in military resources, strengthening its air force and procuring specialized military equipment to enhance deterrence.

At the bilateral level, and from the very beginning, one of the most significant relationships for the UAE has been with the United States, contributing to the UAE's territorial integrity and ensuring safe passage through the Strait of Hormuz. Bilateral security cooperation began to expand since the 1990 Gulf War, and it became formalized in a Defense Cooperation Agreement in 1994 (an updated version came into force in 2019). This agreement provides for joint training and exercises, prepositioning of US military equipment in the UAE, and the transfer of advanced weapons systems (US-UAE Business Council, 2017, p.15), such as the terminal High Altitude Area Defense (THAAD) system (Iddon, 2022).

In this context, the UAE is one of only three countries, and the only Arab nation, to have participated with the United States in six coalition operations over the last 30 years: Afghanistan, Somalia, Bosnia-Kosovo, the 1990 Gulf War, NATO-led intervention in Libya, and the fight against ISIS. The UAE Air Force has played a crucial role in these actions, employing US-made F-16 "*Desert Falcon*" jets. For example, these aircraft participated in enforcing the UN no-fly zone over Libya in 2011 and supported the NATO-led mission in Afghanistan from 2012 to 2014, co-operating with the US 363rd Flying Training Group at Al Dhafra Air Base in Abu Dhabi (Embassy of the United Arab Emirates, 2024).

UAE Air Force F-16 pilots regularly participate in the "Red Flag" aerial combat exercise hosted by the US Air Force at Nellis Air Force Base in Las Vegas, Nevada, which reflects the strong US-UAE security partnership despite the UAE not being a member of NATO. The UAE also hosts the Joint Air Warfare Center and conducts joint training exercises with US forces (Embassy of the United Arab Emirates, 2024). Even though the US sale of F-35 *Lightning II* aircraft and other advanced defense systems to the UAE passed Congressional review in December 2020, this deal has been on hold because of the UAE's growing ties with China (Rumley, 2022), as it will be discussed below.

Regarding non-military tools, and therefore emphasizing its soft power and the ability its resources give it to reach beyond its borders in ways that promote regional stability, the UAE is committed to Iraq's reconstruction, providing significant financial support and other assistance such as medical treatment, humanitarian supplies, and police training. It has also committed to combating terror finance networks by acceding to the International Convention on the Suppression of the Financing of Terrorism since 2005 (Embassy of the United Arab Emirates, 2024).

The UAE also participates in security initiatives such as the Secure Global Energy Supply through Dubai's involvement in the Container Security Initiative (CSI), a multinational program to protect international trade from terrorism. Through this program, US Customs officers operate within Dubai's ports. The UAE plays a significant role in preventing the spread of dangerous nuclear materials as Dubai was the first Middle Eastern entity to join the US Department of Energy's Megaports Initiative, with the purpose of intercepting potential illicit shipments of radioactive material (Embassy of the United Arab Emirates, 2024).

Additionally, the UAE is part of the US-led International Maritime Security Construct (IMSC) created in 2019, to "maintain freedom of navigation, international law, and free flow of commerce to support regional stability and security of the maritime commons" around the Strait of Hormuz (IMSC, 2019). Moreover, the UAE shares information with the US Department of Homeland Security to deal with criminal organizations and terrorist groups (US Department of State, 2021).

In this context, while the UAE is understood to benefit from the US security umbrella as it aligns itself with US strategic priorities in the region, this stance, however, is at odds with extremist non-state actors who reject US involvement in the Middle East. It is important to note that the UAE's allies are governments that are in a *de facto* alliance with Israel, such as France, the United Kingdom and the United States (Davidson, 2009, p.10). This is happening at the same time when the standing of the United States among the Arab population has declined, particularly since the recent events in Gaza (Robbins et al., 2024). The underlying thrust of this effort is to be both a foundational part of the international network of legal protections coming from treaty-based political and economic relations, and a beneficiary of multilateral protections arising from this regime. Given that an international regime is the set of implicit or explicit principles, norms, rules, and decision-making procedures around which actors' expectations converge, the UAE has clearly chosen to be a part of a Sovereignty-based one (Krasner, 1982).

In the multilateral arena, the UAE promotes regional dialogue through the GCC, which is anchored by the UAE's alliance with Saudi Arabia. Founded in 1981 with the instrumental intervention of Sheikh Zayed (Salisbury, p.8), the GCC aims to facilitate economic and security cooperation. The UAE has taken a leading role in global and regional efforts to combat terrorism, implementing an integral strategy that addresses the roots of the problem through various actions. It actively participates in several international and regional alliances against terrorism, such as the Global Counter-Terrorism Forum (GCTF), that is a multilateral platform that focuses on strengthening civilian capacities to prevent and counter terrorism (Permanent Mission, 2017). The UAE has hosted international conferences on counter-terrorism efforts. Moreover, Major General Ahmed Naser Al-Raisi, an Emirati national, was elected as President of Interpol at the 89th General Assembly in Istanbul in November 2021, highlighting the UAE's presence in international law enforcement and security cooperation.

A turning point in UAE's international activism, however, was the 2015 Joint Comprehensive Plan of Action (JCPOA) aimed at addressing Iran's nuclear development plan in exchange for lifting Western economic sanctions. This agreement was supported by the Obama Administration without consulting any of the GCC member states, including the UAE, despite its significant impact on the region (Stickings, 2023). Therefore, while the UAE's relationship with Europe and the US remains stable, UAE interests somewhat diverged from those of its Western allies. This realization underlined the need for the UAE to review its foreign policy, leading to increasing activism and sophistication to address regional instability in the form of building alliances, strengthening its defense capabilities, and diversifying its security partners (Almezani, p.215).

The UAE responded with a more active foreign policy, fostering bilateral and multilateral understandings with regional actors such as Saudi Arabia, Egypt, and Bahrain, and establishing new alliances with countries like Russia and China. In 2019, it signed a defense and military cooperation agreement with China, following a purchase of military hardware for $40 million in 2018, that is precisely the reason why the F-35 II deal has stalled. That same year, the UAE and Russia signed a Declaration of Strategic Partnership, turning the UAE into Russia's biggest military customer (Almezaini, p.211). The UAE ranks 6th globally in military expenditures as a percentage of GDP (5.6%), spending $19.8 billion in defense in 2020; between 2010 and 2019, the UAE allocated between 15-16% of its annual defense budget to procurement from foreign suppliers (International Trade Administration, 2023).

This pragmatic foreign policy has been complemented by the provision of development assistance, positioning the UAE as one of the world's largest donors of humanitarian aid, especially to Muslim states, to promote political stabilization through soft power. For instance, the UAE provided financial support to Egypt for reconstruction after 2011, and the UAE is one of the main investors in the country with $6 billion in the 4 previous years leading to 2019, and the creation, that same year, of a $20 billion fund (Almezaini, p.214). This is how military initiatives have been complemented by financial aid, infrastructure investments, and humanitarian assistance, in the process increasing the sophistication of UEA's foreign policy.

Despite assessments focusing on UAE' presence in Yemen and Libya, these issues often overshadow constructive and investment-oriented initiatives, which were equally instrumental in shaping geopolitical outcomes alongside military actions (Ziadah, 2021). The UAE's agenda incorporates a liberal perspective on international relations with a tolerant Sunni identity that fosters humanitarianism. According to one noteworthy view, the UAE is actually "a case study for how small states can play an outsize role in politics and economics" (Quillam and Vakil, 2023).

3.2. *Domestic*

The UAE promotes a culture of tolerance in the context of a liberal economic model that stands in stark contrast to the ideas of extremist groups. With a multiethnic population, the country welcomes expatriate workers from nations experiencing instability, while ensuring freedom of movement for GCC nationals. The UAE's distinctive socioeconomic model comprehends people of all faiths and cultures peacefully coexisting, not trying to create a "melting pot" but respecting cultural differences.

Given its diverse labor market, there is a concern that extremist organizations may radicalize foreign workers (Al Shaikh, p.75). UAE leaders have dealt with extremism and terrorism using soft power, domestic legislation, and international policies. For instance, the UAE government recognizes the importance of social media in combating terrorism. The country utilizes these networks for this purpose, and its officials have participated in global forums on counter-extremism on online platforms such as the "Tweeps Forum," carried out in Riyadh in 2017, focusing on addressing extremist ideologies (Kawa News, 2017). Additionally, the country has restricted radical websites, funded moderate religious programs, and promoted moderate Islamic leaders to counter extremist ideas.

In terms of legislation, the UAE approved the "Anti-Terrorist Law" that defines terrorism and persons associated with it, imposes convictions, and establishes rehabilitation centers (UAE, 2014). It has also created a law "against hatred, discrimination, and extremism" to reinforce its position against terrorism, by forbidding religious intolerance, racial discrimination, and hate speech (UAE Government Portal, 2023).

Within the government, the Executive Office of Anti-Money Laundering and Counter-Terrorism Financing was established according to Cabinet Resolution No. 10 of 2021, and its main responsibilities are information sharing, integrity, risk management and coordination regarding money laundering (EOAMLCTF, 2024). Besides international collaboration and coordination, this institution has put in place legislation to ban the financing of terrorism, create penalties and fines, all this formalized through memorandums of understanding.

In the field of education, the UAE has established several institutions related to counterterrorism that educate people and benefit from foreign expertise. These include Rabdan Academy, established in 2013, the National Defense College, established that same year, and Zayed Military University created in 2021 as part of the Ministry of Defense. Additional relevant initiatives include the International Institute for Tolerance, launched by the Government of Dubai to deal with extremism, and created the Mohammad Bin Rashid Al Maktoum Tolerance Award to recognize those who contribute to tolerance. The Hedayah Center ("guidance" in Arabic) (Hedayah Website, 2024) was launched in December 2012 in Abu Dhabi to replace the International Centre for Excellence in Countering Violent Extremism (CVE), which between 2018 and 2019 provided support in 20 countries (Rosand, 2020, p.9). The Sawab Center ("right path" in Arabic), launched in July 2015 jointly with the United States, supports the global coalition against extremism as an answer to terrorism and religious misinterpretations being propagated by extremists (UAE's Government portal, 2024). Additionally, the Declaration of Human Fraternity, signed on February 4, 2019, in Abu Dhabi by the Grand Imam Dr. Ahmed Al-

Tayeb, Sheikh of Al-Azhar, and Pope Francis, represents a significant milestone in promoting safe and peaceful coexistence for all people (UAE Ministry of Tolerance and Coexistence, 2024).

In 2023, the UAE inaugurated the Abrahamic Family House in Abu Dhabi, a space containing three Houses of Worship: The Eminence Ahmed El-Tayeb Mosque, St. Francis Church, and Moses Ben Maimon Synagogue. The purpose of this space is to reflect on and learn about the three religions, promoting dialogue and understanding to foster coexistence (Abrahamic Family House, 2024). This institution is unique not only in the region but also unique in the world, reflecting the UAE's strong commitment to tolerance and peace.

Other countries have also followed suit in this regard. For instance, in November 2022, Bahrain organized the "Forum for Dialogue: East and West for Human Coexistence". The objective was to promote mutual understanding among leaders of religions, sects, thought, culture, and media, in cooperation with Al Azhar, the Catholic Church, the Muslim Council of Elders, and other international institutions concerned with dialogue, human coexistence, and tolerance. Pope Francis participated at the closing ceremony against war, advocating for religious freedom, recognition of women's rights, protection of children's rights, and discussing the concept of citizenship (Castellano Lubov, 2024).

In terms of success against terrorism, UAE authorities have dismantled domestic extremist groups and, in 2012, after years of surveillance, disrupted an anti-government organization (Plotkin Boghardt, 2013). In response to these concerns, the UAE authorities have promoted public projects, especially in the northern Emirates that do not attract as much foreign investment as the two bigger Emirates, increased military personnel pensions by 70%, reformed the electoral college, and increased public officials' income (Al Shaikh, p.131).

As seen from abroad, the UAE strategy against extremism has been effective. The US Department of State has recognized the progress made in this regard. In its 2022 Country Report on Terrorism, it stated:

The UAE remained a leader on a global level in CVE narratives, supporting CVE education, and participating in and hosting international fora to promote tolerance and coexistence. The UAE continued valuable support for CT efforts against ISIS, and in Yemen against AQAP, including providing support to local forces in CT operations (US Department of State, 2022).

On the other hand, the EU Parliament also acknowledged the role of the UAE in combatting extremism. In the 2017 Parliamentary session, it praised the UAE's active participation and collaboration against ISIS, its anti-radicalism educational programs, its public awareness campaigns, and intelligence cooperation with the EU (Salama, 2017).

CONCLUSIONS

In contrast to what is absent in other countries, the UAE has a clear pathway to the future as a young and thriving nation. The UAE has made significant progress towards achieving its goals, but the country is in a complicated region characterized by political-military competition and deep structural challenges. According to common understanding, the current security context in the region is partly explained by the 2011 movements. However, the most relevant factors shaping security in the region preceded those movements, namely the 2003 US invasion of Iraq and the civil war in Syria as well as persistent structural problems such as tribal divisions. In this context, which is also characterized by a gradual US withdrawal from the region, the UAE has assumed a more proactive stance to contain the expansion of extreme ideologies in a volatile region. Domestically, the UAE has also neutralized local extremist groups. This dual approach is seen as the right course of action to confront the obstacles to achieving its vision for the future.

In sum, the combination of these factors has prompted the UAE to adopt a more diversified and sophisticated security approach, combining diplomacy, and both hard and soft power in the form of smart power. This shift has complemented the UAE traditional respect for sovereignty posture with a pragmatic approach as an honest broker that allows the country to protect and promote its national interests more efficiently. The goal is to create a stable security and economic foundation to achieve its vision for the future.

So far, the country has been relatively successful in its efforts to promote domestic and regional stability. However, its future success will depend not only on its sustained efforts, but also on several variables beyond the direct control of the UAE's leadership, such as the Palestinian issue as illustrated by the recent Hamas/Hezbollah/Iran-Israel conflict, the confrontation between Saudi Arabia and Iran, the political situation in Syria, and the level of US involvement in the region. In all of these issues, extreme ideologies play a significant role. In contrast to these extreme ideologies, the UAE will continue fostering stability through moderation. According to Sheik Mohammed bin Rashid Al Maktoum, "What makes us proud of our nation is not the height of our buildings, the breadth of our streets, or the magnitude of our shopping malls, but rather the openness and tolerance of our nation. Our pride stems from the fact that we are a country where everyone thrives equally regardless of their differences" (Vogue Arabia, 2024).

REFERENCES

Abrahamic Family House. (2024, June 13). Diverse in our faiths. Common in our humanity. Together in peace. https://www.abrahamicfamilyhouse.ae/

Abu Dhabi Media Office. (2024, April 1). Statistics Centre – Abu Dhabi reports growth of emirate's non-oil economy and real GDP in 2023. https://www.mediaoffice.abudhabi/en/economy/statistics-centre-abu-dhabi-reports-growth-of-emirates-non-oil-economy-and-real-gdp-in-2023

Ahmed, H. M. (2023, November 30). The secret behind UAE's economic miracle. The Halal Times. https://www.halaltimes.com/the-secret-behind-uaes-economic-miracle/

Akbarzadeh, S., & Azizi, H. (2024, April). Iran in the Middle East: Introduction. Middle East Council on Global Affairs. https://mecouncil.org/publication_chapters/iran-in-the-middle-east-introduction/

Al Shaikh, A. B. A. (2022). Securitization theory in the UAE context: Regional instability and shifting security dynamics. The Emirates Center for Strategic Studies and Research (ECSSR).

Almezaini, K. S. (2011). *The UAE and foreign policy: Foreign aid, identities and interests*. Routledge.

Almezaini, K. S. (2020, November). The UAE's security perceptions in the Middle East: Regional challenges, alliances and diversification of partners. In S. Colombo & A. Dessi (Eds.), Fostering a new security architecture in the Middle East (pp. 50–63). Foundation for European Progressive Studies (FEPS) & Istituto Affari Internazionali (IAI). https://www.iai.it/sites/default/files/9788833653501.pdf

Alons, G. C. (2007). Predicting a state's foreign policy: State preferences between domestic and international constraints. *Foreign Policy Analysis*, *3*(3), 211–232.

Antwi-Boateng, O., & Al Jaberi, N. H. S. (2022, April). The post-oil strategy of the UAE: An examination of diversification strategies and challenges. *Politics & Policy*, *50*(2), 341–367. https://www.scopus.com/record/display.uri?eid=2-s2.0-85125657637&origin=inward&txGid=6de433b7f8579f1b0742de9bbd23cb86

Antwi-Boateng, O., & Alhasmi, A. A. (2022). The emergence of the United Arab Emirates as a global soft power: Current strategies and future challenges. *Economic and Political Studies*, *10*(2), 221–240.

Australian Government Department of Foreign Affairs and Trade. (2024). United Arab Emirates country brief. https://www.dfat.gov.au/geo/united-arab-emirates/united-arab-emirates-country-brief

Bassiouni, M. C. (2022). Saudi reforms: Change for survival or for progress? In IEMed Mediterranean Yearbook 2022. European Institute of the Mediterranean. https://www.iemed.org/publication/saudi-reforms-change-for-survival-or-for-progress/

Batrawi, A. (2022, January 17). Drone attack in Abu Dhabi claimed by Yemen's rebels kills 3. Associated Press. https://apnews.com/article/business-dubai-united-arab-emirates-abu-dhabi-yemen-8bdefdf900ce46a6fd6c7bc685bf838a

BBC. (2018, October 31). Yemen war: US presses Saudi Arabia to agree ceasefire. https://www.bbc.com/news/world-middle-east-46040789

Belcher, D. (2024, May 16). Bahrain celebrates its history as a pearling center. The New York Times. https://www.nytimes.com/2024/05/16/fashion/jewelry-bahrain-pearl-path.html

Bertelsmann Stiftung Transformation Index. (2024). United Arab Emirates country report 2024. https://bti-project.org/fileadmin/api/content/en/downloads/reports/country_report_2024_ARE.pdf

Besson, S. (2011, April). Sovereignty. Oxford Public International Law. https://opil.ouplaw.com/display/10.1093/law:epil/9780199231690/law-9780199231690-e1472

Bonesh, F. R. (2022, October 10). UAE's approach to Iraq. Al-Bayan Center for Planning and Studies. https://www.bayancenter.org/en/wp-content/uploads/2022/10/ejbh.pdf

Borger, J. (2023, September 21). Crown prince confirms Saudi Arabia will seek nuclear arsenal if Iran develops one. The Guardian. https://www.theguardian.com/world/2023/sep/21/crown-prince-confirms-saudi-arabia-seek-nuclear-arsenal-iran-develops-one

Bronson, R. (2011, March 13). Saudi Arabia's intervention in Bahrain: A necessary evil or a strategic blunder? Foreign Policy Research Institute. https://www.fpri.org/article/2011/03/saudi-arabias-intervention-in-bahrain-a-necessary-evil-or-a-strategic-blunder/

Castellano Lubov, D. (2022, November 4). Pope at Bahrain dialogue forum: Religious leaders have duty to help humanity. Vatican News. Retrieved from https://www.vaticannews.va/en/pope/news/2022-11/pope-at-bahrain-dialogue-forum-calls-for-peace.html

Central Intelligence Agency. (2024, May 22). United Arab Emirates. The World Factbook. Retrieved from https://www.cia.gov/the-world-factbook/countries/united-arab-emirates/

Conference on Interaction and Confidence Building Measures in Asia. (2024, December). Retrieved from https://www.s-cica.org/index.php?view=press_releases&id=2345

Davidson, C. M. (2009). Dubai and the United Arab Emirates: Security threats. British Journal of Middle Eastern Studies, 36(3), Gulf Security: Legacies of the Past, Prospects for the Future. Retrieved from https://www.jstor.org/stable/40593284

Dubai Airports. (2024, May 13). Retrieved from https://www.dubaiairports.ae/corporate/about-us/dwc-dubai-world-central/

El Kurd, D. (2023, August 31). Assessing the Abraham Accords, three years on. Arab Center Washington DC. Retrieved from https://arabcenterdc.org/resource/assessing-the-abraham-accords-three-years-on/

Embassy of the United Arab Emirates. Washington, DC. (2022, September 16). Abdullah bin Zayed holds official reception in Tel Aviv on second anniversary of Abraham Accords. Retrieved from https://www.wam.ae/en/details/1395303083970

Embassy of the United Arab Emirates. Washington, DC. (2024, June 13). Security. UAE–US Cooperation. Retrieved from https://www.uae-embassy.org/uae-us-cooperation/security

Embassy of the United Arab Emirates. Washington, DC. (n.d.). Occupied UAE islands, unofficial map. For illustrative purposes only. Retrieved from https://www.uae-embassy.org/discover-uae/foreign-policy/occupied-uae-islands

Esfandiary, D. (2021, September 15). The anxiety effect: How 9/11 and its aftermath changed Gulf Arab states' relations with the U.S. Crisis Group. Retrieved from https://www.crisisgroup.org/middle-east-north-africa/gulf-and-arabian-peninsula/united-arab-emirates-united-states-saudi-arabia

Export Council Australia. (2021, September 6). Market information, Middle East. Retrieved from https://export.org.au/united-arab-emirates-looking-beyond-oil/

Ghafoor, A., & Mitchell, P. (2022, August 30). Secret deals ending Britain's control in Gulf revealed. BBC News Arabic. Retrieved from https://www.bbc.com/news/world-middle-east-62713025

Goetschel, L. (1998). The foreign and security policy interests of small states in today's Europe. In Goetschel, L. (Ed.), *Small states inside and outside the European Union* (pp. xx–xx). Springer., DOI: 10.1007/978-1-349-14426-4

Gordon, P. (2018). Great Britain and the Middle East: The rise and fall of a hegemonic power and the pursuit of eternal interests. In Abu-Warda, N., & Rubio-Garcia, D. (Eds.), *La Primavera Árabe y sus perspectivas regionales e internacionales* (pp. xx–xx). Diwan-Mayrit.

Hey, J. A. K. (Ed.). (2003). *Small states in world politics: Explaining foreign policy behavior*. Lynne Rienner.

Hofstede, G., Hofstede, G. J., & Minkov, M. (2010). *Cultures and organizations: Software of the mind* (3rd ed.). McGraw-Hill Professional.

Iddon, P. (2022, January 30). The UAE is bolstering its formidable air defenses. Forbes. Retrieved from https://www.forbes.com/sites/pauliddon/2022/01/30/the-uae-is-bolstering-its-formidable-air-defenses/

International Institute of Strategic Studies. (2019, January). The US withdrawal from Syria. Strategic Comments, 25. Retrieved from https://www.iiss.org/en/publications/strategic-comments/2019/the-us-withdrawal-from-syria/

International Maritime Security Construct. (2019, November 12). Vigilance, surveillance, assurance. Retrieved from https://www.maritimeglobalsecurity.org/media/fasbdek4/2020-01-07-imsc-brochure-tri-fold-version-3.pdf

International Trade Administration. (2023, November 25). United Arab Emirates. U.S. Department of Commerce. Retrieved from https://www.trade.gov/country-commercial-guides/united-arab-emirates-defense#:~:text=The%20UAE%20ranks%20%236%20overall,on%20procurement%20with%20foreign%20suppliers

Iran International. (2023, August 8). UAE expresses concern over Iran's nuclear program. Retrieved from https://www.iranintl.com/en/202308088879

Jacopo, L., Mazzucco, M., & Alexander, K. (2023, August 30). How the United Arab Emirates has promoted tolerance, co-existence and multiculturalism to confront religious violence. Manara Magazine. Retrieved from https://manaramagazine.org/2023/08/uae-tolerance-religious-violence/

Janardhan, N. (2019, April 24). The UAE evolves into a 'smart' power. Gulf Today. Retrieved from https://www.gulftoday.ae/opinion/2019/04/23/the-uae-evolves-into-a-smart-power

Kamrava, M. (2024, April). Iran's neighborhood policy: An assessment. Middle East Council on Global Affairs. Retrieved from https://mecouncil.org/publication_chapters/irans-neighborhood-policy-an-assessment/

Kawa News. (2017, September 28). Tweeps 2017 Forum focuses on the fight against extremist ideologies online. Tech & Business. Retrieved from https://kawa-news.com/en/tweeps-2017-forum-focuses-on-the-fight-against-extremist-ideologies-online/

Keohane, R. O. (1969). Lilliputians' dilemmas: Small states in international politics. *International Organization, 23*(2), 291–310.

Khalil, S. (2020, December 17). Mohamed Bouazizi, 1984–2011: The fire that lit the Arab Spring. The New Arab. Retrieved from https://www.newarab.com/analysis/mohamed-bouazizi-fire-lit-arab-spring

Kissinger, H. (2017). *A world restored: Metternich, Castlereagh, and the problems of peace, 1812–22*. Friedland Books.

Krasner, S. D. (1982). Structural causes and regime consequences: Regimes as intervening variables. *International Organization, 36*(2), 185–205. https://pos-graduacao.uepb.edu.br/ppgri/files/2016/02/Krasner-Structural-Causes-and-Regime-Consequencies-Regime-as-Intervening-Variables.pdf

Labott, E. (2004, May 12). U.S. hits Syria with sanctions. CNN.com. Retrieved from https://edition.cnn.com/2004/WORLD/meast/05/11/us.syria/

Lim, D. J., & Cooper, Z. (2015). Reassessing hedging: The logic of alignment in East Asia. *Security Studies, 24*(4), 696–727. DOI: 10.1080/09636412.2015.1103130

Maceda, C. (2015, August 2). How Google is showing Arabian Gulf on maps. Gulf News. Retrieved from https://gulfnews.com/going-out/society/how-google-is-showing-arabian-gulf-on-maps-1.1560237

Marshall, T. (2015). *Prisoners of geography: Ten maps that tell you everything you need to know about global politics*. Elliott & Thompson.

Mirzaei, A. (2019). Market power among UAE banks: The 2008 financial crisis and its impact. *The Quarterly Review of Economics and Finance, 71*, 187–198. DOI: 10.1016/j.qref.2018.08.008

Morgenthau, H. J. (2005). Politics among nations (7th ed., Rev. by K. Thompson & D. Clinton). McGraw-Hill Education.

Mubadala. (2024). Emirates Global Aluminium: Our portfolio. Retrieved from https://www.mubadala.com/en/what-we-do/emirates-global-aluminium#:~:text=Emirates%20Global%20Aluminium%20is%20the,Emirates%20outside%20oil%20and%20gas

News Wires. (2011, March 14). Gulf states send troops to quell Bahrain protests. France 24. Retrieved from https://www.france24.com/en/20110314-gulf-states-send-troops-bahrain-quell-violent-protests-UAE-Saudi-Arabia

Nyarko, Y. (2010). The United Arab Emirates: Some lessons in economic development (WIDER Working Paper No. 2010/11). United Nations University World Institute for Development Economics Research (UNU-WIDER). Retrieved from https://www.econstor.eu/bitstream/10419/54154/1/636479374.pdf

Nye, J. S. (2008). *The powers to lead: Soft, hard, and smart*. Oxford University Press.

Organization of the Petroleum Exporting Countries. (2022). UAE facts and figures. https://www.opec.org/opec_web/en/about_us/170.htm

Page, M. T., & Vittori, J. (Eds.). (2020). Dubai's role in facilitating corruption and global illicit financial flows. Carnegie Endowment for International Peace. https://carnegie-production-assets.s3.amazonaws.com/static/files/PageVittori_DubaiCorruption_final.pdf

Patel, N. (2019, March 7). How is the UAE diversifying its economy to attract investment? Trade Finance Global. (Last modified December 6, 2023). https://www.tradefinanceglobal.com/posts/how-is-the-uae-diversifying-its-economy-to-attract-investment/

Permanent Mission of the United Arab Emirates to the United Nations. (2017, October 10). UAE reaffirms commitment to combat international terrorism. https://www.un.int/uae/news/uae-reaffirms-commitment-combat-international-terrorism

Plotkin Boghardt, L. (2013, April 12). The Muslim Brotherhood on trial in the UAE (Policy Watch 2064). The Washington Institute for Near East Policy. https://www.washingtoninstitute.org/policy-analysis/muslim-brotherhood-trial-uae

Quilliam, N., & Vakil, S. (2023, December 29). The Medicis of the Middle East? How the United Arab Emirates is plotting its rise. Foreign Affairs. https://www.foreignaffairs.com/united-arab-emirates/medicis-middle-east

Rabinovich, I. (2019, January 24). How Iran's regional ambitions have developed since 1979. Brookings Institution. https://www.brookings.edu/articles/how-irans-regional-ambitions-have-developed-since-1979/

Rafeq, A. K. (2005). A different balance of power: Europe and the Middle East in the eighteenth and nineteenth centuries. In Choueiri, Y. M. (Ed.), *A companion history of the Middle East* (pp. xx–xx). Blackwell Publishing.

Rahman, O. (2023, July 11). Five reasons why the Abraham Accords are ceding ground to Arab-Iranian de-escalation (Issue Brief). Edward P. Djerejian Center for the Middle East, Baker Institute for Public Policy, Rice University. https://www.bakerinstitute.org/research/five-reasons-why-abraham-accords-are-ceding-ground-arab-iranian-de-escalation

Rais, F. R. (2004). Syria under Bashar Al Assad: A profile for power. Strategic Studies (Institute of Strategic Studies Islamabad), 24(3).

Reuters. (2024, April 30). UAE-Iran joint economic commission convenes for first time in 10 years. https://www.reuters.com/world/middle-east/uae-iran-joint-economic-commission-convenes-first-time-10-years-2024-04-30/

Rickli, J. M. (2008). European small states' military policies after the Cold War: From territorial to niche strategies. *Cambridge Review of International Affairs*, *21*(3), 307–325. DOI: 10.1080/09557570802253435

Rickli, J. M., & Almezaini, K. (2016). Theories of small states' foreign and security policies and the Gulf States. In Almezaini, K., & Rickli, J. M. (Eds.), *The small Gulf states: Foreign and security policies before and after the Arab Spring* (1st ed., pp. xx–xx). Routledge.

Rizvi, A. (2020, November 24). Coronavirus: UAE was braced for Covid-19 impact due to long-term investment in services, study finds. The National. https://www.thenationalnews.com/uae/government/coronavirus-uae-was-braced-for-covid-19-impact-due-to-long-term-investment-in-services-study-finds-1.1116950

Robbins, M., Jamal, A. A., & Tessler, M. (2024). America is losing the Arab world and China is reaping the benefits. Foreign Affairs, July/August. https://www.foreignaffairs.com/united-states/america-losing-arab-world

Robinson, K., & Merrow, W. (2020, December 3). The Arab Spring at ten years: What's the legacy of the uprisings? Council on Foreign Relations. https://www.cfr.org/article/arab-spring-ten-years-whats-legacy-uprisings

Robinson, K., & Merrow, W. (2024, April 15). Iran's regional armed network? Council on Foreign Relations. https://www.cfr.org/article/irans-regional-armed-network

Rosand, E. (2020, August). Preparing the Global Counterterrorism Forum for the next decade (Special Report No. 476). United States Institute of Peace. https://www.usip.org/sites/default/files/2020-08/20200817-sr_476-preparing_the_global_counterterrorism_forum_for_the_next_decade-s.pdf

Rumley, G. (2022, February 15). Unpacking the UAE F-35 negotiations (PolicyWatch 3578). The Washington Institute for Near East Policy. https://www.washingtoninstitute.org/policy-analysis/unpacking-uae-f-35-negotiations

Salama, S. (2017, October 29). EU Parliament reaffirms support to UAE in fight against terrorism. Gulf News. https://gulfnews.com/uae/government/eu-parliament-reaffirms-support-to-uae-in-fight-against-terrorism-1.2115176

Salisbury, P. (2020, July). Risk perception and appetite in the UAE foreign and national security policy. Middle East and North Africa Program, Chatham House. https://www.chathamhouse.org/sites/default/files/2020-07-01-risk-in-uae-salisbury.pdf

Scarr, S., Arranz, A., Saul, J., Huang, H., Chowdhury, J., & Kawoosa, V. M. (2024, February 2). Red Sea attacks: How Houthi militants in Yemen are attacking ships in one of the world's busiest maritime trade routes. Reuters. (Last updated March 8, 2024). https://www.reuters.com/graphics/ISRAEL-PALESTINIANS/SHIPPING-ARMS/lgvdnngeyvo/

Slav, I. (2023, May 1). The 10 countries with the largest natural gas reserves. OilPrice.com. https://oilprice.com/Energy/Energy-General/The-10-Countries-With-The-Largest-Natural-Gas-Reserves.html

Stickings, T. (2023, August 7). UAE tells UN of 'profound concern' over Iran's nuclear activities. The National. https://www.thenationalnews.com/world/2023/08/07/uae-tells-un-of-profound-concern-over-irans-nuclear-activities/

Talwar, A. (2022, February 17). From oil to diversification of the UAE: An economic perspective. Diplomacy and Beyond. https://diplomacybeyond.com/from-oil-to-diversification-of-the-uae-an-economic-perspective/

Taulbee, J. L. (2014). Lesser states and niche diplomacy. In Taulbee, J. L., Kelleher, A., & Grosvenor, P. C. (Eds.), *Norway's peace policy* (pp. xx–xx). Palgrave Macmillan.

The Executive Office of Anti-Money Laundering and Counter-Terrorism Financing. (2024). Enhancing the United Arab Emirates' response to fighting money laundering and countering terrorism financing activities. Retrieved from https://amlctf.gov.ae/en

United Arab Emirates. (2014). Federal Law No. (7) of 2014 on combatting terrorism. https://www.adgm.com/documents/financial-crime-prevention-unit/aml-tab/federal-law-no-7-of-2014-on-combatting-terrorism-offences.pdf

United Arab Emirates Government. (n.d.). UAE Centennial Plan 2071. https://uaecabinet.ae/en/uae-centennial-plan-2071

United Arab Emirates Government Portal. (2023). Federal Decree Law No. 34 of 2023 concerning combating discrimination, hatred and extremism. [PDF file]. https://file:///C:/Users/apadilla/Downloads/Federal%20Decree%20Law%20No%2034%20of%202023%20concerning%20combating%20discrimination%20hatred%20and%20extremism%20(1).pdf *(Note: This link appears to be a local file path and not a public URL. Replace with an accessible link if available.)*

United Arab Emirates Government Portal. (2024, June 13). Centres for countering extremism. https://u.ae/en/about-the-uae/culture/tolerance/centers-for-countering-extremism

United Arab Emirates Ministry of Cabinet Affairs. (2024). UAE Centennial Plan 2071. https://uaecabinet.ae/en/uae-centennial-plan-2071

United Arab Emirates Ministry of Tolerance and Coexistence. (2024, June 13). Festival of Human Fraternity. https://www.tolerance.gov.ae/contributing-to-international-efforts-to-promote-tolerance/fhf

United Nations Development Programme. (2024). Human Development Index. https://hdr.undp.org/data-center/human-development-index#/indicies/HDI

United Nations Treaty Collection. (1993). Agreement on the delimitation of boundaries (No. 30250). https://treaties.un.org/doc/publication/unts/volume%201733/i-30250.pdf

U.S. Department of State. (2021). United Arab Emirates. In Country reports on terrorism 2021. https://www.state.gov/reports/country-reports-on-terrorism-2021/united-arab-emirates

U.S. Department of State. (2024, June 13). United Arab Emirates. In Country reports on terrorism 2022. https://www.state.gov/reports/country-reports-on-terrorism-2022/uae

U.S. Energy Information Administration. (2023, November 21). The Strait of Hormuz is the world's most important oil transit chokepoint. https://www.eia.gov/todayinenergy/detail.php?id=61002

US-UAE Business Council. (2019, March). An enduring partnership: The US-UAE defense and security relationship. https://usuaebusiness.org/wp-content/uploads/2019/03/Defense-Report-Final-March-2019.pdf

Vogue Arabia. (2024, July 15). 10 of HH Sheikh Mohammed bin Rashid's wisest quotes to live by. https://en.vogue.me/culture/sheikh-mohammed-bin-rashid-wisest-quotes/

Walt, S. M. (1987). *The origins of alliances*. Cornell University Press.

Waltz, K. N. (1979). *Theory of international politics*. Addison-Wesley.

World Bank. (2022). GDP (current US$) - United Arab Emirates. https://data.worldbank.org/indicator/NY.GDP.MKTP.CD?locations=AE

World Population Review. (2024). Oil reserves by country 2024. https://worldpopulationreview.com/country-rankings/oil-reserves-by-country

Yadlin, A. (2022, May). The attack on Abu Dhabi: Dilemmas, threats, and opportunities. The Jerusalem Strategic Review. https://jstribune.com/yadlin-the-attack-on-abu-dhabi/

Ziadah, R. (2021, October 27). Saudi-UAE interventions: Arms, aid and counter-revolution. Transnational Institute. https://www.tni.org/en/article/saudi-uae-interventions

Chapter 7

The Circular Correlation Between Institutions, Political Marketing, and the Electoral Process

Harry Ph. Sophocleous
Neapolis University, Pafos, Cyprus

Sofia D. Anastasiadou
University of Western Macedonia, Greece

Andreas N. Masouras
https://orcid.org/0000-0001-8989-3930
Neapolis University, Pafos, Cyprus

ABSTRACT

The electoral choices of a nation, combined with the practices of its political establishment and institutions, are a significant factor in the functioning of democracy, prosperity and the overall prospects of the state. Moreover, both political institutions and the surrounding political environment, on the one hand, and the communication intentions and broader political marketing of parties or candidates, on the other, have an impact on electoral behaviour and thus on a country's electoral choices. In this context, the study examines the relationship between institutions, political marketing and the electoral process. Consequently, the specific research considers the impact of political institutions and involves measuring and correlating the elements that make up political marketing with those of electoral motives and perceptions, as well as those of political engagement and measures the cycled relationship between those elements.

DOI: 10.4018/979-8-3693-5583-1.ch007

INTRODUCTION

The research is primarily based on the hypothesis that the voter is a consumer of political marketing /political communication, and thus the ideological output produced by political activities (Sophocleous 2024). The projected research suggests that electoral behaviour can be considered a practice of consumer behaviour, while, at the same time the way in which electorates behave and react is connected with the sense of political security and the way and the way in which they perceived institutions and react to related instructional issues. Therefore, it could be argued that the specific chapter it is connected to the scope of the specific book. Consequently, the voter can be conceptualised as a potential consumer of the "political communication" and the "political marketing mix". The specific study thus attempts to ascertain how the communication and the wider political marketing mix of political parties are produced, perceived, and consumed during the pre-electoral periods by the potential voters.

Furthermore, the proposed research aims to elucidate the manner and perspective in which the average voter consumes political communication. In light of the aforementioned, the consumption of political communication has been examined within the context of this research, as detailed in the following chapters. The research has concentrated on the processes of persuasion, sympathy, attitude formation, and message delivery. In order to achieve the projected research objectives in an appropriate and effective manner, it has been deemed essential to identify the fundamental research principle through an investigative process.

RESEARCH CONTEXT

It is of the utmost importance to justify the selection of the particular topic and the choice of the particular case study before specifying the research aims and objectives. This is essential to provide context for the research conducted.

Why this particular topic

The topic of this study is the electoral behaviour of a nation, which is influenced by the actions of its political establishment and institutions, while as it already been mentioned, the way in which electorates behave and react is connected with the sense of political security and the way and the way in which they perceived institutions and react to related instructional issues. The electoral choice of a nation, along with the course of actions of its political establishment and institutions, is a significant factor in the functioning of democracy, prosperity and the general prospect of the state. In addition, both the political institutions and the surrounding political environment, on the one hand, and the communicational intentions and the wider political marketing of parties or candidates, on the other hand, have an impact on the electoral behaviour and, therefore, the electoral choice of a country. In light of this, it is crucial to examine the interrelationship between the aforementioned notions and to measure, firstly, the electoral effect of political communication and secondly, the influence of the involved institutions throughout the specific communicational process.

Why Cyprus

The rationale behind selecting Cyprus as the case study for this research is based on a number of factors. The majority of current studies in the field of voting behaviour and electoral communication are focused on the US, the UK, Europe and Asia. However, there is a notable absence of significant research activity on Eastern Mediterranean countries, particularly on Cyprus. Secondly, following its independence in 1960, the Republic of Cyprus has experienced a series of political struggles concerning the unity of the two main ethnic groups, the Greek Cypriots and the Turkish Cypriots. These struggles culminated in the Turkish invasion of 1974. Moreover, there is a paucity of examples of relatively newly formed European states that have experienced such diverse political issues, which have affected the institutions, the evolution and the consistency of the political party establishment, and the way in which to anticipate the electoral process within such a short period of time. Consequently, the aforementioned factors present a case worthy of further research in relation to electoral culture, voting behaviour and the consumption of political communication.

The Impact of institutions upon the voting process

Political institutions are the primary coordinators of political choices. (Sniderman and Levendusky, 2007). Consequently, it has been deemed crucial to examine the role and impact of institutions on the perceptions of voters, with a view to evaluating their effects on the process of producing and consuming political communication. Therefore, it is necessary to ascertain the influence of major institutions of the state on perceptions of voting and, consequently, on voting choice. In recent years, a considerable body of research has been devoted to investigating the influence of democratic institutions on campaign behaviour. This includes studies by Alvarez and Sinclair (2012) and Sudulich and Trumm (2019).

Consequently, voting is both the input and the output of the political system, determining the manner in which people participate in collective effect. Nevertheless, the outcome of policy is not solely determined by the distribution of individual decisions. The selected strategy varies depending on the collaboration among distinct electors, each of whom might have distinct choices and form distinct alliances.

RESEARCH MEASURES

It is of great importance to consider the relationship between the research hypotheses and the conceptual framework. Once the research objectives have been established, it is crucial to delineate the structures of the key research variables (Saunders et al.,2003; Gill & Johnson, 1997). This section outlines the research measures of the study and attempts to connect the conceptual framework of the study with the research questions, thereby establishing a clear correspondence between the conceptual framework, research hypotheses and research objectives/aims. Consequently, in order to achieve the proposed objectives, it would be beneficial to define the researchable measures (variables) of the study. In other words, as reflected by the proposed objectives, the proposed research involves the measurement of the following major variables(Sophocleous, 2021, 2023, 2024:

- The marketing mix of the political parties
- The motives the perceptions of the voter
- The Voting involvement
- The impact of institutions upon voting behaviour

2.0 LITERATURE REVIEW

2.1 Social Context, Campaign Effects and Campaign Actions

A substantial corpus of research on electoral campaigns has concentrated on the immediate impact of campaign efforts on the outcome of the political process. This includes the choice of votes cast and the level of voter participation. However, focusing on the "citizen communication process" enables researchers to view voters as active processors of campaign communication and to observe the deliberative nature of political campaigns that has been largely ignored in previous research (Banducci & Karp, J., 2003; Huckfeldt, Sprague, & Levine, 2000; Just et al., 1996; Page, 1996; Pan, Shen, Paek, & Sun, 2006; Hunt, 2018).

The existing body of research indicates that social pressure plays a pivotal role in human behaviour and decision-making. The fundamental aspects of social pressure can be classified as either external or internal. External social pressure is not contingent on social context, whereas internal social pressure is contingent on factors such as family and friends. One significant issue is to determine how to distinguish between social influence from peers and external influences. While a variety of investigational and observational studies have provided insight into this dilemma, the classification of the level of transmission based on large-scale observational data with an unknown grid structure remains unexplored to a great extent. (Baines P.R., Worcester R. M., Jarrett D. and Mortimer R., 2003)

Furthermore, the study of political campaigning has been largely overlooked in the field of political science (Farrell 1996, Schmitt-Beck und Farrell 2002). The erroneous assumption that campaigns have minimal effects can be attributed to the long-held belief that such effects are self-evident. Contemporary research, however, has sought to assess this view of the minimal effect of campaigns. In more specific terms, Iyengar and Simon (2000) posit that campaigns do matter and can be essential. Similarly, the findings of Peterson's (2018) study indicate that the image projected by the candidates in the campaign plays a pivotal role in determining the outcome of the election.

2.2 The Social Context of Electoral Choice

The evolving social landscape and shifting trends have a direct bearing on the role of political communication, making it a crucial aspect of the study. According to Lipset and Rokkan (1967), social conflicts attain political significance when a specific set of conditions is met. Their model, initially outlined in the comprehensive opening chapter of Party Systems and Voter Alignments, is often regarded as the seminal work in the field of political cleavages. In their work Party Systems and Voter Alignments, Lipset and Rokkan define a "cleavage" as a social "fault line," or a prolonged social struggle pitting at least two large groups with conflicting social interests (and defined by their social characteristics) against one another. They posit that European social conflicts can be systematically ordered and divided into four groups, which ultimately trace back to the procedures of modernization. The first two conflicts are primarily cultural in nature and can be traced back to the development of modern nation-states. In contrast, the latter conflicts are predominantly economic in nature and can be attributed to the Industrial Revolution.

Similarly, in a study conducted by Lipset and Rokkan (1967), the context of Cyprus was directly linked to the background and purpose of the specific research. Protopapas (2011) conducted a study that was concerned with the context of Cyprus and that was directly linked to the background and purpose of the specific research. The central hypothesis of the Protopapas (2011) study was Despite the early introduction of modern representation institutions through electoral processes, the unfree nature of the British colonial regime and the redemptive nationalism of the Greek Cypriots delayed the emergence of political parties and influenced their system, with the parties at the heart of its operation. In his 2011 study, Protopapas considers the theory of the party and electoral phenomenon, attempting to determine the applicability of classical interpretive standards in the case of Cyprus. The dominant model of social divisions (cleavages) proposed by Rokkan and Lipset is given greater emphasis, as well as the degraded state of these divisions due to their great resonance.

In a similar context, Katsourides (2011) examines and explains the processes and cleavages through which the foundations of the party system in Cyprus were laid in the late 19th and early 20th century. The primary hypothesis put forth by Katsourides (2009) is that during this period, the formation of a premature party system in the country can be observed, concentring around anti-colonial (ethnic) and class cleavages. Of these, the former emerged as the dominant force. Furthermore, Katsourides (2009) examines the conditions and context in which the party system in Cyprus emerged, as well as the organisational mobilisation of certain cleavages which resulted in political forms of representation. The theoretical framework is largely based on the cleavage theory (Lipset and Rokkan, 1967), taking into account subsequent critiques of this theory and, most importantly, ascribing a pivotal role to political actors (parties and organisations).

Furthermore, in accordance with Blumler and Kavanagh (1999), the current relationships between social change and media change are complex and intertwined. Throughout the post-war era, political communication has been responsive to a series of exogenous/eternal changes, including modernization, secularization, and individualization. It is therefore of paramount importance to recognise that any electoral choice and any campaign that may influence such a choice occurs within a specified context. As Walder (2006: 713) suggests, a theory concerning political preferences is as legitimate as its claims regarding the contexts within which these preferences are expressed.

As proposed by Sniderman and Levendusky (2007), political institutions serve as the 'coordinators of political choices'. In order for individuals to make rational decisions, it is not necessary for society to be based exclusively on the limited cognitive and computational capacities of its members. Alternatively, they receive assistance from political institutions that facilitate the ability to make well-informed decisions (Sniderman and Levendusky, 2007). Kriesi, L. Bernhard and Hänggli (2007) adopt a straightforward approach to the study of campaign strategies employed by political actors. The authors posit that there are three types of actors involved in the communication processes that constitute a political campaign: political actors, the media, and the public. The authors posit that the interface between the three types of actors in a political campaign is approached from the perspective of political actors and their strategies. These actors seek to exert influence over their associated politicians, the media, and the public with the objective of disseminating their message during the campaign, which must contribute to their electoral success.

2.3 Political Institutions and Voting

The act of electing choices can be regarded as two fundamental aspects of the democratic procedure, alongside the institution of the democratic process itself. The act of voting allows the members of a constituency to determine which individuals they entrust with the authority to make decisions on their behalf. The act of voting allows members of a group to collectively determine the course of action they will pursue. In this vein, various researchers have recently addressed the effects of democratic institutions on campaign behaviour (Alvarez and Sinclair, 2012; Sudulich and Trumm, 2019).

Consequently, the act of electing has an impact on both the response and the production of politics. In other words, it affects the manner in which individuals engage in collective outcomes. Nevertheless, the strategy that emerges from the distribution of individual favourites cannot be deduced, as the preferred policy depends on the interaction between different electorates who may have varied preferences and form different coalitions. These issues have been a primary focus of previous scholars in their research.

3.0 METHODOLOGY

3.1 Survey with Cypriot Voters

In order to respond to research objective 2.5.2, it has been considered essential to undertake an empirical survey to assess how Cypriot customers are likely to perceive a foreign franchised brand. As McQuarrie (1996: 52) notes, the term 'survey' can be applied to any procedure in which a fixed set of questions is posed to a sample of respondents. The survey will investigate the voting perceptions of the Cypriot voter in order to examine the impact of electoral campaigns and institutions on the electoral culture of Cypriot voters. Additionally, it will investigate the extent to which priming influences voting behaviour within the context of contemporary Cypriot voting culture. Accordingly, it has been deemed necessary to include a quantitative survey with structured interviews with the electorate of the Republic of Cyprus. A more detailed reference to the proposed survey can be found in the following sub-sections.

Why a Survey questionnaire?

One method that is likely to be suitable for achieving the second principal objective of the specific research is a quantitative survey conducted through the use of structured interviews. Structured interviews or questionnaires are the most suitable method of quantitative research for the project. As Malhorta (1998: 318) states, a questionnaire is a structured technique for data collection consisting of a series of questions, written or verbal, that a respondent answers. Accordingly, the questionnaire has been employed as a tool for quantitative research, fulfilling a descriptive role and facilitating the answering of questions such as "how much?" and "to what extent?" Additionally, structured interviews have been selected over other primary data collection methods (in-depth and semi-structured interviews and observation) due to their capacity to gather information rapidly and efficiently, while simultaneously facilitating quantitative analysis.

3.2.1 The design of the questionnaire

The term 'question design' is used to describe the process of creating questions that elicit reliable and valid responses. This involves considering the type of questions, their wording, and the reliability and validity of responses (Hussey and Hussey, 1997: 162). Accordingly, the proposed questionnaire was administered to a representative sample of Cypriot voters in the form of structured interviews, comprising 10 basic questions plus demographic data.

Furthermore, the questionnaire was fully structured and comprised only closed-ended questions, thus facilitating the analysis of the gathered information. Furthermore, the majority of the questions, especially those of the initial section, were supported by the use of a 'Likert Scale' (Likert, 1932: 140). The Likert scale may be described as: The Likert scale is a measure of attitudes that ranges from very positive to very negative. It allows respondents to indicate how strongly they agree or disagree with carefully constructed statements relating to an attitudinal object (Zikmund, 1997). Consequently, the utilisation of the Likert scale may facilitate a more analytical collection of data and a more effective exploitation of the investigated information.

The manner in which a questionnaire is presented can significantly influence respondents' ability to complete it accurately and can also facilitate subsequent data analysis (Hussey and Hussey, 1997: 162). Accordingly, the layout of the proposed questionnaire has been designed in a way that is easily accessible, not overly time-consuming and avoids any inconvenience. A more detailed view of the layout and content of the proposed questionnaire is provided in Appendix 1, which presents a sample of the proposed questionnaire.

3.2.2 The Actual Design/Content of the Questionnaire

More specifically the given questionnaire includes five major parts of thematic questions, plus some basic demographical questions, which, as has already been mentioned, have been stated in a quantitative manner. Moreover, the questionnaire involved the following Parts:

I. The initial section, comprising 15 items, examined the impact of the political marketing mix. Furthermore, the Political Marketing Mix constitutes the initial of the four principal thematic sections of the questionnaire. This approach is analogous to those previously employed by other researchers, including Widagdo et al. (2014), Chowdhury & Naheed (2018), Chowdhury & Naheed (2019), Sophocleous (2024), and Sophocleous et al. (2024 a,b). These studies have addressed electoral behaviour and comprise four subsections, each addressing one of the four elements (Ps) of the political marketing mix (Place, Product, Price, Promotion). In more specific terms, Question 1 posed the following query: The survey inquired as to the extent to which the following elements might influence the respondents' electoral behaviour. The respondents were asked to indicate their level of agreement with the statements on a five-point Likert scale, with the anchoring points labelled as follows: 1 (Not at all), 2 (A little), 3 (Moderate), 4 (Enough), 5 (Very).
II. The specific thematic part (Question 2 - Question 5B), which involved examining the Decision to Vote Scale (DVS), developed by Muhammad (2013), was a multidimensional measure designed to assess the factors affecting the decision to vote of the general population. The scale consisted of 23 items (Muhammad 2013; Sophocleous ed al 2024, c) and had five sub-scales: reasons to vote (6 items), political identity of a candidate (5 items), personal identity of a candidate (4 items), voter's motive (4 items) and voter's perception (4 items). Voting Involvement/Voting Involvement Scale
III. The specific thematic section (Questions 6A to 7B) involved an examination of various voting scales (Political Involvement, Subjective Knowledge, Political OL, etc.) in a manner adapted from previous research (O'Cass and Pecotich, 2005).

The population and the sample of the survey

In order to be in a position to approach a particular question in a thorough way, it might be necessary to carefully specify the population of the research and clearly identify the sample which represents that population within the actual research process. According to Gill and Johnson (1997: 82): "...questionnaires are concerned with identifying the 'research population', which will provide all the information necessary for tackling the original research problem". It has been considered essential before starting the actual research process to define Cypriot Voters as the targeted research population and to proceed to the selection of a representative sample and a representative sampling method. According to Gay and Diehl (1992: 128), "...selection of a sample is a very important step in conducting a research study because the quality of the sample determines the generalizability of the results". For this reason, it is useful to define a sample representative to the proposed research population.

In this respect, respondents that are likely to form the sample of the proposed survey are to be randomly selected. According to Gay and Diehl (1992: 129), "... random sampling is the process of selecting a sample in such a way that all individuals in the defined population have an equal and independent chance of being selected for the sample".

According to Saunders et al 2003: 162), "...Stratified random sampling is a mortification of random sampling in which you devise the population into, or more relevant and significant strata based on one or a number of attributes." In this respect, the survey involved a structured questionnaire which was allocated through the use Electronic Message and the researcher gained access to the participants through the use of social media platform and in particular Facebook with the use of a particular profile with 5000 connections/friends all taken from the research population, therefore the participants were accessible and was not necessary to imply a consent form. The survey took place during April – May 2024 with Pancyprian Geographical coverage/ spread, the research population of the survey were the Cypriot voters and Sample size of 503 Cypriot Citizens with voting rights. The sampling took place though the use of simple random sampling.

The reason why the 'random sample' has been preferred over any other sampling methods, such as simple random sample and systematic, random sample (Saunders et al, 2003; Gill and Johnson, 1997), is because it gives a very thorough representation of the researchable population, which are the Cypriot voters. More specifically, a random sample is the only sample method which gives a through and comprehensive sample representative to the geographical and demographical spread of the researchable population.

Pilot-testing the questionnaire

As with the semi-structured interviews, it has been considered essential to undertake some pilot-testing of the proposed questionnaire. Pilot-testing involves "... collecting data forms the ultimate subject of the research project to serve as a guide for the larger study." (Zikmund, 1997: 47). Moreover, the proposed questionnaire has been tested twice, once with a smaller sample of interviewees, and once with the actual sample size in a way to reflect the suitability of the given questions and prevent the collection of useless information.

3.2 The researchable model and the originality of the research

It may be worthwhile to articulate the researchable objectives of the project and to elucidate the constructs of the major research variables (Saunders et al., 1997; Gill and Johnson, 1997). In this context, the current section provides a comprehensive overview of the researchable measures of the project and outlines the originality and contribution of the current research to the broader field of electoral behaviour. Consequently, in order to accurately assess the two tested objectives, it was necessary to make a careful selection of the researchable measures (variables). In other words, as reflected by the proposed objectives, the proposed research involved the measurement of the major variables that follow (Sophocleous, 2024).

Furthermore, after addressing the hypotheses and specifying the research measures of the project, it has been considered essential to outline the basic format of the model that is aimed to derive from the project (see Fig..1). Moreover, the aforementioned model is based on the perceptual dimension proposed by Gerbner's model of communication (Gerbner, 1956; 1964) and Maletzke's model of mass communication process (Maletzke, 1963). The model will focus on electoral communication and attempt to map and place the research measures in a circular flow. In other words, the perceptual dimension of political communication and the role of the environment throughout the process of communication, as illustrated in the aforementioned model of communication, indicate that the effects of electoral campaigns, together with the perceptions of those voters upon the principal institutions, may influence and shape the perceptions of the voters. In more specific terms, as illustrated in Figure 1, it is probable for a circular relationship to occur between the political agenda and its ideological clarity, with the pre-electoral campaigns and their effects, as well as with voters' perceptions and electoral choice, and thus with the electoral result. Furthermore, the proposed model, based on the aforementioned hypotheses, seeks to situate instructions at the core of this circle, with the aim of examining and evaluating their interaction and relationship with the other variables/measures of the project. The initial hypothesis is that the way institutions are perceived influences every stage of the electoral cycle, from agenda setting to actual voting action. This is the reason why they are initially placed in the middle of the electoral process (Sophocleous, 2023, 2024).

Figure 1. The Circular Correlation of Communication and Electoral Process

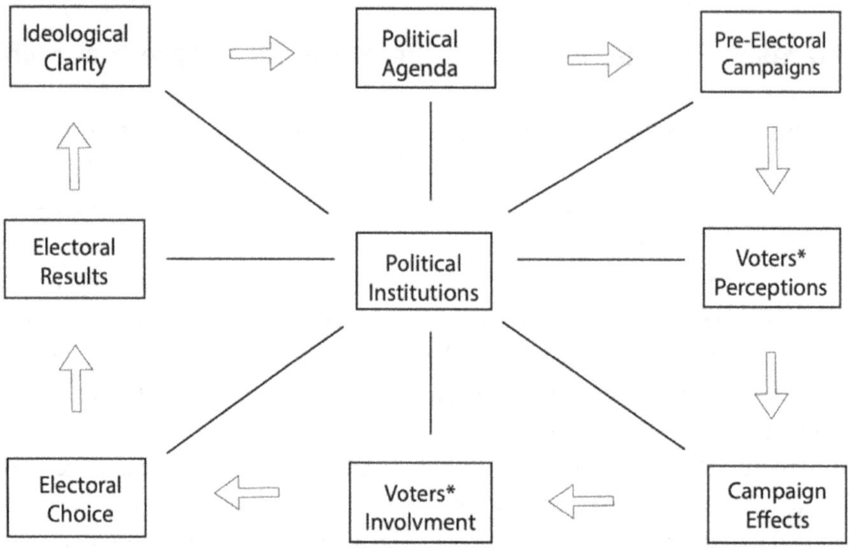

Source: Sophocleous 2024, The Circular correlation of Communication and Electoral Process

The research methodology, the collection and analysis of data, and therefore the discussion and conclusions of the project, will be based on the aforementioned model. The aim is to elaborate and further develop the logic of the specific circular flow and facilitate the interconnection of the formulated research questions. By demonstrating the circular flow, we will gain a comprehensive illustration of the communicational process in relation to the interaction and interrelationship of political campaigns, voting perceptions, campaign effects and institutions.

4.0 RESULTS AND DISCISSION

4.1 The Results of the Survey

Before proceeding to the correlation of the various elements that constitute the researchable model of the circular correlation between communication and electoral causes, it may be essential to make a synopsis of the results gathered.

4.1.1 Political Marketing

The following four points were analysed in relation to the broader element of 'place' as a fundamental component of political marketing: The number of public appearances made by the candidate, the degree of familiarity with the candidate within the region, the candidate's residence within the area, and the extent to which the candidate is accessible. The four items that compose the broader element of "place" present a similar statistical picture, with the majority of respondents indicating that they have at least a moderate impact. (Table 1)

Table 1. Political Marketing Mix / Place Statistics

		Frequent Pub. Appearance	Candidate is known in the area	Candidate lives in the area	Avaliability of Candidate
N	Valid	503	503	503	503
	Missing	0	0	0	0
Mean		2,98	3,16	3,14	3,42
Std. Deviation		1,280	1,267	1,328	1,317

The specific section involved testing three items pertaining to the overarching concept of "product" as a fundamental element of the political marketing mix. The preceding political records of the candidate, the candidate's image as a leader, and the candidate's image as a social entity were also considered. In a manner analogous to the case of "Place," the three items comprising the broader element of "Product" present a comparable statistical profile. The majority of respondents indicated that these three figures exert at least a moderate (3) impact. (Table 2)

Table 2. Political Marketing Mix/Product

		Candidate's Previous Records	Candidate's Leader Image	Candidate's Social Image
N	Valid	503	503	503
	Missing	0	0	0
Mean		3,24	3,60	3,87
Std. Deviation		1,216	1,201	1,097

The specific section involved the testing of three items pertaining to the overarching concept of "price" as a fundamental element of the political marketing mix. The financial cost of the candidate being elected, The psychological cost of the candidate being elected, The candidate's perspective on both genders. In a manner analogous to the cases of "Place" and Product, the three elements comprising the broader element of "Price" exhibited a comparable statistical profile. The majority of respondents indicated that these three figures exert at least a moderate (3) impact. (Table 3)

Table 3. Political Marketing Mix/Price

		Financial Cost of Election	Psychological Cost	Genders' Perspective
N	Valid	503	503	503
	Missing	0	0	0
Mean		3,43	3,64	3,68
Std. Deviation		1,225	1,240	1,253

The particular area of investigation within the study concerned the examination of five items pertaining to the element of "promotion" as a fundamental component of the political marketing mix. The following elements were identified as central to the candidacy: The central slogan of the candidacy, the candidate's election music, and other elements were considered to be central to the candidacy. The utilisation of the candidate's supporters. The candidate's election signs The candidate's meetings/appearances.In contrast to the cases of "Place," "Product," and "Price," only one of the five items pertaining to the broader elements of "Promotion" (i.e., the candidate's meetings/appearances) received a majority response indicating that the figure had at least a moderate (3) impact. (Table 4)

Table 4. Political Marketing Mix Promotion Statistics

		Candidate' s Slogan	Candidate' s Music	Candidate' s Posters	Candidate' s Pre-election Signs	Candidate' s Appearances
N	Valid	503	503	503	503	503
	Missing	0	0	0	0	0
Mean		2,68	1,96	2,10	2,10	3,17
Std. Deviation		1,228	1,037	1,091	1,107	1,251

4.1.2 Voting Behaviour

The specific section under examination considered the following six elements or items in relation to the reasons for voting: Voting is a fundamental right, a way of thinking, a national duty, and a means of bringing about change and representation. The four aforementioned elements present a similar statistical picture, with the vast majority of respondents indicating that they believe these figures have at least some impact. Table 5 presents the results of the survey.

Table 5. Reason to Vote - Statistics

	Voting is a Fund. Right	Voting is a Way of Thinking	Voting is a Responsibility	Voting is a Duty	Voting Brings Change	Voting Brings Repre/tion
Valid	503	503	503	503	503	503
Missing	0	0	0	0	0	0
Mean	4,27	4,16	4,28	4,03	3,63	3,27
Std. Deviation	1,179	1,168	1,175	1,321	1,355	1,357

Items pertaining to the candidate's personal identity. The survey instrument inquired about the respondents' perceptions of the importance of various factors in the context of the election campaign. The factors included in the survey were the candidate's broader pre-election campaign, gender, religion, education, and socio-economic status. The specific question yielded a diversity of statistical images, as each of the five elements elicited a distinct set of responses on the five-point Likert scale. (Table 6)

Table 6. Candidates Personal Identity

	Candidate's Campaign	Candidate's Gender	Candidate's Religion	Candidate's Education	Candidate's Socio Ec. Status
Valid	503	503	503	503	503
Missing	0	0	0	0	0
Mean	3,12	2,00	2,93	3,89	2,91
Std. Deviation	1,262	1,183	1,500	1,261	1,272

The specific section under examination encompassed four elements pertaining to the political identity of the candidate. The respondents were asked to indicate the extent to which their vote was based on the following elements: Candidate's political experience, Candidate's political background, Candidate's pre-election inscriptions and Candidate's broader pre-election campaign (Table 7)

Table 7. Candidates Political identity -Statistics

		Political Experience	Political Background	Pre-election Inscriptions	Candidate's Campaign
N	Valid	503	503	503	503
	Missing	0	0	0	0
Mean		3,16	3,35	2,30	2,51
Std. Deviation		1,193	1,231	1,164	1,157

The section under examination focused on four elements or items pertaining to voters' perceptions. The assumption is that one's vote is contingent upon the political party of the candidate. Moreover, the individual's vote is shaped by their perception of the candidate's integrity. The decision to vote is contingent upon the extent to which the candidate has demonstrated progressive work. Additionally, respondents indicated the extent to which this is influenced by the financial assistance provided by the candidate to the voter. Furthermore, the extent to which the respondents' votes are related to these elements was investigated. The four aforementioned elements were found to present a diversity of statistical pictures, given that each one of them has been considered a basic factor of voting to a completely different extent. (Table 8)

Table 8. Voter's Perceptions -Statistics

		Candidate's Political Party	Candidate's Integrity	Candidate's Prog. Work	Financial Assistance by the Candidate
N	Valid	503	503	503	503
	Missing	0	0	0	0
Mean		2,72	4,45	4,26	2,09
Std. Deviation		1,339	,919	1,001	1,300

The following four elements of voters' motives were taken into account: The personal support of the candidate, The manifesto of the political party/candidate, The decision of parents/relatives and Personal decision/opinion. The extent to which respondents' votes were based on these elements was then examined, and it was found that the four elements mentioned above produced a variety of statistical pictures, as each was considered to be a basic factor in voting to a very different extent. (Table 9)

Table 9. Voter's Motives

	Personal Aid Given by the Candidate	Candidate's Manifesto	Parent's Relatives Decision	Personal Decision
N Valid	503	503	503	503
N Missing	0	0	0	0
Mean	2,42	2,72	1,47	4,55
Std. Deviation	1,332	1,273	,865	,887

4.1.3 Voting Involvement

The specific section examined the following 6 elements/items that measure voter engagement: Politics means a lot to me, Politics is an important part of my life, I am interested in politics, I participate in politics, Elections are an important part of my life, I regularly vote in elections. And asked to what extent respondents agreed with the above statements. (Table 10)

Table 10. Voters' Political Involvement -Statistics

	Politics means a lot to me	Politics is an Important	I am Interested in Politics	I Participate in Politics	Elections are Important	I regularly participate in Elections
N Valid	503	503	503	503	503	503
N Missing	0	0	0	0	0	0
Mean	2,95	2,61	3,02	2,50	2,56	3,41
Std. Deviation	1,377	1,362	1,389	1,400	1,383	1,476

Similarly to the previous section, the following 4 elements/items of voters' subjective knowledge were examined: I know a lot about politics, I am considered an expert in politics, I know more about politics than most people, My vote is related to the financial support of the candidate to the voter, and I have an excellent knowledge of politics, and the extent to which respondents agreed with these statements. (Table 11)

Table 11. Subjective Knowledge -Statistics

	I Know a lot about Politics	I am Expert in Politics	In Comparison to moat I Know More about Politics	I am Excellent Knowledgeable of Politics
N Valid	503	503	503	503
N Missing	0	0	0	0
Mean	3,15	2,15	2,73	2,83
Std. Deviation	1,264	1,213	1,311	1,277

In a more comprehensive way than in the previous sections, the following 5 elements/items measuring voters' political OL were examined: My friends and neighbours ask me about politics, Sometimes I influence the vote of my friends/relatives, they come to me for information about politics, I am seen as a good source of information about politics, I spend a lot of time giving information about politics. And asked to what extent respondents agreed with the above statements. In contrast to the statements in the previous two sections, which presented a variety of statistical pictures, the five statements present an almost identical, regressive chart format. (Table 12)

Table 12. Political O.L. -Statistics

		My friends and neighbours ask me about politics	Sometimes I Influence my Friends	They come to me for Information on Politics	I am considered a good source of information on Politics	I Spend Lot of time giving Information about Politics
N	Valid	503	503	503	503	503
	Missing	0	0	0	0	0
Mean		2,50	2,40	2,38	2,43	2,19
Std. Deviation			1,317	1,364	1,372	1,322

This section examined the following two items/elements relevant to respondents' confidence in their ability to make decisions: I have confidence in my ability to make a good decision, and I have confidence in my ability to decide who/what to vote for. (Table 13).

Table 13. Decision Making Confidence -Statistics

		Confidence About Decision Making	Confidence About Decision Making in Voting
N	Valid	503	503
	Missing	0	0
Mean		4,05	4,19
Std. Deviation		,971	,979

This section examined four elements/characteristics of satisfaction with politics: I am satisfied with the party I voted for in the last election, I am satisfied with the candidate I voted for in the last election, I am satisfied with politics in general and I am satisfied with parties in general (Table 14).

Table 14. Satisfaction -statistics

	Party Satisfaction	Candidate's Satisfaction	Satisfied with Politics	Satisfied with Parties
Í Valid	**503**	503	503	503
Í Missing	**0**	0	0	0
Mean	3,07	3,18	2,02	1,63
Std. Deviation	1,286	1,290	1,055	,899

4.14 The Impact of Institutions upon Consuming Behaviour

The research identifies, evaluates and demonstrates the impact of political institutions on the process of producing and consuming political communication. According to (Sniderman and Levendusky 2007), political institutions are the "coordinators of political decisions". This point of view highlights the fact that campaign impact is not a single concept, but rather a multifaceted and complex issue that requires the consideration of several dimensions. With regard to the perceived influence of institutions on voting criteria, it appears that voters have reached a mean value of influence slightly above the middle of the scale (2.5) for most institutions, with the exception of banks and political parties, which report an average voting influence below 2.0. Figure 2 also illustrates the impact as perceived by the two genders, with women showing significantly higher mean values in almost all of these institutions, with the exception of the Attorney General and the General Inspector. This particular result could be explained by the fact that, at the time the research was carried out, these two particular institutions were represented by two personalities with a purely independent, anti-systemic and objective perspective, who were critical of and in conflict with the central government and the mainstream administrative institutions.

Figure 2. Impact of Institutions by Gender

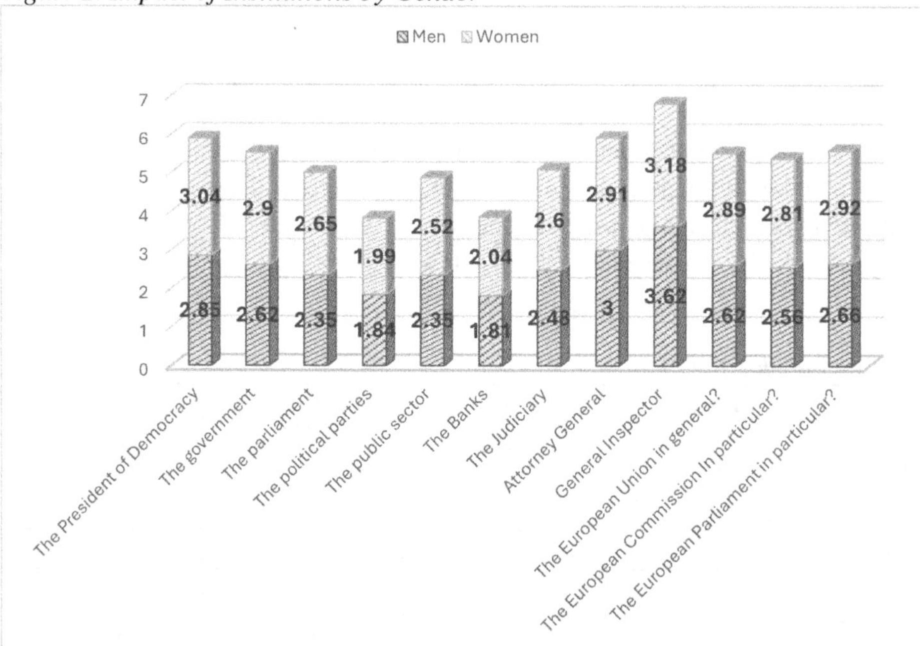

This particular perspective therefore expresses a view that the representation that voters expect to achieve through voting is considered to be narrow and limited as a result of the powerful political establishment. Therefore, in the case of Cyprus, the political institutions and in particular the political party establishment, as reflected in our findings, could be considered as the most influential factors in shaping voters' perceptions and thus the exercise of the right to vote (Sniderman and Levendusky 2007).

4.2 Research Measures and their Cycled Interaction

It can be claimed that the research findings support the circular model of political communication (see Figure 1). In particular, the results show that the level of ideological clarity of a party or candidate has a direct impact on the shaping of the political agenda and consequently on pre-election campaigns. Furthermore, the results of the research indicate that political marketing and political campaigns have a significant impact on voters' perceptions and motives, and thus on campaign effects and overall voting behaviour. The research also suggests that political participation, perceived risk and voting choice, and hence the election outcome, are also influenced by these factors. Finally, the research suggests that electoral outcomes may influence levels of ideological clarity. This is evidenced by the fact that political parties appear to have sacrificed ideological clarity in order to achieve a better electoral result.

In order to achieve the objective of further analysis, it was considered essential to establish correlations between the main variables of each of the three main scales of the survey (Political Marketing Mix, Voter Behaviour and Voter Involvement). In addition, it is essential to establish correlations between some of the variables of subsequent parts of the survey in order to ensure the circular relationship between political marketing/advertising, voting behaviour, voter participation, decision-making confidence and level of satisfaction.

4.2.1 Correlation of variables (Political Marketing / Promotion and Reason to Vote)

Marketing/Promotion and Reason to Vote

In order to examine the correlation between the two variables (Promotion and Reason to Vote), we consider the null and alternative hypotheses. The null hypothesis (Ho) is that the variables Promotion and Reason to Vote do not show a statistically significant linear correlation. The alternative hypothesis (H1) is that the variables show a statistically significant linear correlation. The results of Table 35 are as follows: The Pearson correlation coefficient of the two variables under examination, namely "Promotion" and "Reason to Vote", is $r = 0.307$. Consequently, there is a low and positive linear correlation between the values concerning promotion and reason to vote ($r = 0.307$, $p < 0.01$), which is statistically significant. Therefore, the alternative hypothesis H1, which states that the variables promotion and reason to vote show a statistically significant linear correlation, is accepted.

4.2.2 Correlation of variables (Product and Reason to Vote)

In the same manner, in order to examine the correlation between the two variables (Political Marketing/Product and Reason to Vote), we consider the null and alternative hypotheses. The null hypothesis (Ho) is that the variables Political Marketing/Product and Reason to Vote do not show a statistically significant linear correlation. The alternative hypothesis (H1) is that the variables Political Marketing/Product and Reason to Vote show a statistically significant linear correlation. The results of Table 36 permit the following conclusions to be drawn: The Pearson correlation coefficient for the two variables under examination, namely Political Marketing and Product to Vote, is $r = 0.427$.

4.2.3 Correlation of variables (Reason to Vote and Political Involvement)

Consequently, there is a low and positive linear correlation between the values concerning Political Marketing/Product and Reason to Vote ($r = 0.427$, $p < 0.01$), which is statistically significant. Therefore, the alternative hypothesis H1, which states that the variables Political Marketing/Product and Reason to Vote show a statistically significant linear correlation, is accepted.

Similarly, in order to examine the correlation between the two variables (reason to vote and political involvement), we consider the null and alternative hypotheses. The null hypothesis (Ho) is that there is no statistically significant linear correlation between the variables Reason to Vote and Political Involvement. The alternative hypothesis (H1) is that the variables Reason to Vote and Political Involvement demonstrate a statistically significant linear correlation. In light of the findings presented in Table 37, the following inferences can be drawn: The Pearson correlation coefficient of the two variables under examination, reason to vote and political involvement, is $r = 0.364$. Consequently, there is a low and positive linear correlation between the values concerning reason to vote and political involvement ($r = 0.364$, $p < 0.01$), which is statistically significant. Consequently, the alternative hypothesis H1, which postulates a statistically significant linear correlation between the variables reason to vote and political involvement, is accepted.

4.2.4 Correlation of variables (Voter's Involvement and Information Seeking)

In order to examine the correlation between the two variables (Voter's Involvement and Information Seeking), we consider the null and alternative hypotheses. The null hypothesis is as follows: "Voter's Involvement and Voter's Involvement and Information Seeking variables do not show a statistically significant linear correlation." The alternative hypothesis is as follows: "The variables Voter's Involvement and Voter's Involvement and Information Seeking show a statistically significant linear correlation." The results of Table 38 permit the following conclusions to be drawn: The Pearson correlation coefficient for the two variables under examination, namely Voter's Involvement and Information Seeking, is $r = 0.588$. Consequently, there is a low and positive linear correlation between the values concerning political involvement and information seeking ($r = 0.588$, $p < 0.01$), which is statistically significant. Therefore, the alternative hypothesis H1, which states that the variables voter's involvement and information seeking show a statistically significant linear correlation, is accepted.

4.2.5 Correlation of variables (Voter's Involvement and Decision-Making Confidence)

Correlations Voter's Involvement and Decision-Making Process

In a similar manner, in order to examine the correlation between the two variables (voter involvement and voter involvement and decision-making confidence), we consider the null and alternative hypotheses. The null hypothesis is that the variables "voter involvement" and "voter involvement and decision-making confidence" do not show a statistically significant linear correlation. The alternative hypothesis is that the variables "voter involvement" and "voter involvement and decision-making confidence" show a statistically significant linear correlation. The results of Table 39 permit the following conclusions to be drawn: The Pearson correlation coefficient of the two variables, Voter's Involvement and Decision-Making Confidence, is $r = 0.339$. Consequently, there is a low and positive linear correlation between the values concerning voter involvement and decision-making confidence ($r = 0.339$, $p < 0.01$), which is statistically significant. Therefore, the alternative hypothesis H1, which states that the variables voter involvement and decision-making confidence show a statistically significant linear correlation, is accepted.

4.2.6 Correlation of variables (Satisfaction and Information Seeking)

Likewise, in order to examine the correlation between the two variables (Satisfaction and Information Seeking), we consider the null and alternative hypotheses. The null hypothesis is that the Satisfaction and Information Seeking variables do not show a statistically significant linear correlation. The alternative hypothesis is that the variables Satisfaction and Information Seeking show a statistically significant linear correlation. The results presented in Table 6-18 (Table 40 Correlations) lead to the following conclusions: The Pearson correlation coefficient of the two variables, namely Satisfaction and Information Seeking, is $r = 0.508$. Consequently, there is a low and positive linear correlation between the values concerning satisfaction and information seeking and information seeking ($r = 0.508$, $p < 0.01$), which is statistically significant.

Therefore, the alternative hypothesis H1, which states that the variables satisfaction and information seeking and information seeking show a statistically significant linear correlation, is accepted.

5.0 DISCUSSION & INTERPRETATIONS OF FINDINGS

5.1 The Cycled Interaction of the Research Measures

It could be argued that the research findings confirm the circular model of political communication (see Figure 1). Furthermore, the research suggests that political marketing has a significant impact on voters' perceptions, motives and voting behaviour. This extends to their political engagement, perceived risk, vote choice and ultimately election outcomes. Finally, the research suggests that election outcomes can influence levels of ideological clarity. This is evidenced by the fact that political parties appear to sacrifice ideological clarity in order to achieve better electoral performance.

In order to facilitate further analysis, it was considered essential to develop correlations between the main variables of each of the three main scales of the survey (political marketing mix, voter behaviour and voter involvement). In addition, it was necessary to develop correlations between some variables of subsequent parts of the survey in order to ensure the circular relationship between political marketing/ advertising, voting behaviour, voter involvement, decision making confidence and satisfaction.

5.2 The Impact of Institutions upon Consuming Behaviour

The research findings assess and prove the impact of political institutions on the process of producing and consuming political communication (Sophocleous and Masouras, 2019, Sophocleous 2024). As posited by Sniderman and Levendusky (2007), political institutions serve as 'coordinators of political choices'. This perspective emphasises that the impact of campaigns is not a singular phenomenon, but rather a multifaceted and complex issue that requires consideration of a number of dimensions. In terms of the perceived impact of institutions on voting criteria, the average impact was found to be slightly above the midpoint of the scale (2.5) for the majority of institutions, with the exception of banks and political parties, which reported an average voting impact below 2.0. Figure 2 also illustrates the impact as perceived by the two genders. It can be seen that women have significantly higher mean scores in almost all of these institutions, with the exception of the Attorney General and the General Inspector. The specific result can be attributed to the fact that, at the time of the research, the two institutions in question were represented by two individuals with a distinctly independent, anti-systemic and objective perspective, who were openly critical of and in conflict with the central government and the mainstream administrative institutions.

Accordingly, the specific point of view indicates that the representation expected from voting is perceived as limited and constrained by the powerful political establishment. As a result, the findings of both quantitative and qualitative research suggest that political institutions, and in particular the political party establishment, have a significant impact on voters' perceptions and consequently on the exercise of the right to vote (Sniderman and Levendusky, 2007).

5.3 The campaign Effects

Furthermore, by taking into account that perception is a communicational dimension (Gerbner 1956; 1964), the project aimed to investigate the extent and the way in which electoral campaign influences the voting perceptions and thus campaign effects and the actions of Cypriot voters, together with the method in which electorates observe the clarity and the representativeness of the communication strategies/ campaigns that are produced and are demonstrated by the major political parties. In the same way, the particular research, attempted to give answer to whether and at what extent electorates formulate trade-offs between their personal interest and the collective interest (Descioli et al 2018). Furthermore, the specific study attempts to clarifying the clear relativity among the positions produced by the parties and the ideological/political desires perceived and consumed by the voters both in local, state and European level. A significant outcome of the specified research, in a similar manner to Sophocleous and Masouras (2019) research, is the fact that in general lines the criterion of the average young voter, as it is mirrored by the present research, appears to be improved from the nation-wide average, since it does not reflect the "Customer oriented" relationship that dominates between the Cypriot Voter and the Political Parties.

More precisely, it is about measuring the impact and trustworthiness/representativeness of the communication campaign on voters' perceptions and thus on campaign effects and voting behaviour. On the other hand, it can be said that the way in which the communication mix is perceived by voters illustrates the extent to which political parties are willing to expose/emphasise or modify/adapt their ideological clarity for the sake of a good electoral result. Moreover, as clearly reflected by Sophocleous and Masouras (2019), the participants were asked to indicate the extent to which the electoral campaigns influenced/ shaped their voting criterion. The vast majority placed their answer from the left end to the middle of the scale, indicating that the average assessment of Cypriot young adults is that they are not influenced by the communication campaigns of the parties or the candidates.

However, this may indicate that the 'impact' is not perceived and identified in an accurate and comprehensible way.

6.0 RESEARCH IMPLICATIONS

6.1 Social Context and Institutions vs Voting Behaviour

Theory Vs Research Findings

The relationship between social context and voting behaviour has been the subject of considerable theoretical and empirical investigation. In accordance with the findings of Blumler and Kavanagh (1999), the contemporary movements and associations of social change are inextricably linked to media change, with multiple and reciprocal effects. Political communication has been receptive (though also contributory) to a cycle of external change throughout the post-war era, including processes such as modernisation, secularisation and individualisation.

Consequently, it is of critical importance to consider that any electoral choice and any campaign that may influence such a choice occurs within a specified context. As Walder (2006: 713) suggests, a theory concerning political preferences could be no more legitimate than its claims regarding the contexts within which these preferences are expressed.

As indicated by Lo, Proksch and Slapin (2014), parties in advanced democracies utilise ideological declarations in anticipation of electoral competition. Nevertheless, some parties are more adept at communicating their stance than others. According to their research, parties may present electorates with unclear messages or propose a programme embracing a variety of viewpoints, potentially muddying its ideological content. This doubt may arise in a party's programme for a variety of reasons.

Furthermore, the findings of the specific research indicate that political institutions serve as the primary coordinators of political choices (Sniderman and Levendusky, 2007). The findings of the specific research indicate that, beyond the political party establishment itself, the protagonist institutions of the Republic (including the President of Democracy, Parliament, the Justice, etc.) are also perceived negatively by the majority of respondents. These institutions are therefore considered to be "hostages" of those establishments. In order to make informed decisions, such as those involved in the electoral process, voters do not have to rely solely on their own limited understanding and computational capabilities. Conversely, they are assisted by the political institutions which place them in a position where they can make coherent choices (Sniderman and Levendusky 2007). As outlined by Sniderman and Levendusky (2007), political institutions serve as the 'coordinators of political choices'. In order to formulate rational selections, the society does not have to be based exclusively on their own restricted cognition and computational capacities. In recent years, various researchers have addressed the effects of democratic institutions on pre-election campaign behaviour (Alvarez and Sinclair, 2012; Sudulich and Trumm, 2019). Consequently, the qualitative findings indicate that the political institutions, and in particular the political party establishment, exert the most significant influence on voter perceptions and, consequently, on the right to vote.

The implications of the research context

The implications of the research context can be divided into two categories: the impact of political institutions and the surrounding political environment on electoral behaviour, and the impact of communicational intentions and the wider political marketing of parties or candidates on electoral choice. In light of the aforementioned considerations, the present research builds upon existing academic research by examining the interrelationship between the aforementioned notions and measures. In particular, it examines the impact of political communication on electoral outcomes and the role of institutions involved in the communication process surrounding voting. The majority of current research in the field of voting behaviour and political communication is based on the context of US voting affairs and electoral reality. This fact has important implications for the specific study, which goes beyond the notion of the "Americanization of Political Communication" (Negrine 1996; Negrine and Papathanassopoulos, 1996; R. Negrine, C. Holtz-Bacha, S. Papathanassopoulos, 2007; Papathanassopoulos, 199; Papathanassopoulos and Negrine, 20010).

Another area that has yet to be fully explored is the relationship between electoral behaviour and the party system. A significant proportion of the most comprehensive studies in this field have concentrated on what are known as "critical elections" and "realignments", preceding the era of detailed survey data (Key 1966). Consequently, the specific research contributes to the existing body of knowledge by integrating the theoretical frameworks of voting behaviour and political propositions with those of political marketing and consumer behaviour, specifically in the context of Cyprus.

REFERENCES

Alvarez, R. M., & Sinclair, B. (2012). Electoral Institutions and Legislative Behaviour: The Effects of Primary Processes. *Political Research Quarterly*, *63*, 544–557. DOI: 10.1177/1065912911411098

Baines, P. R., Worcesterb, R. M., Jarrettc, D., & Mortimored, R. (2003). Market Segmentation and Product Differentiation in Political Campaigns: A Technical Feature Perspective. [Westburn Publishers Ltd.]. *Journal of Marketing Management*, •••, 2003.

Banducci, S. A., & Karp, J. A. (2003). How Elections Change the Way Citizens View the Political System: Campaigns, Media Effects and Electoral Outcomes in Comparative Perspective. *British Journal of Political Science* Vol. 33, No. 3 (Jul. 2003), pp. 443-467.Cambridge University Press. DOI: jstor.org/stable/4092306

Blumler, J. G., & Kavanagh, D. (1999). The Third Age of Political Communication: *Influences and Features.Political Communication*, *16*(3), 209–230. DOI: 10.1080/105846099198596

Farrell, A.M. (1996) Roles and behaviours in technology- integrated precalculus classrooms. *The Journal of Mathematical Behaviour* 15 (1):35-53 · March 1996 with 28 Reads · DOI: DOI: 10.1016/S0732-3123(96)90038-3

Gay, L. R., & Diehl, P. L. (1992) *Research Methods for Business and Management*. Mc. Millan Publishing Company, New York.

Gerbner, G. (1956). Toward a general model of communication. *Audio Visual Communication Review*, *4*(3), 171–199.

Gerbner, G. (1964). On Political Message Analysis and Critical Research in Mass Communication. In *Dexter LA and White D.M. People, Society, and Mass Communications Pages: 476 - 500Glencoe*. The Free Press.

Gill, J., & Johnson, P. (1997). *Research methods for managers* (2nd ed.). Paul Chapman Publishing Ltd.

Huckfeldt, R., Sprague, J., & Levine, J. (2000). The dynamic of collective deliberation in the 1996 election: Campaign effects on accessibility, certainty, and accuracy. *The American Political Science Review*, *94*(3), 641–651. DOI: 10.2307/2585836

Hunt, C. R. (2018). When does redistricting matter? Changing conditions and their effects on voter turnout.*Electoral Studies*, *54*(August), 128–138. DOI: 10.1016/j.electstud.2018.05.007

Hussey, J., & Hussey, R. (1997). *Business Research: A Practical Guide for Undergraduate and Postgraduate Students*. Macmillan. DOI: 10.1007/978-1-349-25262-6

Iyengar, S., & Simon, A. F. (2000). New perspectives and evidence on political communication and campaign effects. *Annual Review of Psychology, 51*(1), 149–169. DOI: 10.1146/annurev.psych.51.1.149 PMID: 10751968

Just, M. A., Carpenter, P. A., & Keller, T. A. (1996). The Capacity Theory of Comprehension: New Frontiers of Evidence and Arguments. *Psychological Review, 103*(4), 773–780. DOI: 10.1037/0033-295X.103.4.773 PMID: 8888654

Katsourides, I. (2011). *The party system in Cyprus 1878-1931: structure and peculiarities. Publisher*. University of Cyprus, Faculty of Social Sciences and Education.

Key, V. O. (1966). *The responsible electorate: Rationality in presidential voting 1936–1960*. Harvard University Press.

Likert, R. (1932). A technique for measurement of attitudes. *Archives de Psychologie, 140*, 5–55.

Lipset, S. M., & Rokkan, S. (1967). Cleavage Structures, Party Systems, and Voter Alignments: An Introduction. In Lipset, S. M., & Rokkan, S. (Eds.), *Party Systems and Voter Alignments: Cross-National Perspectives* (pp. 1–64). Collier-Macmillan.

Lo, J., Proksch, S. O., & Slapin, J. B. (2014) Ideological Clarity in Multi-Party Competition: A New Measure and Test Using Election Manifestos. *British Journal of Political Science,* 46 (3). 591 - 610. ISSN 0007-1234

Maletzke, G., (1963) Psychologie der Massenkommunikation, Hamburg In *der Literaturliste für Docupedia-Zeitgeschichte Artikel Propaganda*

Malhotra, Y. (1998) *Compilation of definitions of knowledge management* at www .brint.com

McQuarrie, E., & Mick, D. G. (1996). Figures of Rhetoric in Advertising Language. *The Journal of Consumer Research, 22*(4), 424–438. DOI: 10.1086/209459

Negrine, R., Holtz-Bacha, C., & Papathanassopoulos, S. (2007). *The Professionalization of Political Communication, Changing Media* (Vol. 3). Changing Europe.

Negrine, R., & Papathanassopoulos, S. (1996). The "Americanization" of Political Communication. A Critique. *The Harvard International Journal of Press/Politics, 1*(2), 45–62. DOI: 10.1177/1081180X96001002005

Page, B. I. (1996). *Who deliberates? Mass media in modern democracy*. University of Chicago Press.

Pan, Z., Shen, L., Paek, H., & Sun, Y. (2006). Mobilizing political talk in a presidential campaign: An examination of campaign effects in a deliberative framework. *Communication Research, 33*(5), 315–345. DOI: 10.1177/0093650206291478

Papathanassopoulos S. (1999) The effects of media commercialization on journalism and politics in Greece. *The Communication Review, Volume 3, 199 -Issue 4.* Doi. Org/.DOI: 10.1080/10714429909368591

Papathanassopoulos, S., & Negrine, R. (2010). *Communications Policy: Theories and Issues*. Palgrave. DOI: 10.1007/978-1-137-09447-6

Peterson, D. A. M. (2018). The dynamic construction of candidate image original research. *Electoral Studies*, *54*, 289–296. DOI: 10.1016/j.electstud.2018.04.012

Protopapas, V. *Electoral history of Cyprus: politicians, parties and elections in the British Empire (1878-1960)* Publication Date 2011 University / Publisher National and Kapodistrian University of Athens; URL http://hdl.handle.net/10442/hedi/31045

Saunders, M., Lewis, P., & Thornhill, A. (2003). *Research method for business students* (3rd ed.). Prentice Hall.

Sniderman, P., & Levendusky, M. (2007). *An Institutional Theory of Political Choice. Oxford Handbook of Political Behaviour*. Oxford University Press.

Sophocleous, H. (2024). *Production and Consumption of Political Communication and Voting Behaviour*. Nova Science Publications., DOI: 10.52305/OJBC3507

Sophocleous, H., Anastasiadou, S., Masouras, A., & Apostolopoulos, S. (2024). (b). The Effect of Political Marketing on the Electoral Behavior of Greek Voters. In Kavoura, A., Borges-Tiago, T., & Tiago, F. (Eds.), *Strategic Innovative Marketing and Tourism. ICSIMAT 2023. Springer Proceedings in Business and Economics.* Springer., DOI: 10.1007/978-3-031-51038-0_38

Sophocleous, H., Anastasiadou, S., Masouras, A., & Apostolopoulos, S. (2024). (c). Motives and Perceptions of Greek Voters in National Elections of 2023. In Kavoura, A., Borges-Tiago, T., & Tiago, F. (Eds.), *Strategic Innovative Marketing and Tourism. ICSIMAT 2023. Springer Proceedings in Business and Economics.* Springer., DOI: 10.1007/978-3-031-51038-0_47

Sophocleous, H., & Masouras, A. (2019). "Voters' Behaviour: What Drives Political Consumption in Cyprus? An Analysis of the Behaviour of Young Voters". In: Kavoura, A., Kefallonitis, E., and Giovanis, A., *Strategic Innovative Marketing and Tourism 2018*. Springer. Proceedings in Business and Economics. Springer, Cham.

Sophocleous, H., Masouras, A., & Anastasiadou, S. (2024). (a). The Impact of Political Marketing on Voting Behaviour of Cypriot Voters. *Social Sciences (Basel, Switzerland)*, *2024*(13), 149. DOI: 10.3390/socsci13030149

Sudulich, L., & Trumm, S. (2019). *A Comparative Study of the Effects of Electoral Institutions on Campaigns*. Cambridge University Pres. DOI: 10.1017/S0007123416000570

Walder, A. G. (2006, November). Ambiguity and Choice in Political Movements: The Origins of Beijing Red Guard Factionalism. *American Journal of Sociology*, *112*(3), 710–750. DOI: 10.1086/507854

Zikmund, W. G. (1997). *Exploring Marketing Research* (6th ed.). The Dryden Press.

Chapter 8
Supply Chain Disruptions and Business Resilience:
A Strategic Framework for Corporate Performance

Aristi Karagkouni
https://orcid.org/0000-0003-4596-8069
Democritus University of Thrace, Greece

Dimitrios Dimitriou
https://orcid.org/0000-0002-5744-5110
Democritus University of Thrace, Greece

ABSTRACT

Global supply chains have been increasingly vulnerable to disruption due to geopolitical events like economic sanctions, regional conflict, COVID-19 pandemic and trade wars. Such disruptions result in raw material shortage, high prices, and logistics difficulties, impacting supply chain corporate performance. This chapter addresses strategic frameworks to minimize supply chain risks in terms of supplier diversification, nearshoring, digitalization and crisis management. Supply chain agility and corporate performance can be enabled by utilizing AI-based analytics, ensuring transparency by blockchain technology and real-time monitoring tools. KPI analysis plays a central role in determining effectiveness in resilience strategy. Supply chain management in the future will be characterized by sustainability principles and automation technologies. Organizations employing resilience in corporate strategy actively will be able to respond to uncertainties, ensuring long-term supply chain corporate performance and competitiveness.

DOI: 10.4018/979-8-3693-5583-1.ch008

INTRODUCTION

In contemporary business settings, supply chains provide a fundamental basis for organizational functions, facilitating efficient distribution of raw materials, components, and finished products to international markets. Throughout recent decades, companies have streamlined their supply chain structures through cost-reduction measures, offshoring production processes, and leveraging international trading networks. However, this increased interdependence has simultaneously increased vulnerabilities in supply chains, specifically in terms of geopolitical disruptions. Disruptions in international commerce, economic sanctions, regional unrest, and regulatory changes have risen as important drivers for supply chain volatility, influencing access to strategic resources, increasing production costs, and eroding logistical infrastructures (Christopher, 2016). These disruptions have the potential to create far-reaching implications for corporate performance, affecting important drivers like profitability, operating efficiency, and market positioning (Ivanov and Dolgui, 2020). As such, firms are driven to use proactiveness in their resilience strategies to avoid risks, maintain financial solidity, and maintain their market positioning in an increasingly uncertain international economy.

Geopolitical developments that cause disruptions in supply chains have a significant bearing on business performance, especially in industries with intricate, multi-layered supply chains. Disruptions can occur in many forms, such as shortages in raw materials, transit delays, increased operating costs, and reduced levels of production (Bednarski et al., 2023). A very immediate and pervasive result is the rise in procurement costs due to barriers to trade, tariffs, and sanctions. For instance, the U.S.-China trade conflict-imposed tariffs on a wide range of industrial and consumer products, forcing companies to reassess their reliance on Chinese production and find alternative procurement strategies (Baldwin and Freeman, 2022). This usually results in increased costs and extended lead times, directly affecting profit margins. Another issue with disruptions in supply chains is that logistical clogs and supplier collapses occur. Localized conflicts and barriers to trade can greatly interfere with transport routes, causing shipping delays, increased freight rates, and shortages in raw materials. A relevant example is Russia-Ukraine conflict, which adversely impacted energy and agricultural supplies in international markets, affecting several industries ranging from food production to auto manufacturing (Heckmann et al., 2015). Similarly, the semiconductor crisis, fueled by disruptions in supplies due to the pandemic and geopolitical factors, forced automaker and electronics producers to halt or suspend production, causing revenue drops and market share losses (Sheffi, 2021).

In conjunction with operational disruptions, geopolitical instability creates variations in demand and economic uncertainty as companies strive to adjust to changing market conditions. Organizations operating in uncertain environments are forced to cope with variations in exchange rates, changes in free-trade agreement terms and conditions, and changes in regulatory environments—elements that increase the uncertainty surrounding revenue predictions and investment decisions (Ivanov and Dolgui, 2020). Additionally, frequent disruptions in the supply chain have a negative impact on brand perception and customer satisfaction, mostly in e-commerce and consumer goods sectors, where timely delivery is a defining differentiator. Customers expect reliability and consistency; thus, frequent disruptions in the supply chain could lead to reduced market confidence and lasting reputational damage for companies (Sheffi, 2021). With increased frequency and unpredictability in disruptions in geopolitical supply chains, building resilience in companies has emerged as a strategic imperative. Supply chain resilience is defined as an organization's ability to anticipate, resist, and recover from outside disruptions while maintaining business continuity and economic viability (Ponomarov and Holcomb, 2009). Organizations with highly resilient supply chains have a better ability to cope with geopolitical disruptions and hence avoid economic repercussions and maintain a competitive edge.

Moreover, a fundamental aspect in developing resilience in supply chains is diversification in suppliers alongside regional sourcing strategies, which ensures that reliance on any geographic region is minimized. Several companies have begun to abandon international supply chains for more localized arrangements through the application of nearshoring and dual-sourcing strategies to hedge against risks from trade conflicts and regional instability (Wieland and Durach, 2021). For instance, firms in the semiconductor sector, with disruptions in their supply chains emanating from Asia, have initiated investments in local capabilities in manufacturing and bases for suppliers in a move to diversify their reliance away from a single region. Similarly, the automobile industry has employed multi-sourcing strategies to have a stable supply of essential components, such as lithium-ion batteries for use in electric cars (Jüttner and Maklan, 2011). An additional essential strategy for building resilience involves responsive logistics and inventory optimization, requiring a cautious balance between just-in-time (JIT) supply chain approaches and buffer stock levels. Traditionally, JIT approaches have been favored owing to cost advantages. However, recent disruptions highlighted the dangers of relying too heavily on lean inventory models (Sheffi, 2021). Today, several firms are embracing hybrid inventory strategies, which include maintaining safety stock levels for critical components while using sophisticated forecasting software to manage excess inventory. Additionally, companies are making their logistics operations more responsive using alternative delivery routes, multiple distribution centers, and strategic partnerships with third-party logistics providers to enhance responsiveness in cases of supply chain disruptions. Integration with digital technologies and predictive analytics proves to be a crucial element in building resilience in the supply chain. Sophisticated uses of artificial intelligence (AI), blockchain technologies, and real-time analytics enable companies to track supply chain performance, detect possible disruptions in advance, and implement preemptive contingency measures (Wieland and Durach, 2021). Amazon and Tesla are examples of companies that have made significant investments in digital management of supplies using AI-based forecasting and end-to-end visibility in supply chains to detect vulnerabilities and optimize inventory management processes (Sheffi, 2021). Such technological interventions allow companies to maintain business continuity, reduce downtime, and enhance responsiveness to variations in the supply chain.

The increasing frequency and severity of supply chain disruptions due to geopolitical events have highlighted the need for companies to develop resilience strategies to maintain their operating performance. Such disruptions, ranging from trade wars, economic sanctions, regional conflicts, and changing trading alliances, uncovered vulnerabilities in international supply chains, thus affecting cost structures, operating efficiency, and market positioning. To counter such issues, companies have to develop integrated risk management strategies that promote long-term sustainability in conjunction. This chapter seeks to discuss the relationship between disruptions in the supply chain and business performance and explore how companies can enhance resilience and maintain stability in a highly uncertain international business climate. A primary aim in this chapter is to analyze to what extent geopolitical factors influence disruptions to supply chains, and in turn, business operations and economic performance. This chapter employes empirical illustrations and case studies to present how trade barriers, logistical difficulties, and supplier volatility influence companies in different industries. Such disruptions usually result in increased purchasing costs, production schedule delays, and revenue losses, highlighting the need for companies to have full appreciation for the wider implications linked to weaknesses in their supply chains. Additionally, this chapter will discuss measures that can be taken by organizations to preclude potential risks and develop strategic measures to mitigate them.

The chapter focuses extensively on strategic frameworks for handling disruptions in supply chains. Organizations that integrate proactive steps to improve resilience in their processes for managing supply chains are best placed to sustain performance despite external uncertainties. Fundamental techniques for developing resilience will be discussed, such as supplier diversification, nearshoring, logistical responsiveness, and digital innovation, and their significance in reducing disruption risks will be highlighted. This chapter also discusses how there is a move from conventional just-in-time (JIT) inventory systems to hybrid models that balance cost effectiveness with responsiveness in supply chains. The chapter will continue to discuss in detail how predictive analytics, artificial intelligence (AI), and real-time monitoring systems can be utilized to capture early warning signs and enable quick response systems. The chapter also includes an investigation on how companies can measure the performance of their resilience strategies in supply chains using key performance indicators (KPIs). Using frameworks for performance measurement, companies can continuously improve their resilience strategies, thus promoting long-term competitiveness and economic security. This discourse will, in addition, discuss how companies can integrate sustainability and ethics into decision-making in their supply chains, aiming to balance reducing risks with corporate social responsibility. Overall, the chapter provides a detailed analysis of disruptions in supply chains and their effects on corporate performance, and hence provides business executives, supply chain managers, and policymakers with knowledge to manage geopolitical uncertainties. By understanding inherent risks and utilizing strategic frameworks for resilience, companies can safeguard their supply chain operations while sustaining economic and operating performance in a more complicated international trading system.

BACKGROUND

Supply Chain Disruptions and Corporate Implications Linkage

Supply chain disruptions are defined as unexpected events that hinder normal flows of goods, services, and information along the supply chain, causing inefficiencies in operations, financial losses, and strategic challenges to companies. Such disruptions can result from a wide range of factors, such as, but not limited to, natural disasters, cyberattacks, economic crises, and process failure. Interestingly, recent research in academia has established that geopolitical events have risen to be among the most salient drivers causing disruptions in international supply chains, with different effects on organizational performance (Ivanov and Dolgui, 2020). More frequent and intense trade disputes, regional conflicts, economic sanctions, and changing regulations have impacted business operations, posing risks and strategic challenges to companies reliant on international supply chains (Chopra and Sodhi, 2014).

A fundamental aspect of supply chain disturbances is their cascading nature, whereby a disruption in a point creates a ripple in the overall system. For example, an unexpected trade embargo on raw materials initiated in one nation can result in delayed production processes, heightened costs in purchasing, and shortages in inventory in another nation. This interdependence is indicative of international supply chains with embedded intricate dependencies, rendering firms highly susceptible to geopolitical events (Sheffi, 2021). Moreover, disruptions are usually compounded with globalization as firms pursue cost efficiencies through foreign production and just-in-time (JIT) inventory management. Although such strategies provide economic advantages to firms, in turn, they expose them to external shocks and render them unprepared to manage unforeseen disruptions in their chains (Wieland and Durach, 2021).

The consequences of disruptions in supply chains for businesses are extensive, affecting different aspects of business operations. Financially, disruptions can bring in massive cost hikes, forcing companies to look for alternative suppliers, deal with increased tariffs, or invest in resources for expediting logistics to maintain business. Research carried out by Baldwin and Freeman (2022) shows that companies with major disruptions in their supply chains end up losing an average 25% in shareholders' value due to reduced revenue, inefficiency in operations, and increased cost. Supply chain disruptions can lead to a loss in market share since companies are unable to meet customer orders, and this can result in order cancellation, hence causing reputational loss and customer distrust.

From an operational point of view, disruptions in the supply chain often result in reduced production capacity, forcing companies to delay product launches, scale down production levels, or transfer resources in a bid to mitigate shortages (Christopher, 2016). Disruptions in industries like motor vehicle production and electronics, which are highly dependent on specialized parts, can cause prolonged production halts even from small disruptions (Craighead et al., 2007).

The significant effect of supply chain disruptions has to do with their role in strategic decision-making and planning for resilience in an enterprise. Businesses that face recurrent disruptions have to reassess their supply chain structures, considering alternative sourcing strategies, diversification of suppliers, and localized production methods. The traditional cost management paradigm in supply chains is increasingly being replaced with a resilience-based framework in which companies emphasize business agility, mitigation of risks, and operation adaptability in place of short-term cost cutting (Ivanov and Dolgui, 2020). In summary, disruptions in the supply chain, and in particular those precipitated by geopolitical events, pose significant challenges to organizational performance, negatively influencing economic stability, operational efficiency, and strategic long-term growth. With companies operating in an increasingly uncertain and chaotic arena of international commerce, being able to anticipate, respond to, and recover from disruptions in the supply chain is set to become a paramount driver of business success.

Geopolitical Events as Catalysts for Supply Chain Disruptions

Geopolitical events have become a main contributor to disruptions in modern-day economic global supply chains. Unlike other forms of disruptions like natural disasters, cyberattacks, or process failure, geopolitical disruptions are marked by their prolonged, systemic, and intricate nature, affecting several industries and geographic locations simultaneously. Such disruptions include trade conflicts, economic sanctions, regional instability, political instability, regulatory changes, and pandemics, all with a high capacity to drastically interfere with international supply chains and influence organizational performance (Tang, 2006; Bednarski et al., 2023). With highly integrated features in modern-day economic global supply chains, localized geopolitical disturbances can create extensive ripple effects with far-reaching implications for production, transportation, and market stability (Ivanov and Dolgui, 2020). One major geopolitical disruptor is political ambiguity in respect to regulations in international trade, whereby sudden changes to tariffs, export limitations, and free-trade agreements bring instability to economic global supply chains. The U.S.-China trade conflict triggered a series of tariffs and retaliations that affected industries from consumer electronics to automobile production (Baldwin and Freeman, 2022). Multinational companies have thus redirected their supply chains, diverting production to alternative low-cost centers to counter risks from concentrated trade dependencies (Sheffi, 2021).

Economic sanctions and export controls have increasingly been identified as important tools in the realm of international business, often having unforeseen effects on the stability of supply chains. Sanctioning countries impose restrictions on the exportation or importation of critical commodities, technologies, or raw materials, thus causing disruptions to firms that are dependent on such products. A relevant example is sanctions imposed by Western countries on Russia following the conflict in Ukraine, which resulted in disruptions to international supply chains for oil, gas, agricultural commodities, and industrial metals (Dolgui et al., 2020). This situation generated price volatility in energy, logistical issues, and increased cost of production for firms dependent on such commodities. Additionally, sanctions on the exportation of semiconductor technology to China have had a far-reaching effect on the international electronics industry by restricting access to sophisticated chip technologies and forcing companies to seek alternative sources or develop internal capabilities (Wieland and Durach, 2021). The conflict in Russia and Ukraine is a geopolitical crisis that has affected international supply chains in several aspects. Ukraine, being a major supplier of grain, sunflower oil, and industrial supplies, saw a suspension in its export business, leading to shortages in the world and inflationary pressure (Kim et al., 2015). Additionally, the conflict has affected critical metal supplies like palladium and neon gas, both being essential in semiconductor production, thus worsening chip shortages in the world. Furthermore, disruptions in energy supplies due to sanctions placed on Russian oil and gas have increased production costs for energy-dependent industries. This has forced companies to seek alternative energy sources and adjust their supply chain strategies accordingly.

Moreover, the COVID-19 pandemic has shown how health and geopolitical crises can drastically interfere with international supply chains. This was realized through extensive factory shutdowns, shortages in personnel, shipping delays, and a lack of raw material supplies, all of which impacted sectors like pharmaceuticals, automobiles, and consumer goods extensively (Ivanov and Dolgui, 2020; Ivanov, 2024). Additionally, the pandemic fueled increased international trade protectionism, and many governments responded with export controls on strategic commodities like vaccines and masks, forcing companies to rethink their purchasing strategies and diversify their bases of suppliers. Besides direct limitations in international and regional trade and resultant instability, governments can influence supply chains further with regulatory changes and industrial policies (Lee, 2004).

The tensions in strategic trading areas, for example, in the South China Sea, pose a significant challenge to international supply chains stability. Being one of the most important maritime transit routes, any military conflict escalation in this region has the ability to disturb shipping routes, lead to delivery delays, and raise transport costs. Businesses that rely on smooth international operations have raised concerns about limitations to important shipping routes, particularly against a backdrop of increased geopolitical tensions (Sheffi, 2021). Similarly, Brexit has brought significant ambiguity with respect to trading regulations and policies for businesses operating in the European market, causing increased compliance costs, customs delays, and restructuring UK-EU commerce supply chains (Baldwin and Freeman, 2022). Geopolitical events are inherently uncertain and therefore pose some of the most difficult disruptions to deal with in international supply chains. Compared to other types of disruptions that have recoverable times (e.g., those due to natural disasters) geopolitical disturbances typically bring prolonged periods of uncertainty, requiring companies to develop strategic, long-term strategies to their supply chain structures. Businesses that fail to proactively prepare and mitigate against geopolitical risks can face devastating economic losses, business disruptions, and reputational loss. In response to a more fragmented and uncertain international trading environment, there is a need for companies to develop strategies for resilience to manage risks and maintain business performance. Investments should be made to diversify suppliers, use nearshoring strategies, develop logistics resilience, and enhance digital visibility in their supply chains in order to manage geopolitical risks.

GEOPOLITICAL SUPPLY CHAIN DISRUPTIONS IMPACT MITIGATION THROUGH BUSINESS RESILIENCE

The notion of organizational resilience has developed as a key strategic priority for companies operating in an ever-increasingly dynamic international trading environment. It is defined as a firm's ability to anticipate, withstand, recover from, and adjust to disruptions with stable operations and a sustained competitive position; hence, resilience is a critical vehicle for insulating corporate performance against external disruptions (Ponomarov and Holcomb, 2009). Amidst supply chain disruptions fueled by geopolitical events, resilience is more than a mere defense; rather, it is a forward-thinking strategy that enables companies to stay profitable, save costs, and enhance customer confidence in times of uncertainty (Sheffi, 2021). Disruptions in supply chains have a significant influence on organizational performance in terms of affecting critical business measures like revenue growth, operating efficiency, cost in the supply chain, and customer satisfaction (Ivanov and Dolgui, 2020). Resilient organizations face prolonged recovery times, increased costs, and reputational losses, eventually losing market share. For example, companies affected by the semiconductor crisis due to U.S.-China trade tensions suffered from delayed production times, reduced revenue, and increased procurement costs due to their reliance on a single-source purchasing strategy (Baldwin and Freeman, 2022). However, companies that adopted anticipatory measures to diversify their supplier bases and developed regional production capacities showed a better ability to withstand the crisis and hence avoid economic losses and shortages in products (Kilpatrick and Barter, 2020).

A resilient supply chain is crucial to business continuity, ensures business finance viability, and increases business operational dexterity, especially in times of disruption (Dimitriou and Karagkouni, 2022). Supply chain structures being able to effectively adjust to changing times is a critical element in being able to recover from external disruptions. Organizations with responsive supply networks are able to easily adjust their material sources, production processes, and distribution procedures in response to disruptions. For industries like automobile production, where geopolitical disruptions regularly affect raw material and components supplies, automobile producers have moved away from employing just-in-time inventory systems to using just-in-case inventory systems. By keeping strategic levels of important components in stock, such firms are able to better withstand supply chain disruptions while being cost-effective (Wieland and Durach, 2021).

The expansion of supplier networks has become a crucial element in building organizational resilience, specifically for companies that rely on resources from a specific geographic area. Organizations that have access to critical inputs from a single country or geopolitical area are more susceptible to disruptions from trade conflicts, changes in regulatory environments, and economic sanctions (Sheffi, 2021). By diversifying their supplier networks across different geographic locations, companies can reduce the influence of political unrest in a specific region and promote the sustainability of their supply chains (Baldwin and Freeman, 2022). In the area of supplier diversification, companies are increasingly embracing more responsive inventory and logistics systems to mitigate risks from their supply chains. Conventionally, lean inventory strategies are known for being cost-effective; however, such strategies enhance susceptibility to disruptions in the supply chain. A combined approach that combines lean operations with buffer stock strategies allows companies to maintain adequate stocks of crucial material while keeping costs low (Ivanov and Dolgui, 2020). At the same time, logistical responsiveness has become a crucial driver in promoting business resilience. Companies that establish alternative routes for transport, expand distribution centers within different geographic locations, and improve coordination with third-party logistics companies are better positioned to provide stability in the supply chain in times of crisis (Pettit et al., 2019).

The importance of technological advancements in enhancing supply chain resilience has gained increased relevance. Digitalization and predictive analytics have crucial roles in enabling companies to track their supply chains in real-time, detect early signs of impending disruptions, and develop proactive measures for managing risks. Advances in technologies like artificial intelligence, blockchain, and the Internet of Things have enabled greater visibility in supply chains, thereby enabling companies to detect vulnerabilities and undertake timely interventions to counter external disruptions (Sheffi, 2021). For example, demand forecasting models with artificial intelligence capabilities enable companies to foresee changes in demand and supply patterns and enable them to pre-adjust purchasing and production schedules to counter economic uncertainties (Wieland and Durach, 2021). Alongside technological advancements, improving organizational resilience is highly dependent on interdepartmental coordination and crisis management preparedness (Sartzetaki et al., 2025). Supply chain resilience is not just a simple logistical or purchasing function; it is a strategic imperative that involves all aspects of an organization and requires coordination between different business functions. Business firms that integrate finance, operating, and risk management systems with supply chain management are able to implement coordinated responses to unexpected disruptions (Ponomarov and Holcomb, 2009). Additionally, companies with well-defined crisis management systems that incorporate components such as contingency planning, scenario planning, and stakeholder involvement have a better ability to mitigate disruptions in supply chains, thus reducing downtime and cost implications. By incorporating resilience capabilities into their supply chain approaches, companies can enhance business performance and operational resilience in the face of external uncertainties. Resilient supply chains not only reduce vulnerabilities in terms of geopolitical risks but also enable companies to gain a competitive edge through measures like improving sustainability, building resilient supplier relationships, and improving cost structures (Revilla and Saenz, 2017).

Key Resilience Strategies for Mitigating Supply Chain Disruptions

In light of geopolitical supply chain threats, companies have to implement strategic interventions in an attempt to build resilience with a view to guaranteeing business performance. Supply chain resilience involves planning, flexibility, and organizational responsiveness, factors that minimize risks and guarantee operational effectiveness and economic stability. Companies with resilience interventions in supply chain management processes can effectively withstand disruptions due to barriers to international business, regional conflict, and changing regulation environments. Some of the resilience interventions have been established to be critical tools for companies that desire to insulate supply chains against effects from geopolitical disruptions. One easy method to build resilience involves diversifying with suppliers with a view to minimizing reliance in a nation or country for raw materials and components. Most companies that in the past have relied on foreign production at a low cost have reassessed purchasing plans due to international conflict in international business, economic sanctions, and rising risks from political instability (Baldwin and Freeman, 2022). Having multiple relationships with suppliers from different geographical areas, companies can stop disruptions in a specific region from stopping their whole supply chain activities. This approach not only enhances supply security but also enhances companies' negotiating power and provides them with more room to exercise purchasing.

Beyond the diversification of suppliers, companies have increasingly turned to regionalized and nearshoring strategies to improve management of risks associated with extensive supply chains. Nearshoring is defined as the process of taking production closer to main market centers to reduce reliance on foreign suppliers and mitigate exposure to international conflicts. This has gained particular significance in the automobile and tech manufacturing sectors, where delayed delivery of components can cause massive disruptions in production schedules. For example, automobile producers have increasingly moved the production of batteries and semiconductors to places within their region to break reliance on Asian suppliers and improve the reliability of their supply chains (Macchion et al., 2015). Additionally, regionalized supply chains are characterized by their ability to provide shorter lead times, reduced transport costs, and reduced exposure to currency risks, making them a viable long-term solution to improving resilience in international companies. A vital building block in supply chains is inventory optimization and demand forecasting. The traditional just-in-time (JIT) inventory management system, which strives to reduce storage costs by purchasing materials as and when required, has gained popularity due to cost benefits. However, the vulnerability of JIT systems to supply chain disruptions has led several companies to implement a just-in-case (JIC) strategy, in which companies hold safety stocks to avoid potential shortages (Sheffi, 2021). More and more companies have utilized predictive analytics and AI-based forecasting software to attain balance in inventory levels, having enough stock while simultaneously eliminating unnecessary carrying costs. This data-based approach enables companies to foresee changes in supply patterns, detect impending threats, and develop informed purchasing strategies responsive to geopolitical environments.

Beyond inventory control, logistics agility and transport flexibility are critical elements in building resilience in supply chains. Companies relying on a single shipping route or a single transport entity inherently expose themselves to vulnerabilities, especially when international movements are disrupted by geopolitical events. To mitigate such risks, companies are expanding their logistics systems through multiple transport routes, alternative ports, and multimodal shipping strategies (Ivanov and Dolgui, 2020). Additionally, companies are investing in real-time tracking and blockchain technologies to improve visibility across the supply chain, thus enabling timely redirection of cargo and reducing disruptions caused by geopolitical conflicts. The incorporation of digital technologies in supply chains has proven to be a crucial element in strategies that seek to promote resilience. Sophisticated technologies like blockchain, AI, and IoT provide organizations with timely analytical information that enhances decision-making in operations and enhances risk management strategies. Analytical tools driven by AI have the ability to forecast possible disruptions using historical information and geopolitical events, thus enabling companies to proactively adjust their supply chain strategies (Sheffi, 2021). Blockchain technology, which enables safe and open transaction and commodity tracking, helps companies to validate supplier reliability, track conformity to regulation, and enhance security along the supply chain (Wieland and Durach, 2021). Additionally, digital technologies enable companies to achieve increased visibility along their supply chains and improve their response times, thus reducing their exposure to disruptions from external factors.

Additionally, strategic partnerships and collaborative supply chain structures have proven highly effective in building resilience. Organizations that develop strong relationships with suppliers, logistics firms, and government agencies have a greater ability to manage supplies and handle crises. During the COVID-19 pandemic, companies with strong supplier relationships and developed contingency strategies were able to source critical materials and maintain business continuity in spite of severe disruptions (Handfield et al., 2020; Dimitriou and Sartzetaki, 2022). Collaborative networks enable sharing of information on risks, sharing resources, and collective strategies for overcoming trading barriers and regulation issues. In the current climate for managing supply chain resilience, crisis response planning and corporate frameworks for managing risks have gained added significance. Organizations that regularly evaluate vulnerabilities in their supply chains, conduct stress testing, and conduct scenario analysis are better able to withstand geopolitical disruptions. Several multinational companies have developed geopolitical risk dashboards and early-warning systems to track trade regulations, policy changes, and regional conflicts affecting their supply chains (Ivanov and Dolgui, 2020). Additionally, companies are creating specialized groups to manage crisis response in the supply chain with the ability to implement contingency strategies rapidly in times of disruption. These proactive strategies for managing risks enable companies to reduce downtime in operations, recover from losses in finance, and keep corporate performance stable in times of uncertainty. The adoption of strategic resilience strategies allows companies to insulate their supply chains from geopolitical disruptions while being fiscally responsible and keeping business going. With regard to the increasingly dynamic nature of international supply chains, companies that focus on resilience are better able to weather looming disruptions, improve their bottom lines, and hold a sustainable edge.

Integrating Resilience into Corporate Strategy for Long-Term Performance

The incorporation of business resilience has come to be a major imperative for international supply chain-plagued organizations. Geopolitical instabilities in terms of barriers to international business, regional conflict, regulation adjustments, and economic sanctions have pushed companies to change from a reactive to a resilience-oriented, forward-thinking strategy in managing international supply chains. By embracing resilience in strategic planning, companies can minimize economic burdens and operation risks from supply chain disruption to ensure sustainable performance, competitiveness, and equilibrium in the marketplace. This strategic transformation requires a collaborative partnership between business planning, business management, and corporate governance to develop a unified strategy to ensure business continuity and readiness to respond to likely risks (Sheffi, 2021). A critical aspect in business strategy and resilience integration is that corporate leadership should have a more sophisticated approach to decision-making that considers risk. Business strategies in the past have largely focused on cost cutting and streamlined supply chain designs with a focus on short-term profitability and ignoring long-term exposures to risks. However, disruptions due to geopolitical events have proved that dependency on a single nation or supplier can lead to shortages in supplies, production slowdowns, and overall economic volatility (Ivanov and Dolgui, 2020). Countering such vulnerabilities, companies are increasingly using a balanced approach that balances cost control with investments to improve resilience. This strategy involves geopolitical risk considerations, scenario planning, and impact modeling to guide supply chain decisions in line with overall corporate strategy. Companies using analytics to assess risks as part of strategic planning are better positioned to forecast disruptions in supplies and use proactive measures to maintain corporate performance.

A vital component in a business strategy centered around resilience involves regionalization and diversification of supply chains to allow companies to diversify away from high-risk trading corridors and politically volatile locations (Baldwin and Freeman, 2022). Automotive, pharmaceutical, and electronic manufacturers simultaneously are making investments in regional production bases to deconcentrate supply chains and minimize international business fluctuations to which they are vulnerable (Baldwin and Freeman, 2022). This strategic shift to regionalized supply chains not only enhances supply security, it also leads to logistics savings and responsiveness to geopolitical shocks. A business strategy centered around resilience emphasizes managing risks in finance and implementing measures for managing cost to hedge against supply chain fluctuation. Companies that have embraced risk-adjusted planning in supply chain management have a superior ability to respond to surprise fluctuations in tariffs, raw material shortage, and transport restrictions (Sheffi, 2021). Currency hedging, long-term supplier contracts, and liquidity buffers provide companies with a mechanism to withstand uncertain economic environments and maintain financial stability (Wieland and Durach, 2021). Furthermore, companies are sharpening capital deployment strategy through investment in technologies to develop supply chain resilience, automation, and data-driven platforms to respond to risks to enhance responsiveness in the long term.

The importance of digital transformation and technological advancements in corporate strategies with a focus on resilience is critical. Many companies are using artificial intelligence, blockchain technology, and extensive data analytics to provide greater visibility, enable predictive analytics, and conduct real-time risk assessments along their supply chains (Ivanov and Dolgui, 2020). AI-based software has the ability to simulate disruption scenarios, and through this, companies can identify areas of potential vulnerability and proactively optimize their sourcing, production, and distribution strategies. Utilizing blockchain technology ensures transparency in the supply chain, and companies can track supplier adherence, trading regulations, and conduct cross-border transactions with increased efficiency and security (Sheffi, 2021). Businesses that integrate such digital technologies in their strategic frameworks gain a strategic edge in terms of being responsive, agile, and managing risks, and in this way, position themselves to address geopolitical risks in a timely manner. The alignment of business strategy requires fostering a cross-functional organisational culture with strategic agility. Various organisations are establishing inter-disciplinary task forces for resilience response, which include supply chain managers, finance analysts, regulatory experts, and risk management groups to develop integrated strategies in response to geopolitical disruptions (Ponomarov and Holcomb, 2009). By fostering an organisational climate that focuses on agility and scenario-based decision-making, companies improve their ability to manage supply chain disruptions and maintain business continuity. Leadership groups that regularly undergo risk-awareness training, crisis simulations, and resilience assessments develop a workforce better able to manage ambiguity.

Moreover, the principles of corporate social responsibility and sustainability form integral elements in resilience strategies for supply chains. Growing environmental, social, and governance (ESG) regulations from government and regulatory agencies push firms to integrate their resilience strategies with integrated sustainability strategies and ethical purchasing behavior (Karagkouni and Dimitriou, 2022). Organizations that invest in circular supply chain structures, carbon-neutral logistical processes, and fair labor conditions not only improve the resilience of their supply chains but also improve their corporate reputation and stakeholder trust. ESG-based resilience strategies provide sustainable benefits, ranging from reduced regulatory risks, increased customer loyalty, and improved brand differentiation in competitive marketplaces. In conclusion, integrating resilience in business strategies requires a synchronized and forward-thinking approach that balances cost effectiveness, risk management, technological innovation, and sustainability. Organizations that integrate resilience into the core elements of their supply chain strategies will be better positioned to withstand geopolitical adversity, maintain economic stability, and thrive in the long term. With geopolitical uncertainties continuing to shape the business landscape, companies that focus on resilience-based innovation, diversification strategies, and digital transformation will be best poised to attain leadership in supply chain security and strategic resilience.

STRATEGIC FRAMEWORK FOR IMPROVING CORPORATE PERFORMANCE

In light of current geopolitical factors that pose a significant threat to international supply chains, companies are forced to implement a strategic and proactive approach to mitigate disruptions and maintain operational effectiveness. Clearly defined strategic guidelines provide companies with a structured framework for identifying vulnerabilities, implementing strategies to mitigate risks, crisis management, and linking resiliency programs to business objectives. The strategic framework for managing supply chain disruptions effectively and enhancing corporate performance is outlined in Figure 1.

Figure 1. Strategic Framework for Managing Supply Chain Disruptions

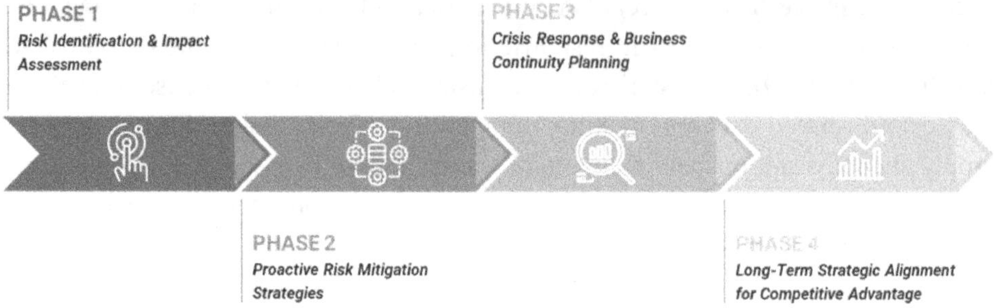

Phase 1: Risk Identification and Impact Assessment

An extensive risk management system commences with a detailed analysis of risks in the supply chain and potential implications because of geopolitical disruptions. Organizations must take into consideration risks associated with suppliers, logistics, inventory management, and demand forecasting because these factors are central to business continuity. One of the key elements in such a process involves supplier risk assessment, whereby companies consider how exposed they are to single-sourcing providers, geographic instability in a particular geographic region, and dependency on specific raw materials. Companies with a short supplier base in high-risk geographic regions are extremely vulnerable to regional conflict, trading prohibitions, and geographical restrictions to trading. Auditorship by providers and geographical risk maps provide companies with a means to determine locations in their supply chains that are most vulnerable to disruption (Ivanov and Dolgui, 2020).

In this regard, logistics risk analyses take into consideration interdependence in transport by looking into how much a supply chain can rely on specific shipping routes, ports, or carriers. Restricted organizational logistics flexibility can make it difficult to respond to disruptions in a timely fashion and will have longer lead times and associated costs. Alternative shipping routes, multimodal transport modes, and adaptive routing can largely enhance logistical responsiveness. Moreover, it's required that companies integrate scenario planning and predictive analysis into risk-identifying processes. Through AI-based forecasting software, companies can model different geopolitical events like embargoes, sanctions, or sudden shifts in regulation environments and analyze probable impacts on effectiveness in supply chains (Sheffi, 2021). This empirical approach enables them to prepare preemptive measures to minimize or alleviate economic and operation impacts from disruptions to supply chains.

Phase 2: Proactive Risk Mitigation Strategies

Upon identifying possible risks, preventive measures should be taken to mitigate possible disruptions and ensure continuity in supply chain processes. Several basic strategies can enhance the resilience of the supply chain and reduce reliance on high-risk areas. The strategy to diversify suppliers and processes has been a strategic move for companies seeking to reduce reliance on a single supplier or geographic area. Organizations are increasingly diversifying their supplier bases in different countries, thus reducing their exposure to political risks in specific locations (Baldwin and Freeman, 2022). Nearshoring and regional sourcing have several advantages in reducing lead times and reducing dependency on foreign suppliers. By having production facilities closer to market hubs, firms can avoid risks associated with extended lead times, border regulations, and currency exchange rate variations (Christopher, 2016). While nearshoring has advantages like faster delivery and reduced transport costs, there are challenges like rising labor costs and infrastructural shortages in specific areas. Organizations have to undertake detailed cost-benefit analyses before shifting their production operations to proximate locations. Methods for inventory optimization are crucial to attaining a symphonic balance between economic efficiency and resilience in supply chains. While just-in-time (JIT) inventory strategy has grown in popularity with its cost advantages, recent disruptions in supply chains have highlighted the role of just-in-case (JIC) inventory systems in which companies consciously maintain safety stock to counteract the effects of unexpected breaks in supplies (Sheffi, 2021). Additionally, automation-based inventory management systems, supplemented with artificial intelligence-based demand forecasting, allow companies to maintain optimal levels of inventory with reduced cost in terms of excess inventory.

Phase 3: Crisis Response and Business Continuity Planning

Notwithstanding the adoption of effective measures for mitigating risks, companies should be in a position to manage unforeseen disruptions through developing flexible crisis management systems. A well-designed business continuity plan (BCP) empowers companies to navigate geopolitical disruptions with ease and stay financially stable while honoring their obligations to customers. An essential element in effective crisis management is having real-time visibility in the supply chain, which enables instant observation of disruptions in real-time, thus making informed decisions to mitigate delays (Ivanov and Dolgui, 2020). Organizations with Internet of Things (IoT) tracking systems, blockchain-based supply chain management, and AI-based alerts for risks can detect bottlenecks, shortages from suppliers, and logistics holdups in real-time, thus making timely corrective measures possible.

Furthermore, it is crucial for companies to develop backup logistics and distribution structures to maintain market presence in times of disruption. Businesses relying on a single shipping channel or distribution point can face extensive disruptions in case geopolitical events restrict such routes. By investing in regional warehousing facilities, multiple shipping carriers, and backup distribution hubs, companies can enhance the robustness of their supply chains and minimize downtime. The interplay between different functional groups is important in formulating crisis response strategies. Coordination of mitigation strategies and communication of contingency plans to stakeholders requires establishing multidisciplinary response groups with legal professionals, finance analysts, supply chain managers, and risk managers (Ponomarov and Holcomb, 2009). Well-coordinated crisis communication procedures are also important in coordinating all response groups in order to reduce uncertainty and shorten recovery times.

Phase 4: Long-Term Strategic Alignment for Competitive Advantage

Supply chain resilience should be thought of not just as a short-term measure, but rather as a strategic asset that maximizes organizational effectiveness in the long term. Organizations that incorporate resilience strategies within their overall corporate strategies, business planning, and operating systems are better positioned to stay profitable in uncertain global trading conditions. A significant benefit of investment in long-term resilience is increased corporate financial stability. Companies that invest in making their supply chains more flexible and diversifying risks are better able to mitigate revenue losses associated with supply chain disruptions and adjust well to changing market conditions (Jüttner and Maklan, 2011). Financial resilience can also allow companies to negotiate better terms from suppliers, receive lower insurance rates, and optimize their procurement spend.

The incorporation of technological innovations and automation greatly enhances the long-term resilience of supply chains. Organizations embracing artificial intelligence, blockchain, automation, and machine learning can enhance predictive analytics, track supplier conformity, and optimize logistics processes (Sheffi, 2021). These digital tools reduce the frequency of man-made mistakes, enhance forecast accuracy, and maximize operating efficiency, thus enabling companies to enhance their agility in an increasingly complex trading environment. An essential building block in sustainable strategic alignment is a commitment to sustainability programs and regulatory guidelines. Governments around the world are increasingly adopting environmental, social, and governance (ESG) regulations that oblige firms to use sustainable procurement procedures, maintain ethical working conditions, and develop strategies to reduce their carbon footprint (Wieland and Durach, 2021). Organizations that proactively integrate sustainable supply chain procedures into their resilience strategies not only meet changing regulations but enhance their brand reputation and develop enduring stakeholder trust.

Strategies for Managing Supply Chain Disruptions and Enhancing Corporate Performance

Disruptions occurring in a global supply chain have different effects on different sectors and thus require sector-specific strategies for improving corporate performance. While ideas like supply chain resilience with features such as supplier diversification, logistical flexibility, and digital connectivity apply to several sectors, their applicability differs depending on the specific structures, regulatory frameworks, and operating interdependencies specific to each sector. This section examines responses from different sectors to disruptions in a supply chain triggered by geopolitical events and evaluates the strategies for resilience adopted to mitigate risks while promoting economic stability in conjunction with operating efficiency.

Strengthening Supply Networks for Operational Stability in Manufacturing Sector

The manufacturing industry has been unprecedentedly challenged due to supply chain disruptions emanating from geopolitical events, specifically due to trade barriers, raw material shortages, and changes in trade flows. Traditionally, companies in this sector have relied on low-cost production in foreign countries, making them susceptible to tariffs, export barriers, and logistics complexities. For instance, the China-US trade conflict hindered industrial components and raw material flows, and many companies began to rethink their dependence on Chinese suppliers (Baldwin and Freeman, 2022). To mitigate such vulnerabilities, companies have increasingly adopted multi-sourcing and nearshoring strategies, thus reducing dependence on a single country or region. This approach ensures disruptions in a particular region do not completely halt production activities. Additionally, companies are investing in resources to establish smart factories and automation technologies to improve production efficiency and lessen dependence on workers, who often experience geopolitical and regulative difficulties. Businesses using digital technologies like real-time supply chain visibility, predictive analytics, and AI-based demand forecasting are in a better position to proactively adjust purchasing and inventory management, thus maintaining continuity in supplies in light of external disruptions (Macchion et al., 2015).

Securing Component Supply Chains Amid Trade Restrictions

The technology and electronics industry is most susceptible to disruptions in supplies due to reliance on specialized components usually sourced from a limited pool of suppliers. The shortages in semiconductors, fueled by economic sanctions between China and America, highlighted the risks inherent in over-reliance on certain centers of production. Technology companies suffered production delays, added costs, and reduced market competition due to limited access to critical chips and electronic components (Sheffi, 2021). To counter such problems, companies in the tech industry have increasingly focused on regionalized supply chains as a critical measure for countering such problems, which involves investments in in-firm production capabilities and diversification of supplier bases(Bednarski et al., 2023). Additionally, companies have enhanced digital tracking systems to improve supply chain resilience and accommodate changing regulations driven by changing international trade policies.

Balancing Lean Manufacturing with Supply Chain Flexibility

The automotive business has witnessed massive supply chain disruptions in recent years, such as witnessing chip shortage in 2021 and 2022 that resulted in production halt. The just-in-time inventory management strategy adopted in such a business has proved to be very vulnerable to such disruptions, such as witnessed in production halt due to chip shortage in 2021 and 2022 (Wieland and Durach, 2021). To balance such disruptions, automobile manufacturers have increasingly turned to just-in-case inventory systems, whereby principal components have safety stock held. Companies have also adopted dual-sourcing methods to source principal materials, such as lithium-ion batteries in electric cars, from more than a single supplier. Through a mix of predictive methods with real-time inventory management, automobile manufacturers have increasingly been improving in terms of forecasting disruptions and readjusting supply chain strategy in advance. The business has also adopted alternative logistics methods, such as diversified transport channels and localized manufacturing hubs, to hedge against possible geopolitical risks.

Adapting to Supply Chain Volatility Through Digitalization

Retail and e-commerce companies experience unique challenges when supply chains get disrupted by geopolitical events like stock shortage, transport prices fluctuation, and consumer demand fluctuation. Retail and e-commerce companies depend much on international sources for electronic and fast-moving consumer goods (FMCG) products and therefore supply chain disruptions can have a huge effect on brand reputation and revenue. The COVID-19 pandemic and international restrictions in foreign markets have exposed supply chains to disruption, such as stockout incidents, delivery delays, and a surge in operational expenditure (Sheffi, 2021). To deal with such disruptions, retailers have implemented omnichannel supply chain strategies to maintain product availability in multiple centers to offset localized disruptions. Moreover, companies apply real-time tracking platforms and utilize artificial intelligence-based demand forecasting to maintain inventory management and reconcile stock level imbalance. Moreover, many companies are consolidating partnerships with local sources to minimize foreign transport reliance, thereby increasing resilience to respond to fluctuating regulations and import restrictions.

Ensuring Supply Chain Continuity for Critical Goods

The pharmaceutical and health industries have very strong supply chains because of complex regulations, long production processes, and absolute priority that such a business has in ensuring public health. Supply chain disruption in such a business in terms of drug shortage, delayed delivery of medicinal devices, and vaccine and essential drug shortage can have widespread ramifications for public health (Queiroz et al., 2020; Sarkis et al., 2020). International pharmaceutical supply chain vulnerabilities were put in focus during the COVID-19 pandemic, in terms of reliance upon a few central production hubs for active pharmaceutical ingredients (APIs) (Baldwin and Freeman, 2022). Increased investments have been made by pharmaceutical firms in regional production hubs and strategic stockpiles for essential drugs due to revealed vulnerabilities. Other firms have partnered with governments to create public-private partnership plans for augmenting emergency distribution of medicinal supplies. Other firms in such a business have adopted blockchain and Internet of Things (IoT) tracking technologies to provide more visibility in supply chains, meet regulations, and reduce risks from counterfeiting.

CORPORATE PERFORMANCE EVALUATION IN DISRUPTED SUPPLY CHAINS

As geopolitical disruptions continue to affect global supply chains, organizations are being forced to implement not only resilience strategies but to establish sound frameworks for business performance assessment and management. A firm's ability to withstand and recover from disruptions in their supply chains has a direct bearing on their economic sustainability, operating efficiency, and market competition position. To enable effective implementation of resilience strategies, firms need to track critical performance measures (KPIs), improve processes for managing supplies, and include processes for ongoing improvement. The proposed assessment framework for corporate performance in terms of supply chain resilience is analytically depicted in Figure 2.

Figure 2. Assessment Framework for Supply Chain Resilience and Corporate Performance

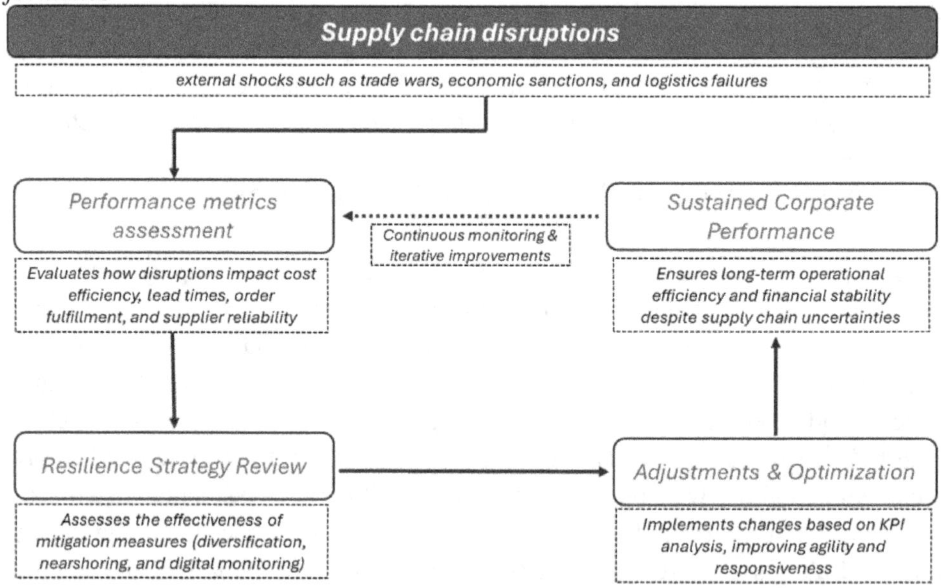

The Role of Key Performance Indicators in Evaluating Corporate Performance During Supply Chain Disruptions

Key Performance Indicators (KPIs) prove useful in monitoring business performance during supply chain disruption because they provide measurable insight into a business's ability to recover and resist disruption from outside. With increasing geopolitical complexity influencing international supply chains, businesses must resort to a data-driven method to measure effectiveness in resilience programs, improve decision-making processes, and promote economic stability. KPIs provide measurable and qualitative frameworks that provide businesses with a platform to keep disruptions in check, measure resilience program effects, and achieve ongoing supply chain effectiveness enhancement. The central function that KPIs have in managing supply chain disruption is to provide real-time visibility into supply chain weakness. Businesses utilize these measures to provide early warning signals for disruption, establish magnitude of supply chain inefficiencies, and develop contingency plans.

Through performance trend analysis, businesses can forecast vulnerable points in supplier network, logistics processes, and inventory management processes, and thus correct them prior to disruption intensification. Having real-time visibility into supply chain performance also enables companies to improve agility, making them respond to changing geopolitical environments in a timely fashion.

Another critical application of KPIs in supply chain resilience is their role in risk assessment and decision-making. Businesses must navigate uncertain trade environments by balancing cost efficiency with operational stability. KPIs provide empirical data that guides strategic choices, such as whether to diversify suppliers, adjust inventory levels, or shift to alternative logistics routes. Instead of making reactive decisions based on short-term disruptions, organizations that systematically track KPI trends can implement evidence-based risk mitigation strategies that align with long-term corporate objectives. Furthermore, by analyzing KPI fluctuations over time, companies can distinguish between temporary supply chain disturbances and systemic risks, enabling them to allocate resources more effectively.

In addition to enabling short-term crisis management, KPIs create a robust framework for strategic resilience planning and continuous improvement in the long term. By evaluating performance across different points in the supply chain, namely pre-disruption, in-disruption, and post-disruption, organizations can measure the effectiveness of their response strategies and identify areas for improvement. This cyclical process allows companies to develop better contingency plans, promote collaboration with suppliers, and integrate innovative technologies like AI analytics to enhance operational effectiveness. Additionally, as companies seek to attain sustainability in their supply chains, KPIs can be used to measure progress in adoption for environmentally responsible sourcing, fair labor practices, and lowering carbon emissions in international supply chains.

The integration of KPI analysis into corporate governance structures further strengthens supply chain resilience by fostering cross-functional collaboration between supply chain management, finance, operations, and risk assessment teams. Supply chain disruptions often have widespread financial and operational implications, requiring coordinated responses across multiple business functions. By establishing standardized KPI reporting mechanisms, organizations can ensure that key stakeholders are aligned in their approach to supply chain risk mitigation and performance optimization. Companies that embed KPI tracking into their broader risk management framework gain a competitive advantage by enhancing transparency, accountability, and strategic agility. Ultimately, the use of KPIs in evaluating corporate performance amid supply chain disruptions enables companies to shift from reactive crisis management to proactive resilience planning. Businesses that continuously monitor and analyze performance data can adapt to geopolitical challenges more effectively, maintain supply chain continuity, and sustain profitability despite market volatility. By leveraging KPIs as a strategic tool, firms can develop a more resilient, agile, and future-proof supply chain model that ensures long-term corporate success in an increasingly uncertain global trade environment.

Strategies for Continuous Performance Optimization

Beyond the measurement of performance, it is crucial for companies to integrate systems for ongoing improvement in order to develop sustainable resilience within their supply chains and gain economic stability. Organizations that regularly perform supply chain-related risk assessments, conduct scenario planning, and focus on process optimization are better able to avoid disruptions and maximize operational effectiveness. One highly effective method for improving performance is digitalizing supply chains. Organizations that use real-time tracking systems, leverage AI-based analytics, and implement transparency programs using blockchain-based systems gain a deeper understanding of their supply chain activities (Sheffi, 2021). Such technological innovations enable companies to anticipate potential risks, optimize purchasing processes, and enhance coordination with suppliers, thus better positioning them to address geopolitical disruptions. An additional strategic aspect involves management of relationships with suppliers. Organizations that develop enduring relationships with their suppliers, establish collaborative risk-sharing structures, and collaborate innovatively along the supply chain can develop a more resilient and stronger supply network. By adopting strategies for diversification with suppliers, nearshoring programs, and sustainability-based approaches to sourcing, companies can reduce reliance on high-risk geographic locations while enhancing supplier stability (Baldwin and Freeman, 2022). Along with supplier-focused strategies, companies need to optimize their distribution and logistics structures to enhance supply chain responsiveness. Organizations that invest in alternative shipping routes, multimodal transport strategies, and sophisticated warehousing technologies can efficiently reduce transit times, reduce freight costs, and avoid disruption risks (Sartzetaki et al., 2025). Additionally, predictive logistics and robotic warehousing management systems improve operating efficiency, enabling companies to manage unexpected changes in market demand and trading conditions effectively.

An essential part is effective management of financial risks. Organizations that face rising commodity costs, currency exchange rate volatility, and import/export levies need to use hedging strategies, negotiate long-term agreements with suppliers, and develop contingency budgets to protect profitability. Companies with large reserves of liquidity, diversified revenue bases, and companies that leverage government programs for promoting innovation in supply chains are better positioned to withstand economic shocks from geopolitical risks (Wieland and Durach, 2021). To create a conducive climate for continuous improvement, companies can create interdisciplinary resilience groups with experts from supply chains, finance analysts, government representatives, and information and communication technologies. Such groups can regularly assess performances, identify inefficiencies, and develop responsive risk management systems. By integrating supply chain resilience into overall corporate governance frameworks, companies can attain sustainable business success and have sustainable market positions. The evolution in business performance in the field of supply chain management will be shaped by changes in geopolitical forces, technological advancements, and increased expectations for sustainability. With governments enacting new regulations in matters regarding trading practice, environmental protection, and digital conformity, responsiveness and agility in the resilience framework are required from organizations. One trend in supply chain resilience is increased emphasis on automation and AI technologies. AI systems have the ability to improve forecasting for demand, optimize inventory management, and provide real-time alerts for potential risks, thus helping organizations to make better decisions (Sheffi, 2021). Additionally, advancements in automation in warehousing processes, use of autonomous systems for logistics, and 3D printing for decentralized production are expected to enhance supply chain resilience.

An important evolution in the sector is towards regionalized and sustainable supply chains. Several companies are investing in circular economy models, renewable energy-based logistics, and purchasing ethically sourced material to meet global sustainability targets (Karagkouni and Dimitriou, 2022; Van Hoek, 2020). Companies that use environmentally responsible supply chain methods, pursue strategies to lower their footprint, and develop purchasing procedures aligned with environmental, social, and governance (ESG) principles will not only mitigate compliance risks but will improve their corporate reputation and appeal to investors who value sustainability (Taraza et al., 2024). Moreover, the use of trading intelligence systems and software for geopolitical risk assessment is going to be a standard operating procedure for companies that engage in international commerce. Organizations using international trading surveillance systems with AI, automation-based verification tools, and international policy forecasting models will gain a strategic edge through real-time information on changing international regulations and tariffs (Baldwin and Freeman, 2022). In conclusion, companies focusing on resilience-based innovation, diversification in approaches to sourcing, and digital innovation will be best positioned to sustain corporate performance and mitigate disruptions in supply chains. The new trade climate will continue to pose challenges to firms; however, those embracing agility, technological innovation, and sustainable operations will be likely to emerge as champions in both supply chain stability and economic sustainability (Dimitriou et al., 2024).

Figure 3. Supply Chain Resilience Strategies for Enhancing Corporate Performance

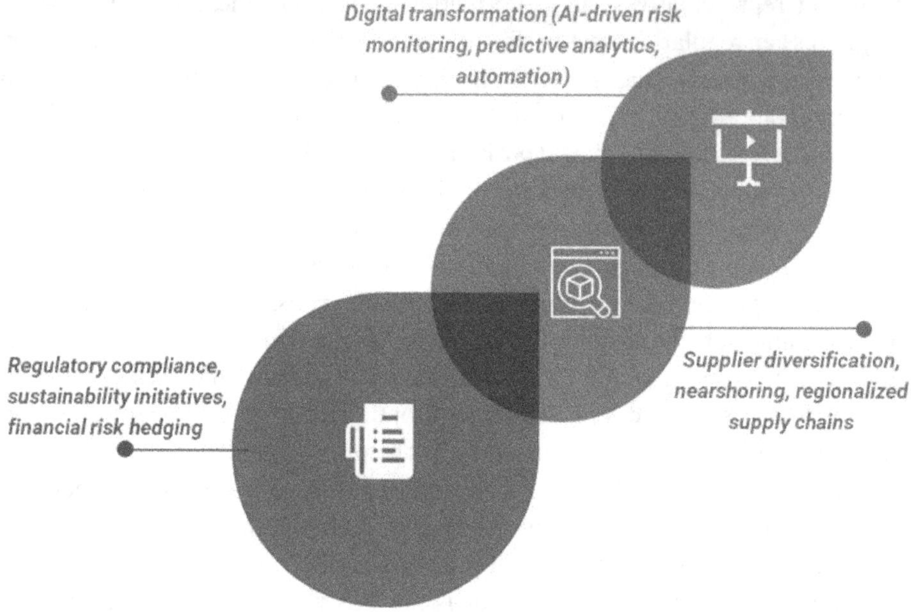

CONCLUDING REMARKS

The increasing complexity surrounding international supply chains, coupled with heightened geopolitical volatility, has made resilience a strategic imperative for companies. Recent disruptions such as U.S.-China trade tensions, Brexit, Russia-Ukraine conflict, and the COVID-19 pandemic have illustrated the fragility of traditional supply chain systems, showcasing that companies are vulnerable to disruptions from suppliers, logistical issues, increased costs, and process inefficiencies. Such disruptions expose the level of interdependence within international supply chains, where localized geopolitical unrest can have far-reaching effects on different industries, thus affecting production schedules, procurement costs, and overall business performance (Dimitriou and Sartzetaki, 2022; Chopra and Sodhi, 2014). To address all this, companies need to move from a crisis management strategy that is highly reactive to a proactive resilience model that involves risk assessment, mitigation strategies, crisis management planning, and alignment with overall strategic business objectives. Identifying vulnerabilities in supply chains, logistics, and regulatory risks is important to anticipate disruptions before their escalation. Businesses that invest in supplier diversification, nearshoring, and inventory optimization can reduce reliance on single-source suppliers and high-risk geographies and increase supply chain responsiveness. Additionally, adoption of digital technologies like AI-based predictive analytics, blockchain-based supply chain transparency, and real-time IoT tracking has proved to be highly effective in improving supply chain visibility, business operations, and risk management measures.

Crisis response planning is a critical element in building resilience in a supply chain. It is crucial for companies to establish responsive response systems, backup distribution routes, and additional sources of supplies in order to maintain business continuity in times of disruption. Utilizing real-time analytics, automating warning systems for risks, and assembling inter-disciplinary crisis management groups can greatly reduce disruption and economic loss and enable a timely and synchronized response to unexpected shocks in a supply chain (Christopher, 2016; Kim et al., 2015). Beyond the requirement to address short-term crises, integration with a wider corporate strategy is critical for companies. Maintaining compatibility with sustainability programs, regulatory compliance, and taking part in digital transformation initiatives is crucial for maintaining stability in a fluid market (Craighead et al., 2007). Additionally, investment in automation, AI-based logistics, and sustainable purchasing practices will enable firms to develop chains that are not only resilient to upcoming challenges but can also develop in response to them.

To assess the efficacy of certain resilience strategies, companies need to track critical performance measures like supply chain cycle time, cost-to-serve, order fill rates, and supplier lead-time variability. By tracking such measures, companies can detect inefficiencies, optimize risk mitigation strategies, and continuously improve their supply chain management processes. By adopting data-based decision-making and encouraging cross-functional collaboration, companies can ensure that supply chain resilience is a core aspect of corporate management and not a marginal issue. In forecasting future trends, it is anticipated that supply chains will be shaped by technological innovations, sustainability demands, and changing international regulations. With companies facing increased pressure to meet Environment, Social, and Governance (ESG) standards, efforts to reduce carbon emissions and set ethical purchasing standards will likely make integrating sustainable processes into supply chains a major differentiating feature (Dimitriou et al., 2024). Additionally, technological advancements, such as automation, AI-based forecasting, and decentralized production, will bring new ways to enhance responsiveness and efficiency in supply chains. In summary, supply chain resilience has evolved from an added value to a basic requirement for business operations. Companies undertaking investments in resource distribution optimization for managing risks, adopting digital transformation, and working towards strategic alignment will most likely be best positioned to weather future disruptions, maintain financial health, and develop a lasting competitive advantage. With international commerce in constant evolution, companies using resilience as a strategic asset will not only survive disruptions but will end up being stronger and more resilient in a more uncertain landscape.

REFERENCES

Baldwin, R., & Freeman, R. (2022). Risks and Global Supply Chains: What We Know and What We Need to Know. *Annual Review of Economics*, *14*(1), 153–180. Advance online publication. DOI: 10.1146/annurev-economics-051420-113737

Bednarski, L., Roscoe, S., Blome, C., & Schleper, M. (2023). Geopolitical disruptions in global supply chains: A state-of-the-art literature review. *Production Planning and Control*, 1–27. Advance online publication. DOI: 10.1080/09537287.2023.2286283

Chopra, S., & Sodhi, M. S. (2014). Reducing the risk of supply chain disruptions. *MIT Sloan Management Review*, *55*(3), 73–80. https://sloanreview.mit.edu/article/reducing-the-risk-of-supply-chain-disruptions

Christopher, M. (2016). *Logistics and Supply Chain Management* (5th ed.). Pearson Education.

Craighead, C., Blackhurst, J., Rungtusanatham, M., & Handfield, R. (2007). The Severity of Supply Chain Disruptions: Design Characteristics and Mitigation Capabilities. *Decision Sciences*, *38*(1), 131–156. DOI: 10.1111/j.1540-5915.2007.00151.x

Dimitriou, D., & Karagkouni, A. (2022). Assortment of Airports' Sustainability Strategy: A Comprehensiveness Analysis Framework. *Sustainability (Basel)*, *14*(7), 4217. DOI: 10.3390/su14074217

Dimitriou, D., & Sartzetaki, M. (2022). Criticality of a regional airport development to mitigate covid-19 economic effects. *Case Studies on Transport Policy*, *10*(1), 581–590. DOI: 10.1016/j.cstp.2022.01.018 PMID: 35106281

Dimitriou, D., Sartzetaki, M., & Karagkouni, A. (2024). *Managing Airport Corporate Performance: Leveraging Business Intelligence and Sustainable Transition*. Elsevier., DOI: 10.1016/C2023-0-51427-2

Dolgui, A., Ivanov, D., & Rozhkov, M. (2020). Does the Ripple Effect Influence the Bullwhip Effect? An Integrated Analysis of Structural and Operational Dynamics in the Supply Chain. *International Journal of Production Research*, *58*(5), 1285–1301. DOI: 10.1080/00207543.2019.1627438

Handfield, R. B., Graham, G., & Burns, L. (2020). Coronavirus, Tariffs, Trade Wars, and Supply Chain Evolutionary Design. *International Journal of Operations & Production Management*, *40*(10), 1649–1660. DOI: 10.1108/IJOPM-03-2020-0171

Heckmann, I., Comes, T., & Nickel, S. (2015). A critical review on supply chain risk – Definition, measure and modeling. *Omega*, *52*, 119–132. DOI: 10.1016/j.omega.2014.10.004

Ivanov, D. (2024). Exiting the COVID-19 pandemic: After-shock risks and avoidance of disruption tails in supply chains. *Annals of Operations Research*, *335*(3), 1627–1644. DOI: 10.1007/s10479-021-04047-7 PMID: 33840871

Ivanov, D., & Dolgui, A. (2020). Viability of Intertwined Supply Networks: Extending the Supply Chain Resilience Angles towards Survivability. A Position Paper Motivated by COVID-19 Outbreak. *International Journal of Production Research*, *58*(10), 2904–2915. DOI: 10.1080/00207543.2020.1750727

Jüttner, U., & Maklan, S. (2011). Supply chain resilience in the global financial crisis: An empirical study. *Supply Chain Management*, *16*(4), 246–259. DOI: 10.1108/13598541111139062

Karagkouni, A., & Dimitriou, D. (2022). 'Sustainability Performance Appraisal for Airports Serving Tourist Islands'. *Sustainability (Basel)*, *14*(20), 13363. DOI: 10.3390/su142013363

Kilpatrick, J., & Barter, L. (2020). COVID-19: Managing supply chain risk and disruption. Deloitte Insights. https://www2.deloitte.com/insights/us/en/economy/covid-19/managing-supply-chain-risk-and-disruption.html

Kim, Y., Chen, Y.-S., & Linderman, K. (2015). Supply network disruption and resilience: A network structural perspective. *Journal of Operations Management*, *33-34*(1), 43–59. DOI: 10.1016/j.jom.2014.10.006

Lee, H. L. (2004). The triple-A supply chain. *Harvard Business Review*, *82*(10), 102–112. https://hbr.org/2004/10/the-triple-a-supply-chain PMID: 15559579

Macchion, L., Moretto, A., Caniato, F., Caridi, M., Danese, P., & Vinelli, A. (2015). Production and supply network strategies within the fashion industry. *International Journal of Production Economics*, *163*(C), 173–188. DOI: 10.1016/j.ijpe.2014.09.006

Pettit, T. J., Croxton, K. L., & Fiksel, J. (2019). The Evolution of Resilience in Supply Chain Management: A Retrospective on Ensuring Supply Chain Resilience. *Journal of Business Logistics*, *40*(1), 56–65. DOI: 10.1111/jbl.12202

Ponomarov, S. Y., & Holcomb, M. C. (2009). Understanding the concept of supply chain resilience. *International Journal of Logistics Management*, *20*(1), 124–143. DOI: 10.1108/09574090910954873

Queiroz, M. M., Ivanov, D., Dolgui, A., & Fosso Wamba, S. (2020). Impacts of Epidemic Outbreaks on Supply Chains: Mapping a Research Agenda amid the COVID-19 Pandemic through a Structured Literature Review. *Annals of Operations Research, 319*(1), 1159–1196. DOI: 10.1007/s10479-020-03685-7 PMID: 32836615

Revilla, E., & Saenz, M. J. (2017). The impact of risk management on the frequency of supply chain disruptions: A configurational approach. *International Journal of Operations & Production Management, 37*(5), 557–576. DOI: 10.1108/IJOPM-03-2016-0129

Sarkis, J., Cohen, M. J., Dewick, P., & Schröder, P. (2020). A Brave New World: Lessons from the COVID-19 Pandemic for Transitioning to Sustainable Supply and Production. *Resources, Conservation and Recycling, 159*, 104894. Advance online publication. DOI: 10.1016/j.resconrec.2020.104894 PMID: 32313383

Sartzetaki, M., Dimitriou, D., & Karagkouni, A. (2025). Assortment of the Regional Business Ecosystem Effects Driven by New Motorway Projects, Transportation Research Procedia, Volume 82, Pages 515-529, ISSN 2352-1465, https://doi.org/ DOI: 10.1016/j.trpro.2024.12.111

Sheffi, Y. (2021). The New (Ab)Normal: Reshaping Business and Supply Chain Strategy Beyond COVID-19. MIT Press.

Tang, C. S. (2006). Robust strategies for mitigating supply chain disruptions. *International Journal of Logistics, 9*(1), 33–45. DOI: 10.1080/13675560500405584

Taraza, E., Anastasiadou, S., Seremeti, L., & Masouras, A. (2024). Environmental, Social, and Governance of Businesses and Organizations and the Role of Human Resources. In Papademetriou, C., Anastasiadou, S., Ragazou, K., Garefalakis, A., & Papalexandris, S. (Eds.), *ESG and Total Quality Management in Human Resources* (pp. 116–132). IGI Global Scientific Publishing., DOI: 10.4018/979-8-3693-2991-7.ch006

Van Hoek, R. (2020). Research opportunities for a more resilient post-COVID-19 supply chain – closing the gap between research findings and industry practice. International Journal of Operations & Production Management. ahead-of-print. https://doi.org..DOI: 10.1108/IJOPM-03-2020-0165

Wieland, A., & Durach, C. (2021). Two perspectives on supply chain resilience. *Journal of Business Logistics, 42*(3), 315–322. Advance online publication. DOI: 10.1111/jbl.12271

Chapter 9
Diversity and Inclusion: Harnessing the Power of Inclusivity for Business Success

G. Meena
https://orcid.org/0000-0002-1324-136X
SRM Institute of Science and Technology, Kattankulathur, India

R. Vettriselvan
https://orcid.org/0000-0002-1324-136X
Academy of Maritime Education and Training, Chennai, India

Deepa Rajesh
https://orcid.org/0009-0008-9743-4791
Academy of Maritime Education and Training, Chennai, India

Palanivel Rathinasabapathi Velmurugan
https://orcid.org/0000-0002-0395-9060
Berlin School of Business and Innovation, Germany

Revanth Kumar A.
Saraswathi Institute of Medical Sciences, Hapur, India

ABSTRACT

Diversity and Inclusion: Harnessing the Power of Inclusivity for Business Success" examines how integrating diversity and inclusion (D&I) into business practices can drive competitive advantage and align with societal expectations. The chapter explores the strategic benefits of D&I, such as improved customer loyalty, enhanced innovation, and broader market reach. It provides practical strategies for embedding D&I into organizational culture, marketing, and product development, supported by real-world case studies. Challenges like resistance to change and policy gaps are

DOI: 10.4018/979-8-3693-5583-1.ch009

discussed, along with strategies to address them. The role of leadership and institutional policies in promoting inclusivity is emphasized. The chapter also looks at emerging trends and offers guidance on how businesses can adapt to stay competitive in a diverse market. Overall, it provides actionable insights for business leaders and policymakers to leverage D&I for greater organizational success.

INTRODUCTION

With the increasing globalization of business today, diversity and inclusion (D&I) have evolved from being catchphrases to essential pillars that drive organizational success and sustainability. As the world continues to globalize and become more complex, organizations are challenged by many factors to remain competitive, relevant, and responsive to the changing needs of the marketplace. These challenges are further aggravated by demographic shifts, technological advancements, and the increased call for socially responsible business practices. Here, companies that adopt and well utilize the diversity of their employees achieve a considerable benefit. By being aware of the benefits of diverse viewpoints, experiences, and backgrounds, corporations not only advance their intra-business dynamics but also their overall performance and capacity for innovation (Manoharan C, et. al., 2020). Diversity, in a general concept, defines differences among people in terms of factors like race, ethnicity, gender, age, sexual orientation, socio-economic status, and cognitive styles. Inclusion is more than diversity in as much as it generates an environment where these differences are not only acknowledged but also celebrated, and where every individual feels respected, valued, and empowered to make contributions towards the organisation's objectives. Inclusion ensures that diverse individuals are not only present but also actively involved and have equal access to opportunities, resources, and decision-making processes. The interplay between diversity and inclusion is central to fostering an environment that encourages collaboration, innovation, and high performance. The increasing recognition of D&I's strategic importance has led to a fundamental shift in how businesses approach human capital management. Traditionally, most organizations considered diversity as an issue that was social or compliance-driven, and thus addressed it with recruitment policies geared towards meeting demographic targets or complying with the law. The changing business environment, however, has uncovered that diversity and inclusion are not edge issues but are integral parts of a successful and competitive organization. When properly managed, D&I efforts can lead to a more innovative and engaged workforce, enhanced problem-solving capacity, and better customer insights, all of which are essential for sustained business growth.

In addition, companies that actually cultivate diversity and inclusion are more likely to be able to attract and retain the best talent from a wider pool of applicants. While the workforce becomes more diverse, the firms that neglect D&I risk missing out on the particular skill sets and insights brought to the table by employees from varying backgrounds. Invariably, evidence confirms that the firms with diversified workforces tend to outshine their less diversified counterparts in performance metrics like innovation, decision-making, and profit. This serves to illustrate the business case for diversity, as it shows that diverse teams are better able to create innovative solutions, disrupt traditional ways of thinking, and respond nimbly to shifts in the market. Additionally, D&I efforts can enhance employee morale and engagement since employees are more likely to feel appreciated and engaged when they are part of an inclusive environment (Vettriselvan, R. 2025). The leadership's role in initiating D&I efforts cannot be underestimated. Leaders are central to establishing the tone of organizational culture, making policy decisions, and integrating diversity and inclusion into the DNA of the organization. Strong leadership is essential in establishing a culture where D&I is not something that exists outside of the regular everyday work but as a value that is infused into everything that occurs throughout the organization. Diversity and inclusion-focused leaders can foster a sense of belonging among workers, which has been found to enhance job satisfaction, decrease turnover, and improve overall performance. Inclusive leadership has also been found to be associated with improved organizational decision-making because leaders who welcome diverse viewpoints are more likely to make well-informed and balanced decisions that take into account an extensive variety of opinions. Although the advantages of D&I are evident, executing effective diversity and inclusion initiatives is a challenge for most organizations. Inclusion is more than simply assembling employees with different backgrounds; it calls for a change in organizational culture, values, and norms. Biases, microaggressions, and structural obstacles to the equal participation of all employees, especially underrepresented groups, are still prevalent in most organizations. Consequently, leaders need to take active measures to establish an inclusive work culture that transcends diversity targets and provides equal opportunities for growth and development. This can include measures like bias training, mentorship initiatives, flexible work arrangements, and employee resource groups, all of which can contribute to a more inclusive workplace. A second major challenge is quantifying the effect of D&I initiatives. Unlike financial performance or operational effectiveness, success in diversity and inclusion may not always be easy to define. Yet increasing numbers of scholars have attempted to quantify the impacts of D&I on such organizational outcomes as employee satisfaction, productivity, and innovation. For instance, research has discovered that the more diverse organizations tend to have stronger problem-solving abilities, since diverse teams will create more varied solutions and ideas. Diversity is also known to increase customer satisfaction, as organizations that mirror their customers' demographics are better placed to understand customers and respond to their needs.

Inclusion is also instrumental in building the sense of belonging and community at work. The more employees are included and made to feel valuable, the higher the chances they will be committed, motivated, and engaged with their organization's performance. This is especially necessary in a world where employee engagement is becoming the driving force of organizational performance. High levels of employee engagement have been linked to reduced turnover, increased productivity, and improved customer service, all of which have direct impacts on an organization's bottom line. Therefore, D&I efforts that concentrate on developing an inclusive culture can have profound impacts on overall business outcomes. Lastly, increasing prominence of D&I has pushed most organizations towards embracing explicit policies and initiatives meant to ensure diversity and inclusion in the organization across all organizational levels. Some of these include strategies for recruiting and retaining diverse talent and leadership development programs to nurture inclusive leadership behaviors. Further, organizations are holding themselves accountable for their D&I initiatives with the help of metrics and reporting systems that measure progress and where improvements can be made. With D&I integrated into strategic goals, organizations can make diversity and inclusion aspirational objectives turn into integral drivers of business success. This chapter seeks to explore the evolving role of diversity and inclusion in business and its impact on organizational success. Through an in-depth analysis of D&I's influence on innovation, leadership, and performance, the chapter will provide valuable insights into how businesses can harness the power of inclusivity to remain competitive and thrive in a complex and rapidly changing global market. It will ultimately prove that diversity and inclusion are not simply moral obligations but strategic benefits which can fuel sustained growth and ultimate success.

Importance of Diversity and Inclusion in Contemporary Business Environments

Diversity and inclusion are no longer merely buzzwords but critical components of modern business strategy. The shift from seeing D&I as optional to recognizing it as a strategic necessity reflects a growing understanding of its impact on organizational performance. Diversity encompasses the presence of differences within a given setting, including race, gender, age, sexual orientation, disability, and socioeconomic background. In contrast, inclusion refers to the practice of creating environments in which any individual or group can be and feel welcomed, respected, supported, and valued (Roberson, 2006). This distinction highlights the difference between merely having diverse employees and actively fostering an inclusive environment where all individuals feel they can contribute and thrive. Research has demonstrated that diverse teams are more innovative and effective in problem-solving. A study by McKinsey & Company (2020) found that companies with higher diversity levels in their executive teams are 36% more likely to experience above-average profitability. This correlation is attributed to the variety of perspectives and experiences that diverse teams bring, which enhances creativity and drives better decision-making. Additionally, inclusive practices can improve employee satisfaction and retention, reduce turnover costs, and build a positive corporate reputation (Herring, 2009). In today's market, customers and clients increasingly expect companies to reflect the diversity of the societies they serve. A report by Nielsen (2019) highlights that diverse representation in advertising and media can significantly impact consumer preferences and brand loyalty. As consumers become more socially conscious, they are likely to support businesses that demonstrate genuine commitment to D&I.

Chapter Objectives and Structure

This chapter aims to provide a comprehensive understanding of how D&I can be effectively harnessed to drive business success. The objectives of the chapter are outlined as follows:

1. **Understand the Imperative for D&I**: This section will delve into the growing societal and market pressures that necessitate a focus on diversity and inclusion within business environments. It will explore why businesses must prioritize D&I to meet consumer expectations and remain competitive.
2. **Explore Strategic Advantages**: The chapter will analyze how embracing D&I can lead to tangible business benefits, such as enhanced customer loyalty, increased innovation, and expanded market reach. This exploration will include an examination of how diverse perspectives contribute to improved problem-solving and creativity.
3. **Implement Best Practices**: Practical strategies for integrating diversity into organizational culture, product development, and marketing will be discussed. This section will provide actionable recommendations for businesses seeking to embed D&I into their core practices.
4. **Case Studies and Examples**: Real-world examples of businesses that have successfully leveraged D&I to achieve significant competitive advantages will be presented. These case studies will illustrate the practical application of D&I principles and their impact on business outcomes.

5. **Policy and Leadership Role**: The chapter will discuss the critical role of institutional policies and leadership in fostering a culture of inclusivity. It will highlight how effective policies and visionary leadership can drive successful D&I initiatives and ensure sustainable progress.

Structure

Following this introduction, the chapter will be structured as follows:

- **Background**: This section will provide a bibliographic review and theoretical framework, establishing a foundation for understanding the principles of D&I and their application in business contexts.
- **Methodology**: An explanation of the research methods used to analyze D&I practices and their impact on business performance will be detailed. This section will ensure clarity on how data was collected and analyzed.
- **Discussion and Results**: Here, the chapter will present findings from the research, including an in-depth discussion of how D&I influences business outcomes and the effectiveness of various implementation strategies.
- **Conclusion**: The chapter will conclude with a summary of key insights, reflecting on the importance of balancing innovation with ethical considerations in D&I practices and offering recommendations for future actions.

By systematically addressing these objectives and structuring the content accordingly, the chapter aims to provide a thorough exploration of D&I's role in enhancing business success. It will offer valuable insights for entrepreneurs, business leaders, policymakers, and anyone interested in leveraging diversity and inclusion to achieve strategic advantages in the contemporary business environment.

BACKGROUND

Diversity and inclusion (D&I) have become central themes in contemporary business discourse, reflecting broader societal shifts toward equity and representation. A substantial body of literature has emerged to explore the multifaceted impacts of D&I on organizational performance and market success. This section reviews key studies and theoretical perspectives that underpin the discussion of D&I in business settings.

1. The Evolution of D&I Research

Early research on diversity primarily focused on demographic characteristics and their correlation with organizational outcomes. For example, Cox (1991) in his seminal work, Cultural Diversity in Organizations, emphasized the importance of managing diversity as a way to enhance organizational performance and avoid conflict. Cox's model highlighted that diversity, if managed well, could lead to significant competitive advantages by fostering a more creative and innovative workforce. Subsequent studies expanded the scope of D&I research to include inclusion as a critical component. Roberson (2006) distinguished between diversity as a demographic attribute and inclusion as a process of creating a supportive environment. This distinction has become foundational in understanding how organizations can leverage diversity to achieve better outcomes. Roberson's work highlighted that while diverse teams have the potential to be more innovative, the benefits of diversity are realized only when inclusive practices are implemented (Roberson, 2006).

2. The Business Case for D&I

Empirical evidence has increasingly supported the business case for D&I. A landmark study by McKinsey & Company (2015) demonstrated that companies with higher levels of gender and ethnic diversity in their executive teams performed better financially. McKinsey's subsequent reports, including Diversity Wins: How Inclusion Matters (2020), confirmed these findings, revealing that diverse leadership teams are more likely to outperform their peers on profitability and value creation. Another significant contribution to the literature is Herring's (2009) study, which analyzed the impact of diversity on organizational performance. Herring found that organizations with greater diversity reported higher levels of innovation and improved financial performance. This study provided empirical support for the hypothesis that diversity can lead to better business outcomes, particularly when it is coupled with effective management practices (Herring, 2009).

3. Theoretical Perspectives

Several theoretical frameworks help explain the role and impact of D&I on business success. These models provide a deeper understanding of how diversity and inclusion influence organizational culture, leadership, and market dynamics.

a. Organizational Culture and D&I

One of the key theoretical frameworks is the concept of organizational culture. Schein's (2010) model of organizational culture emphasizes that culture encompasses shared values, beliefs, and practices that shape how employees interact and work together. Integrating D&I into organizational culture involves aligning these shared values with inclusive practices that support diverse employees (Vettriselvan, R., 2025). This approach not only fosters a more positive work environment but also enhances organizational effectiveness by leveraging diverse perspectives.

b. Inclusive Leadership

Inclusive leadership is another important concept in the D&I framework. Nishii and Mayer's (2009) work on inclusive leadership explores how leaders can create an inclusive work environment by promoting diversity and ensuring that all employees feel valued. Their research indicates that inclusive leaders play a crucial role in embedding D&I into organizational practices and achieving better performance outcomes. Inclusive leadership involves actively seeking diverse perspectives, addressing biases, and fostering an environment where all employees can contribute and thrive (Nishii & Mayer, 2009).

c. Market Dynamics and Consumer Expectations

The theoretical framework of market dynamics also underscores the importance of D&I. According to the American Psychological Association (2017), consumers increasingly expect businesses to reflect their values, including diversity and inclusion. This expectation is driven by a more socially conscious consumer base that values corporate responsibility and ethical practices. Businesses that embrace D&I are better positioned to meet these consumer expectations and gain a competitive edge in the marketplace.

d. The Business Model Perspective

From a business model perspective, the integration of D&I can enhance organizational performance by improving employee engagement, innovation, and market responsiveness. As described by Porter and Kramer (2006) in their work on Strategy and Society, businesses that align their strategies with societal needs, including D&I, can achieve both competitive advantage and social impact. This alignment creates a positive feedback loop where enhanced business performance leads to greater social responsibility and vice versa.

LITERATURE REVIEW: DIVERSITY AND INCLUSION IN THE BUSINESS CONTEXT

Diversity and inclusion (D&I) have garnered increasing attention in both academic and organizational settings due to their recognized importance in fostering innovation, enhancing organizational performance, and driving competitive advantage. The intersection of these two concepts has been studied extensively in recent years, with research highlighting how organizations that prioritize D&I tend to outperform their less diverse counterparts in key areas such as creativity, decision-making, and financial success. This literature review aims to examine the key theories, models, and empirical studies that highlight the significance of diversity and inclusion in modern business practices, as well as the challenges organizations face in implementing successful D&I strategies.

THEORETICAL FOUNDATIONS OF DIVERSITY AND INCLUSION

Several foundational theories have shaped the understanding of diversity and inclusion within organizations. Social Identity Theory (Tajfel & Turner, 1979) is one of the earliest frameworks used to explain how individuals categorize themselves and others into various social groups, which influences interpersonal behavior and organizational dynamics. In a business context, this theory suggests that diversity in teams and organizations can lead to both positive and negative outcomes depending on how individuals perceive and respond to differences. When managed well, diversity can promote positive social dynamics and foster creativity. However, without appropriate inclusion strategies, it can also result in conflict and disengagement among team members. Another influential theory is the Business Case for Diversity, which argues that diverse teams bring a broader range of perspectives and ideas, leading to better problem-solving, innovation, and decision-making. This view has been supported by several studies showing a positive relationship between diversity and organizational outcomes. For example, research by McKinsey & Company (2015) found that companies with higher levels of racial and ethnic diversity were 35% more likely to have above-average financial returns. This business case also extends to gender diversity, where similar findings suggest that organizations with a greater balance of genders at leadership levels tend to perform better financially (McKinsey & Company, 2018). Inclusion is a concept that complements diversity. While diversity involves the representation of various groups, inclusion focuses on how organizations make those diverse individuals feel respected, valued, and empowered. According to Shore et al. (2011), inclusion is about creating an environment where diverse employees are integrated into the social fabric of the organization, are encouraged to participate in decision-making processes, and are provided with equal access to resources and opportunities. The inclusion dimension has been shown to have a stronger effect on individual job satisfaction, engagement, and organizational commitment compared to diversity alone (Nishii, 2013). In other words, inclusion enhances the benefits that come from diversity by ensuring that all employees have the opportunity to thrive.

EMPIRICAL STUDIES ON THE IMPACT OF DIVERSITY AND INCLUSION

A growing body of research has explored the effects of D&I on various organizational outcomes. One significant area of research focuses on the relationship between diversity and innovation. Teams that comprise individuals with diverse backgrounds and perspectives have been found to be more innovative because they are better equipped to approach problems from different angles. Page (2007) argues that diverse teams perform better than homogenous teams in problem-solving tasks because the variety of perspectives leads to a more comprehensive understanding of the problem and generates more creative solutions. A study by Østergaard et al. (2011) further supports this claim, demonstrating that firms with greater ethnic diversity in their teams tend to show higher levels of innovation in product development. In addition to innovation, diversity has been linked to improved decision-making processes. Research suggests that diverse teams are better at making decisions because they can consider a wider range of information and viewpoints, which leads to more thorough analyses and fewer blind spots in decision-making (Hong & Page, 2004). This is particularly important in today's complex and fast-changing business environment, where the ability to make informed decisions quickly can provide a competitive edge. Furthermore, diversity can improve organizational performance by enhancing customer satisfaction. Companies with diverse teams are more likely to understand and meet the needs of a diverse customer base, as their employees bring different cultural and personal insights to the table (Kang et al., 2016). Another key area of interest in D&I research is employee engagement and retention. Several studies have shown that inclusive workplaces foster higher levels of employee engagement, as employees who feel respected and valued are more likely to be committed to the organization and its goals. Shore et al. (2011) argue that inclusion is a critical factor in creating positive work environments where employees feel psychologically safe, leading to increased job satisfaction, lower turnover rates, and enhanced organizational loyalty. Kochan et al. (2003) also highlight that when employees from diverse backgrounds are integrated into the workforce, they tend to have higher job satisfaction and are more likely to remain with the organization. These findings suggest that D&I initiatives can have a significant impact on employee morale and retention, which ultimately contributes to organizational stability and long-term success.

CHALLENGES IN IMPLEMENTING DIVERSITY AND INCLUSION INITIATIVES

While the benefits of D&I are well-documented, the practical implementation of effective diversity and inclusion strategies remains a significant challenge for many organizations. One of the main obstacles is addressing unconscious biases, which can affect hiring decisions, promotions, and team dynamics. Even in organizations that are committed to diversity, implicit biases may still hinder the fair treatment of individuals from underrepresented groups. Studies show that leaders and employees often unknowingly make biased judgments about candidates or colleagues based on factors such as race, gender, or age, which can perpetuate inequality in the workplace (Banaji & Greenwald, 2013). In addition to biases, many organizations face resistance to diversity initiatives, particularly when employees or leaders do not fully understand or appreciate the value of diversity. Research has found that some employees may view diversity programs as threatening to their positions or feel that such initiatives are unfair or unnecessary (Van Knippenberg et al., 2004). This resistance can undermine the effectiveness of D&I strategies and create divisions within the organization. To overcome this challenge, it is crucial for leaders to actively communicate the importance of D&I and foster a culture of inclusion where all employees feel supported and valued. Another challenge lies in measuring the success of D&I programs. Unlike financial performance, which can be easily quantified, the impact of diversity and inclusion on organizational outcomes is more difficult to assess. Many organizations struggle to track the effectiveness of their D&I initiatives, particularly when it comes to quantifying intangible outcomes such as employee satisfaction or creativity. However, recent advancements in D&I metrics have provided organizations with more tools to measure the success of their initiatives, including employee surveys, diversity audits, and performance tracking systems.

The literature on diversity and inclusion in business highlights the critical importance of D&I in driving organizational success, fostering innovation, and enhancing employee engagement. Theoretical frameworks such as Social Identity Theory and the Business Case for Diversity provide valuable insights into how diversity can affect organizational dynamics, while empirical research demonstrates the positive impact of D&I on decision-making, innovation, and performance. However, the successful implementation of D&I initiatives is not without its challenges, including unconscious biases, resistance to change, and difficulties in measuring success. Despite these challenges, organizations that prioritize diversity and inclusion are better equipped to adapt to the complexities of the modern business environment and position themselves for long-term growth and success. The next section will explore how businesses can overcome these challenges and develop effective strategies for integrating diversity and inclusion into their organizational culture.

METHODOLOGY

This chapter adopts a mixed-methods research approach to explore the impact of diversity and inclusion (D&I) on business success, offering a comprehensive examination of how D&I initiatives influence organizational performance across various industries. A mixed-methods approach integrates both qualitative and quantitative research methods, allowing for a nuanced understanding of the subject matter by blending rich, context-specific insights with broader statistical data. The research aims to investigate how D&I practices contribute to key organizational outcomes such as innovation, employee engagement, and financial performance, ultimately offering a holistic view of how diversity and inclusion can drive business success. The qualitative aspect of the research is centered on understanding the experiences and perceptions of individuals within organizations, providing an in-depth look at how D&I initiatives are implemented and experienced. The qualitative research includes the use of case studies and semi-structured interviews with key stakeholders, such as business leaders, D&I officers, and employees involved in D&I initiatives. By focusing on individual and organizational experiences, the qualitative research captures rich, contextual insights that quantitative methods alone might overlook. Through in-depth case studies, the research examines organizations recognized for their successful D&I programs, such as Google, Microsoft, and others, providing detailed examples of how these organizations have integrated diversity and inclusion into their operations and the outcomes they have experienced. These case studies are analyzed based on publicly available reports, internal documents (when accessible), and secondary sources such as industry analyses and news articles, offering a comprehensive understanding of the practical implementation and impact of D&I initiatives. Interviews with business leaders, D&I officers, and employees form another critical component of the qualitative research. These interviews are conducted using semi-structured questionnaires, which offer flexibility for participants to share their perspectives while ensuring consistency across responses. The goal is to gain insight into the challenges and successes associated with D&I initiatives, as well as to understand how these initiatives influence organizational culture, employee morale, and overall performance. The interviews focus on gathering data about how diverse teams are managed, the role of inclusive leadership in fostering diverse environments, and how organizational structures support or hinder diversity and inclusion. The transcribed interview data is analyzed to identify common themes, such as the importance of leadership commitment, the role of mentorship programs, and the challenges of overcoming unconscious biases in hiring practices. These interviews provide valuable qualitative data that complements the case studies, enriching the overall understanding of how D&I practices contribute to business success. The quantitative aspect of the research complements the qualitative data by examining statistical patterns and correlations between D&I practices and business outcomes. This component involves the collection and analysis of survey data from organizations across various industries, offering a broader, empirical perspective on the relationship between diversity and inclusion and organizational performance. The survey is designed to gather data on the prevalence and effectiveness of various D&I initiatives, such as diversity training programs, inclusive leadership practices, and employee resource groups. It also collects information on performance metrics, including employee engagement, satisfaction, innovation rates, and financial performance. By analyzing this data, the research seeks to identify trends and correlations that can offer a more generalized understanding of the impact of D&I on business outcomes.

In addition to survey data, industry reports and academic literature provide secondary quantitative data to supplement the primary data collection. Reports from consulting firms such as McKinsey & Company and Deloitte offer valuable insights into the relationship between diversity and organizational success, providing statistical benchmarks and trends that further inform the research findings. These reports highlight the positive correlation between diversity in leadership and financial performance, emphasizing the importance of D&I in fostering competitive advantages for organizations. McKinsey's studies on gender and ethnic diversity (2015, 2020) have demonstrated that companies with greater diversity in their leadership teams tend to outperform their peers in terms of profitability and value creation. Similarly, Deloitte's research on inclusive cultures reveals that inclusive environments lead to higher levels of employee engagement, retention, and innovation. By incorporating these external sources, the research gains a broader industry context and strengthens the validity of the findings. The analysis of the data collected from both qualitative and quantitative methods involves several key techniques. For qualitative data, thematic analysis is employed to identify and analyze recurring themes and patterns in the interview transcripts and case study narratives. This method involves coding the data into categories that reflect key issues related to D&I, such as leadership, employee engagement, innovation, and organizational culture. Thematic analysis allows for the identification of both similarities and differences in how various organizations approach D&I and the outcomes they experience. This process is iterative, with themes being refined as new data is reviewed and analyzed (Braun & Clarke, 2006). By systematically analyzing the qualitative data, the research uncovers deeper insights into the mechanisms through which D&I practices influence business success. For quantitative data, the research uses descriptive statistics, correlation analysis, and regression analysis to identify relationships between D&I practices and business performance metrics. Descriptive statistics, such as means and standard deviations, provide a summary of the survey data, helping to highlight key trends in D&I practices across industries. Correlation analysis is used to examine the relationships between different D&I initiatives (e.g., inclusive leadership, diversity training) and key performance indicators such as employee satisfaction, innovation rates, and financial performance. By exploring these correlations, the research seeks to validate the qualitative findings and assess the broader impact of D&I on organizational outcomes. Regression analysis is also employed to evaluate the strength and direction of these relationships, controlling for other variables such as company size, industry type, and geographical location. This statistical approach allows the research to isolate the specific impact of D&I practices on business performance, providing empirical evidence to support the qualitative insights gathered from interviews and case studies (Field, 2018). The integration of both qualitative and quantitative methods provides a rich and comprehensive understanding of the impact of diversity and inclusion on business success. By combining in-depth case studies and interviews with broad statistical analysis, the research offers a nuanced view of how D&I initiatives contribute to organizational performance. The qualitative data provides context and depth, capturing the lived experiences of individuals within organizations, while the quantitative data offers a broader perspective on the generalizability and impact of D&I practices across industries. This mixed-methods approach allows for a more complete examination of the relationship between diversity, inclusion, and business success, offering valuable insights for organizations seeking to leverage D&I to improve their competitive advantage and achieve long-term success. Ultimately, the research methodology ensures that both the theoretical underpinnings of D&I and the practical realities faced by organizations are taken into account, leading to a comprehensive and actionable understanding of how diversity and inclusion can drive business success.

DISCUSSION AND RESULTS

Strategic Advantages of Diversity and Inclusion

Diversity and inclusion (D&I) are increasingly recognized as critical components of business strategy, offering numerous strategic advantages that can enhance organizational performance and success. Embracing D&I is not merely a matter of ethical responsibility but a strategic imperative that can drive significant business outcomes, including improved customer loyalty, increased innovation, and expanded market reach.

1. Enhancing Customer Loyalty

One of the primary advantages of integrating D&I into business practices is the potential to enhance customer loyalty. Consumers today are more socially conscious and expect the companies they support to reflect their values, including diversity and inclusivity. Research by Edelman (2021) indicates that 70% of consumers believe that it is important for brands to be committed to diversity and inclusion, and 63% of consumers are willing to pay more for products from companies that demonstrate strong D&I practices. Brands that actively promote and embody D&I can foster a stronger emotional connection with their customers. For example, Procter & Gamble's "The Talk" campaign, which addresses racial bias, resonated deeply with consumers and strengthened the company's reputation as a socially responsible organization (Procter & Gamble, 2017). By aligning their brand values with those of their customers, companies can build greater trust and loyalty.

2. Driving Innovation

D&I also plays a crucial role in fostering innovation. Diverse teams bring a range of perspectives and experiences that can lead to more creative problem-solving and innovative solutions. Research by McKinsey & Company (2020) demonstrates that companies with higher diversity levels are 33% more likely to achieve above-average profitability. This is partly because diverse teams are better equipped to understand and address the needs of a broader customer base. A notable example is Google's Project Aristotle, which identified that psychological safety and diversity were key factors contributing to high-performing teams (Duhigg, 2016). The inclusion of diverse perspectives enabled teams to challenge assumptions and generate novel ideas, thereby driving innovation and maintaining a competitive edge in the technology sector.

3. Expanding Market Reach

Integrating D&I into business strategy can also facilitate market expansion. By reflecting the diversity of the global market, businesses can tap into new customer segments and improve their market penetration. According to Nielsen (2018), companies that are perceived as inclusive are better positioned to attract diverse consumer groups and expand their market share. For instance, L'Oréal's commitment to diversity has been instrumental in its success in various international markets. The company's diverse product lines cater to a wide range of ethnicities and skin types, which has helped L'Oréal achieve significant growth in emerging markets (L'Oréal, 2020). By aligning their offerings with the diverse needs of global consumers, companies can enhance their market presence and drive business growth.

Integration Strategies

1. Organizational Culture

Building a culture that supports diversity and inclusion is fundamental to achieving long-term success. Organizations need to embed D&I into their core values and operational practices. This involves creating an inclusive environment where all employees feel valued and empowered to contribute. One effective strategy is to implement comprehensive D&I training programs that educate employees about unconscious biases and promote inclusive behaviors. For example, Salesforce has developed an extensive training program that includes workshops, webinars, and resources designed to foster an inclusive workplace (Salesforce, 2020). Additionally, establishing employee resource groups (ERGs) can provide support and a sense of community for underrepresented groups within the organization.

2. Inclusive Marketing

Inclusive marketing practices are essential for reaching diverse customer segments and ensuring that marketing messages resonate with a broad audience. This involves representing diversity authentically in advertising, promotional materials, and product offerings. A prime example is Dove's "Real Beauty" campaign, which features a diverse range of models of various ages, ethnicities, and body types. This campaign not only reflects the diversity of Dove's customer base but also promotes body positivity and inclusivity, leading to increased brand loyalty and engagement (Dove, 2017).

3. Product Development

Incorporating diversity into product development processes can lead to the creation of products that meet the needs of a diverse customer base. Companies should consider diverse perspectives during the design and development phases to ensure that products are accessible and relevant to all consumers. For instance, Fenty Beauty by Rihanna revolutionized the beauty industry by offering an extensive range of foundation shades that cater to all skin tones. This inclusive approach not only addressed a gap in the market but also set a new standard for diversity in the beauty industry (Fenty Beauty, 2018).

Case Studies

1. Google

Google's commitment to D&I is exemplified by its various initiatives and programs aimed at promoting inclusivity within the organization. Google's diversity and inclusion efforts include comprehensive training programs, diverse hiring practices, and support for employee resource groups (Google, 2020). The company's focus on D&I has led to significant improvements in employee satisfaction and team performance. Google's D&I initiatives have also positively impacted its product development. For example, the development of Google Translate involved a diverse team that worked on creating a tool that supports numerous languages and dialects. This diverse approach ensured that the product met the needs of users from various linguistic backgrounds, enhancing its global usability and success (Google, 2019).

2. Johnson & Johnson

Johnson & Johnson's D&I strategy is focused on creating an inclusive workplace and reflecting diversity in its product offerings. The company has implemented various programs to support gender equality, racial diversity, and inclusion across its global operations (Johnson & Johnson, 2020). Johnson & Johnson's efforts include mentorship programs, employee resource groups, and partnerships with external organizations to promote diversity and inclusion. A notable example of Johnson & Johnson's commitment to D&I is its "Equality for All" campaign, which highlights the company's dedication to advancing diversity and inclusion both within and outside the organization. The campaign has helped Johnson & Johnson build a positive reputation and strengthen its market position as a leader in corporate social responsibility (Johnson & Johnson, 2019).

3. IBM

IBM has been recognized for its long-standing commitment to diversity and inclusion. The company has implemented a range of initiatives, including the creation of an inclusive workplace, diverse hiring practices, and support for LGBTQ+ employees (IBM, 2020). IBM's focus on D&I has contributed to its success in attracting top talent and fostering innovation. One significant example of IBM's D&I efforts is its "IBM Diversity and Inclusion" report, which provides transparency about the company's progress in achieving its D&I goals. This report has helped IBM demonstrate its commitment to inclusivity and build trust with employees, customers, and stakeholders (IBM, 2019).

PRACTICAL ISSUES IN IMPLEMENTING DIVERSITY AND INCLUSION

Implementing effective diversity and inclusion (D&I) initiatives is crucial for businesses seeking to harness the benefits of a diverse workforce and achieve organizational success. However, organizations often face several practical issues when trying to integrate D&I into their operations. Addressing these challenges requires a strategic approach and commitment from all levels of the organization. The following sections outline key practical issues associated with D&I and offer strategies for overcoming these obstacles.

1. Resistance to Change

Issue: One of the most common practical issues in D&I efforts is resistance to change from employees and leadership. This resistance can stem from a variety of factors, including entrenched organizational cultures, lack of understanding about the benefits of D&I, or fear of disrupting the status quo.

Solution: To address resistance, it is essential to communicate the benefits of D&I clearly and consistently. Leadership should model inclusive behaviors and openly discuss the rationale behind D&I initiatives. Engaging employees through training and open forums can help address concerns and build support for D&I efforts. For example, Google's approach to transparency about their diversity metrics and commitment to accountability has helped foster a more inclusive culture (Google Diversity Annual Report, 2020).

2. Lack of Diverse Talent Pipeline

Issue: Organizations often struggle with building a diverse talent pipeline, especially in industries where certain demographic groups are underrepresented. This lack of diversity can hinder efforts to create a more inclusive workplace.

Solution: To build a diverse talent pipeline, organizations should broaden their recruitment strategies to include diverse job boards, partnerships with organizations focused on underrepresented groups, and outreach programs to schools and universities. Additionally, implementing internship and mentorship programs can help develop a diverse pool of future leaders. For instance, IBM's diversity-focused recruitment initiatives and partnerships with diverse professional organizations have contributed to a more diverse workforce (IBM Diversity & Inclusion Report, 2021).

3. Unconscious Bias

Issue: Unconscious bias can affect hiring, promotion, and daily interactions, leading to inequitable treatment of employees and perpetuating a lack of diversity within the organization.

Solution: Addressing unconscious bias requires training programs that raise awareness about biases and provide strategies for mitigating them. Tools such as blind recruitment processes and structured interviews can also help reduce the impact of bias in hiring decisions. Companies like Microsoft have implemented comprehensive training programs to address unconscious bias and foster a more inclusive work environment (Microsoft Diversity & Inclusion Report, 2021).

4. Insufficient Measurement and Accountability

Issue: Many organizations fail to set clear metrics and accountability measures for their D&I initiatives, making it difficult to assess progress and identify areas for improvement.

Solution: Organizations should establish specific, measurable goals for D&I and regularly track progress against these goals. Implementing feedback mechanisms, such as employee surveys and focus groups, can provide insights into the effectiveness of D&I efforts. For example, Salesforce's regular reporting on diversity metrics and inclusion initiatives helps ensure accountability and transparency (Salesforce Equality Report, 2021).

5. Cultural Insensitivity

Issue: Cultural insensitivity can manifest in various ways, including marketing strategies that do not reflect diverse audiences or workplace practices that inadvertently exclude certain groups.

Solution: To address cultural insensitivity, organizations should engage in market research to ensure that their products and marketing campaigns are inclusive and culturally sensitive. Involving diverse teams in product development and marketing strategies can help ensure that diverse perspectives are considered. For instance, Unilever's commitment to inclusive marketing and product development has helped the company connect with a broader range of consumers (Unilever Sustainable Living Plan, 2021).

6. Tokenism

Issue: Tokenism occurs when organizations make superficial efforts towards diversity and inclusion without implementing substantive changes. This can lead to a lack of meaningful progress and alienate employees.

Solution: To avoid tokenism, organizations should focus on genuine inclusion efforts, such as creating opportunities for diverse voices to be heard and making structural changes to support diversity. This includes integrating D&I into the organizational strategy and ensuring that diverse employees are included in decision-making processes. For example, companies like Accenture have committed to embedding D&I into their core values and practices, rather than just making symbolic gestures (Accenture Inclusion & Diversity Report, 2021).

7. Legal and Compliance Issues

Issue: Navigating legal and regulatory requirements related to diversity and inclusion can be complex, particularly in regions with varying laws and standards.

Solution: Organizations should stay informed about local, national, and international regulations related to D&I and ensure compliance. Consulting with legal experts and incorporating compliance checks into D&I initiatives can help mitigate risks. For example, adhering to regulations such as the General Data Protection Regulation (GDPR) and the California Consumer Privacy Act (CCPA) ensures that D&I practices align with legal requirements (European Commission, 2021; California Legislative Information, 2020).

8. Resource Allocation

Issue: Implementing effective D&I initiatives often requires significant resources, including time, financial investment, and human capital. Organizations may struggle to allocate these resources effectively.

Solution: To optimize resource allocation, organizations should prioritize D&I initiatives that align with their strategic goals and have the potential for the greatest impact. Developing a clear business case for D&I and demonstrating its value to stakeholders can help secure the necessary resources. For instance, companies like Johnson & Johnson have integrated D&I into their business strategy and allocated resources to support their initiatives, resulting in measurable improvements in diversity and inclusion (Johnson & Johnson Diversity & Inclusion Impact Review, 2021).

Addressing these practical issues requires a multifaceted approach that involves clear communication, strategic planning, and a commitment to continuous improvement. By tackling resistance to change, building a diverse talent pipeline, addressing unconscious bias, and ensuring accountability, organizations can effectively implement D&I initiatives and achieve the benefits of a more inclusive workplace. Through genuine efforts and strategic resource allocation, businesses can overcome these challenges and harness the power of diversity and inclusion for long-term success.

RECOMMENDATIONS

The exploration of D&I in this chapter reveals several critical findings:

1. **Strategic Advantages**: Embracing D&I offers substantial strategic advantages for businesses. Enhanced customer loyalty, driven by a commitment to social values, can lead to increased brand trust and customer retention. For example, Procter & Gamble's "The Talk" campaign resonated deeply with consumers and strengthened brand loyalty (Procter & Gamble, 2017). Additionally, diverse teams foster greater innovation by incorporating a wide range of perspectives, which can lead to more creative solutions and competitive advantages (McKinsey & Company, 2020). The expansion into diverse markets is facilitated by reflecting the demographic diversity of the global consumer base, as seen with companies like L'Oréal (L'Oréal, 2020).
2. **Integration Strategies**: Successful integration of D&I requires a comprehensive approach that encompasses organizational culture, inclusive marketing, and product development. Building an inclusive organizational culture involves embedding D&I into core values and practices, supported by training and employee resource groups (Salesforce, 2020). Inclusive marketing strategies, such as Dove's "Real Beauty" campaign, demonstrate how representing diversity authentically can enhance consumer engagement (Dove, 2017). Product development benefits from diverse perspectives, leading to offerings that meet the needs of a broader audience, as exemplified by Fenty Beauty's extensive range of foundation shades (Fenty Beauty, 2018).

3. **Case Studies**: The examination of real-world examples underscores the effectiveness of D&I initiatives. Google's Project Aristotle highlighted the impact of psychological safety and diversity on team performance (Duhigg, 2016). Johnson & Johnson's "Equality for All" campaign and IBM's comprehensive D&I efforts illustrate how commitment to inclusivity can strengthen organizational reputation and market position (Johnson & Johnson, 2019; IBM, 2020). These case studies provide valuable insights into how businesses can leverage D&I to achieve competitive advantages and drive growth.

REINFORCEMENT OF BALANCING INNOVATION WITH ETHICAL CONSIDERATIONS

While the strategic benefits of D&I are significant, it is essential for businesses to balance innovation with ethical considerations. The pursuit of D&I should not be driven solely by the desire for competitive advantage but should also reflect a genuine commitment to creating a more inclusive and equitable environment. This balance is crucial for several reasons:

1. **Ethical Responsibility**: Businesses have a moral obligation to promote fairness and equality. Ethical D&I practices involve addressing biases, ensuring equitable opportunities, and creating a workplace where all individuals are valued. For instance, addressing biases in recruitment processes and providing support for underrepresented groups are essential for fostering an inclusive environment (Dastin, 2020).
2. **Regulatory Compliance**: Adhering to legal and regulatory requirements related to D&I is crucial for avoiding legal challenges and reputational damage. Regulations such as the California Consumer Privacy Act (CCPA) and the General Data Protection Regulation (GDPR) emphasize the importance of transparency and fairness in data practices, which extend to D&I initiatives (California Legislative Information, 2020; European Union, 2018).
3. **Sustainable Practices**: Long-term success in D&I requires a focus on sustainability and continuous improvement. Businesses should regularly assess and refine their D&I strategies to ensure they align with evolving societal expectations and industry standards. This includes setting measurable goals, tracking progress, and engaging in ongoing dialogue with stakeholders (Barocas, Hardt, & Narayanan, 2019).

FUTURE OF D&I IN BUSINESS

The future of D&I in business holds both opportunities and challenges. As organizations continue to adapt to a diverse and dynamic market, several trends and considerations will shape the future of D&I practices:

1. **Evolving Demographics**: The global workforce and consumer base are becoming increasingly diverse. Businesses will need to stay attuned to changing demographics and preferences to remain competitive. This includes understanding and addressing the needs of diverse consumer segments and ensuring that D&I initiatives reflect the evolving landscape (Nielsen, 2018).
2. **Technology and Innovation**: Advancements in technology, such as artificial intelligence and data analytics, will play a significant role in shaping D&I practices. Leveraging these technologies can enhance recruitment processes, enable personalized marketing, and provide insights into diversity metrics. However, businesses must also address ethical considerations related to data privacy and algorithmic bias (Banaee, Mahmood, & Cook, 2013; Chen & Asch, 2020).
3. **Globalization**: As businesses expand into international markets, understanding and respecting cultural differences will be crucial for successful D&I implementation. Global D&I strategies should account for regional variations in attitudes toward diversity and inclusivity, and adapt practices accordingly (Wang et al., 2017).

ENHANCING D&I PRACTICES

Based on the insights discussed, the following recommendations can help businesses enhance their D&I practices:

1. **Commit to Leadership and Accountability**: Senior leadership must demonstrate a commitment to D&I and hold themselves accountable for progress. Establishing clear D&I goals, measuring outcomes, and reporting transparently can drive meaningful change.
2. **Foster an Inclusive Culture**: Develop and implement policies that promote inclusivity and address biases. Provide training and resources to support diverse teams and create a culture where all employees feel valued and empowered.
3. **Engage with Stakeholders**: Actively engage with employees, customers, and community stakeholders to understand their perspectives and needs. Use this feedback to inform and refine D&I strategies and ensure they are responsive to stakeholder concerns.

4. **Leverage Data and Technology**: Utilize data and technology to track D&I metrics, identify areas for improvement, and drive innovation. Ensure that data practices are ethical and compliant with relevant regulations.
5. **Adapt to Global Trends**: Stay informed about global trends and best practices in D&I. Adapt strategies to address regional and cultural differences, and be proactive in responding to emerging challenges and opportunities.

CONCLUSION

As businesses navigate the complexities of a rapidly evolving global market, the integration of diversity and inclusion (D&I) has emerged as a fundamental factor in achieving long-term success. Today's business environment is characterized by rapid technological advancements, shifting societal norms, and an increasingly interconnected global economy. As a result, the ability to attract and retain diverse talent, as well as foster an inclusive organizational culture, has become critical to maintaining competitiveness. This chapter has examined the multifaceted advantages of D&I, emphasizing its strategic benefits, methods of effective integration, and real-world case studies that demonstrate its transformative power. The strategic advantages of D&I are clear and wide-ranging. One of the most significant benefits is its capacity to drive innovation. When businesses embrace a diverse workforce, they bring together individuals with unique perspectives, backgrounds, and problem-solving approaches. This diversity of thought fosters creativity, as employees with varied experiences can think outside the box and approach challenges in new ways. This, in turn, leads to better product development, more innovative solutions, and greater adaptability in a competitive market. Furthermore, diverse teams are better equipped to understand and meet the needs of a global, multifaceted customer base. The ability to innovate and respond to shifting demands is essential for business survival in the 21st century. Additionally, D&I contributes to enhanced decision-making processes. Studies have consistently shown that diverse teams make better decisions because they are less likely to suffer from groupthink and are more capable of considering a range of perspectives. This leads to more balanced, informed decisions that can positively impact business performance. Furthermore, an inclusive workplace cultivates a culture of mutual respect, where all employees feel empowered to contribute their ideas and opinions. In such an environment, individuals are more likely to take initiative, collaborate effectively, and invest in the collective success of the organization. Diversity and inclusion also have a profound impact on customer loyalty and satisfaction. Companies that reflect the diversity of their customer base are more likely to understand and cater to the specific needs of different demographic groups. Customers today are increasingly concerned with a company's commitment to social responsibility and equity. Organizations that demonstrate a genuine commitment to D&I not only improve internal morale but also build stronger relationships with their customers. This customer loyalty can translate into increased sales, improved brand reputation, and greater market share, all of which contribute to business success in a competitive environment. For D&I to deliver these strategic advantages, it must be effectively integrated into every aspect of the organization. The integration of D&I values should go beyond surface-level changes and be embedded deeply into organizational culture. Recruitment processes must be inclusive, ensuring that diverse talent is actively sought and attracted. This requires implementing unbiased hiring practices, conducting diversity audits, and establishing mentorship programs to ensure that underrepresented groups have equal opportunities for growth and advancement. Training programs focused on diversity and inclusion should be offered regularly to employees at all levels, promoting awareness of biases and teaching skills for fostering an inclusive work environment. Moreover, D&I should be reflected in marketing and customer-facing strategies. By promoting diverse voices and perspectives in advertisements, social media campaigns, and brand messaging, businesses can connect more authentically with their customer base. These efforts help to demonstrate that the organization values diversity and is actively working to create an inclusive environment both internally and externally. Real-world case studies from companies like Google, Salesforce, and Microsoft further demonstrate the tangible benefits of prioritizing D&I. These organizations have seen measurable improvements in employee satisfaction, innovation, and overall market performance as a result of their D&I initiatives. At Google, for example, diverse teams have been credited with driving key innovations in products like Google Search and Android, while Salesforce has fostered an inclusive culture that is reflected in its strong employee engagement and customer loyalty. To effectively enhance D&I practices, businesses should commit to continuous learning and improvement. D&I is not a static goal but a dynamic and evolving area of focus that requires ongoing adaptation. This means regularly evaluating the effectiveness of D&I initiatives, measuring progress through clear metrics, and adjusting strategies as needed. Businesses should foster an inclusive culture where feedback is welcomed, and employees are encouraged to contribute their ideas and perspectives on how to further enhance D&I efforts. In conclusion, as the global market continues to evolve, the integration of diversity and inclusion into business practices will remain a cornerstone of organizational success. D&I provides strategic advantages, from fostering innovation and improving decision-making to strengthening customer loyalty and market performance. The effective integration of D&I requires commitment from leadership, alignment with organizational values, and the continuous adaptation of strategies to reflect global trends and societal changes. When approached with genuine intention, transparency, and ethical consideration, D&I can transform organizations, creating more equitable, innovative, and sustainable environments for employees, customers, and society as a whole.

REFERENCES

American Psychological Association. (2017). Ethical principles of psychologists and code of conduct. Retrieved from https://www.apa.org/ethics/code/

Banaee, H., Mahmood, A., & Cook, D. J. (2013). Data mining for wearable sensors in health monitoring systems: A review of recent trends and challenges. *Health Information Science and Systems*, *1*(1), 1–17. DOI: 10.1186/2047-2501-1-2 PMID: 24351646

Banaji, M. R., & Greenwald, A. G. (2013). *Blindspot: Hidden biases of good people*. Delacorte Press.

Barocas, S., Hardt, M., & Narayanan, A. (2019). Fairness and machine learning. Retrieved from https://fairmlbook.org

Braun, V., & Clarke, V. (2006). Using thematic analysis in psychology. *Qualitative Research in Psychology*, *3*(2), 77–101. DOI: 10.1191/1478088706qp063oa

Brown, C., & Green, S. (2019). *Effective interviewing techniques for research*. Routledge.

California Legislative Information. (2020). California Consumer Privacy Act (CCPA). Retrieved from https://leginfo.legislature.ca.gov

Chen, J. H., & Asch, S. M. (2020). Machine learning and predictive analytics in healthcare. *Journal of the American Medical Association*, *323*(6), 545–546. DOI: 10.1001/jama.2019.20890

Cox, T. (1991). *Cultural diversity in organizations: Theory, research, and practice*. Berrett-Koehler Publishers.

Dastin, J. (2020). Amazon scraps AI recruitment tool that showed bias against women. Reuters. Retrieved from https://www.reuters.com

Deloitte. (2019). Diversity and inclusion in the workplace. Retrieved from https://www2.deloitte.com/global/en/pages/about-deloitte/articles/diversity-and-inclusion.html

Dove. (2017). Dove real beauty campaign. Retrieved from https://www.dove.com/us/en/stories/campaigns/real-beauty.html

Duhigg, C. (2016). What Google learned from its quest to build the perfect team. The New York Times. Retrieved from https://www.nytimes.com/2016/02/28/magazine/what-google-learned-from-its-quest-to-build-the-perfect-team.html

Edelman. (2021). 2021 Edelman trust barometer. Retrieved from https://www.edelman.com/trustbarometer

European Union. (2018). General data protection regulation (GDPR). Retrieved from https://eur-lex.europa.eu

Fenty Beauty. (2018). Fenty Beauty by Rihanna. Retrieved from https://www.fentybeauty.com

Field, A. (2018). *Discovering statistics using IBM SPSS statistics*. Sage Publications.

Google. (2019). Google Translate. Retrieved from https://translate.google.com

Google. (2020). Diversity and inclusion at Google. Retrieved from https://diversity.google

Herring, C. (2009). Does diversity pay?: Race, gender, and the business case for diversity. *American Sociological Review*, *74*(2), 208–224. DOI: 10.1177/000312240907400203

Hong, L., & Page, S. E. (2004). Groups of diverse problem solvers can outperform groups of high-ability problem solvers. *Proceedings of the National Academy of Sciences of the United States of America*, *101*(46), 16385–16389. DOI: 10.1073/pnas.0403723101 PMID: 15534225

IBM. (2019). IBM diversity and inclusion report. Retrieved from https://www.ibm.com/employment/inclusion/

IBM. (2020). IBM's commitment to diversity and inclusion. Retrieved from https://www.ibm.com/employment/inclusion/

Johnson & Johnson. (2019). Equality for all. Retrieved from https://www.jnj.com/our-approach/equality-for-all

Johnson & Johnson. (2020). Diversity and inclusion. Retrieved from https://www.jnj.com/diversity-inclusion

Jones, A. (2021). Innovations in diversity: Case studies of successful organizations. *Harvard Business Review*.

Kang, S. K., DeCelles, K. A., Tilcsik, A., & Jun, S. (2016). Whistle while you work: The impact of affective and cognitive diversity on team creativity. *Organization Science*, *27*(3), 928–944. DOI: 10.1287/orsc.2016.1070

Kochan, T. A., Bezrukova, K., Ely, R., Jackson, S. E., Joshi, A., & Youndt, M. A. (2003). The effects of diversity on business performance: Report of the Diversity Research Network. *Human Resource Management*, *42*(1), 3–21. DOI: 10.1002/hrm.10061

L'Oréal. (2020). Diversity and inclusion at L'Oréal. Retrieved from https://www.loreal.com/group/diversity-inclusion

Manoharan, C., Poongavanam, S., Arivazhagan, D., Divyaranjani, R., & Vetri Selvan, R. (2020). Cognition and emotions during the teaching/learning process. *International Journal of Scientific and Technology Research*, *9*(2), 267–269.

McKinsey & Company. (2015). Why diversity matters. Retrieved from https://www.mckinsey.com/business-functions/organization/our-insights/why-diversity-matters

McKinsey & Company. (2018). Delivering through diversity. https://www.mckinsey.com/business-functions/organization/our-insights/delivering-through-diversity

McKinsey & Company. (2020). Diversity wins: How inclusion matters. Retrieved from https://www.mckinsey.com/business-functions/organization/our-insights/diversity-wins-how-inclusion-matters

Nielsen. (2018). The inclusion imperative: Why diversity is good for business. Retrieved from https://www.nielsen.com/us/en/insights/report/2018/the-inclusion-imperative/

Nielsen. (2019). The power of consumer diversity. Retrieved from https://www.nielsen.com/us/en/insights/report/2019/the-power-of-consumer-diversity/

Nishii, L. H. (2013). The benefits of climate for inclusion for gender-diverse groups. *Academy of Management Journal*, *56*(6), 1754–1774. DOI: 10.5465/amj.2009.0823

Nishii, L. H., & Mayer, D. M. (2009). Do inclusive leaders help improve the quality of the workplace? *Academy of Management Journal*, *52*(1), 123–140. DOI: 10.5465/amj.2009.36461930

Østergaard, C. R., Timmermans, B., & Kristinsson, K. (2011). Does a different view create something new? The effect of employee diversity on innovation. *Research Policy*, *40*(3), 500–509. DOI: 10.1016/j.respol.2010.11.004

Page, S. E. (2007). *The difference: How the power of diversity creates better groups, firms, schools, and societies*. Princeton University Press.

Porter, M. E., & Kramer, M. R. (2006). Strategy and society: The link between competitive advantage and corporate social responsibility. *Harvard Business Review*, *84*(12), 78–92. PMID: 17183795

Procter & Gamble. (2017). The Talk. Retrieved from https://www.pg.com/en_US/brands/talk

Roberson, Q. M. (2006). Disentangling the meanings of diversity and inclusion in organizations. *Group & Organization Management*, *31*(2), 212–236. DOI: 10.1177/1059601104273064

Salesforce. (2020). Salesforce's commitment to diversity and inclusion. Retrieved from https://www.salesforce.com/company/careers/diversity/

Schein, E. H. (2010). *Organizational culture and leadership*. Jossey-Bass.

Shore, L. M., Cleveland, J. N., & Sanchez, D. (2011). Inclusive workplaces: A review and model. *Human Resource Management Review*, *21*(4), 266–280. DOI: 10.1016/j.hrmr.2011.03.001

Smith, J. (2020). Diversity and inclusion: Practices and outcomes in major tech firms. *Journal of Business Research*, *112*, 123–134. DOI: 10.1016/j.jbusres.2020.03.005

Tajfel, H., & Turner, J. C. (1979). An integrative theory of intergroup conflict. In Austin, W. G., & Worchel, S. (Eds.), *The social psychology of intergroup relations* (pp. 33–47). Brooks/Cole.

Van Knippenberg, D., Haslam, S. A., & Platow, M. J. (2004). Diversity and leadership in organizations: An overview. *European Journal of Social Psychology*, *34*(4), 345–359. DOI: 10.1002/ejsp.215

Vettriselvan, R. (2025). Harnessing Innovation and Digital Marketing in the Era of Industry 5.0: Resilient Healthcare SMEs. In Olubiyi, T., Suppiah, S., & Chidoko, C. (Eds.), *The Future of Small Business in Industry 5.0* (pp. 163–186). IGI Global Scientific Publishing., DOI: 10.4018/979-8-3693-7362-0.ch007

Vettriselvan, R., Deepa, R., Gautam, R., Suresh, N. V., & Cathrine, S. (2025). Bridging Academia and Industry Through Technology and Entrepreneurial Innovation: Enhancing Supply Chain Efficiency. In Mahalle, P. (Ed.), *Bridging Academia and Industry Through Cloud Integration in Education* (pp. 145–174). IGI Global Scientific Publishing., DOI: 10.4018/979-8-3693-6705-6.ch006

Wang, F., Casalino, L. P., & Khullar, D. (2017). The role of predictive analytics in health care: A review of current literature and future directions. *Health Affairs*, *36*(3), 421–428. DOI: 10.1377/hlthaff.2016.1103

KEY TERMS AND DEFINITIONS

Diversity: Diversity refers to the presence of differences within a given setting. This includes a broad range of characteristics such as race, ethnicity, gender, age, sexual orientation, disability, socioeconomic background, and more. In the context of a workplace or business environment, diversity signifies a mix of individuals with varying attributes and perspectives.

Inclusion: Inclusion is the practice of creating environments where any individual or group can feel welcomed, respected, supported, and valued. While diversity focuses on the composition of a group, inclusion pertains to the quality of interactions and the culture within an organization. An inclusive environment ensures that all members have equal opportunities to contribute and participate.

Organizational Culture: Organizational culture encompasses the shared values, beliefs, norms, and practices that influence how employees within an organization interact and conduct their work. It shapes the behavior and attitudes of individuals within the organization, affecting everything from communication styles to decision-making processes.

Competitive Advantage: Competitive advantage refers to the attributes or capabilities that enable an organization to outperform its competitors. These advantages can stem from various sources, including unique business processes, innovative products, superior technology, or exceptional customer service.

Market Expansion: Market expansion is the strategy of increasing sales and reach into new markets or customer segments. This can involve entering new geographical regions, targeting different demographic groups, or introducing new products and services. Effective market expansion often requires a deep understanding of diverse consumer needs and preferences.

Inclusive Marketing: Inclusive marketing refers to marketing strategies that reflect and address the diverse needs and preferences of various consumer groups. This involves creating marketing campaigns, messages, and materials that resonate with a wide range of audiences, ensuring that they are represented and considered in promotional efforts.

Leadership: Leadership is the process of influencing and guiding others to achieve organizational goals. In the context of D&I, effective leadership involves promoting and championing diversity and inclusion within the organizational structure.

Strategic Advantage: A strategic advantage is a long-term benefit gained by an organization through the implementation of effective practices that enhance its competitive position. In relation to D&I, strategic advantages are achieved by integrating diversity and inclusion into core business strategies and operations.

Chapter 10
Local Entrepreneurial Ecosystems for Global Market Diversification

Amvrosios Prodromou
https://orcid.org/0009-0008-4787-6292
Neapolis University, Pafos, Cyprus

Marilia Kountouridou
European University, Cyprus

ABSTRACT

Consecutive economic and health crises have reshaped the global markets with their impact to be clearly visible on small and medium enterprises (SMEs) which are facing serious obstacles in the attempt to ensure sustainable development. These problems are clearly identified at a larger scale in SMEs than large companies as the latter have the appropriate knowhow as well as the relevant productive resources to overcome these challenges and increase their market resilience. Further, several geopolitical developments such as the war in Ukraine have put more pressure on SMEs on both microeconomic and macroeconomic levels requiring from national authorities to provide the appropriate support in order to ensure uninterrupted supply chain management which leads to a major impact on food security.

INTRODUCTION

Consecutive economic (Lacina & Vavřina, 2013) and health crises (Eggers, 2020) have reshaped the global markets with their impact to be clearly visible on small and medium enterprises (SMEs) which are facing serious obstacles in the attempt to

DOI: 10.4018/979-8-3693-5583-1.ch010

ensure sustainable development (Steinerowska-Streb, et al., 2022). These problems are clearly identified at a larger scale in SMEs than large companies as the latter have the appropriate knowhow as well as the relevant productive resources to overcome these challenges and increase their market resilience (Bvirindi & Inalegwu, 2023). Further, several geopolitical developments such as the war in Ukraine have put more pressure on SMEs on both microeconomic and macroeconomic levels, (Alhitmi & Ndambuki, 2024) requiring from national authorities to provide the appropriate support in order to ensure the uninterrupted supply chain management which leads to a major impact on food security (Leal Filho et al., 2023).

The current chapter will focus on examining the existing business modelling applied by SMEs in the Republic of Cyprus and the European Union that enable them to remain competitive (Ibarra et al., 2020). Further, the examination the challenges and the opportunities that exist in the global market that require establishment of survival strategies through extrovert approaches (Naradda Gamage et al., 2020) will enable the creation of a sustainable business modelling based on elements such as creativity and innovation (Li et al., 2022). The examination of the geopolitical changes requires from SMEs to ensure business modelling diversification (Asgary et al., 2020) through the incorporation of sophisticated technology which will enable them to expand their market potentials (de Mattos et al., 2023). The increased impact of artificial intelligence (AI) calls for SMEs to re-examine, and possibly revise, the way that thy operate, with the role of human and technological infrastructure to be viewed as a core element for sustainable development in a highly competitive market (Oldemeyer et al., 2024). This should be viewed within the increasing impact of green human resource management which to a large scale is reshaping the overall operations of businesses and provides new opportunities for sustainable development (Papademetriou et al., 2024).

As a result of all the above-mentioned elements, a new business modelling shall be proposed in order to effectively reflect to the emerging geopolitical challenges, enabling entrepreneurs and national authorities to operate and develop based on a more resilient basis.

1. GEOPOLITICAL CHANGES AND ECONOMIC IMPACT

1.1. The International Political Context and the Impact on Business Environment

Continuous geopolitical changes across the world have led to a massive impact on the global economy with the free trade and open markets to be under constant threat leading to potential economic decline (Goes & Bekker, 2023). Such developments have reshaped the way businesses develop their strategic approach and business modelling as they need to adapt to the changing business and operational environment (Aagaard, & Nielsen, 2021). Highlby sensitive and hypercompetitive sectors such as that of Big Tech are under constant pressure to evaluate and reshape their business models in order to increase their competitiveness and ability to implement innovation as a major requirement for sustainable development (Jacobides, 2020).

Zhang (2023) highlights the increasing role of Asian economies, especially that of China and suggests that this element has reshaped the overall architecture of both the political and economic environment, leading several industries and businesses to innovation and digital transformation. To this identification, one should consider the increasing role of BRICS within the international business arena which has enabled businesses from the five participating countries (Brazil, Russia, India, China, and South Africa) to expand their strategic role in the global economy, and therefore, become more competitive (Reivan-Ortiz et al., 2023). Despite the slow start, BRICS bloc has become a powerful political and economic organisation which is increasingly providing incentives to several industries and businesses, such as that of high-tech, in order to ensure a sustainable development based on a diversified model that will lead to a competitive environment (Chatterjee & Naka, 2022). This political and economic 'experiment' and the incentives provided to the economy for economic development should be considered as an example to follow as "…drivers of entrepreneurship in a given environment can render entrepreneurship policies defective and cause them to miss their targets. They can also be cautiously applied in other developing economies since the BRICS economies are the fastest growing emerging markets in the world" (Matenda & Sibanda, 2023). Statista (2023) reveals the historical economic importance of the BRICS bloc, with all five nations to enjoy a healthy growth and China to hold the lion's share. Despite minor fluctuations, the economic results should be viewed from a critical point of view, especially in terms of economic prospects.

Figure 1. BRICS GDP from 2000 – 2028

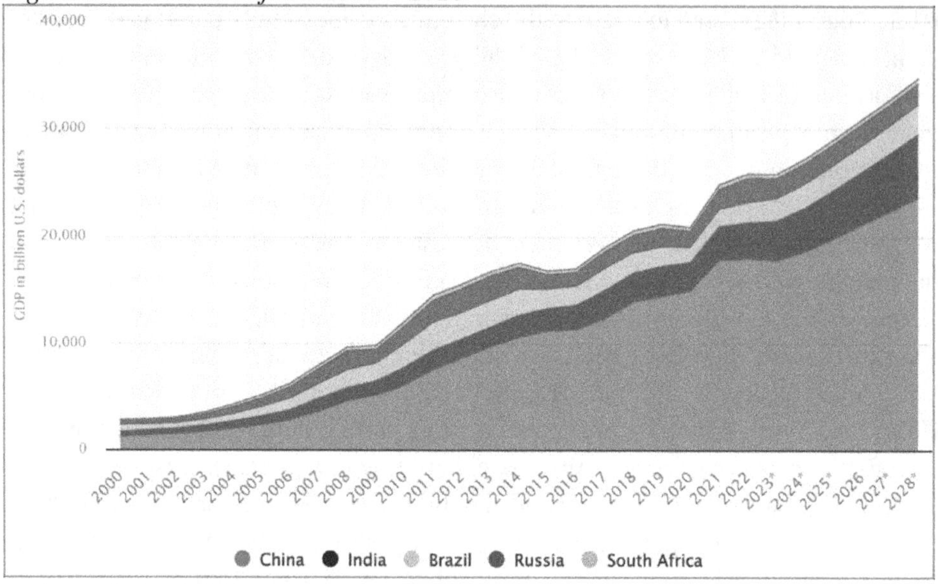

Source: Statista (2023)

Iqbal (2022) identifies the increasing strategic role of BRICS within the global economy by suggesting that the group has provided enormous opportunities for growth, with its role to be crucial during the recent pandemic and to have established measures that were a lot more focused and fairer, compared to other large global organisations, for both the citizens and businesses, hence creating opportunities for smoother problem confrontation in the long-term horizon. Zhu et al. (2022) add to this argument and suggest that despite obvious differences between the BRICS's countries, the latter have managed to respond effectively and provide the appropriate support to their citizens. BRICS have in recent years paid exceptional attention in establishing a powerful network that would promote greener energy, gas emissions' reduction, more effective water treatment and reuse, as well as policies for sustainable growth and innovation, especially in mutually beneficial sectors, such as inventory management, SC and Logistics (Miranda et al., 2021). Kıprızlı and Köstem (2022) add to the previous approach by stating that BRICS are taking advantage of their increasing impact on political and economic levels by developing a diversified approach towards climate change through the development of strategic planning that will contribute towards mitigating the gas emissions problems.

1.2. Climate Change and Global Economy

The increasing impact of climate change has reshaped the political and economic environment as both national governments and industries/businesses are forced to adapt accordingly in order to ensure sustainable growth and implement strategies that will enable them to overcome competition (Tol, 2018). Climate change has been a topic of discussion for several years with the United Nations (UN, 2024) to define that "Climate Change is the defining issue of our time, and we are at a defining moment. From shifting weather patterns that threaten food production, to rising sea levels that increase the risk of catastrophic flooding, the impacts of climate change are global in scope and unprecedented in scale."

Several crucial primary production sectors such as agricultural and livestock have in recent years been highly exposed to the negative consequences of climate change, affecting producers' ability in developing a sustainable business model and focus on innovative practices that will enable them to diversify in a competitive environment (Abbass et al., 2022). Climate change and innovation should be linked to strategic actions undertaken by both national governments and the private sector, and should also consider aspects such as behavioural change, socio-technical drivers, and emerging digital technologies, in order to ensure a blend of legitimate power and innovation approach (Matos et el., 2022). Within this context, the role of Artificial Intelligence (AI) should be seen as a major driver for innovation, entrepreneurship, and confronting climate change as it enables deeper understanding of the related trends, therefore, help businesses to take the appropriate decisions that will help them establish a more sustainable and resilient business model (Cowls et al., 2023).

1.3. The Impact of BREXIT

United Kingdom's (UK) decision to exit (best known as BREXIT) the European Union (EU) has established a brand new political and economic environment which businesses were called upon evaluating it in order to adjust accordingly (Oliver, 2023). Brown et al. (2019) suggest that BREXIT has led to a massive negative impact on the majority of the country's SMEs, with the problem to be escalating in most sectors, calling for the country's government to provide the appropriate support in order to ensure their long-term resilience.

However, further research on UK's SMEs has linked the recent pandemic to their ability to overcome the problems developed as a result of the overall measures in the country's economy, which mostly affected SMEs, as the latter were extremely vulnerable to such difficult situation (Gupta et al., 2023). This is in consistency with the work of Bissoondeeal et al. (2023, p. 1825) who suggest that BREXIT has negatively impacted the country's ability to focus on issues such as "… investment, economic growth, trade, unemployment, and financial markets." This raises the importance of providing the appropriate support to SMEs in order to overcome such problems (Belitski et al., 2022).

The case of Scotland is an interesting one as this part of UK has voted against BREXIT (Billing et al., 2019), with the majority of the SMEs; owners to be fearful of the possible impacts, especially amongst young innovators and entrepreneurs (Brown et al., 2020). Considering UK's political distribution and local government powers on several economic aspects, the measurement of BREXIT's effects should take into consideration such variations that will enable deeper examination of the consequences and provide more accurate information and support measures, especially to those that are in more vulnerable conditions (Soroka et al., 2020). Johnson et al. (2020) support that the Welsh SMEs are under pressure as a result of BREXIT with the problems to have further increased as a result of the Covid-19 pandemic outbreak, creating a challenging business environment which requires from the regional Welsh government to strategically focus on mitigating the impact. In Northern Ireland, SMEs faced similar problems during the pandemic with governmental support to be limited, hence, adding to the negative BREXIT consequence, hence, negatively impacting entrepreneurship (Belghitar et al., 2022).

Moradlou et al. (2021) support that the majority of UK's companies are facing Supply Chain Management (SCM) issues, therefore, considering the relocation of the warehouse and SC facilities in more convenient Distributions Centers (DC) in order to be closer to their target-market and mitigate the transportation and management cost as a result of BREXIT. However, Sindakis and Aggarwal (2022) see BREXIT as an opportunity for the country's SMEs to diversify their existing product and services portfolio and strategically focus on innovation, especially in highly competitive industries. Further, they evaluate this as an opportunity for UK's SMEs to eliminate their dependence from external stakeholders.

1.4. Ukraine vs Russia – Economic Consequences

The war between Ukraine and Russia has intensified the negative economic spillovers leading to high level of uncertainty which is essential in maintain a stable environment for continuous entrepreneurship and innovation (Balbaa et al., 2022). Further, the authors suggest that the war impact was further enhanced as a result of the ongoing pandemic which caused serious problems in the global economy, with Ukraine to pay a high price due to its exposure to several external factors such as the weather which has intensified the problem, especially during the winter period

(Shishkin et al., 2023). These consequences have been identified in Russian Federation, with the impact to be clearly visible in inflation (Semenenko et al., 2024).

The International Monetary Fund (IMF, 2024) adds to the issue by suggesting that the Ukraine war led to extensive problems, both economic and social, with businesses, especially SMEs, and people, to confront serious problems (Prodromou, 2019). IMF suggests that since the dawn of the war in the eastern part of Europe has disrupted the smooth supply chain and led to increased poverty across the world. Rojas-Romagosa (2024) adds to IMF's reporting by suggesting that the war is causing serious medium and macroeconomic consequences on the global economy, affecting several business operations, such as energy supply and security, innovation, and entrepreneurship, increase of gas emissions. Importantly, the author clarifies that these consequences are affecting both large and SMEs, calling for governmental support.

The impact of the Ukraine war has affected several other crucial fields, such as the academic which is essential for developing economic activities, innovation, and entrepreneurship, especially in developing economies (de Rassenfosse et al., 2023). The impact of the Ukraine war has not only affected the two countries' economies, but has also impacted other powerful economies, such as that of Germany, which finds it difficult to come in terms with the long-term effects, especially in areas such as energy and innovation, both important for sustainable development (de Rassenfosse et al., 2023; Masouras, 2019). Vlados and Chatzinikolaou (2024) take a different approach towards the long-term impact of the war by suggesting that this is leading to a change of the global economic system, impacting the way industries and businesses are operating.

1.5. SMEs Access to Financial Support

Access to the appropriate financial support has long been a serious problem for SMEs, creating serious obstacles, affecting their ability to focus on innovation and market diversification as an essential tool for sustainable growth (Harel et al., 2020). Such problems can be eased through the collaboration of banking institutions and the national authorities, as the latter can act as guarantees, therefore, enabling SMEs to obtain access to the relevant support, especially during crises in which SMEs are in a vulnerable position (Crawford et al., 2023).

The exclusion of SMEs in terms of access to financial support, either by national or private funding can potentially lead SMEs towards collapsing, inability to enjoy a healthy growth, negatively impacting creativity and innovation, poor business, and operational model, as well as lack of introducing technological changes (IMF, 2020). In order to ease such problems, the European Investment Bank (EIB, 2024) has developed several programs such as the latest SME Access to Finance Initiative that "... that aims to enhance access to finance for small and medium businesses (SMEs), as well as financial inclusion of underserved segments, such as start-ups or youth- and women-led businesses." Such programs are of a greater importance as a result of the recent pandemic which has created serious problems to SMEs, especially in terms of entrepreneurship and innovation as well as threatening their overall survival (Adam & Alarifi, 2021; Hossain et al., 2022). Further, the pandemic and inability to access financial support has led to serious problems in terms of environmental protection, an issue that was enhanced by poor political decisions (Makris et al., 2025; Du et al., 2023). Such problems were obvious in several industries such as the automotive which required strong support from both the private and public sectors in order to overcome the pandemic's serious challenges (Prodromou, 2021).

The EU SBA Fact Sheet 2022-2023 (2024) adds to these concerns and states that the problem of access to financial support remains a long-term issue for the Union's SMEs, with the problem to have been substantially increased as a result of massive increase of energy cost, extreme inflation, and increase of interest rates, all raising a silo between SMEs and financial support. At a European Level, the European Central Bank (ECB, 2020) had reacted proactively during the pandemic developing specific programs such as 'Pandemic Emergency Purchase Programme' (PEPP) and the 'Asset Purchase Programme' (APP). According to ECB both programs are complementary to other ECB actions and political decisions undertaken by EU.

Gyamfi et al. (2024) identify the increasing problem of access to financial support by SME in EU, as well as the negative consequences on their operational and competitiveness ability, calling for national and EU authorities to design and deliver a comprehensive set of financial and non-financial measures that will ease the problem. Further, the authors suggest that innovation and entrepreneurship should be at the core of such planning in order to ensure a more sustainable and resilient business ecosystem. Such measures should be clearly targeted towards specific groups of the population, such as female entrepreneurs, as the latter confront serious obstacles in obtaining the appropriate financial support and developing their business ideas, with governmental subsidies to constitute an effective tool, especially at the early stages at which newly established businesses are more vulnerable (Bonanno et al., 2023; Masouras et al., 2021).

The issue of female entrepreneurship should be viewed from as part of a broader concept of social policies which affects the entire local and global business ecosystem, with political and social consequences to be clearly visible (Martínez-Rodríguez et al., 2021). Despite positive steps towards this direction by several economies, including EU, USA, and other emerging regions, the problem of gender gap in relation to entrepreneurship remains a sad reality, causing long-term concerns over the current applied policies (Cardella et al., 2020). Critically approaching the specific problem, this should be examined and linked to the problem of gender pay gap that exists in the entire European economy, including both EU and non-EU member states, consequently, creating a negative entrepreneurial ecosystem, affecting the economy's ability to focus on sustainability and innovation (Iwasaki & Satogami, 2023), as well as promoting the much-needed social cohesion (Ballet et al., 2020).

The problems of access to financial support by SMEs creates several other problems in emerging economies, such as that of South Africa. Lack of access to technology, poor management and leadership development, limited HR training, and inability to incorporate the appropriate technological solutions, are amongst the problems confronted by SMEs, calling for a close collaboration with the national authorities in order to provide the much-desired support (Ogujiuba et al., 2023). Such problems within the broader African economy led to other 'alternative solutions' such as informal finance, which can potentially lead to operational as well as social problems Sawitri (2023).

1.6. Supply Chain Disruptions

The consecutive crises such as the banking meltdown of 2007 which started from the USA as a result of the collapse of Lehman's Brothers which impacted the global economy with enormous financial and social consequences (Burkhanov, 2011); the Covid-19 pandemic which created serious health and economy concerns (Younis et al., 2023), and the energy crisis which has impacted the operational costs (Zhao et al., 2023), have all impacted the smooth Supply Chain Management (SCM) and Logistics. All these consecutive crises require managers, especially those dealing with SCM, to strategically identify the existing obstacles and develop sustainable policies that will mitigate the negative effects (Durugbo & Al-Balushi, 2022).

Incorporating the appropriate technological tools can substantially contribute towards mitigating the negative SCM and Logistics disruptions and help companies towards establishing a more sustainable and resilient business model (Katsaliaki et al., 2021). The digitalisation of SCM and Logistics seems to be a necessity for contemporary businesses of all sizes as such transformation can enable them to become more resilient, achieve improved inventory management, avoid potential market pitfalls, and consequently, lead to improved productivity and performance (Zhao, 2023). Further, the authors suggest that this is of an increasing importance following the recent Covid-19 pandemic during which the SCM has been greatly damaged, with the consequences to be visible in crucial industries across the world, such as the automotive, affecting not only the producers, but also to most companies linked to them, with the problems to expand to the HR (Rokicki et al., 2023).

SC disruptions have led to a negative impact on SMEs' product quality as they were forced to use substitute products in order to ensure survival, with the uncertainty as a result of consecutive lockdowns to be their major concern (Canwat, 2024).

The problems in terms of SC disruptions during the pandemic were significantly higher amongst SMEs, as over 65% of them faced serious problems, compared to an approximately 40% which was observed amongst large enterprises, requiring more resilient and risk management strategies (Cagri Gurbuz et al., 2023). Importantly, the authors identify that the role of national authorities is of vital importance and can provide the appropriate know-how in this process.

The recognition and implementation of the appropriate disruption management strategies constitutes a necessity which SMEs must focus on in order to avoid future unlikely situations that can threaten their survival (Moosavi et al., 2022). However, it is important that such decisions that affect entrepreneurship and innovation, must consider the broader political and decision-making environment in order to ensure that the development of such strategies will follow the relevant political trends and requirements (Fan et al., 2022). Further to the political decisions, companies must ensure that they also take into serious consideration several other factors such as the "...the perceived intensity of institutional pressures; (2) the relative mobility of suppliers and supply chain assets; and (3) the perceived severity of the potential disruption risk" (Roscoe et al., 2022, p. 1407).

The protection of SC is vital in fundamental industries, such as that of the agriculture and food supply, namely Agriculture Supply Chain (ASC) as this is directly related to the protection not only of the relevant businesses, but most importantly, the people that rely on its smooth operations, hence, leading to a broader social dimension (Khandelwal et al., 2021). Within this context, the Food and Agriculture Organisation (FAO, 2019) of the United Nations, pays exceptional attention to the role and impact of the "Directive (EU) 2019/633 of the European Parliament and of the Council on unfair trading practices in business-to-business relationships in the agricultural and food supply chain." According to FAO, the specific Directive constitutes a powerful legal tool that protects both SMEs and people, as it enforces minimum requirements, therefore, protecting the SC at all stages, and protecting those within it that are in a more vulnerable situation.

Taylor (2023) suggests that the EU's efforts in protecting the entire SC, and consequently, all businesses and people within this process, has intensified following the catastrophic consequences experienced as a result of the recent pandemic during which businesses went through difficult times. The EU's legislative efforts to protect the both the SC and the ASC go far beyond the Union itself and expand to other markets, such as that of Africa in which companies are forced to apply specific rules and regulations applied within the EU in order to ensure that the EU shall be protected in both quality and quantity, as well as protecting its businesses participating in the process (Akande et al., 2023).

2. ENTREPRENEURSHIP AND SOCIAL CULTURAL CHANGES

2.1. Entrepreneurship in the Current Business Environment

Entrepreneurship in contemporary business environment is directly associated with the development of political changes and ability of organisations to design and develop the appropriate culture that will enable them to become more resilient, especially in emerging economies due to their special economic and political characteristics (Farias et al., 2019). The social dimensions of entrepreneurship, such as job creation, social cohesion, and fair income distribution should also be taken into serious consideration, as all these elements contribute to the development of an overall sustainable development (Weiss et al., 2023). Importantly, the authors suggest that in order to ensure an improved entrepreneurship environment, societies must strategically focus on several elements, such as improving the entrepreneurship pedagogy, view entrepreneurship as a social phenomenon, avoid possible social biases, and identify alternative models; all crucial in order to expand entrepreneurship' social impact.

Elements such as existence of appropriate information technology, professional consulting, continuous training, and development of a holistic e-marketing approach which can contribute to the conventional marketing activities, are vital for ensuring innovation and sustainable development for SMEs (Sophocleous & Prodromou, 2024). This calls for a close collaboration with the national authorities and other institutions such as the relevant Chambers (Alawamleh et al., 2023). Ricciardi et al. (2022) add to the above argument and suggest that emerging problems such as poverty, income inequality, extensive environmental pollution, and climate change, are negatively impacting businesses, especially SMEs, ability to strategically focus on innovative processes that will help them to become more resilient. Apostolopoulos et al. (2021) clarify that the long-term existence of such problems can lead towards a dual negatively impact; poor entrepreneurship and innovation behalf the businesses as well as lack of added value for the customers, hence, leading towards declined competitiveness which can potentially harm business long-term operational vision. Sadly, such problems have substantially increased following the recent pandemic which caught businesses, especially SMEs, by surprise, as they were not ready to confront such extreme situation, leading to several problems, including both poor innovation and bankruptcies (Ratten, 2023).

2.2. Cultural Shifts and Consumer Preferences

Globalisation and change of consumer preferences has attracted researchers' attention since the dawn of the millennium, calling for organisations, especially those operating within highly competitive industries, to strategically focus on extensive market research and innovation in order to ensure sustainable growth (James, 2000; Reed et al., 2012). These changes have intensified as a result of the negative consequences of the Covid-19 pandemic outbreaks which forced consumers towards new behaviour patterns to which businesses need to adapt their operations (Fandrejewska et al., 2022).

The shift of consumers' preferences is highly affected by heterogenous elements such as the societal structure, age, lifestyle, and increasing impact of technology, with all these dimensions to require from businesses to adjust their operational and entrepreneurship approach accordingly (Afzal et al., 2019). Such rapid changes require from businesses to clearly identify the continuously changing global environment, with the need to implement marketing segmentation, targeting, and positioning strategies to be a major necessity that will enable them to gain an improved market performance (Salnikova & Grunert, 2020).

The emerging services industry is facing serious challenges in relation to cultural shifts and consumer preferences, as a result of consumers' ability to obtain broad range of choices from both local and global markets (Ambos et al., 2019). This brings into the discussion the concept of globalisation vs localization, and how this can potentially affect consumer's final decision making, with the higher education to be amongst one of the industries that have experienced such consumers' shifts during the last decades (Tijssen et al., 2020). The technological advancements, especially those relate to AI, have enabled companies that have previously been 'isolated' in their domestic markets, to expand their entrepreneurial activities into the global environment, hence, taking advantage the enormous opportunities, and grow into international businesses (Nambisan, 2020). Wang and Sun (2021) take a different approach towards this issue and suggest that the Covid-19 pandemic has revealed an alternative to globalisation and localization, that of Regionalization in which companies are able to obtain better market and cost control and develop more innovative products and services.

2.3. Technology and Social Media Influence

The role and impact of technology and social media have experienced massive growth in the fields of entrepreneurship and marketing in recent years, forcing companies to diversify their overall market strategic approach (Singh et al., 2023). Taking advantage of the social media can become a major driver for rapid operational development as well as reaching out to new markets that will enable them to become more competitive through a set of extrovert policies (Blanco-González-Tejero et al., 2024). Investing in such contemporary technology should be treated as a major investment that will enable businesses to develop based on a more sustainable and competitive model (Chen & Liu, 2023).

Technology and social media should be viewed as a tool for entrepreneurship and innovation for young female university graduates, as the latter have limited opportunities for developing their business dreams (Emmanuel et al., 2022). Importantly, the authors suggest that such actions are indeed crucial in emerging economies, such as those of Asia, in which several political decisions do not enable effective female entrepreneurship based on a sustainable business model. Ahmetaj et al. (2023) add to this argument by suggesting that despite positive development in terms of political decisions, Albania's female entrepreneurs are still facing serious obstacles that hold them back from fully developing their plans, with the technology and social media to mitigate the problem. Abdulla and Ahmad (2023, p. 71) expand the issue and identify that six major obstacles are faced by female entrepreneurs compared to their male counterparts in order to be able to develop their business ideas, namely "... financial challenges, lack of knowledge and experience, work-life balance, gender discrimination, sociocultural factors, and lack of government support."

Figure 2 (Statista, 2024) provides some important information as it outlines the overall percentage of female entrepreneurs within the Organisation for Economic Co-operation and Development (OECD). The average of 9.3% with the maximum of 26.1% in Colombia and the lowest of 1.6% in Poland are indeed considered as a worrying fact that should be mitigated through the establishment of governmental support (Simarasl et al., 2024). Critically evaluating these issues, it is obvious that a lot must be done in order to mitigate such a massive gap.

Figure 2. Share of women in OECD countries who are entrepreneurs in 2023.

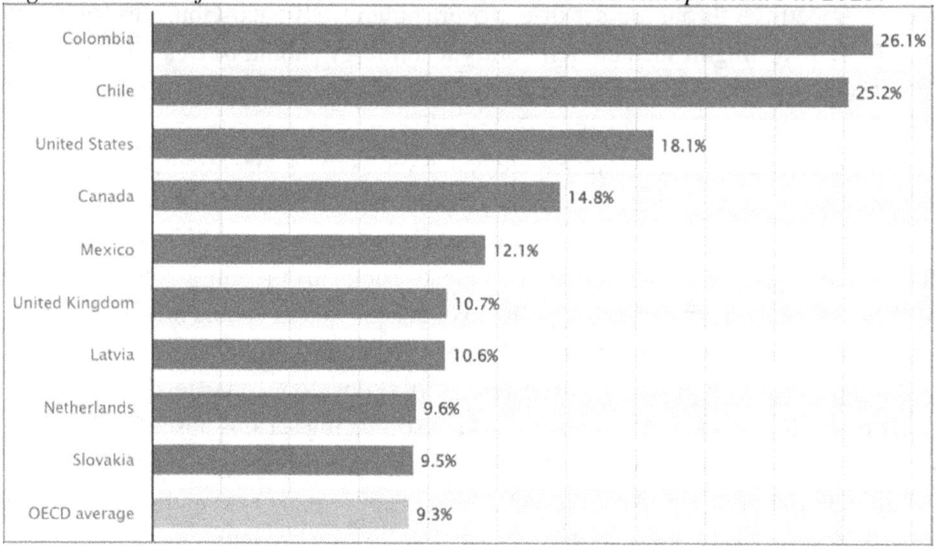

Source: Statista (2024)

2.4. Evolving Family Structures in SMEs

The impact of SMEs in global economy has been significant in recent decades contributing massively towards job creation, especially in emerging economies that face serious challenges in terms of innovation and entrepreneurship (Pasnicu, 2018). The SMEs' role within the broader context of job creation is directly linked to two major elements; ability to provide innovation in products, services, and processes, as well as establishing an effective organizational structure at all levels that will enable them to focus on sustainable growth (Inegbedion et al., 2024). Heijs et al. (2019) expand on the issue by suggesting that innovation and job creation within SMEs are directly related to the latter's ability to strategically focus on Research & Development (R&D) which constitutes a major requirement for overcoming operational challenges on both local and global levels. The specific issue should be examined in the light of extensive poverty that has prevailed in several low and medium-income countries that are facing serious challenges, with the job creation behalf the SMEs, with the role of national governments to be a major requirement (Abisuga-Oyekunle et al., 2019).

The EU has in recent years been paying exceptional attention towards the proper operations of SMEs, as these are related to the emerging issue of Circular Economy (CE) which can provide several economic and social benefits to its economic development and confronting the climate change impact (Bassi & Guidolin, 2021).

SMEs' ability to transform their operations from a conventional business model to a more sustainable one, that of CE, requires from SMEs to restructure their organisational chart and focus on micro, meso, and macro-operational levels, all important for overcoming the emerging challenges (Ahmadov et al., 2023).

Family structure is essential in order to ensure longevity and promoting sustainable growth in highly competitive environments (Lambrecht & Lievens, 2008), therefore, this should become a major requirement for operational continuity and contribution to further job creation and social creation (Dettori & Floris, 2022). Family continuity is affected by several other factors such as ability to examine the external macro-environmental trends, with the role of technology to be of a primary importance as it enables SMEs to identify opportunities and become more competitive through a set of diversified products, services, and processes (Minola et al., 2022).

2.5. Workforce Dynamics – The New Reality in Entrepreneurship

Workforce Dynamics (WD) refers to the changing environment in which people within an organisation are called to adjust, considering several internal factors, such as training and motivation, as well as external factors such as the adjustment to the technological developments and consumer behaviour (Vantilborgh et al., 2018). WD are directly associated with an organisation's ability to design and implement an effective communication system that will encompass both internal and external factors, especially in highly competitive industries in which interaction constitutes a key element towards productivity (Neill & Kang, 2024).

WD are essential in establishing a balance between productivity and profitability for the organisation, as well as Work-life Balance for the employees, as both of them are essential in order to ensure a sustainable working environment for all participants (Kountouridou & Domic, 2022; Gragnano et al., 2020). Further, the authors identify that this is essential as it enables employees to focus on balancing between work and family, hence, avoiding potential social isolation.

The role of WD is of a strategic importance for SMEs, as they provide incentives for extensive market diversification and identification of opportunities in both internal and external operational environments, with the HR to have a key role in this process (Harney et al., 2022). Wang et al. (2024) expand the strategic role of HR within the context of WD by suggesting that this is affected by several factors such as the operational competitive climate, digital capabilities, organisational learning, employee digital performance, and employee dynamic capabilities. Further, the authors suggest that these factors are interrelated, therefore, SMEs should strategically focus on involving their human assets in such operations. This is in consistency with the work of Civelek et al. (2023) who point out the need for developing a holistic approach towards digital transformation, digital literacy, and cyber-security, as a set of means that can substantially improve entrepreneurship within SMEs.

The need for enhancing digital transformation and digitalization, as part of SMEs WD has emerged as a result of the recent pandemic outbreak which established a brand-new business environment and has created several opportunities for the SMEs, employees, and the entire economy (Viswanathan & Telukdarie, 2021). de Lucas et al. (2023) add to this argument and suggest that the working environment will never be the same as both employers and employees have indeed identified a new way of interaction between them, which however, carries both advantages and disadvantages that need to be assessed. Such crises can potentially trigger opportunities for expanding extrovert entrepreneurial activities and contribute towards a diversified and a more sustainable business model which is essential in order for SMEs to retain their competitiveness and brand image (Malousis et al., 2023).

The International Labor Office (ILO, 2021) is in alignment with the previous comments, clarifying that such actions are essential and calls for employers to strategically focus on delivering continuous and quality training to their employees in order to ensure that the latter will be able to overcome the existing challenges and develop a sustainable competitive environment. Further, ILO (2024) strongly recommends that in order for SMEs to develop innovative entrepreneurial approach, hence, achieving their long-term goals, they must focus on working closely with the national authorities, as the latter possess the appropriate knowhow that will enable them to become more competitive.

2.6. Urbanisation and Threats for Entrepreneurial Ecosystem

Kuddus et al. (2021, p. 1) have defined that "Urbanisation refers to the mass movement of populations from rural to urban settings and the consequent physical changes to urban settings." Further, the authors suggest that increasing urbanisation is increasingly leading towards social and economic inequalities, with the impact on the overall economy and business activity to be visible in most economies across the world. Such problems, especially those related to peoples' health in urbanized areas can be eased through the development of a series of programs that are essential in contemporary societies (Zhang et al., 2023). However, such programs should be carefully designed and implemented in order to ensure monetary and macro-economic stability and avoid possible long-term problems (Shao et al., 2022).

According to Eurostat (2022) "In 2021, some 38.9% of the EU population was living in a city, with lower shares living in towns and suburbs (35.9%) and in rural areas (25.2%). Designing effective policies requires a good understanding of the socioeconomic conditions that exist in urban and rural areas, which in turn depends on building a solid base of knowledge about people, their activities, communities, well-being, and interaction with the environment." Figure 3 outlines the percentage of people living in rural, towns and suburbs, and cities, in EU and other selected countries. The increasing percentage should create concerns in terms of sustainability of the economy and social cohesion (Sakketa, 2023).

Figure 3. Population Distribution in EU and Selected Countries

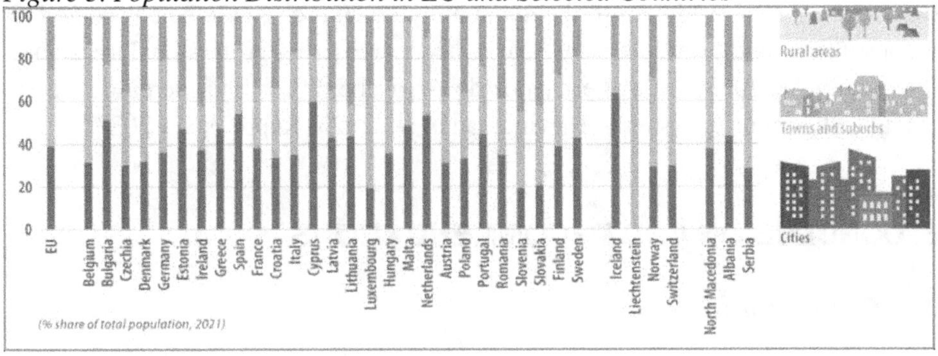

Source: Eurostat (2022)

Urbanisation has experienced a massive growth during the last decades, leading to some serious challenges such as the need to secure the availability of the relevant water and food, in both quality and quantity terms (Kookana et al., 2020). Importantly, the authors identify that over 80% of the wasted water is poorly treated, consequently, leading to serious social and economic challenges that need to be identified and confronted through the implementation of a Solid Waste Management (SWM), with the impact on health to be considered as the most important issue in this process (Abubakar et al., 2022). In the light of all the above, a holistic social sustainability and water/food management approach behalf both the private and public sectors should be established (Santos & Moreira, 2021).

The development of SMEs in rural areas can have a significant impact on mitigating urbanization's negative effects, therefore, national authorities should strategically focus on this direction, as it can lead to job creation and entrepreneurship behalf people with limited access to opportunities (Ranman & Kabir, 2021). Steady development of SMEs in rural areas can provide alternatives to people that find it difficult to compete in highly intense urban business environment, with the benefits to be clearly associated to both financial and non-financial issues, calling for the local and national authorities to invest heavily towards identifying and developing such opportunities (Manzoor et al., 2021). Tackling the negative effects of urbanisation and transferring entrepreneurship into rural, remote, and possibly disadvantaged areas, should be viewed as an opportunity for collaboration between SMEs in these areas, as working together can potentially minimize the overall operational cost, establish economies of scale, and therefore, create opportunities for sustainable development and social cohesion (Beckmann et al., 2021).

Digital transition and transformation can become a key success factor for promoting entrepreneurial activities in rural areas, as sophisticated digital tools can enable SMEs in rural areas to minimize their operational cost, improve their productivity, and gain access to more market segments, in both global and domestic markets (Morris et al., 2022). However, the threat of cyber-attacks should be considered as it constitutes a major problem for SMEs, hence, requiring professional assistance (Fernandez De Arroyabe & Fernandez de Arroyabe, 2021) and increase of their overall cybersecurity systems (Rawindaran et al., 2023; Kappe et al., 2023).

3. CONCLUSION AND RECOMMENDATIONS

3.1. Conclusion

As a result of the rapidly changing business environment, SMEs around the world have been significantly impacted by consecutive economic and health crises, coupled with geopolitical developments (Lacina & Vavřina, 2013; Eggers, 2020). These changes have significantly affected the business ecosystem, putting SMEs in a difficult position how to ensure their sustainable growth and competitiveness (Steinerowska-Streb, et al., 2022). This necessitates the need for SMEs to establish a more robust approach to overcome these challenges. Therefore, the aim of this chapter was two-fold; first to investigate the current business models applied by SMEs in the Republic of Cyprus, and the European Union that will allow them to ensure their sustainable development and competitiveness. Secondly to develop a new business model for SMEs to effectively reflect emerging geopolitical challenges and strategies that can be integrated, allowing entrepreneurs and national authorities to operate and grow on a more resilient basis. In light of this examination, a new business model (Figure 4) namely GESME (Geopolitical Entrepreneurial Sustainability for SMEs) has been developed and presented below.

Figure 4. GESME - Geopolitical Entrepreneurial Sustainability for SMEs

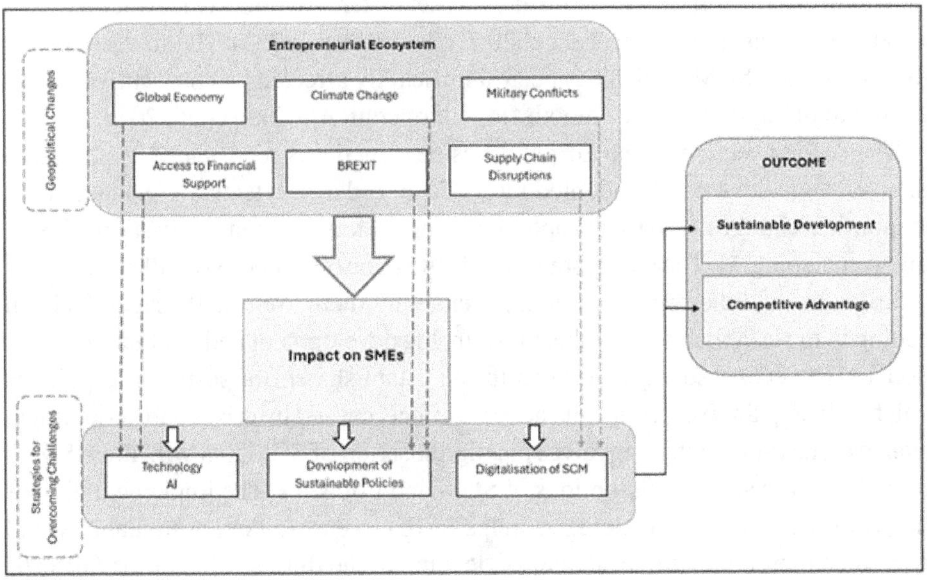

The model delineates the geopolitical changes within the business ecosystem which have a significant negative impact on SMEs. Further, the model suggests three main strategies that can be adopted by SMEs, leading to their sustainable development and competitiveness. The proposed model is divided into three interrelated sections namely, (1) geopolitical changes, (2) strategies for overcoming challenges and (3) the outcome on the SMEs. This model can be applied by SMEs in order to effectively manage these changes. The analysis of the geopolitical changes revealed important challenges which have fundamentally altered the global markets causing a significant impact on the sustainable development and competitiveness of SMEs. Six major changes have been identified from the analysis. The first geopolitical change refers to the impact of global economy as a result of the consecutives crises leading to economic decline (Goes & Bekker, 2023). These changes necessitate the need for developing their strategies to adapt to the rapidly changing business environment (Aagaard, & Nielsen, 2021). The second shift in the business ecosystem pertains to the impact of climate change. This factor affected the political and economic environment (Tol, 2018). The third geopolitical challenge is represented by BREXIT, which has negatively affected the vast majority of the country's SMEs (Oliver, 2023; Brown et al., 2019). The fourth geopolitical shift refers to military conflicts and more specifically to the war between Russia and Ukraine which has intensified the negative economic effects leading to high level of uncertainty (Balbaa et al., 2022). Access to the appropriate financial support constitutes the fifth geopolitical change. This challenge persistently poses a formidable issue for SMEs and hinders their ability to prioritize innovation and market differentiation, critical elements for sustainable expansion (Harel et al., 2020; Crawford et al., 2023). The sixth challenge revolves around SCM, which has been significantly affected by consecutive crises, leading to disruptions in the smooth flow of operations (Zhao et al., 2023).

The second section of the GESME business model is represented by the three main strategies that can be adopted by SMEs in order to effectively manage these geopolitical changes. The first proposed strategy refers to the incorporation of technology including AI. The incorporation and utilisation of technology will allow SMEs to further expand their market potentials enabling them to make the right decision leading to the establishment of their sustainable development and resilient business model. The second strategy pertains to the establishment of sustainable policies which will help them to reduce the adverse effects caused by crises and geopolitical changes. The third strategy involves the digitalisation of SCM that will allow SMEs to minimize the adverse disruptions of SCM and Logistics. The implementation of the previously mentioned strategies helps SMEs to ensure their sustainability and strengthen their competitive advantage, leading to the third section of the GESME business model, i.e. the outcome on the SMEs.

3.2. Recommendations

The extensive analysis of the existing business modelling applied by SMEs in the Republic of Cyprus and the European Union conducted in this chapter leads to four main recommendations. By considering these recommendations, SMEs can effectively manage the geopolitical challenges in the business ecosystem in order to address the previously mentioned challenges. The first strategy refers to the significant role of business consulting since will enable SMEs to develop their strategic plan accordingly aiming to mitigate any risk resulted from the geopolitical changes. The role of industry experts is of paramount importance since can share valuable insights, enabling SMEs to develop a comprehensive strategy that will allow them to enhance their resilience, ensure their competitiveness and sustainable development. Second, SMEs can develop collaborations with professional non-profit organisations such as the Chamber of Commerce. This will enable them to develop Public-Private Partnerships (PPP), allowing them to leverage shared resources, expertise, and network to enhance their sustainability and resilience. Third, SMEs should focus on the appropriate technological tools, particularly AI to enhance their operational efficiency and competitiveness. The fourth recommendation highlights the need for SMEs to establish sustainable policies that will allow them to mitigate the adverse outcomes caused by geopolitical changes. By implementing these recommendations,

SMEs can effectively manage the geopolitical shifts in the business ecosystem and ensure their competitive advantage and sustainable development.

REFERENCES

Aagaard, A., & Nielsen, C. (2021). The Fifth Stage of Business Model Research: The Role of Business Models in Times of Uncertainty. *Journal of Business Models*, *9*(1), 77–90. DOI: 10.5278/jbm.v9i1.4246

Abbass, K., Qasim, M. Z., Song, H., Murshed, M., Mahmood, H., & Younis, I. (2022). A review of the global climate change impacts, adaptation, and sustainable mitigation measures. *Environmental Science and Pollution Research International*, *29*(28), 42539–42559. DOI: 10.1007/s11356-022-19718-6 PMID: 35378646

Abdulla, F. S., & Ahmad, A. (2023). Challenges Faced by Women Entrepreneurs of 21st Century. *Journal of Management & Science*, *21*(1), 71–86. DOI: 10.57002/jms.v21i1.368

Abisuga-Oyekunle, O. A., Patra, S. K., & Muchie, M. (2019). SMEs in sustainable development: Their role in poverty reduction and employment generation in sub-Saharan Africa. *African Journal of Science, Technology, Innovation and Development*, *12*(4), 405–419. DOI: 10.1080/20421338.2019.1656428

Abubakar, I. R., Maniruzzaman, K. M., Dano, U. L., AlShihri, F. S., AlShammari, M. S., Ahmed, S. M. S., Al-Gehlani, W. A. G., & Alrawaf, T. I. (2022). Environmental Sustainability Impacts of Solid Waste Management Practices in the Global South. *International Journal of Environmental Research and Public Health*, *19*(19), 12717. DOI: 10.3390/ijerph191912717 PMID: 36232017

Adam, N. A., & Alarifi, G. (2021). Innovation practices for survival of small and medium enterprises (SMEs) in the COVID-19 times: The role of external support. *Journal of Innovation and Entrepreneurship*, *10*(1), 15. Advance online publication. DOI: 10.1186/s13731-021-00156-6 PMID: 34075328

Afzal, F., Yunfei, S., Sajid, M., & Afzal, F. (2019). Market Sustainability: A Globalization and Consumer Culture Perspective in the Chinese Retail Market. *Sustainability (Basel)*, *11*(3), 575. DOI: 10.3390/su11030575

Ahmadov, T., Durst, S., Gerstlberger, W., & Kraut, E. (2023). *SMEs on the way to a circular economy: insights from a multi-perspective review*. Management Review Quarterly., DOI: 10.1007/s11301-023-00380-2

Ahmetaj, B., Kruja, A. D., & Hysa, E. (2023). Women Entrepreneurship: Challenges and Perspectives of an Emerging Economy. *Administrative Sciences*, *13*(4), 111. DOI: 10.3390/admsci13040111

Akande, Y. B., Tijani, A. A., Kehinde, A. D., & Oyenpemi, L. O. (2023). Impact of compliance with European Union (EU) regulations on the income of actors along the cocoa supply chain in Osun state, Nigeria. *Sustainable Futures : An Applied Journal of Technology, Environment and Society*, *6*, 100120. DOI: 10.1016/j.sftr.2023.100120

Alawamleh, M., Francis, Y. H., & Alawamleh, K. J. (2023). Entrepreneurship challenges: The case of Jordanian start-ups. *Journal of Innovation and Entrepreneurship*, *12*(1), 21. Advance online publication. DOI: 10.1186/s13731-023-00286-z PMID: 37034301

Alhitmi, H. K., & Ndambuki, D. (2024). Examining the impact of Russia-Ukraine conflict and China support on the supply chain of German family-owned SMEs in 2022. *Asian Journal of Political Science*, •••, 1–14. DOI: 10.1080/02185377.2023.2285921

Ambos, T. C., Cesinger, B., Eggers, F., & Kraus, S. (2019). How does de-globalization affect location decisions? A study of managerial perceptions of risk and return. *Global Strategy Journal*, *10*(1), 210–236. DOI: 10.1002/gsj.1335

Apostolopoulos, N., Ratten, V., Petropoulos, D., Liargovas, P., & Anastasopoulou, E. (2021). Agri-food sector and entrepreneurship during the COVID-19 crisis: A systematic literature review and research agenda. *Strategic Change*, *30*(2), 159–167. DOI: 10.1002/jsc.2400

Asgary, A., Ozdemir, A. I., & Özyürek, H. (2020). Small and Medium Enterprises and Global Risks: Evidence from Manufacturing SMEs in Turkey. *International Journal of Disaster Risk Science*, *11*(1), 59–73. DOI: 10.1007/s13753-020-00247-0

Balbaa, M. E., Eshov, M. P., & Ismailova, N. (2022). The Impacts of Russian Ukrainian War on the Global Economy in the frame of digital banking networks and cyber attacks. *Proceedings of the 6th International Conference on Future Networks & Distributed Systems*. https://doi.org/DOI: 10.1145/3584202.3584223

Ballet, J., Bazin, D., & Mahieu, F. (2020). A policy framework for social sustainability: Social cohesion, equity and safety. *Sustainable Development (Bradford)*, *28*(5), 1388–1394. DOI: 10.1002/sd.2092

Bansal, S., Garg, I., & Sharma, G. (2019). Social Entrepreneurship as a Path for Social Change and Driver of Sustainable Development: A Systematic Review and Research Agenda. *Sustainability (Basel)*, *11*(4), 1091. DOI: 10.3390/su11041091

Bassi, F., & Guidolin, M. (2021). Resource Efficiency and Circular Economy in European SMEs: Investigating the Role of Green Jobs and Skills. *Sustainability (Basel)*, *13*(21), 12136. DOI: 10.3390/su132112136

Beckmann, M., Garkisch, M., & Zeyen, A. (2021). Together we are strong? A systematic literature review on how SMEs use relation-based collaboration to operate in rural areas. *Journal of Small Business and Entrepreneurship*, *35*(4), 515–549. DOI: 10.1080/08276331.2021.1874605

Belitski, M., Guenther, C., Kritikos, A. S., & Thurik, R. (2022). Economic effects of the COVID-19 pandemic on entrepreneurship and small businesses. *Small Business Economics*, *58*(2), 593–609. DOI: 10.1007/s11187-021-00544-y PMID: 38624899

Billing, C., McCann, P., & Ortega-Argilés, R. (2019). Interregional inequalities and UK sub-national governance responses to Brexit. *Regional Studies*, *53*(5), 741–760. DOI: 10.1080/00343404.2018.1554246

Bissoondeeal, R. K., Binner, J. M., & Milas, C. (2023). Brexit and coronavirus: Financial perspectives and future prospects. *European Journal of Finance*, *29*(16), 1825–1834. DOI: 10.1080/1351847X.2023.2249961

Blanco-González-Tejero, C., Ulrich, K., & Ribeiro-Navarrete, S. (2024). Can Social Media Be a Key Driver to Becoming an Entrepreneur? *Journal of the Knowledge Economy*, *15*(4), 16780–16798. Advance online publication. DOI: 10.1007/s13132-024-01764-9

Bonanno, G., Fiorino, N., Garzarelli, G., & Rossi, S. P. S. (2023). Public subsidies for credit support, democracy and European female-led SMEs. *Journal of Economic Studies (Glasgow, Scotland)*, *50*(8), 1908–1925. DOI: 10.1108/JES-11-2022-0599

Brown, R., Kalafsky, R. V., Mawson, S., & Davies, L. (2020). Shocks, uncertainty and regional resilience: The case of Brexit and Scottish SMEs. *Local Economy*, *35*(7), 655–675. DOI: 10.1177/0269094220979261

Brown, R., Liñares-Zegarra, J., & Wilson, J. O. S. (2019). The (potential) impact of Brexit on UK SMEs: Regional evidence and public policy implications. *Regional Studies*, *53*(5), 761–770. DOI: 10.1080/00343404.2019.1597267

Burkhanov, U. (2011). The Big Failure: Lehman Brothers' Effects On Global Markets. *European Journal of Business and Economics*, *2*. Advance online publication. DOI: 10.12955/ejbe.v2i0.93

Bvirindi, T. C., & Inalegwu, O. I. (2023). The impact of the global financial crisis and the European sovereign debt crisis on the capital structure of firms in Europe: Do SMEs, and listed firms respond the same? *European Journal of Finance*, •••, 1–25.

Cagri Gurbuz, M., Yurt, O., Ozdemir, S., Sena, V., & Yu, W. (2023). Global supply chains risks and COVID-19: Supply chain structure as a mitigating strategy for small and medium-sized enterprises. *Journal of Business Research, 155*, 113407. DOI: 10.1016/j.jbusres.2022.113407 PMID: 36408443

Canwat, V. (2024). COVID-19-related supply chain disruptions: Resilience and vulnerability of micro, small and medium enterprises. *Cogent Business & Management, 11*(1), 2315691. Advance online publication. DOI: 10.1080/23311975.2024.2315691

Cardella, G. M., Hernández-Sánchez, B. R., & Sánchez-García, J. C. (2020). Women Entrepreneurship: A Systematic Review to Outline the Boundaries of Scientific Literature. *Frontiers in Psychology, 11*, 1557. DOI: 10.3389/fpsyg.2020.01557 PMID: 32765357

Chatterjee, M., & Naka, I. (2022). Twenty years of BRICS: Political and economic transformations through the lens of land. *Oxford Development Studies, 50*(1), 2–13. DOI: 10.1080/13600818.2022.2033191

Chen, J., & Liu, L. (2023). Social media usage and entrepreneurial investment: An information-based view. *Journal of Business Research, 155*, 113423. DOI: 10.1016/j.jbusres.2022.113423

Civelek, M., Krajčík, V., & Ključnikov, A. (2023). The impacts of dynamic capabilities on SMEs' digital transformation process: The resource-based view perspective. *Oeconomia Copernicana, 14*(4), 1367–1392. DOI: 10.24136/oc.2023.019

Cowls, J., Tsamados, A., Taddeo, M., & Floridi, L. (2023). The AI gambit: Leveraging artificial intelligence to combat climate change-opportunities, challenges, and recommendations. *AI & Society, 38*(1), 283–307. DOI: 10.1007/s00146-021-01294-x PMID: 34690449

Crawford, J., Cui, Z. Y. A., & Kewley, D. (2023). Government finance, loans, and guarantees for small and medium enterprises (SMEs) (2000–2021): A systematic review. *Journal of Small Business Management*, •••, 1–31. DOI: 10.1080/00472778.2023.2246061

de Lucas Ancillo, A., Gavrila Gavrila, S., & Del Val Núñez, M. T. (2023). Workplace change within the COVID-19 context: The new (next) normal. *Technological Forecasting and Social Change, 194*, 122673. DOI: 10.1016/j.techfore.2023.122673 PMID: 37293385 de Mattos, C. S., Pellegrini, G., Hagelaar, G., & Dolfsma, W. (2023). *Systematic literature review on technological transformation in SMEs: a transformation encompassing technology assimilation and business model innovation*. Management Review Quarterly., DOI: 10.1007/s11301-023-00327-7

de Rassenfosse, G., Murovana, T., & Uhlbach, W. H. (2023). The effects of war on Ukrainian research. *Humanities & Social Sciences Communications*, *10*(1), 856. Advance online publication. DOI: 10.1057/s41599-023-02346-x

Dettori, A., & Floris, M. (2022). Improving continuity by simplifying the structure of family firms: A replication study. *Management Review Quarterly*, *73*(2), 635–660. DOI: 10.1007/s11301-021-00255-4

Du, L., Razzaq, A., & Waqas, M. (2023). The impact of COVID-19 on small- and medium-sized enterprises (SMEs): Empirical evidence for green economic implications. *Environmental Science and Pollution Research International*, *30*(1), 1540–1561. DOI: 10.1007/s11356-022-22221-7 PMID: 35917071

Eggers, F. (2020). Masters of disasters? Challenges and opportunities for SMEs in times of crisis. *Journal of Business Research*, *116*, 199–208. DOI: 10.1016/j.jbusres.2020.05.025 PMID: 32501306

Emmanuel, C. P., Qin, S., Hossain, S. F. A., & Hussain, K. (2022). Factors influencing social-media-based entrepreneurship prospect among female students in China. *Heliyon*, *8*(12), e12041. DOI: 10.1016/j.heliyon.2022.e12041 PMID: 36483305

European Central Bank. (2020).. . *Economic Bulletin*, *2020*(4), •••. https://www.ecb.europa.eu/press/economic-bulletin/html/eb202004.en.html

European Commission. (2024). *SME Performance Review*. Available at: https://single-market-economy.ec.europa.eu/smes/sme-strategy/sme-performance-review_en

Eurostat (2022). *Urban-rural Europe – introduction*. Available at: https://ec.europa.eu/eurostat/statistics-explained/index.php?title=Urban-rural_Europe_-_introduction

Fan, D., Yeung, A. C. L., Tang, C. S., Lo, C. K. Y., & Zhou, Y. (2022). Global operations and supply-chain management under the political economy. *Journal of Operations Management*, *68*(8), 816–823. DOI: 10.1002/joom.1232

Fandrejewska, A., Chmielarz, W., & Zborowski, M. (2022). The Impact of the COVID-19 Pandemic on the Perception of Globalization and Consumer Behavior. *Sustainability (Basel)*, *14*(15), 9575. DOI: 10.3390/su14159575

Farias, C., Fernandez, P., Hjorth, D., & Holt, R. (2019). Organizational entrepreneurship, politics and the political. *Entrepreneurship and Regional Development, 31*(7–8), 555–566. DOI: 10.1080/08985626.2019.1599186

Fernandez De Arroyabe, I., & Fernandez de Arroyabe, J. C. (2021). The severity and effects of Cyber-breaches in SMEs: A machine learning approach. *Enterprise Information Systems, 17*(3), 1942997. Advance online publication. DOI: 10.1080/17517575.2021.1942997

Food and Agriculture Organisation. (2019). *FAOLEX Database Directive (EU) 2019/633 of the European Parliament and of the Council on unfair trading practices in business-to-business relationships in the agricultural and food supply chain."* Available at: https://www.fao.org/faolex/results/details/en/c/LEX-FAOC185638/

Goes, C., & Bekker, E. (2023). The Impact of Geopolitical Conflicts on Trade, Growth, and Innovation. *WTO Working Papers.* https://doi.org/DOI: 10.30875/4445c521-en

Gragnano, A., Simbula, S., & Miglioretti, M. (2020). Work-Life Balance: Weighing the Importance of Work-Family and Work-Health Balance. *International Journal of Environmental Research and Public Health, 17*(3), 907. DOI: 10.3390/ijerph17030907 PMID: 32024155

Gupta, R., Hasan, M. M., Islam, S. Z., Yasmin, T., & Uddin, J. (2023). Evaluating the Brexit and COVID-19's influence on the UK economy: A data analysis. *PLoS One, 18*(6), e0287342. DOI: 10.1371/journal.pone.0287342 PMID: 37319267

Gyamfi, S., Gerstlberger, W., Prokop, V., & Stejskal, J. (2024). A new perspective for European SMEs' innovative support analysis: Does non-financial support matter? *Heliyon, 10*(1), e23796. DOI: 10.1016/j.heliyon.2023.e23796 PMID: 38192801

Harel, R., Schwartz, D., & Kaufmann, D. (2020). Funding Access and Innovation in Small Businesses. *Journal of Risk and Financial Management, 13*(9), 209. DOI: 10.3390/jrfm13090209

Harney, B., Gilman, M., Mayson, S., & Raby, S. (2022). Advancing understanding of HRM in small and medium-sized enterprises (SMEs): Critical questions and future prospects. *International Journal of Human Resource Management, 33*(16), 3175–3196. DOI: 10.1080/09585192.2022.2109375

Heijs, J., Díaz, G. A., & Reyes, D. M. V. (2019). *Impact of innovation on employment in quantitative terms: review of empirical literature based on micro data.* Munich Personal RePEc Archive. No. 95326:1–31 https://mpra.ub.uni-muenchen.de/95326/1/MPRA_paper_95326.pdf

Hossain, M. R., Akhter, F., & Sultana, M. M. (2022). SMEs in Covid-19 Crisis and Combating Strategies: A Systematic Literature Review (SLR) and A Case from Emerging Economy. *Operations Research Perspectives*, *9*, 100222. DOI: 10.1016/j.orp.2022.100222

Ibarra, D., Bigdeli, A. Z., Igartua, J. I., & Ganzarain, J. (2020). Business Model Innovation in Established SMEs: A Configurational Approach. *Journal of Open Innovation*, *6*(3), 76. DOI: 10.3390/joitmc6030076

Inegbedion, H. E., Thikan, P. R., David, J. O., Ajani, J. O., & Peter, F. O. (2024). Small and medium enterprise (SME) competitiveness and employment creation: The mediating role of SME growth. *Humanities & Social Sciences Communications*, *11*(1), 11. Advance online publication. DOI: 10.1057/s41599-023-02434-y

International Labour Office. (2021). *Strategic Staff Management in SMEs to Support Lifelong Learning: A Literature Review.* Available at: https://shorturl.at/dBMV9

International Labour Office. (2024). *Small and Medium Enterprises.* Available at: https://shorturl.at/bioyQ

International Monetary Fund. (2020). *Unlocking Access to Finance for SMEs: A Cross-Country Analysis.* Available at: https://www.imf.org/en/Publications/WP/Issues/2020/03/13/Unlocking-Access-to-Finance-for-SMEs-A-Cross-Country-Analysis-49243

International Monetary Fund. (2024). *The Long-lasting Economic Shock of War*. Available at: https://www.imf.org/en/Publications/fandd/issues/2022/03/the-long-lasting-economic-shock-of-war

Iqbal, B. A. (2022). BRICS as a Driver of Global Economic Growth and Development. *Global Journal of Emerging Market Economies*, *14*(1), 7–8. DOI: 10.1177/09749101211067096

Iwasaki, I., & Satogami, M. (2023). Gender wage gap in European emerging markets: A meta-analytic perspective. *Journal for Labour Market Research*, *57*(1), 9. Advance online publication. DOI: 10.1186/s12651-023-00333-y

Jacobides, M. G. (2020). Regulating Big Tech in Europe: Why, so what, and how understanding their business models and ecosystems can make a difference. SSRN *Electronic Journal*. https://doi.org/DOI: 10.2139/ssrn.3765324

James, J. (2000). Globalization, Preference Change and Consumer Welfare in Developing Countries. In: *Consumption, Globalization and Development.* Palgrave Macmillan, London. https://doi.org/DOI: 10.1057/9780230510951_2

Johnson, G., Price, J., & Tilley, H. (2020). The implications of the European transition for key Welsh economic sectors. *Wales Centre for Public Policy*.https://shorturl.at/jopzQ

Kappe, M., Härting, R. C., Karg, C., & Deffner, D. (2023). Cybersecurity in SMEs – Drivers of Cybercrime, Insufficient Equipment and Prevention. *Procedia Computer Science*, *225*, 3631–3640. DOI: 10.1016/j.procs.2023.10.358

Katsaliaki, K., Galetsi, P., & Kumar, S. (2021). Supply chain disruptions and resilience: A major review and future research agenda. *Annals of Operations Research*, *319*(1), 965–1002. DOI: 10.1007/s10479-020-03912-1 PMID: 33437110

Khandelwal, C., Singhal, M., Gaurav, G., Dangayach, G., & Meena, M. (2021). Agriculture Supply Chain Management: A Review (2010–2020). *Materials Today: Proceedings*, *47*, 3144–3153. DOI: 10.1016/j.matpr.2021.06.193

Kıprızlı, G., & Köstem, S. (2022). Understanding the BRICS framing of climate change: The role of collective identity formation. *International Journal (Toronto, Ont.)*, *77*(2), 270–291. DOI: 10.1177/00207020221135300

Kookana, R. S., Drechsel, P., Jamwal, P., & Vanderzalm, J. (2020). Urbanisation and emerging economies: Issues and potential solutions for water and food security. *The Science of the Total Environment*, *732*, 139057. DOI: 10.1016/j.scitotenv.2020.139057 PMID: 32438167

Kountouridou, M., & Domic, D. (2022). The impact of a positive visualisation course in brand identity on freshmen students' perceptions of university brand image. *Iranian. Journal of Management Studies*, *15*(4), 945–962. DOI: 10.22059/ijms.2022.326021.674612

Kuddus, M. A., Tynan, E., & McBryde, E. (2020). Urbanization: A problem for the rich and the poor? *Public Health Reviews*, *41*(1), 1. Advance online publication. DOI: 10.1186/s40985-019-0116-0 PMID: 31908901

Lacina, L., & Vavřina, J. (2013). The impact of financial and economic crisis on SME's in Greece and Ireland. *Acta Universitatis Agriculturae et Silviculturae Mendelianae Brunensis*, *61*(4), 1005–1016. DOI: 10.11118/actaun201361041005

Lambrecht, J., & Lievens, J. (2008). Pruning the family tree: An unexplored path to family business continuity and family harmony. *Family Business Review*, *21*(4), 295–313. DOI: 10.1177/08944865080210040103

Leal Filho, W., Fedoruk, M., Paulino Pires Eustachio, J. H., Barbir, J., Lisovska, T., Lingos, A., & Baars, C. (2023). How the War in Ukraine Affects Food Security. *Foods*, *12*(21), 3996. DOI: 10.3390/foods12213996 PMID: 37959115

Li, Y., Li, B., & Lu, T. (2022). Founders' Creativity, Business Model Innovation, and Business Growth. *Frontiers in Psychology*, *13*, 892716. Advance online publication. DOI: 10.3389/fpsyg.2022.892716 PMID: 35756233

Makris, I. A., Apostolopoulos, S., & Masouras, A. (2025). EU policies and female entrepreneurship in Greek rural areas in relation to digital challenges. In *Real-World Tools and Scenarios for Entrepreneurship Exploration* (pp. 203–222). IGI Global.

Malousis, A. T., Zefkilis, P. N., & Daglis, T. (2023). Employment in the 21st Century: Pre- and Post-COVID-19 Changes. *Encyclopedia*, *3*(3), 853–869. DOI: 10.3390/encyclopedia3030061

Manzoor, F., Wei, L., & Sahito, N. (2021). The role of SMEs in rural development: Access of SMEs to finance as a mediator. *PLoS One*, *16*(3), e0247598. DOI: 10.1371/journal.pone.0247598 PMID: 33684146

Martínez-Rodríguez, I., Quintana-Rojo, C., Gento, P., & Callejas-Albiñana, F. E. (2021). Public policy recommendations for promoting female entrepreneurship in Europe. *The International Entrepreneurship and Management Journal*, *18*(3), 1235–1262. DOI: 10.1007/s11365-021-00751-9

Masouras, A. (2019). Young entrepreneurship in Cyprus. *Zeszyty Naukowe Małopolskiej Wyższej Szkoły Ekonomicznej w Tarnowie, 42*(2), 27-42. https://doi.org/DOI: 10.25944/znmwse.2019.02.2742

Masouras, A., Pistikou, V., & Komodromos, M. (2021). Innovation analysis in cypriot small and medium-sized enterprises and the role of the European Union. In *Entrepreneurship, Institutional Framework and Support Mechanisms in the EU* (pp. 115-131). Emerald Publishing Limited. DOI: 10.1108/978-1-83909-982-320211011

Matenda, F. R., & Sibanda, M. (2023). The influence of entrepreneurship on economic growth in BRICS economies. *Ekonomska Istrazivanja*, *36*(3), 2275582. Advance online publication. DOI: 10.1080/1331677X.2023.2275582

Matos, S., Viardot, E., Sovacool, B. K., Geels, F. W., & Xiong, Y. (2022). Innovation and climate change: A review and introduction to the special issue. *Technovation*, *117*, 102612. DOI: 10.1016/j.technovation.2022.102612

Minola, T., Baù, M., Brumana, M., & De Massis, A. (2022). Under which circumstances do family SMES achieve high growth? A behavioural perspective. *International Small Business Journal*, *40*(6), 768–798. DOI: 10.1177/02662426221102859

Miranda, I. T. P., Moletta, J., Pedroso, B., Pilatti, L. A., & Picinin, C. T. (2021). A Review on Green Technology Practices at BRICS Countries: Brazil, Russia, India, China, and South Africa. *SAGE Open, 11*(2), 21582440211013780. Advance online publication. DOI: 10.1177/21582440211013780

Moosavi, J., Fathollahi-Fard, A. M., & Dulebenets, M. A. (2022). Supply chain disruption during the COVID-19 pandemic: Recognizing potential disruption management strategies. *International journal of disaster risk reduction. International Journal of Disaster Risk Reduction, 75*, 102983. DOI: 10.1016/j.ijdrr.2022.102983 PMID: 35475018

Moradlou, H., Reefke, H., Skipworth, H., & Roscoe, S. (2021). Geopolitical disruptions and the manufacturing location decision in multinational company supply chains: A Delphi study on Brexit. *International Journal of Operations & Production Management, 41*(2), 102–130. DOI: 10.1108/IJOPM-07-2020-0465

Morris, J., Morris, W., & Bowen, R. (2022). Implications of the digital divide on rural SME resilience. *Journal of Rural Studies, 89*, 369–377. DOI: 10.1016/j.jrurstud.2022.01.005

Nambisan, S. (2020). Digital innovation and international business. *Innovation (North Sydney, N.S.W.), 24*(1), 86–95. DOI: 10.1080/14479338.2020.1834861

Naradda Gamage, S. K., Ekanayake, E., Abeyrathne, G., Prasanna, R., Jayasundara, J., & Rajapakshe, P. (2020). A Review of Global Challenges and Survival Strategies of Small and Medium Enterprises (SMEs). *Economies, 8*(4), 79. DOI: 10.3390/economies8040079

Neill, M. S., & Kang, M. (2024). Guest editorial: Shifting role and challenges of internal communication in an age of workplace turbulence/disruption. *Corporate Communications, 29*(3), 285–290. DOI: 10.1108/CCIJ-05-2024-182

Ogujiuba, K. K., Eggink, M., & Olamide, E. (2023). Impact of Elements of Finance and Business Support on the SME Business Ecosystem in South Africa: An Econometric Analysis. *Sustainability (Basel), 15*(11), 8461. DOI: 10.3390/su15118461

Oldemeyer, L., Jede, A., & Teuteberg, F. (2024). *Investigation of artificial intelligence in SMEs: a systematic review of the state of the art and the main implementation challenges*. Management Review Quarterly., DOI: 10.1007/s11301-024-00405-4

Oliver, T. (2023). Reflections: The UK after Brexit. *International Politics*. Advance online publication. DOI: 10.1057/s41311-023-00472-6

Papademetriou, C., Ragazou, K., Belias, D., Anastasiadou, S., Garefalakis, A., & Prodromou, A. (2024). The Importance of Green Human Resources: Green Ambidexterity and Environmental Performance. In *Sustainability Through Green HRM and Performance Integration* (pp. 83–100). IGI Global., DOI: 10.4018/979-8-3693-5981-5.ch004

Pasnicu, D. (2018). Supporting SMEs in creating jobs. *Journal of Economic Development. Environment and People*, *7*(1), 15. DOI: 10.26458/jedep.v7i1.575

Prodromou, A. (2019). *Business Ethics and Corporate Social Responsibility: A Necessity for Contemporary Businesses. Examples to Follow in the Globalised Environment* (Vol. 9). The Cyprus Research Facts., http://cdacollege.com/new-uploaded_files/147.pdf

Prodromou, A. (2021). The Impact of Covid-19 on the Global Automotive Industry - Future Challenges. *American International Journal of Social Science*, *10*(1), 1–11. DOI: 10.30845/aijss.v10n1p1

Ranman, S. M. T., & Kabir, M. A. (2021). Role of Small and Medium Enterprise Clusters in Urban–Rural Linkage: A Study Based on Manufacturing SMEs of Khulna City, Bangladesh. *Environment & Urbanization Asia*, *12*(1), 27–39. DOI: 10.1177/0975425321990385

Ratten, V. (2023). Entrepreneurship: Definitions, opportunities, challenges, and future directions. *Global Business and Organizational Excellence*, *42*(5), 79–90. DOI: 10.1002/joe.22217

Rawindaran, N., Nawaf, L., Alarifi, S., Alghazzawi, D., Carroll, F., Katib, I., & Hewage, C. (2023). Enhancing Cyber Security Governance and Policy for SMEs in Industry 5.0: A Comparative Study between Saudi Arabia and the United Kingdom. *Digital*, *3*(3), 200–231. DOI: 10.3390/digital3030014

Reed, A.II, Forehand, M. R., Puntoni, S., & Warlop, L. (2012). Identity-based consumer behavior. *International Journal of Research in Marketing*, *29*(4), 310–321. DOI: 10.1016/j.ijresmar.2012.08.002

Reivan-Ortiz, G. G., Cong, P. T., Wong, W. K., Ali, A., Thu, H. T. T., & Akhter, S. (2023). Role of geopolitical risk, currency fluctuation, and economic policy on tourist arrivals: Temporal analysis of BRICS economies. *Environmental Science and Pollution Research International*, *30*(32), 78339–78352. DOI: 10.1007/s11356-023-27736-1 PMID: 37269525

Ricciardi, F., Rossignoli, C., & Zardini, A. (2021). Grand challenges and entrepreneurship: Emerging issues, research streams, and theoretical landscape. *The International Entrepreneurship and Management Journal, 17*(4), 1673–1705. DOI: 10.1007/s11365-021-00771-5

Rojas-Romagosa, H. (2024). Medium-term Macroeconomic Effects of Russia's War in Ukraine and How it Affects Energy Security and Global Emission Targets. *IMF Working Paper, 2024*(039), 1. DOI: 10.5089/9798400264269.001

Rokicki, T., Bórawski, P., & Bełdycka-Bórawska, A. (2023). Disruptions in the COVID-19 Pandemic in the Supply Chains of the Automotive Industry as Crucial for the Polish Economy. *Sustainability (Basel), 16*(1), 269. DOI: 10.3390/su16010269

Roscoe, S., Aktas, E., Petersen, K. J., Skipworth, H. D., Handfield, R. B., & Habib, F. (2022). Redesigning global supply chains during compounding geopolitical disruptions: The role of supply chain logics. *International Journal of Operations & Production Management, 42*(9), 1407–1434. DOI: 10.1108/IJOPM-12-2021-0777

Sakketa, T. (2023). *Urbanisation and social cohesion: Theory and empirical evidence from Africa* (IDOS Discussion Paper 16/2023). Bonn: German Institute of Development and Sustainability (IDOS). https://doi.org/DOI: 10.23661/idp16.2023

Salnikova, E., & Grunert, K. G. (2020). The role of consumption orientation in consumer food preferences in emerging markets. *Journal of Business Research, 112*, 147–159. DOI: 10.1016/j.jbusres.2020.03.006

Santos, E., & Moreira, J. (2021). Social Sustainability of Water and Waste Management Companies in Portugal. *Sustainability (Basel), 14*(1), 221. DOI: 10.3390/su14010221

Sawitri, N. N. (2023). Financial Funding for Small and Medium-sized Enterprises (SMEs). *East Asian Journal of Multidisciplinary Research, 2*(11), 4605–4614. DOI: 10.55927/eajmr.v2i11.6815

Semenenko, O., Sliusarenko, M., Onofriichuk, A., Onofriichuk, V., & Remez, A. (2024). Impact of the Russian–Ukrainian War on the National Economy of Russia. *Journal of Interdisciplinary Economics, 36*(1), 41–57. DOI: 10.1177/02601079231207489

Shao, Q., Tao, R., & Luca, M. M. (2022). The Effect of Urbanization on Health Care Expenditure: Evidence From China. *Frontiers in Public Health, 10*, 850872. Advance online publication. DOI: 10.3389/fpubh.2022.850872 PMID: 35242736

Shishkin, A., Lhewa, P., Yang, C., Gankin, Y., Chowell, G., Norris, M., Skums, P., & Kirpich, A. (2023). Excess mortality in Ukraine during the course of COVID-19 pandemic in 2020-2021. *Scientific Reports*, *13*(1), 6917. DOI: 10.1038/s41598-023-33113-2 PMID: 37106001

Simarasl, N., Tabesh, P., Munyon, T. P., & Marzban, Z. (2024). Unveiled confidence: Exploring how institutional support enhances the entrepreneurial self-efficacy and performance of female entrepreneurs in constrained contexts. *European Management Journal*, *42*(1), 33–45. DOI: 10.1016/j.emj.2022.07.003

Simpson, R. (1999). Urbanization, urban problems. In *Environmental Geology. Encyclopedia of Earth Science*. Springer. DOI: 10.1007/1-4020-4494-1_342

Sindakis, S., & Aggarwal, S. (2022). The Implications of Brexit for Small Businesses in the UK. *Small Business Management and Control of the Uncertain External Environment*, 179–196. https://doi.org/DOI: 10.1108/978-1-83909-624-220211011

Singh, S., Singh, S., & Dhir, S. (2023). The evolving relationship of entrepreneurship, technology, and innovation: A topic modeling perspective. *International Journal of Entrepreneurship and Innovation*, 14657503231179597. Advance online publication. DOI: 10.1177/14657503231179597

Sophocleous, H., & Prodromou, A. (2024). A Marketing - Business Plan and competition analysis for the Cyprus specialized /wellness tourism services / market. In *Real-World Tools and Scenarios for Entrepreneurship Exploration* (pp. 379–412). IGI Global., DOI: 10.4018/979-8-3693-3100-2.ch014

Soroka, A., Bristow, G., Naim, M., & Purvis, L. (2019). Measuring regional business resilience. *Regional Studies*, *54*(6), 838–850. DOI: 10.1080/00343404.2019.1652893

Statista (2023). *Gross domestic product (GDP) of the BRICS countries from 2000 to 2028 (in billion U.S. dollars).* Available at: https://rb.gy/ow8pyu

Statista (2024). Share of women in OECD countries who are entrepreneurs in 2023. Available at: https://shorturl.at/aeK15

Steinerowska-Streb, I., Glod, G., & Steiner, A. (2022). What do we know about small and medium enterprises' survival in a post-global economic crisis context? *Local Economy*, *37*(4), 259–278. DOI: 10.1177/02690942221112042

Taylor, M. (2023). EU endeavors to secure and strengthen its supply chain. *MRS Bulletin*, *48*(5), 1–6. Advance online publication. DOI: 10.1557/s43577-023-00526-3 PMID: 37361858

Tijssen, R., van de Klippe, W., & Yegros, A. (2020). Localization, regionalization and globalization of university-business research co-operation in the United Kingdom. *Papers in Regional Science*, *99*(5), 1215–1237. DOI: 10.1111/pirs.12531

Tol, R. S. J. (2018). The Economic Impacts of Climate Change. *Review of Environmental Economics and Policy*, *12*(1), 4–25. DOI: 10.1093/reep/rex027

Vantilborgh, T., Hofmans, J., & Judge, T. A. (2018). The time has come to study dynamics at work. *Journal of Organizational Behavior*, *39*(9), 1045–1049. https://www.jstor.org/stable/26610780. DOI: 10.1002/job.2327

Viswanathan, R., & Telukdarie, A. (2021). A systems dynamics approach to SME digitalization. *Procedia Computer Science*, *180*, 816–824. DOI: 10.1016/j.procs.2021.01.331

Vlados, C., & Chatzinikolaou, D. (2024). Russo-Ukrainian War and the emerging new globalization: a critical review of relevant research. *The Japanese Political Economy*, 1–23. https://doi.org/DOI: 10.1080/2329194X.2024.2309594

Wang, G., Niu, Y., Mansor, Z. D., Leong, Y. C., & Yan, Z. (2024). Unlocking digital potential: Exploring the drivers of employee dynamic capability on employee digital performance in Chinese SMEs-moderation effect of competitive climate. *Heliyon*, *10*(4), e25583. DOI: 10.1016/j.heliyon.2024.e25583 PMID: 38379974

Wang, Z., & Sun, Z. (2020). From Globalization to Regionalization: The United States, China, and the Post-Covid-19 World Economic Order. *Journal of Chinese Political Science*, *26*(1), 69–87. DOI: 10.1007/s11366-020-09706-3 PMID: 33144822

Weiss, T., Eberhart, R., Lounsbury, M., Nelson, A., Rindova, V., Meyer, J., Bromley, P., Atkins, R., Ruebottom, T., Jennings, J., Jennings, D., Toubiana, M., Shantz, A. S., Khorasani, N., Wadhwani, D., Tucker, H., Kirsch, D., Goldfarb, B., Aldrich, H., & Aldrich, D. (2023). The Social Effects of Entrepreneurship on Society and Some Potential Remedies: Four Provocations. *Journal of Management Inquiry*, *32*(4), 251–277. DOI: 10.1177/10564926231181555

Younis, H., Alsharairi, M., Younes, H., & Sundarakani, B. (2023). The impact of COVID-19 on supply chains: Systematic review and future research directions. *Operations Research*, *23*(3), 48. Advance online publication. DOI: 10.1007/s12351-023-00790-w

Zhang, S. (2023). The Impact of Changes in Geopolitical Patterns on Global Economy and Trade. *Social Sciences in Business and Policy Analysis*, *1*(1). Advance online publication. DOI: 10.62220/j.ssbpa.2023.01.007

Zhang, Z., Zhao, M., Zhang, Y., & Feng, Y. (2023). How does urbanization affect public health? New evidence from 175 countries worldwide. *Frontiers in Public Health*, *10*, 1096964. DOI: 10.3389/fpubh.2022.1096964 PMID: 36684862

Zhao, N., Hong, J., & Lau, K. H. (2023). Impact of supply chain digitalization on supply chain resilience and performance: A multi-mediation model. *International Journal of Production Economics*, *259*, 108817. DOI: 10.1016/j.ijpe.2023.108817 PMID: 36852136

Zhao, Z. Y., Hao, Y. X., Chang, R. D., & Wang, Q. C. (2023). Assessing the vulnerability of energy supply chains: Influencing factors and countermeasures. *Sustainable Energy Technologies and Assessments*, *56*, 103018. DOI: 10.1016/j.seta.2023.103018

Zhu, J., Yan, W., Zhu, L., & Liu, J. (2021). COVID-19 pandemic in BRICS countries and its association with socio-economic and demographic characteristics, health vulnerability, resources, and policy response. *Infectious Diseases of Poverty*, *10*(1), 97. DOI: 10.1186/s40249-021-00881-w PMID: 34238368

Chapter 11
Empowering Social Entrepreneurship and Social Enterprises Through Digital Technologies:
Opportunities and Challenges

Panagiota Xanthopoulou
https://orcid.org/0000-0003-2503-3901
University of West Attica, Greece

Alexandros Sahinidis
University of West Attica, Greece

Vassilis Vyttas
Neapolis University, Pafos, Cyprus

Sofoklis Papakonstantinou
https://orcid.org/0009-0002-5403-5869
Neapolis University, Pafos, Cyprus

Vassilis Zakopoulos
National and Kapodistrian University of Athens, Greece

Ioannis Antoniadis
University of Western Macedonia, Greece

ABSTRACT

This chapter examines how digital technologies transform social entrepreneurship, creating opportunities and challenges. Social entrepreneurship addresses societal issues by merging social and economic goals but often faces regulatory and resource limitations. Digital tools such as AI, big data, and blockchain enhance efficiency, transparency, and value co-creation, helping social enterprises expand their reach and financial sustainability. Case studies from Greece and beyond highlight how digitalization fosters resilience and collaboration, particularly during crises like

DOI: 10.4018/979-8-3693-5583-1.ch011

COVID-19. While digital transformation offers new growth pathways, it also raises ethical concerns about access, privacy, and disparities. This study proposes a framework linking digitalization, value co-creation, and social entrepreneurship, offering insights for policymakers, researchers, and practitioners seeking innovative and sustainable business models.

INTRODUCTION

Social entrepreneurship (SE) refers to activities related to social trends, organizational structures, and individual initiatives (Corner & Ho, 2010). This is a means by which people and entrepreneurs try to solve societal problems and advance both social and economic development (Nicholls, 2010). Social entrepreneurship seeks to address social issues and benefit communities, in contrast to traditional entrepreneurship, which concentrates on satisfying consumer demands for products and services (Mair & Martí, 2005). However, it has been criticized for its utopian orientation, bias in favor of social activities, high coordination costs, operational efficiency challenges, and performance-monitoring issues (Boone & Özcan, 2016; Kenny et al., 2020). Furthermore, depending on the capitalist model, there are differences in how social entrepreneurship is implemented. For example, social entrepreneurs in developed economies typically focus on collectively organizing for the benefit of the community (Shrivastava & Kennelly, 2013). Developing nations, however, encounter obstacles such as institutional weaknesses (Kaufmann et al., 2008) and a lack of support, which makes it difficult to obtain resources and adjust (Muñoz et al., 2020). Low regulatory quality, high levels of corruption, and ineffective public administration are characteristics of emerging economies' inadequate institutional environment (Kaufmann et al. 2008).

Digital technology usage has been suggested as a resilience and adaptation method to deal with these issues, particularly during emergencies or crises like the Covid-19 pandemic crisis (Cavallo et al., 2019; Osabohien et al., 2022; Ramos-Villagrasa et al., 2019). Digitization —the process of switching from analog to digital tools and technologies—is essential to a company's ability to survive, compete, and expand (Abou-foul et al., 2022; Skare et al., 2023). It is important to boost corporate growth (Bohan et al., 2024) and maintain competitiveness (Powell & Dent-Micallef, 1997). Digitalization has been shown to improve corporate value (Salvi et al., 2021), productivity, environmental performance (Avelar et al., 2024), and business performance (Atienza-Barba et al., 2025). According to a study by Salvi et al. (2020), digitalization is also essential for sustainable development and generating social and environmental effect. The strategic integration of digital technologies and hybrid business models offers a competitive edge, particularly for social businesses. This allows for the simultaneous expansion of economic development and social impacts (Skare et al., 2022).

Although their economic and social significance cannot be denied, there are few empirical studies on the variables driving the growth of social companies (Kotiranta et al., 2020). Although there is a dearth of scientific research demonstrating the advantages of digitization in this field, it is thought to be essential for generating both economic and social value (Yáñez-Valdés et al., 2023). Digitalization and value co-creation in social businesses have been extensively studied separately, but little is known about how digitalization affects value co-creation, and what little is known about it is restricted to traditional manufacturing firms (Abou-Foul et al., 2020). Furthermore, from a practical standpoint, social entrepreneurs may believe that the industry is not making sufficient use of digitalization for value co-creation and may use more technologies to create value; however, many still do not have a thorough understanding of this concept. Therefore, more studies are required to fully comprehend the impact of digitalization and how it relates to value co-creation from a fresh angle, using various social approaches and in the framework of social entrepreneurship. Thus, our goal is to link value co-creation and digitization to the advancement of social entrepreneurship. We attempt to respond to the following research question by taking this goal into account: How is value co-creation for social entrepreneurship made possible by digitalization?

The main topics of this study are the influence of digital innovation on the growth of sustainable business practices and the difficulties social enterprises and social entrepreneurs face when using digital technology. Additionally, it examines how digitalization might help social enterprises become more flexible and collaborative (Mursalzade, 2024). Using the content analysis approach, this study focuses on examples of social enterprises from Greece and the global environment, highlighting the advantages and difficulties of digital transformation. These results will close the knowledge gap on how digitalization impacts the growth of social entrepreneurship by offering theoretical insights and suggesting a framework and research agenda on digitalization and value co-creation for social entrepreneurship. In addition, it offers practitioners and policymakers helpful knowledge that promotes creative and sustainable business strategies (Antonizzi & Smuts, 2020).

BACKGROUND

Building on the conceptual foundations of social entrepreneurship, this section elaborates on the contextual background that frames the present analysis.

Scholars continue to characterize SE in a number of ways, some of which are comparable and others less so, which is explained by the lack of agreement in explanations of the phenomena (García-Jurado et al., 2021). According to Dwivedi and Weerawardena (2018), SE entails taking initiative and having the capacity to control risk while adhering to sustainability and environmental and social goals. Alvord et al. (2004), SE provides innovative solutions to social issues and produces long-lasting, constructive social change. According to Monteiro et al. (2022), SE is the creative production of social value that includes readiness to disseminate social value despite potential hazards and a perceived lack of resources. According to other explanations (Gupta et al., 2020; Rodríguez-Ramírez et al., 2022), the two SE primary drivers are social purpose and financial sustainability. Sustainable development is another recurrent issue in SE research (Hein, 2022; Pérez-Barea, 2025; Gouveia et al., 2024), although asserting that SE contributes to sustainable development, Pérez-Barea (2025) confirmed that SE and sustainable development are directly related. Instead of looking for a long-term edge for their companies, they try to offer lasting solutions to the issues that they tackle (Teasdale et al., 2022). As a result, social entrepreneurs prioritize local problems with global implications and offer long-term solutions in their efforts to benefit society (Monteiro et al., 2022; Teasdale et al., 2022). After analyzing the content of these different definitions of social entrepreneurship (SE), the authors aimed to visualize the key themes in a diagram presented as follows (Figure 1).

Figure 1. Content analysis of social entrepreneurship definitions

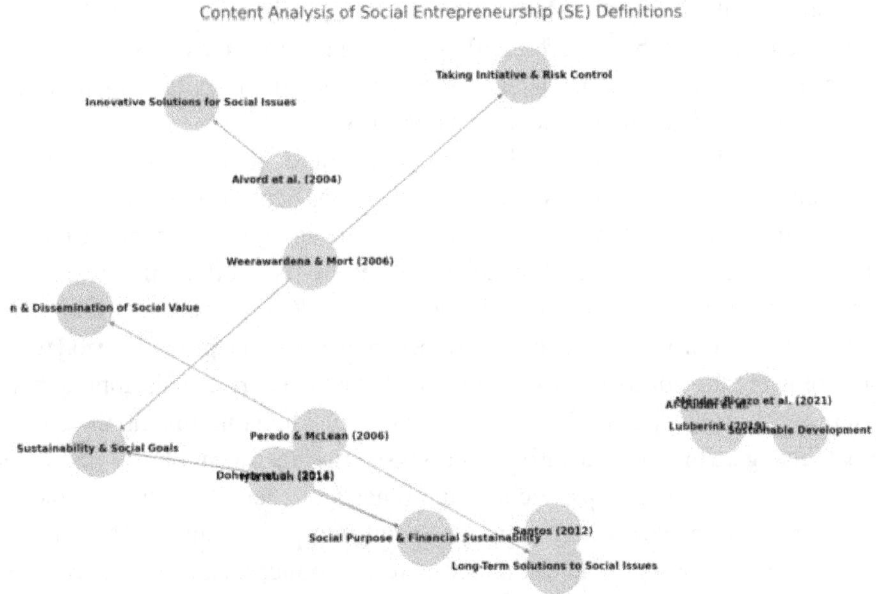

Various academic researchers highlight several recurring elements in their Social Entrepreneurship (SE) definitions based on content analysis. Dwivedi and Weerawardena (2018) define SE as a process with leadership capabilities and uncertain risk management to achieve sustainability objectives. The important topic of sustainability and social goals receives extensive discussion from Dwivedi and Weerawardena (2018), Gupta et al. (2020), and Rodríguez-Ramírez et al. (2022) because these authors demonstrate how SE embeds environmental awareness and social results into its fundamental business framework. The essential characteristic of Social Enterprise includes generating innovative solutions for social issues because García-Jurado et al. (2021) prove that social entrepreneurship involves developing modern approaches to address social challenges and sustain lasting positive change.

Social entrepreneurs according to Monteiro et al. (2022) strive to develop and share social value even when facing challenging situations through their initiatives to distribute the benefits they create. The concept of achieving financial sustainability through social mission objectives forms the essence of SE according to Gupta et al. (2020) and Rodríguez-Ramírez et al. (2022). SE literature continuously emphasizes sustainable development through works of Hein (2022), Pérez-Barea (2025), and Gouveia et al. (2024), thereby demonstrating that social entrepreneurship directly contributes to long-lasting sustainability goals.

Social entrepreneurs use strategies that resolve current social issues according to Teasdale et al. (2022) and Monteiro et al. (2022) by implementing solutions that produce enduring global effects. Different scholar definitions of social entrepreneurship still produce four persistent themes that include sustainability, innovation, social value creation, and financial sustainability.

From the above-mentioned definitions, it could be understood that social entrepreneurship is a business activity that emphasizes solving social, cultural, or environmental problems. Social entrepreneurs integrate innovation into their actions to achieve their goals. Financial profitability is not the ultimate goal but a means. According to the Brundtland Commission's 'Our Common Future' (1987), sustainability is defined as the ability to meet the needs of the present period without compromising the ability to meet future needs that may arise. This approach helps to improve the quality of life and eradicate poverty while minimizing the effects of climate change. Through innovative solutions such as green technologies and services targeted at vulnerable groups, social entrepreneurs are helping to create a more equitable and sustainable economic model. Social entrepreneurship and sustainability are based on common principles that promote economic, social, and environmental well-being. Environmental responsibility refers to the commitment of businesses to reduce their negative impact on the environment through resource conservation. Social justice refers to ensuring equal opportunities for all members of society and promoting equality. Finally, economic sustainability focuses on creating economic strategies to make the business profitable and support sustainability.

At this point it is important to clarify the differences between the two terms of social entrepreneurship and social enterprises. Social enterprises are social economy actors whose main objective is to create social impact rather than profit, and whose operation is based on the production of goods and services and the management of their commercial activities by their stakeholders (European Commission, 2019). On the other hand, social entrepreneurship is a broad concept and covers a range of activities and ventures that do not necessarily involve the production of goods and may show diversity over the years (Monteiro et al., 2022). Another difference is that social entrepreneurship focuses on the characteristics of people who start new ventures, such as their responsibility and resourcefulness. In contrast, the social enterprise sector tends to focus on organisations and their activities (e.g. commercial etc.) (Díaz-Foncea & Marcuello, 2022).

Today people appreciate social entrepreneurship as a vital instrument to generate helpful social change. A new type of entrepreneur now exists because people criticize businesses that only care about making money and neglecting planet and community needs. Social entrepreneurs combine a strong desire to address social and environmental problems with the creation of lasting business systems. Their business know-how serves as a foundation for their dedication to solving major societal problems and environmental issues. Technology has made people interconnected and easy to reach, which supports why social entrepreneurship is expanding.

Some examples that promote social and environmental responsibility are recycling and the circular economy, where companies use recycled materials to produce new products, and the so-called "fair trade," a trade network specifically built to fight poverty, globally and locally, through a sustainable, fair, and ethical approach to the production, purchase, and consumption of products. Sustainable development was originally defined in the 1987 Brundtland Report of the International Commission on Environment and Development and is a form of development that meets the needs of the present generation without compromising the ability of future generations to meet their own needs. It is based on conservation between three pillars (Figure 2):

Figure 2. The three pillars of sustainable development

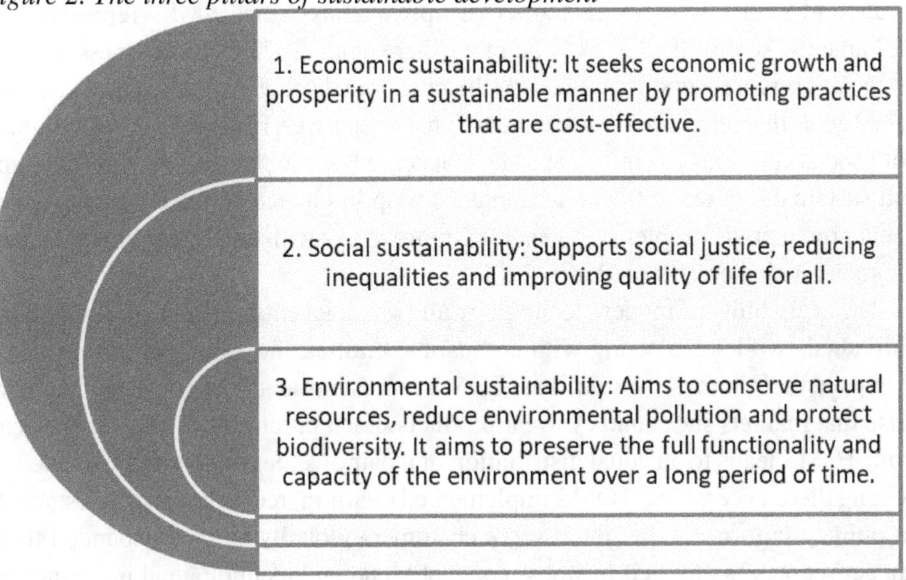

Social entrepreneurship produces this foundation which operates as the essential principle for developing a fairer planet.

The increase of social entrepreneurship stems from increasing consumer interest in businesses that actually make positive social impacts. Both social understanding and impact-based values drive millennials along with Generation Z members to select companies first. The changing consumer preferences have established market demand for ethical businesses so social entrepreneurs can build sustainable business frameworks that express their organizational purpose.

Social entrepreneurship grows rapidly while technology acts as an essential tool for social entrepreneurs who aim to create positive change. Social entrepreneurs use technological capabilities to expand their influence and establish worldwide alliances with progressive individuals and develop revolutionary answers for worldwide problems.

Digital technology and its impact on entrepreneurship

Transitioning from conceptual understanding, the current section explores how digital technologies influence entrepreneurship and innovation dynamics.

Businesses achieve innovation development by implementing digital transformation while expanding their outward perspective together with operational improvements. Digital technologies provide SMEs with opportunities to improve production levels and gain international market competitiveness since SMEs represent the fundamental part of the Greek economy (Skare et al., 2022). The business models of social entrepreneurship align with the concept of achieving environmental and social goals that function outside standard profit measures. Business operations unite with social missions to create ventures that serve both social welfare enhancement and sustainability aims. Social entrepreneurship in Greece appeared as an answer to economic crisis problems to generate improved growth and better opportunities for social inclusion (Pérez-Barea, 2025).

The availability of modern technology allows social entrepreneurs to reach more individuals while connecting with compatible entities and using digital resources to expand their innovative solutions. TOMS represents an outstanding social enterprise that markets shoes and eyewear products. Each purchase of shoes or eyewear from TOMS leads to an equal distribution of a pair of shoes or eyewear to someone lacking these necessities. TOMS implemented e-commerce technology to establish an online platform that let them serve customers globally so they expanded their impact scope. Due to their business concept blend and technological implementation, TOMS has provided more than 100 million pairs of footwear to disadvantaged individuals (Gouveia et al., 2024).

Digital technologies, such as the Internet of Things (IoT), big data, and artificial intelligence, offer social enterprises the opportunity to improve their operational efficiency and deliver more efficient and targeted services (Abou-Foul et al., 2022). Their integration enables the creation of advanced collaboration networks and the interconnection of information in real time, enhancing the efficiency of processes and quality of services provided. At the same time, the use of these technologies helps to improve transparency and accountability, promoting trust and accountability within organizations and the communities with which they interact (Mursalzade, 2024).

Digital technologies enable businesses to implement digital solutions that address issues such as recycling and social inequalities, achieve highly environmentally friendly production and energy savings, and successfully shape the true meaning of social value. Moreover, through the use of data and artificial intelligence, companies can optimize their processes and significantly enhance their efficiency (Akram et al., 2024). E-commerce platforms, for example, enable small businesses to carry out projects with social and environmental impacts, thus reducing barriers to market entry (Adam et al., 2025). Thus, the integration of digital innovation not only improves the competitiveness of businesses, but also helps create a more sustainable economic environment.

Digital innovation plays an important role in the development of sustainable business practices because it enables companies to reassess their operations and strategies with greater resource efficiency, environmental responsibility, and social sensitivity (Gouveia et al., 2024). Moreover, through digital transformation, businesses can adapt more quickly to changing market demands by addressing challenges related to climate and social disruption (Bachmann et al., 2025).

It is very important to note that today's technology is growing exponentially, and in 2018, there was a high level of activity in businesses using technologies such as artificial intelligence (AI), blockchain, Internet of Things (IoT), and 3D printing (Abou-Foul et al., 2022). For the development of artificial intelligence (AI) computers, algorithms, that is, self-contained sequences of instructions and actions, are used (Atienza-Barba et al., 2025). The computer starts from an initial state, and after being fed with initial data describing the computational steps, it executes them and passes through new states until it reaches the final phase. Applications in supply chains are of particular interest in the business world. Maersk transports millions of containers and places temperature and humidity detectors on them, that is, a mechanism that enables appropriate control of conditions that prevent damage or loss of goods due to unfavorable and unsuitable conditions (Bal & Erkan, 2019). According to Abou-Foul et al. (2020), technological breakthroughs are the first important factor, as the development of social networks, laptops, the ability to process large datasets, and cloud computing, among many others, has grown exponentially in recent years and provides individuals and businesses with countless possibilities.

Innovation plays an important role in promoting business sustainability, particularly in promoting sustainable growth in various sectors. Innovation enables businesses to integrate environmental, social and economic considerations into their activities. Theories related to this, such as Systems Thinking and Sustainable Innovation, highlight how businesses can create value while facing global challenges, such as climate change, inequality, and resource scarcity. This integration of sustainability with innovation is essential to developing new business models and processes that not only enhance profitability but also contribute to greater social good. Integrating sustainability and innovation creates practices that not only minimize negative impacts, but also actively create value through the introduction of innovative products, services, and processes that contribute to the well-being of both society and the environment.

Social Entrepreneurship and Digital Technologies use

Following the exploration of digital influence in entrepreneurship, this section focuses specifically on how social enterprises utilize digital technologies for social impact.

The adoption of digital technology serves as a trigger that enhances social entrepreneurship practice. The Internet of Things (IoT) technology enables instant data acquisitions which supports organizations in making strategic business choices (Bachmann et al., 2025). Big data functions to foresee market developments and recognize business possibilities yet artificial intelligence (AI) assists by creating automatic processes for customized solutions (Abou-Foul et al., 2022). Social enterprises find enhanced audience engagement through e-commerce and social network platforms that enable better communication and blockchain delivers secure reliable business operations (Adam et al., 2025). Digital technology integration within social entrepreneurship has become the key element which led to better sustainability and operational efficiency (Akram et al., 2024).

The operational transformations of social enterprises can be achieved by implementing Internet of Things (IoT) and Big Data technology in addition to Artificial Intelligence and e-commerce platforms. Big Data enables sound decision-making through extensive data analysis and IoT enables analysis and improvement of physical resources management (Abou-Foul et al., 2020). The combination of e-commerce platforms enables social enterprises to reach more potential buyers and increase revenue since AI creates smart operational systems that enhance service quality (Antonizzi & Smuts, 2020). Businesses should focus on innovation since it enables them to adapt effectively to changing market conditions and achieve strong market competition (Gouveia et al., 2024).

The 'Triple Bottom Line' (TBL) theory serves as a reliable instrument for analyzing sustainable development by understanding economic-social-environmental performance alignment (Chandra & Kerlin, 2020). Social entrepreneurs employ unique solutions to deal with social difficulties such as joblessness or destitution by uniting business targets with their social impact objectives (Monteiro et al., 2022). Unemployed people can benefit from digital tech training programs delivered through a social enterprise which helps them find work opportunities (Paul et al., 2022).

Digital technologies emerge as critical enablers of sustainable development because they serve beyond operational tool functionality within social enterprises as per the presented theoretical framework and illustrative examples (Fischer et al., 2023). Social awareness regarding sustainability grows through digital technology operations because they stimulate new collaborative initiatives and sustainable solutions which produce an economy that is both fair and environmentally friendly (Teasdale et al., 2022).

Social entrepreneurship understands fully the digital technologies' ability to achieve its social targets. Modern platforms such as the Internet of Things (IoT) and major data artificial intelligence (AI) together with e-commerce platforms enable social enterprises to build solutions that achieve higher efficiency and economic sustainability and better results (Gupta et al., 2022). Social business strategies promoting sustainability and social responsibility are increasingly developed with the help of AI technology and the ChatGPT (Upadhyay et al., 2021).

The functionality of ChatGPT enables social enterprises to build real-time user communication while automating processes and generating personalized solutions for different problems. These tools decrease operational expenses and boost operational effectiveness through their ability to extend service reach to numerous people especially within regions which lack technological infrastructure. Bignumerical data serves as a useful digital technology for social entrepreneurship because it allows organizations to examine social trends alongside social needs. These data help businesses discover social issues which they use to create solutions that produce better operational efficiency and better relations with the community. By using e-commerce platforms social enterprises can enhance both their sustainability initiatives and social mission by enabling market expansion of products that support these causes.

Shaping social entrepreneurship during the Covid-19 pandemic

This section reflects on the unique challenges and adaptations of social entrepreneurship in response to the Covid-19 pandemic.

The Covid-19 crisis occurred in December 2019 resulted in border closures, economic breakdowns, significant human casualties, and other repercussions (Abou-Foul et al., 2022). The epidemic affected companies and disrupted industries (Chandra & Kerlin, 2020), caused shortages of food and shelter, and worsened pre-existing societal issues while creating new ones (García-Jurado et al., 2021). Given the effect of COVID-19 on SE, it is critical to understand how SE enterprises perform their duties (Díaz-Foncea & Marcuello, 2022).

According to Boone and Özcan (2015) and Kotiranta et al. (2020), SE firms face several difficulties as a result of the pandemic, such as maintaining communication networks throughout the value chain, adjusting to new technologies, accepting new working methods, coping with lockdowns, restricted mobility, and service withdrawals. Given their ability to reach important stakeholders (governments, markets, and institutions) and provide platforms that bring stakeholders' interests together, SE firms are well positioned to address the issues brought on by the pandemic, despite these obstacles (Gouveia et al., 2024; Fischer et al., 2023). SE involves increasingly intricate relationships between players whose primary duty is to promote constructive social change, although it is expected that SE will become more complex beyond COVID-19.

It is significant that SE companies have reported positive outcomes from the COVID-19 pandemic. Pérez-Barea (2025) emphasizes how they modernized their service delivery and used resources to help society's most disadvantaged members. These initiatives have led to new SE models, such as digital social entrepreneurship (DSE) (Adam et al., 2025; Mursalzade, 2024), which has facilitated the development of technical solutions to social problems (Monteiro et al., 2022; Osabohien et al., 2022). However, there are national differences in the technology used and institutional support that SE enterprises receive (Skare et al., 2022).

Entrepreneurship, especially SE, is crucial to mitigate the negative consequences of crises (Gupta et al., 2020). By providing the resources needed in the aftermath of crises (Monteiro et al., 2022; Díaz-Foncea & Marcuello, 2022; Fischer et al., 2023), building positive emotions for community well-being in post-disaster recovery (Monteiro et al., 2022), rearranging social and economic infrastructure (Cavallo et al., 2018), and filling institutional gaps where disaster recovery systems fail (Teasdale et al., 2022), SE reduces the effects of crises. Nonetheless, the main focus of these studies is how entrepreneurship contributes to building resilience for recovery after a disaster. Little information has been provided on how SE firms, mostly tiny businesses, handle disruptions. According to previous research, small businesses respond to crises with more innovation, adaptability, and flexibility than large corporations (Rodríguez-Ramírez et al., 2022; Skare et al., 2022). The ability of smaller business owners to handle crises is based on their interpersonal skills (Rodríguez-Ramírez et al., 2022; Gouveia et al., 2024; Xanthopoulou et al., 2022; Xanthopoulou, et al., 2023; García-Jurado et al., 2021). This emphasizes how SE enterprises must use a variety of tools to respond to new issues and opportunities while expanding the idea of social improvisation (Mursalzade, 2024; Pérez-Barea, 2025).

Consequently, digital tools have become essential to social enterprises. García-Jurado et al. (2021) highlight how SE enterprises use digital platforms to overcome financial constraints and legitimacy concerns, as well as how they speed up the adoption of new methods. Given that crises deplete resources and affect resilience, this is crucial for SE. Based on García-Jurado et al. (2021), Paul et al. (2022) concur that digital technology provides new avenues for SE that benefit everyone, particularly those who are less fortunate. Paul et al. (2022) present an opposing viewpoint, arguing that digital technologies are major contributors to growing pay disparities and inequality. Skare et al. (2022) show that varying degrees of digital transformation among nations affect the ability for SE in order to comprehend the negative effects of digital technologies as stated by Paul et al. (2022). Thus, a nation's power to intervene in society is strengthened by advancements in the digital sphere. To accomplish societal good and long-lasting improvements, Mursalzade (2024) emphasized the necessity of institutionalizing adaptation through digitalization and SE, acknowledging the potential benefits of interactions between SE and digital technology. However, little is known about how much digital technology is used by decision-makers and businesses (Gouveia et al., 2024). Therefore, more focus should be placed on the relationship between (digital technological) innovation and SE resilience (Pérez-Barea, 2025).

The next section examines the landscape and institutional environment of social enterprises across Europe.

Social Enterprises in Europe

Social entrepreneurship is promoted through organizational structures and institutional social economy environments. However, it is not based on specific organizational forms or specific types of activities. It is motivated by the need to seek new and/or alternative forms of entrepreneurship and identify individuals who share this need (Díaz-Foncea & Marcuello, 2022). According to the European Commission (2019), social entrepreneurship aims to address social challenges and meet social needs in innovative ways, creating a positive social impact for vulnerable population groups. Its purpose is not to maximize profit but to contribute to sustainable development (European Commission, 2019). The social economy organizations operating in European countries have been active in the Union countries, including non-profit organizations, cooperatives, companies, associations, mutual aid societies, associations and foundations, and social enterprises with the common goal of creating a positive social impact and pursuing a social purpose. Social economy business models have, as their main objective, reinvesting most of their profits in the organisation/business and/or in the achievement of the social mission, as well as having a participatory and democratic form of governance. There are 2.8 million social economy enterprises in the EU, representing around 10% of all enterprises in the EU. Their paid workforce amounts to 13.6 million - about 6.2% of the EU workforce - while volunteers amount to 5.5 million. Table 1 shows the main characteristics of social economy enterprises in Europe according to the European Commission (European Commission, 2019).

Table 1. Characteristics of social economy enterprises in Europe

Members	≤ 160 million (mainly retail, banking and agricultural cooperatives, mutuals)
Objectives	Enhancing employment Social cohesion Local development Environmental protection Consumer protection Rural development Development of third countries Social security policies
Size	Small Small and medium-sized enterprises (SMEs)

Financial tools for the digitization of social enterprises

To support digital transformation, this section outlines the financial mechanisms available to social enterprises.

As mentioned above, a social enterprise is a social economy entity whose main objective is to create social impact rather than generate profit for its owners and/or shareholders. Thus, social enterprises are considered (mainly by investors) to be high-risk enterprises, a perception that creates obstacles and difficulties in their financing (Díaz-Foncea & Marcuello, 2022), thereby threatening their financial viability. Financial viability highlights the firm's ability to meet its production and financial obligations while continuing to operate in the near future. Social enterprises additionally have a social mission to fulfill, so financial sustainability enhances their ability to continue serving the vulnerable in the long term (García-Jurado et al., 2021). Globally, there has been a recognized need for financial instruments that take into account the social dimensions of social enterprises and the slower growth rate of their business models. This has resulted in an increase in social investment, social investment programs, financing schemes, and financial instruments for social enterprises.

The European Union, in order to strengthen the financing of social enterprises, has promoted funded programs. At the same time, private organizations such as companies through CSR programs, foundations, individual investors, and municipalities (mainly through public procurement) are supporting social enterprises both at the start-up and development stages, providing both capital and advisory services to address business challenges and achieve a balance between creating social impact and achieving financial sustainability. In addition to these sources of finance, a social enterprise can raise capital from members' cooperative shares, donations, loans, reserves, surplus, profits from the sale of products/services, as well as subsidies, grants, and equity investments.

The European Commission provides specific funding and investment instruments to support social enterprises in creating social impact and social innovation through programs related to innovation, business development, digitization, rural development, and the circular economy. Resources such as the EN Funding Toolkit from the Euclid Network provide concise information on available funding and how to access it (Yaghil & Schmidt, 2022). The European Commission launched the EU Social Economy Action Plan (SEAP) in December 2021, announcing funding programs for improving access to finance for social enterprises and social economy organizations that support them. The plan consists of ten action initiatives aimed at strengthening the social economy by 2030 and includes actions (European Commission, 2019):

- Developing policy and legal frameworks
- Developing state aid mechanisms
- Enhancing access to markets
- Promoting the social economy at local and international levels
- Supporting and developing the capacities of members
- Improving access to finance
- Facilitating green and digital transitions

Access to finance is the final stage of the process, requiring organizations to submit applications. The funding requested by organizations can take the form of grants, loans, and guarantees, as well as opportunities to tender for public procurement contracts.

Types of European Commission Financial Support (Funding Grants, 2022)

- Grants: Provides funding in various forms. They are awarded to organizations (and occasionally individuals), usually based on project proposals submitted in response to relevant calls for proposals.
- Financial Instruments: Loans, guarantees, and equity investments provided to enterprises.
- Financial Prizes: In the context of organized competitions, companies often benefit from free publicity and promotion.
- Procurement of Services: Projects and products are acquired through public procurement tenders.

The financial programs available under the EU Action Plan are outlined in Table 5. However, it should be noted that the new EU Multiannual Financial Framework (MFF) has brought changes to programs related to social economy organizations since 2022 (European Parliament, 2022):

- The EaSI program now falls under the ESF+ program.
- COSME has been transferred to the InvestEU program.

- Erasmus+ has remained but expanded, incorporating key updates linked to the Skills Pact and digitalization for the green economy.
- Horizon 2020 has transitioned to Horizon Europe.

These funding opportunities (Table 2) and financial instruments demonstrate the European Union's commitment to supporting social enterprises through increased access to finance, digital transformation, and social innovation

Table 2. Financial programs available under the Action Plan of the EU[1]

	Sustainable Development and Green Transition	**Social Integration**	**Labour Employment and Skills**	**Digitization**	**International Cooperation and Development**	**Access to finance**
ESF+						
Horizon Europe	●			●	●	
InvestEU						●
The European Single Market Programme	●		●			●
Erasmus+	●	●	●	●	●	
Interreg	●					
European Neighbourhood Instrument			●			●
European Regional Development Fund	●					
Citizens, Equality, Rights & Values		●	●			
Global Europe			●		●	
AMIF		●			●	
Digital Europe (DIGITAL)			●			
EEA & Norway Grants			●	●		

These programs reflect the European Union's commitment to fostering digital transformation, financial access, and social innovation for social enterprises. In addressing financial challenges, the next section explores crowdfunding as an alternative financing method tailored to social enterprises.

Social entrepreneurship: Unique crowdfunding needs

Social entrepreneurship serves as an essential field of study although it remains within its initial phases of development. Most definitions of social entrepreneurship center on four key aspects related to social entrepreneurs and their operations, which include their personal characteristics and operational field, as well as their mission and resource utilization (Gupta, Chauhan, Paul, & Jaiswal, 2020). Social entrepreneurship focuses on developing social value through business methods, which serve to implement this valuable creation. The main purpose aims to enhance the entire system's condition while benefiting both target groups and every member of society (Dwivedi & Weerawardena, 2018).

Social-enterprise ventures represent companies that both create social value and execute mission purposes. This is not like the traditionally sought-after goals of financial gain or some kind of personal benefit. However, while the primary mission of social entrepreneurs may be social, the goal of creating social value does not preclude an economic focus, which may still be part of social entrepreneurship and is actually beneficial from a strategic sustainability perspective (Hein, 2022). Thus, both social entrepreneurs and for-profit entrepreneurs are motivated by their visions, the pursuit of opportunities identified by them, and non-financial goals such as satisfaction or the successful realization of their idea.

The distinguishing characteristic of social entrepreneurship, therefore, lies in its primary mission or purpose of social impact (Teasdale et al., 2022). Over the past decade, the field of social entrepreneurship has garnered a great deal of attention. Such goals stand apart from what society usually considers the most desirable benefits, including financial rewards and personal advantages. Social entrepreneurs focus first on social missions while their aim to generate social value does not impede economic considerations that serve social entrepreneurship strategies for strategic sustainability (García-Jurado, Pérez-Barea, & Nova, 2021; Xanthopoulou, 2020).

Social entrepreneurs, along with their for-profit counterparts, experience motivation through specific visions coupled with the identification of novel opportunities and beyond-financial goals that emphasize satisfaction or the successful implementation of their creative ideas (Chatterjee, Cornelissen, & Wincent, 2020). The main characteristic marking social entrepreneurship exists in its core objective to create meaningful social change. Over the previous decade, the social entrepreneurship sector has caught substantial interest (Mair & Martí, 2005).

A business owner faces their biggest challenge when they lack sufficient capital to operate their venture. The financial problems keep profitable ideas from transitioning beyond the planning stage. Crowdfunding makes its appearance at this moment to serve companies through generous liquidity resources. Through crowdfunding platforms one can interpret market reception for their products or services. Startups receive funding opportunities and industry pattern insights through both the crowdfunding process and the participating platforms to obtain business partnership support.

P2P consumer lending is a form of consumer finance where individuals borrow money directly from other individuals, usually through an online platform. In P2P consumer lending, the borrower typically submits a loan application to an online platform, and investors choose which loans to fund based on the information provided about the borrower and the risk assessment performed by the platform (Yáñez-Valdés & Guerrero, 2023).

P2P business lending is a form of financing for SMEs, where private investors provide loans to these businesses through an online social network. Unlike traditional banking, where businesses need to apply for a loan and have their credit checked, P2P business lending allows businesses to receive funding from investors who are willing to invest in those businesses with greater ease and lower costs (Gouveia, De La Iglesia, Abrantes, & Rivero, 2024).

There is a wide variety of fundraising platforms, each of which has its own strengths and specializations. Kickstarter, Indiegogo, and GoFundMe are the largest in terms of user base and are considered among the most flexible platforms on the market. Based on crowdfunding platform statistics, Kickstarter is the ideal choice among the three for successful campaigns. But the projects with the most funding often come from Indiegogo (Antonizzi & Smuts, 2020). As it can been observed from Figure 5 below, Wefunder crowdfunding platform leads with $70.89 million, followed closely by StartEngine ($68.6 million) and Republic ($37.65 million). Other platforms, such as Netcapital ($8.18 million), Microventures ($5.71 million), and SeedInvest ($5.09 million), raised significantly lower amounts. Smaller platforms like MainVest ($3.97 million), NextSeed ($3.73 million), Equifund CFP ($2.97 million), and TruCrowd ($2.08 million) contributed to the crowdfunding ecosystem. The data from KingsCrowd 2021 showcases the growing impact of regulated crowdfunding in the US, offering startups and businesses alternative financing.

The challenges faced by social entrepreneurs tend to evolve over time. Some of the most persistent challenges include the leadership issues facing social-enterprise entrepreneurs, as leaders in these positions must balance both social and business aspects with great skill and expertise (Nicholls, 2010). Moreover, in most social-business environments, there is a strong social component alongside the profit component, leading to competing institutional logics. Despite the blurred boundaries and the intertwined nature of the social and entrepreneurial aspects, it is important that social entrepreneurs have a clearly defined mission, planned outcomes, and measurable goals (Chatterjee, Cornelissen, & Wincent, 2020). The scaling of the social-entrepreneurial venture from its fledgling roots to a larger enterprise is fraught with ethical concerns in addition to operational and financial issues, making this one of the most challenging aspects of social entrepreneurship (Bohan et al., 2023). The abilities to raise capital, remain attractive to investors, and leverage resources as required are dependent on legitimacy, and this is an issue that often plagues social-enterprise ventures, particularly start-ups. This also relates to the challenge of institutional support, as social-enterprise ventures often do not have access to the institutional support they desire (Rodríguez-Ramírez, Zapata-Domínguez, & Ramírez-Plazas, 2022).

The role of digital platforms

Digital technologies combined with updated methods of interaction and collaboration and alternative opportunity-seeking approaches have generated a novel competitive business environment that presents different challenges to all types of business ventures. Digital technology development enables social entrepreneurship expansion since these tools help social ventures become more visible and discover new opportunities (Paul, Alhassan, Binsaif, & Singh, 2022). The absence of capital access has been replaced by crowdfunding. The natural progression of crowdsourcing led to crowdfunding that acts as the successor through its approach of obtaining innovative ideas from numerous members while fixing perception problems with groupthink (Mursalzade, 2024). Through crowdfunding, social entrepreneurs secure valuable funding since banks will not extend financing to them like conventional businesses (Pérez-Barea, 2025).

Social entrepreneurs who lack experience can gather various small donations from global supporters across the world to construct a significant funding base (Zhiyang, Chenfang, & Bin, 2020). Social entrepreneurs demonstrate innate entrepreneurial strength and leadership in their mission, which makes them natural seekers of new technology from early on. New technology does not serve as a barrier that limits social entrepreneurship growth. Social enterprises began adopting crowdfunding platforms recently, which serve as critical elements for new social-enterprise success (Monteiro, Sánchez-García, Hernández-Sánchez, & Cardella, 2022). Social-enterprise ventures would directly perish from lack of funding support because traditional funding institutions view them as unattractive investment opportunities due to their non-profit orientation (Chatterjee, Cornelissen, & Wincent, 2020).

Figure 3. Digital Technology Adoption in Social Enterprises vs SMEs (Source: Authors' own work)

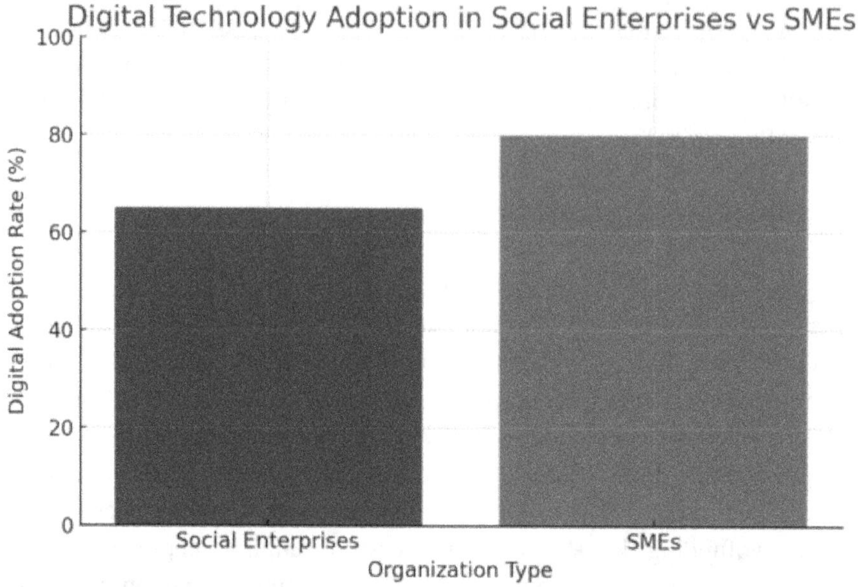

Table 3 below presents the structured data for digital technologies and their impact on social enterprises:

Table 3. Impact of Digital Technology on Social Enterprises (Source: Authors' own work)

Digital Technology	Impact on Social Enterprises
AI (Artificial Intelligence)	Improves efficiency, predictive analytics for impact measurement
Big Data Analytics	Enhances decision-making and impact assessment
Cloud Computing	Reduces operational costs, improves accessibility
E-commerce Platforms	Expands market reach and sales revenue
Social Media Marketing	Boosts customer engagement and brand visibility
ERP (Enterprise Resource Planning) Software	Optimizes resource management and financial planning
Automation & Chatbots	Increases response speed and operational efficiency
Blockchain for Transparency	Enhances trust and transparency in transactions
Remote Collaboration Tools	Improves teamwork and productivity across locations

Digital technologies and social entrepreneurship now operate together to reshape business models of social enterprises so they can handle social issues more efficiently. Modern technologies allow social enterprises to make social and sustainability value in addition to financial achievements (Gouveia, De La Iglesia, Abrantes, & Rivero, 2024). Social enterprises felt compelled to develop new business models that use digital platforms due to the COVID-19 pandemic's speeded-up digitalization needs for better resilience and expansion capabilities (Skare, De Las Mercedes De Obesso, & Ribeiro-Navarrete, 2022).

Digital transformation enables new ways to practice social entrepreneurship, but it creates various obstacles as well. Financial restrictions prevent numerous social enterprises from adopting modern digital tools, and limitation of technological expertise makes it challenging to maximize digital systems (Antonizzi & Smuts, 2020). Safety and privacy of data alongside automation systems and digital platform dependence demand serious ethical reviews because digital platform usage continues expanding (Hein, 2022). Digitalization functions as an essential force of social innovation that enables businesses to work with stakeholders and increase transparency while expanding their reach to larger audiences, even though it poses implementation difficulties (Mursalzade, 2024).

Social enterprises maintain financial sustainability as their primary core challenge. Social enterprises experience funding barriers because they prioritize social value creation over maximizing profits, which leads to rejection by typical investment channels (Díaz-Foncea & Marcuello, 2022). The lack of financial sustainability encourages social enterprises to explore alternative funding mechanisms consisting of crowdfunding, impact investing, and European funding programs (European Commission, 2019). Through different financial instruments such as grants and social investment programs, the social entrepreneurship sector achieves digital transformation (Paul, Alhassan, Binsaif, & Singh, 2022).

Social entrepreneurship will develop toward sustainable ethical business methods due to substantial requests from younger generations like Millennials and Gen Z (Teasdale, Bellazzecca, De Bruin, & Roy, 2022). These socially conscious consumers deliberately choose enterprises that match their values, thus offering social businesses an opportunity to apply digital tools for both social goal achievement and industry competitiveness (Gupta, Chauhan, Paul, & Jaiswal, 2020). Social enterprises need to transform their operations through digital tools development because digital tools will continue expanding in the coming years (Skare, De Las Mercedes De Obesso, & Ribeiro-Navarrete, 2022). Digital transformation is now an essential development for social entrepreneurship to achieve their mission of creating sustainable and inclusive business models (Gouveia, De La Iglesia, Abrantes, & Rivero, 2024).

Social entrepreneurship development will be driven by growing market demand for sustainable ethical practices because this mindset is popular among social consumers, including Millennials and Gen Z (Monteiro, Sánchez-García, Hernández-Sánchez, & Cardella, 2022). Sustainable business customers now prefer companies matching their social values, which creates a business opportunity for social enterprises to combine digital solutions that both grow their competitive advantage and advance their social cause (Mursalzade, 2024). Social enterprises need to transform their operations by incorporating new digital tools because the tools will continue to develop in the future to maintain both their extended performance and social goals (Antonizzi & Smuts, 2020). Social entrepreneurship needs digital technology integration to advance its mission of creating sustainable and inclusive business systems (Pérez-Barea, 2025).

To consolidate the insights presented throughout this chapter, Figure 4 below illustrates the interconnected role of digital inputs, enabling conditions, transformation processes, and resulting outcomes in social enterprises. This conceptual model offers a visual summary of how digital innovation can support value co-creation and sustainable impact in the context of social entrepreneurship.

Figure 4. Digital Innovation Framework for Social Enterprises

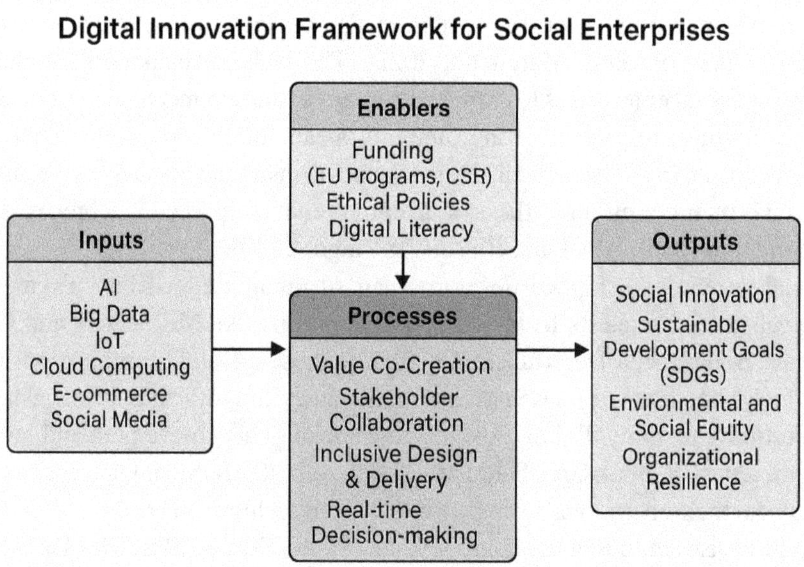

CONCLUSIONS

This chapter has investigated the transformative role of digital technologies in advancing the mission of social entrepreneurship, with a specific emphasis on value co-creation and sustainability. Through an integrative analysis of theoretical perspectives and empirical evidence, we have demonstrated how digitalization supports social enterprises in navigating complex socio-economic challenges, enhancing operational efficiency, and fostering innovative, inclusive solutions. From a theoretical standpoint, the application of digital tools within social entrepreneurship benefits from the inclusion of established frameworks such as the Technology-Organization-Environment (TOE) model and the Diffusion of Innovation Theory. These models can provide a structured lens through which to analyze the adoption and integration of digital technologies in varied socio-institutional contexts, thereby enriching the academic rigor of the discussion.

On a practical level, digital technologies enable social enterprises to expand their reach, scale impact, and improve service delivery. Nonetheless, this transformation is not without challenges. Issues such as digital inequality, limited technological literacy, ethical risks, and governance concerns must be critically addressed. Moreover, while successful case studies are often highlighted, greater attention should be paid to failure narratives and the barriers that hinder technological adoption, particularly in under-resourced regions.

To support these initiatives, policy interventions and targeted funding mechanisms, such as those provided by the European Commission, play a critical role. These instruments facilitate digital adoption, improve financial sustainability, and empower social enterprises to innovate in alignment with societal needs. In light of these findings, we advocate for future research that employs both qualitative and quantitative approaches to explore the long-term effects of digital transformation on social enterprise models. Areas of inquiry should include ethical considerations, regional disparities, stakeholder engagement processes, and resilience in times of crisis.

While the integration of digital technologies offers significant benefits for social entrepreneurship, it also raises a number of ethical concerns that must be addressed. These include issues related to data privacy, algorithmic bias, and unequal access to digital infrastructure—especially in marginalized or underserved communities. Over-reliance on automation and platform economies may inadvertently exclude the very groups social enterprises aim to empower. Therefore, ethical governance and inclusive digital strategies are critical to ensuring that technology serves as a tool for empowerment rather than exclusion.

Ultimately, while digitalization is not a panacea, it serves as a powerful enabler for social entrepreneurship when aligned with inclusive practices and sustainable development goals. By addressing both opportunities and constraints, stakeholders can harness digital innovation to build resilient, equitable, and socially impactful business ecosystems. In light of the findings discussed, this final section proposes key areas for future academic inquiry in the field of digital social entrepreneurship.

Recommendations for Further Research

Academic research on digital social entrepreneurship continues to expand, but researchers need to fill multiple knowledge gaps. Research needs to prioritize systematic investigation between digitalization and value co-creation relationships in social enterprises (Mursalzade, 2024). The majority of studies in traditional entrepreneurship exist, but research about how digital transformation supports stakeholder collaboration and social enterprise value co-generation remains relatively scarce (Zhiyang, Chenfang, & Bin, 2020). Future academic research needs to use mixed approaches of qualitative and quantitative methods to examine how digital adoption boosts co-creation operations in diverse social enterprise types (Monteiro, Sánchez-García, Hernández-Sánchez, & Cardella, 2022).

Research must track digital social businesses over many years to determine how well they remain viable (Paul, Alhassan, Binsaif, & Singh, 2022). Business digitalization helps social enterprises grow, but it is difficult to predict how this method will affect their ability to keep operating over extended periods (Pérez-Barea, 2025). Research needs to examine whether digital technology supports steady business performance while allowing change and growth for social enterprises in different economic environments (Skare, De Las Mercedes De Obesso, & Ribeiro-Navarrete, 2022). The examination of digital technology use in social enterprises needs to happen across multiple areas and nations to identify effective methods and regional difficulties (Gouveia, De La Iglesia, Abrantes, & Rivero, 2024).

Digital transformation in social entrepreneurship faces problems related to both ethical standards and privacy protection requirements (Upadhyay, Upadhyay, & Dwivedi, 2021). Social enterprises require additional research to determine methods of digitally transformed implementation that protect privacy while supplying equal access to technology (Gupta, Chauhan, Paul, & Jaiswal, 2020). Leaders in policy-making and business need to create systems that will maintain proper digital innovation levels while ensuring ethical practices remain a priority (Teasdale, Bellazzecca, De Bruin, & Roy, 2022).

Digital transformation in social entrepreneurship creates ethical and privacy issues that deserve attention (Hein, 2022). Social enterprises face challenges regarding digital tool safety aspects as well as biases and ethical standards of their governance systems while using digital tools for data collection, consumer interaction tasks, and impact measurement activities (Mair & Martí, 2005). Additional research must examine the methods through which social enterprises can implement digital solutions to protect privacy while providing equal technological access (Díaz-Foncea & Marcuello, 2022). Government officials and business executives need to establish rules that combine the advantages of digital progress with ethical practices (European Commission, 2019).

Research should expand to evaluate how policymaking together with institutional support assists digital social enterprises achieve wider growth. The growth of digital social enterprises became possible through several financial instruments including EU funding programs and impact investing and corporate social responsibility initiatives. Additional assessment must occur to understand the accessibility along with effectiveness and long-term working capacity of these digital social enterprises. The study of funding models that shape digital transformation within social entrepreneurship provides essential knowledge to policymaking bodies who want to create sustainable and inclusive economic systems.

Researchers should study how frequent use of artificial intelligence and automation technologies will affect social enterprises in forthcoming years. The implementation of AI-driven solutions generates productivity improvements and automatic process execution and improved decision-making although workers might lose their positions while ethical challenges emerge about monitoring systems and responsible decision-making methods. Research needs to determine how artificial intelligence can join social entrepreneurship operations without compromising its core values of inclusiveness and environmental sustainability.

Research gaps enable scholars to build a better comprehension of digital social entrepreneurship so they can develop sustainable and ethical and innovative social enterprise models.

REFERENCES

Abou-Foul, M., Ruiz-Alba, J. L., & López-Tenorio, P. J. (2022). The impact of artificial intelligence capabilities on servitization: The moderating role of absorptive capacity-A dynamic capabilities perspective. *Journal of Business Research, 157*, 113609. DOI: 10.1016/j.jbusres.2022.113609

Abou-Foul, M., Ruiz-Alba, J. L., & Soares, A. (2020). The impact of digitalization and servitization on the financial performance of a firm: An empirical analysis. *Production Planning and Control, 32*(12), 975–989. DOI: 10.1080/09537287.2020.1780508

Adam, S., Fuzi, N. M., Ramdan, M. R., & Ismail, A. F. M. F. (2025). The Effectiveness of Digital Entrepreneurship ecosystem toward enriching income generation: The moderating role of entrepreneurial intention. *SAGE Open, 15*(1), 21582440241305361. Advance online publication. DOI: 10.1177/21582440241305361

Akram, R., Li, Q., Srivastava, M., Zheng, Y., & Irfan, M. (2024). Nexus between green technology innovation and climate policy uncertainty: Unleashing the role of artificial intelligence in an emerging economy. *Technological Forecasting and Social Change, 209*, 123820. DOI: 10.1016/j.techfore.2024.123820

Antonizzi, J., & Smuts, H. (2020). The Characteristics of Digital Entrepreneurship and Digital Transformation: A Systematic Literature review. In *Lecture notes in computer science* (pp. 239–251). DOI: 10.1007/978-3-030-44999-5_20

. Atienza-Barba, M., Álvarez-García, J., Meseguer-Martínez, Á., & Barba-Sánchez, V. (2025). The family business in the digital era: advancing towards artificial intelligence. *Journal of Family Business Management*. DOI: 10.1108/JFBM-09-2024-0215

Bachmann, N., Thienemann, A., Tüzün, A., Brunner, M., Tripathi, S., Pöchtrager, S., & Jodlbauer, H. (2025). The evolution of the business model Canvas for digital sustainability. *Procedia Computer Science, 253*, 1012–1023. DOI: 10.1016/j.procs.2025.01.163

Bohan, S., Tippmann, E., Levie, J., Igoe, J., & Bowers, B. (2023). What is scaling? *Journal of Business Venturing, 39*(1), 106355. DOI: 10.1016/j.jbusvent.2023.106355

Boone, C., & Özcan, S. (2015). Strategic Choices at Entry and Relative Survival Advantage of Cooperatives versus Corporations in the US Bio-Ethanol Industry, 1978-2015. *Journal of Management Studies, 53*(7), 1113–1140. DOI: 10.1111/joms.12168

Cavallo, A., Ghezzi, A., & Balocco, R. (2018). Entrepreneurial ecosystem research: Present debates and future directions. *The International Entrepreneurship and Management Journal*, *15*(4), 1291–1321. DOI: 10.1007/s11365-018-0526-3

Chandra, Y., & Kerlin, J. A. (2020). Social entrepreneurship in context: Pathways for new contributions in the field. *Journal of Asian Public Policy*, *14*(2), 135–151. DOI: 10.1080/17516234.2020.1845472

Chatterjee, I., Cornelissen, J., & Wincent, J. (2020). Social entrepreneurship and values work: The role of practices in shaping values and negotiating change. *Journal of Business Venturing*, *36*(1), 106064. DOI: 10.1016/j.jbusvent.2020.106064

Corner, P. D., & Ho, M. (2010). How opportunities develop in social entrepreneurship. *Entrepreneurship Theory and Practice*, *34*(4), 635–659. DOI: 10.1111/j.1540-6520.2010.00382.x

COSME. (n.d.). Internal Market, Industry, Entrepreneurship and SMEs. Retrieved March 8, 2025, from https://single-market-economy.ec.europa.eu/smes/cosme_en

Díaz-Foncea, M., & Marcuello, C. (2022). Social Enterprises: Conceptual Debates and Approaches. In *Springer eBooks* (pp. 133–151). DOI: 10.1007/978-3-031-14216-1_7

Dwivedi, A., & Weerawardena, J. (2018). Conceptualizing and operationalizing the social entrepreneurship construct. *Journal of Business Research*, *86*, 32–40. DOI: 10.1016/j.jbusres.2018.01.053

European Commission. (2019). *Funding opportunities*. Research and Innovation. Retrieved March 8, 2025, from https://research-and-innovation.ec.europa.eu/funding/funding-opportunities_en

Eurostat. (2022, June 29). More than half of EU enterprises use social media. *Eurostat*. https://ec.europa.eu/eurostat/web/products-eurostat-news/-/edn-20220629-1

Fischer, M., Foord, D., Frecè, J., Hillebrand, K., Kissling-Näf, I., Meili, R., Peskova, M., Risi, D., Schmidpeter, R., & Stucki, T. (2023). Social innovation (or why we need the civil society). In *SpringerBriefs in business* (pp. 77–89). DOI: 10.1007/978-3-031-25397-3_5

García-Jurado, A., Pérez-Barea, J. J., & Nova, R. J. (2021). A New Approach to Social Entrepreneurship: A Systematic Review and Meta-Analysis. *Sustainability (Basel)*, *13*(5), 2754. DOI: 10.3390/su13052754

Gouveia, S., De La Iglesia, D. H., Abrantes, J. L., & Rivero, A. J. L. (2024). Transforming strategy and value creation through digitalization? *Administrative Sciences*, *14*(11), 307. DOI: 10.3390/admsci14110307

Gupta, B. B., Gaurav, A., Panigrahi, P. K., & Arya, V. (2022). Analysis of artificial intelligence-based technologies and approaches on sustainable entrepreneurship. *Technological Forecasting and Social Change*, *186*, 122152. DOI: 10.1016/j.techfore.2022.122152

Gupta, P., Chauhan, S., Paul, J., & Jaiswal, M. (2020). Social entrepreneurship research: A review and future research agenda. *Journal of Business Research*, *113*, 209–229. DOI: 10.1016/j.jbusres.2020.03.032

Hein, R. (2022). Beyond a Balanced View of Social Entrepreneurship within a Social–Commercial Dichotomy: Towards a Four-Dimensional Typology. *Sustainability (Basel)*, *14*(8), 4454. DOI: 10.3390/su14084454

Kaufmann, D., Kraay, A., & Mastruzzi, M. (2011). The Worldwide Governance Indicators: Methodology and analytical issues. *Hague Journal on the Rule of Law*, *3*(02), 220–246. DOI: 10.1017/S1876404511200046

Kenny, N., McCoy, S., & Mihut, G. (2020). Special education reforms in Ireland: Changing systems, changing schools. *International Journal of Inclusive Education*, •••, 1–20. DOI: 10.1080/13603116.2020.1821447

Kotiranta, A., Tykkyläinen, S., & Puumalainen, K. (2020). Growth of social and commercial SMEs: a comparative study. In *Edward Elgar Publishing eBooks*. DOI: 10.4337/9781839109690.00018

Mair, J., & Martí, I. (2005). Social entrepreneurship research: A source of explanation, prediction, and delight. *Journal of World Business*, *41*(1), 36–44. DOI: 10.1016/j.jwb.2005.09.002

Mair, J., & Sharma, S. (2012). Performance measurement and social entrepreneurship. In *Gabler Verlag eBooks* (pp. 175–189). DOI: 10.1007/978-3-8349-7093-0_9

Monteiro, A. A., Sánchez-García, J. C., Hernández-Sánchez, B. R., & Cardella, G. M. (2022). Social Entrepreneurship Conceptual Approaches. *Encyclopedia*, *2*(2), 1004–1018. DOI: 10.3390/encyclopedia2020066

Muñoz, P., Naudé, W., Williams, N., Williams, T., & Frías, R. (2020). Reorienting entrepreneurial support infrastructure to tackle a social crisis: A rapid response. *Journal of Business Venturing Insights*, *14*, e00181. DOI: 10.1016/j.jbvi.2020.e00181

Mursalzade, H. (2024). Digital social entities, valuable communities: How digitalization enables value co-creation for social enterprises. *Society and Economy*, *46*(4), 423–440. Advance online publication. DOI: 10.1556/204.2024.00015

Nicholls, A. (2010). The Legitimacy of Social Entrepreneurship: Reflexive Isomorphism in a Pre–Paradigmatic Field. *Entrepreneurship Theory and Practice*, *34*(4), 611–633. DOI: 10.1111/j.1540-6520.2010.00397.x

Osabohien, R., Worgwu, H., & Al-Faryan, M. S. (2022). Social entrepreneurship, technology diffusion and future employment in Nigeria. *Social Enterprise Journal*, *19*(1), 40–50. DOI: 10.1108/SEJ-03-2022-0032

Paul, J., Alhassan, I., Binsaif, N., & Singh, P. (2022). Digital entrepreneurship research: A systematic review. *Journal of Business Research*, *156*, 113507. DOI: 10.1016/j.jbusres.2022.113507

Pérez-Barea, J. J. (2025). The Evolution of Social Entrepreneurship: Broadening the framework for the digital and sustainable era. *Administrative Sciences*, *15*(2), 55. DOI: 10.3390/admsci15020055

Powell, T. C., & Dent-Micallef, A. (1997). Information technology as competitive advantage: The role of human, business, and technology resources. *Strategic Management Journal*, *18*(5), 375–405. DOI: 10.1002/(SICI)1097-0266(199705)18:5<375::AID-SMJ876>3.0.CO;2-7

Ramos-Villagrasa, P. J., Barrada, J. R., Fernández-Del-Río, E., & Koopmans, L. (2019). Assessing job performance using brief self-report scales: The case of the individual work performance Questionnaire. *Journal of Work and Organizational Psychology*, *35*(3), 195–205. DOI: 10.5093/jwop2019a21

Rodríguez-Ramírez, A., Zapata-Domínguez, Á., & Ramírez-Plazas, E. (2022). Theoretical analysis of the social entrepreneur's mode of being. *Journal of Social Entrepreneurship*, *15*(3), 1183–1205. DOI: 10.1080/19420676.2022.2128393

Salvi, A., Vitolla, F., Rubino, M., Giakoumelou, A., & Raimo, N. (2020). Online information on digitalisation processes and its impact on firm value. *Journal of Business Research*, *124*, 437–444. DOI: 10.1016/j.jbusres.2020.10.025

Shrivastava, P., & Kennelly, J. J. (2013). Sustainability and Place-Based enterprise. *Organization & Environment*, *26*(1), 83–101. DOI: 10.1177/1086026612475068

Skare, M., De Las Mercedes De Obesso, M., & Ribeiro-Navarrete, S. (2022). Digital transformation and European small and medium enterprises (SMEs): A comparative study using digital economy and society index data. *International Journal of Information Management*, *68*, 102594. DOI: 10.1016/j.ijinfomgt.2022.102594

Teasdale, S., Bellazzecca, E., De Bruin, A., & Roy, M. J. (2022). The (R)evolution of the Social Entrepreneurship Concept: A Critical Historical Review. *Nonprofit and Voluntary Sector Quarterly*, *52*(1, suppl), 212S–240S. DOI: 10.1177/08997640221130691

Upadhyay, N., Upadhyay, S., & Dwivedi, Y. K. (2021). Theorizing artificial intelligence acceptance and digital entrepreneurship model. *International Journal of Entrepreneurial Behaviour & Research, 28*(5), 1138–1166. DOI: 10.1108/IJEBR-01-2021-0052

Xanthopoulou, P. (2020). From e-government to public value creation. [IJSR]. *International Journal of Scientific Research, 9*(3), 927–933. https://www.researchgate.net/profile/Panagiota_Xanthopoulou4/publication/341930864_From_e-Government_to_Public_Value_Creation/links/638361a9554def6193793485/From-e-Government-to-Public-Value-Creation.pdf

Xanthopoulou, P., Antoniadis, I., & Avlogiaris, G. (2023). Unveiling the drivers of digital governance adoption in public administration. *Problems and Perspectives in Management, 21*(4), 454–467. DOI: 10.21511/ppm.21(4).2023.35

Xanthopoulou, P., Antoniadis, I., & Triantari, S. (2022, July). Managing public sector in the digital reform era: Organizational factors and their impact on the digital transformation at the Greek public administration. In *International Conference on Applied Economics* (pp. 947-962). Cham: Springer International Publishing. DOI: 10.1007/978-3-031-22749-3_59

Yaghil, A., & Schmidt, G. (Eds.). (2022). *EN Funding Toolkit*. Euclid Network. https://euclidnetwork.eu/wp-content/uploads/2022/12/eu-funding-toolkit_final_2022.pdf

Yáñez-Valdés, C., & Guerrero, M. (2023). Assessing the organizational and ecosystem factors driving the impact of transformative FinTech platforms in emerging economies. *International Journal of Information Management, 73*, 102689. DOI: 10.1016/j.ijinfomgt.2023.102689

Zhiyang, L., Chenfang, Z., & Bin, L. (2020). Digital Social Entrepreneurship: Theoretical Framework and Research Outlook. *Waiguo Jingji Yu Guanli, 42*(04), 3–18. DOI: 10.16538/j.cnki.fem.20200228.402

KEY TERMS AND DEFINITIONS

Social entrepreneurship: The entrepreneurial approach of social entrepreneurship combines equal importance between social and environmental impact alongside economic sustainability. Social enterprises operate differently from usual businesses because they tackle societal issues with mission-based innovative approaches. The enterprise channels its profits toward its social mission regardless of whether it meets traditional financial standards.

Social enterprises: Organizations known as social enterprises have positive social or environmental change as their main operating goal. These organizations work within the social economy framework by merging profit-based activities into their structures which combine social responsibility projects.

Digitalization: Digitalization exists as a procedure that merges digital technologies with operational business processes to deliver increased efficiency along with innovation and extended scalability. The implementation of artificial intelligence together with big data and blockchain makes up digitalization which enables companies to revolutionize their established business practices.

Value co-creation: Businesses or consumers and stakeholders unite through value co-creation as a collaborative process to jointly create value for each other. For social entrepreneurship to create social and economic value it requires active involvement between communities and policymakers and investors.

Artificial intelligence (AI): Through AI development computer systems attain capabilities for executing human-intelligence-based activities which entail decisions and data assessments along with problem resolution. AI systems integrate into social enterprises because they help these organizations improve their efficiency as well as their ability to evaluate their impact.

Big data analytics: Organizations use the data analytics method to study extensive datasets for discovering marketing patterns which generate strategic choices. Through big data analysis social enterprises explore social patterns and evaluate their organizational effects to enhance service quality.

Blockchain technology: Blockchain technology serves social enterprises through tracking metrics of impact and handling supply chain operations with ethical practice monitoring.

Crowdfunding: Crowdfunding provides social enterprises with an online-based alternative financing method to obtain capital from numerous donors through digital platforms. This funding mechanism enables organizations to obtain financial resources from numerous donors even though they do not meet standard investment qualifications.

Sustainable development: Sustainable development describes progress which fulfills present requirements while preserving the future generations' capacity to satisfy their needs. The goals of sustainable development match those of social enterprises because they work to bring together economic development with protection of the environment and fairness for all members of society.

The triple bottom line (TBL): Through this approach organizations can assess their achievement by validating more than financial data.

The Internet of Things (IoT): Through IoT networks devices achieve real-time data collection and data exchange capabilities. The IoT helps social enterprises to manage resources and conduct sustainability monitoring while improving their service operations.

Digital social entrepreneurship (DSE): Social entrepreneurship principles united with digital technology form the business model of Digital social entrepreneurship (DSE) to tackle social problems. Mission-based business entities use digital tools to increase accessibility as well as efficiency and scalability.

Resilience: The ability of social enterprises to survive and grow through economic changes along with social and technological transformations makes up their organizational resilience. Flexible and scalable digital tools serve as important tools to build resilience because they deliver effective solutions for social initiatives.

Green technologies: People consider green technology a collection of innovative practices that aim to minimize environmental destruction through clean energy methods and sustainable production systems combined with environment-friendly business operations. The adoption of green technologies depends heavily on social enterprises for achieving sustainable development goals.

ENDNOTE

1 Using data from Yaghil and Schmidt, (2022).

Chapter 12
Total Quality Management (TQM): A Linkage to Customer Satisfaction Through Academic Quality Services

Despina Konstantinides
Neapolis University, Pafos, Cyprus

Anastasia Athanasoula-Reppa
Neapolis University, Pafos, Cyprus

Panagiota Chatzimichailidou
https://orcid.org/0000-0002-7241-3678
Neapolis University, Pafos, Cyprus

ABSTRACT

This chapter explores the linkage between the Total Quality Management (TQM) and customer satisfaction, in the context of academic service quality. Using Deming's theory as a theoretical background, this study examines how TQM principles can improve academic quality services, with the goal of increased customer satisfaction. It is sought to reveal the possible impact of TQM in upgrading academic services through the empowerment of academic community members, students, faculty and staff. From the literature review path, it seems that there is strong evidence of the positive impact of TQM on academic services, with an emphasis on long-term benefits for all members involved. TQM offers a powerful framework for the improvement of academic quality services, while, concurrently, achieving high levels of customer satisfaction. The successful implementation of TQM seems to have a beneficial effect on all members, contributing to the overall effectiveness of the academic

DOI: 10.4018/979-8-3693-5583-1.ch012

organization. The study concludes with recommendations on the dynamics of TQM in enhancing academic services.

INTRODUCTION

Total Quality Management (TQM) is considered a key framework in various sectors and is mainly linked to continuous improvement and customer satisfaction. In the field of academic institutions, TQM principles can significantly improve educational quality, fostering improved outcomes for students, staff and the institution in general. This chapter explores further the understanding of the relationship between TQM and customer satisfaction, specifically through the lens of higher education.

Although TQM is rooted in the manufacturing sector, its application extends to other fields, such as education. Integrated management that leads to the improvement of quality of products and services through systemic processes is at the core of TQM and this calls for a commitment to continuous improvement. These practices tend to involve all members of an organization in pursuing excellence. This study endorses the idea that TQM can be utilized for serving the students' needs, perceived as the customers, enhancing, at the same time, the quality of educational services and the administrative procedures.

The aim of the chapter is to discuss aspects of TQM that lead to customer satisfaction and the impact it has on the context of service quality matters, as well as the extent to which this relationship occurs. Might this approach succeed in services' effectiveness and achieve customer satisfaction, is a query this study seeks to answer. Basic strategic steps signpost the structure of the chapter, to serve the objectives of this study:

i. Depict the definition of the TQM; a foundational understanding of TQM principles and their evolution are discussed, as well as the theoretical underpinnings, essential components, such as customer focus, continuous improvement and employee involvement. By depicting TQM concepts, a preliminary stage for a deeper exploration of its integration in academic settings is revealed.
ii. Investigate the linkage to customer satisfaction through academic quality services and bridge the gap between TQM principles and customer satisfaction. In academic institutions, customer satisfaction can be measured through various ways, including student satisfaction, retention rates and academic performance. Hereby, we try to examine how implementing TQM practices in educational services may lead to enhanced satisfaction among the members of the academic community, by demonstrating the positive impact of TQM in terms of academic quality and customer satisfaction.

iii. Discuss sides of TQM and enlighten the relationship between customer satisfaction and customer empowerment, delving into insights in the context of higher education. Empowering means involving all members of the academic community in decision-making processes, providing them with the necessary resources, support, with an environment that fosters self-directed learning. All these are studied in order to lead to satisfaction and more effective educational outcomes, through the active roles of the staff in supporting and implementing empowerment strategies.
iv. Discuss the TQM approaches in Academic Quality Services, to understand the way it can be applied to various academic services. Academic institutions can ensure that their services are consistently aligned with the needs and expectations of students as customers and sustain improvements in quality and performance.
v. Extract the conclusions of the study through a comprehensive exploration of how TQM principles may be effectively applied to enhance academic quality services and customer satisfaction in higher education. By examining the theoretical foundations, practical dimensions and evidence, the chapter can contribute to the growing body of research on TQM in education. The main aim is to offer valuable insights for educators, administrators and policymakers that strive to improve the quality of educational services and achieve higher levels of satisfaction among all members of their organization.

The inclusion of TQM in academic institutions is an innovative way of managing quality. Inculcating a learning culture that advances the principles of TQM in these institutions will improve their service provision and thus enhance education quality which will result to better outcomes for students, faculty and the entire institution. This chapter presents findings from this integrative approach, pointing towards some possible features of TQM leading to substantial improvement in academic quality plus consumer satisfaction as well; thereby preparing a more efficient and competitive higher education system.

THE TOTAL QUALITY MANAGEMENT (TQM)

TQM is related to the philosophy of seeking to meet customer needs, constantly improving quality and performance. One of the most important elements (Montgomery, 2012) in favor of the success of TQM in various fields is the measurement of quality performance (Prajogo & Brown 2004; Prajogo, 2005; Prajogo & Mcdermott, 2005; Prajogo & Sohal, 2006; Prajogo & Mcdermott, 2005) that is of high importance. It has been considered as an approach to improve the effectiveness, flexibility and competitiveness of enterprises to meet customer requirements

(Oakland, 2014). By focusing on the customers' needs, the operational practices are performed in accordance with the requirements of excellence. This might be the reason that TQM has been recognized as a viable way to achieve excellence, acquire efficient business solutions and enchant customers and suppliers (Mohanty & Behera, 1996). Conceptualizing over the *excellence in quality* as a part of TQM, this chapter initiates a service quality perspective in the process of customer satisfaction, which (perspective) is being examined on a bibliographical level.

TQM is an outward customer-based approach (Deming, 1986) and has been considered as "a management approach that ensures mutual cooperation of everyone in an organization and associated business processes to produce products and services that meet and hopefully exceed the needs and expectations of customers" (Dale, 2003). TQM has become an essential management philosophy used for improving quality and productivity in organizations (Karia and Asaari, 2006) and is the process of changing the basic culture of an organization and forwarding it towards advanced product or service quality (Gaither,1996).

TQM rapidly became a top priority in many organizations due to the globalization age and highly competitive environment forcing customers to search for better products and services (Thiagaragan, Zairi and Dale, 2001). In 1980 the notion of TQM was considered as a strategic policy which had been implemented by focusing all the resources of an organization to achieve quality excellence (Benavides-Velasco, et al., 2014). Entrepreneurs adopt TQM in their attempt to move towards quality. On a literature review level, it is argued that TQM principles are not universally applicable across all contexts but are contingent on contextual factors (Brinbaum and Deshotels, 1999; Brinbaum, 2000) and that the way the definition of quality is given based on the customers' needs and expectations in business and industry environments is not at all appropriate for education (Houston, 2008).

Successful TQM implementation is often linked with the CSFs, which are responsible for achieving business excellence (Talib and Rahman, 2010). TQM practices have been classified by researchers as hard and soft phase; some practices are considered to be hard elements of TQM (i.e. fewer human factors involved, like quality control, quality measurements, etc.), while others are considered as soft elements of TQM (i.e. human factors are involved, like quality control, quality measurement, etc.) (Ali, et al., 2018). According to a research that aimed to examine the relationship between critical success factors (CSFs) of TQM, strategic goals and organizational performance in India TQM practices have a significant impact on financial and operational performance (Zehir & Zehir, 2023). Thus, performance should not be considered as an objective; it is orientated by the efficacy and efficiency of the outcomes of well-organized and strategic goals.

TQM can be interpreted as a holistic approach to long-term success through customer satisfaction. This means that all members of an organization are actively involved in participating for improving processes, products, services and the organizational cultural framework. The basic principles of TQM include customer focus, total employee involvement, process-centered approaches, strategic and systematic policies, integrated systems, continuous improvement, fact-based decision making, as well as communication; understanding is required and meeting customer needs and expectations (Evans & Lindsay, 2020), engaging all employees in the pursuit of quality improvements (Goetsch & Davis, 2014), improving processes to enhance quality and efficiency (Oakland, 2014), ensuring all parts of the organization work together towards quality goals (Dale, 2015), planning and managing quality initiatives systematically (Hoyle, 2009), continuous efforts to improve products, services, and processes (Besterfield et al., 2013), using data and analysis to guide decisions (Juran & De Feo, 2010), promoting open and effective communication within the organization (Deming, 1986).

LINKING TQM WITH ACADEMIC QUALITY SERVICES ACCORDING TO DEMING'S THEORY

Dr. W. Edwards Deming's theory emphasizes the importance of continuous improvement and the role of management in fostering a culture of quality. Deming's 14 Points are empowered by the main idea that academic institutions can develop a culture of quality that enhances academic services and leads to higher customer satisfaction. Academic quality services are aligned to this point of view and mainly focus on the following aspects (Deming, 1986): Academic organizations are required to align with strategic planning as opposed to short-term objectives, focusing on continuous enhancement of education quality; Culture inculcation is centered on enhancing quality and constant improvement in educational services; The emphasis should be on improving procedures to ensure high worth rather than relying exclusively upon inspections and audits; When making decisions, those concerned should not only consider costs but also quality and value; Endeavor always to enhance academic programs, administrative processes, and student services; Continuously offer training to faculty members and employees so that they can improve their skills; The direction from academic leaders is necessary for quality improvements initiatives; Create an atmosphere where all staff members are able to express their worries about the system's state; Foster collaboration among departments and between faculty and administrative staff. Focus on meaningful actions rather than empty slogans or motivational posters; Avoid setting arbitrary targets; instead, focus on improving processes; Ensure that faculty and staff have the resources and support they need to do their jobs well; Encourage continuous learning and professional development. Engage all members of the academic community in quality improvement efforts.

According to Deming's theory, the thorough role of continuous improvement and the central management of influence is emphasized in order to promote the creation of a quality culture. These core management components provide a fertile ground for integrating TQM into academic quality services. A focus on strategic, long-term, rather than short term goals is advocated. The first point, "Creating constancy of purpose", is attributed to the priority for academic institutions to emphasize enduring goals, aimed at continuous improvement of quality in education (Deming, 1986).

This framework suggests formulating and promoting a vision that transcends immediate pressures, ensuring that the academic institution remains committed to its strategic educational mission and student success through long-term perspectives. The characteristic of strategic planning helps to implement the additional value of complexity of the educational requirements and to maintain a focus on quality improvement (Oakland, 2014). Academic organizations, with these practices, might align their efforts with continuous improvement, by embedding quality more deeply into the overall academic ethos of their organization. Deming's second point, "Adopt the new philosophy", is based on a cultural inclination to value quality, based on the axis of continuous improvement in all aspects of service delivery (Deming, 1986).

This philosophical approach presupposes a fundamental change in attitude and practices, whereby quality is not seen as a continuous pursuit. Adopting this philosophical perspective can help institutions adapt to changing educational landscapes and responds to stakeholders expectations (Prajogo & Brown, 2004; Prajogo & Mcdermott, 2005; Prajogo & Sohal, 2006). This form of shift can assist the academic institutions to respond further to the students' needs and remain competitive. A notable aspect of Deming's theory is the focus on the process improvement over dependencies on inspections, that is actually included in the third point "Breaking Dependence on Inspection" (Deming, 1986).

Academic institutions often rely very much on audits and inspections to ensure quality, however, Deming's approach is more proactive, since the suggested processes are continuously improved to naturally produce higher quality outcomes. This proactive stance reduces the need for frequent inspections and allows a more efficient educational environment. Research findings focusing on process improvements, rather than inspections concluded to better overall performance and quality outcomes (Prajogo & Brown, 2004). Deming's fourth point, "Ending the practice of price-tag-only outsourcing" is that academic institutions should consider quality and value rather than the entirely cost in their decision-making procedures (Deming, 1986). This is particularly important in processes, sush as the recruitment of academic staff, the procurement of educational equipment and materials and the selection of service providers.

Emphasizing and prioritizing quality can help the institutions enhance their educational offerings and provide a greater value to their students, thereby empower and further enrich their learning experiences (Prajogo, 2005). These foundational points underscore the importance of a strategic, quality-focused approach to management in academic environments, promoting a culture where continuous improvement is ingrained in the institution's operations and ethos.

The subsequent points of Deming's theory further elucidate the path towards ingraining a culture of quality within academic institutions. The fifth point, "Improve Constantly and Forever," encapsulates the essence of continuous improvement, urging institutions to relentlessly seek enhancements in academic programs, administrative processes, and student services (Deming, 1986). This continuous quest for improvement ensures that educational institutions remain dynamic and responsive to changes, therefore maintaining high standards of educational quality. Research indicates that continuous improvement efforts contribute significantly to institutional effectiveness and student satisfaction (Mohanty & Behera, 1996). Deming's sixth point, "Institute Training on the Job," highlights the necessity of ongoing professional development for faculty and staff (Deming, 1986). By providing continuous training opportunities, institutions can ensure that their staff remain proficient in the latest educational methodologies and technologies, thereby enhancing the overall quality of education; This commitment to training fosters a knowledgeable and skilled workforce capable of delivering high-quality education and services (Karia & Asaari, 2006).

Leadership plays a crucial role in the successful implementation of TQM in the academic framework, as articulated in Deming's seventh point, "Institute Leadership" (Deming, 1986). Academic leaders should guide and support quality improvement initiatives, in the context of a creative environment that encourages innovation and excellence. Effective leadership involves setting clear goals, providing necessary resources, and fostering a culture of collaboration and trust (Talib & Rahman, 2010). The eighth point, "Drive Out Fear," emphasizes the importance of creating a safe and supportive environment, where staff and students feel empowered to express concerns and suggest improvements without fear of retribution (Deming, 1986). This open communication channel is vital for identifying and addressing issues promptly, thereby fostering a culture of continuous improvement. By eliminating fear, institutions can tap into the collective potential of their academic community, driving innovation and quality enhancements across all areas of operation (Thiagarajan, Zairi, & Dale, 2001).

Deming's theory highlights the importance of collaboration and meaningful action in achieving quality improvements. The ninth point, "Break Down Barriers," advocates for fostering collaboration among departments and between faculty and administrative staff (Deming, 1986). Breaking down silos within the institution can lead to more integrated and cohesive efforts towards quality improvement, leveraging diverse perspectives and expertise (Brinbaum & Deshotels, 1999). This collaborative approach ensures that all aspects of the educational process are aligned and working towards common goals. Deming's tenth point, "Eliminate Slogans," cautions against relying on empty slogans or motivational posters, instead urging institutions to focus on meaningful actions that drive real improvements (Deming, 1986). This point emphasizes the importance of substance over form, advocating for genuine efforts to enhance quality rather than superficial gestures. Research supports that meaningful actions and practical improvements yield better results than symbolic gestures (Zehir & Zehir, 2023).

In alignment with a focus on genuine improvement, Deming's eleventh point, "Eliminate Management by Objectives," advises against setting arbitrary targets and instead encourages a focus on improving processes (Deming, 1986). This approach ensures that goals are realistic and aligned with the institution's capacity and capabilities, fostering sustainable improvements. The twelfth point, "Remove Barriers to Pride in Workmanship," emphasizes the importance of ensuring that faculty and staff have the resources and support they need to perform their jobs well (Deming, 1986). By removing obstacles that hinder performance, institutions can enhance job satisfaction and productivity, leading to better educational outcomes. Finally, Deming's thirteenth and fourteenth points, "Institute a Vigorous Program of Education and Self-Improvement" and "Put Everybody in the Company to Work," respectively, underscore the importance of continuous learning and active engagement of all members of the academic community in quality improvement efforts (Deming, 1986). Encouraging professional development and involving everyone in the institution in the quest for quality ensures that the pursuit of excellence becomes a collective endeavour, ingrained in the institution's culture and practices (Prajogo & Brown, 2004).

Deming's Points for Management provide a comprehensive framework for integrating TQM into academic quality services, emphasizing continuous improvement, effective leadership and a supportive educational environment. By focusing on long-term goals, fostering a culture of quality and encouraging collaboration and professional development, academic institutions could enhance further their educational offerings and achieve excellence. The implementation of these principles requires a strategic approach, ensuring that quality is deeply embedded in the institution's operations and ethos, ultimately leading to more effective educational outcomes and greater students' satisfaction.

TQM AND THE CONNECTION OF CUSTOMER SATISFACTION WITH CUSTOMER EMPOWERMENT

Customer satisfaction can be defined as the measure of how products or services provided by a company meet or surpass customer expectations (Oliver, 2010). It is a subjective metric that can vary widely among customers because of individual expectations and perceptions. Therefore, understanding and managing these expectations is essential for businesses aiming to enhance customer satisfaction (Homburg, Koschate, & Hoyer, 2006). Improving customer satisfaction requires a proactive approach. Businesses should focus on understanding their customers' needs and expectations through regular feedback and market research (Kumar & Reinartz, 2018). Personalizing the customer experience, offering high-quality products and services, and ensuring excellent customer support are considered as critical strategies. Additionally, resolving complaints swiftly and effectively can turn a dissatisfied customer into a loyal one (Hart, Heskett, & Sasser, 1990).

Various factors might influence customer satisfaction, including product quality, service quality, price and overall customer experience. In essence, product quality means how well a product works, how long it lasts, and how dependable it is. Products that work well and don't break easily usually make people happier (Zeithaml, Bitner, & Gremler, 2013). Service quality is strongly related to the way customers are treated by the company's staff. Fast paced, polite and helpful service can greatly improve the level of customers' satisfaction (Parasuraman, Zeithaml, & Berry, 1988).

Price also plays a pivotal role. People often judge their satisfaction by the factor of feeling that they feel they got their money's worth (Kotler & Keller, 2016). Also, the whole experience of being a customer, including how easy it is to buy, getting help after buying, and how user-friendly the product is, is very important for how satisfied customers feel (Meyer & Schwager, 2007). There are several ways to measure customers' satisfaction, such as surveys, feedback forms and net promoter scores (NPS). Surveys and feedback forms usually have a scale where customers extract the level of customers' satisfaction, i.e. how satisfied they are, from very unsatisfied to very satisfied (Hayes, 2008). The NPS, created by Fred Reichheld requires from customers to express how likely they are by telling others about a company's product or service. This provides us with a simple way to measure how loyal and happy customers are (Reichheld, 2003).

Customer satisfaction is closely connected to customer loyalty and retention. It is more likely for satisfied people to come back to a business and make repeat purchases, while not satisfied customers might take their business elsewhere. Additionally, satisfied customers often become brand advocates, share their positive experiences with others and contribute to positive word-of-mouth marketing (Anderson, Fornell, & Lehmann, 1994).

The key for a company to survive in this competitive world of business is to find the best ways to be wanted; business competition is implemented on three major levels: price, delivery, and quality (Farida & Setiawan, 2022). With multi-dimensional demand and challenges of globalization, organizations are forced to re-engineer their operations and systems to be more customer-centric to improve service quality and remain competitive (Rodie and Martin, 2001; Tan et al., 2010).

Although maintaining the lowest price is one necessary element in the business competition, in the long term, companies that choose the low-cost approach may find themselves facing the bitter fact of losing premium business to competitors while retaining the low margin (Porter, 1980). The concept is not restricted to the manufacturing sector; it has been extended to service companies and non-profit organizations, such as healthcare, government services, education, and financial institutions (Sirvanci, 2004; Lakhe and Mohanty, 1995; Yaya et al., 2011). Customers are the ultimate judges of service or product quality (Sakthivel et al., 2005). The prominence of quality is further manifested by the growing recognition that the delivery of high-quality services can often lead to a sustainable competitive advantage (Sureshchandar et al., 2002). Thus, it is not surprising that quality of service has become the forefront for planning strategy in service organizations (Khamalah and Lingaraj, 2007).

Therefore, offering the best quality is one of the unsurpassed and essential ways for companies to survive. From various previous studies, it is noted that TQM has become the key element for improving the performance of companies and the satisfaction of customers (Terziovski, 2006; Sakthivel et al., 2005; Lagrosen, 2001). Total Quality Management (TQM) emerged for the management of service and product quality (Ayers, 1993; Juran, 1993; Schonberger, 1992). One of the major goals of TQM is to improve customer satisfaction (Jablonski, 1992; Tennor and DeToro, 1992). Additionally, there are studies in this area where customer satisfaction is introduced as the outcome of TQM (Choi and Eboch, 1998; Forza and Filippini, 1998). Maintaining a high level of customer satisfaction needs to be one of the goals of every company and can be achieved through TQM (Jones and Crowe, 1996). In addition, customer value anticipation, which leads to customer satisfaction, is reachable by TQM and its tools. It is a strong leader of customer satisfaction and consequently customer loyalty (Flint et al., 2011). The concept of service quality has been considered one of the most debated subjects in the services literature due to the lack of consensus on how to define it (Babakus and Boller, 1992; Gupta et al., 2005). Based on voluminous previous studies, Parasuraman et al. (1985) proposed three underlying themes on service quality: a) it is more complicated and difficult for customers to evaluate as compared to tangible goods quality; b) the perceptions of service quality are the outcomes of actual service performance vs. consumer expectations; c) the evaluations of quality are not solely focused on the outcome of the service; they also involve evaluations of the process of service delivery.

As mentioned, TQM is a measurement of value (Deming, 1986); it is about a strategic, integrated management system that focuses on achieving customer satisfaction and seeking continuous improvement of processes (Bisho & Sam, 2022). The most important dimensions of customer-focused performance are service quality, customer value and customer satisfaction (Wang and Lo, 2003). We have already explained that customer satisfaction should be made the goal and the measure of service quality (Milakovich, 1995). TQM approaches focus on improving the effectiveness of the processes and the responsiveness in meeting the customer requirement as part of organization excellence goals in achieving customer satisfaction (Ramlawati and Putra, 2018). This can be facilitated through customer empowerment.

Empowering customers means that they are provided with the necessary tools and information in order to be able to make informed decisions, while controlling their interactions with companies (Hawkins, Best, & Mothersbaugh, 2010; Hawkins, Best, & Coney, 2001). The customer empowerment can be interpreted as a remarkable tool to achieve customer satisfaction. In the context of academic quality service, such an empowerment of students and other community members can lead to improved satisfaction and outcomes. In general, customer empowerment acquires many benefits, both for consumers and businesses. Concerning the consumers, this empowerment leads to a more satisfying experience of purchasing, as they feel that they are able to make decisions that meet better their needs and preferences (Prahalad & Ramanswamy, 2004). In product companies, positive feedback from empowered and satisfied customers can provide valuable insights that drive product development and service improvements. Thus, these factors contribute to competitiveness and innovation. Empowered customers are often more loyal to products and services, making them advocates for that particular brand, by spreading positive words of mouth and attracting more new customers (Kendall & Bodinson, 2017).

Customer empowerment involves the elements of information, choices, participation and support by: ensuring students have access to the information they need to make informed decisions about their education (Kendall & Bodinson, 2017); allowing students to have a say in their learning experiences, such as choosing elective courses or participating in extracurricular activities (Hawkins, Best, & Mothersbaugh, 2010; Hawkins, Best, & Coney, 2001); involving students in decision-making processes related to academic programs and services (Trowler, 2010); helping students develop the skills to advocate for themselves and their needs (Seale, 2013).

Empowering customers offers positive insights, however, there are also many challenges. Practices of managing customers' expectations and ensuring that empowerment strategies do not lead to overloaded information, or decision fatigue are crucial (Van Herpen, Pieters & Zeelenberg, 2009). Businesses must be very careful to strike the proper balance between providing adequate information and empowering customers without exhausting them. Additionally, organizations should be well prepared in order to meet the increased scrutiny and transparency requirements that characterize the empowered clients.

Several companies have successfully deployed customer empowerment strategies. Many representative examples of customer empowerment strategies can be found in the literature, such as: Dell's customization options for their computers and Zappos' customer service approaches (Pine, Peppers & Rogers, 2011). Such approaches enhance customer satisfaction and also create a strong, loyal customer basis that contributes to long-term success. Empowered students of Academic Institutions are more likely to be engaged and satisfied with their educational experiences. This is, probably, due to the factor that they are led to a better academic performance, higher retention rates and a high index of positive institutional reputation.

TQM IN ACADEMIC QUALITY SERVICES: IDEAL PRACTICES

Implementing TQM in academic quality services involves applying its principles to various aspects of the educational experience for the students, the faculty and the staff. The students have the benefit for feedback mechanisms, by establishing robust systems for collecting and acting on student feedback to improve academic programs and services (Harvey, 2003). They can also use data to tailor their educational experiences to their individual needs and preferences (Ubell, 2010). Academic Institutions can strengthen further the student support services sector. This can be effectively undertaken through continuous improvement of services, such as academic tutoring and advising and career services, to promote further student success (Drake, 2011). Although there have been controversial opinions, research discussions conclude that "TQM is credibly compatible with education". Nevertheless, in this connection the remark of Sousa and Voss is quite thought provoking; they comment that TQM principles are not universally applicable across all contexts but are contingent on contextual factors. It implies that TQM tools and techniques are subject to fine tuning while applying in education" (Sohel-Uz-Zaman & Anjalin, 2016).

Adopting TQM in academic quality services lead the faculty members to strive for professional development, collaborative culture and research support. Providing ongoing training and development opportunities helps faculty stay current with best practices in teaching and research (Guskey, 2002), while encouraging collaboration among faculty members to share knowledge and improve teaching practices (Hargreaves & Fullan, 2012). Support is enhanced for faculty research via improved resources, funding opportunities and administrative assistance (Brew & Lucas, 2009).

The Staff members, also, benefit from TQM practices, as they start walking in a path of continuous improvement, high rate of involvement and resource allocation. Streamlining administrative processes reduces inefficiencies and enhances service quality (Lientz & Rea, 2001). The staff is engaged in quality improvement initiatives and their contributions are being recognized (Cameron & Green, 2019). TQM practices require that it has to be ensured that staff have the necessary resources to perform their duties effectively (Spreitzer, 2008).

Practices that revolve around the axis of commitment to leadership, training and development; involvement of all stakeholders; data-driven decision making; continuous feedback; collaboration, communication, recognition and reward might lead to high levels of efficacy. Thus, academic leaders should: demonstrate commitment to quality and continuous development (Sallis, 2014); provide regular training to faculty, general staff and administrators on TQM principles and practices (Oakland, 2014); to involve students, academics, staff and other stakeholders in initiatives aimed at improving quality (Evans & Lindsay, 2020), using data and metrics to guide decisions and measuring progress (Juran & De Feo, 2010); create systems for collecting and acting on feedback from all involved members (Harvey, 2003). Thus, open communication and collaboration between departments and levels of the institution is promoted (Deming, 1986). Contributions and efforts to improve quality are, also, recognized and rewarded (Spreitzer, 2008).

Regarding the curriculum design, TQM principles adopt a systematic approach that obtains main elements like the continuous feedback from all members, such as students, faculty and professionals, to ensure that the program remains relevant, up to date and fully aligned with the recent developments and demands of the labor market (Deming, 1986). This is mainly related to iterative reviews and iterative modifications of the curriculum based on empirical data and feedback. It is ensured that students acquire the necessary and proper knowledge and skills to succeed in their optional fields (Oakland, 2014).

Applying TQM to curriculum design fosters a proactive educational environment that responds to the dynamic prospective demands of the labor market and technological developments, meaning that graduates are well prepared for their professional endeavours. The benefits for teaching methodologies are, also, vibrant because of the application of TQM principles. By implementing a student-cantered approach, academic staff can continually improve their teaching strategies and facilitate deeper learning by enabling active student participation. This includes regularly collecting and analysing data on student performance and satisfaction, experimenting with innovative teaching techniques and incorporating technology to improve the learning experiences (Juran & Godfrey, 1998). For instance, implementing active learning techniques and leveraging digital tools have the ability to foster more interactive and participatory classroom environments, that improve student outcomes (Goetsch & Davis, 2014).

Also, continuous professional development for educators, guided by TQM principles, ensures that teachers remain competent and effective in delivering high-quality education (Evans & Dean, 2003). By fostering a culture of continuous improvement, academic institutions can ensure that teaching methodologies evolve to meet the changing needs of students and the educational landscape. These approaches trigger the effectiveness of teaching practices and contribute to a more engaging and supportive learning environment that leads to improved student satisfaction and academic success.

Evaluation practices consist of another notable area, where applied TQM can lead to significant improvements. Traditional evaluation methods are often characterized as lacking in reliability and validity and can be improved through TQM applications that emphasize accuracy, fairness and continuous improvement (Crosby, 1979). This is accomplished by designing assessments that accurately measure student learning outcomes, while providing timely constructive feedback and using assessment data to inform instructional practices and curriculum adjustments (Talib, Rahman & Qureshi, 2011).

Furthermore, TQM encourages the use of alternative assessment methods that serve the capture of a comprehensive review of student learning, such as formative assessments, peer assessments and self-assessments. Thus, it ensures that assessment practices are much more fair, transparent and strongly connected to learning objectives and that academic institutions can function better and in a more supportive way for student learning and development (Zairi, 1991).

TQM practices appear to have a positive impact on the administrative processes of academic institutions and the field of academic advising services. It seems that factors such as continuous assessment and improvement lead to a streamlining of these practices, ensuring that they are effective for students and help them meet the needs of the academic community (Sallis, 2014). The adoption and diffusion of TQM in the overall becoming aspects of academic quality services show the path for the institutions to excellence and promote success and efficiency.

CONCLUSION

The effective and successful diffusion of Total Quality Management (TQM) in the services of academic institutions can make a significant contribution to improving student outcomes, staff performance and efficiency. this chapter shows that the principles of TQM, such as the tendency for continuous improvement, customer-centric approaches and the active participation of all members can be seamlessly integrated into the training processes and ultimately promote a culture of excellence and long-term growth.

The implementation of aspects of TQM in academic institutions needs a systemic approach that includes all members and employees from the top of the hierarchy level pyramid to its base. The ideal practices of commitment to quality should permeate all services levels of the academic institutions, ensuring that they are implemented in full alliance with the goal of ongoing improvement. In this way, academic organizations will be led to a new culture of quality and continuous improved environments that eventually reflect these norms as common practices.

One of the main findings of this research is the importance of customer satisfaction in higher education. Students, who are considered as the clients, have a set of requirements, desires and expectations that must be met to ensure their satisfaction. Total Quality Management (TQM) provides an appropriate framework for identifying and managing these requirements, using various methods such as feedback channels, quality assessments and customer empowerment initiatives.

The utilization of these mechanisms can be further improved to keep up with the needs of the students. This chapter presents practical dimensions of these issues and tries to deal with the theory behind them. It shows ways of how using TQM can increase quality and overall good performance.

The holistic application of TQM in institutional academic effectiveness can achieve high levels of performance. Universities, through a quality culture, can improve their operational efficiency, management mechanisms and strategic planning processes. High level points of the institution's competitiveness can be detected in those practices, that ensure long-term continuity and sustainable development. This leads to better students learning outcomes, fostering a more vibrant academic environment. The integration of aspects of TQM, as presented in this chapter, also presupposes a thorough review and renewal of academic services, teaching and administrative in nature. The ideal practices that emerge illustrate the transformative potential of TQM in the academic context; successful integration into academic services can lead to improved student outcomes and faculty performance, as well as greater institutional effectiveness. By adopting TQM principles, academic institutions might create a customer centric culture of continuous improvement and empowerment, resulting in a more efficient and competitive education system.

The chapter's contribution to research is highlighted by bringing to the surface dimensions that reflect the stigma of valuable guidance for academic staff, managers and policy makers. The main and key objective is to guide assistance in favor of the quality of educational services and achievement of high levels of satisfaction in the academic community.

REFERENCES

Al-Qahtani, N. D., Alsehri, S. S., & Aziz, A. A. (2015). The impact of total quality management on organizational performance. *European Journal of Business and Management, 7*(36), 119–127.

Anderson, E. W., Fornell, C., & Lehmann, D. R. (1994). Customer satisfaction, market share, and profitability: Findings from Sweden. *Journal of Marketing, 58*(3), 53–66. DOI: 10.1177/002224299405800304

Babakus, E., & Boller, G. W. (1992). An empirical assessment of the SERVQUAL scale. *Journal of Business Research, 24*(3), 253–268. DOI: 10.1016/0148-2963(92)90022-4

Benavides-Velasco, C. A., Quintana-García, C., & Marchante-Lara, M. (2014). Total quality management, corporate social responsibility and performance in the hotel industry. *International Journal of Hospitality Management, 41*, 77–87. DOI: 10.1016/j.ijhm.2014.05.003

Besterfield, D. H., Besterfield-Michna, C., Besterfield, G. H., & Besterfield-Sacre, M. (2013). *Total quality management*. Pearson.

Birnbaum, R. (2000). The life cycle of academic management fads. *The Journal of Higher Education, 71*(1), 1–16. DOI: 10.1080/00221546.2000.11780813

Birnbaum, R., & Deshotels, J. (1999). Has the academy adopted TQM? *Planning for Higher Education, 27*(3), 29–37.

Bisho, A. H. A. I., & Sam, M. F. M. (2022). Total Quality Management Integrated Strategy: Its Implication to Organizational Success. *Proceedings on Engineering Sciences, 4*(3), 371–378. DOI: 10.24874/PES04.03.014

Bon, A. T., & Mustafa, E. M. A. (2013). Impact of total quality management on innovation in service organizations: Literature review and new conceptual framework. *Procedia Engineering, 53*, 516–529. DOI: 10.1016/j.proeng.2013.02.067

Brew, A., & Lucas, L. (2009). *Academic research and researchers: Policy and Practice*. McGraw-Hill Education.

Cameron, E., & Green, M. (2019). *Making sense of change management: A complete guide to the models, tools, and techniques of organizational change*. Kogan Page.

Cameron, K. S., & Quinn, R. E. (2011). *Diagnosing and changing organizational culture: Based on the competing values framework* (3rd ed.). John Wiley & Sons.

Choi, T. Y., & Eboch, K. (1998). The TQM paradox: Relations among TQM practices, plant performance, and customer satisfaction. *Journal of Operations Management, 17*(1), 59–75. DOI: 10.1016/S0272-6963(98)00031-X

Crosby, P. B. (1979). *Quality is Free: The Art of Making Quality Certain*. McGraw-Hill.

Dale, B. G. (2003). *Managing quality* (4th ed.). Blackwell Publishing.

Dale, B. G. (2015). Total quality management: An overview. In Dale, B. G. (Ed.), *Managing quality* (6th ed., pp. 1–40). Wiley.

Dale, B. G., Zairi, M., & Thiagarajan, T. (2001). A proposed model of TQM implementation based on an empirical study of Malaysian industry. *International Journal of Quality & Reliability Management, 18*(3), 289–306. DOI: 10.1108/02656710110383539

Deming, W. E. (1986). *Out of the crisis*. MIT Press.

Demirel, D. (2022). The effect of service quality on customer satisfaction in digital age: Customer satisfaction based examination of digital CRM. *Journal of Business Economics and Management, 23*(3), 1–25. DOI: 10.3846/jbem.2022.15328

Drake, J. K. (2011). The role of academic advising in student retention and persistence. *About Campus: Enriching the Student Learning Experience, 16*(3), 8–12. DOI: 10.1002/abc.20062

Evans, J. R., & Dean, J. W. (2003). *Total Quality: Management, Organization, and Strategy*. Thomson.

Evans, J. R., & Lindsay, W. M. (2020). *Managing for quality and performance excellence* (11th ed.). Cengage Learning.

Farida, I., & Setiawan, D. (2022). Business Strategies and Competitive Advantage: The Role of Performance and Innovation. *Journal of Open Innovation, 8*(3), 163. DOI: 10.3390/joitmc8030163

Flint, D. J., Blocker, C. P., & Boutin, P. J.Jr. (2011). Customer value anticipation, customer satisfaction and loyalty: An empirical examination. *Industrial Marketing Management, 40*(2), 219–230. DOI: 10.1016/j.indmarman.2010.06.034

Forza, C., & Filippini, R. (1998). TQM impact on quality conformance and customer satisfaction: A causal model. *International Journal of Production Economics, 55*(1), 1–20. DOI: 10.1016/S0925-5273(98)00007-3

Furtasan, A. Y. (2023). Total Quality Management (TQM) and Quality of Higher Education: A Meta-Analysis Study. *International Journal of Instruction, 16*(2), 161–178. DOI: 10.29333/iji.2023.16210a

Gaither, N. (1996). *Production and operations management* (6th ed.). Dryden Press.

George, S. & Weimerskirch. (1998). *Total Quality Management: Strategies and Techniques Proven at Today's Most Successful Companies* (2nd ed.). Wiley.

Goetsch, D. L., & Davis, S. B. (2014). *Quality management for organizational excellence: Introduction to total quality* (7th ed.). Pearson.

Gupta, A., McDaniel, J. C., & Herath, S. K. (2005). Quality management in service firms: Sustaining structures of total quality service. *Managing Service Quality, 15*(4), 389–402. DOI: 10.1108/09604520510606853

Guskey, T. R. (2002). Professional development and teacher change. *Teachers and Teaching, 8*(3), 381–391. DOI: 10.1080/135406002100000512

Hargreaves, A., & Fullan, M. (2012). *Professional capital: Transforming teaching in every school.* Teachers College Press.

Hart, C. W., Heskett, J. L., & Sasser, W. E. (1990). The profitable art of service recovery. *Harvard Business Review, 68*(4), 148–156. PMID: 10106796

Harvey, L. (2003). Student feedback. *Quality in Higher Education, 9*(1), 3–20. DOI: 10.1080/13538320308164

Hawkins, D. I., Best, R. J., & Coney, K. A. (2001). *Consumer behavior: Building marketing strategy.* Irvin/McGraw-Hill.

Hawkins, D. I., Best, R. J., & Mothersbaugh, D. L. (2010). *Consumer behavior: Building marketing strategy* (11th ed.). McGraw-Hill Education.

Hayes, B. E. (2008). *Measuring customer satisfaction and loyalty* (3rd ed.). ASQ Quality Press.

Homburg, C., Koschate, N., & Hoyer, W. D. (2006). The role of cognition and affect in the formation of customer satisfaction: A dynamic perspective. *Journal of Marketing, 70*(3), 21–31. DOI: 10.1509/jmkg.70.3.021

Houston, D. (2008). Rethinking quality and improvement in higher education. *Quality Assurance in Education, 16*(1), 61–79. DOI: 10.1108/09684880810848413

Hoyle, D. (2009). *ISO 9000 quality systems handbook* (6th ed.). Butterworth-Heinemann.

Ibrahim, I., Amer, A., & Omar, F. (2011). The total quality management practices and quality performance: A case study of Pos Malaysia Berhad, Kota Kinabalu, Sabah. *Proceedings of the 2nd International Conference on Business and Economic Research (2nd ICBER 2011)*, 1–10.

Jablonski, J. R. (1992). *Implementing Total Quality Management: An Overview*. Technical Management Consortium, Inc.

Jones, B., & Crowe, T. J. (1996). The new definition of quality. *Quality Progress*, *29*(2), 55–62.

Juran, J. M. (1993). Made in USA: A Renaissance in Quality. *Harvard Business Review*, *71*(4), 42–50. PMID: 10127039

Juran, J. M., & De Feo, J. A. (2010). *Juran's quality handbook: The complete guide to performance excellence* (6th ed.). McGraw-Hill Education.

Juran, J. M., & Godfrey, A. B. (1999). *Juran's Quality Handbook*. McGraw-Hill.

Karia, N., & Asaari, M. H. A. H. (2006). The effects of total quality management practices on employees' work-related attitudes. *The TQM Magazine*, *18*(1), 30–43. DOI: 10.1108/09544780610637677

Kendall, K., & Bodinson, G. (2017). *Leading the Malcolm Baldrige way: how world-class leaders align their organizations to deliver exceptional results* (1st ed.). McGraw-Hill.

Khamalah, J. N., & Lingaraj, B. P. (2007). TQM in the service sector: A survey of small businesses. *Total Quality Management & Business Excellence*, *18*(9), 973–982. DOI: 10.1080/14783360701592059

Kotler, P., & Keller, K. L. (2016). *Marketing management* (15th ed.). Pearson.

Kucuk, S. U. (2009). Consumer empowerment model: From unspeakable to redress. *Direct Marketing (Bradford)*, *3*(4), 327–342. DOI: 10.1108/17505930911000892

Kumar, V., & Reinartz, W. (2018). *Customer relationship management: Concept, strategy, and tool* (3rd ed.). Springer.

Lagrosen, S. (2001). Strengthening the weakest link of TQM–from customer focus to customer understanding. *The TQM Magazine*, *13*(5), 348–354. DOI: 10.1108/09544780110401916

Lakhe, R. R., & Mohanty, R. P. (1995). Understanding TQM in service systems. *International Journal of Quality & Reliability Management*, *12*(9), 139–153. DOI: 10.1108/02656719510101240

Lientz, B. P., & Rea, K. P. (2001). *Breakthrough technology project management*. Academic Press.

Lovelock, C., & Wirtz, J. (2023). *Services marketing: People, technology, strategy* (9th ed.). World Scientific Publishing.

Meyer, C., & Schwager, A. (2007). Understanding customer experience. *Harvard Business Review*, *85*(2), 116–126. PMID: 17345685

Milakovich, M. E. (1995). *Improving service quality: Achieving high performance in the public and private sectors*. St. Lucie Press.

Mohanty, R. P., & Behera, A. K. (1996). TQM in the service sector. *Work Study*, *45*(3), 13–17. DOI: 10.1108/00438029610115479

Montgomery, D. C. (2012). *Statistical Quality Control: A modern Introduction* (7th ed.). John Wiley and Sons.

Oakland, J. S. (2014). *Total quality management and operational excellence: text and cases* (4th ed.). Routledge. DOI: 10.4324/9781315815725

Oliver, R. L. (2010). *Satisfaction: A behavioral perspective on the consumer* (2nd ed.). M.E. Sharpe.

Parasuraman, A., Zeithaml, V. A., & Berry, L. L. (1985). A conceptual model of service quality and its implications for future research. *Journal of Marketing*, *49*(4), 41–50. DOI: 10.1177/002224298504900403

Parasuraman, A., Zeithaml, V. A., & Berry, L. L. (1988). SERVQUAL: A multiple-item scale for measuring consumer perceptions of service quality. *Journal of Retailing*, *64*(1), 12–40.

Pine, B. J., Peppers, D., & Rogers, M. (2011). *Do you want to keep your customers forever?* Harvard Business Review Press.

Porter, M. E. (1980). *Competitive strategy: Techniques for analyzing industries and competitors*. Free Press.

Powell, T. C. (1995). Total quality management as competitive advantage: A review and empirical study. *Strategic Management Journal*, *16*(1), 15–37. DOI: 10.1002/smj.4250160105

Prahalad, C. K., & Ramaswamy, V. (2004). *The future of competition: Co-creating unique value with customers*. Harvard Business School Press.

Prajogo, D. I. (2005). The comparative analysis of TQM practices and quality performance between manufacturing and service firms. *International Journal of Service Industry Management*, *16*(3), 217–228. DOI: 10.1108/09564230510601378

Prajogo, D. I., & Brown, A. (2004). The relations between TQM practices and Quality Performance and the Role of Forman TQM Programs: An Australia Empirical Study. *The Quality Management Journal*, *11*(4), 31–42. Advance online publication. DOI: 10.1080/10686967.2004.11919131

Prajogo, D. I., & McDermott, C. M. (2005). The relationship between total quality management practices and organizational culture. *International Journal of Operations & Production Management*, *25*(11), 1101–1122. DOI: 10.1108/01443570510626916

Prajogo, D. I., & Sohal, A. S. (2006). The integration of TQM and technology/R&D management in determining quality and innovation performance. *Omega*, *34*(3), 296–312. DOI: 10.1016/j.omega.2004.11.004

Ramlawati, R., & Putra, A. H. P. K. (2018). Total quality management as the Key of the Company to Gain the Competitiveness, Performance Achievement and Consumer Satisfaction. *International Review of Management and Marketing*. *EconJournals*, *8*(5), 60–69.

Rasheed, F. A. K. (2017). Impact of Total Quality Management on Customer Satisfaction. *International Journal of Management and Commerce Innovations*, *4*(2), 702–709.

Reichheld, F. F. (2003). The one number you need to grow. *Harvard Business Review*, *81*(12), 46–55. PMID: 14712543

Rodie, A. R., & Martin, C. L. (2001). Competing in the service sector: The entrepreneurial challenge. *International Journal of Entrepreneurial Behaviour & Research*, *7*(1), 5–21. DOI: 10.1108/13552550110385718

Sakthivel, R., Rajendran, C., & Anantharaman, R. N. (2005). TQM implementation and students' satisfaction of academic performance. *The TQM Magazine*, *17*(6), 573–589. DOI: 10.1108/09544780510627660

Sallis, E. (2014). *Total quality management in education* (3rd ed.). Routledge. DOI: 10.4324/9780203417010

Schonberger, R. J. (1992). Total Quality Management Cuts a Broad Swath: Through Manufacturing and Beyond. *Organizational Dynamics*, *20*(4), 16–28. DOI: 10.1016/0090-2616(92)90072-U

Seale, J. (2013). *E-learning and disability in higher education: Accessibility research and practice* (2nd ed.). Routledge. DOI: 10.4324/9780203095942

Sila, I., & Ebrahimpour, M. (2002). An investigation of the total quality management survey-based research published between 1989 and 2000: A literature review. *International Journal of Quality & Reliability Management, 19*(7), 902–970. DOI: 10.1108/02656710210434801

Sirvanci, M. B. (2004). TQM implementation: Critical issues for TQM in higher education. *The TQM Magazine, 16*(6), 382–386. DOI: 10.1108/09544780410563293

Sohel-Uz-Zaman, A., & Anjalin, U. (2016). Implementing total quality management in education: Compatibility and challenges. *Open Journal of Social Sciences, 4*(11), 207–217. DOI: 10.4236/jss.2016.411017

Sousa, R., & Voss, C. A. (2002). Quality management re-visited: A reflective review and agenda for future research. *Journal of Operations Management, 20*(1), 91–109. DOI: 10.1016/S0272-6963(01)00088-2

Spreitzer, G. M. (2008). Taking stock: A review of more than twenty years of research on empowerment at work. In Cooper, C., & Barling, J. (Eds.), *Volume one - Micro approaches* (pp. 54–72). The SAGE handbook of organizational behavior. SAGE Publications. DOI: 10.4135/9781849200448.n4

Šteta-Ćerimović, N., & Mekic, E. (2020). The effects of Quality Management Practices and Organizational Learning on Organizational Performance: A proposed research framework. *Open Journal for Research in Economics, 3*(1), 9–20. DOI: 10.32591/coas.ojre.0301.02009s

Sureshchandar, G. S., Rajendran, C., & Anantharaman, R. N. (2002). The relationship between service quality and customer satisfaction – A factor-specific approach. *Journal of Services Marketing, 16*(4), 363–379. DOI: 10.1108/08876040210433248

Talib, F., & Rahman, Z. (2010). Critical success factors of TQM in service organizations: A proposed model. *Services Marketing Quarterly, 31*(3), 363–380. DOI: 10.1080/15332969.2010.486700

Talib, F., Rahman, Z., & Qureshi, M. N. (2011). A study of total quality management and supply chain management practices. *International Journal of Productivity and Performance Management, 60*(3), 268–288. DOI: 10.1108/17410401111111998

Talib, F., Rahman, Z., & Qureshi, M. N. (2011). Analysis of interaction among the barriers to total quality management implementation using interpretive structural modeling approach. *Benchmarking, 18*(4), 563–587. DOI: 10.1108/14635771111147641

Tan, K. C., Lyman, S. B., & Wisner, J. D. (2002). Supply chain management: A strategic perspective. *International Journal of Operations & Production Management, 22*(6), 614–631. DOI: 10.1108/01443570210427659

Taraza, E., Anastasiadou, S., & Masouras, A. (2023, September). *Malcolm Baldrige National Quality Award (MBNQA) Quality Tool in Education: A Systematic Literature Review*. In ECIE 2023 18th European Conference on Innovation and Entrepreneurship Vol 1. Academic Conferences and publishing limited.

Taraza, E., Anastasiadou, S., Papademetriou, C., & Masouras, A. (2024). Evaluation of quality and equality in education using the European foundation for quality management excellence model—A literature review. *Sustainability (Basel), 16*(3), 960. DOI: 10.3390/su16030960

Terziovski, M. (2006). Quality management practices and their relationship with customer satisfaction and productivity improvement. *Management Research News, 29*(7), 414–424. DOI: 10.1108/01409170610690871

Trowler, V. (2010). *Student engagement literature review*. The Higher Education Academy.

Ubell, R. (Ed.). (2010). *Virtual teamwork: Mastering the art and practice of online learning and corporate collaboration*. John Wiley & Sons. DOI: 10.1002/9780470615782

Van Herpen, E., Pieters, R., & Zeelenberg, M. (2009). When demand accelerates demand: Trailing the bandwagon. *Journal of Consumer Psychology, 19*(3), 302–331. DOI: 10.1016/j.jcps.2009.01.001

Wang, Y., & Lo, H.-P. (2003). Customer-focused performance and the dynamic model for competence building and leveraging: A resource-based view. *Journal of Management Development, 22*(6), 483–526. DOI: 10.1108/02621710310478486

Yaya, L. H. P., Marimon, F., & Casadesus, M. (2011). Customer's loyalty and perception of ISO 9001 in online banking. *Industrial Management & Data Systems, 111*(8), 1194–1213. DOI: 10.1108/02635571111170767

Zairi, M. (1991). *Total quality management for engineers*. Woodhead Publishing.

Zairi, M. (1995). Total quality management: What is it really? Definition, core concepts and impact. *The TQM Magazine, 7*(3), 8–15.

Zehir, S., & Zehir, C. (2023). Effects of Total Quality Management Practices on Financial and Operational Performance of Hospitals. *Sustainability (Basel), 15*(21), 15430. Advance online publication. DOI: 10.3390/su152115430

Zeithaml, V. A., Bitner, M. J., & Gremler, D. D. (2013). *Services marketing: Integrating customer focus across the firm* (6th ed.). McGraw-Hill Education.

Chapter 13
Women Empowerment Through CSR in India:
A Review of Indian CSR Initiatives and Framework Development

Sreelal Bhagyabhavanam
Indian Institute of Management, Ranchi, India

Shilpee A. Dasgupta
https://orcid.org/0000-0002-2298-1570
Indian Institute of Management, Ranchi, India

Prashant Maurya
https://orcid.org/0000-0001-9661-0353
Indian Institute of Management, Ranchi, India

Shubh Majumdarr
https://orcid.org/0000-0003-3951-3367
Indian Institute of Management, Ranchi, India

ABSTRACT

In this chapter, the authors examine Corporate Social Responsibility initiatives to empower Indian women, emphasizing that sustainable development is unattainable without their active participation. The study employs a non-probability purposive sampling technique to analyze secondary data from CSR reports of Indian companies from 2014 to 2018, including sources such as the High-Level Committee-2015 (HLC-2015), the CSR Reporting Survey 2019, the National Health Survey of Families Health, and the top 10 women empowerment projects through CSR initiatives in 2018-19. Utilizing percentage analysis, the chi-square test, and ANOVA, the study assesses the impact of CSR initiatives on women's personal and professional growth

DOI: 10.4018/979-8-3693-5583-1.ch013

in both social and economic spheres. Furthermore, the chapter proposes a conceptual framework to enhance women's development through CSR. This chapter contributes valuable insights into the role of CSR in fostering women's empowerment in a developing economy like India.

1. INTRODUCTION

Over the past two decades, Corporate Social Responsibility (CSR) has received immense global interest from businesses, academia, policymakers, and financial investors (Boubakri et al., 2021). The topic has grown over time, and the definition has progressed, Carroll (1991) defining CSR as the complete range of company responsibilities towards the society and community with economic, legal, ethical, and discretionary obligations. The European Commission (2001) defines CSR as a "concept whereby companies integrate social and environmental concerns in their business operations and their interaction with their stakeholders voluntarily". For Vogel (2007) CSR enhances the workplace and provides society with benefits beyond what companies must do as per the norms. In comparison, Carroll (2016) states that CSR is an organizational legal and ethical responsibility to improve society, environment, and economic conditions and meet stakeholders' expectations. Despite different interpretations, CSR's objectives regarding contributing to and benefitting society have remained firm.

In recent decades, there have been significant changes in the global CSR scenario, where the paradigm shift happened from CSR being the trend to its becoming practice, particularly in medium and large organizations (Lichtenstein et al., 2004). The scope of CSR, however, is not only restricted to supply chain activities (Frankental, 2001); it is also being considered a strategic tool to improve business (Jamali, 2008), transforming brand reputation into brand equity (A. Mahmood & Bashir, 2020), and even acting as a competitive advantage over competition (S. Mahmood & Khan, 2023). It has also encompassed various programs, such as women empowerment. (Marshall, 2011; Spence, 2016) argues that CSR scholarship and practice have neglected women for years. However, a significant change is visible in contemporary times as women's empowerment has become an integral part of CSR programs (Grosser, 2016; ICRW et al., 2014; Mogaji et al., 2021). Recent CSR activities have focused significantly on women, such as Coca-Cola and Walmart, which have financially empowered millions of women across many countries through their CSR initiatives (Johnstone-Louis, 2017). CSR has attempted to enhance women's personal and professional growth in the social and economic spheres. However, economic empowerment has always been at the center of CSR (McCarthy, 2017; Roberts, 2015). India is the second largest populated country with a vast women population, becoming a potential site for the intersection of women's empowerment and gender equality. Previous studies (Jatana & Crowther, 2007; Larrieta-Rubín de Celis et al., 2015; Mogaji et al., 2021; Narwal & Singh, 2013) have dealt with CSR and women's empowerment. However, a comprehensive study of Indian CSR initiatives and their role and impact on women's empowerment is missing. This chapter fills the lacuna in the existing literature on CSR and women empowerment in the Indian scenario. It focuses on the Indian CSR initiatives to determine the impact on women's empowerment.

2. LITERATURE REVIEW

2.1 CSR and Women Empowerment

A CSR and women empowerment review is discussed, further narrowing to country-specific developments and initiatives. To ensure rigor, the present review is further supported by a bibliometric analysis on the subject. The bibliometric analysis was sourced from the Scopus database, which offers more coverage than Wos (Rahman et al., 2022) with keywords from past studies (Kumar et al., 2020) and (Zhao et al., 2023), focusing on 'women empowerment' and 'corporate social responsibility'. The search results covered publications from 2007-20222 from the relevant domains of Business, Management and Accounting, Social Sciences, Economics, Econometrics, and Finance and Arts and Humanities. The document types were limited to articles, book chapters, and conference papers in English, in line with past studies (Donthu et al., 2021). For data visualization, the study opted Vosviewer (van Eck & Waltman, 2010) and conducted co-occurrence keyword and bibliographic coupling analysis aligned with past research (Amankwaa et al., 2022) to provide a bird's eye view of the literature.

As shown in Figure 1, the co-occurrence network analysis (author keywords) of 42 publications reveals corporate social responsibility and women empowerment as a well-researched and theoretically connected relationship with 4 diverse clusters. Furthermore, a lack of review reflects the need for knowledge updating and the researcher's motivation for the study.

Figure 1. Co-occurrence of Network Analysis

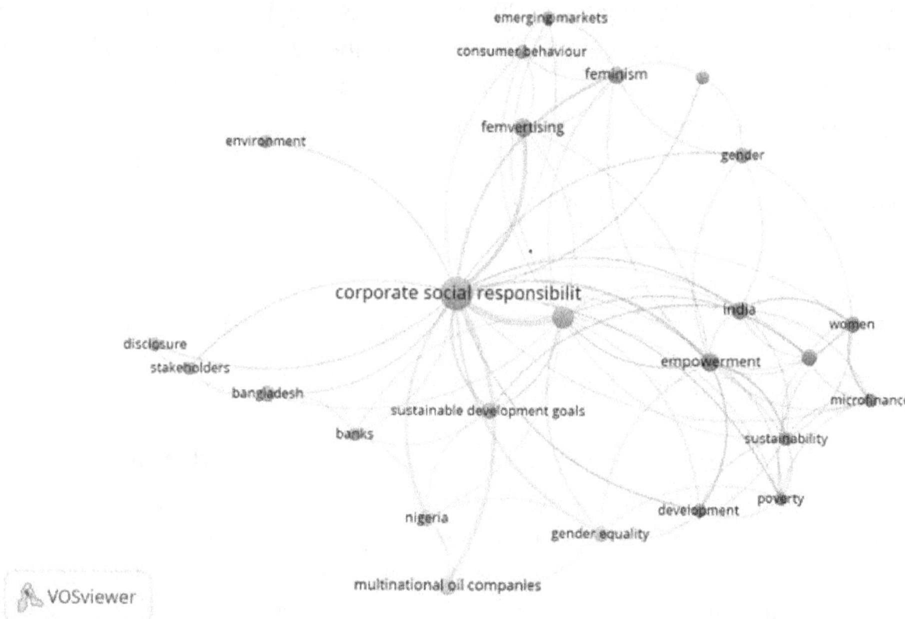

Source: Analysis done by the authors using Vosviewer

Figure 2 demonstrates the bibliographic coupling analysis network on corporate social responsibility and women empowerment. The Companies Act 2013 mandates CSR expenditure from public sector units (PSUs) and private companies, and 'India' as a prime node in the network showcases its importance in the domain and provides further justification for the present studies.

Figure 2. Bibliographic Coupling Network Analysis (countries)

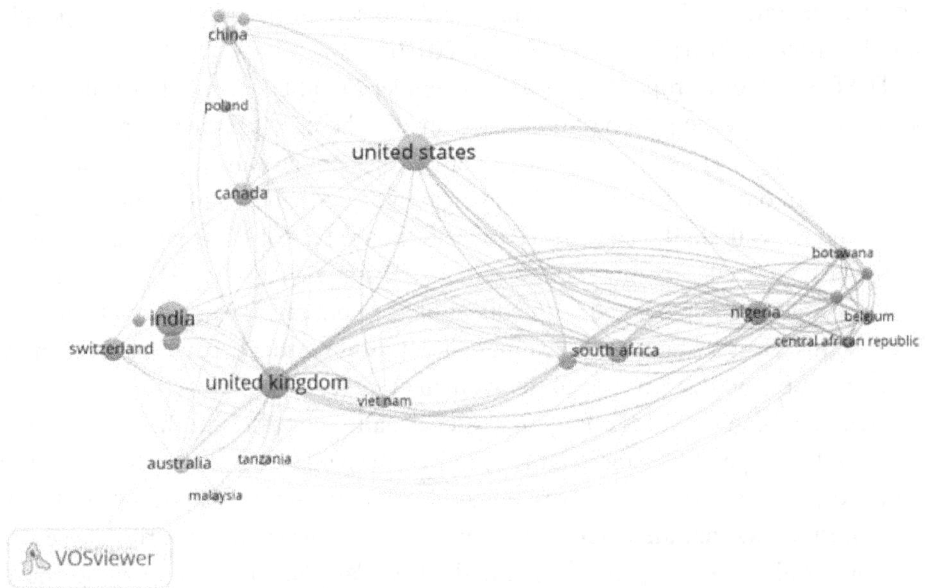

Source: Analysis done by the authors using Vosviewer

2.2 CSR and Women Empowerment in India

CSR gained popularity in India only in the new millennium despite originating in the USA in the 1950s (Abraham, 2013). Through the Companies Act 2013, the CSR requirement has been made mandatory for Public Sector Units (PSUs) and private companies. According to this act, companies meeting specific size or profit thresholds must spend at least 2% of their net profit on CSR (Dharmapala & Khanna, 2018). In 2017, over 1000 companies contributed about Rs. 9000 crores in various CSR initiatives in education, skill-building, rural development, and environmental sustainability. The focus of CSR initiatives has recently diverted toward women empowerment and gender equality (Ernst & Young, 2020). Kabeer (2001) states that in India, one of the efficient methods adopted to improve women's empowerment, particularly in the rural and semi-urban areas, is forming Self-Help Groups (SHGs), particularly for providing credit and support to the development of microenterprises. These SHGs help the women gain expertise in the micro-enterprise activities, enabling sustainable economic development for the women engaging in these activities (Kannabiran, 2009; Kapoor, 2019). Moreover, these micro-enterprise activities are extended into various self-employment activities like tailors, artisans, blacksmiths, carpenters, and off-farm activities (Versluysen, 1999). However, suitable CSR initiatives should have ethical and philosophical dimensions, as there is a huge gap between income levels, gender equality, and the socio-economic status of people in India (Bajpai, 2001; Gautam & Singh, 2010).

The Council of Europe (1998) defines Gender Equality as 'equal visibility, empowerment and participation of both sexes in all spheres of public and private life'. (Babu & Sahay, 2018) refer to women's empowerment as enhancing and uplifting women's economic, social, political, and legal rights so that they are assured of equal rights and show them the confidence to avail themselves of those rights. Women's empowerment is vital for any society's social uplifting and economic development, where women are empowered with educational, economic, health, social, and political status. Besides benefitting women, it provides remote benefits to the society or community and the families of the women at large.

India has been one of the lowest gender equality countries in the world in the recent past. Compared to some leading countries, the percentage of women employees in the corporate sector is the lowest, as the Corporate Gender Gap report in India. The report shows that the percentage of women employees in the corporate sector in India is only 23% compared to that in the US, Canada, and Finland, which have 52%, 46%, and 44% of women employees, respectively (Zahidi & Ibarra, 2010).

Table 1. Percentage of women employees in the corporate sector

Sr. No	Country	Percentage of women employees
1	US	52%
2	Canada	46%
3	Finland	44%
4	India	23%

This insists on women's empowerment in India with an overall approach to health, social, and politics so that women can have increased access to occupation, education, health care, and political and economic decision-making. World Economic Forum (2022) ranks India 135th among the 146 countries on the gender equality index. This means India did not provide an encouraging environment for women and girls to exhibit their full potential. One of the potential reasons could be that patriarchal attitudes and norms make it hard to have equal rights in education, employment, and decision-making.

However, in recent times, India has made considerable progress in the activities related to empowering women, particularly in bringing gender equality to the workplace. The liberalization policy of the Indian economy launched three decades ago enabled many multinational companies to start their operations in India, giving plenty of employment opportunities to women in India (Khurana, 2020). In most BSE 100 companies in India, the percentage of women as permanent employees was less than 10%, the percentage of companies which has at least one women director on the board was 98%, and the percentage of companies that have more than three women board members was 15%. This shows the acceptance of increased women's participation in the corporate sector.

Table 2. Percentage of women participation in the corporate sector

Sr. No	Criteria	Percentage
1	Permanent women workforce	< 10%
2	At least one women director on the board	98%
3	More than three women board members	15%

In the recent past, worldwide CSR activities have focused more on women empowerment initiatives, which can bring economic development, sustainable societies, and enhanced business performance. By engaging more women in their organizational structure, companies have started witnessing improved effectiveness of the firms. Many organizations have included women empowerment initiatives in their CSR initiative portfolio. The main focus areas of women empowerment activities shown by these firms are education (Haski-Leventhal, 2022), skill development (Poddar et al., 2019), and entrepreneurship training for women and girls (Agrawal et al., 2021). Many Indian companies have collaborated with non-profit organizations to implement CSR activities, particularly in women empowerment CSR initiatives (Kabeer & Mahmud, 2010). In recent decades, it has been observed that there is increased participation of girls in education (Gupta, 2012; Sahni & Kalyan Shankar, 2012) and women in employment in various sectors (Bhardwaj, 2022). Among the CSR initiatives related to women empowerment, 68% focused on vocational training, 42% focused on Self-Help Group (SHG) creation, and 30% focused on entrepreneurship development.

Table 3. CSR initiatives related to women's empowerment

Sr. No	Criteria	Percentage
1	Vocational training	68%
2	SHG creation	42%
3	entrepreneurship development	33%

2.3 Top 10 CSR Projects for Women Empowerment in India in 2018-19

1. Targeting the Hardcore Poor, a Program by Bandhan Bank

This CSR program launched by Bandhan Bank aims at eradicating poverty among poor women. The target destitute women are supported through free assets, not direct monetary benefits, except for some weekly allowances for basic living. The women will be given training, counseling, and mentoring to generate income from these assets to sustain their living. This program has helped destitute women uplift themselves from poverty and link themselves to the other streams of society. This program has been introduced in 12 states and 10,009 villages, where 1,29,390 households have benefitted from this program.

2. Economic Empowerment of Women, ITC Limited

This CSR initiative aims to provide a range of fruitful employment opportunities through various activities to more than 64,000 poor women, including 22,700 extremely needy women. This initiative provides provisions to help people gain a sustainable income via non-farm livelihood activities. One of the capacity-building training given to the women was an inclusion project with financial literacy in about 765 villages across 11 districts in the state of Madhya Pradesh with the partnership of CRISIL Foundation and Madhya Pradesh Rural Livelihood Mission (MPSRLM).

3. Salon-i, Godrej

It is an in-house vocational training program for young women to provide basic skills in skin and hair care and beauty, as well as modules on life skills and entrepreneurship to encourage self-employment. The program focuses on entrepreneurship, employability, and the development of women. It helps increase the number of women entrepreneurs in micro sectors like beauty and wellness through 'Beautypreneuer' start-ups. It also trains young girls to expand the enterprise, apart from their regular salon business. The project assessment shows that 50% of the trainees have taken up employment, and about 25% work from home in the beauty and wellness business. Both avenues provide monthly earnings of around Rs. 1000 to Rs. 5000 depending on the location, the number of working hours, and skillset in the early career period.

4. 'Main Kuch Bhi Kar Sakti Hoon' ('I can do anything), REC Limited

REC Limited, a power sector financing organization, has launched this program in partnership with the Population Foundation of India (PFI), a population and advocacy research organization. This awareness project propagates the Swachh Bharat Mission (Clean India Mission) through a TV-based show as mass communication media. The program creates an understanding of safe and sustained sanitation practices and focuses on women's health issues and empowerment.

5. Sakhi, Hindustan Zinc Ltd.,

This women empowerment project is aimed at rural women, making them form self-help groups (SHGs) and providing training and skill development on leadership, saving, and entrepreneurship. Through this project, 1922 SHGs have been formed with 23,954 members. About 18,053 women, so far, availed loans for various livelihood purposes and education, expanding their micro-enterprises. This program was made in collaboration with one more CSR initiative program, Kushi–a 'Khushi Baatiye 'campaign, to stitch uniforms for 60000 Anganwadi children.

6. Empowerment of Women through various media, HeroMotoCorp Limited

This women empowerment initiative was launched associating with the Department of Police to provide two-wheelers to women police so they could move freely after responding to distressed calls. This project was launched in 8 states, and 960 women police benefitted from this initiative. Besides, this initiative also provided short-term courses on tailoring, beauty care, and hospitality to improve the employability of girls and women from the marginalized section of society to enable them to earn a decent livelihood. This initiative also aims to promote community development and socio-economic awareness through all means and media

7. Swayam, CEAT Limited.

This women empowerment initiative aims to provide driving skills to women in driving two-wheelers, three-wheelers, and four-wheelers and assists them in getting a driving license to get them employment as taxi drivers, autos, and school vans. Under this initiative, 1279 women benefitted from the driving training, with 250 women in a four-wheeler, 360 women in a three-wheeler, and 728 women in a two-wheeler, and got permanent driving licenses. This company also provided training to 719 underprivileged women as Patient Care Assistants so that they could get a livelihood.

8. Jeewan Jyoti Women Empowerment Programme, Sterlite Technologies

This women empowerment initiative aims to provide vocational skill development to rural women in nursing, computer training, tailoring, and beauty care to make them financially independent. Besides, to use these training skills efficiently, they are also provided with public speaking skills and confidence building. In the year 2019 there, 421 women benefitted from this program. Transport facilities are available for women in remote villages to attend the training programs.

9. Cummins Powers Women program, Cummins India Limited

This women empowerment initiative aims to support women and girls in getting advanced education, opportunity, equity, and social justice in association with the Rise Up initiative in Mumbai. This initiative is part of the gender equity initiative, which focuses on improving laws, programs, and funding for women's education.

10. Education program for Empowerment, Tata Technologies Limited

This women empowerment initiative aims to empower girls to be financially independent and capable individuals by providing scholarships and mentoring to the 70 commendable girls students from below-poverty-line families. This scholarship program sponsors girls for Engineering degree courses based on their academic performance. The purpose is to increase women's representation in science, Technology, and engineering careers. In addition, benefactors are also given training through various personality development programs.

Table 4. Summaries of the Top 10 Women Empowerment Initiatives in India 2019

Sr.No	Name of the scheme	Company (Industry type)	CSR Locations	Total Expenditure on the Project Rs (Crores)	Total Prescribed CSR in FY 2018-19 Rs (Crores)	Origin	Area
1	Targeting the Hardcore Program	Bandhan Bank Limited (Banking)	West Bengal, Jharkhand Odisha, Bihar,	12.95	27.83	Indian	Women poverty eradication
2	Economic Empowerment of Women	ITC Limited (FMCG)	Andhra Pradesh, Tamil Nadu, Karnataka, Maharashtra, Bihar, Telangana, Uttar Pradesh, Uttarakhand, Madhya Pradesh, Assam, Rajasthan, West Bengal, Himachal Pradesh.	12.02	306.55	Indian	Employment for poor women
3	Project Salon-i	Godrej Consumer Products Limited (FMCG)	Pan-India	8.10	21.87	Indian	Women Skill development (Vocational training in Beauty and Styling)
4	'Main Kuch Bhi Kar Sakti Hoon' Season 3	REC Limited (Power)	Pan-India	5.41	157.29	Indian	Women health and hygiene
5	SAKHI Project	Hindustan Zinc Limited (Metal)	Rajasthan	5.40	203.93	Indian	Women skill development, entrepreneurship
6	Empowering Women through various media.	HeroMotoCorp Limited (Automobile)	Pan-India	5.36	93.72	Indian	Women Police empowerment, Women Skill development, entrepreneurship
7	Project Swayam & Project Sanjeevani:	CEAT Limited (Tyre)	Madhya Pradesh, Rajasthan, Maharashtra, Tamil Nadu, Delhi, Gujarat,	2.39	10.509	Indian	Women skill development and employment (Driving skills)

continued on following page

Table 4. Continued

Sr.No	Name of the scheme	Company (Industry type)	CSR Locations	Total Expenditure on the Project Rs (Crores)	Total Prescribed CSR in FY 2018-19 Rs (Crores)	Origin	Area
8	Jeewan Jyoti Women Empowerment Programme	Sterlite Technologies Limited (Telecom and Digital Technology)	Maharashtra	1.94	5.37	Indian	Women Skill development
9	Cummins Powers Women Program	Cummins India Limited (Power)	Pan-India	1.74	16.16	Non-Indian	Women (Girl) Education and Gender Equity
10	Empowerment Via Education Program	Tata Technologies Limited (Engineering & IT services)	Maharashtra	1.25	5.13	Indian	Women Education (Scholarships)

3. CONCEPTUAL FRAMEWORK FOR WOMEN'S EMPOWERMENT

The CSR women empowerment initiatives launched by various organizations provide women empowerment in a particular area but do not comprehensively empower women in various areas and solve their problems and challenges. Though various studies have been conducted on women's issues and challenges and their impact on women's empowerment, there is a need to develop a model that comprehensively empowers women in all areas or disciplines. Sahay & Kumar (2014) suggested a framework that focuses not only on one issue but includes various issues related to women and complex problems that must be solved.

Based on the above review, a conceptual framework for women's empowerment through CSR has been developed as follows:

Figure 3. Conceptual Framework for Women's Empowerment

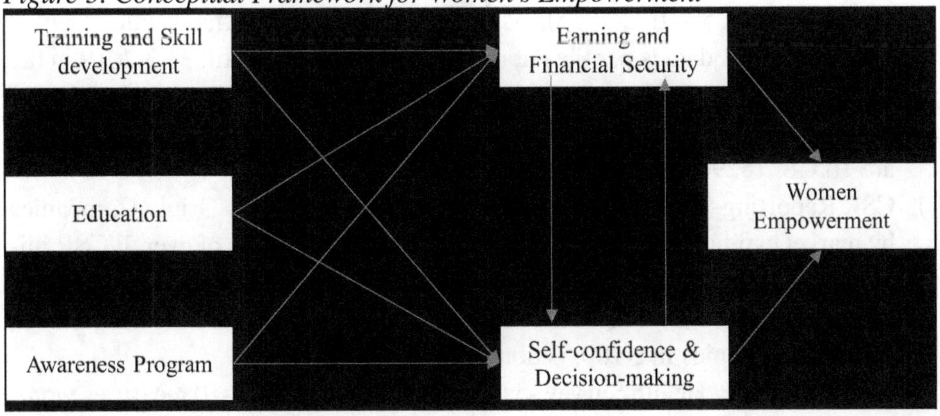

Source: Developed by the authors

The major underlying factors influencing women's empowerment are providing training & skill development, education, and awareness programs for women. The factor training & skill development includes developing communication, leadership, managerial, and other skill sets. The factor education includes educating women in the general areas of discipline, including finance, accounting, marketing, and specific technical areas like textiles and home science, based on their specific needs. The factor awareness program includes providing awareness to women on various areas and issues like health and hygiene, atrocities and a crime against women, and understanding women's rights and laws. All these above factors will positively influence earnings and provide financial security for women. Also, the underlying factors will increase the self-confidence & the decision-making capability of the women. The earnings & financial security and self-confidence & decision-making capability factor will influence each other. In other words, a woman with more self-confidence & decision-making capability can improve their earnings & financial security. Likewise, women who gain more earnings & financial security will have increased self-confidence & decision-making capability. All these factors have a positive influence on women's empowerment. So, this framework covers most factors related to issues and challenges women face in their empowerment.

4. METHODS

The research design of this study is mainly descriptive. Data were collected using secondary data from the CSR reports. This study is mainly done on the secondary data analysis using the secondary data from the following data sources:

1) CSR reporting of Indian companies from 2014 to 2018 by the High-Level Committee-2105 (HLC-2015), Ministry of Corporate Affairs, published in 2019. The CSR data is per the data filed by the companies till 31.3.2019 in the MCA21 registry (Ministry of Corporate Affairs, 2019). The sample sizes of the companies in this CSR report for 2014-15, 2015-16, 2016-17, and 2017-18 are 16548, 18290, 19532, and 21337, respectively.
2) CSR Reporting Survey 2019 in the 100 largest listed Indian Origin Companies by market capitalization (KPMG, 2020), where the analysis of overall CSR initiatives concerning women empowerment through CSR initiatives and women empowerment in CSR activities, i.e., the role of women in CSR activities of top 100 companies in N100, is done.
3) National Family Health Survey -5 (NFHS) in India in 2019-20 measures women's empowerment, albeit narrowly (Ministry of Health and Family Welfare, 2020). It measures six factors—three related to ownership of physical assets (mobile phones, bank accounts, land, and housing), access to menstrual hygiene products, participation in three key household decisions (healthcare for herself, visits to family or relatives, household purchases, and), and employment status over the last year.
4) Top 10 women empowerment projects by CSR initiatives in India during the year 2018-19 (CSR Box, 2020)

The sampling technique adopted in this study was a non-probability, purpose sampling technique, wherein the above reports on gender equality and women empowerment were analyzed. Data analysis techniques are simple percentage analysis, chi-square test, and ANOVA.

5. DATA ANALYSIS

5.1 CSR reporting of Indian companies from 2014 to 2018 by the High-Level Committee-2105 (HLC-2015)

Table 5 shows that, in 2014-15, out of the total CSR amount, the amount spent on gender equality was 0.55%, women empowerment was 0.72%, and 0.09% was on setting up hostels and homes for women. The overall amount spent on women empowerment activities was 1.36%.

In the year 2015-16, out of the total CSR amount, the amount spent for gender equality was 0.51%, for women empowerment was 0.84%, and 0.20% was to set up hostels and homes for women, and the overall amount spent for women empowerment activities was 1.55%.

In the year 2016-17, out of the total CSR amount, the amount spent for gender equality was 0.51%, for women empowerment was 0.99%, and 0.43% was to set up hostels and homes for women, and the overall amount spent for women empowerment activities was 1.93%.

In the year 2017-18, out of the total CSR amount, the amount spent for gender equality was 0.15%, for women empowerment was 1.46%, and 0.51% was to set up hostels and homes for women, and the overall amount spent for women empowerment activities was 2.12%.

From 2014-15 to 2017-18, an increase was observed in the total amount spent on overall women empowerment activities, from 1.36% to 2.12%. However, the average percentage spent on overall women empowerment activities from 2014-15 to 2017-18 was 1.76% of the total CSR amount.

Table 5. CSR expenditure for gender equality, women empowerment and setting up accommodation facilities

Sr. No	Year	Total CSR Amount Rs. (crores)	Amount spent on						Total amount spent on overall activities of women empowerment	
			Gender Equality		Women Empowerment		Setting up homes and hostels for women			
			Rs. (crores)	%	Rs. (crores)	%	Rs. (crores)	%	Rs. (crores)	%
1	**2014-15**	**10065.93**	**55.21**	**0.55**	**72.87**	**0.72**	**8.74**	**0.09**	**136.82**	**1.36**
2	2015-16	14503.65	73.85	0.51	121.94	0.84	29.28	0.20	**225.07**	**1.55**
3	2016-17	14312.03	72.60	0.51	141.61	0.99	61.97	0.43	**276.18**	**1.93**
4	2017-18	13,326.69	20.17	0.15	194.84	1.46	67.63	0.51	**282.64**	**2.12**
	Total	**52208.33**	**221.83**	**0.42**	**531.26**	**1.02**	**167.62**	**0.32**	**920.71**	**1.76**

Source: Analysis done by the authors using SPSS

5.2 Role of Women in CSR Committees

Gender equality in the CSR committees is one of the steps toward women's empowerment. Out of the N100 companies, it has been observed that there is a significant improvement in the percentage of women members in the CSR committee. i.e., from 52% in 2017-18, it has increased to 62% in 2018-19. Also, in the above CSR committees where women members are present, there is a slight increase in the percentage of women as the chairperson of the CSR committee, i.e., from 36%

in the year 2017-18, it has increased to 38% in the year 2018-19. Moreover, the expenditure by companies on reducing inequality with a woman as chairperson in the CSR committee has increased from 14% in 2016-17 to 42% in 2018-19, almost three times higher.

Table 6. Role of Women in CSR Committee from 2016 to 2019

Category	2016-17	2017-18	2018-19
Women as a member of the CSR committee	53%	53%	62%
Women as a chairperson of the CSR committee	37%	36%	38%
Expenditure by companies on gender equality with women as Chairpersons	14%	-	42%

Source: (KPMG, 2020)

When we see the role of women in CSR activities in the Public Sector Units (PSU) and Non-Public Sector units (non-PSUs), the percentage of women members in the CSR committee is higher in PSUs at 69% than in non-PSUs at 62%. Nevertheless, in the case of women as chairpersons of the CSR committees, the percentage is higher in non-PSUs at 38% than in PSUs at 33%. It shows that though women's participation in CSR committees is higher in PSUs, women's empowerment in CSR committees is higher in non-PSUs.

Table 7. Role of women in CSR committee: PSU Vs. Non-PSU

Category	PSU	Non-PSU
Women as a member of the CSR committee	69%	62%
Women as a chairperson of the CSR committee	33%	38%

Source: (KPMG, 2020)

Similarly, when we see the role of women in CSR activities in Indian companies and non-Indian companies, the percentage of women members in the CSR committee is higher in non-Indian companies at 88% than in Indian companies at 59%. Also, among women as chairpersons of the CSR committees, the percentage is higher in non-Indian companies at 50% than in Indian companies at 21%. This shows that women's participation in CSR committees is higher in non-Indian companies than in Indian companies.

Table 8. Role of women in CSR committee: Indian Vs. Non-Indian

Category	Indian	Non-Indian
Women as a member of the CSR committee	59%	88%
Women as a chairperson of the CSR committee	21%	50%

Source: (KPMG, 2020)

5.3 National Family Health Survey Data (NFHS)

Table 9 provides data on NHFS comparisons from 2015 to 2020.

Table 9. NFHS Women Empowerment Parameters data from 2015 to 2020

Sr.No	Parameters	Criteria	2015	2020
1	Educational Attainment	Share of women with more than 10 years of education	+5.5%	
		The gender gap in education	11.5%	8%
2	Health and Survival	Share of women using hygienic methods like sanitary napkins, etc.	60%	78%
3	Economic participation	Bank account ownership	10%	28%
		Share of married women who are employed and getting paid	26%	28%
4	Social empowerment	participation in household decisions	85%	89%
		Land House ownership	45%	45%
		% of women experiencing spousal violence	32%	30%
		% of women using modern methods of contraception	50%	70%

Source: (NFHS, 2020)

Table 9 shows that in the educational attainment parameter, the share of women with more than 10 years of education has increased by 5.5%, and the gender gap in education has reduced from 11.5% to 8% from 2015 to 2020.

In the health and survival parameter, the share of women using hygienic methods like sanitary napkins has increased from 68% to 78% from 2015 to 2020.

In the economic participation parameter, bank account ownership by women has increased from 10% to 28%, and the share of married women who are employed and getting paid has increased from 26% to 28% from 2015 to 2020.

In the social empowerment parameter, women's participation in household decisions has increased from 85% to 89%; women owning land and the house remains the same at 45%; the percentage of women facing spousal violence has reduced from 32% to 30%, and the percentage of women using modern methods of contraception has increased from 50% to 70% from the year 2015 to 2020.

Figure 4. Trend observed across social empowerment indicators

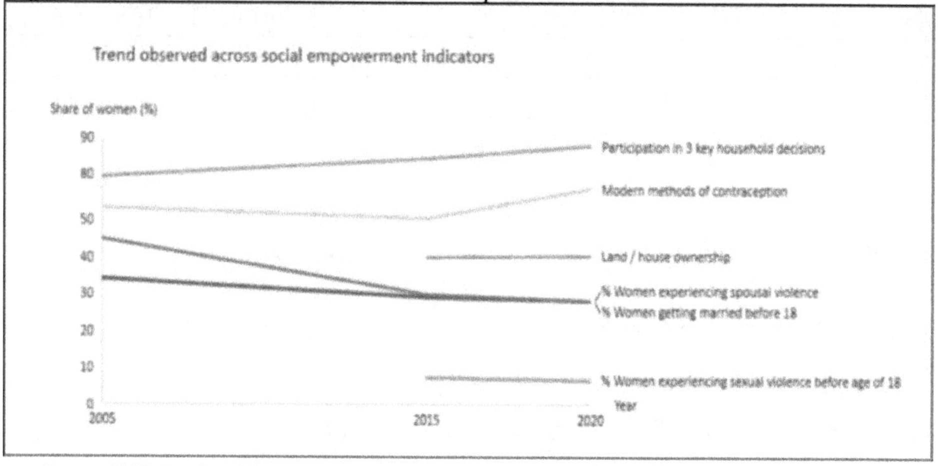

Source: 5th National and Family Health Survey (NFHS)

5.4 Analysis of Top 10 CSR Women Empowerment Initiatives in India

5.4.1 Descriptive Statistics

Table 10 shows that in the top 10 CSR women empowerment initiatives, FMCG & Power companies contribute 20% each; Banking, Automobile, Metal, Tyre, Telecom & Digital Services, and Engineering & IT services contribute 10% each. So, most of the contributions come from FMCG and power companies in the top 10 CSR women empowerment initiatives.

Table 10. Industry type-wise contributions

Industry Type	Frequency	Percent
Banking	1	10.0
FMCG	2	20.0
Power	2	20.0
Automobile	1	10.0
Metal	1	10.0
Tyre	1	10.0
Telecom and Digital Services	1	10.0

continued on following page

Table 10. Continued

Industry Type	Frequency	Percent
Engineering and IT services	1	10.0
Total	**10**	**100.0**

Source: Analysis done by the authors using SPSS

Table 11 shows that in the top 10 CSR women empowerment initiatives, 90% of the contribution comes from Indian companies, and 10% of the contribution comes from non-Indian companies. So. the majority of the contribution comes from Indian companies in the top 10 CSR women empowerment initiatives.

Table 11. Company Origin wise contribution

Company Origin	Frequency	Percent
Indian	9	90.0
Non-Indian	1	10.0
Total	**10**	**100.0**

Source: Analysis done by the authors using SPSS

From Table 12, it is observed that in the top 10 CSR women empowerment initiatives, 40% of the initiatives are related to women's skill development and entrepreneurship; 20% of the initiatives are related to both each women's employment and women's education, and 10% of the initiatives are related to both each women poverty eradication and women health & hygiene. So the majority of the initiatives are women's skill development and entrepreneurship in the top 10 CSR women empowerment initiatives.

Table 12. Area of Women Empowerment focused on CSR initiatives

Area of Women Empowerment	Frequency	Percent
Women Poverty Eradication	1	10.0
Women Employment	2	20.0
Women Skill Development and Entrepreneurship	4	40.0
Women Education	2	20.0
Women Health and Hygiene	1	10.0
Total	**10**	**100.0**

Source: Analysis done by the authors using SPSS

From Table 13, it is observed that in the top 10 CSR women empowerment initiatives, 40% of the initiatives have spent less than 10% of their CSR expenses on women empowerment; 30% of the initiatives have spent above 30% of their CSR expenses on women empowerment; 20% of the initiatives have spent 21% - 30% of their CSR expenses on women empowerment; and 10% of the initiatives have spent 11% - 20% of their CSR expenses on women empowerment. So, most companies have spent less than 10% of their CSR expenses on women's empowerment in the top 10 CSR women's empowerment initiatives.

Table 13. Percentage of CSR Expenses on Women Empowerment

Percentage of CSR Expenses on Women Empowerment	Frequency	Percent
Less than 10%	4	40.0
11% to 20%	1	10.0
21% to 30%	2	20.0
Above 30%	3	30.0
Total	**10**	**100.0**

Source: Analysis done by the authors using SPSS

From Table 14, it is observed that in the top 10 CSR women empowerment initiatives, 50% of the initiatives have been launched in more than 10 states, 40% of the initiatives have been launched in less than five states, and 10% of the initiatives have been launched in 5-10 states. So, the majority of the CSR women empowerment initiatives were launched in more than 10 states or on a pan-India basis in the top 10 CSR women empowerment initiatives.

Table 14. Geographical Distribution of CSR Women Empowerment Initiatives

Geographical Distribution	Frequency	Percent
Less than 5 states	4	40.0
5 to 10 states	1	10.0
Above 10 states	5	50.0
Total	**10**	**100.0**

Source: Analysis done by the authors using SPSS

5.4.2 Chi-square Test

Chi-square Test between categories

The chi-square test of association is done to understand any association between the company categories in the top 10 CSR women empowerment initiatives.

Table 15. Chi-square between categories

Categories	Chi-Square Value	df	Asymp. Sig. (2-sided)
Industry type Vs. origin	4.444	7	0.727
Origin Vs. CSR area	4.444	4	0.349
Industry type Vs. CSR	28.750	28	0.425

Source: Analysis done by the authors using SPSS

From the table, it is observed that,

Category industry type (χ^2= 4.444, p > .05) is not associated with category origin; Category origin (χ^2= 4.444, p > .05) is not associated with category CSR area; and Category industry type (χ^2= 28.75, p > .05) is not associated with the category CSR area. So, no company categories are associated with each other in the top 10 CSR women empowerment initiatives.

Chi-square Test Categories Vs. Geographical Distribution

Table 16. Categories Vs. Geographical distribution

Categories	Chi-Square Value	df	Asymp. Sig. (2-sided)
Industry type	20.000	14	0.123
CSR area	7.250	8	0.510
Industry type Vs. CSR	1.111	2	0.574

Source: Analysis done by the authors using SPSS

From Table 16, it is observed that for the category.

Industry type (χ^2= 20.000, p > .05), there is no association with the geographical distribution. CSR area (χ^2= 7.250, p > .05) has no association with the geographical distribution. Origin (χ^2= 1.111, p > .05), there is no association with the geographical distribution. So, no categories are associated with geographical distribution in the top 10 CSR women empowerment initiatives.

5.4.3 ANOVA

ANOVA test is done to understand any difference between the company categories in CSR women empowerment project expenditure and the percentage of CSR expenditure in the top 10 CSR women empowerment initiatives.

ANOVA: Categories Vs. Project Expenditure

Table 17. ANOVA: Categories Vs. Project Expenditure

Category	Project Expenditure	Sum of Squares	df	Mean Square	F	Sig.
Industry Type	Between Groups	144.695	7	20.671	2.867	0.283
	Within Groups	14.418	2	7.209		
	Total	159.113	9			
Origin	Between Groups	17.039	1	17.039	0.959	0.356
	Within Groups	142.074	8	17.759		
	Total	159.113	9			
CSR Area	Between Groups	93.521	4	23.38	1.782	0.269
	Within Groups	65.592	5	13.118		
	Total	159.113	9			

Source: Analysis done by the authors using SPSS

From Table 17, it is observed that with project expenditure as the dependent variable for the categories, Industry type ($F= 2.867; p> .05$), there is no significant difference in project expenditure; Origin ($F= 0.959; p> .05$), there is no significant difference in project expenditure; and there is no significant difference in project expenditure in the CSR area ($F= 1.782; p> .05$). The analysis shows no significant difference in the CSR women empowerment project expenditure among the industry category types.

ANOVA: Categories Vs. Percentage Expenditure

Table 18. ANOVA: Categories Vs. Percentage Expenditure

Category	Percentage of Expenditure	Sum of Squares	df	Mean Square	F	Sig.
Industry Type	Between Groups	1824.11	7	260.587	0.906	0.617
	Within Groups	575.332	2	287.666		
	Total	2399.442	9			

continued on following page

Table 18. Continued

Category	Percentage of Expenditure	Sum of Squares	df	Mean Square	F	Sig.
	Between Groups	81.434	1	81.434	0.281	0.61
	Within Groups	2318.008	8	289.751		
Origin	Total	2399.442	9			
	Between Groups	1074.979	4	268.745	1.015	0.48
	Within Groups	1324.463	5	264.893		
CSR Area	Total	2399.442	9			

Source: Analysis done by the authors using SPSS

From Table 18, it is observed that with the percentage of CSR women empowerment project expenditure as the dependent variable for the categories Industry type (F= 0.906; p> .05), there is no significant difference in project expenditure; Origin (F= 0.281; p> .05), there is no significant difference in project expenditure; and There is no significant difference in percentage expenditure in the CSR area (F= 1.015; p> .05). The analysis shows no significant difference in the CSR women empowerment project expenditure percentage among the industry category types.

6. FINDINGS AND DISCUSSIONS

The findings of this study show that out of the N100 companies, there has been a significant improvement in the percentage of women members in the CSR committee. Also, in the above CSR committees where women members are present, there is a slight increase in the percentage of women elevated as the chairperson of these CSR committees. Also, in companies where the chairperson of the CSR committee is a woman, the spending on CSR women empowerment initiatives has increased thrice over the past few years. The average percentage of the total amount spent on overall women empowerment activities from 2014-15 to 2017-18 was 1.76% of the total CSR amount.

The descriptive statistics it was found that in the top 10 CSR women empowerment initiatives, the majority of the contribution comes from FMCG and Power sector companies; the majority of the contribution comes from Indian companies; the majority of the initiatives are women skill development and entrepreneurship; the majority of the companies have spent less than 10% of their CSR expenses on the activities for women empowerment, and the majority of the CSR empowerment of women initiatives were launched in more than 10 states or pan-India basis.

The findings of the Chi-square test show no association between the company categories in their CSR women empowerment initiatives, and there is no association with the categories and geographical distributions related to CSR women empowerment initiatives.

The ANOVA analysis shows no significant difference in the expenditure on CSR women empowerment projects among the industry category types, and no significant difference exists in the percentage of expenditure on CSR women empowerment projects among the industry category types.

The percentage of the total amount of CSR women empowerment initiative spending should be increased by at least 5% of the total CSR amount allocated by the companies. More women should be enrolled as members of the CSR committees, and more companies should engage women as their CSR committee chairpersons so that the women empowerment initiatives will be executed efficiently and effectively.

Like FMCG and power sector companies, other companies should more actively engage in women empowerment initiatives in their overall CSR initiatives. Companies involved in CSR initiatives should spend at least 25% of their CSR expenditure on women empowerment initiatives. If more companies get engaged in the CSR women empowerment initiatives, they should try to launch on a pan-India basis so that women in each state get an equal chance to be empowered. India has a lot of foreign-origin multinational companies. These companies should include women empowerment initiatives in their CSR initiatives portfolio.

7. CONCLUSION

In India, CSR acts as a medium for empowering women. In India, the private sector has started contributing more to CSR activities, where women empowerment initiatives are one of the essential parts of the CSR portfolio. However, compared to other developed countries, there is a long way to go. Likewise, there is a need to explore more interventions where women's empowerment can be achieved through domestic philanthropy. In the case of many developed countries, the contribution of domestic philanthropy is higher in CSR activities compared to that of Indian domestic philanthropy (Biasco & Adrian, 2018). Moreover, at levels, enough steps are to be taken to realize the importance of increasing social awareness so that the gaps can be narrowed down in the future. Though CSR acts as a good platform for firms to give back to society and the community, the firms also should modify their internal policies and policies favoring the women empowerment principles as detailed by the UN Global Compact's Women's Empowerment Principles, empowering women in corporate leadership, HR policies, procurement practices, career development, etc., towards the gender equality achievement at the workplace. Representation of women at corporate leadership levels will positively impact the initiatives for women's empowerment, apart from the higher profits of the organizations (Abraham, 2012). The corporate sector's role in women's economic empowerment is inevitable. They should develop long-term CSR women empowerment initiatives with a lifecycle approach that is highly impactful and can be measurable. Creating a supportive environment based on shared responsibilities and values is necessary, where equitable inclusion of women at all levels of the organization, society, and nation is envisaged.

11. LIMITATION AND FUTURE IMPLICATION

One limitation of this research is its reliance on secondary data, which may not fully capture the on-ground realities of women's empowerment through CSR initiatives. While reports and surveys provide valuable insights, they may not reflect the direct experiences, challenges, and long-term impacts on beneficiaries. The practical implication of this chapter's findings is that they support the development of a framework encouraging businesses to integrate CSR strategies for sustainable and inclusive growth. By prioritizing women's empowerment, companies can contribute meaningfully to gender equality, workforce diversity, and overall social and economic development in India.

11. REFERENCES

Abraham, D. T. (2013). *CSR and empowerment of women: the way forward.* AIMA Journal of Management and Research.

Agrawal, A., Gandhi, P., & Khare, P. (2021). Women empowerment through entrepreneurship: Case study of a social entrepreneurial intervention in rural India. *The International Journal of Organizational Analysis.* Advance online publication. DOI: 10.1108/IJOA-03-2021-2659

Amankwaa, A., Seet, P.-S., & Susomrith, P. (2022). Tackling hotel employees' turnover: A moderated-mediation analysis of transformational leadership, organisational embeddedness, and community embeddedness. *Journal of Hospitality and Tourism Management, 51*, 67–78. DOI: 10.1016/j.jhtm.2022.02.029

Babu, A., & Sahay, M. (2018). Impact of Corporate Social Responsibility on Women Empowerment. *International Journal of Pure and Applied Mathematics.*

Bajpai, G. N. (2001). *Corporate social responsibility in India and Europe: Cross-cultural perspective.* http://www.ficci.com

Bhardwaj, N. (2022). *Women and Work in India: Trends and Analysis.* India Briefing. https://www.india-briefing.com/news/women-and-work-in-india-trends-and-analysis-24758.html/

Boubakri, N., El Ghoul, S., Guedhami, O., & Wang, H. (2021). Corporate social responsibility in emerging market economies: Determinants, consequences, and future research directions. *Emerging Markets Review, 46*, 100758. DOI: 10.1016/j.ememar.2020.100758

Box, C. S. R. (2020). *Top 10 Women empowerment projects through CSR in India in the financial Year 2018-19.* https://csrbox.org/India_CSR_news_Top-10-Women%09Empowerment-Projects-through-CSR-in-India-in-the-Financial-Year-2018-19_540

Carroll, A. B. (1991). The pyramid of corporate social responsibility: Toward the moral management of organizational stakeholders. *Business Horizons, 34*(4), 39–48. DOI: 10.1016/0007-6813(91)90005-G

Carroll, A. B. (2016). Carroll's pyramid of CSR: Taking another look. *International Journal of Corporate Social Responsibility, 1*(1), 3. DOI: 10.1186/s40991-016-0004-6

Council of Europe. (1998). *Gender mainstreaming: conceptual framework, methodology and presentation of good practices.*

Dharmapala, D., & Khanna, V. (2018). The impact of mandated corporate social responsibility: Evidence from India's Companies Act of 2013. *International Review of Law and Economics*, *56*, 92–104. DOI: 10.1016/j.irle.2018.09.001

Donthu, N., Kumar, S., Mukherjee, D., Pandey, N., & Lim, W. M. (2021). How to conduct a bibliometric analysis: An overview and guidelines. *Journal of Business Research*, *133*, 285–296. DOI: 10.1016/j.jbusres.2021.04.070

Ernst & Young. (2020). *Corporate social responsibility in India: re-engineering compliance and fraud mitigation strategies*. https://assets.ey.com/content/dam/ey-sites/ey-com/en_in/topics/forensic/ey-csr-survey-2020.pdf

European Commission. (2001). *Green Paper, Promoting a European framework for Corporate Social Responsibility COM(2001)366 final*.

Frankental, P. (2001). Corporate social responsibility – a PR invention? *Corporate Communications*, *6*(1), 18–23. DOI: 10.1108/13563280110381170

Gautam, R., & Singh, A. (2010). Corporate social responsibility practices in India: A study of top 500 companies. *Global Business and Management Research*, *2*(1), 41–56.

Grosser, K. (2016). Corporate Social Responsibility and Multi-Stakeholder Governance: Pluralism, Feminist Perspectives and Women's NGOs. *Journal of Business Ethics*, *137*(1), 65–81. DOI: 10.1007/s10551-014-2526-8

Gupta, N. (2012). Women Undergraduates in Engineering Education in India: A Study of Growing Participation. *Gender, Technology and Development*, *16*(2), 153–176. DOI: 10.1177/097185241201600202

Haski-Leventhal, D. (2022). Editorial: CSR in Asia. *Society and Business Review*, *17*(1), 1–2. DOI: 10.1108/SBR-02-2022-156

Jamali, D. (2008). A Stakeholder Approach to Corporate Social Responsibility: A Fresh Perspective into Theory and Practice. *Journal of Business Ethics*, *82*(1), 213–231. DOI: 10.1007/s10551-007-9572-4

Jatana, R., & Crowther, D. (2007). Corporate Social Responsibility and the Empowerment of Women: An Indian Perspective. *Social Responsibility Journal*, *3*(4), 40–48. DOI: 10.1108/17471110710840224

Johnstone-Louis, M. (2017). Corporate Social Responsibility and Women's Entrepreneurship: Towards a More Adequate Theory of "Work.". *Business Ethics Quarterly*, *27*(4), 569–602. DOI: 10.1017/beq.2017.6

Kabeer, N. (2001). Conflicts Over Credit: Re-Evaluating the Empowerment Potential of Loans to Women in Rural Bangladesh. *World Development*, *29*(1), 63–84. DOI: 10.1016/S0305-750X(00)00081-4

Kabeer, N., & Mahmud, S. (2010). Microfinance and social mobilization: alternative pathways to grassroots democracy? In *Mobilizing for democracy*. Zed Books Ltd., DOI: 10.5040/9781350221413.ch-003

Kannabiran, G. (2009). Sustainable stakeholder engagement through innovative supply chain strategy: An exploratory study of an Indian organization. *Asian Business & Management*, *8*(2), 205–223. DOI: 10.1057/abm.2009.6

Kapoor, S. (2019). Entrepreneurship for economic and social empowerment of women: A case study of a self help credit program in Nithari Village, Noida, India. *Australasian Accounting. Business and Finance Journal*, *13*(2), 123–142.

Khurana, A. (2020). *Understanding how CSR can become catalyst to women empowerment in India*. Crossbarriers. https://crossbarriers.org/women-empowerment-in

KPMG. (2020). *India's CSR reporting survey 2019*. https://assets.kpmg.com/content/dam/kpmg/in/pdf/2020/02/india-s-csr-reporting-survey-2019.pdf

Kumar, A., Reddy, K. G., & P S, V. (2020). A scientometric analysis of the women empowerment (1985-2018). *Australian Journal of Business and Management Research*, 09–27. DOI: 10.52283/NSWRCA.AJBMR.20200511A02

Larrieta-Rubín de Celis, I., Velasco-Balmaseda, E., Fernández de Bobadilla, S., Alonso-Almeida, M. del M., & Intxaurburu-Clemente, G. (2015). Does having women managers lead to increased gender equality practices in corporate social responsibility? *Business Ethics (Oxford, England)*, *24*(1), 91–110. DOI: 10.1111/beer.12081

Lichtenstein, D. R., Drumwright, M. E., & Braig, B. M. (2004). The Effect of Corporate Social Responsibility on Customer Donations to Corporate-Supported Nonprofits. *Journal of Marketing*, *68*(4), 16–32. DOI: 10.1509/jmkg.68.4.16.42726

Mahmood, A., & Bashir, J. (2020). How does corporate social responsibility transform brand reputation into brand equity? Economic and noneconomic perspectives of CSR. *International Journal of Engineering Business Management*, *12*, 184797902092754. DOI: 10.1177/1847979020927547

Mahmood, S., & Khan, Z. (2023). CSR and customer orientation: A sustainable pathway towards competitive advantage? A customer's perspective. *Social Responsibility Journal*, *19*(4), 741–755. DOI: 10.1108/SRJ-04-2020-0139

Marshall, J. (2011). En-gendering Notions of Leadership for Sustainability. *Gender, Work and Organization, 18*(3), 263–281. DOI: 10.1111/j.1468-0432.2011.00559.x

McCarthy, L. (2017). Empowering Women Through Corporate Social Responsibility: A Feminist Foucauldian Critique. *Business Ethics Quarterly, 27*(4), 603–631. DOI: 10.1017/beq.2017.28

Mogaji, E., Hinson, R. E., Nwoba, A. C., & Nguyen, N. P. (2021). Corporate social responsibility for women's empowerment: A study on Nigerian banks. *International Journal of Bank Marketing, 39*(4), 516–540. DOI: 10.1108/IJBM-04-2020-0195

Narwal, M., & Singh, R. (2013). Corporate social responsibility practices in India: A comparative study of MNCs and Indian companies. *Social Responsibility Journal, 9*(3), 465–478. DOI: 10.1108/SRJ-11-2011-0100

Poddar, A., Narula, S. A., & Zutshi, A. (2019). A study of corporate social responsibility practices of the top Bombay Stock Exchange 500 companies in India and their alignment with the Sustainable Development Goals. *Corporate Social Responsibility and Environmental Management*, csr.1741. DOI: 10.1002/csr.1741

Rahman, S. U., Faisal, F., & Ali, A. (2022). Financial Development and Shadow Economy: A Bibliometric Analysis Using the Scopus Database (1985–2021). *Journal of the Knowledge Economy*. Advance online publication. DOI: 10.1007/s13132-022-00980-5

Roberts, A. (2015). The Political Economy of "Transnational Business Feminism.". *International Feminist Journal of Politics, 17*(2), 209–231. DOI: 10.1080/14616742.2013.849968

Sahay, M., & Kumar, K. (2014). Enhancing the corporate performance through system dynamics modelling. *Corporate Ownership & Control, 167*.

Sahni, R., & Kalyan Shankar, V. (2012). Girls' higher education in India on the road to inclusiveness: On track but heading where? *Higher Education, 63*(2), 237–256. DOI: 10.1007/s10734-011-9436-9

Spence, L. J. (2016). Small Business Social Responsibility. *Business & Society, 55*(1), 23–55. DOI: 10.1177/0007650314523256

van Eck, N. J., & Waltman, L. (2010). Software survey: VOSviewer, a computer program for bibliometric mapping. *Scientometrics, 84*(2), 523–538. DOI: 10.1007/s11192-009-0146-3 PMID: 20585380

Versluysen, E. (1999). *Defying the odds: Banking for the poor*. Kumarian Press West Hartford.

Vogel, D. (2007). *The market for virtue: The potential and limits of corporate social responsibility*. Brookings Institution Press.

World Economic Forum. (2022). *Global Gender Gap Report 2022*. https://www3.weforum.org/docs/WEF_GGGR_2022.pdf

Zahidi, S., & Ibarra, H. (2010). *The Corporate Gender Gap Report 2010*. https://alba.acg.edu/media/2492/coporategendergap_report.pdf

Zhao, L., Yang, M. M., Wang, Z., & Michelson, G. (2023). Trends in the Dynamic Evolution of Corporate Social Responsibility and Leadership: A Literature Review and Bibliometric Analysis. *Journal of Business Ethics*, *182*(1), 135–157. DOI: 10.1007/s10551-022-05035-y

Chapter 14
Applying Strategic Models in Distance Education and Educational Communication

Stalo Georgiou
https://orcid.org/0009-0003-5004-0481
Neapolis University, Paphos, Cyprus

ABSTRACT

In the rapidly evolving landscape of education, distance learning has emerged as a pivotal modality, necessitating the strategic application of educational frameworks to ensure effectiveness, engagement, and communication. This article explores the integration of strategic models within distance education and educational communication to optimize learning outcomes. Among these models, the Community of Inquiry (CoI) framework emphasizes the importance of cognitive presence, social presence, and teaching presence in creating an interactive and meaningful learning experience. Additionally, the ADDIE instructional design model provides a systematic approach to course development, ensuring that learning objectives, content delivery, and assessment are aligned with student needs. The blended learning model offers a flexible solution, combining online and face-to-face instruction, while Competency-Based Education (CBE) shifts the focus toward mastery of specific skills, providing learners with a more personalized pace.

DOI: 10.4018/979-8-3693-5583-1.ch014

INTRODUCTION

In a period characterized by swift technological progress and enhanced global interconnectedness, the landscape of education has moved beyond conventional classroom limitations, transforming into a dynamic and adaptable framework that increasingly depends on distance education methodologies. Distance education, defined by the temporal and spatial separation between instructors and students, enables individuals from diverse geographical locations and backgrounds to engage with educational opportunities at their own convenience. The transition from traditional face-to-face instruction to virtual learning environments necessitates a comprehensive reassessment of pedagogical approaches and communication frameworks. Strategic models in distance education and educational communication are essential for facilitating effective, engaging, and student-centered learning experiences (Morrison, et al, 2013).

The utilization of strategic models in distance education offers a systematic framework that aids educational institutions and educators in enhancing the effectiveness of their program delivery. These models are informed by a diverse array of fields, such as business, communication theory, and pedagogy, thereby facilitating informed decision-making and the design of instructional practices (O'Connor, et al, 2013). The implementation of these models enables educators to foresee and tackle the distinct challenges associated with distance learning, including the absence of physical interaction, the diverse needs of learners, technological obstacles, and the need to sustain student motivation and engagement. As distance education expands, the integration of strategic models is essential to ensure that educational experiences remain consistent, adaptable, and capable of fulfilling the expectations of both learners and educational institutions (O'Connor, et al, 2013).

These frameworks highlight the necessity of consistent and organized communication, the significance of interactive and adaptive learning technologies, and the incorporation of AI-driven analytics to customize educational content according to individual student requirements and learning speeds. The strategies under consideration encompass encryption techniques, the implementation of two- factor authentication, adherence to secure Wi-Fi protocols, and the utilization of virtual private networks (VPNs) by both students and faculty to ensure the integrity of data transmission. Furthermore, the study includes a comprehensive examination of the adoption of end-to-end encryption in video conferencing solutions, analyzing its implications for both functionality and security. This study presents a comprehensive framework aimed at assisting educational institutions in the systematic evaluation and integration of technological tools within their distance education programs (Shea et al, 2010).

The proposed framework seeks to reconcile security considerations with the educational advantages presented by emerging technologies. It advocates for continuous training for both educators and students regarding the utilization of these tools, as well as for implementing strategies that prioritize data privacy and security. In summary, although distance education technologies provide substantial opportunities for enhancing access to education, they also require meticulous attention to security measures and strategic communication models to guarantee their effective and secure application. The results presented in this paper seek to advance the ongoing discourse surrounding educational technology by proposing a strategic framework that educational institutions can implement to improve security measures and learning outcomes in remote education environments.

The Goal of the Article

This article aims to introduce and explain various strategic models that are relevant to distance education, such as the Community of Inquiry (CoI) framework, blended learning, and flipped classrooms, as well as communication theories like Shannon and Weaver's model. The article will also discuss the unique challenges posed by distance learning, such as lack of physical interaction, maintaining student engagement, and technological barriers, and show how strategic models can help address these issues.

A key goal is to emphasize the importance of effective communication in distance education, examining how strategic approaches can facilitate clear, purposeful, and interactive communication between students and instructors. Moreover, the article intends to provide practical insights on how educational institutions and instructors can implement these models to create more engaging, flexible, and supportive learning environments, ensuring that the goals of distance education are met.

The article will also encourage a flexible, adaptive approach to applying these models, acknowledging that ongoing changes in technology and learner needs require dynamic strategies to ensure success in distance education.

Ultimately, the article seeks to contribute to a better understanding of how to strategically manage and optimize distance education, helping educators design effective, meaningful, and sustainable learning experiences.

Methodology

This article shall utilize a descriptive analysis of the existing scholarly literature. The examination of relevant research and texts aims to guide the development of the research question, based on the most credible and pertinent information accessible. Moreover, it is imperative to systematically document and critically assess the methodologies and procedures utilized by other researchers who have explored the same or analogous topics. This process is vital for identifying both similarities and differences in relation to the current hypothesis. Such a comparative analysis will enable the formulation of well-informed conclusions and the possible integration of effective research methods and approaches.

2. DEFINITION OF TERMS

Strategic Models: Frameworks or structured approaches used to plan, organize, and optimize educational processes and communication, particularly in distance learning environments.

Distance Education: A method of delivering education to students who are not physically present in a traditional classroom setting, often utilizing online platforms to bridge the gap.

Educational Communication: The exchange of information and ideas between teachers and students, focusing on clear, purposeful, and effective communication to facilitate learning, especially in remote environments.

Community of Inquiry (CoI) Framework: A model for creating meaningful educational experiences in online environments through three elements: cognitive presence, social presence, and teaching presence.

Learning Management Systems (LMS): Digital platforms, such as Moodle or Blackboard, used to deliver, track, and manage educational content and communication in online and distance education.

3. REVIEW OF LITERATURE

Distance Education Strategy

Research on DE (distance education) strategies has predominantly concentrated on three overarching themes: the objectives and aspirations of distance education initiatives, the obstacles and challenges that impede their success, and the various responses or strategies employed to address these barriers. Additionally, another significant area of focus has been the perceptions and attitudes of faculty members and administrators towards distance education, as these viewpoints can greatly influence the effectiveness and implementation of DE programs. Lastly, the planning processes and associated issues surrounding distance education have also been a critical area of investigation, as effective planning is essential for the successful integration and sustainability of distance education within educational institutions. In 1998, Smith posed a critical question regarding the rationale for providing distance education (DE). He delineated five key objectives that institutions might aim to achieve through the implementation of DE programs. First and foremost, he emphasized the importance of improving access to education, ensuring that learners from various backgrounds and locations could engage with educational opportunities. Secondly, he highlighted the potential for institutions to expand their geographic reach, allowing them to serve a broader audience beyond their immediate vicinity. Thirdly, Smith pointed out the potential for enhancing the overall quality of education, suggesting that DE could foster innovative teaching methods and learning experiences. Fourth, he addressed the need for increased efficiency, both for educational institutions and for the students themselves, streamlining processes and making learning more effective. Lastly, Smith stressed the significance of achieving customer satisfaction, which entails meeting the needs and expectations of students and stakeholders involved in the educational process.

Additionally, Berge and Muilenburg (2001) contributed to the discourse on distance education by conducting a comparative analysis of the various "barriers to distance education" against the concept of "stages of organizational maturity." This study aimed to identify the challenges that institutions face in adopting DE while also examining how the maturity of an organization influences its ability to effectively implement and sustain distance education initiatives. Through these explorations, the researchers sought to shed light on the complexities surrounding the adoption of distance education and the multifaceted factors that institutions must navigate in order to successfully integrate DE into their educational offerings. In a related study, Fornaciari, Forte, and Mathews (1999) put forth a framework consisting of four distinct strategies for distance education. They emphasized that the appropriate strategy for an institution should be guided by key factors such as its overall size, its reputation within the academic community, and the financial implications of implementing these DE initiatives. This suggests that a tailored approach, considering these critical variables, is essential for effectively navigating the complexities of distance education and optimizing its success within different institutional contexts.

In a related study, Schifter (2000) examined the various factors that either encouraged or discouraged faculty members from participating in asynchronous learning networks (ALNs). His research revealed that there were three primary motivating factors that drove faculty engagement in ALNs. Firstly, the personal motivation to embrace and utilize technology played a significant role. Many faculty members found the integration of technology into their teaching practices to be a compelling reason to participate. Secondly, the opportunity to develop and explore new ideas was another key motivator. Faculty members were often eager to innovate and expand their pedagogical approaches through engagement with ALNs. Lastly, the desire to enhance their teaching effectiveness served as a strong incentive for faculty participation. By engaging with ALNs, educators sought to refine their instructional methods, thereby improving the overall quality of education they could provide to their students. The authors proposed that larger regional universities, which often struggle with lower reputations, should consider implementing cost leadership strategies as a means to attract out-of-state students. One effective approach they suggested is to offer these out-of-state students the same tuition rates as in-state residents. This strategy could potentially enhance the appeal of these institutions to a broader student base. On the other hand, they recommended that smaller national institutions, which tend to enjoy higher reputations, should adopt differentiation strategies.

This could involve placing a strong emphasis on developing and promoting highly selective distance degree programs that cater to specific niches in the educational market. In her 2000 study, Armstrong identified two distinct categories of factors that drive faculty members to participate in distance education (DE). The first category consists of institutional factors, which include elements such as strong administrative support, a positive organizational culture, and a firm institutional commitment to enhancing access to education for all students. These institutional factors create an environment that encourages faculty engagement in DE initiatives. On the other hand, primary personal factors that motivate faculty include a sense of curiosity about new teaching methodologies, the chance to interact with students who are already practicing professionals in their fields, and the convenience that DE offers in terms of flexible scheduling.

Furthermore, it is noteworthy that while some colleges and universities implement comprehensive and formal strategic planning processes for their distance education programs, as highlighted by Hache (1998) and Berge & Schrum (1998), there are also many institutions that adopt a more organic approach. In these cases, DE initiatives may emerge predominantly from faculty-driven efforts and experimental practices, as discussed by Adams (2001). This divergence in approaches underscores the varied strategies that institutions employ to develop and enhance their distance education offerings, reflecting the unique contexts and priorities of each institution. Ultimately, the interplay between institutional support and individual faculty motivation plays a crucial role in shaping the landscape of distance education at higher education institutions. In this study, the colleges adopted a comprehensive approach to formulating their Distance Education (DE) strategies, reflecting a deliberate and thoughtful planning process.

This methodology aligns with the principles put forth by several scholars who have explored various aspects of DE planning. Notable contributions from authors such as Bates and Pole (2003), Compora (2003), and Levy (2003) have provided valuable insights into the complexities and dynamics of developing effective DE strategies. Their work has significantly influenced the framework that will be discussed, which consists of a strategic 3 out of 13 choices model that serves as a foundation for decision-making in this context. To further elaborate, the concept of Strategic Mental Models plays a crucial role in this research, as it incorporates three essential ideas derived from strategic cognition theory. These mental models help to shape how educational leaders and decision-makers conceptualize and navigate the challenges associated with implementing DE initiatives. By understanding these cognitive frameworks, stakeholders can enhance their strategic planning processes, ensuring that their approaches are not only innovative but also aligned with the evolving needs of learners in a digital environment. In essence, the integration of these theoretical perspectives into the colleges' DE strategies underscores the importance of informed decision-making and strategic foresight in the ever-changing landscape of education.

By utilizing these frameworks, leaders can more readily identify patterns, predict outcomes, and make informed decisions in an increasingly complex business landscape. The formation of these mental models is not merely an individual phenomenon; rather, it is influenced by the shared experiences, knowledge, and cultural contexts of the industry in which these leaders operate. As a result, we often see a convergence in the mental models adopted by leaders from similar sectors, which can lead to a homogenization of strategic thought and action within those groups. This phenomenon highlights the importance of understanding how collective cognitive frameworks shape strategic behavior in organizational contexts. Ultimately, the interplay between individual and collective strategic mental models plays a vital role in shaping an organization's strategic vision and operational effectiveness.

By continuously refining these models and ensuring they are grounded in both experience and collaborative insights, managers can enhance their decision-making capabilities and drive their organizations toward sustained competitive advantage. Moreover, the process of developing these mental models is not solely an individual endeavor; it often involves significant collaboration among team members. As leaders come together, they engage in discussions and share insights, which leads to the formation of common mental models. This collaborative approach is crucial for addressing key challenges and aligning on strategic priorities. When leaders possess a shared understanding of the organization's direction and the external factors at play, they are better equipped to implement strategies that are cohesive and effective. In essence, the strategic mental models that managers create serve as cognitive tools that shape their understanding of the business environment.

These models help leaders navigate complex situations by providing a framework through which they can interpret various data points and trends. For instance, a manager's perception of industry trends, competitor actions, and customer preferences will significantly influence their decision-making process. This cognitive framework allows managers to anticipate challenges and opportunities, guiding them toward informed choices that align with their organization's goals. Moreover, leaders operating within cohesive industry groups often find themselves developing analogous strategic mental models. This phenomenon occurs as these leaders compete with one another while simultaneously learning from each other's experiences and strategies, a concept explored by Huff (1982).

The interplay of competition and collaboration within these groups contributes to the establishment of shared understandings and frameworks that guide decision-making processes. As such, the dynamics of industry collaboration and rivalry can significantly influence how leaders conceptualize and navigate their strategic landscapes. Through various professional and social interactions, such as networking events, conferences, and informal gatherings, managers share their perspectives and experiences, which can lead to the cross-pollination of strategic concepts. Furthermore, the movement of individuals between organizations—whether through job changes, consultancy roles, or collaborations—facilitates the transfer of innovative ideas and strategic practices. This fluidity in the labor market allows for a rich exchange of knowledge and methodologies, enabling leaders to refine their own approaches while simultaneously responding to the competitive landscape. Thus, the interplay between leaders and their external environments is characterized by a dynamic relationship, where strategies are not only influenced by external factors but are also actively reshaped through ongoing dialogue and experiential learning.

The Community of Inquiry

The Community of Inquiry (CoI) framework is a widely recognized model in the field of online and distance education. Developed by Garrison, Anderson, and Archer in 2000, it provides a robust conceptual foundation for understanding and facilitating meaningful learning experiences in virtual environments. The framework is centered on the idea that effective online learning arises through the interaction of three core elements: cognitive presence, social presence, and teaching presence (Garrison et al., 2000).

Cognitive presence refers to the extent to which learners are able to construct and confirm meaning through sustained reflection and discourse. It is grounded in the theory of critical thinking and practical inquiry. Cognitive presence develops across four phases: triggering events, exploration, integration, and resolution (Garrison et al., 2001). The process begins with a triggering event that sparks interest or a problem to be solved, followed by exploration as learners seek information and share ideas. In the integration phase, learners synthesize the information and ideas, constructing meaning and insights. Finally, resolution involves applying new knowledge to solve problems or answer questions.

In the context of distance education, cognitive presence is fostered through discussions, reflection activities, problem-solving tasks, and collaborative projects. The framework highlights that creating opportunities for learners to engage deeply with content is essential for developing critical thinking and knowledge construction, which are fundamental to higher education (Akyol & Garrison, 2011).

Social presence is the ability of learners to project themselves socially and emotionally in a community of inquiry, creating an environment where students feel connected to their peers and instructors. Social presence is critical for reducing the sense of isolation that can occur in online learning environments, as it facilitates open communication, group cohesion, and the development of interpersonal relationships (Garrison & Anderson, 2003). Social presence is supported through three dimensions: affective expression, open communication, and group cohesion.

In online education, social presence is established through the use of discussion boards, group projects, video conferences, and collaborative activities that encourage students to interact, share ideas, and build relationships. The use of personalized communication, such as addressing students by name, providing timely and constructive feedback, and using emotive language, enhances social presence and promotes a supportive online community (Lowenthal, 2010).

Teaching presence involves the design, facilitation, and direction of cognitive and social processes for the purpose of realizing educationally meaningful outcomes. It is the element that helps guide and sustain the learning community through course design, facilitation of discussion, and direct instruction. Teaching presence has three primary functions: instructional design and organization, facilitating discourse, and direct instruction (Anderson, Rourke, Garrison, & Archer, 2001).

In distance education, teaching presence begins with clear course design, including the creation of learning objectives, materials, assessments, and communication guidelines. Instructors facilitate discourse by encouraging active participation, asking probing questions, and ensuring that discussions remain focused on course content. Finally, direct instruction involves providing content expertise, clarifying misunderstandings, and offering feedback to guide learning (Shea et al., 2010).

The three elements of the CoI framework—cognitive presence, social presence, and teaching presence—are interdependent and mutually reinforcing. Cognitive presence is enhanced when students feel socially connected and when instructors provide effective facilitation and guidance. Similarly, social presence is strengthened by teaching presence, which sets the tone for open communication and community building. When the three elements are balanced, learners are more likely to engage meaningfully with the content and their peers, leading to a more effective and fulfilling educational experience (Garrison, 2017).

ADDIE Model

The ADDIE model is a widely used instructional design framework that is particularly effective for distance education. It stands for Analysis, Design, Development, Implementation, and Evaluation, representing the five phases of the instructional design process.

- Analysis: This phase involves identifying the needs of learners, defining learning objectives, and understanding the context in which the learning will occur. For distance education, this might include assessing students' access to technology, their familiarity with online learning platforms, and their learning preferences.
- Design: In the design phase, instructors develop a plan for how the course will be structured and delivered. This includes creating a course outline, determining the sequence of learning activities, selecting appropriate instructional methods (e.g., videos, readings, quizzes), and designing assessments.
- Development: The development phase is where the actual course materials are created. In distance education, this might involve recording lectures, developing interactive activities, creating multimedia content, and setting up the course on a Learning Management System (LMS).
- Implementation: During the implementation phase, the course is delivered to students. In distance education, this involves ensuring that all students have access to the materials and are able to navigate the online learning environment effectively. Instructors may also provide orientation sessions to help students get accustomed to the technology.
- Evaluation: The final phase involves assessing the effectiveness of the course and identifying areas for improvement. This includes evaluating student performance, gathering feedback from learners, and making adjustments to the course content and structure for future iterations (O'Connor, et al, 2013)

The ADDIE model's systematic approach ensures that distance education courses are well-planned, well-implemented, and continuously improved. Its iterative nature allows instructors to refine their courses based on feedback and evolving student needs (Graham, 2016).

Blended Learning Model

Blended learning is a strategic model that combines online and face-to-face instruction. While it is not exclusively a distance education model, it offers a flexible approach that can be particularly effective in hybrid or semi-distance learning scenarios.

Blended learning leverages the strengths of both traditional and online learning. It allows students to engage with course materials at their own pace online while also providing opportunities for synchronous, in-person interaction. This model is especially beneficial in contexts where full distance learning is not feasible but where students still require flexibility due to work, family, or other commitments (Graham, 2006).

In blended learning environments, strategic planning is essential to ensure that online and in-person components are integrated seamlessly. Instructors must carefully balance asynchronous and synchronous activities, ensuring that both complement each other and contribute to the overall learning objectives. Blended learning models often use flipped classroom strategies, where students are introduced to new concepts online and then engage in interactive, hands-on activities during in-person sessions.

Competency-Based Education (CBE)

Competency-Based Education (CBE) is another strategic model gaining popularity in distance education. CBE focuses on students' demonstration of mastery of specific skills and knowledge, rather than the amount of time spent in class. This model is particularly suited to distance education, where students often work independently and at their own pace.

In CBE, the curriculum is organized around clearly defined competencies that students must demonstrate. Assessments are designed to measure these competencies, and students can progress through the course as they master each competency, rather than being tied to a fixed schedule. This approach provides greater flexibility for learners, allowing them to accelerate through material they already understand and spend more time on areas where they need additional support (Morrison et al, 2013).

CBE requires careful instructional design to ensure that competencies are clearly defined, assessments are aligned with those competencies, and students receive adequate support and feedback. The use of technology, including adaptive learning systems and digital assessments, plays a critical role in facilitating CBE in distance education (Hodges, & Fowler, 2020).

Learning Management Systems (LMS)

A Learning Management System (LMS) is not a strategic model per se but serves as the backbone for implementing strategic models in distance education. LMS platforms such as Moodle, Blackboard, and Canvas provide the infrastructure for delivering course content, managing communication, and tracking student progress.

An effective LMS allows for the seamless integration of strategic models like the CoI framework, ADDIE, and CBE by offering tools for content delivery, assessment, discussion forums, and real-time communication. The LMS also provides analytics that help instructors monitor student engagement and performance, enabling them to make data-driven decisions to improve course delivery.

Strategically, the choice of LMS and how it is utilized can significantly impact the success of distance education programs. A well-chosen and well-implemented LMS can enhance both the teaching presence and social presence within an online course, creating a more cohesive and engaging learning experience for students (Garrison, 2017).

Taraza et al. (2024) explore the evaluation of quality and equality in education through the European Foundation for Quality Management (EFQM) Excellence Model, highlighting its role in assessing institutional performance and promoting sustainable educational practices. Their literature review emphasizes the importance of structured quality frameworks in ensuring equitable learning opportunities. Similarly, Taraza, Anastasiadou, and Masouras (2023) analyze the Malcolm Baldrige National Quality Award (MBNQA) Quality Tool in the educational sector, providing a systematic review of its application in enhancing institutional effectiveness and innovation. Their research underscores the relevance of quality management models in fostering continuous improvement and excellence in education.

Practical Implications

In addition to theoretical models, practical strategic approaches like blended learning and flipped classrooms have become prevalent in distance education. Blended learning integrates online educational materials with traditional in-person methods, providing a more flexible learning environment. The flipped classroom model, on the other hand, involves delivering instructional content outside of the classroom, often through online platforms, while classroom time is reserved for interactive, hands-on activities. These models enhance the efficacy of distance education by leveraging the advantages of both online and offline learning environments. They allow students to engage with materials at their own pace while fostering interactive and collaborative activities that reinforce learning during synchronous sessions (Bonk, & Graham, 2012).

Strategic models also play an essential role in addressing communication in distance education. Educational communication extends beyond the simple exchange of information; it involves the development of relationships, fostering a sense of community, and creating an environment conducive to learning. Effective communication is critical for bridging the gap created by the absence of face-to-face interaction in distance education. Shannon and Weaver's communication model, a foundational theory in communication studies, can be adapted to the context of distance education to help instructors and institutions design communication channels that are clear, efficient, and adaptable. By understanding the process of encoding, transmission, and decoding messages, educators can reduce misunderstandings and improve the quality of communication with students (Hodges, and Fowler, 2020).

Furthermore, the role of strategic models in educational communication is evident in the development of digital tools and platforms that facilitate interaction between students and instructors. Learning Management Systems (LMS) such as Moodle, Blackboard, and Canvas serve as comprehensive platforms that allow for the seamless integration of educational materials, assessments, and communication channels. The use of synchronous communication tools like video conferencing, webinars, and real-time chats, combined with asynchronous methods such as discussion boards and emails, ensures that students have multiple avenues for interaction and support (Anderson, et al, 2001).

However, applying strategic models in distance education and educational communication is not without challenges. The diversity of learners in terms of technological proficiency, learning styles, and personal circumstances necessitates a flexible approach to model implementation. Educators must continuously adapt and refine their strategies to address emerging needs and challenges, including accessibility, digital equity, and maintaining student engagement over extended periods of remote learning (Garrison, 2017).

In conclusion, applying strategic models in distance education and educational communication is essential for creating a supportive and effective learning environment. These models provide a roadmap for navigating the complexities of remote learning, ensuring that educational experiences are not only accessible but also meaningful and engaging. As the landscape of education continues to evolve, the strategic application of these models will be crucial for shaping the future of learning and communication in a digital age (Anderson, et al, 2001).

Critique

The chapter provides a substantial amount of background information and a literature review on the topic of strategic models in distance education and educational communication. The discussion of key frameworks, such as the Community of Inquiry (CoI), ADDIE, Blended Learning, Competency-Based Education (CBE), and Learning Management Systems (LMS), is well-structured and supported by relevant academic references.

However, while the literature review is extensive, there are areas where it could be further strengthened:

Depth of Analysis on Historical Development

The chapter provides insights into strategic models but lacks a comprehensive historical evolution of distance education. A discussion of early distance education methods (e.g., correspondence courses, radio, and television-based education) would help frame how modern strategic models emerged in response to technological advancements.

Recommendation: The author(s) should integrate a section that traces the evolution of distance education, including key milestones, technological advancements, and paradigm shifts in pedagogical approaches.

Comparative Analysis of Strategic Models

The chapter presents multiple frameworks but does not critically compare their strengths, weaknesses, and applicability across different contexts (e.g., higher education, corporate training, K-12 education).

Recommendation: A comparative analysis table or discussion that contrasts these models based on factors like student engagement, scalability, flexibility, and effectiveness in different learning environments would enhance clarity.

Limited Discussion on Challenges and Gaps in Existing Research

The chapter discusses challenges such as student engagement and communication barriers but does not sufficiently explore gaps in existing research on strategic models.

Recommendation: The author(s) should include a section that identifies open research questions and unresolved challenges in applying strategic models to distance education, such as issues related to digital equity, accessibility, and technological infrastructure in underdeveloped regions.

Integration of Emerging Technologies and AI in Distance Education

While the chapter touches on Learning Management Systems (LMS) and security concerns, there is minimal discussion of the impact of Artificial Intelligence (AI), adaptive learning, and data analytics in shaping modern strategic models.

Recommendation: Including recent developments such as AI-driven personalized learning, blockchain for credentialing, and gamification in distance education would make the chapter more forward-looking.

The Impact of COVID-19 on Distance Education and Lessons Learned

The global pandemic accelerated the adoption of online learning models. The chapter does not analyze how institutions adapted strategic models in response to COVID-19 and what lessons can be applied moving forward.

Suggested Addition: A section examining emergency remote teaching (ERT) vs. planned distance education, lessons learned from the pandemic, and how institutions are shaping future-ready online learning strategies.

Overall,

- The chapter is well-researched and provides a strong theoretical foundation for strategic models in distance education. However, it would benefit from a more critical analysis, comparative discussion, and integration of emerging trends in online learning. To augment the manuscript, the author(s) should:
- Expand the historical context and evolution of distance education.
- Provide a comparative analysis of strategic models, highlighting their applicability and limitations.
- Address gaps in current research, including accessibility challenges, digital equity, and pedagogical training for educators.
- Integrate discussions on AI, data analytics, and emerging educational technologies to enhance the relevance of the chapter.
- Explore assessment strategies, faculty development, and lessons from the COVID-19 era to provide a more comprehensive understanding of the strategic landscape in distance education.

4. CONCLUSION

Strategic models in the realm of distance education serve as critical frameworks that facilitate the organization, delivery, and assessment of educational experiences within online and remote learning environments. These models are designed to address the unique challenges and opportunities presented by distance learning, enabling educators and institutions to create structured and effective learning experiences for students who may be geographically dispersed. By employing these strategic frameworks, educators can ensure that the curriculum is not only well-organized but also accessible, engaging, and aligned with the diverse needs of learners. Furthermore, these models guide the implementation of assessment strategies that accurately measure student learning and progress, thereby enhancing the overall effectiveness of the educational experience in a virtual context.

Ultimately, strategic models in distance education play a pivotal role in shaping the quality and impact of online learning initiatives, ensuring that they meet the evolving demands of both learners and educational institutions. Moreover, blended learning presents a versatile educational strategy that effectively merges the advantages of both online and in-person instruction. This approach allows for a more personalized learning experience by accommodating different learning styles and preferences, enabling students to engage with the material in a way that best suits them. By integrating face-to-face interactions with digital resources, blended learning cultivates a richer educational experience, encouraging greater engagement and participation from learners.

Additionally, Competency-Based Education (CBE) focuses on the mastery of skills and knowledge, offering learners the flexibility to progress at their own pace. This model prioritizes individual learning outcomes over traditional time-based measures, allowing students to advance once they have demonstrated a sufficient level of understanding and proficiency. CBE emphasizes the importance of personalized learning pathways, empowering learners to take ownership of their educational journeys and ensuring that they acquire the competencies necessary for success in their chosen fields. Together, these educational frameworks and models create a dynamic landscape that supports a diverse range of learning needs and preferences, ultimately enhancing the overall quality of education. The Community of Inquiry (CoI) framework highlights the critical role that three distinct yet interrelated presences—cognitive, social, and teaching—play in fostering engaging and effective online learning experiences. This framework posits that for learners to achieve meaningful learning outcomes, it is essential to cultivate an environment where these three presences interact harmoniously. Cognitive presence refers to the degree to which learners are able to construct and confirm meaning through sustained reflection and discourse. Social presence emphasizes the importance of establishing a sense of community and connection among participants, enabling them to engage with one another in a supportive and collaborative manner.

Finally, teaching presence involves the design, facilitation, and direction of cognitive and social processes to achieve learning outcomes. In parallel, the ADDIE model serves as a comprehensive and systematic approach to instructional design, ensuring that educational courses are not only meticulously planned but also subject to ongoing evaluation and enhancement. The ADDIE acronym stands for Analysis, Design, Development, Implementation, and Evaluation, each stage contributing to the overall effectiveness and relevance of the instructional materials and experiences provided to learners. By following this structured framework, educators can create courses that are tailored to meet the specific needs of their learners while continuously refining and improving the instructional process based on feedback and assessment.

The successful execution of these strategic models is significantly dependent on the integration of technology, with Learning Management Systems (LMS) playing a pivotal role as the foundational framework for the delivery and administration of online educational programs. In an era where distance education is gaining increasing prominence and relevance, the thoughtful application of these strategic models becomes essential in guaranteeing that online learning opportunities are not only accessible to a wide range of students but also effective and engaging for a diverse array of learners. As more individuals turn to online platforms for their educational needs, it is imperative that these strategic frameworks are meticulously designed and implemented to foster an enriching learning experience that caters to the unique requirements of each learner. The evolution of educational technology and its application within these models will undoubtedly shape the future of online education, making it crucial for educators and institutions to prioritize this integration to meet the demands of an increasingly digital learning landscape.

REFERENCES

Adams, J. (2001, November). Strategic distance education planning: Crossing boarders, boundaries and frontiers. Paper presented at the meeting of the Society for College and University Planning, Monterrey, Mexico.

Adams, J. (2003). Community college distance education strategy: A multi-case study of strategic mental models and strategic choices. Unpublished doctoral dissertation, University of Nebraska – Lincoln.

Akyol, Z., & Garrison, D. R. (2011). Assessing metacognition in an online community of inquiry. *The Internet and Higher Education*, *14*(3), 183–190. DOI: 10.1016/j.iheduc.2011.01.005

Anderson, T., Rourke, L., Garrison, D. R., & Archer, W. (2001). Assessing teaching presence in a computer conferencing context. *Journal of Asynchronous Learning Networks*, *5*(2), 1–17.

Armstrong, R. (2000). Faculty strategies for learning to teach at a distance with instructional technology. DEOSNEWS, 11(1). Retrieved from https://www.ed.psu.edu/acsde/deosnews/deosnews11_1.asp

Berge, Z., & Schrum, L. (1998). Linking strategic planning with program implementation for distance education. Cause/Effect, 21(3). Retrieved from https://www.educause.edu/pub/

Berge, Z. L., & Muilenburg, L. (2001). Obstacles faced at various stages of capability regarding distance education in institutions of higher education: Survey results. *TechTrends*, *45*(4), 40–45.

Bonk, C. J., & Graham, C. R. (Eds.). (2012). *The Handbook of Blended Learning: Global Perspectives, Local Designs*. Wiley.

Compora, D. (2003). Current trends in distance education: An administrative model. *Online Journal of Distance Learning Administration*, *6*(2). https://www.westga.edu/~distance/ojdla/summer62/compora62.html

Fornaciari, C., Forte, M., & Mathews, C. (1999). Distance education strategy: How can your school complete? [H]. *Journal of Management Education*, *23*(6), 703–718. DOI: 10.1177/105256299902300608

Garrison, D. R. (2017). *E-Learning in the 21st Century: A Community of Inquiry Framework for Research and Practice* (3rd ed.). Routledge.

Garrison, D. R., Anderson, T., & Archer, W. (2000). Critical inquiry in a text-based environment: Computer conferencing in higher education. *The Internet and Higher Education*, *2*(2-3), 87–105. DOI: 10.1016/S1096-7516(00)00016-6

Graham, C. R. (2006). Blended learning systems: Definition, current trends, and future directions. In Bonk, C. J., & Graham, C. R. (Eds.), *Handbook of Blended Learning: Global Perspectives, Local Designs* (pp. 3–21). Pfeiffer.

Hache, D. (1998). Strategic planning of distance education in the age of teleinformatics. *Journal of Distance Learning Administration*, *1*(2). https://www.westga.edu/~distance/Hache12.html

Hodges, C. B., & Fowler, D. J. (2020). The use of learning management systems in the United States. In Khine, M. S., & Areepattamannil, S. (Eds.), *Handbook of Research on Blended Learning Pedagogies and Professional Development in Higher Education* (pp. 12–35). IGI Global.

Levy, S. (2003). Six factors to consider when planning online distance learning programs in higher education. *Online Journal of Distance Learning Administration*, *6*(1).

Lowenthal, P. R. (2010). The evolution and influence of social presence theory on online learning. In Kidd, T. T., & Keengwe, J. (Eds.), *Adult learning in the digital age: Perspectives on online technologies and outcomes* (pp. 124–139).

Merrill, M. D. (2002). First principles of instruction. *Educational Technology Research and Development*, *50*(3), 43–59. DOI: 10.1007/BF02505024

Morrison, G. R., Ross, S. M., Kemp, J. E., & Kalman, H. K. (2013). *Designing Effective Instruction* (7th ed.). Wiley.

O'Connor, S. J., & D'Angelo, J. D. (2013). Applying the ADDIE instructional design model to online continuing education for an international audience. *The Journal of Continuing Education in the Health Professions*, *33*(3), 216–224.

Shea, P., Hayes, S., Vickers, J., Gozza-Cohen, M., Uzuner, S., Mehta, R., & Rangan, P. (2010). A re-examination of the Community of Inquiry framework: Social network and content analysis. *The Internet and Higher Education*, *13*(1-2), 10–21. DOI: 10.1016/j.iheduc.2009.11.002

Swan, K., Garrison, D. R., & Richardson, J. C. (2009). A constructivist approach to online learning: The Community of Inquiry framework. In Howard, C. (Eds.), *Encyclopedia of Distance Learning* (2nd ed., pp. 352–360). IGI Global.

Taraza, E., Anastasiadou, S., & Masouras, A. (2023, September). Malcolm Baldrige National Quality Award (MBNQA) Quality Tool in Education: A Systematic Literature Review. In ECIE 2023 18th European Conference on Innovation and Entrepreneurship Vol 1. Academic Conferences and publishing limited.

Taraza, E., Anastasiadou, S., Papademetriou, C., & Masouras, A. (2024). Evaluation of quality and equality in education using the European foundation for quality management excellence model—A literature review. *Sustainability (Basel)*, *16*(3), 960. DOI: 10.3390/su16030960

Compilation of References

Aagaard, A., & Nielsen, C. (2021). The Fifth Stage of Business Model Research: The Role of Business Models in Times of Uncertainty. *Journal of Business Models*, *9*(1), 77–90. DOI: 10.5278/jbm.v9i1.4246

Abbass, K., Qasim, M. Z., Song, H., Murshed, M., Mahmood, H., & Younis, I. (2022). A review of the global climate change impacts, adaptation, and sustainable mitigation measures. *Environmental Science and Pollution Research International*, *29*(28), 42539–42559. DOI: 10.1007/s11356-022-19718-6 PMID: 35378646

Abdulla, A. (2013). The Arab Gulf moment. In *The Transformation of the Gulf* (pp. 106–124). Routledge.

Abdulla, F. S., & Ahmad, A. (2023). Challenges Faced by Women Entrepreneurs of 21st Century. *Journal of Management & Science*, *21*(1), 71–86. DOI: 10.57002/jms.v21i1.368

Abisuga-Oyekunle, O. A., Patra, S. K., & Muchie, M. (2019). SMEs in sustainable development: Their role in poverty reduction and employment generation in sub-Saharan Africa. *African Journal of Science, Technology, Innovation and Development*, *12*(4), 405–419. DOI: 10.1080/20421338.2019.1656428

Abou-Foul, M., Ruiz-Alba, J. L., & López-Tenorio, P. J. (2022). The impact of artificial intelligence capabilities on servitization: The moderating role of absorptive capacity-A dynamic capabilities perspective. *Journal of Business Research*, *157*, 113609. DOI: 10.1016/j.jbusres.2022.113609

Abou-Foul, M., Ruiz-Alba, J. L., & Soares, A. (2020). The impact of digitalization and servitization on the financial performance of a firm: An empirical analysis. *Production Planning and Control*, *32*(12), 975–989. DOI: 10.1080/09537287.2020.1780508

Abraham, D. T. (2013). *CSR and empowerment of women: the way forward.* AIMA Journal of Management and Research.

Abrahamic Family House. (2024, June 13). Diverse in our faiths. Common in our humanity. Together in peace. https://www.abrahamicfamilyhouse.ae/

Abu Dhabi Media Office. (2024, April 1). Statistics Centre – Abu Dhabi reports growth of emirate's non-oil economy and real GDP in 2023. https://www.mediaoffice.abudhabi/en/economy/statistics-centre-abu-dhabi-reports-growth-of-emirates-non-oil-economy-and-real-gdp-in-2023

Abubakar, I. R., Maniruzzaman, K. M., Dano, U. L., AlShihri, F. S., AlShammari, M. S., Ahmed, S. M. S., Al-Gehlani, W. A. G., & Alrawaf, T. I. (2022). Environmental Sustainability Impacts of Solid Waste Management Practices in the Global South. *International Journal of Environmental Research and Public Health*, *19*(19), 12717. DOI: 10.3390/ijerph191912717 PMID: 36232017

Adam, N. A., & Alarifi, G. (2021). Innovation practices for survival of small and medium enterprises (SMEs) in the COVID-19 times: The role of external support. *Journal of Innovation and Entrepreneurship*, *10*(1), 15. Advance online publication. DOI: 10.1186/s13731-021-00156-6 PMID: 34075328

Adams, J. (2001, November). Strategic distance education planning: Crossing boarders, boundaries and frontiers. Paper presented at the meeting of the Society for College and University Planning, Monterrey, Mexico.

Adams, J. (2003). Community college distance education strategy: A multi-case study of strategic mental models and strategic choices. Unpublished doctoral dissertation, University of Nebraska – Lincoln.

Adam, S., Fuzi, N. M., Ramdan, M. R., & Ismail, A. F. M. F. (2025). The Effectiveness of Digital Entrepreneurship ecosystem toward enriching income generation: The moderating role of entrepreneurial intention. *SAGE Open*, *15*(1), 21582440241305361. Advance online publication. DOI: 10.1177/21582440241305361

Afzal, F., Yunfei, S., Sajid, M., & Afzal, F. (2019). Market Sustainability: A Globalization and Consumer Culture Perspective in the Chinese Retail Market. *Sustainability (Basel)*, *11*(3), 575. DOI: 10.3390/su11030575

Agoraki, K. K., Deirmentzoglou, G. A., Psychalis, M., & Apostolopoulos, S. (2024). Types of innovation and sustainable development: Evidence from medium-and large-sized firms. *International Journal on Management of Innovation & Technology*, *21*(02), 2450013. DOI: 10.1142/S0219877024500135

Agoraki, K. K., Deirmentzoglou, G. A., & Triantopoulos, C. (2024). Cultural Values as Catalysts of Technological Innovation for a Sustainable Future. *Sustainability (Basel)*, *16*(5), 2064. DOI: 10.3390/su16052064

Agrawal, A., Gandhi, P., & Khare, P. (2021). Women empowerment through entrepreneurship: Case study of a social entrepreneurial intervention in rural India. *The International Journal of Organizational Analysis*. Advance online publication. DOI: 10.1108/IJOA-03-2021-2659

Aguas del Tunari SA v Bolivia ICSID Case No ARB/02/3 Letter by NGO to Petition to Participate as Amici Curiae. (2003).

Agubamah, E., & Theresa, O. S. (2025). Hezbollah Involvement in Israel-Hamas War: Causes and Implications 2023-2024. *Kashere Journal of Politics and International Relations*, *3*(1), 15–21.

Agues Argentinas SA Suez Sodedad General de Aguas de Barcelona SA and Vivendi Universal SA v Algerine Republic ICSID Case No ARB/03/19 Order in Response to a Petition for Participation as Amicus Curiae. (2005).

Ahmadov, T., Durst, S., Gerstlberger, W., & Kraut, E. (2023). *SMEs on the way to a circular economy: insights from a multi-perspective review*. Management Review Quarterly., DOI: 10.1007/s11301-023-00380-2

Ahmed, H. M. (2023, November 30). The secret behind UAE's economic miracle. The Halal Times. https://www.halaltimes.com/the-secret-behind-uaes-economic-miracle/

Ahmetaj, B., Kruja, A. D., & Hysa, E. (2023). Women Entrepreneurship: Challenges and Perspectives of an Emerging Economy. *Administrative Sciences*, *13*(4), 111. DOI: 10.3390/admsci13040111

Akande, Y. B., Tijani, A. A., Kehinde, A. D., & Oyenpemi, L. O. (2023). Impact of compliance with European Union (EU) regulations on the income of actors along the cocoa supply chain in Osun state, Nigeria. *Sustainable Futures : An Applied Journal of Technology, Environment and Society*, *6*, 100120. DOI: 10.1016/j.sftr.2023.100120

Akbarzadeh, S., & Azizi, H. (2024, April). Iran in the Middle East: Introduction. Middle East Council on Global Affairs. https://mecouncil.org/publication_chapters/iran-in-the-middle-east-introduction/

Akram, R., Li, Q., Srivastava, M., Zheng, Y., & Irfan, M. (2024). Nexus between green technology innovation and climate policy uncertainty: Unleashing the role of artificial intelligence in an emerging economy. *Technological Forecasting and Social Change*, *209*, 123820. DOI: 10.1016/j.techfore.2024.123820

Akyol, Z., & Garrison, D. R. (2011). Assessing metacognition in an online community of inquiry. *The Internet and Higher Education*, *14*(3), 183–190. DOI: 10.1016/j.iheduc.2011.01.005

Al Shaikh, A. B. A. (2022). Securitization theory in the UAE context: Regional instability and shifting security dynamics. The Emirates Center for Strategic Studies and Research (ECSSR).

Alawamleh, M., Francis, Y. H., & Alawamleh, K. J. (2023). Entrepreneurship challenges: The case of Jordanian start-ups. *Journal of Innovation and Entrepreneurship*, *12*(1), 21. Advance online publication. DOI: 10.1186/s13731-023-00286-z PMID: 37034301

Alhitmi, H. K., & Ndambuki, D. (2024). Examining the impact of Russia-Ukraine conflict and China support on the supply chain of German family-owned SMEs in 2022. *Asian Journal of Political Science*, •••, 1–14. DOI: 10.1080/02185377.2023.2285921

Allison, G. (2017). *Destined for War: Can America and China Escape Thucydides's Trap?* Houghton Mifflin Harcourt.

Almezaini, K. S. (2020, November). The UAE's security perceptions in the Middle East: Regional challenges, alliances and diversification of partners. In S. Colombo & A. Dessi (Eds.), Fostering a new security architecture in the Middle East (pp. 50–63). Foundation for European Progressive Studies (FEPS) & Istituto Affari Internazionali (IAI). https://www.iai.it/sites/default/files/9788833653501.pdf

Almezaini, K. S. (2011). *The UAE and foreign policy: Foreign aid, identities and interests*. Routledge.

Alons, G. C. (2007). Predicting a state's foreign policy: State preferences between domestic and international constraints. *Foreign Policy Analysis*, *3*(3), 211–232.

Al-Qahtani, N. D., Alsehri, S. S., & Aziz, A. A. (2015). The impact of total quality management on organizational performance. *European Journal of Business and Management*, *7*(36), 119–127.

Alvarez, R. M., & Sinclair, B. (2012). Electoral Institutions and Legislative Behaviour: The Effects of Primary Processes. *Political Research Quarterly*, *63*, 544–557. DOI: 10.1177/1065912911411098

Amado, J. D., Kern, J. S., & Doe Rodriguez, M. (2018). *Arbitrating the Conduct of International Investors*. Cambridge University Press., DOI: 10.1017/9781108235051

Amankwaa, A., Seet, P.-S., & Susomrith, P. (2022). Tackling hotel employees' turnover: A moderated-mediation analysis of transformational leadership, organisational embeddedness, and community embeddedness. *Journal of Hospitality and Tourism Management*, *51*, 67–78. DOI: 10.1016/j.jhtm.2022.02.029

Ambos, T. C., Cesinger, B., Eggers, F., & Kraus, S. (2019). How does de-globalization affect location decisions? A study of managerial perceptions of risk and return. *Global Strategy Journal, 10*(1), 210–236. DOI: 10.1002/gsj.1335

American Psychological Association. (2017). Ethical principles of psychologists and code of conduct. Retrieved from https://www.apa.org/ethics/code/

Amiti, M., Redding, S. J., & Weinstein, D. E. (2019). The impact of the 2018 tariffs on prices and welfare. *The Journal of Economic Perspectives, 33*(4), 187–210. DOI: 10.1257/jep.33.4.187

Amnesty International. Actionaid, ECCJ, Campaign, C. C., Anti-Slavery, & FIDH. (2018). *Suggested Elements for an EU Action Plan on Business and Human Rights*. https://www.amnesty.eu/wp-content/uploads/2018/11/suggested-elements-for-an-eu-action-plan-on-business-and-human-rights_8-june.pdf

Anderson, E. W., Fornell, C., & Lehmann, D. R. (1994). Customer satisfaction, market share, and profitability: Findings from Sweden. *Journal of Marketing, 58*(3), 53–66. DOI: 10.1177/002224299405800304

Anderson, T., Rourke, L., Garrison, D. R., & Archer, W. (2001). Assessing teaching presence in a computer conferencing context. *Journal of Asynchronous Learning Networks, 5*(2), 1–17.

Antonizzi, J., & Smuts, H. (2020). The Characteristics of Digital Entrepreneurship and Digital Transformation: A Systematic Literature review. In *Lecture notes in computer science* (pp. 239–251). DOI: 10.1007/978-3-030-44999-5_20

Antwi-Boateng, O., & Al Jaberi, N. H. S. (2022, April). The post-oil strategy of the UAE: An examination of diversification strategies and challenges. *Politics & Policy, 50*(2), 341–367. https://www.scopus.com/record/display.uri?eid=2-s2.0-85125657637&origin=inward&txGid=6de433b7f8579f1b0742de9bbd23cb86

Antwi-Boateng, O., & Alhasmi, A. A. (2022). The emergence of the United Arab Emirates as a global soft power: Current strategies and future challenges. *Economic and Political Studies, 10*(2), 221–240.

Apostolopoulos, N., Ratten, V., Petropoulos, D., Liargovas, P., & Anastasopoulou, E. (2021). Agri-food sector and entrepreneurship during the COVID-19 crisis: A systematic literature review and research agenda. *Strategic Change, 30*(2), 159–167. DOI: 10.1002/jsc.2400

Apotex Inc v The United States of America ICSID Case No UNCT/10/2 Procedural Order No 2. (2011).

Arcuri, A., & Montanaro, F. (2018). Justice for All? Protecting the Public Interest in Investment Treaties. *Boston College Law Review. Boston College. Law School, 59*(8), 2791–2824.

Armstrong, R. (2000). Faculty strategies for learning to teach at a distance with instructional technology. DEOSNEWS, 11(1). Retrieved from https://www.ed.psu.edu/acsde/deosnews/deosnews11_1.asp

Asgary, A., Ozdemir, A. I., & Özyürek, H. (2020). Small and Medium Enterprises and Global Risks: Evidence from Manufacturing SMEs in Turkey. *International Journal of Disaster Risk Science, 11*(1), 59–73. DOI: 10.1007/s13753-020-00247-0

Attinasi, M. G., Ioannou, D., Lebastard, L., & Morris, R. 2023. Global production and supply chain risks: insights from a survey of leading companies. https://www.ecb.europa.eu/press/economic-bulletin/focus/2023/html/ecb.ebbox202307_01~2a0bcf0b48.en.html?utm_

Augutis, J., Krikštolaitis, R., Pečiulytė, S., & Konstantinavičiūtė, I. (2011). Sustainable development and energy security level after Ignalina NPP shutdown. *Technological and Economic Development of Economy, 17*(1), 5–21. DOI: 10.3846/13928619.2011.553930

Australian Government Department of Foreign Affairs and Trade. (2024). United Arab Emirates country brief. https://www.dfat.gov.au/geo/united-arab-emirates/united-arab-emirates-country-brief

Autor, D. H., Dorn, D., & Hanson, G. H. (2016). The China shock: Learning from labor-market adjustment to large changes in trade. *Annual Review of Economics, 8*(1), 205–240. DOI: 10.1146/annurev-economics-080315-015041

Babakus, E., & Boller, G. W. (1992). An empirical assessment of the SERVQUAL scale. *Journal of Business Research, 24*(3), 253–268. DOI: 10.1016/0148-2963(92)90022-4

Babu, A., & Sahay, M. (2018). Impact of Corporate Social Responsibility on Women Empowerment. *International Journal of Pure and Applied Mathematics.*

Bachmann, N., Thienemann, A., Tüzün, A., Brunner, M., Tripathi, S., Pöchtrager, S., & Jodlbauer, H. (2025). The evolution of the business model Canvas for digital sustainability. *Procedia Computer Science, 253*, 1012–1023. DOI: 10.1016/j.procs.2025.01.163

Baines, P. R., Worcesterb, R. M., Jarrettc, D., & Mortimored, R. (2003). Market Segmentation and Product Differentiation in Political Campaigns: A Technical Feature Perspective. [Westburn Publishers Ltd.]. *Journal of Marketing Management*, •••, 2003.

Bajpai, G. N. (2001). *Corporate social responsibility in India and Europe: Cross-cultural perspective*. http://www.ficci.com

Balbaa, M. E., Eshov, M. P., & Ismailova, N. (2022). The Impacts of Russian Ukrainian War on the Global Economy in the frame of digital banking networks and cyber attacks. *Proceedings of the 6th International Conference on Future Networks & Distributed Systems*. https://doi.org/DOI: 10.1145/3584202.3584223

Baldwin, R., & Freeman, R. (2022). Risks and Global Supply Chains: What We Know and What We Need to Know. *Annual Review of Economics*, *14*(1), 153–180. Advance online publication. DOI: 10.1146/annurev-economics-051420-113737

Ballet, J., Bazin, D., & Mahieu, F. (2020). A policy framework for social sustainability: Social cohesion, equity and safety. *Sustainable Development (Bradford)*, *28*(5), 1388–1394. DOI: 10.1002/sd.2092

Baltag, C., & Dautaj, Y. (2021). Promoting, Regulating, and Enforcing Human Rights Through International Investment Law and ISDS. *Fordham International Law Journal*, *45*(1). https://www.fordhamilj.org/volume-45-issue-1/2021/10/19/promoting-regulating-and-enforcing-human-rights-through-international-investment-law-and-isds

Banaee, H., Mahmood, A., & Cook, D. J. (2013). Data mining for wearable sensors in health monitoring systems: A review of recent trends and challenges. *Health Information Science and Systems*, *1*(1), 1–17. DOI: 10.1186/2047-2501-1-2 PMID: 24351646

Banaji, M. R., & Greenwald, A. G. (2013). *Blindspot: Hidden biases of good people*. Delacorte Press.

Banducci, S. A., & Karp, J. A. (2003). How Elections Change the Way Citizens View the Political System: Campaigns, Media Effects and Electoral Outcomes in Comparative Perspective. *British Journal of Political Science* Vol. 33, No. 3 (Jul. 2003), pp. 443-467.Cambridge University Press. DOI: jstor.org/stable/4092306

Banerjee, S., & Singh, S. (2024). Examining the India-Middle East-Europe Economic Corridor (IMEC) as a collaborative infrastructure for transcontinental policymaking: An ICIO-LP analysis. *Asia Europe Journal*, *22*(4), 481–506. DOI: 10.1007/s10308-024-00712-1

Bansal, S., Garg, I., & Sharma, G. (2019). Social Entrepreneurship as a Path for Social Change and Driver of Sustainable Development: A Systematic Review and Research Agenda. *Sustainability (Basel), 11*(4), 1091. DOI: 10.3390/su11041091

Bardalai, A. K. (2024). On the Geoeconomics Drivers of International Conflicts Global Political Economy, Geopolitics and International Security: The World in Permacrisis. In Mishra, O., & Sen, S. (Eds.), (pp. 93–112). Springer Nature Singapore., DOI: 10.1007/978-981-97-2231-0_6

Barocas, S., Hardt, M., & Narayanan, A. (2019). Fairness and machine learning. Retrieved from https://fairmlbook.org

Barteková, E., & Kemp, R. (2016). National strategies for securing a stable supply of rare earths in different world regions. *Resources Policy, 49*, 153–164. DOI: 10.1016/j.resourpol.2016.05.003

Bassi, F., & Guidolin, M. (2021). Resource Efficiency and Circular Economy in European SMEs: Investigating the Role of Green Jobs and Skills. *Sustainability (Basel), 13*(21), 12136. DOI: 10.3390/su132112136

Bassiouni, M. C. (2022). Saudi reforms: Change for survival or for progress? In IEMed Mediterranean Yearbook 2022. European Institute of the Mediterranean. https://www.iemed.org/publication/saudi-reforms-change-for-survival-or-for-progress/

Batrawi, A. (2022, January 17). Drone attack in Abu Dhabi claimed by Yemen's rebels kills 3. Associated Press. https://apnews.com/article/business-dubai-united-arab-emirates-abu-dhabi-yemen-8bdefdf900ce46a6fd6c7bc685bf838a

BBC. (2018, October 31). Yemen war: US presses Saudi Arabia to agree ceasefire. https://www.bbc.com/news/world-middle-east-46040789

BBC. (2020). US China tariffs "incosistent" with trade rules says TWO. https://www.bbc.com/news/business-54168419

Beckmann, M., Garkisch, M., & Zeyen, A. (2021). Together we are strong? A systematic literature review on how SMEs use relation-based collaboration to operate in rural areas. *Journal of Small Business and Entrepreneurship, 35*(4), 515–549. DOI: 10.1080/08276331.2021.1874605

Bednarski, L., Roscoe, S., Blome, C., & Schleper, M. (2023). Geopolitical disruptions in global supply chains: A state-of-the-art literature review. *Production Planning and Control*, 1–27. Advance online publication. DOI: 10.1080/09537287.2023.2286283

Belcher, D. (2024, May 16). Bahrain celebrates its history as a pearling center. The New York Times. https://www.nytimes.com/2024/05/16/fashion/jewelry-bahrain-pearl-path.html

Belitski, M., Guenther, C., Kritikos, A. S., & Thurik, R. (2022). Economic effects of the COVID-19 pandemic on entrepreneurship and small businesses. *Small Business Economics*, *58*(2), 593–609. DOI: 10.1007/s11187-021-00544-y PMID: 38624899

Bell, D. A. (2025). The Age of Trump and Musk: Reflections on the Election of 2024. *Society*, *62*(1), 109–111. DOI: 10.1007/s12115-024-01045-w

Benavides-Velasco, C. A., Quintana-García, C., & Marchante-Lara, M. (2014). Total quality management, corporate social responsibility and performance in the hotel industry. *International Journal of Hospitality Management*, *41*, 77–87. DOI: 10.1016/j.ijhm.2014.05.003

Berge, Z., & Schrum, L. (1998). Linking strategic planning with program implementation for distance education. Cause/Effect, 21(3). Retrieved from https://www.educause.edu/pub/

Berge, Z. L., & Muilenburg, L. (2001). Obstacles faced at various stages of capability regarding distance education in institutions of higher education: Survey results. *TechTrends*, *45*(4), 40–45.

Bertelsmann Stiftung Transformation Index. (2024). United Arab Emirates country report 2024. https://bti-project.org/fileadmin/api/content/en/downloads/reports/country_report_2024_ARE.pdf

Besson, S. (2011, April). Sovereignty. Oxford Public International Law. https://opil.ouplaw.com/display/10.1093/law:epil/9780199231690/law-9780199231690-e1472

Besterfield, D. H., Besterfield-Michna, C., Besterfield, G. H., & Besterfield-Sacre, M. (2013). *Total quality management*. Pearson.

Bhardwaj, N. (2022). *Women and Work in India: Trends and Analysis*. India Briefing. https://www.india-briefing.com/news/women-and-work-in-india-trends-and-analysis-24758.html/

Billing, C., McCann, P., & Ortega-Argilés, R. (2019). Interregional inequalities and UK sub-national governance responses to Brexit. *Regional Studies*, *53*(5), 741–760. DOI: 10.1080/00343404.2018.1554246

Birnbaum, R. (2000). The life cycle of academic management fads. *The Journal of Higher Education*, *71*(1), 1–16. DOI: 10.1080/00221546.2000.11780813

Birnbaum, R., & Deshotels, J. (1999). Has the academy adopted TQM? *Planning for Higher Education*, *27*(3), 29–37.

Bisho, A. H. A. I., & Sam, M. F. M. (2022). Total Quality Management Integrated Strategy: Its Implication to Organizational Success. *Proceedings on Engineering Sciences*, *4*(3), 371–378. DOI: 10.24874/PES04.03.014

Bissoondeeal, R. K., Binner, J. M., & Milas, C. (2023). Brexit and coronavirus: Financial perspectives and future prospects. *European Journal of Finance*, *29*(16), 1825–1834. DOI: 10.1080/1351847X.2023.2249961

Biwater Gauff Ltd v Tanzania ICSID Case No ARB/05/22 Award. (2008).

Blanco-González-Tejero, C., Ulrich, K., & Ribeiro-Navarrete, S. (2024). Can Social Media Be a Key Driver to Becoming an Entrepreneur? *Journal of the Knowledge Economy*, *15*(4), 16780–16798. Advance online publication. DOI: 10.1007/s13132-024-01764-9

Blenkinsop, Ph. (2018). EU expands WTO case against Chinese technology transfers. https://www.reuters.com/article/us-eu-china-wto/eu-expands-wto-case-against-chinese-technology-transfers-idUSKCN1OJ1AP/

Blumler, J. G., & Kavanagh, D. (1999). The Third Age of Political Communication: *Influences and Features.Political Communication*, *16*(3), 209–230. DOI: 10.1080/105846099198596

Bockmann, M. W. (2024). *China, Russia ships get free pass from Houthis to transit Red Sea*. https://www.lloydslist.com/LL1150561/China-Russia-ships-get-free-pass-from-Houthis-to-transit-Red-Sea

Bohan, S., Tippmann, E., Levie, J., Igoe, J., & Bowers, B. (2023). What is scaling? *Journal of Business Venturing*, *39*(1), 106355. DOI: 10.1016/j.jbusvent.2023.106355

Bon, A. T., & Mustafa, E. M. A. (2013). Impact of total quality management on innovation in service organizations: Literature review and new conceptual framework. *Procedia Engineering*, *53*, 516–529. DOI: 10.1016/j.proeng.2013.02.067

Bonanno, G., Fiorino, N., Garzarelli, G., & Rossi, S. P. S. (2023). Public subsidies for credit support, democracy and European female-led SMEs. *Journal of Economic Studies (Glasgow, Scotland)*, *50*(8), 1908–1925. DOI: 10.1108/JES-11-2022-0599

Bonesh, F. R. (2022, October 10). UAE's approach to Iraq. Al-Bayan Center for Planning and Studies. https://www.bayancenter.org/en/wp-content/uploads/2022/10/ejbh.pdf

Bonk, C. J., & Graham, C. R. (Eds.). (2012). *The Handbook of Blended Learning: Global Perspectives, Local Designs*. Wiley.

Boone, C., & Özcan, S. (2015). Strategic Choices at Entry and Relative Survival Advantage of Cooperatives versus Corporations in the US Bio-Ethanol Industry, 1978-2015. *Journal of Management Studies, 53*(7), 1113–1140. DOI: 10.1111/joms.12168

Borger, J. (2023, September 21). Crown prince confirms Saudi Arabia will seek nuclear arsenal if Iran develops one. The Guardian. https://www.theguardian.com/world/2023/sep/21/crown-prince-confirms-saudi-arabia-seek-nuclear-arsenal-iran-develops-one

Born, G., & Forrest, S. (2019). Amicus Curiae Participation in Investment Arbitration. *ICSID Review*, *34*(3), 626–665. DOI: 10.1093/icsidreview/siz020

Boubakri, N., El Ghoul, S., Guedhami, O., & Wang, H. (2021). Corporate social responsibility in emerging market economies: Determinants, consequences, and future research directions. *Emerging Markets Review*, *46*, 100758. DOI: 10.1016/j.ememar.2020.100758

Bown, C. P. (2020). How the United States marched the semiconductor industry into its trade war with China. *East Asian Economic Review*, *24*(4), 349–388. DOI: 10.11644/KIEP.EAER.2020.24.4.384

Bown, C. P. (2021). The US–China trade war and Phase One agreement. *Journal of Policy Modeling*, *43*(4), 805–843. DOI: 10.1016/j.jpolmod.2021.02.009

Bown, C. P., & Crowley, M. A. (2013). Import protection, business cycles, and exchange rates: Evidence from the Great Recession. *Journal of International Economics*, *90*(1), 50–64. DOI: 10.1016/j.jinteco.2012.12.001

Box, C. S. R. (2020). *Top 10 Women empowerment projects through CSR in India in the financial Year 2018-19*. https://csrbox.org/India_CSR_news_Top-10-Women%09Empowerment-Projects-through-CSR-in-India-in-the-Financial-Year-2018-19_540

Brands, H., & Gavin, F. J. (2020). *COVID-19 and world order*. Johns Hopkins University Press. DOI: 10.1353/book.77593

Braun, V., & Clarke, V. (2006). Using thematic analysis in psychology. *Qualitative Research in Psychology*, *3*(2), 77–101. DOI: 10.1191/1478088706qp063oa

Brautigam, D. (2020). A critical look at Chinese 'debt-trap diplomacy': The rise of a meme. *Area Development and Policy*, *5*(1), 1–14. DOI: 10.1080/23792949.2019.1689828

Bretschger, L., & Pittel, K. (2020). Twenty Key Challenges in Environmental and Resource Economics. *Environmental and Resource Economics*, *77*(4), 725–750. DOI: 10.1007/s10640-020-00516-y PMID: 33082623

Brew, A., & Lucas, L. (2009). *Academic research and researchers: Policy and Practice*. McGraw-Hill Education.

Bronson, R. (2011, March 13). Saudi Arabia's intervention in Bahrain: A necessary evil or a strategic blunder? Foreign Policy Research Institute. https://www.fpri.org/article/2011/03/saudi-arabias-intervention-in-bahrain-a-necessary-evil-or-a-strategic-blunder/

Brown, C., & Green, S. (2019). *Effective interviewing techniques for research*. Routledge.

Brown, R., Kalafsky, R. V., Mawson, S., & Davies, L. (2020). Shocks, uncertainty and regional resilience: The case of Brexit and Scottish SMEs. *Local Economy*, *35*(7), 655–675. DOI: 10.1177/0269094220979261

Brown, R., Liñares-Zegarra, J., & Wilson, J. O. S. (2019). The (potential) impact of Brexit on UK SMEs: Regional evidence and public policy implications. *Regional Studies*, *53*(5), 761–770. DOI: 10.1080/00343404.2019.1597267

Buchwald, E. 2025. Tariffs on cars from Mexico and Canada delayed by one month. https://edition.cnn.com/2025/03/05/business/tariffs-autos-mexico-canada-paused/index.html

Burke-White, W., & Staden, A. V. (2010). The Need for Public Law Standards of Review in Investor-State Arbitrations. In Schill, S. W. (Ed.), *International Investment Law and Comparative Public Law*. Oxford University Press. DOI: 10.1093/acprof:oso/9780199589104.003.0022

Burkhanov, U. (2011). The Big Failure: Lehman Brothers' Effects On Global Markets. *European Journal of Business and Economics*, *2*. Advance online publication. DOI: 10.12955/ejbe.v2i0.93

Butler, P. (2017). Red Riding Hood: Is Investor State Arbitration the Big Bad Wolf? *Penn State Journal of Law & International Affairs*, *5*(2), 328–373. https://elibrary.law.psu.edu/jlia/vol5/iss2/5

Bvirindi, T. C., & Inalegwu, O. I. (2023). The impact of the global financial crisis and the European sovereign debt crisis on the capital structure of firms in Europe: Do SMEs, and listed firms respond the same? *European Journal of Finance*, •••, 1–25.

Cagri Gurbuz, M., Yurt, O., Ozdemir, S., Sena, V., & Yu, W. (2023). Global supply chains risks and COVID-19: Supply chain structure as a mitigating strategy for small and medium-sized enterprises. *Journal of Business Research, 155*, 113407. DOI: 10.1016/j.jbusres.2022.113407 PMID: 36408443

California Legislative Information. (2020). California Consumer Privacy Act (CCPA). Retrieved from https://leginfo.legislature.ca.gov

Callahan, W. A. (2016). China's "Asia Dream": The Belt Road Initiative and the new regional order. *Asian Journal of Comparative Politics, 1*(3), 226–243. DOI: 10.1177/2057891116647806

Cameron, E., & Green, M. (2019). *Making sense of change management: A complete guide to the models, tools, and techniques of organizational change*. Kogan Page.

Cameron, K. S., & Quinn, R. E. (2011). *Diagnosing and changing organizational culture: Based on the competing values framework* (3rd ed.). John Wiley & Sons.

Canwat, V. (2024). COVID-19-related supply chain disruptions: Resilience and vulnerability of micro, small and medium enterprises. *Cogent Business & Management, 11*(1), 2315691. Advance online publication. DOI: 10.1080/23311975.2024.2315691

Cardella, G. M., Hernández-Sánchez, B. R., & Sánchez-García, J. C. (2020). Women Entrepreneurship: A Systematic Review to Outline the Boundaries of Scientific Literature. *Frontiers in Psychology, 11*, 1557. DOI: 10.3389/fpsyg.2020.01557 PMID: 32765357

Carroll, A. B. (1991). The pyramid of corporate social responsibility: Toward the moral management of organizational stakeholders. *Business Horizons, 34*(4), 39–48. DOI: 10.1016/0007-6813(91)90005-G

Carroll, A. B. (2016). Carroll's pyramid of CSR: Taking another look. *International Journal of Corporate Social Responsibility, 1*(1), 3. DOI: 10.1186/s40991-016-0004-6

Cassese, A. (1990). *Human Rights in a Changing World*. Cambridge University Press.

Castellano Lubov, D. (2022, November 4). Pope at Bahrain dialogue forum: Religious leaders have duty to help humanity. Vatican News. Retrieved from https://www.vaticannews.va/en/pope/news/2022-11/pope-at-bahrain-dialogue-forum-calls-for-peace.html

Cavallo, A., Ghezzi, A., & Balocco, R. (2018). Entrepreneurial ecosystem research: Present debates and future directions. *The International Entrepreneurship and Management Journal, 15*(4), 1291–1321. DOI: 10.1007/s11365-018-0526-3

Central Intelligence Agency. (2024, May 22). United Arab Emirates. The World Factbook. Retrieved from https://www.cia.gov/the-world-factbook/countries/united-arab-emirates/

Cerdeiro, D. A., Mano, R., Eugster, J., & Peiris, M. S. J. (2021). *Sizing up the effects of technological decoupling*. International Monetary Fund.

Chan, A.-W., Tetzlaff, J. M., Gotzsche, P. C., Altman, D. G., Mann, H., Berlin, J. A., Dickersin, K., Hrobjartsson, A., Schulz, K. F., Parulekar, W. R., Krleza-Jeric, K., Laupacis, A., & Moher, D. (2013). SPIRIT 2013 explanation and elaboration: Guidance for protocols of clinical trials. Volume(346), e7586-e7586. *BMJ (Clinical Research Ed.), 346*(jan08 15), e7586. Advance online publication. DOI: 10.1136/bmj.e7586 PMID: 23303884

Chandra, Y., & Kerlin, J. A. (2020). Social entrepreneurship in context: Pathways for new contributions in the field. *Journal of Asian Public Policy, 14*(2), 135–151. DOI: 10.1080/17516234.2020.1845472

Charpin, R., & Cousineau, M. (2024). Friendshoring: How geopolitical tensions affect foreign sourcing, supply base complexity, and sub-tier supplier sharing. *International Journal of Operations & Production Management*. Advance online publication. DOI: 10.1108/IJOPM-01-2024-0067

Chatterjee, I., Cornelissen, J., & Wincent, J. (2020). Social entrepreneurship and values work: The role of practices in shaping values and negotiating change. *Journal of Business Venturing, 36*(1), 106064. DOI: 10.1016/j.jbusvent.2020.106064

Chatterjee, M., & Naka, I. (2022). Twenty years of BRICS: Political and economic transformations through the lens of land. *Oxford Development Studies, 50*(1), 2–13. DOI: 10.1080/13600818.2022.2033191

Chen, J. H., & Asch, S. M. (2020). Machine learning and predictive analytics in healthcare. *Journal of the American Medical Association, 323*(6), 545–546. DOI: 10.1001/jama.2019.20890

Chen, J., & Liu, L. (2023). Social media usage and entrepreneurial investment: An information-based view. *Journal of Business Research, 155*, 113423. DOI: 10.1016/j.jbusres.2022.113423

Chivvis, C. S., & Keating, J. (2024). How Evil? Deconstructing the New Russia–China–Iran–North Korea Axis. In *Survival: December 2024–January 2025* (pp. 51-66). Routledge. DOI: 10.1080/00396338.2024.2432198

Choi, T. Y., & Eboch, K. (1998). The TQM paradox: Relations among TQM practices, plant performance, and customer satisfaction. *Journal of Operations Management*, *17*(1), 59–75. DOI: 10.1016/S0272-6963(98)00031-X

Chopra, S., & Sodhi, M. S. (2014). Reducing the risk of supply chain disruptions. *MIT Sloan Management Review*, *55*(3), 73–80. https://sloanreview.mit.edu/article/reducing-the-risk-of-supply-chain-disruptions

Cho, S. (2004). A dual catastrophe of protectionism. *Nw. J. Int'l L. & Bus.*, *25*, 315.

Christopher, M. (2016). *Logistics and Supply Chain Management* (5th ed.). Pearson Education.

Chukwuma, N. A., Ngoc, L. M., & Mativenga, P. (2024). The US-China trade war: Interrogating globalisation of technology. *Cogent Social Sciences*, *10*(1), 2365509. DOI: 10.1080/23311886.2024.2365509

Civelek, M., Krajčík, V., & Ključnikov, A. (2023). The impacts of dynamic capabilities on SMEs' digital transformation process: The resource-based view perspective. *Oeconomia Copernicana*, *14*(4), 1367–1392. DOI: 10.24136/oc.2023.019

Cochrane, L., & Zaidan, E. (2024). Shifting global dynamics: An empirical analysis of BRICS + expansion and its economic, trade, and military implications in the context of the G7. *Cogent Social Sciences*, *10*(1), 2333422. DOI: 10.1080/23311886.2024.2333422

Codish, S., Frenkel, A., Klein, M., Geftler, A., Dreiher, J., & Schwarzfuchs, D. (2024). October 7th 2023 attacks in Israel: Frontline experience of a single tertiary center. *Intensive Care Medicine*, *50*(2), 308–310. DOI: 10.1007/s00134-023-07293-4 PMID: 38172298

Columbia Center on Sustainable Development. (2019). *Third Party Rights in Investor-State Dispute Settlement: Options for Reform*. UNCITRAL. https://uncitral.un.org/sites/uncitral.un.org/files/media-documents/uncitral/en/wgiii_reformoptions_0.pdf

Comments, S. (2018). Strategic rivalries around the Bab el-Mandeb Strait. *Strategic Comments*, *24*(4), viii–x. DOI: 10.1080/13567888.2018.1485341

Compora, D. (2003). Current trends in distance education: An administrative model. *Online Journal of Distance Learning Administration*, *6*(2). https://www.westga.edu/~distance/ojdla/summer62/compora62.html

Conference on Interaction and Confidence Building Measures in Asia. (2024, December). Retrieved from https://www.s-cica.org/index.php?view=press_releases&id=2345

Conroy, G. (2024). How 'Made in China 2025' helped supercharge scientific development in China's cities. https://www.nature.com/articles/d41586-024-03522-y#:~:text=The%20overarching%20goal%20of%20MIC2025,ocean%20engineering%20and%20aerospace%20equipment

Core Writing Team, P. (2014). Climate change 2014: synthesis report. Contribution of working groups I, II and III to the fifth assessment report of the intergovernmental panel on climate change, 151.

Corner, P. D., & Ho, M. (2010). How opportunities develop in social entrepreneurship. *Entrepreneurship Theory and Practice*, *34*(4), 635–659. DOI: 10.1111/j.1540-6520.2010.00382.x

COSME. (n.d.). Internal Market, Industry, Entrepreneurship and SMEs. Retrieved March 8, 2025, from https://single-market-economy.ec.europa.eu/smes/cosme_en

Council of Europe. (1998). *Gender mainstreaming: conceptual framework, methodology and presentation of good practices.*

Council of Europe. (2021). *What are Human Rights*. https://www.coe.int/en/web/compass/what-are-human-rights-

Council of the European Union. (2025). *Where does the EU's gas come from?* Retrieved [date], from https://www.consilium.europa.eu/en/infographics/where-does-the-eu-s-gas-come-from/

Cowls, J., Tsamados, A., Taddeo, M., & Floridi, L. (2023). The AI gambit: Leveraging artificial intelligence to combat climate change-opportunities, challenges, and recommendations. *AI & Society*, *38*(1), 283–307. DOI: 10.1007/s00146-021-01294-x PMID: 34690449

Cox, T. (1991). *Cultural diversity in organizations: Theory, research, and practice.* Berrett-Koehler Publishers.

Cragg, W. (2012). Business and human rights: A principle and value-based analysis. In Cragg, W. (Ed.), *Business and Human Rights*. Edward Elgar Publishing Limited. DOI: 10.4337/9781781005774.00007

Craighead, C., Blackhurst, J., Rungtusanatham, M., & Handfield, R. (2007). The Severity of Supply Chain Disruptions: Design Characteristics and Mitigation Capabilities. *Decision Sciences*, *38*(1), 131–156. DOI: 10.1111/j.1540-5915.2007.00151.x

Crawford, J., Cui, Z. Y. A., & Kewley, D. (2023). Government finance, loans, and guarantees for small and medium enterprises (SMEs) (2000–2021): A systematic review. *Journal of Small Business Management*, •••, 1–31. DOI: 10.1080/00472778.2023.2246061

Crosby, P. B. (1979). *Quality is Free: The Art of Making Quality Certain.* McGraw-Hill.

Crownhart, C. (2024). China banned exports of a few rare minerals to the US. Things could get messier. https://www.technologyreview.com/2024/12/12/1108568/china-export-bans/

CRS – Congressional Research Service. (2022). Russia's Nord Stream 2 Natural Gas Pipeline to Germany Halted. https://crsreports.congress.gov/product/pdf/IF/IF11138#:~:text=On%20January%2019%2C%202021%2C%20the,in%202020%20(PEESA%3B%2022%20U.S.C.

Dale, B. G. (2003). *Managing quality* (4th ed.). Blackwell Publishing.

Dale, B. G., Zairi, M., & Thiagarajan, T. (2001). A proposed model of TQM implementation based on an empirical study of Malaysian industry. *International Journal of Quality & Reliability Management*, *18*(3), 289–306. DOI: 10.1108/02656710110383539

Das, D. (2024). Revisiting the contours of the evolving Middle Eastern order through the India-Middle East-EU Corridor: Mapping India's scopes and limitations. *Asian Journal of Political Science*, *32*(1), 35–56. DOI: 10.1080/02185377.2024.2322498

Dastin, J. (2020). Amazon scraps AI recruitment tool that showed bias against women. Reuters. Retrieved from https://www.reuters.com

David, M., Lyth, S. M., Lindner, R., & Harrington, G. F. (2021). Critical Raw Materials Future-Proofing Fuel Cells: Critical Raw Material Governance in Sustainable Energy. In David, M., Lyth, S. M., Lindner, R., & Harrington, G. F. (Eds.), (pp. 15–33). Springer International Publishing., DOI: 10.1007/978-3-030-76806-5_2

Davidson, C. M. (2009). Dubai and the United Arab Emirates: Security threats. British Journal of Middle Eastern Studies, 36(3), Gulf Security: Legacies of the Past, Prospects for the Future. Retrieved from https://www.jstor.org/stable/40593284

De Brabandere, E. (2011). NGOs and the Public Interest: The Legality and Rationale of Amicus Curiae Interventions in International Economic and Investment Disputes. *Chicago Journal of International Law*, *12*(1), 85–114. https://ssrn.com/abstract=1992939

De Brabandere, E. (2014). *Investment Treaty Arbitration as Public International Law: Procedural Aspects and Implications*. Cambridge University Press., DOI: 10.1017/CBO9781107589216

de Lucas Ancillo, A., Gavrila Gavrila, S., & Del Val Núñez, M. T. (2023). Workplace change within the COVID-19 context: The new (next) normal. *Technological Forecasting and Social Change*, *194*, 122673. DOI: 10.1016/j.techfore.2023.122673 PMID: 37293385

de Mattos, C. S., Pellegrini, G., Hagelaar, G., & Dolfsma, W. (2023). *Systematic literature review on technological transformation in SMEs: a transformation encompassing technology assimilation and business model innovation*. Management Review Quarterly., DOI: 10.1007/s11301-023-00327-7

de Rassenfosse, G., Murovana, T., & Uhlbach, W. H. (2023). The effects of war on Ukrainian research. *Humanities & Social Sciences Communications*, *10*(1), 856. Advance online publication. DOI: 10.1057/s41599-023-02346-x

Deirmentzoglou, G. A., & Deirmentzoglou, E. A. (2022) September. Pest analysis of the e-commerce industry: The case of Greece. In *Business Development and Economic Governance in Southeastern Europe:13th International Conference on the Economies of the Balkan and Eastern European Countries (EBEEC),Pafos, Cyprus,2021* (pp. 315-323). Cham: Springer International Publishing.

Deirmentzoglou, G. A., Agoraki, K. K., & Patsoulis, P. (2024). The nexus between cultural values and perceptions of corporate sustainable development. *Social Responsibility Journal*, *20*(2), 224–242. DOI: 10.1108/SRJ-09-2022-0373

Deirmentzoglou, G. A., Anastasopoulou, E. E., & Sklias, P. (2024). International economic relations and energy security in the European Union: A systematic literature review. *International Journal of Sustainable Energy*, *43*(1), 2385682.

Deirmentzoglou, G. A., Vlassi, E., & Anastasopoulou, E. E. (2024). DDMMO Website Quality, Destination Image and Intention to Use Metaverse Platforms. *Platforms*, *2*(4), 180–192. DOI: 10.3390/platforms2040012

Dejonghe, M., Van de Graaf, T., & Belmans, R. (2023). From natural gas to hydrogen: Navigating import risks and dependencies in Northwest Europe. *Energy Research & Social Science*, *106*, 103301. DOI: 10.1016/j.erss.2023.103301

Deloitte. (2019). Diversity and inclusion in the workplace. Retrieved from https://www2.deloitte.com/global/en/pages/about-deloitte/articles/diversity-and-inclusion.html

Deming, W. E. (1986). *Out of the crisis*. MIT Press.

Demirel, D. (2022). The effect of service quality on customer satisfaction in digital age: Customer satisfaction based examination of digital CRM. *Journal of Business Economics and Management*, *23*(3), 1–25. DOI: 10.3846/jbem.2022.15328

Dettori, A., & Floris, M. (2022). Improving continuity by simplifying the structure of family firms: A replication study. *Management Review Quarterly*, *73*(2), 635–660. DOI: 10.1007/s11301-021-00255-4

DFAT – Australian Government – Department of Foreign Affairs and Trade. (2025). *Comprehensive and Progressive Agreement for Trans-Pacific Partnership*. CPTPP.

Dharmapala, D., & Khanna, V. (2018). The impact of mandated corporate social responsibility: Evidence from India's Companies Act of 2013. *International Review of Law and Economics*, *56*, 92–104. DOI: 10.1016/j.irle.2018.09.001

Díaz-Foncea, M., & Marcuello, C. (2022). Social Enterprises: Conceptual Debates and Approaches. In *Springer eBooks* (pp. 133–151). DOI: 10.1007/978-3-031-14216-1_7

Díaz, S., Settele, J., Brondízio, E. S., Ngo, H. T., Agard, J., Arneth, A., Balvanera, P., Brauman, K. A., Butchart, S. H. M., Chan, K. M. A., Garibaldi, L. A., Ichii, K., Liu, J., Subramanian, S. M., Midgley, G. F., Miloslavich, P., Molnár, Z., Obura, D., Pfaff, A., & Zayas, C. N. (2019). Pervasive human-driven decline of life on Earth points to the need for transformative change. Volume(366). *Science*, *366*(6471), eaax3100. Advance online publication. DOI: 10.1126/science.aax3100 PMID: 31831642

Dimitriou, D., & Karagkouni, A. (2022). Assortment of Airports' Sustainability Strategy: A Comprehensiveness Analysis Framework. *Sustainability (Basel)*, *14*(7), 4217. DOI: 10.3390/su14074217

Dimitriou, D., & Sartzetaki, M. (2022). Criticality of a regional airport development to mitigate covid-19 economic effects. *Case Studies on Transport Policy*, *10*(1), 581–590. DOI: 10.1016/j.cstp.2022.01.018 PMID: 35106281

Dimitriou, D., Sartzetaki, M., & Karagkouni, A. (2024). *Managing Airport Corporate Performance: Leveraging Business Intelligence and Sustainable Transition*. Elsevier., DOI: 10.1016/C2023-0-51427-2

Directorate-General for Trade and Economic Security. (2020). EU, US and Japan agree on new ways to strengthen global rules on industrial subsidies. https://policy.trade.ec.europa.eu/news/eu-us-and-japan-agree-new-ways-strengthen-global-rules-industrial-subsidies-2020-01-14_en

Dolgui, A., Ivanov, D., & Rozhkov, M. (2020). Does the Ripple Effect Influence the Bullwhip Effect? An Integrated Analysis of Structural and Operational Dynamics in the Supply Chain. *International Journal of Production Research, 58*(5), 1285–1301. DOI: 10.1080/00207543.2019.1627438

Donthu, N., Kumar, S., Mukherjee, D., Pandey, N., & Lim, W. M. (2021). How to conduct a bibliometric analysis: An overview and guidelines. *Journal of Business Research, 133*, 285–296. DOI: 10.1016/j.jbusres.2021.04.070

Dove. (2017). Dove real beauty campaign. Retrieved from https://www.dove.com/us/en/stories/campaigns/real-beauty.html

Drake, J. K. (2011). The role of academic advising in student retention and persistence. *About Campus: Enriching the Student Learning Experience, 16*(3), 8–12. DOI: 10.1002/abc.20062

Dubai Airports. (2024, May 13). Retrieved from https://www.dubaiairports.ae/corporate/about-us/dwc-dubai-world-central/

Duhigg, C. (2016). What Google learned from its quest to build the perfect team. The New York Times. Retrieved from https://www.nytimes.com/2016/02/28/magazine/what-google-learned-from-its-quest-to-build-the-perfect-team.html

Du, L., Razzaq, A., & Waqas, M. (2023). The impact of COVID-19 on small- and medium-sized enterprises (SMEs): Empirical evidence for green economic implications. *Environmental Science and Pollution Research International, 30*(1), 1540–1561. DOI: 10.1007/s11356-022-22221-7 PMID: 35917071

Dupuy, P.-M. (2009). Unification Rather than Fragmentation in International Law? The Case of International Investment Law and Human Rights. In Dupuy, P.-M., Petersmann, E.-U., & Francioni, F. (Eds.), *Human Rights in International Investment Law and Arbitration* (pp. 45–62). Oxford University Press. DOI: 10.1093/acprof:oso/9780199578184.003.0002

Dwivedi, A., & Weerawardena, J. (2018). Conceptualizing and operationalizing the social entrepreneurship construct. *Journal of Business Research, 86*, 32–40. DOI: 10.1016/j.jbusres.2018.01.053

Dwivedi, S. L., Van Bueren, E. L., Ceccarelli, S., Grando, S., Upadhyaya, H. D., & Ortíz, R. (2017). Diversifying Food Systems in the Pursuit of Sustainable Food Production and Healthy Diets. Volume(22), 842-856. *Trends in Plant Science.* Advance online publication. DOI: 10.1016/j.tplants.2017.06.011 PMID: 28716581

Dwivedi, Y. K., Hughes, L., Baabdullah, A. M., Ribeiro-Navarrete, S., Giannakis, M., Al-Debei, M. M., & Dennehy, D.. (2022). Metaverse beyond the hype: Multidisciplinary perspectives on emerging challenges, opportunities, and agenda for research, practice and policy. Volume(66), 102542-102542. *International Journal of Information Management*. Advance online publication. DOI: 10.1016/j.ijinfomgt.2022.102542

Dwyer, P. G. (2008). Self-Interest versus the Common Cause: Austria, Prussia and Russia against Napoleon. *The Journal of Strategic Studies*, *31*(4), 605–632. DOI: 10.1080/01402390802088440

Economic Impact. (2025). Europe's path to resilience and responsibility in a fragmented world. https://impact.economist.com/projects/trade-in-transition/regional-analysis-europe/

Edelman. (2021). 2021 Edelman trust barometer. Retrieved from https://www.edelman.com/trustbarometer

Efthymiopoulos, M. P. (2019). Hybrid Alliances: Efficiency, Business Continuity and Future Foresight in a World of Challenges. In Smart Technologies and Innovation for a Sustainable Future: Proceedings of the 1st American University in the Emirates International Research Conference—Dubai, UAE 2017 (pp. 187-193). Springer International Publishing.

Eggers, F. (2020). Masters of disasters? Challenges and opportunities for SMEs in times of crisis. *Journal of Business Research*, *116*, 199–208. DOI: 10.1016/j.jbusres.2020.05.025 PMID: 32501306

Eichengreen, B. (2002). The political economy of the Smoot-Hawley tariff. In *International Political Economy* (pp. 37–46). Routledge.

El Kurd, D. (2023, August 31). Assessing the Abraham Accords, three years on. Arab Center Washington DC. Retrieved from https://arabcenterdc.org/resource/assessing-the-abraham-accords-three-years-on/

El-Hosseny, F. (2018). *Civil Society in Investment Treaty Arbitration*. Brill Nijhoff., DOI: 10.1163/9789004349131

Embassy of the United Arab Emirates. Washington, DC. (2022, September 16). Abdullah bin Zayed holds official reception in Tel Aviv on second anniversary of Abraham Accords. Retrieved from https://www.wam.ae/en/details/1395303083970

Embassy of the United Arab Emirates. Washington, DC. (2024, June 13). Security. UAE–US Cooperation. Retrieved from https://www.uae-embassy.org/uae-us-cooperation/security

Embassy of the United Arab Emirates. Washington, DC. (n.d.). Occupied UAE islands, unofficial map. For illustrative purposes only. Retrieved from https://www.uae-embassy.org/discover-uae/foreign-policy/occupied-uae-islands

Emerson, K., Nabatchi, T., & Balogh, S. (2011). An Integrative Framework for Collaborative Governance. Volume(22), 1-29. *Journal of Public Administration: Research and Theory*. Advance online publication. DOI: 10.1093/jopart/mur011

Emmanuel, C. P., Qin, S., Hossain, S. F. A., & Hussain, K. (2022). Factors influencing social-media-based entrepreneurship prospect among female students in China. *Heliyon*, *8*(12), e12041. DOI: 10.1016/j.heliyon.2022.e12041 PMID: 36483305

Ernst & Young. (2020). *Corporate social responsibility in India: re-engineering compliance and fraud mitigation strategies*. https://assets.ey.com/content/dam/ey-sites/ey-com/en_in/topics/forensic/ey-csr-survey-2020.pdf

Esfandiary, D. (2021, September 15). The anxiety effect: How 9/11 and its aftermath changed Gulf Arab states' relations with the U.S. Crisis Group. Retrieved from https://www.crisisgroup.org/middle-east-north-africa/gulf-and-arabian-peninsula/united-arab-emirates-united-states-saudi-arabia

EU. (2025a). *An EU critical raw materials act for the future of EU supply chains*. https://www.consilium.europa.eu/en/infographics/critical-raw-materials/

EU. (2025b). *EUNAVFOR ASPIDES*. https://www.eeas.europa.eu/eunavfor-aspides_en?s=410381

European Central Bank. (2020).. . *Economic Bulletin*, *2020*(4), •••. https://www.ecb.europa.eu/press/economic-bulletin/html/eb202004.en.html

European Commission. (2001). *Green Paper, Promoting a European framework for Corporate Social Responsibility COM(2001)366 final*.

European Commission. (2019). *Funding opportunities*. Research and Innovation. Retrieved March 8, 2025, from https://research-and-innovation.ec.europa.eu/funding/funding-opportunities_en

European Commission. (2022). A Hydrogen Strategy for a Climate-Neutral Europe. https://energy.ec.europa.eu/ system/files/2020-07/hydrogen_strategy_0.pdf

European Commission. (2024). *SME Performance Review*. Available at: https://single-market-economy.ec.europa.eu/smes/sme-strategy/sme-performance-review_en

European Union. (2018). General data protection regulation (GDPR). Retrieved from https://eur-lex.europa.eu

Eurostat (2022). *Urban-rural Europe – introduction.* Available at: https://ec.europa.eu/eurostat/statistics-explained/index.php?title=Urban-rural_Europe_-_introduction

Eurostat. (2022, June 29). More than half of EU enterprises use social media. *Eurostat.* https://ec.europa.eu/eurostat/web/products-eurostat-news/-/edn-20220629-1

Evans, J. R., & Dean, J. W. (2003). *Total Quality: Management, Organization, and Strategy*. Thomson.

Evans, J. R., & Lindsay, W. M. (2020). *Managing for quality and performance excellence* (11th ed.). Cengage Learning.

Export Council Australia. (2021, September 6). Market information, Middle East. Retrieved from https://export.org.au/united-arab-emirates-looking-beyond-oil/

Fajgelbaum, P. D., Goldberg, P. K., Kennedy, P. J., & Khandelwal, A. K. (2020). The return to protectionism. *The Quarterly Journal of Economics*, *135*(1), 1–55. DOI: 10.1093/qje/qjz036

Fan, D., Yeung, A. C. L., Tang, C. S., Lo, C. K. Y., & Zhou, Y. (2022). Global operations and supply-chain management under the political economy. *Journal of Operations Management*, *68*(8), 816–823. DOI: 10.1002/joom.1232

Fan, D., Zhou, Y., Yeung, A. C., Lo, C. K., & Tang, C. (2022). Impact of the US–China trade war on the operating performance of US firms: The role of outsourcing and supply base complexity. *Journal of Operations Management*, *68*(8), 928–962. DOI: 10.1002/joom.1225

Fandrejewska, A., Chmielarz, W., & Zborowski, M. (2022). The Impact of the COVID-19 Pandemic on the Perception of Globalization and Consumer Behavior. *Sustainability (Basel)*, *14*(15), 9575. DOI: 10.3390/su14159575

Farber, S. (2019). The Amicus Curiae Phenomenon—Theory, Causes and Meanings. *Transnational Law and Contemporary Problems, 29*(1). https://ssrn.com/abstract=3341963

Farias, C., Fernandez, P., Hjorth, D., & Holt, R. (2019). Organizational entrepreneurship, politics and the political. *Entrepreneurship and Regional Development*, *31*(7–8), 555–566. DOI: 10.1080/08985626.2019.1599186

Farida, I., & Setiawan, D. (2022). Business Strategies and Competitive Advantage: The Role of Performance and Innovation. *Journal of Open Innovation*, *8*(3), 163. DOI: 10.3390/joitmc8030163

Farrell, A.M. (1996) Roles and behaviours in technology- integrated precalculus classrooms. *The Journal of Mathematical Behaviour* 15 (1):35-53 · March 1996 with 28 Reads · DOI: DOI: 10.1016/S0732-3123(96)90038-3

Fawzy, S., Osman, A. I., Doran, J., & Rooney, D. W. (2020). Strategies for mitigation of climate change: A review. Volume(18), 2069-2094. *Environmental Chemistry Letters*. Advance online publication. DOI: 10.1007/s10311-020-01059-w

Fayet, H., Futter, A., Kühn, U., Kulesa, Ł., van Hooft, P., & Bruusgaard, K. V. (2025). Forum: European Nuclear Deterrence and Donald Trump. *Survival, 67*(1), 123–142. DOI: 10.1080/00396338.2025.2459011

Fenty Beauty. (2018). Fenty Beauty by Rihanna. Retrieved from https://www.fentybeauty.com

Fernandez De Arroyabe, I., & Fernandez de Arroyabe, J. C. (2021). The severity and effects of Cyber-breaches in SMEs: A machine learning approach. *Enterprise Information Systems, 17*(3), 1942997. Advance online publication. DOI: 10.1080/17517575.2021.1942997

Ferreira, F. H., Messina, J., Rigolini, J., López-Calva, L. F., Lugo, M. A., Vakis, R., & Ló, L. F. (2012). *Economic mobility and the rise of the Latin American middle class*. World Bank Publications.

Field, A. (2018). *Discovering statistics using IBM SPSS statistics*. Sage Publications.

Fioretti, M., Saint-Jean, V., & Smith, S. C. (2024). *NGO Activism: Exposure vs. Influence*. In. https://arxiv.org/abs/2411.06875

Fischer, M., Foord, D., Frecè, J., Hillebrand, K., Kissling-Näf, I., Meili, R., Peskova, M., Risi, D., Schmidpeter, R., & Stucki, T. (2023). Social innovation (or why we need the civil society). In *SpringerBriefs in business* (pp. 77–89). DOI: 10.1007/978-3-031-25397-3_5

Flint, D. J., Blocker, C. P., & Boutin, P. J.Jr. (2011). Customer value anticipation, customer satisfaction and loyalty: An empirical examination. *Industrial Marketing Management, 40*(2), 219–230. DOI: 10.1016/j.indmarman.2010.06.034

Food and Agriculture Organisation. (2019). *FAOLEX Database Directive (EU) 2019/633 of the European Parliament and of the Council on unfair trading practices in business-to-business relationships in the agricultural and food supply chain."* Available at: https://www.fao.org/faolex/results/details/en/c/LEX-FAOC185638/

Fornaciari, C., Forte, M., & Mathews, C. (1999). Distance education strategy: How can your school complete? [H]. *Journal of Management Education, 23*(6), 703–718. DOI: 10.1177/105256299902300608

Forza, C., & Filippini, R. (1998). TQM impact on quality conformance and customer satisfaction: A causal model. *International Journal of Production Economics, 55*(1), 1–20. DOI: 10.1016/S0925-5273(98)00007-3

Frankental, P. (2001). Corporate social responsibility – a PR invention? *Corporate Communications, 6*(1), 18–23. DOI: 10.1108/13563280110381170

Furtasan, A. Y. (2023). Total Quality Management (TQM) and Quality of Higher Education: A Meta-Analysis Study. *International Journal of Instruction, 16*(2), 161–178. DOI: 10.29333/iji.2023.16210a

Gaither, N. (1996). *Production and operations management* (6th ed.). Dryden Press.

Gao, R. (2021). Bridging Separate Worlds—Application of Human Rights Law in Investment Treaty Arbitration. *SSRN, 42*(1), 1. DOI: 10.2139/ssrn.4075407

García-Jurado, A., Pérez-Barea, J. J., & Nova, R. J. (2021). A New Approach to Social Entrepreneurship: A Systematic Review and Meta-Analysis. *Sustainability (Basel), 13*(5), 2754. DOI: 10.3390/su13052754

Garrison, D. R. (2017). *E-Learning in the 21st Century: A Community of Inquiry Framework for Research and Practice* (3rd ed.). Routledge.

Garrison, D. R., Anderson, T., & Archer, W. (2000). Critical inquiry in a text-based environment: Computer conferencing in higher education. *The Internet and Higher Education, 2*(2-3), 87–105. DOI: 10.1016/S1096-7516(00)00016-6

Gautam, R., & Singh, A. (2010). Corporate social responsibility practices in India: A study of top 500 companies. *Global Business and Management Research, 2*(1), 41–56.

Gavriil, E. (2024). Protection of Property under Human Rights and International Investment Law: A Case-Law Analysis. *Laws, 13*(1), 1. Advance online publication. DOI: 10.3390/laws13010006

Gay, L. R., & Diehl, P. L. (1992) *Research Methods for Business and Management.* Mc. Millan Publishing Company, New York.

George, S. & Weimerskirch. (1998). *Total Quality Management: Strategies and Techniques Proven at Today's Most Successful Companies* (2nd ed.). Wiley.

Gerbner, G. (1956). Toward a general model of communication. *Audio Visual Communication Review*, *4*(3), 171–199.

Gerbner, G. (1964). On Political Message Analysis and Critical Research in Mass Communication. In *Dexter LA and White D.M. People, Society, and Mass Communications Pages: 476 - 500Glencoe*. The Free Press.

Ghafoor, A., & Mitchell, P. (2022, August 30). Secret deals ending Britain's control in Gulf revealed. BBC News Arabic. Retrieved from https://www.bbc.com/news/world-middle-east-62713025

Gill, J., & Johnson, P. (1997). *Research methods for managers* (2nd ed.). Paul Chapman Publishing Ltd.

Gilpin, R. (2001). *Global political economy: Understanding the international economic order*. Princeton university press. DOI: 10.1515/9781400831272

Global Data. (2018). Is the biopharma industry safe from the US-China trade war? https://www.pharmaceutical-technology.com/comment/biopharma-industry-safe-us-china-trade-war/?utm_source=chatgpt.com&cf-view

Goes, C., & Bekker, E. (2023). The Impact of Geopolitical Conflicts on Trade, Growth, and Innovation. *WTO Working Papers*.https://doi.org/DOI: 10.30875/4445c521-en

Goetsch, D. L., & Davis, S. B. (2014). *Quality management for organizational excellence: Introduction to total quality* (7th ed.). Pearson.

Goetschel, L. (1998). The foreign and security policy interests of small states in today's Europe. In Goetschel, L. (Ed.), *Small states inside and outside the European Union* (pp. xx–xx). Springer., DOI: 10.1007/978-1-349-14426-4

Goldstein, J. (2017). Bringing BITs Back from the Brink. *Denver Journal of International Law and Policy*, *45*(3). https://digitalcommons.du.edu/djilp/vol45/iss3/5

Goldthau, A., & Sitter, N. (2021). Power, authority and security: the EU's Russian gas dilemma. In *Renegotiating Authority in EU Energy and Climate Policy* (pp. 107–123). Routledge. DOI: 10.4324/9781003173106-7

Gomez, T. (2025). Philipine defense chief warns allies will fight if China restricts flights over South China Sea. https://apnews.com/article/philippines-south-china-sea-defense-secretary-gilberto-teodoro-air-defense-zone-4c63b28b674c63b1730a22d-c9faa5f22

Gomez, J. F., & Basterra, M. L. (2024). Critical Raw Materials and Strategic Relations between the EU and China: The Role of the EU Critical Raw Materials Act. In Li, Y., & Leandro, S. (Eds.), *The Palgrave Handbook on China-Europe-Africa Relations*. Palgrave. DOI: 10.1007/978-981-97-5640-7_13

Gomez, K. F. (2012). Rethinking the Role of Amicus Curiae in International Investment Arbitration: How to Draw the Line Favorably for the Public Interest. *Fordham International Law Journal*, *35*(2), 510–564. https://ir.lawnet.fordham.edu/ilj/vol35/iss2/3

Goodman, P. (2020, April 1). New York Times. Retrieved April 1, 2020, from https://www.nytimes.com/2020/04/01/business/economy/coronavirus-recession.html

Google. (2019). Google Translate. Retrieved from https://translate.google.com

Google. (2020). Diversity and inclusion at Google. Retrieved from https://diversity.google

Gordon, P. (2018). Great Britain and the Middle East: The rise and fall of a hegemonic power and the pursuit of eternal interests. In Abu-Warda, N., & Rubio-Garcia, D. (Eds.), *La Primavera Árabe y sus perspectivas regionales e internacionales* (pp. xx–xx). Diwan-Mayrit.

Götz, E., & Staun, J. (2022). Why Russia attacked Ukraine: Strategic culture and radicalized narratives. *Contemporary Security Policy*, *43*(3), 482–497. DOI: 10.1080/13523260.2022.2082633

Gouveia, S., De La Iglesia, D. H., Abrantes, J. L., & Rivero, A. J. L. (2024). Transforming strategy and value creation through digitalization? *Administrative Sciences*, *14*(11), 307. DOI: 10.3390/admsci14110307

Gragnano, A., Simbula, S., & Miglioretti, M. (2020). Work-Life Balance: Weighing the Importance of Work-Family and Work-Health Balance. *International Journal of Environmental Research and Public Health*, *17*(3), 907. DOI: 10.3390/ijerph17030907 PMID: 32024155

Graham, C. R. (2006). Blended learning systems: Definition, current trends, and future directions. In Bonk, C. J., & Graham, C. R. (Eds.), *Handbook of Blended Learning: Global Perspectives, Local Designs* (pp. 3–21). Pfeiffer.

Grant, W. (2024). How Chinese firms are using Mexico as a backdoor to the US. https://www.bbc.com/news/business-68825118

Grieco, J. M. (1988). Anarchy and the limits of cooperation: A realist critique of the newest liberal institutionalism. *International Organization*, *42*(3), 485–507. DOI: 10.1017/S0020818300027715

Groitl, G. (2025). *The good, the bad, and the ugly: What Donald Trump's return to the White House means for US strategic competition with Russia and China.* Z Politikwiss., DOI: 10.1007/s41358-025-00403-2

Grosser, K. (2016). Corporate Social Responsibility and Multi-Stakeholder Governance: Pluralism, Feminist Perspectives and Women's NGOs. *Journal of Business Ethics*, *137*(1), 65–81. DOI: 10.1007/s10551-014-2526-8

Gupta, A., McDaniel, J. C., & Herath, S. K. (2005). Quality management in service firms: Sustaining structures of total quality service. *Managing Service Quality*, *15*(4), 389–402. DOI: 10.1108/09604520510606853

Gupta, B. B., Gaurav, A., Panigrahi, P. K., & Arya, V. (2022). Analysis of artificial intelligence-based technologies and approaches on sustainable entrepreneurship. *Technological Forecasting and Social Change*, *186*, 122152. DOI: 10.1016/j.techfore.2022.122152

Gupta, N. (2012). Women Undergraduates in Engineering Education in India: A Study of Growing Participation. *Gender, Technology and Development*, *16*(2), 153–176. DOI: 10.1177/097185241201600202

Gupta, P., Chauhan, S., Paul, J., & Jaiswal, M. (2020). Social entrepreneurship research: A review and future research agenda. *Journal of Business Research*, *113*, 209–229. DOI: 10.1016/j.jbusres.2020.03.032

Gupta, R., Hasan, M. M., Islam, S. Z., Yasmin, T., & Uddin, J. (2023). Evaluating the Brexit and COVID-19's influence on the UK economy: A data analysis. *PLoS One*, *18*(6), e0287342. DOI: 10.1371/journal.pone.0287342 PMID: 37319267

Gur, N., & Dilek, S. (2023). US–China economic rivalry and the reshoring of global supply chains. *The Chinese Journal of International Politics*, *16*(1), 61–83. DOI: 10.1093/cjip/poac022

Guskey, T. R. (2002). Professional development and teacher change. *Teachers and Teaching*, *8*(3), 381–391. DOI: 10.1080/135406002100000512

Gyamfi, S., Gerstlberger, W., Prokop, V., & Stejskal, J. (2024). A new perspective for European SMEs' innovative support analysis: Does non-financial support matter? *Heliyon*, *10*(1), e23796. DOI: 10.1016/j.heliyon.2023.e23796 PMID: 38192801

Hache, D. (1998). Strategic planning of distance education in the age of teleinformatics. *Journal of Distance Learning Administration, 1*(2). https://www.westga.edu/~distance/Hache12.html

Hall, N. (2025). With the Fall of Assad, Can Syria Rise? *Survival, 67*(1), 45–54. DOI: 10.1080/00396338.2025.2459015

Handfield, R. B., Graham, G., & Burns, L. (2020). Coronavirus, Tariffs, Trade Wars, and Supply Chain Evolutionary Design. *International Journal of Operations & Production Management, 40*(10), 1649–1660. DOI: 10.1108/IJOPM-03-2020-0171

Handley, K., & Limão, N. (2017). Policy uncertainty, trade, and welfare: Theory and evidence for China and the United States. *The American Economic Review, 107*(9), 2731–2783. DOI: 10.1257/aer.20141419

Harel, R., Schwartz, D., & Kaufmann, D. (2020). Funding Access and Innovation in Small Businesses. *Journal of Risk and Financial Management, 13*(9), 209. DOI: 10.3390/jrfm13090209

Hargreaves, A., & Fullan, M. (2012). *Professional capital: Transforming teaching in every school.* Teachers College Press.

Harney, B., Gilman, M., Mayson, S., & Raby, S. (2022). Advancing understanding of HRM in small and medium-sized enterprises (SMEs): Critical questions and future prospects. *International Journal of Human Resource Management, 33*(16), 3175–3196. DOI: 10.1080/09585192.2022.2109375

Hart, C. W., Heskett, J. L., & Sasser, W. E. (1990). The profitable art of service recovery. *Harvard Business Review, 68*(4), 148–156. PMID: 10106796

Harvey, L. (2003). Student feedback. *Quality in Higher Education, 9*(1), 3–20. DOI: 10.1080/13538320308164

Hasan, R. (2013). Reflections on Foreign Direct Investment and Development with Reference to Non-Governmental Organizations and Corporate Social Responsibility. *Critical Sociology, 39*(1), 37–43. DOI: 10.1177/0896920511414067

Haski-Leventhal, D. (2022). Editorial: CSR in Asia. *Society and Business Review, 17*(1), 1–2. DOI: 10.1108/SBR-02-2022-156

Hawkins, D. I., Best, R. J., & Coney, K. A. (2001). *Consumer behavior: Building marketing strategy*. Irvin/McGraw-Hill.

Hayes, B. E. (2008). *Measuring customer satisfaction and loyalty* (3rd ed.). ASQ Quality Press.

Heckmann, I., Comes, T., & Nickel, S. (2015). A critical review on supply chain risk – Definition, measure and modeling. *Omega*, *52*, 119–132. DOI: 10.1016/j.omega.2014.10.004

Heijs, J., Díaz, G. A., & Reyes, D. M. V. (2019). *Impact of innovation on employment in quantitative terms: review of empirical literature based on micro data.* Munich Personal RePEc Archive. No. 95326:1–31 https://mpra.ub.uni-muenchen.de/95326/1/MPRA_paper_95326.pdf

Hein, R. (2022). Beyond a Balanced View of Social Entrepreneurship within a Social–Commercial Dichotomy: Towards a Four-Dimensional Typology. *Sustainability (Basel)*, *14*(8), 4454. DOI: 10.3390/su14084454

Herring, C. (2009). Does diversity pay?: Race, gender, and the business case for diversity. *American Sociological Review*, *74*(2), 208–224. DOI: 10.1177/000312240907400203

Hey, J. A. K. (Ed.). (2003). *Small states in world politics: Explaining foreign policy behavior*. Lynne Rienner.

Hirsch, M. (2010). Investment Tribunals and Human Rights Treaties: A Sociological Perspective. In Baetens, F. (Ed.), *Investment Law Within International Law: Integrationist Perspectives* (pp. 85–105). Cambridge University Press., DOI: 10.1017/CBO9781139855921.008

Hobfoll, S. E., Halbesleben, J. R. B., Neveu, J.-P., & Westman, M. (2017). Conservation of Resources in the Organizational Context: The Reality of Resources and Their Consequences. Volume(5), 103-128. *Annual Review of Organizational Psychology and Organizational Behavior*. Advance online publication. DOI: 10.1146/annurev-orgpsych-032117-104640

Hodges, C. B., & Fowler, D. J. (2020). The use of learning management systems in the United States. In Khine, M. S., & Areepattamannil, S. (Eds.), *Handbook of Research on Blended Learning Pedagogies and Professional Development in Higher Education* (pp. 12–35). IGI Global.

Hofstede, G., Hofstede, G. J., & Minkov, M. (2010). *Cultures and organizations: Software of the mind* (3rd ed.). McGraw-Hill Professional.

Homburg, C., Koschate, N., & Hoyer, W. D. (2006). The role of cognition and affect in the formation of customer satisfaction: A dynamic perspective. *Journal of Marketing*, *70*(3), 21–31. DOI: 10.1509/jmkg.70.3.021

Hong, L., & Page, S. E. (2004). Groups of diverse problem solvers can outperform groups of high-ability problem solvers. *Proceedings of the National Academy of Sciences of the United States of America, 101*(46), 16385–16389. DOI: 10.1073/pnas.0403723101 PMID: 15534225

Hosoe, N. (2023). The cost of war: Impact of sanctions on Russia following the invasion of Ukraine. *Journal of Policy Modeling, 45*(2), 305–319. DOI: 10.1016/j.jpolmod.2023.04.001

Hossain, M. R., Akhter, F., & Sultana, M. M. (2022). SMEs in Covid-19 Crisis and Combating Strategies: A Systematic Literature Review (SLR) and A Case from Emerging Economy. *Operations Research Perspectives, 9*, 100222. DOI: 10.1016/j.orp.2022.100222

Houston, D. (2008). Rethinking quality and improvement in higher education. *Quality Assurance in Education, 16*(1), 61–79. DOI: 10.1108/09684880810848413

Hoyle, D. (2009). *ISO 9000 quality systems handbook* (6th ed.). Butterworth-Heinemann.

Huckfeldt, R., Sprague, J., & Levine, J. (2000). The dynamic of collective deliberation in the 1996 election: Campaign effects on accessibility, certainty, and accuracy. *The American Political Science Review, 94*(3), 641–651. DOI: 10.2307/2585836

Hunt, C. R. (2018). When does redistricting matter? Changing conditions and their effects on voter turnout.*Electoral Studies, 54*(August), 128–138. DOI: 10.1016/j.electstud.2018.05.007

Hussey, J., & Hussey, R. (1997). *Business Research: A Practical Guide for Undergraduate and Postgraduate Students*. Macmillan. DOI: 10.1007/978-1-349-25262-6

Ibarra, D., Bigdeli, A. Z., Igartua, J. I., & Ganzarain, J. (2020). Business Model Innovation in Established SMEs: A Configurational Approach. *Journal of Open Innovation, 6*(3), 76. DOI: 10.3390/joitmc6030076

IBM. (2019). IBM diversity and inclusion report. Retrieved from https://www.ibm.com/employment/inclusion/

IBM. (2020). IBM's commitment to diversity and inclusion. Retrieved from https://www.ibm.com/employment/inclusion/

Ibrahim, I., Amer, A., & Omar, F. (2011). The total quality management practices and quality performance: A case study of Pos Malaysia Berhad, Kota Kinabalu, Sabah. *Proceedings of the 2nd International Conference on Business and Economic Research (2nd ICBER 2011)*, 1–10.

Iddon, P. (2022, January 30). The UAE is bolstering its formidable air defenses. Forbes. Retrieved from https://www.forbes.com/sites/pauliddon/2022/01/30/the-uae-is-bolstering-its-formidable-air-defenses/

Inegbedion, H. E., Thikan, P. R., David, J. O., Ajani, J. O., & Peter, F. O. (2024). Small and medium enterprise (SME) competitiveness and employment creation: The mediating role of SME growth. *Humanities & Social Sciences Communications*, *11*(1), 11. Advance online publication. DOI: 10.1057/s41599-023-02434-y

International Energy Agency. (2025). *Hydrogen*. https://www.iea.org/energy-system/low-emissions-fuels/hydrogen

International Institute of Strategic Studies. (2019, January). The US withdrawal from Syria. Strategic Comments, 25. Retrieved from https://www.iiss.org/en/publications/strategic-comments/2019/the-us-withdrawal-from-syria/

International Labour Office. (2021). *Strategic Staff Management in SMEs to Support Lifelong Learning: A Literature Review.* Available at: https://shorturl.at/dBMV9

International Labour Office. (2024). *Small and Medium Enterprises.* Available at: https://shorturl.at/bioyQ

International Maritime Security Construct. (2019, November 12). Vigilance, surveillance, assurance. Retrieved from https://www.maritimeglobalsecurity.org/media/fasbdek4/2020-01-07-imsc-brochure-tri-fold-version-3.pdf

International Monetary Fund. (2020). *Unlocking Access to Finance for SMEs: A Cross-Country Analysis.* Available at: https://www.imf.org/en/Publications/WP/Issues/2020/03/13/Unlocking-Access-to-Finance-for-SMEs-A-Cross-Country-Analysis-49243

International Monetary Fund. (2024). *The Long-lasting Economic Shock of War.* Available at: https://www.imf.org/en/Publications/fandd/issues/2022/03/the-long-lasting-economic-shock-of-war

International Trade Administration. (2023, November 25). United Arab Emirates. U.S. Department of Commerce. Retrieved from https://www.trade.gov/country-commercial-guides/united-arab-emirates-defense#:~:text=The%20UAE%20ranks%20%236%20overall,on%20procurement%20with%20foreign%20suppliers

Iqbal, B. A. (2022). BRICS as a Driver of Global Economic Growth and Development. *Global Journal of Emerging Market Economies*, *14*(1), 7–8. DOI: 10.1177/09749101211067096

Iran International. (2023, August 8). UAE expresses concern over Iran's nuclear program. Retrieved from https://www.iranintl.com/en/202308088879

Ivanov, D. (2024). Exiting the COVID-19 pandemic: After-shock risks and avoidance of disruption tails in supply chains. *Annals of Operations Research, 335*(3), 1627–1644. DOI: 10.1007/s10479-021-04047-7 PMID: 33840871

Ivanov, D., & Dolgui, A. (2020). Viability of Intertwined Supply Networks: Extending the Supply Chain Resilience Angles towards Survivability. A Position Paper Motivated by COVID-19 Outbreak. *International Journal of Production Research, 58*(10), 2904–2915. DOI: 10.1080/00207543.2020.1750727

Iwasaki, I., & Satogami, M. (2023). Gender wage gap in European emerging markets: A meta-analytic perspective. *Journal for Labour Market Research, 57*(1), 9. Advance online publication. DOI: 10.1186/s12651-023-00333-y

Iyengar, S., & Simon, A. F. (2000). New perspectives and evidence on political communication and campaign effects. *Annual Review of Psychology, 51*(1), 149–169. DOI: 10.1146/annurev.psych.51.1.149 PMID: 10751968

Jablonski, J. R. (1992). *Implementing Total Quality Management: An Overview*. Technical Management Consortium, Inc.

Jacobides, M. G. (2020). Regulating Big Tech in Europe: Why, so what, and how understanding their business models and ecosystems can make a difference. SSRN *Electronic Journal*. https://doi.org/DOI: 10.2139/ssrn.3765324

Jacopo, L., Mazzucco, M., & Alexander, K. (2023, August 30). How the United Arab Emirates has promoted tolerance, co-existence and multiculturalism to confront religious violence. Manara Magazine. Retrieved from https://manaramagazine.org/2023/08/uae-tolerance-religious-violence/

Jamali, D. (2008). A Stakeholder Approach to Corporate Social Responsibility: A Fresh Perspective into Theory and Practice. *Journal of Business Ethics, 82*(1), 213–231. DOI: 10.1007/s10551-007-9572-4

James, J. (2000). Globalization, Preference Change and Consumer Welfare in Developing Countries. In: *Consumption, Globalization and Development*. Palgrave Macmillan, London. https://doi.org/DOI: 10.1057/9780230510951_2

Janardhan, N. (2019, April 24). The UAE evolves into a 'smart' power. Gulf Today. Retrieved from https://www.gulftoday.ae/opinion/2019/04/23/the-uae-evolves-into-a-smart-power

Jatana, R., & Crowther, D. (2007). Corporate Social Responsibility and the Empowerment of Women: An Indian Perspective. *Social Responsibility Journal*, *3*(4), 40–48. DOI: 10.1108/17471110710840224

Jha, S., Bhushan, S., & Nirola, N. (2024). Is geopolitical risk always detrimental to economic growth? *Economic Change and Restructuring*, *57*(2), 25. DOI: 10.1007/s10644-024-09585-1

Jinji, N., & Ozawa, S. (2024). Economic consequences of US-China technological decoupling: An illustrative quantitative analysis. https://cepr.org/voxeu/columns/economic-consequences-us-china-technological-decoupling-illustrative-quantitative

Johnson & Johnson. (2019). Equality for all. Retrieved from https://www.jnj.com/our-approach/equality-for-all

Johnson & Johnson. (2020). Diversity and inclusion. Retrieved from https://www.jnj.com/diversity-inclusion

Johnson, G., Price, J., & Tilley, H. (2020). The implications of the European transition for key Welsh economic sectors. *Wales Centre for Public Policy*.https://shorturl.at/jopzQ

Johnstone-Louis, M. (2017). Corporate Social Responsibility and Women's Entrepreneurship: Towards a More Adequate Theory of "Work.". *Business Ethics Quarterly*, *27*(4), 569–602. DOI: 10.1017/beq.2017.6

Jones, A. (2021). Innovations in diversity: Case studies of successful organizations. *Harvard Business Review*.

Jones, B., & Crowe, T. J. (1996). The new definition of quality. *Quality Progress*, *29*(2), 55–62.

Jopp, M., & Pollak, J. (2024). Introduction: The EU's Geopolitics—Where Ambition Exceeds Ability. In Jopp, M., & Pollak, J. (Eds.), *The European Union's Geopolitics. The Future of Europe*. Springer., DOI: 10.1007/978-3-031-74587-4_1

Juneau, T. (2024). How War in Yemen Transformed the Iran-Houthi Partnership. *Studies in Conflict and Terrorism*, *47*(3), 278–300. DOI: 10.1080/1057610X.2021.1954353

Juran, J. M. (1993). Made in USA: A Renaissance in Quality. *Harvard Business Review*, *71*(4), 42–50. PMID: 10127039

Juran, J. M., & De Feo, J. A. (2010). *Juran's quality handbook: The complete guide to performance excellence* (6th ed.). McGraw-Hill Education.

Juran, J. M., & Godfrey, A. B. (1999). *Juran's Quality Handbook*. McGraw-Hill.

Just, M. A., Carpenter, P. A., & Keller, T. A. (1996). The Capacity Theory of Comprehension: New Frontiers of Evidence and Arguments. *Psychological Review, 103*(4), 773–780. DOI: 10.1037/0033-295X.103.4.773 PMID: 8888654

Jüttner, U., & Maklan, S. (2011). Supply chain resilience in the global financial crisis: An empirical study. *Supply Chain Management, 16*(4), 246–259. DOI: 10.1108/13598541111139062

Kabeer, N. (2001). Conflicts Over Credit: Re-Evaluating the Empowerment Potential of Loans to Women in Rural Bangladesh. *World Development, 29*(1), 63–84. DOI: 10.1016/S0305-750X(00)00081-4

Kabeer, N., & Mahmud, S. (2010). Microfinance and social mobilization: alternative pathways to grassroots democracy? In *Mobilizing for democracy*. Zed Books Ltd., DOI: 10.5040/9781350221413.ch-003

Kaim, M., & Stanzel, A. (2022). The rise of China and NATO's Strategic Concept. *04*.

Kamrava, M. (2024, April). Iran's neighborhood policy: An assessment. Middle East Council on Global Affairs. Retrieved from https://mecouncil.org/publication_chapters/irans-neighborhood-policy-an-assessment/

Kang, S. K., DeCelles, K. A., Tilcsik, A., & Jun, S. (2016). Whistle while you work: The impact of affective and cognitive diversity on team creativity. *Organization Science, 27*(3), 928–944. DOI: 10.1287/orsc.2016.1070

Kannabiran, G. (2009). Sustainable stakeholder engagement through innovative supply chain strategy: An exploratory study of an Indian organization. *Asian Business & Management, 8*(2), 205–223. DOI: 10.1057/abm.2009.6

Kapoor, S. (2019). Entrepreneurship for economic and social empowerment of women: A case study of a self help credit program in Nithari Village, Noida, India. *Australasian Accounting. Business and Finance Journal, 13*(2), 123–142.

Kappe, M., Härting, R. C., Karg, C., & Deffner, D. (2023). Cybersecurity in SMEs – Drivers of Cybercrime, Insufficient Equipment and Prevention. *Procedia Computer Science, 225*, 3631–3640. DOI: 10.1016/j.procs.2023.10.358

Karagkouni, A., & Dimitriou, D. (2022). 'Sustainability Performance Appraisal for Airports Serving Tourist Islands'. *Sustainability (Basel), 14*(20), 13363. DOI: 10.3390/su142013363

Karia, N., & Asaari, M. H. A. H. (2006). The effects of total quality management practices on employees' work-related attitudes. *The TQM Magazine, 18*(1), 30–43. DOI: 10.1108/09544780610637677

Katsaliaki, K., Galetsi, P., & Kumar, S. (2021). Supply chain disruptions and resilience: A major review and future research agenda. *Annals of Operations Research, 319*(1), 965–1002. DOI: 10.1007/s10479-020-03912-1 PMID: 33437110

Katsourides, I. (2011). *The party system in Cyprus 1878-1931: structure and peculiarities. Publisher.* University of Cyprus, Faculty of Social Sciences and Education.

Kaufmann, D. (2024). *Rising shipping costs hit global trade hard.* https://www.dw.com/en/rising-shipping-costs-hit-global-trade-hard/a-69586965

Kaufmann, D., Kraay, A., & Mastruzzi, M. (2011). The Worldwide Governance Indicators: Methodology and analytical issues. *Hague Journal on the Rule of Law, 3*(02), 220–246. DOI: 10.1017/S1876404511200046

Kawa News. (2017, September 28). Tweeps 2017 Forum focuses on the fight against extremist ideologies online. Tech & Business. Retrieved from https://kawa-news.com/en/tweeps-2017-forum-focuses-on-the-fight-against-extremist-ideologies-online/

Kendall, K., & Bodinson, G. (2017). *Leading the Malcolm Baldrige way: how world-class leaders align their organizations to deliver exceptional results* (1st ed.). McGraw-Hill.

Kennedy, R. (2025). US government raises tariffs on Chinese solar polysilicon, wafers, cells to 60%. https://www.pv-magazine.com/2025/02/05/us-government-raises-solar-polysilicon-wafer-and-cell-tariffs-from-china-to-60/#:~:text=Imported%20solar%20energy%20resources%2C%20including,from%2025%25%20to%2050%25

Kenny, N., McCoy, S., & Mihut, G. (2020). Special education reforms in Ireland: Changing systems, changing schools. *International Journal of Inclusive Education*, •••, 1–20. DOI: 10.1080/13603116.2020.1821447

Keohane, R. O. (1969). Lilliputians' dilemmas: Small states in international politics. *International Organization, 23*(2), 291–310.

Keohane, R. O., & Nye, J. S. (1997). *Power and Interdependence: World Politics in Transition*. Longman.

Key, V. O. (1966). *The responsible electorate: Rationality in presidential voting 1936–1960.* Harvard University Press.

Khalil, S. (2020, December 17). Mohamed Bouazizi, 1984–2011: The fire that lit the Arab Spring. The New Arab. Retrieved from https://www.newarab.com/analysis/mohamed-bouazizi-fire-lit-arab-spring

Khamalah, J. N., & Lingaraj, B. P. (2007). TQM in the service sector: A survey of small businesses. *Total Quality Management & Business Excellence, 18*(9), 973–982. DOI: 10.1080/14783360701592059

Khandelwal, C., Singhal, M., Gaurav, G., Dangayach, G., & Meena, M. (2021). Agriculture Supply Chain Management: A Review (2010–2020). *Materials Today: Proceedings, 47*, 3144–3153. DOI: 10.1016/j.matpr.2021.06.193

Khan, S. M. (2020). *US Semiconductor Exports to China: Current Policies and Trends*. Center for Security and Emerging Technology, October. DOI: 10.51593/20200039

Khurana, A. (2020). *Understanding how CSR can become catalyst to women empowerment in India*. Crossbarriers. https://crossbarriers.org/women-empowerment-in

Kilpatrick, J., & Barter, L. (2020). COVID-19: Managing supply chain risk and disruption. Deloitte Insights. https://www2.deloitte.com/insights/us/en/economy/covid-19/managing-supply-chain-risk-and-disruption.html

Kim, Y., Chen, Y.-S., & Linderman, K. (2015). Supply network disruption and resilience: A network structural perspective. *Journal of Operations Management, 33-34*(1), 43–59. DOI: 10.1016/j.jom.2014.10.006

King, G., Pan, J., & Roberts, M. E. (2013). How Censorship in China Allows Government Criticism but Silences Collective Expression. Volume(107), 326-343. *The American Political Science Review*. Advance online publication. DOI: 10.1017/S0003055413000014

Kıprızlı, G., & Köstem, S. (2022). Understanding the BRICS framing of climate change: The role of collective identity formation. *International Journal (Toronto, Ont.), 77*(2), 270–291. DOI: 10.1177/00207020221135300

Kissinger, H. (2017). *A world restored: Metternich, Castlereagh, and the problems of peace, 1812–22*. Friedland Books.

Knahr, C. (2011). The New Rules on Participation of Non-Disputing Parties in ICSID Arbitration: Blessing or Curse? In Brown, C., & Miles, K. (Eds.), *Evolution in Investment Treaty Law and Arbitration* (pp. 319–338). Oxford University Press. DOI: 10.1017/CBO9781139043809.022

Kochan, T. A., Bezrukova, K., Ely, R., Jackson, S. E., Joshi, A., & Youndt, M. A. (2003). The effects of diversity on business performance: Report of the Diversity Research Network. *Human Resource Management, 42*(1), 3–21. DOI: 10.1002/hrm.10061

Kookana, R. S., Drechsel, P., Jamwal, P., & Vanderzalm, J. (2020). Urbanisation and emerging economies: Issues and potential solutions for water and food security. *The Science of the Total Environment*, *732*, 139057. DOI: 10.1016/j.scitotenv.2020.139057 PMID: 32438167

Koster, M., Simaens, A., & Vos, B. (2019). The Advocate's Own Challenges to Behave in a Sustainable Way: An Institutional Analysis of Advocacy NGOs. *Journal of Business Ethics*, *157*(2), 483–501. DOI: 10.1007/s10551-017-3674-4

Kotiranta, A., Tykkyläinen, S., & Puumalainen, K. (2020). Growth of social and commercial SMEs: a comparative study. In *Edward Elgar Publishing eBooks*. DOI: 10.4337/9781839109690.00018

Kotler, P., & Keller, K. L. (2016). *Marketing management* (15th ed.). Pearson.

Kountouridou, M., & Domic, D. (2022). The impact of a positive visualisation course in brand identity on freshmen students' perceptions of university brand image. *Iranian. Journal of Management Studies*, *15*(4), 945–962. DOI: 10.22059/ijms.2022.326021.674612

Kourkoumelis, A., Anastasopoulou, E., Deirmentzoglou, G., Masouras, A., & Anastasiadou, S. 2024, September. Artificial Intelligence and Managerial Decision-Making in International Business. In *European Conference on Innovation and Entrepreneurship* (pp. 363-369). Academic Conferences International Limited. DOI: 10.34190/ecie.19.1.2573

Koyama, T. (2024). Who Restarts Violent Conflict? Post-Conflict Government Policy and Two Types of Conflict Recurrence. *Defence and Peace Economics*, *36*(2), 200–226. DOI: 10.1080/10242694.2024.2308473

KPMG. (2020). *India's CSR reporting survey 2019*. https://assets.kpmg.com/content/dam/kpmg/in/pdf/2020/02/india-s-csr-reporting-survey-2019.pdf

Kraay, A., Kaufmann, D., & Mastruzzi, M. (2010). The worldwide governance indicators: Methodology and analytical issues. *World Bank Policy Research Working Paper*. Advance online publication. DOI: 10.1596/1813-9450-5430

Krasner, S. D. (1982). Structural causes and regime consequences: Regimes as intervening variables. *International Organization*, *36*(2), 185–205. https://pos-graduacao.uepb.edu.br/ppgri/files/2016/02/Krasner-Structural-Causes-and-Regime-Consequencies-Regime-as-Intervening-Variables.pdf

Kriebaum, U. (2014). The Rompetrol Group N.V. v. Romania. *The Journal of World Investment & Trade*, *15*(5-6), 1022–1031. DOI: 10.1163/22119000-01506011

Kroet, C. (2024). *Eleven EU countries took 5G security measures to ban Huawei, ZTE*. https://www.euronews.com/next/2024/08/12/eleven-eu-countries-took-5g-security-measures-to-ban-huawei-zte

Krugman, P. R. (1987). Is free trade passé? *The Journal of Economic Perspectives, 1*(2), 131–144. DOI: 10.1257/jep.1.2.131

Kruk, M. E., Gage, A., Arsenault, C., Jordan, K., Leslie, H. H., Roder-DeWan, S., Adeyi, O., Barker, P., Daelmans, B., Doubova, S. V., English, M., García-Elorrio, E., Guanais, F., Gureje, O., Hirschhorn, L. R., Jiang, L., Kelley, E., Lemango, E. T., Liljestrand, J., & Pate, M. (2018). High-quality health systems in the Sustainable Development Goals era: Time for a revolution. Volume(6), e1196-e1252. *The Lancet. Global Health, 6*(11), e1196–e1252. Advance online publication. DOI: 10.1016/S2214-109X(18)30386-3 PMID: 30196093

Kucuk, S. U. (2009). Consumer empowerment model: From unspeakable to redress. *Direct Marketing (Bradford), 3*(4), 327–342. DOI: 10.1108/17505930911000892

Kuddus, M. A., Tynan, E., & McBryde, E. (2020). Urbanization: A problem for the rich and the poor? *Public Health Reviews, 41*(1), 1. Advance online publication. DOI: 10.1186/s40985-019-0116-0 PMID: 31908901

Kumar, A., Reddy, K. G., & P S, V. (2020). A scientometric analysis of the women empowerment (1985-2018). *Australian Journal of Business and Management Research*, 09–27. DOI: 10.52283/NSWRCA.AJBMR.20200511A02

Kumar, V., & Reinartz, W. (2018). *Customer relationship management: Concept, strategy, and tool* (3rd ed.). Springer.

L'Oréal. (2020). Diversity and inclusion at L'Oréal. Retrieved from https://www.loreal.com/group/diversity-inclusion

Labott, E. (2004, May 12). U.S. hits Syria with sanctions. CNN.com. Retrieved from https://edition.cnn.com/2004/WORLD/meast/05/11/us.syria/

Lacina, L., & Vavřina, J. (2013). The impact of financial and economic crisis on SME's in Greece and Ireland. *Acta Universitatis Agriculturae et Silviculturae Mendelianae Brunensis, 61*(4), 1005–1016. DOI: 10.11118/actaun201361041005

Lagrosen, S. (2001). Strengthening the weakest link of TQM–from customer focus to customer understanding. *The TQM Magazine, 13*(5), 348–354. DOI: 10.1108/09544780110401916

Lakhe, R. R., & Mohanty, R. P. (1995). Understanding TQM in service systems. *International Journal of Quality & Reliability Management, 12*(9), 139–153. DOI: 10.1108/02656719510101240

Lambert, L. A., Tayah, J., Lee-Schmid, C., Abdalla, M., Abdallah, I., Ali, A. H., Esmail, S., & Ahmed, W. (2022). The EU's natural gas Cold War and diversification challenges. *Energy Strategy Reviews, 43*, 100934. DOI: 10.1016/j.esr.2022.100934

Lambrecht, J., & Lievens, J. (2008). Pruning the family tree: An unexplored path to family business continuity and family harmony. *Family Business Review, 21*(4), 295–313. DOI: 10.1177/08944865080210040103

Lammert, C. (2025). *The USA after the election: economic and social policy implications*. Z Politikwiss., DOI: 10.1007/s41358-025-00400-5

Landesz, T. (2023). Future of Geopolitics. In *Future Intelligence*. https://library.oapen.org/bitstream/handle/20.500.12657/76732/1/978-3-031-36382-5.pdf#page=50

Larrieta-Rubín de Celis, I., Velasco-Balmaseda, E., Fernández de Bobadilla, S., Alonso-Almeida, M. del M., & Intxaurburu-Clemente, G. (2015). Does having women managers lead to increased gender equality practices in corporate social responsibility? *Business Ethics (Oxford, England), 24*(1), 91–110. DOI: 10.1111/beer.12081

Le Monde. (2024). Western sanctions on Russian oil have too many loopholes. https://www.lemonde.fr/en/opinion/article/2024/10/31/western-sanctions-on-russian-oil-have-too-many-loopholes_6731133_23.html

Leal Filho, W., Fedoruk, M., Paulino Pires Eustachio, J. H., Barbir, J., Lisovska, T., Lingos, A., & Baars, C. (2023). How the War in Ukraine Affects Food Security. *Foods, 12*(21), 3996. DOI: 10.3390/foods12213996 PMID: 37959115

Lee, H. L. (2004). The triple-A supply chain. *Harvard Business Review, 82*(10), 102–112. https://hbr.org/2004/10/the-triple-a-supply-chain PMID: 15559579

Leruth, B. (2024). Political long-termism and the European Union: Five research questions for the future. *Contemporary European Politics, 2*(2), e70000. DOI: 10.1002/cep4.70000

Levitan, N., Reich, A., & Rynhold, J. From Conflict to Connectivity: The India-Middle East-Europe Corridor Amidst Geopolitical Turbulence (January 30, 2025). Bar Ilan University Faculty of Law Research Paper No. 5117805, Available at SSRN: https://ssrn.com/abstract=5117805 or DOI: 10.2139/ssrn.5117805

Levy, J. S., & Mulligan, W. (2017). Shifting power, preventive logic, and the response of the target: Germany, Russia, and the First World War. *The Journal of Strategic Studies*, *40*(5), 731–769. DOI: 10.1080/01402390.2016.1242421

Levy, S. (2003). Six factors to consider when planning online distance learning programs in higher education. *Online Journal of Distance Learning Administration*, *6*(1).

Lichtenstein, D. R., Drumwright, M. E., & Braig, B. M. (2004). The Effect of Corporate Social Responsibility on Customer Donations to Corporate-Supported Nonprofits. *Journal of Marketing*, *68*(4), 16–32. DOI: 10.1509/jmkg.68.4.16.42726

Lientz, B. P., & Rea, K. P. (2001). *Breakthrough technology project management*. Academic Press.

Likert, R. (1932). A technique for measurement of attitudes. *Archives de Psychologie*, *140*, 5–55.

Lim, D. J., & Cooper, Z. (2015). Reassessing hedging: The logic of alignment in East Asia. *Security Studies*, *24*(4), 696–727. DOI: 10.1080/09636412.2015.1103130

Lindberg, L. N. (1970). Political Integration as a Multidimensional Phenomenon Requiring Multivariate Measurement. *International Organization*, *24*(4), 648–731. DOI: 10.1017/S0020818300017501

Lipset, S. M., & Rokkan, S. (1967). Cleavage Structures, Party Systems, and Voter Alignments: An Introduction. In Lipset, S. M., & Rokkan, S. (Eds.), *Party Systems and Voter Alignments: Cross-National Perspectives* (pp. 1–64). Collier-Macmillan.

Liu, R., Zhang, J. J., & Vortherms, S. A. (2022). In the middle: American multinationals in China and trade war politics. *Business and Politics*, *24*(4), 348–376. DOI: 10.1017/bap.2022.14

Li, Y., Li, B., & Lu, T. (2022). Founders' Creativity, Business Model Innovation, and Business Growth. *Frontiers in Psychology*, *13*, 892716. Advance online publication. DOI: 10.3389/fpsyg.2022.892716 PMID: 35756233

Lo, J., Proksch, S. O., & Slapin, J. B. (2014) Ideological Clarity in Multi-Party Competition: A New Measure and Test Using Election Manifestos. *British Journal of Political Science,* 46 (3). 591 - 610. ISSN 0007-1234

Lovelock, C., & Wirtz, J. (2023). *Services marketing: People, technology, strategy* (9th ed.). World Scientific Publishing.

Lowenthal, P. R. (2010). The evolution and influence of social presence theory on online learning. In Kidd, T. T., & Keengwe, J. (Eds.), *Adult learning in the digital age: Perspectives on online technologies and outcomes* (pp. 124–139).

Macchion, L., Moretto, A., Caniato, F., Caridi, M., Danese, P., & Vinelli, A. (2015). Production and supply network strategies within the fashion industry. *International Journal of Production Economics, 163*(C), 173–188. DOI: 10.1016/j.ijpe.2014.09.006

Maceda, C. (2015, August 2). How Google is showing Arabian Gulf on maps. Gulf News. Retrieved from https://gulfnews.com/going-out/society/how-google-is-showing-arabian-gulf-on-maps-1.1560237

Mackinder, H. J. (1904). The Geographical Pivot of History. *The Geographical Journal, 23*(4), 421–437. DOI: 10.2307/1775498

Mahmood, A., & Bashir, J. (2020). How does corporate social responsibility transform brand reputation into brand equity? Economic and noneconomic perspectives of CSR. *International Journal of Engineering Business Management, 12*, 184797902092754. DOI: 10.1177/1847979020927547

Mahmood, S., & Khan, Z. (2023). CSR and customer orientation: A sustainable pathway towards competitive advantage? A customer's perspective. *Social Responsibility Journal, 19*(4), 741–755. DOI: 10.1108/SRJ-04-2020-0139

Mair, J., & Sharma, S. (2012). Performance measurement and social entrepreneurship. In *Gabler Verlag eBooks* (pp. 175–189). DOI: 10.1007/978-3-8349-7093-0_9

Mair, J., & Martí, I. (2005). Social entrepreneurship research: A source of explanation, prediction, and delight. *Journal of World Business, 41*(1), 36–44. DOI: 10.1016/j.jwb.2005.09.002

Makris, I. A., Apostolopoulos, S., & Masouras, A. (2025). EU policies and female entrepreneurship in Greek rural areas in relation to digital challenges. In *Real-World Tools and Scenarios for Entrepreneurship Exploration* (pp. 203–222). IGI Global.

Maletzke, G., (1963) Psychologie der Massenkommunikation, Hamburg In *der Literaturliste für Docupedia-Zeitgeschichte Artikel Propaganda*

Malhotra, Y. (1998) *Compilation of definitions of knowledge management* at www.brint.com

Malousis, A. T., Zefkilis, P. N., & Daglis, T. (2023). Employment in the 21st Century: Pre- and Post-COVID-19 Changes. *Encyclopedia, 3*(3), 853–869. DOI: 10.3390/encyclopedia3030061

Mann, H. (2011). Civil Society Perspectives: What Do Key Stakeholders Expect from the International Investment Regime? In Alvarez, J. E., & Sauvant, K. P. (Eds.), *The Evolving International Investment Regime: Expectations, Realities, Options* (pp. 22–29). Oxford University Press., DOI: 10.1093/acprof:oso/9780199793624.003.0004

Manoharan, C., Poongavanam, S., Arivazhagan, D., Divyaranjani, R., & Vetri Selvan, R. (2020). Cognition and emotions during the teaching/learning process. *International Journal of Scientific and Technology Research*, *9*(2), 267–269.

Manzoor, F., Wei, L., & Sahito, N. (2021). The role of SMEs in rural development: Access of SMEs to finance as a mediator. *PLoS One*, *16*(3), e0247598. DOI: 10.1371/journal.pone.0247598 PMID: 33684146

Mao, H., & Görg, H. (2020). Friends like this: The impact of the US–China trade war on global value chains. *World Economy*, *43*(7), 1776–1791. DOI: 10.1111/twec.12967

Marshall, J. (2011). En-gendering Notions of Leadership for Sustainability. *Gender, Work and Organization*, *18*(3), 263–281. DOI: 10.1111/j.1468-0432.2011.00559.x

Marshall, T. (2015). *Prisoners of geography: Ten maps that tell you everything you need to know about global politics*. Elliott & Thompson.

Martínez-Rodríguez, I., Quintana-Rojo, C., Gento, P., & Callejas-Albiñana, F. E. (2021). Public policy recommendations for promoting female entrepreneurship in Europe. *The International Entrepreneurship and Management Journal*, *18*(3), 1235–1262. DOI: 10.1007/s11365-021-00751-9

Masouras, A., Pistikou, V., & Komodromos, M. (2021). Innovation analysis in cypriot small and medium-sized enterprises and the role of the European Union. In *Entrepreneurship, Institutional Framework and Support Mechanisms in the EU* (pp. 115-131). Emerald Publishing Limited. DOI: 10.1108/978-1-83909-982-320211011

Masouras, A. (2019). Young entrepreneurship in Cyprus. *Zeszyty Naukowe Małopolskiej Wyższej Szkoły Ekonomicznej w Tarnowie, 42*(2), 27-42. https://doi.org/DOI: 10.25944/znmwse.2019.02.2742

Matenda, F. R., & Sibanda, M. (2023). The influence of entrepreneurship on economic growth in BRICS economies. *Ekonomska Istrazivanja*, *36*(3), 2275582. Advance online publication. DOI: 10.1080/1331677X.2023.2275582

Matos, S., Viardot, E., Sovacool, B. K., Geels, F. W., & Xiong, Y. (2022). Innovation and climate change: A review and introduction to the special issue. *Technovation*, *117*, 102612. DOI: 10.1016/j.technovation.2022.102612

Mavroidis, P.C. and Sapir, A. (2021). China and the WTO: why multilateralism still matters.

McCarthy, L. (2017). Empowering Women Through Corporate Social Responsibility: A Feminist Foucauldian Critique. *Business Ethics Quarterly*, *27*(4), 603–631. DOI: 10.1017/beq.2017.28

McGee, R. W. (1992). An economic analysis of protectionism in the United states with implications for international trade in Europe. *Geo. Wash. J. Int'l L. & Econ.*, *26*, 539.

McKinsey & Company. (2015). Why diversity matters. Retrieved from https://www.mckinsey.com/business-functions/organization/our-insights/why-diversity-matters

McKinsey & Company. (2018). Delivering through diversity. https://www.mckinsey.com/business-functions/organization/our-insights/delivering-through-diversity

McKinsey & Company. (2020). Diversity wins: How inclusion matters. Retrieved from https://www.mckinsey.com/business-functions/organization/our-insights/diversity-wins-how-inclusion-matters

McQuarrie, E., & Mick, D. G. (1996). Figures of Rhetoric in Advertising Language. *The Journal of Consumer Research*, *22*(4), 424–438. DOI: 10.1086/209459

Meckling, J., Kelsey, N., Biber, E., & Zysman, J. (2015). Winning coalitions for climate policy. *Science*, *349*(6253), 1170–1171. DOI: 10.1126/science.aab1336 PMID: 26359392

Merrill, M. D. (2002). First principles of instruction. *Educational Technology Research and Development*, *50*(3), 43–59. DOI: 10.1007/BF02505024

Methanex Corporation v United States of America UNCITRAL Final Award. (2005).

Meyer, C., & Schwager, A. (2007). Understanding customer experience. *Harvard Business Review*, *85*(2), 116–126. PMID: 17345685

Mikadze, K. (2016). Uninvited Guests: NGOs, Amicus Curiae Briefs, and the Environment in Investor-State Dispute Settlement. *Journal of International Law and International Relations*, *12*(1), 35.

Milakovich, M. E. (1995). *Improving service quality: Achieving high performance in the public and private sectors*. St. Lucie Press.

Miles, K. (2013). *The Origins of International Investment Law*. Cambridge University Press., DOI: 10.1017/CBO9781139600279

Milner, H. V. (1999). The political economy of international trade. *Annual Review of Political Science*, *2*(1), 91–114. DOI: 10.1146/annurev.polisci.2.1.91

Minola, T., Baù, M., Brumana, M., & De Massis, A. (2022). Under which circumstances do family SMES achieve high growth? A behavioural perspective. *International Small Business Journal*, *40*(6), 768–798. DOI: 10.1177/02662426221102859

Miranda, I. T. P., Moletta, J., Pedroso, B., Pilatti, L. A., & Picinin, C. T. (2021). A Review on Green Technology Practices at BRICS Countries: Brazil, Russia, India, China, and South Africa. *SAGE Open*, *11*(2), 21582440211013780. Advance online publication. DOI: 10.1177/21582440211013780

Mirzaei, A. (2019). Market power among UAE banks: The 2008 financial crisis and its impact. *The Quarterly Review of Economics and Finance*, *71*, 187–198. DOI: 10.1016/j.qref.2018.08.008

Mogaji, E., Hinson, R. E., Nwoba, A. C., & Nguyen, N. P. (2021). Corporate social responsibility for women's empowerment: A study on Nigerian banks. *International Journal of Bank Marketing*, *39*(4), 516–540. DOI: 10.1108/IJBM-04-2020-0195

Mohanty, R. P., & Behera, A. K. (1996). TQM in the service sector. *Work Study*, *45*(3), 13–17. DOI: 10.1108/00438029610115479

Monteiro, A. A., Sánchez-García, J. C., Hernández-Sánchez, B. R., & Cardella, G. M. (2022). Social Entrepreneurship Conceptual Approaches. *Encyclopedia*, *2*(2), 1004–1018. DOI: 10.3390/encyclopedia2020066

Montgomery, D. C. (2012). *Statistical Quality Control: A modern Introduction* (7th ed.). John Wiley and Sons.

Moosavi, J., Fathollahi-Fard, A. M., & Dulebenets, M. A. (2022). Supply chain disruption during the COVID-19 pandemic: Recognizing potential disruption management strategies. *International journal of disaster risk reduction. International Journal of Disaster Risk Reduction*, *75*, 102983. DOI: 10.1016/j.ijdrr.2022.102983 PMID: 35475018

Moradlou, H., Reefke, H., Skipworth, H., & Roscoe, S. (2021). Geopolitical disruptions and the manufacturing location decision in multinational company supply chains: A Delphi study on Brexit. *International Journal of Operations & Production Management*, *41*(2), 102–130. DOI: 10.1108/IJOPM-07-2020-0465

Morgan, S., Arita, S., Beckman, J., Ahsan, S., Russell, D., Jarrell, P. and Kenner, B. (2022). The Economic Impacts of Retaliatory Tariffs on US Agriculture.

Morgenthau, H. J. (2005). Politics among nations (7th ed., Rev. by K. Thompson & D. Clinton). McGraw-Hill Education.

Mori, S. (2019). US technological competition with China: The military, industrial and digital network dimensions. *Asia-Pacific Review, 26*(1), 77–120. DOI: 10.1080/13439006.2019.1622871

Morris, J., Morris, W., & Bowen, R. (2022). Implications of the digital divide on rural SME resilience. *Journal of Rural Studies, 89*, 369–377. DOI: 10.1016/j.jrurstud.2022.01.005

Morrison, G. R., Ross, S. M., Kemp, J. E., & Kalman, H. K. (2013). *Designing Effective Instruction* (7th ed.). Wiley.

Mubadala. (2024). Emirates Global Aluminium: Our portfolio. Retrieved from https://www.mubadala.com/en/what-we-do/emirates-global-aluminium#:~:text=Emirates%20Global%20Aluminium%20is%20the,Emirates%20outside%20oil%20and%20gas

Muñoz, P., Naudé, W., Williams, N., Williams, T., & Frías, R. (2020). Reorienting entrepreneurial support infrastructure to tackle a social crisis: A rapid response. *Journal of Business Venturing Insights, 14*, e00181. DOI: 10.1016/j.jbvi.2020.e00181

Mursalzade, H. (2024). Digital social entities, valuable communities: How digitalization enables value co-creation for social enterprises. *Society and Economy, 46*(4), 423–440. Advance online publication. DOI: 10.1556/204.2024.00015

Mutschler, M., Bales, M., & Meininghaus, E. (2024). The impact of precision strike technology on the warfare of non-state armed groups: Case studies on Daesh and the Houthis. *Small Wars & Insurgencies, 35*(7), 1123–1150. DOI: 10.1080/09592318.2024.2319216

Nambisan, S. (2020). Digital innovation and international business. *Innovation (North Sydney, N.S.W.), 24*(1), 86–95. DOI: 10.1080/14479338.2020.1834861

Naradda Gamage, S. K., Ekanayake, E., Abeyrathne, G., Prasanna, R., Jayasundara, J., & Rajapakshe, P. (2020). A Review of Global Challenges and Survival Strategies of Small and Medium Enterprises (SMEs). *Economies, 8*(4), 79. DOI: 10.3390/economies8040079

Narine, S. (2023). The problem of a "rules-based international order": The significance of the non-Western world's restrained response to the Russia-Ukraine war. *Canadian Foreign Policy, 29*(3), 301–316. DOI: 10.1080/11926422.2023.2193420

Narwal, M., & Singh, R. (2013). Corporate social responsibility practices in India: A comparative study of MNCs and Indian companies. *Social Responsibility Journal*, *9*(3), 465–478. DOI: 10.1108/SRJ-11-2011-0100

Nazarenko, S., Sharyi, V., & Kifin, O. (2024) Prospects for the Integration of Ukraine's National Security Mechanisms with the Collective Security Systems of the EU and NATO. Economic scope. doi: https://www.semanticscholar.org/paper/7185f2e034463f4b11b8caa56f232a0f0091014b

Nazir, S., Sohag, K., & Mariev, O. (2025). Geopolitical Risk and Trade Reorientation Dynamics: A Comparative Study. *Emerging Markets Finance & Trade*, •••, 1–22. DOI: 10.1080/1540496X.2025.2451188

Neep, D. (2025). Rebuilding the State in Post-Assad Syria. *Journal of Democracy*, *36*(2), 68–77. DOI: 10.1353/jod.2025.a954564

Negrine, R., Holtz-Bacha, C., & Papathanassopoulos, S. (2007). *The Professionalization of Political Communication, Changing Media* (Vol. 3). Changing Europe.

Negrine, R., & Papathanassopoulos, S. (1996). The "Americanization" of Political Communication. A Critique. *The Harvard International Journal of Press/Politics*, *1*(2), 45–62. DOI: 10.1177/1081180X96001002005

Neill, M. S., & Kang, M. (2024). Guest editorial: Shifting role and challenges of internal communication in an age of workplace turbulence/disruption. *Corporate Communications*, *29*(3), 285–290. DOI: 10.1108/CCIJ-05-2024-182

News Wires. (2011, March 14). Gulf states send troops to quell Bahrain protests. France 24. Retrieved from https://www.france24.com/en/20110314-gulf-states-send-troops-bahrain-quell-violent-protests-UAE-Saudi-Arabia

Nicholls, A. (2010). The Legitimacy of Social Entrepreneurship: Reflexive Isomorphism in a Pre–Paradigmatic Field. *Entrepreneurship Theory and Practice*, *34*(4), 611–633. DOI: 10.1111/j.1540-6520.2010.00397.x

Nielsen. (2018). The inclusion imperative: Why diversity is good for business. Retrieved from https://www.nielsen.com/us/en/insights/report/2018/the-inclusion-imperative/

Nielsen. (2019). The power of consumer diversity. Retrieved from https://www.nielsen.com/us/en/insights/report/2019/the-power-of-consumer-diversity/

Nishii, L. H. (2013). The benefits of climate for inclusion for gender-diverse groups. *Academy of Management Journal*, *56*(6), 1754–1774. DOI: 10.5465/amj.2009.0823

Nishii, L. H., & Mayer, D. M. (2009). Do inclusive leaders help improve the quality of the workplace? *Academy of Management Journal, 52*(1), 123–140. DOI: 10.5465/amj.2009.36461930

Nivola, P. S. (1986). The new protectionism: US trade policy in historical perspective. *Political Science Quarterly, 101*(4), 577–600. DOI: 10.2307/2150795

Nordenfelt, J. (1987). Human Rights—What They Are and What They Are Not. *Nordic Journal of International Law, 56*(3), 3–8. DOI: 10.1163/157181087X00093

Norton, B. (2025). *BRICS expands to 54.6% of world population by adding Nigeria, Africa's most populous country*. https://geopoliticaleconomy.com/2025/01/19/brics-expands-population-nigeria-africa/

Nyarko, Y. (2010). The United Arab Emirates: Some lessons in economic development (WIDER Working Paper No. 2010/11). United Nations University World Institute for Development Economics Research (UNU-WIDER). Retrieved from https://www.econstor.eu/bitstream/10419/54154/1/636479374.pdf

Nye, J. S. (2008). *The powers to lead: Soft, hard, and smart*. Oxford University Press.

Nye, J. S. (2023). *Soft power and great-power competition: Shifting sands in the balance of power between the United States and China*. Springer Nature. DOI: 10.1007/978-981-99-0714-4

O'Connor, S. J., & D'Angelo, J. D. (2013). Applying the ADDIE instructional design model to online continuing education for an international audience. *The Journal of Continuing Education in the Health Professions, 33*(3), 216–224.

O'Neill, B. C., Kriegler, E., Riahi, K., Ebi, K. L., Hallegatte, S., Carter, T. R., & Mathur, R.. (2013). A new scenario framework for climate change research: The concept of shared socioeconomic pathways. Volume(122), 387-400. *Climatic Change*. Advance online publication. DOI: 10.1007/s10584-013-0905-2

O'Neill, B. C., Tebaldi, C., Van Vuuren, D. P., Eyring, V., Friedlingstein, P., Hurtt, G., & Sanderson, B. M. (2016). The scenario model intercomparison project (ScenarioMIP) for CMIP6. *Geoscientific Model Development, 9*(9), 3461–3482.

Oakland, J. S. (2014). *Total quality management and operational excellence: text and cases* (4th ed.). Routledge. DOI: 10.4324/9781315815725

Obadia, E. (2007). Extension of Proceedings Beyond the Original Parties: Non-Disputing Party Participation in Investment Arbitration. *ICSID Review, 22*(2), 349–379. DOI: 10.1093/icsidreview/22.2.349

Ogujiuba, K. K., Eggink, M., & Olamide, E. (2023). Impact of Elements of Finance and Business Support on the SME Business Ecosystem in South Africa: An Econometric Analysis. *Sustainability (Basel), 15*(11), 8461. DOI: 10.3390/su15118461

Oğurlu, E. (2024). Changing Nature of the European Union - Turkey Relations: From Civilizational Project to Transactional Cooperation. *Ankara Hacı Bayram Veli Üniversitesi İktisadi Ve İdari Bilimler Fakültesi Dergisi, 26*(1), 33–54. DOI: 10.26745/ahbvuibfd.1363956

Oldemeyer, L., Jede, A., & Teuteberg, F. (2024). *Investigation of artificial intelligence in SMEs: a systematic review of the state of the art and the main implementation challenges*. Management Review Quarterly., DOI: 10.1007/s11301-024-00405-4

Oliver, R. L. (2010). *Satisfaction: A behavioral perspective on the consumer* (2nd ed.). M.E. Sharpe.

Oliver, T. (2023). Reflections: The UK after Brexit. *International Politics*. Advance online publication. DOI: 10.1057/s41311-023-00472-6

Organization of the Petroleum Exporting Countries. (2022). UAE facts and figures. https://www.opec.org/opec_web/en/about_us/170.htm

Osabohien, R., Worgwu, H., & Al-Faryan, M. S. (2022). Social entrepreneurship, technology diffusion and future employment in Nigeria. *Social Enterprise Journal, 19*(1), 40–50. DOI: 10.1108/SEJ-03-2022-0032

Osiatynski, W. (2014). The Historical Development of Human Rights. In Sheeran, S., & Rodlev, N. (Eds.), *Routledge Handbook of International Human Rights Law* (pp. 9–24). Taylor and Francis., DOI: 10.4324/9780203481417-4

Østergaard, C. R., Timmermans, B., & Kristinsson, K. (2011). Does a different view create something new? The effect of employee diversity on innovation. *Research Policy, 40*(3), 500–509. DOI: 10.1016/j.respol.2010.11.004

Overland, I. (2019). The geopolitics of renewable energy: Debunking four emerging myths. *Energy Research & Social Science, 49*, 36–40. DOI: 10.1016/j.erss.2018.10.018

Page, M. T., & Vittori, J. (Eds.). (2020). Dubai's role in facilitating corruption and global illicit financial flows. Carnegie Endowment for International Peace. https://carnegie-production-assets.s3.amazonaws.com/static/files/PageVittori_DubaiCorruption_final.pdf

Page, B. I. (1996). *Who deliberates? Mass media in modern democracy*. University of Chicago Press.

Page, S. E. (2007). *The difference: How the power of diversity creates better groups, firms, schools, and societies*. Princeton University Press.

Pan, Z., Shen, L., Paek, H., & Sun, Y. (2006). Mobilizing political talk in a presidential campaign: An examination of campaign effects in a deliberative framework. *Communication Research, 33*(5), 315–345. DOI: 10.1177/0093650206291478

Papademetriou, C., Ragazou, K., Belias, D., Anastasiadou, S., Garefalakis, A., & Prodromou, A. (2024). The Importance of Green Human Resources: Green Ambidexterity and Environmental Performance. In *Sustainability Through Green HRM and Performance Integration* (pp. 83–100). IGI Global., DOI: 10.4018/979-8-3693-5981-5.ch004

Papathanassopoulos S. (1999) The effects of media commercialization on journalism and politics in Greece. *The Communication Review, Volume 3, 199 -Issue 4*. Doi. Org/.DOI: 10.1080/10714429909368591

Papathanassopoulos, S., & Negrine, R. (2010). *Communications Policy: Theories and Issues*. Palgrave. DOI: 10.1007/978-1-137-09447-6

Parasuraman, A., Zeithaml, V. A., & Berry, L. L. (1985). A conceptual model of service quality and its implications for future research. *Journal of Marketing*, *49*(4), 41–50. DOI: 10.1177/002224298504900403

Parasuraman, A., Zeithaml, V. A., & Berry, L. L. (1988). SERVQUAL: A multiple-item scale for measuring consumer perceptions of service quality. *Journal of Retailing*, *64*(1), 12–40.

Pascariu, G. C. (2025). Resilience: From Theoretical Thinking to a New Paradigm and Normative Approaches in EU' Foreign and Security Policy. In Rouet, G., & Pascariu, G. C. (Eds.), *Resilience and the EU's Eastern Neighbourhood Countries*. Palgrave Macmillan., DOI: 10.1007/978-3-031-73379-6_2

Pasnicu, D. (2018). Supporting SMEs in creating jobs. *Journal of Economic Development. Environment and People*, *7*(1), 15. DOI: 10.26458/jedep.v7i1.575

Patel, N. (2019, March 7). How is the UAE diversifying its economy to attract investment? Trade Finance Global. (Last modified December 6, 2023). https://www.tradefinanceglobal.com/posts/how-is-the-uae-diversifying-its-economy-to-attract-investment/

Patrice, C., & Mamadou, T. (2024). How does consumer quality misperception change European Union antidumping actions? *Review of World Economics*, *160*(4), 1247–1275. DOI: 10.1007/s10290-024-00553-5

Patsoulis, P., Psychalis, M., & Deirmentzoglou, G. A. (2022). Stability and Growth Pact: Too Young to Die, Too Old to Rock 'n'Roll. *Journal of Risk and Financial Management, 15*(12), 608. DOI: 10.3390/jrfm15120608

Paul, J., Alhassan, I., Binsaif, N., & Singh, P. (2022). Digital entrepreneurship research: A systematic review. *Journal of Business Research, 156*, 113507. DOI: 10.1016/j.jbusres.2022.113507

Payne, J. (2024). EU energy ministers discuss Ukraine energy crisis, Russian LNG. https://www.reuters.com/business/energy/eu-energy-ministers-discuss-ukraine-energy-crisis-russian-lng-2024-10-15/

Perera, C., Zaslavsky, A., Christen, P., & Georgakopoulos, D. (2013). Context Aware Computing for The Internet of Things: A Survey. Volume(16), 414-454. *IEEE Communications Surveys and Tutorials*. Advance online publication. DOI: 10.1109/SURV.2013.042313.00197

Pérez-Barea, J. J. (2025). The Evolution of Social Entrepreneurship: Broadening the framework for the digital and sustainable era. *Administrative Sciences, 15*(2), 55. DOI: 10.3390/admsci15020055

Permanent Mission of the United Arab Emirates to the United Nations. (2017, October 10). UAE reaffirms commitment to combat international terrorism. https://www.un.int/uae/news/uae-reaffirms-commitment-combat-international-terrorism

Peterson, D. A. M. (2018). The dynamic construction of candidate image original research. *Electoral Studies, 54*, 289–296. DOI: 10.1016/j.electstud.2018.04.012

Pettit, T. J., Croxton, K. L., & Fiksel, J. (2019). The Evolution of Resilience in Supply Chain Management: A Retrospective on Ensuring Supply Chain Resilience. *Journal of Business Logistics, 40*(1), 56–65. DOI: 10.1111/jbl.12202

Pine, B. J., Peppers, D., & Rogers, M. (2011). *Do you want to keep your customers forever?* Harvard Business Review Press.

Piroska, D., & Epstein, R. A. (2023). Stalled by design: New paradoxes in the European Union's single financial market. *Journal of European Integration, 45*(1), 181–201. DOI: 10.1080/07036337.2022.2154344

Plotkin Boghardt, L. (2013, April 12). The Muslim Brotherhood on trial in the UAE (Policy Watch 2064). The Washington Institute for Near East Policy. https://www.washingtoninstitute.org/policy-analysis/muslim-brotherhood-trial-uae

Poddar, A., Narula, S. A., & Zutshi, A. (2019). A study of corporate social responsibility practices of the top Bombay Stock Exchange 500 companies in India and their alignment with the Sustainable Development Goals. *Corporate Social Responsibility and Environmental Management*, csr.1741. DOI: 10.1002/csr.1741

Ponomarov, S. Y., & Holcomb, M. C. (2009). Understanding the concept of supply chain resilience. *International Journal of Logistics Management, 20*(1), 124–143. DOI: 10.1108/09574090910954873

Porter, M. E. (1980). *Competitive strategy: Techniques for analyzing industries and competitors*. Free Press.

Porter, M. E., & Kramer, M. R. (2006). Strategy and society: The link between competitive advantage and corporate social responsibility. *Harvard Business Review, 84*(12), 78–92. PMID: 17183795

Powell, T. C. (1995). Total quality management as competitive advantage: A review and empirical study. *Strategic Management Journal, 16*(1), 15–37. DOI: 10.1002/smj.4250160105

Powell, T. C., & Dent-Micallef, A. (1997). Information technology as competitive advantage: The role of human, business, and technology resources. *Strategic Management Journal, 18*(5), 375–405. DOI: 10.1002/(SICI)1097-0266(199705)18:5<375::AID-SMJ876>3.0.CO;2-7

Prahalad, C. K., & Ramaswamy, V. (2004). *The future of competition: Co-creating unique value with customers*. Harvard Business School Press.

Prajogo, D. I. (2005). The comparative analysis of TQM practices and quality performance between manufacturing and service firms. *International Journal of Service Industry Management, 16*(3), 217–228. DOI: 10.1108/09564230510601378

Prajogo, D. I., & Brown, A. (2004). The relations between TQM practices and Quality Performance and the Role of Forman TQM Programs: An Australia Empirical Study. *The Quality Management Journal, 11*(4), 31–42. Advance online publication. DOI: 10.1080/10686967.2004.11919131

Prajogo, D. I., & McDermott, C. M. (2005). The relationship between total quality management practices and organizational culture. *International Journal of Operations & Production Management, 25*(11), 1101–1122. DOI: 10.1108/01443570510626916

Prajogo, D. I., & Sohal, A. S. (2006). The integration of TQM and technology/R&D management in determining quality and innovation performance. *Omega, 34*(3), 296–312. DOI: 10.1016/j.omega.2004.11.004

Procter & Gamble. (2017). The Talk. Retrieved from https://www.pg.com/en_US/brands/talk

Prodromou, A. (2019). *Business Ethics and Corporate Social Responsibility: A Necessity for Contemporary Businesses. Examples to Follow in the Globalised Environment* (Vol. 9). The Cyprus Research Facts., http://cdacollege.com/new-uploaded_files/147.pdf

Prodromou, A. (2021). The Impact of Covid-19 on the Global Automotive Industry - Future Challenges. *American International Journal of Social Science*, *10*(1), 1–11. DOI: 10.30845/aijss.v10n1p1

Protopapas, V. *Electoral history of Cyprus: politicians, parties and elections in the British Empire (1878-1960)* Publication Date 2011 University / Publisher National and Kapodistrian University of Athens; URL http://hdl.handle.net/10442/hedi/31045

Puvimanasinghe, S. F. (2007). *Foreign Investment, Human Rights and the Environment*. Brill | Nijhoff.

Queiroz, M. M., Ivanov, D., Dolgui, A., & Fosso Wamba, S. (2020). Impacts of Epidemic Outbreaks on Supply Chains: Mapping a Research Agenda amid the COVID-19 Pandemic through a Structured Literature Review. *Annals of Operations Research*, *319*(1), 1159–1196. DOI: 10.1007/s10479-020-03685-7 PMID: 32836615

Quilliam, N., & Vakil, S. (2023, December 29). The Medicis of the Middle East? How the United Arab Emirates is plotting its rise. Foreign Affairs. https://www.foreignaffairs.com/united-arab-emirates/medicis-middle-east

Rabinovich, I. (2019, January 24). How Iran's regional ambitions have developed since 1979. Brookings Institution. https://www.brookings.edu/articles/how-irans-regional-ambitions-have-developed-since-1979/

Race, M., & Espiner, T. (2025). How is China hitting back against US tariffs? https://www.bbc.com/news/articles/czj31l4p7vzo

Radi, Y. (2012). Realising Human Rights in Investment Treaty Arbitration: A Perspective from within the International Investment Law Toolbox. *North Carolina Journal of International Law and Commercial Regulation*, *37*(4), 1108–1185. DOI: 10.1525/sp.2007.54.1.23

Radi, Y. (2018). Introduction: Taking Stock of the Societal and Legal Interplay between Human Rights and Investment. In Radi, Y. (Ed.), *Research Handbook on Human Rights and Investment* (pp. 1–11). Edward Elgar Publishing., DOI: 10.4337/9781782549123.00007

Rafeq, A. K. (2005). A different balance of power: Europe and the Middle East in the eighteenth and nineteenth centuries. In Choueiri, Y. M. (Ed.), *A companion history of the Middle East* (pp. xx–xx). Blackwell Publishing.

Rahman, O. (2023, July 11). Five reasons why the Abraham Accords are ceding ground to Arab-Iranian de-escalation (Issue Brief). Edward P. Djerejian Center for the Middle East, Baker Institute for Public Policy, Rice University. https://www.bakerinstitute.org/research/five-reasons-why-abraham-accords-are-ceding-ground-arab-iranian-de-escalation

Rahman, S. U., Faisal, F., & Ali, A. (2022). Financial Development and Shadow Economy: A Bibliometric Analysis Using the Scopus Database (1985–2021). *Journal of the Knowledge Economy*. Advance online publication. DOI: 10.1007/s13132-022-00980-5

Rais, F. R. (2004). Syria under Bashar Al Assad: A profile for power. Strategic Studies (Institute of Strategic Studies Islamabad), 24(3).

Ramlawati, R., & Putra, A. H. P. K. (2018). Total quality management as the Key of the Company to Gain the Competitiveness, Performance Achievement and Consumer Satisfaction. *International Review of Management and Marketing. EconJournals*, *8*(5), 60–69.

Ramos-Villagrasa, P. J., Barrada, J. R., Fernández-Del-Río, E., & Koopmans, L. (2019). Assessing job performance using brief self-report scales: The case of the individual work performance Questionnaire. *Journal of Work and Organizational Psychology*, *35*(3), 195–205. DOI: 10.5093/jwop2019a21

Ranman, S. M. T., & Kabir, M. A. (2021). Role of Small and Medium Enterprise Clusters in Urban–Rural Linkage: A Study Based on Manufacturing SMEs of Khulna City, Bangladesh. *Environment & Urbanization Asia*, *12*(1), 27–39. DOI: 10.1177/0975425321990385

Rasheed, F. A. K. (2017). Impact of Total Quality Management on Customer Satisfaction. *International Journal of Management and Commerce Innovations*, *4*(2), 702–709.

Ratten, V. (2023). Entrepreneurship: Definitions, opportunities, challenges, and future directions. *Global Business and Organizational Excellence*, *42*(5), 79–90. DOI: 10.1002/joe.22217

Rawindaran, N., Nawaf, L., Alarifi, S., Alghazzawi, D., Carroll, F., Katib, I., & Hewage, C. (2023). Enhancing Cyber Security Governance and Policy for SMEs in Industry 5.0: A Comparative Study between Saudi Arabia and the United Kingdom. *Digital*, *3*(3), 200–231. DOI: 10.3390/digital3030014

Reed, A.II, Forehand, M. R., Puntoni, S., & Warlop, L. (2012). Identity-based consumer behavior. *International Journal of Research in Marketing*, *29*(4), 310–321. DOI: 10.1016/j.ijresmar.2012.08.002

Reichheld, F. F. (2003). The one number you need to grow. *Harvard Business Review*, *81*(12), 46–55. PMID: 14712543

Reivan-Ortiz, G. G., Cong, P. T., Wong, W. K., Ali, A., Thu, H. T. T., & Akhter, S. (2023). Role of geopolitical risk, currency fluctuation, and economic policy on tourist arrivals: Temporal analysis of BRICS economies. *Environmental Science and Pollution Research International*, *30*(32), 78339–78352. DOI: 10.1007/s11356-023-27736-1 PMID: 37269525

Reuters. (2024). *Greek military ship intercepts two Houthi drones in the Red Sea*. https://www.reuters.com/world/greek-military-ship-intercepts-two-houthi-drones-red-sea-2024-04-25/

Reuters. (2024, April 30). UAE-Iran joint economic commission convenes for first time in 10 years. https://www.reuters.com/world/middle-east/uae-iran-joint-economic-commission-convenes-first-time-10-years-2024-04-30/

Revilla, E., & Saenz, M. J. (2017). The impact of risk management on the frequency of supply chain disruptions: A configurational approach. *International Journal of Operations & Production Management*, *37*(5), 557–576. DOI: 10.1108/IJOPM-03-2016-0129

Ricardo, D. (1817). *On the Principles of Political Economy and Taxation*. John Murray.

Ricciardi, F., Rossignoli, C., & Zardini, A. (2021). Grand challenges and entrepreneurship: Emerging issues, research streams, and theoretical landscape. *The International Entrepreneurship and Management Journal*, *17*(4), 1673–1705. DOI: 10.1007/s11365-021-00771-5

Rickli, J. M. (2008). European small states' military policies after the Cold War: From territorial to niche strategies. *Cambridge Review of International Affairs*, *21*(3), 307–325. DOI: 10.1080/09557570802253435

Rickli, J. M., & Almezaini, K. (2016). Theories of small states' foreign and security policies and the Gulf States. In Almezaini, K., & Rickli, J. M. (Eds.), *The small Gulf states: Foreign and security policies before and after the Arab Spring* (1st ed., pp. xx–xx). Routledge.

Rizvi, A. (2020, November 24). Coronavirus: UAE was braced for Covid-19 impact due to long-term investment in services, study finds. The National. https://www.thenationalnews.com/uae/government/coronavirus-uae-was-braced-for-covid-19-impact-due-to-long-term-investment-in-services-study-finds-1.1116950

Robbins, M., Jamal, A. A., & Tessler, M. (2024). America is losing the Arab world and China is reaping the benefits. Foreign Affairs, July/August. https://www.foreignaffairs.com/united-states/america-losing-arab-world

Roberson, Q. M. (2006). Disentangling the meanings of diversity and inclusion in organizations. *Group & Organization Management*, *31*(2), 212–236. DOI: 10.1177/1059601104273064

Roberts, A. (2015). The Political Economy of "Transnational Business Feminism.". *International Feminist Journal of Politics*, *17*(2), 209–231. DOI: 10.1080/14616742.2013.849968

Robinson, K., & Merrow, W. (2020, December 3). The Arab Spring at ten years: What's the legacy of the uprisings? Council on Foreign Relations. https://www.cfr.org/article/arab-spring-ten-years-whats-legacy-uprisings

Robinson, K., & Merrow, W. (2024, April 15). Iran's regional armed network? Council on Foreign Relations. https://www.cfr.org/article/irans-regional-armed-network

Rodie, A. R., & Martin, C. L. (2001). Competing in the service sector: The entrepreneurial challenge. *International Journal of Entrepreneurial Behaviour & Research*, *7*(1), 5–21. DOI: 10.1108/13552550110385718

Rodríguez-Ramírez, A., Zapata-Domínguez, Á., & Ramírez-Plazas, E. (2022). Theoretical analysis of the social entrepreneur's mode of being. *Journal of Social Entrepreneurship*, *15*(3), 1183–1205. DOI: 10.1080/19420676.2022.2128393

Rojas-Romagosa, H. (2024). Medium-term Macroeconomic Effects of Russia's War in Ukraine and How it Affects Energy Security and Global Emission Targets. *IMF Working Paper*, *2024*(039), 1. DOI: 10.5089/9798400264269.001

Rokicki, T., Bórawski, P., & Bełdycka-Bórawska, A. (2023). Disruptions in the COVID-19 Pandemic in the Supply Chains of the Automotive Industry as Crucial for the Polish Economy. *Sustainability (Basel)*, *16*(1), 269. DOI: 10.3390/su16010269

Rosand, E. (2020, August). Preparing the Global Counterterrorism Forum for the next decade (Special Report No. 476). United States Institute of Peace. https://www.usip.org/sites/default/files/2020-08/20200817-sr_476-preparing_the_global_counterterrorism_forum_for_the_next_decade-s.pdf

Roscoe, S., Aktas, E., Petersen, K. J., Skipworth, H. D., Handfield, R. B., & Habib, F. (2022). Redesigning global supply chains during compounding geopolitical disruptions: The role of supply chain logics. *International Journal of Operations & Production Management*, *42*(9), 1407–1434. DOI: 10.1108/IJOPM-12-2021-0777

Rosenberg, M. (2024). Geopolitics and Business Strategy The Palgrave Handbook of Contemporary Geopolitics. In Cope, Z. (Ed.), (pp. 1037–1054). Springer Nature Switzerland., DOI: 10.1007/978-3-031-47227-5_52

Rumley, G. (2022, February 15). Unpacking the UAE F-35 negotiations (PolicyWatch 3578). The Washington Institute for Near East Policy. https://www.washingtoninstitute.org/policy-analysis/unpacking-uae-f-35-negotiations

Sahay, M., & Kumar, K. (2014). Enhancing the corporate performance through system dynamics modelling. *Corporate Ownership & Control, 167.*

Sahni, R., & Kalyan Shankar, V. (2012). Girls' higher education in India on the road to inclusiveness: On track but heading where? *Higher Education*, *63*(2), 237–256. DOI: 10.1007/s10734-011-9436-9

Sakketa, T. (2023). *Urbanisation and social cohesion: Theory and empirical evidence from Africa* (IDOS Discussion Paper 16/2023). Bonn: German Institute of Development and Sustainability (IDOS). https://doi.org/DOI: 10.23661/idp16.2023

Sakthivel, R., Rajendran, C., & Anantharaman, R. N. (2005). TQM implementation and students' satisfaction of academic performance. *The TQM Magazine*, *17*(6), 573–589. DOI: 10.1108/09544780510627660

Salama, S. (2017, October 29). EU Parliament reaffirms support to UAE in fight against terrorism. Gulf News. https://gulfnews.com/uae/government/eu-parliament-reaffirms-support-to-uae-in-fight-against-terrorism-1.2115176

Salesforce. (2020). Salesforce's commitment to diversity and inclusion. Retrieved from https://www.salesforce.com/company/careers/diversity/

Salisbury, P. (2020, July). Risk perception and appetite in the UAE foreign and national security policy. Middle East and North Africa Program, Chatham House. https://www.chathamhouse.org/sites/default/files/2020-07-01-risk-in-uae-salisbury.pdf

Sallis, E. (2014). *Total quality management in education* (3rd ed.). Routledge. DOI: 10.4324/9780203417010

Salnikova, E., & Grunert, K. G. (2020). The role of consumption orientation in consumer food preferences in emerging markets. *Journal of Business Research, 112*, 147–159. DOI: 10.1016/j.jbusres.2020.03.006

Salvi, A., Vitolla, F., Rubino, M., Giakoumelou, A., & Raimo, N. (2020). Online information on digitalisation processes and its impact on firm value. *Journal of Business Research, 124*, 437–444. DOI: 10.1016/j.jbusres.2020.10.025

Santos, E., & Moreira, J. (2021). Social Sustainability of Water and Waste Management Companies in Portugal. *Sustainability (Basel), 14*(1), 221. DOI: 10.3390/su14010221

Saravanan, A., & Subramanian, S. R. (2016). The Participation of Amicus Curiae in Investment Treaty Arbitration. *Journal of Civil & Legal Sciences, 5*(4). https://ssrn.com/abstract=2840614

Sarkis, J., Cohen, M. J., Dewick, P., & Schröder, P. (2020). A Brave New World: Lessons from the COVID-19 Pandemic for Transitioning to Sustainable Supply and Production. *Resources, Conservation and Recycling, 159*, 104894. Advance online publication. DOI: 10.1016/j.resconrec.2020.104894 PMID: 32313383

Sarpong, S. (2021). Geopolitics of Natural Resources The Palgrave Handbook of Corporate Social Responsibility. In Crowther, D., & Seifi, S. (Eds.), (pp. 1131–1151). Springer International Publishing., DOI: 10.1007/978-3-030-42465-7_15

Sartzetaki, M., Dimitriou, D., & Karagkouni, A. (2025). Assortment of the Regional Business Ecosystem Effects Driven by New Motorway Projects, Transportation Research Procedia, Volume 82, Pages 515-529, ISSN 2352-1465, https://doi.org/ DOI: 10.1016/j.trpro.2024.12.111

Saunders, M., Lewis, P., & Thornhill, A. (2003). *Research method for business students* (3rd ed.). Prentice Hall.

Sawitri, N. N. (2023). Financial Funding for Small and Medium-sized Enterprises (SMEs). *East Asian Journal of Multidisciplinary Research, 2*(11), 4605–4614. DOI: 10.55927/eajmr.v2i11.6815

Scarr, S., Arranz, A., Saul, J., Huang, H., Chowdhury, J., & Kawoosa, V. M. (2024, February 2). Red Sea attacks: How Houthi militants in Yemen are attacking ships in one of the world's busiest maritime trade routes. Reuters. (Last updated March 8, 2024). https://www.reuters.com/graphics/ISRAEL-PALESTINIANS/SHIPPING-ARMS/lgvdnngeyvo/

Schadendorf, S. (2015). Investor-State Arbitrations and the Human Rights of the Host State's Population: An Empirical Approach to the Impact of Amicus Curiae Submissions. In Weiss, N., & Thouvenin, J.-M. (Eds.), *The Influence of Human Rights on International Law* (pp. 167–181). Springer. DOI: 10.1007/978-3-319-12021-8_12

Schein, E. H. (2010). *Organizational culture and leadership*. Jossey-Bass.

Scheu, J. (2017). Trust Building, Balancing, and Sanctioning: Three Pillars of A Systematic Approach to Human Rights in International Investment Law and Arbitration. *Georgetown Journal of International Law*, *48*, 449–504.

Schill, S. W., & Djanic, V. (2018). Wherefore Art Thou? Towards a Public Interest-Based Justification of International Investment Law. *ICSID Review - Foreign Investment Law Journal, 33*(1), 29–55. https://doi.org/DOI: 10.1093/icsidreview/six025

Schill, S. W. (2010). Crafting the International Economic Order: The Public Function of Investment Treaty Arbitration and Its Significance for the Role of the Arbitrator. *Leiden Journal of International Law*, *23*(2), 401–430. DOI: 10.1017/S0922156510000117

Schonberger, R. J. (1992). Total Quality Management Cuts a Broad Swath: Through Manufacturing and Beyond. *Organizational Dynamics*, *20*(4), 16–28. DOI: 10.1016/0090-2616(92)90072-U

Schulze, J. L., & Pupcenoks, J. (2025). Securitizing Russian-speakers in Estonia and Latvia: The Frame-Policy Nexus before and after Russia's Invasion of Ukraine. *Nationalities Papers*, •••, 1–25. DOI: 10.1017/nps.2024.97

Seale, J. (2013). *E-learning and disability in higher education: Accessibility research and practice* (2nd ed.). Routledge. DOI: 10.4324/9780203095942

Semenenko, O., Sliusarenko, M., Onofriichuk, A., Onofriichuk, V., & Remez, A. (2024). Impact of the Russian–Ukrainian War on the National Economy of Russia. *Journal of Interdisciplinary Economics*, *36*(1), 41–57. DOI: 10.1177/02601079231207489

Shao, Q., Tao, R., & Luca, M. M. (2022). The Effect of Urbanization on Health Care Expenditure: Evidence From China. *Frontiers in Public Health*, *10*, 850872. Advance online publication. DOI: 10.3389/fpubh.2022.850872 PMID: 35242736

Shea, P., Hayes, S., Vickers, J., Gozza-Cohen, M., Uzuner, S., Mehta, R., & Rangan, P. (2010). A re-examination of the Community of Inquiry framework: Social network and content analysis. *The Internet and Higher Education*, *13*(1-2), 10–21. DOI: 10.1016/j.iheduc.2009.11.002

Sheffi, Y. (2021). The New (Ab)Normal: Reshaping Business and Supply Chain Strategy Beyond COVID-19. MIT Press.

Shen, M., & Yang, M. (2024). Are Geopolitical Risks Fuelling Trade Protectionism? *Defence and Peace Economics*, *35*(8), 1120–1140. DOI: 10.1080/10242694.2024.2364320

Shishkin, A., Lhewa, P., Yang, C., Gankin, Y., Chowell, G., Norris, M., Skums, P., & Kirpich, A. (2023). Excess mortality in Ukraine during the course of COVID-19 pandemic in 2020-2021. *Scientific Reports*, *13*(1), 6917. DOI: 10.1038/s41598-023-33113-2 PMID: 37106001

Shore, L. M., Cleveland, J. N., & Sanchez, D. (2011). Inclusive workplaces: A review and model. *Human Resource Management Review*, *21*(4), 266–280. DOI: 10.1016/j.hrmr.2011.03.001

Shrivastava, P., & Kennelly, J. J. (2013). Sustainability and Place-Based enterprise. *Organization & Environment*, *26*(1), 83–101. DOI: 10.1177/1086026612475068

Sila, I., & Ebrahimpour, M. (2002). An investigation of the total quality management survey-based research published between 1989 and 2000: A literature review. *International Journal of Quality & Reliability Management*, *19*(7), 902–970. DOI: 10.1108/02656710210434801

Silva, J. D. (2025). *Trade war escalates as Trump metal tariffs take effect*. https://www.bbc.com/news/articles/cx2r3md0j84o

Simarasl, N., Tabesh, P., Munyon, T. P., & Marzban, Z. (2024). Unveiled confidence: Exploring how institutional support enhances the entrepreneurial self-efficacy and performance of female entrepreneurs in constrained contexts. *European Management Journal*, *42*(1), 33–45. DOI: 10.1016/j.emj.2022.07.003

Simpson, R. (1999). Urbanization, urban problems. In *Environmental Geology. Encyclopedia of Earth Science*. Springer. DOI: 10.1007/1-4020-4494-1_342

Sindakis, S., & Aggarwal, S. (2022). The Implications of Brexit for Small Businesses in the UK. *Small Business Management and Control of the Uncertain External Environment*, 179–196. https://doi.org/DOI: 10.1108/978-1-83909-624-220211011

Singh, S., Singh, S., & Dhir, S. (2023). The evolving relationship of entrepreneurship, technology, and innovation: A topic modeling perspective. *International Journal of Entrepreneurship and Innovation*, 14657503231179597. Advance online publication. DOI: 10.1177/14657503231179597

Sirvanci, M. B. (2004). TQM implementation: Critical issues for TQM in higher education. *The TQM Magazine, 16*(6), 382–386. DOI: 10.1108/09544780410563293

Skare, M., De Las Mercedes De Obesso, M., & Ribeiro-Navarrete, S. (2022). Digital transformation and European small and medium enterprises (SMEs): A comparative study using digital economy and society index data. *International Journal of Information Management, 68*, 102594. DOI: 10.1016/j.ijinfomgt.2022.102594

Slav, I. (2023, May 1). The 10 countries with the largest natural gas reserves. OilPrice.com. https://oilprice.com/Energy/Energy-General/The-10-Countries-With-The-Largest-Natural-Gas-Reserves.html

Smith, J. (2020). Diversity and inclusion: Practices and outcomes in major tech firms. *Journal of Business Research, 112*, 123–134. DOI: 10.1016/j.jbusres.2020.03.005

Smyth, S. (2012). NGOs and Legitimacy in International Development. *Kansas Law Review, 61*(2), 377–440. https://ssrn.com/abstract=2129399

Sniderman, P., & Levendusky, M. (2007). *An Institutional Theory of Political Choice. Oxford Handbook of Political Behaviour.* Oxford University Press.

Sohel-Uz-Zaman, A., & Anjalin, U. (2016). Implementing total quality management in education: Compatibility and challenges. *Open Journal of Social Sciences, 4*(11), 207–217. DOI: 10.4236/jss.2016.411017

Sophocleous, H., & Masouras, A. (2019). "Voters' Behaviour: What Drives Political Consumption in Cyprus? An Analysis of the Behaviour of Young Voters". In: Kavoura, A., Kefallonitis, E., and Giovanis, A., *Strategic Innovative Marketing and Tourism 2018*. Springer. Proceedings in Business and Economics. Springer, Cham.

Sophocleous, H. (2024). *Production and Consumption of Political Communication and Voting Behaviour.* Nova Science Publications., DOI: 10.52305/OJBC3507

Sophocleous, H., Anastasiadou, S., Masouras, A., & Apostolopoulos, S. (2024). (b). The Effect of Political Marketing on the Electoral Behavior of Greek Voters. In Kavoura, A., Borges-Tiago, T., & Tiago, F. (Eds.), *Strategic Innovative Marketing and Tourism. ICSIMAT 2023. Springer Proceedings in Business and Economics.* Springer., DOI: 10.1007/978-3-031-51038-0_38

Sophocleous, H., Masouras, A., & Anastasiadou, S. (2024). (a). The Impact of Political Marketing on Voting Behaviour of Cypriot Voters. *Social Sciences (Basel, Switzerland), 2024*(13), 149. DOI: 10.3390/socsci13030149

Sornarajah, M. (2010). *The International Law on Foreign Investment.* Cambridge University Press., DOI: 10.1017/CBO9780511841439

Sornarajah, M. (2015). *Resistance and Change in the International Law on Foreign Investment.* Cambridge University Press., DOI: 10.1017/CBO9781316156339

Soroka, A., Bristow, G., Naim, M., & Purvis, L. (2019). Measuring regional business resilience. *Regional Studies*, *54*(6), 838–850. DOI: 10.1080/00343404.2019.1652893

Sousa, R., & Voss, C. A. (2002). Quality management re-visited: A reflective review and agenda for future research. *Journal of Operations Management*, *20*(1), 91–109. DOI: 10.1016/S0272-6963(01)00088-2

Spence, L. J. (2016). Small Business Social Responsibility. *Business & Society*, *55*(1), 23–55. DOI: 10.1177/0007650314523256

Spiro, P. J. (2008). NGOs and Civil Society. In Hey, E., Bodansky, D., & Brunnée, J. (Eds.), *The Oxford Handbook of International Environmental Law*. Oxford University Press., DOI: 10.1093/law/9780199552153.001.0001

Spreitzer, G. M. (2008). Taking stock: A review of more than twenty years of research on empowerment at work. In Cooper, C., & Barling, J. (Eds.), *Volume one - Micro approaches* (pp. 54–72). The SAGE handbook of organizational behavior. SAGE Publications. DOI: 10.4135/9781849200448.n4

Spykman, N. J. (2007). *America's Strategy in World Politics: The United States and the Balance of Power* (1st ed.). Routledge., https://doi.org/https://doi.org/10.4324/9781315082431

Statista (2023). *Gross domestic product (GDP) of the BRICS countries from 2000 to 2028 (in billion U.S. dollars).* Available at: https://rb.gy/ow8pyu

Statista (2024). Share of women in OECD countries who are entrepreneurs in 2023. Available at: https://shorturl.at/aeK15

Steinerowska-Streb, I., Glod, G., & Steiner, A. (2022). What do we know about small and medium enterprises' survival in a post-global economic crisis context? *Local Economy*, *37*(4), 259–278. DOI: 10.1177/02690942221112042

Stephan, H. (2019). Human Rights, Role of Non-Governmental Organizations. In *Max Planck Encyclopedia of Public International Law*. Oxford University Press., DOI: 10.1093/law:epil/9780199231690/e816

Stern, R. (2024). Technology Combats Supply Chain Disruptions. *Research Technology Management*, *67*(5), 2–4. DOI: 10.1080/08956308.2024.2370224

Šteta-Ćerimović, N., & Mekic, E. (2020). The effects of Quality Management Practices and Organizational Learning on Organizational Performance: A proposed research framework. *Open Journal for Research in Economics*, *3*(1), 9–20. DOI: 10.32591/coas.ojre.0301.02009s

Sticher, V. (2024). War and peace in the age of AI. *British Journal of Politics and International Relations*, •••, 1–9. DOI: 10.1177/13691481241293066

Stickings, T. (2023, August 7). UAE tells UN of 'profound concern' over Iran's nuclear activities. The National. https://www.thenationalnews.com/world/2023/08/07/uae-tells-un-of-profound-concern-over-irans-nuclear-activities/

Stuenkel, O., & Treadwell, M. (2024). *Why Is Saudi Arabia Hedging Its BRICS Invite?*https://carnegieendowment.org/emissary/2024/11/brics-saudi-arabia-hedging-why?lang=en

Sudulich, L., & Trumm, S. (2019). *A Comparative Study of the Effects of Electoral Institutions on Campaigns*. Cambridge University Pres. DOI: 10.1017/S0007123416000570

Suez and Vivendi v Argentina ICSID Case No ARB/03/19 Decision on Liability. (2010).

Sureshchandar, G. S., Rajendran, C., & Anantharaman, R. N. (2002). The relationship between service quality and customer satisfaction – A factor-specific approach. *Journal of Services Marketing*, *16*(4), 363–379. DOI: 10.1108/08876040210433248

Swan, K., Garrison, D. R., & Richardson, J. C. (2009). A constructivist approach to online learning: The Community of Inquiry framework. In Howard, C. (Eds.), *Encyclopedia of Distance Learning* (2nd ed., pp. 352–360). IGI Global.

Tajfel, H., & Turner, J. C. (1979). An integrative theory of intergroup conflict. In Austin, W. G., & Worchel, S. (Eds.), *The social psychology of intergroup relations* (pp. 33–47). Brooks/Cole.

Talib, F., & Rahman, Z. (2010). Critical success factors of TQM in service organizations: A proposed model. *Services Marketing Quarterly*, *31*(3), 363–380. DOI: 10.1080/15332969.2010.486700

Talib, F., Rahman, Z., & Qureshi, M. N. (2011). A study of total quality management and supply chain management practices. *International Journal of Productivity and Performance Management*, *60*(3), 268–288. DOI: 10.1108/17410401111111998

Talib, F., Rahman, Z., & Qureshi, M. N. (2011). Analysis of interaction among the barriers to total quality management implementation using interpretive structural modeling approach. *Benchmarking, 18*(4), 563–587. DOI: 10.1108/14635771111147641

Talwar, A. (2022, February 17). From oil to diversification of the UAE: An economic perspective. Diplomacy and Beyond. https://diplomacybeyond.com/from-oil-to-diversification-of-the-uae-an-economic-perspective/

Tan, K. W. K. (2025). The US has been watching DeepSeek since late 2023 and still has a way to beat it, Biden's former AI advisory says. https://www.businessinsider.com/biden-ai-advisor-us-watching-deepseek-since-late-2023-2025-3?utm_

Tang, C. S. (2006). Robust strategies for mitigating supply chain disruptions. *International Journal of Logistics, 9*(1), 33–45. DOI: 10.1080/13675560500405584

Tan, K. C., Lyman, S. B., & Wisner, J. D. (2002). Supply chain management: A strategic perspective. *International Journal of Operations & Production Management, 22*(6), 614–631. DOI: 10.1108/01443570210427659

Taraza, E., Anastasiadou, S., & Masouras, A. (2023, September). *Malcolm Baldrige National Quality Award (MBNQA) Quality Tool in Education: A Systematic Literature Review*. In ECIE 2023 18th European Conference on Innovation and Entrepreneurship Vol 1. Academic Conferences and publishing limited.

Taraza, E., Anastasiadou, S., Papademetriou, C., & Masouras, A. (2024). Evaluation of quality and equality in education using the European foundation for quality management excellence model—A literature review. *Sustainability (Basel), 16*(3), 960. DOI: 10.3390/su16030960

Taraza, E., Anastasiadou, S., Seremeti, L., & Masouras, A. (2024). Environmental, Social, and Governance of Businesses and Organizations and the Role of Human Resources. In Papademetriou, C., Anastasiadou, S., Ragazou, K., Garefalakis, A., & Papalexandris, S. (Eds.), *ESG and Total Quality Management in Human Resources* (pp. 116–132). IGI Global Scientific Publishing., DOI: 10.4018/979-8-3693-2991-7.ch006

Taulbee, J. L. (2014). Lesser states and niche diplomacy. In Taulbee, J. L., Kelleher, A., & Grosvenor, P. C. (Eds.), *Norway's peace policy* (pp. xx–xx). Palgrave Macmillan.

Taylor, M. (2023). EU endeavors to secure and strengthen its supply chain. *MRS Bulletin, 48*(5), 1–6. Advance online publication. DOI: 10.1557/s43577-023-00526-3 PMID: 37361858

Teasdale, S., Bellazzecca, E., De Bruin, A., & Roy, M. J. (2022). The (R)evolution of the Social Entrepreneurship Concept: A Critical Historical Review. *Nonprofit and Voluntary Sector Quarterly, 52*(1, suppl), 212S–240S. DOI: 10.1177/08997640221130691

Terziovski, M. (2006). Quality management practices and their relationship with customer satisfaction and productivity improvement. *Management Research News, 29*(7), 414–424. DOI: 10.1108/01409170610690871

The Executive Office of Anti-Money Laundering and Counter-Terrorism Financing. (2024). Enhancing the United Arab Emirates' response to fighting money laundering and countering terrorism financing activities. Retrieved from https://amlctf.gov.ae/en

The Gurdian. (2019). US government to pay farmers hurt by China trade war $16bn. https://www.theguardian.com/business/2019/jul/26/us-government-to-pay-farmers-hurt-by-china-trade-war-16bn

Tijssen, R., van de Klippe, W., & Yegros, A. (2020). Localization, regionalization and globalization of university-business research co-operation in the United Kingdom. *Papers in Regional Science, 99*(5), 1215–1237. DOI: 10.1111/pirs.12531

Tol, R. S. J. (2018). The Economic Impacts of Climate Change. *Review of Environmental Economics and Policy, 12*(1), 4–25. DOI: 10.1093/reep/rex027

Tomuschat, C. (2009). The European Court of Human Rights and Investment Protection. In Binder, C., Kriebaum, U., Reinisch, A., & Wittich, S. (Eds.), *International Investment Law for the 21st Century: Essays in Honour of Christoph Schreuer* (pp. 636–656). Oxford University Press. DOI: 10.1093/acprof:oso/9780199571345.003.0034

Towfighi, J. (2024). Manufacturing in Mexico is having its moment. The US is buying in — and so is China. https://edition.cnn.com/2024/04/28/business/us-china-mexico-manufacturing-nearshoring-hnk-intl/index.html

Trakman, L. E., & Ranieri, N. W. (2013). Foreign Direct Investment: A Historical Perspective. In Trakman, L. E., & Ranieri, N. W. (Eds.), *Regionalism in International Investment Law* (pp. 14–26). Oxford University Press., DOI: 10.1093/acprof:oso/9780195389005.003.0002

Trowler, V. (2010). *Student engagement literature review*. The Higher Education Academy.

Tuathail, G. Ó. (1996). *Critical Geopolitics The Politics of Writing Global Space*. Routledge.

Tyler, B. (2025, June). Parker, Accepting Appreciation: Partner Perceptions and Major Non-NATO Ally Designations. *Journal of Global Security Studies, 10*(2), ogae047. Advance online publication. DOI: 10.1093/jogss/ogae047

U.S. Department of Commerce. (2023). Biden-Harris Administration Launches First CHIPS for America Funding Opportunity. https://www.commerce.gov/news/press-releases/2023/02/biden-harris-administration-launches-first-chips-america-funding

U.S. Department of State. (2021). United Arab Emirates. In Country reports on terrorism 2021. https://www.state.gov/reports/country-reports-on-terrorism-2021/united-arab-emirates

U.S. Department of State. (2024, June 13). United Arab Emirates. In Country reports on terrorism 2022. https://www.state.gov/reports/country-reports-on-terrorism-2022/uae

U.S. Energy Information Administration. (2023, November 21). The Strait of Hormuz is the world's most important oil transit chokepoint. https://www.eia.gov/todayinenergy/detail.php?id=61002

Ubell, R. (Ed.). (2010). *Virtual teamwork: Mastering the art and practice of online learning and corporate collaboration*. John Wiley & Sons. DOI: 10.1002/9780470615782

Underwood, E., & Paul, T. (2025, January 22). Rising India. *Oxford Research Encyclopedia of Politics.* Retrieved 6 Apr. 2025, from https://oxfordre.com/politics/view/10.1093/acrefore/9780190228637.001.0001/acrefore-9780190228637-e-2163

United Arab Emirates Government Portal. (2023). Federal Decree Law No. 34 of 2023 concerning combating discrimination, hatred and extremism. [PDF file]. https://file:///C:/Users/apadilla/Downloads/Federal%20Decree%20Law%20No%2034%20of%202023%20concerning%20combating%20discrimination%20hatred%20and%20extremism%20(1).pdf *(Note: This link appears to be a local file path and not a public URL. Replace with an accessible link if available.)*

United Arab Emirates Government Portal. (2024, June 13). Centres for countering extremism. https://u.ae/en/about-the-uae/culture/tolerance/centers-for-countering-extremism

United Arab Emirates Government. (n.d.). UAE Centennial Plan 2071. https://uaecabinet.ae/en/uae-centennial-plan-2071

United Arab Emirates Ministry of Cabinet Affairs. (2024). UAE Centennial Plan 2071. https://uaecabinet.ae/en/uae-centennial-plan-2071

United Arab Emirates Ministry of Tolerance and Coexistence. (2024, June 13). Festival of Human Fraternity. https://www.tolerance.gov.ae/contributing-to-international-efforts-to-promote-tolerance/fhf

United Arab Emirates. (2014). Federal Law No. (7) of 2014 on combatting terrorism. https://www.adgm.com/documents/financial-crime-prevention-unit/aml-tab/federal-law-no-7-of-2014-on-combatting-terrorism-offences.pdf

United Nations Development Programme. (2024). Human Development Index. https://hdr.undp.org/data-center/human-development-index#/indicies/HDI

United Nations Treaty Collection. (1993). Agreement on the delimitation of boundaries (No. 30250). https://treaties.un.org/doc/publication/unts/volume%201733/i-30250.pdf

United Nations. (2011). Guiding Principles on Business and Human Rights: Implementing the United Nations "Protect, Respect and Remedy" Framework A/HRC/8/5.

Upadhyay, N., Upadhyay, S., & Dwivedi, Y. K. (2021). Theorizing artificial intelligence acceptance and digital entrepreneurship model. *International Journal of Entrepreneurial Behaviour & Research*, *28*(5), 1138–1166. DOI: 10.1108/IJEBR-01-2021-0052

Urbaser SA and Consorcio de Aguas Bilbao Bizkaia, Bilbao Biskaia Ur Partzuergoa v Argentina ICSID Case No ARB/07/26 Award. (2016). **Secondary Sources**

US-UAE Business Council. (2019, March). An enduring partnership: The US-UAE defense and security relationship. https://usuaebusiness.org/wp-content/uploads/2019/03/Defense-Report-Final-March-2019.pdf

Vadi, V. (2018). *Proportionality, Reasonableness and Standards of Review in International Investment Law and Arbitration*. Edward Elgar Publishing. DOI: 10.4337/9781785368585

Valdevelde, K. (2009). A Brief History of International Investment Agreements. In Sauvant, K. P., & Sachs, L. E. (Eds.), *The Effect of Treaties on Foreign Direct Investment: Bilateral Investment Treaties, Double Taxation Treaties and Investment Flows* (pp. 3–36). Oxford University Press. DOI: 10.1093/acprof:oso/9780195388534.003.0001

Van Boeckel, T. P., Brower, C., Gilbert, M., Grenfell, B. T., Levin, S. A., Robinson, T. P., Teillant, A., ... (2015) Global trends in antimicrobial use in food animals. Volume(112), 5649-5654. Proceedings of the National Academy of Sciences. DOI: 10.1073/pnas.1503141112 van Eck, N. J., & Waltman, L. (2010). Software survey: VOSviewer, a computer program for bibliometric mapping. *Scientometrics*, *84*(2), 523–538. DOI: 10.1007/s11192-009-0146-3 PMID: 20585380

Van Herpen, E., Pieters, R., & Zeelenberg, M. (2009). When demand accelerates demand: Trailing the bandwagon. *Journal of Consumer Psychology*, *19*(3), 302–331. DOI: 10.1016/j.jcps.2009.01.001

Van Hoek, R. (2020). Research opportunities for a more resilient post-COVID-19 supply chain – closing the gap between research findings and industry practice. International Journal of Operations & Production Management. ahead-of-print. https://doi.org..DOI: 10.1108/IJOPM-03-2020-0165

Van Knippenberg, D., Haslam, S. A., & Platow, M. J. (2004). Diversity and leadership in organizations: An overview. *European Journal of Social Psychology*, *34*(4), 345–359. DOI: 10.1002/ejsp.215

Vantilborgh, T., Hofmans, J., & Judge, T. A. (2018). The time has come to study dynamics at work. *Journal of Organizational Behavior*, *39*(9), 1045–1049. https://www.jstor.org/stable/26610780. DOI: 10.1002/job.2327

Versluysen, E. (1999). *Defying the odds: Banking for the poor*. Kumarian Press West Hartford.

Vettriselvan, R. (2025). Harnessing Innovation and Digital Marketing in the Era of Industry 5.0: Resilient Healthcare SMEs. In Olubiyi, T., Suppiah, S., & Chidoko, C. (Eds.), *The Future of Small Business in Industry 5.0* (pp. 163–186). IGI Global Scientific Publishing., DOI: 10.4018/979-8-3693-7362-0.ch007

Vettriselvan, R., Deepa, R., Gautam, R., Suresh, N. V., & Cathrine, S. (2025). Bridging Academia and Industry Through Technology and Entrepreneurial Innovation: Enhancing Supply Chain Efficiency. In Mahalle, P. (Ed.), *Bridging Academia and Industry Through Cloud Integration in Education* (pp. 145–174). IGI Global Scientific Publishing., DOI: 10.4018/979-8-3693-6705-6.ch006

Vicuña, F. O. (2025). "Chapter 15 International Law and World Order: In Search of Rebalance". In International Law in Search of Rebalance. Leiden, The Netherlands: Brill | Nijhoff. DOI: 10.1163/9789004721388_016

Vihma, A., & Wigell, M. (2016). Unclear and present danger: Russia's geoeconomics and the Nord Stream II pipeline. *Global Affairs*, *2*(4), 377–388. DOI: 10.1080/23340460.2016.1251073

Viswanathan, R., & Telukdarie, A. (2021). A systems dynamics approach to SME digitalization. *Procedia Computer Science*, *180*, 816–824. DOI: 10.1016/j.procs.2021.01.331

Vlados, C., & Chatzinikolaou, D. (2024). Russo-Ukrainian War and the emerging new globalization: a critical review of relevant research. *The Japanese Political Economy*, 1–23. https://doi.org/DOI: 10.1080/2329194X.2024.2309594

Vogel, D. (2007). *The market for virtue: The potential and limits of corporate social responsibility*. Brookings Institution Press.

Vogue Arabia. (2024, July 15). 10 of HH Sheikh Mohammed bin Rashid's wisest quotes to live by. https://en.vogue.me/culture/sheikh-mohammed-bin-rashid-wisest-quotes/

Walder, A. G. (2006, November). Ambiguity and Choice in Political Movements: The Origins of Beijing Red Guard Factionalism. *American Journal of Sociology*, *112*(3), 710–750. DOI: 10.1086/507854

Walterskirchen, J., Mangott, G., & Wend, C. (2022). Sanction dynamics in the cases of North Korea, Iran, and Russia. *Objectives, Measures and Effect*. Springer.

Walt, S. M. (1987). *The origins of alliances*. Cornell University Press.

Waltz, K. N. (1979). *Theory of international politics*. Addison-Wesley.

Waltz, K. N. (1979). *Theory of International Politics*. Addison-Wesley.

Wang, F., Casalino, L. P., & Khullar, D. (2017). The role of predictive analytics in health care: A review of current literature and future directions. *Health Affairs*, *36*(3), 421–428. DOI: 10.1377/hlthaff.2016.1103

Wang, G., Niu, Y., Mansor, Z. D., Leong, Y. C., & Yan, Z. (2024). Unlocking digital potential: Exploring the drivers of employee dynamic capability on employee digital performance in Chinese SMEs-moderation effect of competitive climate. *Heliyon*, *10*(4), e25583. DOI: 10.1016/j.heliyon.2024.e25583 PMID: 38379974

Wang, Y., & Lo, H.-P. (2003). Customer-focused performance and the dynamic model for competence building and leveraging: A resource-based view. *Journal of Management Development*, *22*(6), 483–526. DOI: 10.1108/02621710310478486

Wang, Z., & Sun, Z. (2020). From Globalization to Regionalization: The United States, China, and the Post-Covid-19 World Economic Order. *Journal of Chinese Political Science*, *26*(1), 69–87. DOI: 10.1007/s11366-020-09706-3 PMID: 33144822

Weeks, J. (2008). Autocratic Audience Costs: Regime Type and Signaling Resolve. Volume(62). *International Organization*, *62*(1). Advance online publication. DOI: 10.1017/S0020818308080028

Wegner, B. (1990). The road to defeat: The German campaigns in Russia 1941–43. *The Journal of Strategic Studies*, *13*(1), 105–127. DOI: 10.1080/01402399008437403

Weible, C. M., Nohrstedt, D., Cairney, P., Carter, D., Crow, D. A., Durnová, A., & Heikkila, T.. (2020). COVID-19 and the policy sciences: Initial reactions and perspectives. Volume(53), 225-241. *Policy Sciences*. Advance online publication. DOI: 10.1007/s11077-020-09381-4 PMID: 32313308

Weiss, T., Eberhart, R., Lounsbury, M., Nelson, A., Rindova, V., Meyer, J., Bromley, P., Atkins, R., Ruebottom, T., Jennings, J., Jennings, D., Toubiana, M., Shantz, A. S., Khorasani, N., Wadhwani, D., Tucker, H., Kirsch, D., Goldfarb, B., Aldrich, H., & Aldrich, D. (2023). The Social Effects of Entrepreneurship on Society and Some Potential Remedies: Four Provocations. *Journal of Management Inquiry*, *32*(4), 251–277. DOI: 10.1177/10564926231181555

Wendt, A. (1999). *Social Theory of International Politics*. Cambridge University Press. DOI: 10.1017/CBO9780511612183

Wieland, A., & Durach, C. (2021). Two perspectives on supply chain resilience. *Journal of Business Logistics*, *42*(3), 315–322. Advance online publication. DOI: 10.1111/jbl.12271

Wiik, A. (2018). *Amicus Curiae Before International Courts and Tribunals*. Nomos., DOI: 10.5771/9783845275925

Woodward, B. K. (2011). The Role of International NGOs: An Introduction. *Willamette Journal of International Law and Dispute Resolution*, 19(2), 203–231. https://www.jstor.org/stable/26211687

World Association of Non-Governmental Organizations. (2021). *Overview of NGOs—NGO Handbook*. https://www.wangohandbook.org//index.php?title=NGO_Overview

World Bank. (1995). *Working with NGOs A Practical Guide to Operational Collaboration between the World Bank and Non-Governmental Organizations*. Operational Policy Department.

World Bank. (2022). GDP (current US$) - United Arab Emirates. https://data.worldbank.org/indicator/NY.GDP.MKTP.CD?locations=AE

World Bank. (2024). *Growth in the Middle East and North Africa: MENA upadate*. https://www.worldbank.org/en/region/mena/publication/middle-east-and-north-africa-economic-update

World Economic Forum. (2022). *Global Gender Gap Report 2022*. https://www3.weforum.org/docs/WEF_GGGR_2022.pdf

World Population Review. (2024). Oil reserves by country 2024. https://worldpopulationreview.com/country-rankings/oil-reserves-by-country

Xanthopoulou, P. (2020). From e-government to public value creation. [IJSR]. *International Journal of Scientific Research*, *9*(3), 927–933. https://www.researchgate.net/profile/Panagiota_Xanthopoulou4/publication/341930864_From_e-Government_to_Public_Value_Creation/links/638361a9554def6193793485/From-e-Government-to-Public-Value-Creation.pdf

Xanthopoulou, P., Antoniadis, I., & Avlogiaris, G. (2023). Unveiling the drivers of digital governance adoption in public administration. *Problems and Perspectives in Management*, *21*(4), 454–467. DOI: 10.21511/ppm.21(4).2023.35

Xanthopoulou, P., Antoniadis, I., & Triantari, S. (2022, July). Managing public sector in the digital reform era: Organizational factors and their impact on the digital transformation at the Greek public administration. In *International Conference on Applied Economics* (pp. 947-962). Cham: Springer International Publishing. DOI: 10.1007/978-3-031-22749-3_59

Yadlin, A. (2022, May). The attack on Abu Dhabi: Dilemmas, threats, and opportunities. The Jerusalem Strategic Review. https://jstribune.com/yadlin-the-attack-on-abu-dhabi/

Yaghil, A., & Schmidt, G. (Eds.). (2022). *EN Funding Toolkit*. Euclid Network. https://euclidnetwork.eu/wp-content/uploads/2022/12/eu-funding-toolkit_final_2022.pdf

Yáñez-Valdés, C., & Guerrero, M. (2023). Assessing the organizational and ecosystem factors driving the impact of transformative FinTech platforms in emerging economies. *International Journal of Information Management*, *73*, 102689. DOI: 10.1016/j.ijinfomgt.2023.102689

Yaya, L. H. P., Marimon, F., & Casadesus, M. (2011). Customer's loyalty and perception of ISO 9001 in online banking. *Industrial Management & Data Systems*, *111*(8), 1194–1213. DOI: 10.1108/02635571111170767

Younis, H., Alsharairi, M., Younes, H., & Sundarakani, B. (2023). The impact of COVID-19 on supply chains: Systematic review and future research directions. *Operations Research*, *23*(3), 48. DOI: 10.1007/s12351-023-00790-w

Zahidi, S., & Ibarra, H. (2010). *The Corporate Gender Gap Report 2010*. https://alba.acg.edu/media/2492/coporategendergap_report.pdf

Zairi, M. (1991). *Total quality management for engineers*. Woodhead Publishing.

Zairi, M. (1995). Total quality management: What is it really? Definition, core concepts and impact. *The TQM Magazine*, *7*(3), 8–15.

Zehir, S., & Zehir, C. (2023). Effects of Total Quality Management Practices on Financial and Operational Performance of Hospitals. *Sustainability (Basel)*, *15*(21), 15430. Advance online publication. DOI: 10.3390/su152115430

Zeithaml, V. A., Bitner, M. J., & Gremler, D. D. (2013). *Services marketing: Integrating customer focus across the firm* (6th ed.). McGraw-Hill Education.

Zhang, K. H. (2023). US-China economic links and technological decoupling. *Chinese Economy*, *56*(5), 353–365. DOI: 10.1080/10971475.2023.2173399

Zhang, S. (2023). The Impact of Changes in Geopolitical Patterns on Global Economy and Trade. *Social Sciences in Business and Policy Analysis*, *1*(1). Advance online publication. DOI: 10.62220/j.ssbpa.2023.01.007

Zhang, Z., Zhao, M., Zhang, Y., & Feng, Y. (2023). How does urbanization affect public health? New evidence from 175 countries worldwide. *Frontiers in Public Health*, *10*, 1096964. DOI: 10.3389/fpubh.2022.1096964 PMID: 36684862

Zhao, L., Yang, M. M., Wang, Z., & Michelson, G. (2023). Trends in the Dynamic Evolution of Corporate Social Responsibility and Leadership: A Literature Review and Bibliometric Analysis. *Journal of Business Ethics*, *182*(1), 135–157. DOI: 10.1007/s10551-022-05035-y

Zhao, N., Hong, J., & Lau, K. H. (2023). Impact of supply chain digitalization on supply chain resilience and performance: A multi-mediation model. *International Journal of Production Economics*, *259*, 108817. DOI: 10.1016/j.ijpe.2023.108817 PMID: 36852136

Zhao, Z. Y., Hao, Y. X., Chang, R. D., & Wang, Q. C. (2023). Assessing the vulnerability of energy supply chains: Influencing factors and countermeasures. *Sustainable Energy Technologies and Assessments*, *56*, 103018. DOI: 10.1016/j.seta.2023.103018

Zhiyang, L., Chenfang, Z., & Bin, L. (2020). Digital Social Entrepreneurship: Theoretical Framework and Research Outlook. *Waiguo Jingji Yu Guanli*, *42*(04), 3–18. DOI: 10.16538/j.cnki.fem.20200228.402

Zhu, J., Yan, W., Zhu, L., & Liu, J. (2021). COVID-19 pandemic in BRICS countries and its association with socio-economic and demographic characteristics, health vulnerability, resources, and policy response. *Infectious Diseases of Poverty*, *10*(1), 97. DOI: 10.1186/s40249-021-00881-w PMID: 34238368

Ziadah, R. (2021, October 27). Saudi-UAE interventions: Arms, aid and counter-revolution. Transnational Institute. https://www.tni.org/en/article/saudi-uae-interventions

Zikmund, W. G. (1997). *Exploring Marketing Research* (6th ed.). The Dryden Press.

About The Contributors

Marios Panagiotis Efthymiopoulos. is Associate Professor of International Security and Strategy. Head of Department of History, Politics and International Studies, Neapolis University Pafos. CEO of Strategy International (SI). Former Dean and now advisory board member of the college of Security and Global Studies at the American University in the Emirates. Former professional positions include, the Emirates Center for Strategic Studies and Research (ECSSR) Abu Dhabi UAE,Member of the Geostrategic Council of Cyprus, Harriman Institute,Columbia University, New York,Johns Hopkins University Center for Transatlantic Relations,George Washington University Business School, the Woodrow Wilson Center for International Scholars, Washington DC USA. Awarded his PhD from the University of Crete, as Alexander S. Onassis Scholar. Obtained NATO's Defense College Diploma,Rome Italy, Masters in Advanced International Studies, Diplomatic Academy of Vienna Austria, BA (Hons) International Relations and Politics,University of Lincoln UK.

Andreas Masouras is Associate Professor at Neapolis University Pafos in the fields of Marketing and Communication. He holds a PhD (Honors) from the Department of Political Science and International Relations of the University of the Peloponnese. The title of his doctoral dissertation is "Entrepreneurship and Competitiveness through the lens of the Institutional Analysis: The Case of Cyprus". His doctoral thesis is posted in the National Archive of Doctoral Theses. Also, he holds an MPhil from Brighton University (Media Management). He is pursuing his postdoctoral research at the University of Western Macedonia in the field of entrepreneurship. He studied at the Department of Communication and Mass Media of the National and Kapodistrian University of Athens (BA). He then continued his postgraduate studies at the University of South Wales, where he received a MSc in Globalisation, Media and Culture. Also, he holds a Postgraduate Certificate (PgCert) in Research Methodologies from Brighton University and Postgraduate

Diploma (PgDip) in Management from the Northern Council for Further Education (NCFE). He holds a degree in Law (LLB) with Honors. Member of the Cyprus Bar Association. He is a founding member and Head of the Research Institute of Applied Communication in Cyprus. Andreas has been a Visiting Research Fellow at Antwerp University in Belgium, at the Central European University in Hungary and at Fordham University, NY. He is a visiting researcher at several other universities. Main researcher of the Centre of International & European Political Economy & Governance – CIEPEG of the University of Peloponnese. Member of the Scientific Council, as an external visitor, of the Centre of the Study of Media and Culture in Small Nations of the University of South Wales. He is a distance tutor of Webster University (Missouri, USA) and the Hellenic Open University. Dr Masouras actively writes a series of scientific articles while he is constantly involved in remarkable international conferences where he presents his research. His latest book, "Entrepreneurship in Small and Medium-Sized Enterprises," is released by the American publishing house Nova (Scopus indexed).

***

R. Vettriselvan, an Associate Professor, AMET University, specialized in HRM and Marketing. He is acting as Mentor, Saraswathi Institute of Medical Sciences, Hapur. He served as Review Board member, National Council for Higher Education, Malawi, Head of the Department, School of Commerce and Management Studies, St. Eugene University, Zambia, and Director, Research and Publication, St. John the Baptist University, Malawi. He has published 25 books and 94 articles in peer reviewed journals and edited book chapters. Under his guidance two have completed and five are pursuing their PhD.

Alexandros Sahinidis is a professor of Management and Entrepreneurship at University of West Attica, Greece. He received his Doctoral Degree from University of Pireaus (Greece). His research interests include Motivation, Leadership, Organizational Change, Organizational Culture, Entrepreneurship etc. He published in international and local refereed journals and presented his work in a number of conferences.

Ioannis Antoniadis has received an MSc Degree in Marketing from Reading University, UK and a PhD Degree in Corporate Governance from Aristotle University of Thessaloniki, Greece. His research interests focus on social media marketing, governance, blockchain and strategy. He has participated in international conferences and has published various papers in international journals and book chapters, including the International Journal of Internet Marketing and Advertising,

International Journal of Retail & Distribution Management and the International Journal of Technology Marketing. He is currently is a Professor in the Department of Management Science and Technology of the University of Western Macedonia in the field of Corporate Governance and Marketing. Dr. Antoniadis is also the Director of the MSc. in e-Business and Digital Marketing, and the Head of the Department.

Panagiota Chatzimichailidou is a researcher in Neapolis University Pafos. She holds a Ph.D. in Adult Education and Economic Development. She has worked as Adjunct Teaching Staff and as Educator for Neapolis University Pafos and the Agricultural University of Athens. She is an accredited Trainer for Adults from the National Organization for the Certification of Qualifications & Vocational Guidance (EOPPEP). Her research interests include sustainable economic development, ESG Standards and adult education.

Shilpee A Dasgupta teaches Business Communication at the Indian Institute of Management Ranchi. She had won two gold medals in her graduation for standing first in order of merit in the university. She earned her Ph. D. in Communication Studies from IIT Kharagpur. Her research publications in peer-reviewed international journals have been highly cited in national and international repute manuscripts. A communication consultant, Dr Dasgupta, has been involved in various training programmes.

Georgios A. Deirmentzoglou is an Assistant Professor in International Entrepreneurship, Technology, and Sustainable Development at Neapolis University Pafos (Cyprus). He holds a PhD in Business Administration from the University of Piraeus, where he also earned an MBA with a specialization in Total Quality Management (MBA-TQM) and a Bachelor's degree in Industrial Management and Technology. Additionally, he has pursued studies in film and music production. Before joining Neapolis University Pafos, Georgios served as an Adjunct Lecturer and Academic Fellow at the University of Piraeus and other colleges in Greece in partnership with UK and French universities. His research interests focus on entrepreneurship, technological innovation, human-computer interaction, sustainable development, and tourism. His research has been published in high-impact international peer-reviewed journals and presented at more than 30 international peer-reviewed conferences. Georgios has extensive experience as a Principal Investigator and Researcher in EU-funded projects, primarily focusing on digital transformation and sustainable development. Beyond academia, he has practical expertise in e-commerce, including the creation and management of online stores, and is the co-founder of a consulting firm specializing in information systems and software.

Josef Demergis, (BA, MA, MSc, MRes, PhD) is an Adjunct Professor at the Department of History, Politics and International Studies, Neapolis University Pafos. He is the Research & Analysis Director of Strategy International (SI) Ltd. He has lectured extensively in various academic environments about international relations, strategic studies, security, hybrid warfare, information operations and the use of social media to further political aims. He also specializes in the use of Structural Equation Modelling to create behavioral models, useful for information operations, behavioral analysis of states and other political actors and of the efficacy of changes in field strategy. He has published various books and articles.

Dimitrios Dimitriou educational background includes Doctorate in econometric modelling for quantitative demand forecasting, MSc in Airport Planning and Management, MSc in Infrastructures Environmental Management, and Diploma (equivalent to 4 years BA and 1-year MSc) in Civil Engineering (transportation sector). His specialization deals with the subjects of large investment appraisal, project financing, business planning, project management, transport and supply chain economics, corporate management performance, decision making for organizations/ enterprises, investment economic impact assessment and Sustainable planning, management and economics for large projects. His direction focused on sector of energy, transport, logistics and supply chain.

Eleni Gavriil is a Lecturer in International Economic Law and Human Rights at the Department of History, Politics and International Studies of the Neapolis University Pafos. She is an Attorney-at-Law with the Athens Bar Association. Her research interests include the fields of International Economic Law and European Law with an emphasis on foreign direct investments, human rights and inclusivity. She is the director of the research institute NUP Human Rights Observatory.

Agustin Maciel-Padilla is an Independent Researcher with extensive experience both in academia and public service in the field of security studies and intelligence. Dr. Agustin holds a B.A. in International Relations from El Colegio de Mexico, an M.A. in National Security Studies from the Department of Government, Georgetown University, and a Ph.D in War Studies from King's College London. Dr. Agustin research interests are related to the development and evolution of the concept of national security, trans-border issues, border security, and intelligence. He is a lecturer of security, intelligence, and security in U.S.-Mexican Relations at diploma courses in several universities in Mexico, and has participated in a wide variety of conferences as well as a guest speaker at both civilian and military institutions. He has written and contributed to a number of articles and books, and his most recent publication is Understanding Mexico's Security Conundrum by Routledge, Taylor &Francis Group, which was released in 2021.

Shubh Majumdarr is currently pursuing a doctoral degree in General Management at the Indian Institute of Management in Ranchi, India. He earned his B. Tech in Electronics and Communication with a Distinction grade from Birla Vishvakarma Mahavidyalaya, India.

Prashant Maurya is an assistant professor of English and teaches literature and communication courses at the Indian Institute of Management Ranchi. His academic interests include Business Communication, Popular Media and Culture, Postcolonial Literature, and Cultural Studies.

Deepa Rajesh, Vice President (Academics) and Executive Director of AMET Business School, AMET University, Chennai has rich academic, research and administrative experience. She specialized in Human Resources and System and completed her Doctorate in University of Madras, Chennai. She also serve as a Director, Human Resource Development Centre, AMET University and Nodal officer for AMET University Academic and Administrative Development Centre (AADC), Association of Indian University.

Meena G, is a Ph.D. Candidate in the Faculty of Management of the SRM Institute of Science and Technology. She has a BBA degree in Business Administration (2007) an MBA degree in Human Resources (2009) and a D-tech in Teaching Professional Courses (2017). Her research involves the Intellectual innovation capital and technology adaptation of employees. She has work experience of 9 years as a Team leader in E-publishing at Scientific Publishing Services (P) Ltd. She has worked on the 2018-2022 teaching experiences at Seventh-Day Adventists Matriculation Higher Secondary School. She proudly presents her research at prestigious institutions, including IIM Nagpur and the Indian Academic Researchers Association, where she received the Best Researcher Award in 2023. Star Global Excellence Awards She was Awarded for Achievements in Innovation Research in 2023. In the 2024 Asia Research Award for Certificate of Achievements in International Young Research Award, Science International publishing house she received the Best Young Intellectual Property Rights (IPR) holder Award. In the Journal publication of the Scopus index journals, ABDC, B& C Category journals were also published. Her research contributions extend to Commerce, Management & Economics, UGC care journals and Emerald book chapters, earning her recognition for innovative research at the Hailing from Chennai, Tamil Nādu, India, she stands as a promising scholar in the field.

Palanivel Rathinasabapathi Velmurugan is associated with BSBI, Berlin, as a Professor in the Human Resource Management & Finance Stream. Prior to joining BSBI, he held the designation of "Head" of the Faculty of Management in Uzbekistan, Central Asia, and Dean of Arts in Malawi, Central Africa. Additionally, he has been associated (currently) with various universities in the United States, United Kingdom, Italy, Cyprus, Switzerland, and various engineering colleges in India. He earned his Ph.D. in Management from India. Besides this, he holds an MBA and BE in Chemical Engineering from India. He has also completed six NPTEL Certificate Programs conducted by various IITs in India. He brings with him 16 years of rich experience in teaching and research. Furthermore, he has a keen interest in the case method of teaching and research. He is an academic out of passion and takes a keen interest in guiding Ph.D. students. He has supervised three Ph.D. research scholars from Zambia. Currently, he is supervising 12 more PhD/DBA Scholars across the globe. Dr. Palanivel has actively involved himself in research and publications, with over 50 research papers in international and national journals and conferences. He has also authored two textbooks in Strategic Management and TQM. Dr. Palanivel has been invited as an expert in SPSS and Research Methodology workshops and conferences around the globe. He has participated in conferences and faculty development programs at leading B-schools in India and abroad. He also holds an active membership in ISTE.

Anastasia Athanasoula-Reppa is Professor of Educational Management and Organizational Behavior at Neapolis University Pafos (NUP) in Cyprus.She is the depute head of the departmetn of Economics and Bussines and coordinator of the direction Educational Administration in Master Programme Public Administration. She also is the head of the Distance Learning Unit (DLU) NUP. She holds a PhD and a Master's degree from Panteion University (1992 and 1980 respectively), as well as three basic degrees from the same university: Political Science (1977), Public Administration (1979) and Sociology (1986). She also holds a Master's Degree in Open and Distance Education from the Hellenic Open University (2001) and a Degree from the School of Education SELETE / now ASPETE (1979), in which she later served as a professor and from 1-9-02 until 21/05/04 she was a member of the Administrative Committee of ASPETE, and from 6-2-09 until 2-7-2010 (date of her retirement) President of the Department of Education. She was also responsible for ASPETE's Branches in Crete, Ioannina, Sapes/Komotini, and North Aegean (Mytilene). Since 2005 and for regular periods he has offered teaching and research work at the Department of Education Sciences of the University of Cyprus as a Visiting Professor, as well as at other universities in Greece and abroad (Roehampton, England and Donou Austria) as a collaborator in Postgraduate Programs of Educational Administration. She has 14 years of experience in distance education as an Collaborating Teaching Staff of the Hellenic Open University and 6 years in the Open University of Cyprus. She is a certified trainer of trainers in Greece and Cyprus and a Certified Evaluator for the Qualification of Vocational Training Trainer by HRDA Cyprus. In 2004 she was a trainer for the Police officers for the qualification of adult educator during the Olympic Games and a volunteer driver for the President of the Lithuanian Olympic Committee. She has also been a trainer in various Regional Training Centres (PEK) for teachers throughout Greece and for teachers of schools of the Holy Metropolis of Toronto, Canada, as well as in various VTCs in Greece and Cyprus. It also collaborated for the production of educational and teaching material, as well as training activities with the Pedagogical Institutes of Greece and Cyprus. She has a rich reachersh and academic work in her academic field . selected:Kazi, M., Charalambous, M., Athanasoula – Reppa, A. & Reppa G. (2023) Entrepreneurial education: An overview of alternative and effective school practices and actions in Cyprus and Greece educational system. International Journal of Educational Administration and Policy Studies Vol.15(1), pp. 9-18. Georgiou, S. & Reppa, A. (2023). Sign Language as a Universal Language of Communication. An Alternative Approach to Nation Branding. IGI Global Publisher of Timely Knowledge Konstantinides, D. & Athanasoula-Reppa, A. (2022) Multimedia Tools in Online Teaching Process. Journal of Modern Education Review, ISSN 2155-7993, USA June 2022, Volume 12, No. 6, pp. 431–447 Doi:10.15341/jmer(2155-7993)/06.12.2022/002 © Academic Star Publishing Company, 2022

Eldar Saljic is a Professor of Criminal Justice and Security at the College of Security and Global Studies, at the American University in the Emirates.. He graduated from the Faculty of Criminology, (BA) in Criminalistics and Security Studies, University of Sarajevo in Bosnia and Herzegovina (BiH) with Cum Laude. He holds a Master's degree in Criminology. Policing and Security and a PhD in Terrorism from Department of Law of the University of Novi Pazar. Dr. Eldar has been working at the Department of Law of the University of Novi Pazar in Serbia. During the course of his work, he published three books in the field of terrorism and security, and one dealing with the issues of victimization. Has published over 60 scientific papers in the field of terrorism and security. He participated on over 60 scientific expert conferences. He was also the first administrator of the Legal Clinic at the University of Novi Pazar, which was engaged in providing free legal aid.

Dusko Tomic, is a full Professor in the College of Security and Global Studies, American University in the Emirates. His research interests include security and risk management, where he has more than 20 years of experience in the area of disaster and risk prevention and sanitation, and risk management of emergency situations.. He completed his Doctoral degree in Political Sciences and graduated from Belgrade University in 2009. Professor Tomic is the author of nine monography and published books and over 30 peer-reviewed journal articles and book chapters related to security, terrorism, intelligence system and emergency management. He is a member of the International Police Association and the Commercial Crime Bureau at the World Commercial Organization since 2001 He was also the chief risk manager of Universidad 2009 in Belgrade, Serbia.

Saul Sandoval Perea is a professor in the Department of Business and Management at CETYS University in Tijuana, Mexico. His research interests lie at the intersections of politics, economics, and business. He has published works on economic and political development, as well as on public policy, particularly in the area of public security. He holds graduate degrees from Claremont Graduate University (California) and Carleton University (Canada), and a B.A. in International Trade from ITESM (Monterrey).

Harry Ph. Sophocleous is a Visiting Lecturer and PHD Researcher at Neapolis University Pafos. With a background as a Marketing and Strategy Consultant at Strategico Consulting Group, Harry has a strong foundation in strategic planning, market research, and marketing. Education credentials include a PhD in Political Communication, MPhil in Social Sciences, MSc in Marketing, and B.A. in Business Administration.

A Revanth Kumar, Associate Professor, Department of Community Medicine, Saraswathi Institute of Medical Sciences, Hapur, UP

Panagiota Xanthopoulou is a Postdoctoral Researcher and Academic Fellow of the Department of Business Administration at University of West Attica. Her teaching and research interests include Public Administration, Entrepreneurship & Innovation and Distance Education. Her research has been published in international and Greek scientific journals and has also been presented at international scientific conferences.

Index

T

U

V

W

www.ingramcontent.com/pod-product-compliance
Lightning Source LLC
LaVergne TN
LVHW080611300926
849162LV00005B/1122
* 9 7 9 8 3 6 9 3 5 5 8 3 1 *